Principles of Service Marketing and Management

Principles of Service Marketing and Management

Second Edition

CHRISTOPHER LOVELOCK
Adjunct Professor, Yale School of Management

LAUREN WRIGHT
Professor, California State University, Chico

Prentice Hall

Pearson Education International, Inc.

Acquisitions Editor: Bruce Kaplan
Editor-in-Chief: Jeff Shelstad
Assistant Editor: Anthony Palmiotto
Media Project Manager: Cindy Harford
Marketing Manager: Shannon Moore
Marketing Assistant: Christine Genneken
Managing Editor (Production): John Roberts
Production Editor: Renata Butera
Production Assistant: Diane Falcone
Permissions Coordinator: Suzanne Grappi
Associate Director, Manufacturing: Vincent Scelta
Production Manager: Arnold Vila
Manufacturing Buyer: Arnold Vila
Design Manager: Pat Smythe
Interior Design: Proof Positive/Farrowlyne Associates, Inc.
Designer: Steven Frim
Cover Design: Steven Frim
Cover Illustration and Chapter Illustration: Proof Positive/Farrowlyne Associates, Inc.
Manager, Print Production: Christina Mahon
Composition: UG / GGS Information Services, Inc
Full-Service Project Management: UG / GGS Information Services, Inc
Printer/Binder: Courier Kendalville

Credits and acknowledgments borrowed from other sources and reproduced, with permission, in this textbook appear on page 429.

This edition may be sold only in those countries to which it is consigned by Pearson Education International. It is not to be re-exported and it is not for sale in the U.S.A., Mexico, or Canada.

Pearson Education LTD.
Pearson Education Australia PTY, Limited
Pearson Education Singapore, Pte. Ltd.
Pearson Education North Asia Ltd.
Pearson Education Canada, Ltd.
Pearson Educación de Mexico, S.A. de C.V.
Pearson Education—Japan
Pearson Education Malaysia, Pte. Ltd.
Pearson Education, Upper Saddle River, New Jersey

10 9 8 7 6 5 4 3 2
ISBN 0-13-095012-2

Brief Contents

Contents

Preface

The service sector of the economy can best be characterized by its diversity. No single conceptual model can serve to embrace organizations ranging in size from huge international corporations (in fields such as airlines, banking, insurance, telecommunications, hotel chains, and freight transportation) to locally owned and operated small businesses such as restaurants, laundries, taxis, optometrists, and many business-to-business services. So, the goal of this book is to provide a carefully designed toolbox for service managers, teaching students how different frameworks and analytical procedures can best be used to examine the varied challenges faced by managers in different service settings.

WHAT'S NEW IN THE SECOND EDITION?

Responding to reviewer suggestions, new research findings, and continuing rapid changes in technology and the environment of the service sector, the content of the second edition of *Principles of Service Marketing and Management* incorporates many changes and refinements. The book comprises seventeen chapters, grouped into five parts, each of which is preceded by an overview of the issues to be addressed in the constituent chapters. There are also nine relatively short cases of varying levels of difficulty.

Key changes from the first edition—described in more detail later in this preface—include:

> ➤ A restructuring of chapter sequence and content, plus two new chapters.

> ➤ Significant updating, including the addition of many new examples and research findings.

> ➤ Improved approaches to pedagogy, designed to enhance student learning, including a service decision framework that provides a "roadmap" for the book.

> ➤ Revised and enhanced supplements, including an instructor's manual, enlarged and improved test bank, and more than 200 PowerPoint transparencies.

Target Courses

The text presents an integrated approach to studying services that places marketing issues within a broader general management context. Managers working in service organizations have to understand and acknowledge the close ties that link the marketing, operations, and human resource functions. They also need a realistic understanding of the potential (and limitations) of technology—especially information technology—to facilitate creation and delivery of services. As the experience of the "dot-com" meltdown of 2000–2001 suggests, not every new concept is commercially viable or creates useful value for consumers. With these perspectives in mind, this book has been designed so that instructors can make selective use of chapters and cases to teach courses of different lengths and formats in either Services Marketing or Service Management.

Books are necessarily printed in a linear sequence. However, this text has been designed to give instructors the flexibility to depart from the printed order if they wish. For instance, both Chapter 15, "Employee Roles in Service Organizations," and Chapter 16, "The Impact of Technology on Services," can easily be moved up in the course sequence.

Distinguishing Features of the Book

Key features of this book include its strong managerial orientation and strategic focus, use of memorable and relevant conceptual frameworks, references to both recent and classic research findings, use of interesting examples to link theory to practice, and inclusion of nine classroom-tested cases to accompany the text chapters.

Principles of Service Marketing and Management, Second Edition, is designed to complement the materials found in traditional marketing principles texts. It avoids sweeping and often misleading generalizations about services, recognizing explicitly that the differences between specific categories of services (based on the nature of the underlying service process) may be as important to student understanding as the broader differences between goods marketing and services marketing.

The book shows how different technologies—and information technology in particular—are changing the nature of service delivery and can offer innovative ways for service providers and customers to relate to each other (the people side of the business). The text makes use of recent research in such areas as service encounters, customer expectations and satisfaction, loyalty and relationship marketing, service quality, service recovery, managing demand and capacity, productivity improvement in services, pricing and yield management, new service development, technology, and service leadership.

New Chapter Content in the Second Edition

Changes and enhancements to the chapters include the following:

> ➤ Use of a new service decision framework, featured in each of the five part openers (and also in Chapters 1 and 2), to provide a roadmap for the book and to highlight the questions that service managers need to ask. This framework is sufficiently flexible to allow instructors to treat topics in different sequences and with different levels of emphasis.

> ➤ Explicit linkage between the service decision framework and the 8Ps model of integrated service management, which modifies elements of the traditional 7Ps framework of service marketing (for instance, describing service delivery systems in terms of "Place, Cyberspace, and Time" instead of the outdated "Place" terminology) and adds Productivity and Quality as linked concepts.

> ➤ Addition of two new chapters, one focusing on technology in services and the other on service leadership.

> ➤ Restructuring of chapter sequence and content, together with better integration between chapters to tighten the linkages between them and facilitate their use in alternative sequences.

> ➤ A revision and updating of all text materials, including addition of numerous examples and references from the period 1999–2001.

> ➤ An enhanced treatment of service pricing, designed to capture student interest and including such topics as activity-based costing, yield management, and introduction of new types of service fees.

➤ A more balanced treatment of marketing communication, describing its role in educating service customers in addition to promoting sales.

➤ Coverage of technology issues throughout the book, with a thoughtful discussion of the role and potential of Internet and Web applications in the "post-dot-com-meltdown" era, supplemented by in-depth treatment in Chapter 16 of how technological change impacts services.

➤ Discussion of ethical issues facing service managers, introduced as appropriate in specific and relevant contexts.

➤ Use of international examples throughout the book.

➤ Inclusion of references at the end of each chapter.

New and Improved Pedagogical Aids

The *Instructor's Resource Manual* for the book includes:

1. Detailed course design and teaching hints, plus sample course outlines.

2. Chapter-by-chapter teaching suggestions, plus discussion of learning objectives and sample responses to study questions and exercises.

3. A description of sixteen suggested student exercises and five comprehensive projects (designed for either individual or team use).

4. Detailed teaching notes for each of the nine cases, plus suggestions for possible chapters with which they might be paired.

5. More than 200 new and revised PowerPoint transparencies, keyed to each chapter, and contained as electronic files in a CD-ROM.

A new Test Bank features an enlarged and enhanced set of questions for use in quizzes and exams.

The Companion Web site for this book includes:

1. An online study guide and additional resources for students.

2. Faculty resources including an online version of the Instructor's Manual and PowerPoints.

ACKNOWLEDGMENTS

Over the years, many colleagues in both the academic and business worlds have provided us with valuable insights into the management and marketing of services, through their writings and in conference or seminar discussions. We have also benefited greatly from in-class and after-class discussions with our students and from their feedback on assignments and exercises.

It's with sadness that we acknowledge the contributions of two friends who have died recently, the late Eric Langeard of the Université d'Aix-Marseille III in France and the late Liam Glynn of University College, Dublin, Ireland. Both played an important role in stimulating international debate among service scholars and are much missed.

Although it's impossible to mention everyone who has influenced our thinking, we particularly want to express our appreciation to the following individuals: John Bateson of Gemini Consulting; Leonard Berry of Texas A&M University; Mary Jo Bitner and Steven Brown of Arizona State University; David Bowen of the Thunderbird Graduate School of International Management; Richard Chase of the University of Southern California; John Deighton, James Heskett, Theodore Levitt, Earl Sasser, and Leonard Schlesinger, all currently or formerly of Harvard Business School; Pierre Eiglier of Université d'Aix-Marseille III; Ray Fisk of the University of New Orleans; Christian

Grönroos of the Swedish School of Economics in Finland; Stephen Grove of Clemson University; Evert Gummesson of Stockholm University; Christopher Hart of Spire; Denis Lapert of Reims Management School; Jean-Claude Larréché of INSEAD; Barbara Lewis of the Manchester School of Management; David Maister of Maister Associates; "Parsu" Parasuraman of the University of Miami; Paul Patterson of the University of New South Wales; Fred Reichheld of Bain & Co; Javier Reynoso of ITESM, Monterrey, Mexico; Roland Rust and Benjamin Schneider of the University of Maryland; Sandra Vandermerwe of Imperial College, London; Rhett Walker of the Royal Melbourne Institute of Technology; Charles Weinberg of the University of British Columbia; Jochen Wirtz of the National University of Singapore; and Valarie Zeithaml of the University of North Carolina.

We're also pleased to acknowledge the insightful and helpful comments of the following reviewers for the second edition: Jack Forrest, Cumberland University; Richard S. Jacobs, Adams State College; Kenneth R. Laird, Southern Connecticut State University; Anil Mathur, Hofstra University; Kim A. Nelson, University of Arizona; Jim Stephens, Emporia State University; and Stephen Tax, University of Victoria. We also would like to thank the reviewers of the previous edition: Eileen Bridges of Kent State University; Tom Brown of Oklahoma State University; Douglas Dalrymple of Indiana University; Dawn Iacobucci of Northwestern University; and Surendra N. Singh of Oklahoma State University. They challenged our thinking and, through their critiques and suggestions, stimulated us to make many significant improvements to the second edition.

Warm thanks are due, too, to Tim Lovelock, who helped design and prepare many of the PowerPoint graphics developed as teaching aids. And, of course, we're very appreciative of all the hard work put in by the editing and production staff in helping to transform our manuscript into a handsome published text. They include Renata Butera and Terri O'Prey. Finally, we're most grateful to our editor, Bruce Kaplan, for his friendly support and encouragement.

Christopher Lovelock

Lauren Wright

About the Authors

Christopher Lovelock is one of the pioneers of services marketing. Based in Massachusetts, he gives seminars and workshops for managers around the world and also teaches an MBA service marketing course at the Yale School of Management. His distinguished academic career has included 11 years on the faculty of the Harvard Business School and two years as a visiting professor at IMD in Switzerland. He has also held appointments at Berkeley, Stanford, and the Sloan School at MIT, as well as visiting professorships at The University of Queensland in Australia and at both INSEAD and Theseus Institute in France. Christopher obtained a BCom and an MA in economics from the University of Edinburgh, then worked in advertising with the London office of J. Walter Thompson Co. and in corporate planning with Canadian Industries Ltd. in Montreal. Later, he obtained an MBA from Harvard and a PhD from Stanford. Author or coauthor of over 60 articles, more than 100 teaching cases, and 26 books, he serves on the editorial review boards of the *International Journal of Service Industry Management*, *Journal of Service Research*, and *Service Industries Journal*. He is a recipient of the American Marketing Association's Award for Career Contributions to the Services Discipline and a best article award from the *Journal of Marketing*. He has also been recognized for excellence in case writing and in 2000 won the *Business Week* European Case Award.

Lauren Wright is a professor and former marketing department chair at California State University, Chico. In 1998, she was a visiting faculty fellow at the University of Canterbury in Christchurch, New Zealand. Winner of several awards for outstanding undergraduate teaching, Lauren has been recognized as a Master Teacher at CSU Chico and consults with faculty campus-wide on effective teaching techniques. Her name is listed in the 1998 publication *Who's Who Among America's Teachers* and *Strathmore's Who's Who* for 1999–2000. She is past chair of the American Marketing Association's Special Interest Group for Services Marketing (SERVSIG), founded the annual SERVSIG Doctoral Consortium, and has served as research director for the International Service Quality Association. She has published numerous articles on service quality, new service success, business process redesign, and innovative teaching pedagogies and has presented her research findings at many national and international conferences. She holds a BS from the University of Oregon and MBA and PhD degrees from Pennsylvania State University, where she won the Marketing Science Doctoral Dissertation Award for her work on the factors affecting new service success.

Principles of Service
Marketing and Management

partone

Understanding Services

This text is designed to introduce you to effective strategies for marketing and managing many different types of service organizations. To help organize your thinking, we've structured the book around the service management decision framework, a series of strategic questions depicted in Figure I.1.

A Framework for Making Service Management Decisions

The decision framework begins with the question: *What business are we in?* The answer is critical to the development of effective marketing strategy. Determining the nature of the business goes beyond just specifying the industry in which the organization is usually classified. Competition may come from outside as well as within that industry. Managers should examine what other services and goods offer alternative ways to meet a customer's needs.

Central to strategy formulation in services is the question: *What service processes can be used in our operation?* The processes used to create and deliver services help define (1) the role of customers in service delivery, (2) the nature of customers' service experiences, (3) the availability of alternative delivery methods, and (4) the application of information technology.

The third question asks: *Who are our customers and how should we relate to them?* It addresses such issues as which types of customers to target, the nature of consumer decision making, and relationship marketing strategies. We demonstrate how consumer behavior concepts apply in a service setting.

The next component of the framework is: *What should be the core and supplementary elements of our service product?* The response to this question requires managers to define the core product, which is a function of the nature of the business (the first strategic question in Figure I.1). They must also identify the supplementary service elements that enhance this core product. It's important to know what differentiates a company's service offering from that of the competition and what adds value for customers.

Another critical issue is: *What price should we charge for our service?* The answer depends on the perceived value of the service, the price of competing alternatives, and the customer's willingness and/or ability to pay. To put pricing in perspective, we also need to know what additional outlays customers incur in using our service, ranging from out-of-pocket expenses to investments of time and effort. Pricing decisions should reflect the costs to be recovered by the firm and its need to make a profit.

The next element in the framework revolves around the question: *How should we communicate what our service has to offer?* Managers need to determine how target customers view the firm, its brand names, and its services—if, indeed, they are even aware of them. We discuss the many tools available to service marketers for promotional and educational purposes.

What are the options for delivering our service? is a topic for vigorous debate in the age of the Internet. Physical channels can deliver services to a specific place, but require time to do so. Electronic channels, by contrast, allow information-based services to be delivered in cyberspace instantaneously, giving customers access to these services where and when it suits them. The choice of channel may change the nature of the service experience. Marketers also have opportunities to use third-party intermediaries to perform certain tasks in any given delivery channel.

Operational priorities don't always coincide with marketing ones, raising the question: *How can we balance productivity and quality?* The challenge for many service businesses is to operate as efficiently as possible without spoiling the appeal of the service for customers. The goal should be to achieve synergies between productivity and quality strategies so that value can be created for both customers and the firm. Marketers need to share information across other functional areas about what customers expect. Hence, service standards should reflect both productivity and quality goals.

One distinctive aspect of service management is the perishability of the product. There are no inventories of completed services to buffer productive capacity from sharp swings in demand. The question therefore arises: *How should we match demand and productive capacity?* We discuss demand management strategies including: (1) using price and promotion to increase or reduce demand at specific times, and (2) varying the level of available

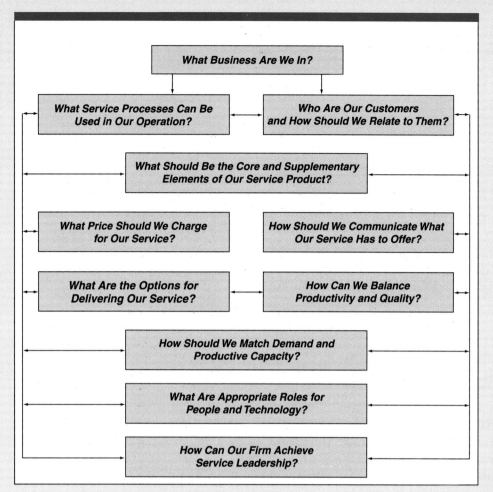

FIGURE I.1

A Framework for Making Service Management Decisions

The boxes in the figure contain the following:

What Business Are We In?

What Service Processes Can Be Used in Our Operation?

Who Are Our Customers and How Should We Relate to Them?

What Should Be the Core and Supplementary Elements of Our Service Product?

What Price Should We Charge for Our Service?

How Should We Communicate What Our Service Has to Offer?

What Are the Options for Delivering Our Service?

How Can We Balance Productivity and Quality?

How Should We Match Demand and Productive Capacity?

What Are Appropriate Roles for People and Technology?

How Can Our Firm Achieve Service Leadership?

capacity. Subsequently, we look at ways of inventorying demand by managing waiting lines and using reservations systems.

A significant issue for all service strategists is: *What are appropriate roles for people and technology?* To answer this question, managers need to know how important it is for customers to receive high-contact service with a human touch. When employees constitute a key aspect of the service experience, a well-trained and motivated workforce can offer a major competitive advantage. In many businesses, a variety of technologies—notably information technology—are available to help the firm automate service delivery, replacing employees with self-service by customers.

The final question in our framework is: *How can our firm achieve service leadership?* To be recognized as a leader in its field, a firm must offer services that are known for superior value and quality. It must have marketing strategies that beat the competition, yet still be viewed as a trustworthy organization that does business in ethical ways. The company should be seen as a leader in operations, too—respected for its superior operational processes and innovative use of technology. Finally, the firm should be recognized as an outstanding place to work, leading its industry in human resource management practices and creating loyal, productive, and customer-oriented employees.

Using the Framework

The service management decision framework shapes the structure of this book and guides the coverage of individual chapters. At the beginning of Parts II through V, you'll find an overview. In each instance, we reproduce the framework and expand the content of certain boxes to include more detailed questions that are especially relevant to the topics raised in the chapters. We hope this material will help you become aware of some basic questions facing service managers as they address specific issues.

chapter one

Why Study Services?

Learning from Service Leaders

Modern service industries are in an almost constant state of change. In particular, we hear a lot today about the "knowledge economy," reflecting both the increasing proportion of jobs that require a high level of education and the widespread application of information technology in business.

Services have been profoundly influenced by these and other trends, making the task of managing them very challenging. Traditional services can now be delivered through new channels, marketers can offer customers useful new features, and new services have sprung up to take advantage of the Internet. In fact, innovators are continually launching new ways to satisfy customers' existing wants and to meet needs that people did not even know they had. How many people ten to fifteen years ago foresaw a personal need for electronic mail? Although most new start-up ventures eventually fail—a trend from which "dot-com" companies have not been exempt—a few survive and succeed. Many long-established firms are also struggling. However, others are making spectacular progress by continually rethinking the way in which they do business and re-evaluating how they can add value for their customers. Consider the following examples of innovative companies that you will encounter again in subsequent chapters.

Charles Schwab, America's largest discount broker, got its start in 1975 when fixed commission rates were abolished in the United States. Its low prices attracted a lot of investors away from full-service brokers. The company was always quick to take advantage of new developments in information technology. Growth was fueled by early investments in automation, which allowed Schwab to expand its offerings through a primarily telephone-based channel. In 1995, it introduced software that allowed clients to trade through their own computers. With the growth of the Internet and the advent of other online brokers, Schwab actively sought to move much of its business online. By the year 2000, approximately half its accounts were trading through the Internet.

Southwest Airlines is the most consistently profitable airline in America. From its original base in Texas, it has successfully positioned itself as a low-cost, no-frills carrier emphasizing short- and medium-haul routes across the United States. Underlying its success are punctual, frequent flights that offer excellent value for customers, an easy-to-use online reservations service, a low-cost operations strategy that runs counter to established industry traditions, and human resource policies that have created an extraordinarily loyal and hardworking group of employees. Airlines from around the world have studied Southwest's marketing, operations, and human resource strategies, but none has yet been able to achieve their finely tuned balance.

Intrawest Corporation has spread from its Canadian base in Vancouver, British Columbia, to become one of the largest operators of ski resorts in North America. Its properties include Whistler, British Columbia; Mammoth, California; Copper Mountain, Colorado; and Killington, Vermont. Intrawest's expertise includes a multi-step strategy of enhancing the skiing experience, building an appealing resort community that will encourage people to stay longer, and expansion into year-round activities at each resort.

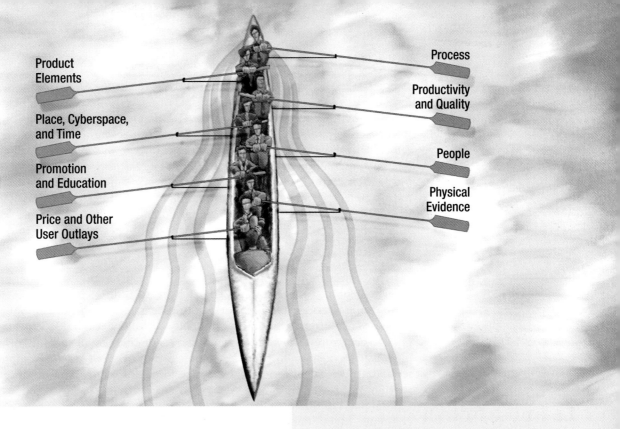

Product Elements

Place, Cyberspace, and Time

Promotion and Education

Price and Other User Outlays

Process

Productivity and Quality

People

Physical Evidence

Aggreko describes itself as "the world's power rental leader." Headquartered in the United Kingdom, it rents mobile electricity generators and temperature control equipment from 70 depots in 20 countries. Large companies and government agencies dominate its customer base. Much of the firm's business comes from backup operations or special events such as the Olympics, but it is also poised to respond rapidly to emergency situations, such as natural disasters that knock out normal power supplies. Speed, flexibility, reliability, and environmental sensitivity are among Aggreko's strengths.

eBay defines its mission as "to help people trade practically anything on earth." Founded in 1995, eBay has no physical presence other than its corporate offices, which customers never see. Instead, it uses the power of the Web to bring buyers and sellers together, on a national or regional basis, in a cyberspace auction format. Targeting individual customers—not businesses—the company enables people to offer and bid for items in more than 4,300 categories, including cars, antiques, toys, dolls, jewelry, sports memorabilia, books, pottery, glass, coins, stamps, and much more. Part of eBay's appeal is simply that it is the world's largest person-to-person trading site, offering more new items for sale every day and more potential buyers than any other auction site on the Web.

Learning Objectives

After reading this chapter, you should be able to

⟹ describe what kinds of businesses are classified as services

⟹ recognize the major changes occurring in the service sector

⟹ identify the characteristics that make services different from goods

⟹ understand the 8Ps of integrated services management

⟹ explain why service businesses need to integrate the marketing, operations, and human resource functions

SERVICES IN THE MODERN ECONOMY

As consumers, we use services every day. Turning on a light, watching TV, talking on the telephone, riding a bus, visiting the dentist, mailing a letter, getting a haircut, refueling a car, writing a check, or sending clothes to the cleaners are all examples of service consumption at the individual level. The institution at which you are studying is itself a complex service organization. In addition to educational services, today's college facilities usually include libraries and cafeterias, counseling, a bookstore, placement offices, copy services, telecommunications, and even a bank. If you are enrolled at a residential university, campus services are also likely to include dormitories, health care, indoor and outdoor athletic facilities, a theater, and perhaps a post office.

Customers are not always happy with the quality and value of the services they receive. People complain about late deliveries, rude or incompetent personnel, inconvenient service hours, poor performance, and needlessly complicated procedures. They grumble about the difficulty of finding sales clerks to help them in retail stores, express frustration about mistakes on their credit card bills or bank statements, shake their heads over the complexity of new self-service equipment, mutter about poor value, and sigh as they are forced to wait in line almost everywhere they go.

Suppliers of services often seem to have a very different set of concerns than the consumer. Many suppliers complain about how difficult it is to make a profit, how hard it is to find skilled and motivated employees, or how difficult it has become to please customers. Some firms seem to believe that the surest route to financial success lies in cutting costs and eliminating "unnecessary" frills. A few even give the impression that they could run a much more efficient operation if it weren't for all the stupid customers who keep making unreasonable demands and messing things up!

Fortunately, in almost every industry there are service suppliers who know how to please their customers while also running a productive, profitable operation staffed by pleasant and competent employees. By studying organizations such as Charles Schwab, Intrawest, Aggreko, Southwest Airlines, eBay, and the many others featured in this book, we can draw important insights about the most effective ways to manage the different types of services found in today's economy.

What Is a Service?

service: an act or performance that creates benefits for customers by bringing about a desired change in—or on behalf of—the recipient.

Because of their diversity, services have traditionally been difficult to define. The way in which services are created and delivered to customers is often hard to grasp since many inputs and outputs are intangible. Most people have little difficulty defining manufacturing or agriculture, but defining **service** can elude them. Here are two approaches that capture the essence of the word.

➢ A service is an act or performance offered by one party to another. Although the process may be tied to a physical product, the performance is essentially intangible and does not normally result in ownership of any of the factors of production.

benefit: an advantage or gain that customers obtain from performance of a service or use of a physical good.

➢ Services are economic activities that create value and provide **benefits** for customers at specific times and places, as a result of bringing about a desired change in—or on behalf of—the recipient of the service.

More humorously, service has also been described as "something that may be bought and sold, but which cannot be dropped on your foot."

Understanding the Service Sector

Services make up the bulk of today's economy, not only in the United States and Canada where they account for 73 percent and 67 percent of the gross domestic product (GDP), respectively, but also in other developed industrial nations throughout the world.[1] Figure 1.1 shows how service industries contribute to the economy of the United States relative to manufacturing, government (itself mostly services), agriculture, mining, and construction.

The **service sector** accounts for most of the new job growth in developed countries. In fact, unless you are already predestined for a career in a family manufacturing or agricultural business, the probability is high that you will spend your working life in companies (or public agencies and nonprofit organizations) that create and deliver services.

As a nation's economy develops, the share of employment between agriculture, industry (including manufacturing and mining), and services changes dramatically. Figure 1.2 shows how the evolution to a service-dominated employment base is likely to take place over time as per capita income rises. Service jobs now account for 76 percent of private sector payrolls in the United States, with wages growing at a faster pace than in manufacturing jobs.[2] In most countries, the service sector of the economy is very diverse and includes a wide array of different industries, ranging in size from huge enterprises that operate on a global basis to small entrepreneurial firms that serve a single town.

It comes as a surprise to most people to learn that the dominance of the service sector is not limited to highly developed nations. For instance, World Bank statistics show that in many Latin American and Caribbean nations the service sector accounts

service sector: the portion of a nation's economy represented by services of all kinds, including those offered by public and non-profit organizations.

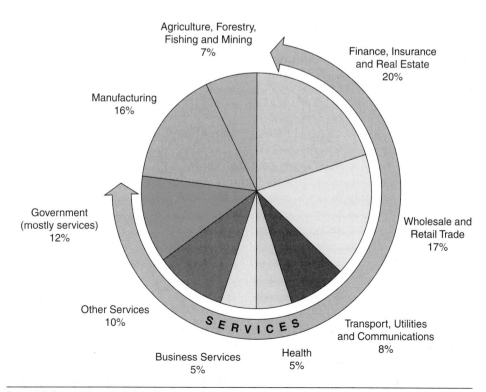

Agriculture, Forestry, Fishing and Mining
7%

Finance, Insurance and Real Estate
20%

Manufacturing
16%

Government (mostly services)
12%

Wholesale and Retail Trade
17%

Other Services
10%

SERVICES

Transport, Utilities and Communications
8%

Business Services
5%

Health
5%

Source: U.S. Bureau of Economic Analysis, *Survey of Current Business*, December 2000, Table 1, p. 29.

FIGURE 1.1

Services in the U.S. Economy: Share of GDP by Industry, 1999

FIGURE 1.2

Changing Structure of
Employment as an Economy
Develops

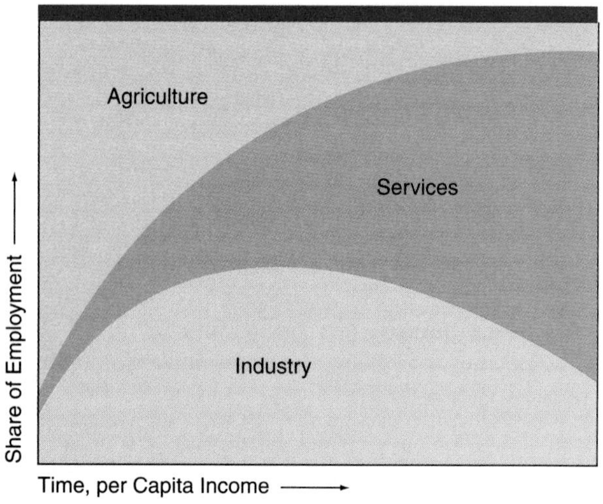

Source: International Monetary Fund, *World Economic Outlook*, Washington, D.C.: International Monetary Fund, May 1997.

for more than half the gross national product (GNP) and employs more than half the labor force.[3] These countries often have a large "underground economy" that is not captured in official statistics. In Mexico, for instance, it has been estimated that as much as 40 percent of trade and commerce is "informal."[4] Significant service output is created by undocumented work in domestic jobs (e.g., cook, housekeeper, gardener) or in small, cash-based enterprises such as restaurants, laundries, rooming houses, and taxis.

Service organizations range in size from huge international corporations like airlines, banking, insurance, telecommunications, hotel chains, and freight transportation to a vast array of locally owned and operated small businesses, including restaurants, laundries, taxis, optometrists, and numerous business-to-business ("B2B") services. Franchised service outlets—in fields ranging from fast foods to bookkeeping—combine the marketing characteristics of a large chain that offers a standardized product with local ownership and operation of a specific facility. Some firms that create a time-sensitive physical product, such as printing or photographic processing, are now describing themselves as service businesses because speed, customization, and convenient locations create much of the value added.

internal services: service elements within any type of business that facilitate creation of, or add value to, its final output.

There's a hidden service sector, too, within many large corporations that are classified by government statisticians as being in manufacturing, agricultural, or natural resources industries. So-called **internal services** cover a wide array of activities including recruitment, publications, legal and accounting services, payroll administration, office cleaning, landscape maintenance, freight transport, and many other tasks. To a growing extent, organizations are choosing to outsource those internal services that can be performed more efficiently by a specialist subcontractor.[5] As these tasks are outsourced, they become part of the competitive marketplace and are therefore categorized as contributing to the service component of the economy. Even when such services are not outsourced, managers of the departments that supply them would do well to think in terms of providing good service to their internal customers.

Governments and nonprofit organizations are also in the business of providing services, although the extent of such involvement may vary widely from one country to another, reflecting both tradition and political values. In many countries, colleges, hospitals, and museums are publicly owned or operate on a not-for-profit basis, but for-profit versions of each type of institution also exist.

MARKETING SERVICES VERSUS PHYSICAL GOODS

The dynamic environment of services today places a premium on effective marketing. Although it's still very important to run an efficient operation, it no longer guarantees success. The service product must be tailored to customer needs, priced realistically, distributed through convenient channels, and actively promoted to customers. New market entrants are positioning their services to appeal to specific market segments through their pricing, communication efforts, and service delivery, rather than trying to be all things to all people. But are the marketing skills that have been developed in manufacturing companies directly transferable to service organizations? The answer is often no, because marketing management tasks in the service sector tend to differ from those in the manufacturing sector in several important respects.

Basic Differences Between Goods and Services

Every **product**—a term used in this book to describe the core output of any type of industry—delivers benefits to the customers who purchase and use them. **Goods** can be described as physical objects or devices and services are actions or performances.[6] Early research into services sought to differentiate them from goods, focusing particularly on four generic differences, referred to as intangibility, heterogeneity (or variability), perishability of output, and simultaneity of production and consumption.[7] Although these characteristics are still cited, they have been criticized for over-simplifying the real-world environment. More practical insights are provided in Figure 1.3, which lists nine basic differences that can help us to distinguish the tasks associated with service marketing and management from those involved with physical goods.

product: the core output (either a service or a manufactured good) produced by a firm.

goods: physical objects or devices that provide **benefits** for customers through ownership or use.

It's important to note that in identifying these differences we're still dealing with generalizations that do not apply equally to all services. In Chapter 2, we classify services into distinct categories, each of which presents somewhat different challenges for marketers and other managers. We also need to draw a distinction between *marketing of services* and *marketing goods through service.* In the former, it's the service itself that is being sold and in the latter, service is added—usually free of charge—to enhance the appeal of a manufactured product. Now, let's examine each of the nine differences in more detail.

Customers Do Not Obtain Ownership   Perhaps the key distinction between goods and services lies in the fact that customers usually derive value from services without obtaining permanent ownership of any substantial tangible elements. In many instances, service marketers offer customers the opportunity to rent the use of a physical object like a car or hotel room, or to hire the labor and skills of people whose expertise ranges from brain surgery to knowing how to check customers into a hotel. As a

- customers do not obtain ownership of services
- service products are intangible performances
- there is greater involvement of customers in the production process
- other people may form part of the product
- there is greater variability in operational inputs and outputs
- many services are difficult for customers to evaluate
- there is typically an absence of inventories
- the time factor is relatively more important
- delivery systems may involve both electronic and physical channels

FIGURE 1.3

Basic Differences Between Goods and Services

Checking in: People are part of the product in hotel services, so customer satisfaction depends on both employee performance and the behavior of the other customers.

purchaser of services yourself, you know that while your main interest is in the final output, the way in which you are treated during service delivery can also have an important impact on your satisfaction.

intangible: something that is experienced and cannot be touched or preserved.

Service Products as Intangible Performances   Although services often include tangible elements—such as sitting in an airline seat, eating a meal, or getting damaged equipment repaired—the service performance itself is basically an intangible. The benefits of owning and using a manufactured product come from its physical characteristics (although brand image may convey benefits, too). In services, the benefits come from the nature of the performance. The notion of service as a performance that cannot be wrapped up and taken away leads to the use of a theatrical metaphor for service management, visualizing service delivery as similar to the staging of a play with service personnel as the actors and customers as the audience.

Some services, such as rentals, include a physical object like a car or a power tool. But marketing a car rental performance is very different from attempting to market the physical object alone. For instance, in car rentals, customers usually reserve a particular category of vehicle, rather than a specific brand and model. Instead of worrying about styling, colors, and upholstery, customers focus on price, location and appearance of pickup and delivery facilities, extent of insurance coverage, cleanliness and maintenance of vehicles, provision of free shuttle buses at airports, availability of 24-hour reservations service, hours when rental locations are staffed, and quality of service provided by customer-contact personnel. By contrast, the core benefit derived from owning a physical good normally comes specifically from its tangible elements, even though it may provide intangible benefits, too. An interesting way to distinguish between goods and services is to place them on a scale from tangible dominant to intangible dominant (illustrated in Figure 1.4).[8]

Customer Involvement in the Production Process   Performing a service involves assembling and delivering the output of a combination of physical facilities and mental or physical labor. Often, customers are actively involved in helping create

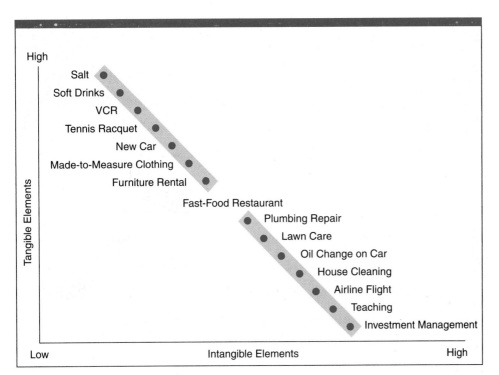

FIGURE 1.4

Value Added by Tangible versus Intangible Elements in Goods and Services

the service product, either by serving themselves (as in using a laundromat or ATM) or by cooperating with service personnel in settings such as hair salons, hotels, colleges, or hospitals. As we will see in Chapter 2, services can be categorized according to the extent of contact that the customer has with the service organization.

People as Part of the Product   In high-contact services, customers not only come into contact with service personnel, but they may also rub shoulders with other customers (literally so, if they ride a bus or subway during the rush hour). The difference between service businesses often lies in the quality of employees serving the customers. Similarly, the type of customers who patronize a particular service business helps to define the nature of the service experience. As such, people become part of the product in many services. Managing these service encounters—especially those between customers and service employees—is a challenging task.

Greater Variability in Operational Inputs and Outputs   The presence of personnel and other customers in the operational system makes it difficult to standardize and control **variability** in both service inputs and outputs. Manufactured goods can be produced under controlled conditions, designed to optimize both productivity and quality, and then checked for conformance with quality standards long before they reach the customer. (Of course, their subsequent use by customers will vary widely, reflecting customer needs and skills, as well as the nature of the usage occasion.) However, when services are consumed as they are produced, final "assembly" must take place under real-time conditions, which may vary from customer to customer and even from one time of the day to another. As a result, mistakes and shortcomings are both more likely and harder to conceal. These factors make it difficult for service organizations to improve productivity, control quality, and offer a consistent product. As

variability: a lack of consistency in inputs and outputs during the service production process.

a former packaged goods marketer observed some years ago after moving to a new position at Holiday Inn:

> *We can't control the quality of our product as well as a Procter and Gamble control engineer on a production line can. . . . When you buy a box of Tide, you can reasonably be 99 and 44/100ths percent sure that this stuff will work to get your clothes clean. When you buy a Holiday Inn room, you're sure at some lesser percentage that it will work to give you a good night's sleep without any hassle, or people banging on the walls and all the bad things that can happen in a hotel.*[9]

Not all variations in service delivery are necessarily negative. Modern service businesses are recognizing the value of customizing at least some aspects of the service offering to the needs and expectations of individual customers. In some fields, like health care, customization is essential.[10]

Harder for Customers to Evaluate   Most physical goods tend to be relatively high in "search attributes." These are characteristics that a customer can determine prior to purchasing a product, such as color, style, shape, price, fit, feel, and smell. Other goods and some services, by contrast, may emphasize "experience attributes" that can only be discerned after purchase or during consumption (e.g., taste, wearability, ease of handling, quietness, and personal treatment). Finally, there are "credence attributes"—characteristics that customers find hard to evaluate even after consumption. Examples include surgery and auto repairs, where the results of the service delivery may not be readily visible.[11]

No Inventories for Services   Because a service is a deed or performance, rather than a tangible item that the customer keeps, it is "perishable" and cannot be inventoried. Of course, the necessary facilities, equipment, and labor can be held in readiness to create the service, but these simply represent productive capacity, not the product itself. Having unused capacity in a service business is rather like running water into a sink without a stopper. The flow is wasted unless customers (or possessions requiring service) are present to receive it. When demand exceeds capacity, customers may be sent away disappointed, since no inventory is available for backup. An important task for service marketers, therefore, is to find ways of smoothing demand levels to match capacity.

Importance of the Time Factor   Many services are delivered in real time. Customers have to be physically present to receive service from organizations such as airlines, hospitals, haircutters, and restaurants. There are limits as to how long customers are willing to be kept waiting and service must be delivered fast enough so that customers do not waste time receiving service. Even when service takes place in the back office, customers have expectations about how long a particular task should take to complete—whether it is repairing a machine, completing a research report, cleaning a suit, or preparing a legal document. Today's customers are increasingly time sensitive and speed is often a key element in good service.

Different Distribution Channels   Unlike manufacturers that require physical distribution channels to move goods from factory to customers, many service businesses either use electronic channels (as in broadcasting or electronic funds transfer) or combine the service factory, retail outlet, and point of consumption at a single location. In the latter instance, service firms are responsible for managing customer-contact personnel. They may also have to manage the behavior of customers in the service factory to ensure smoothly running operations and to avoid situations in which one person's behavior irritates other customers who are present at the same time.

AN INTEGRATED APPROACH TO SERVICE MANAGEMENT

This book is not just about service marketing. Throughout the chapters, you'll find continuing reference to two other important functions: service operations and human resource management. Imagine yourself as the manager of a repair garage. Or think big, if you like, as the CEO of a major airline. In either instance, you need to be (1) concerned on a day-to-day basis that your customers are satisfied, (2) your operational systems are running smoothly and efficiently, and (3) your employees are not only working productively but are also doing a good job either of serving customers directly or of helping other employees to deliver good service. Even if you see yourself as a middle manager with specific responsibilities in marketing, operations, or human resources, your success in your job will often involve the understanding of these other functions and periodic meetings with colleagues working in these areas. In short, integration of activities between functions is the name of the game. Problems in any one of these three areas may signal financial difficulties ahead.

The Eight Components of Integrated Service Management

When discussing strategies to market manufactured goods, marketers usually address four basic strategic elements: product, price, place (or distribution), and promotion (or communication). Collectively, these four categories are often referred to as the "4Ps" of the marketing mix.[12] However, the distinctive nature of service performances, especially such aspects as customer involvement in production and the importance of the time factor, requires that other strategic elements be included. To capture the nature of this challenge, we will be using the "8Ps" of **integrated service management**, which describe eight decision variables facing managers of service organizations.[13]

Our visual metaphor for the 8Ps is the racing "eight," a lightweight boat or shell powered by eight rowers, made famous by the Oxford and Cambridge boat race that has taken place annually on the River Thames near London for almost 150 years. Today, similar races involving many different teams are a staple of rowing competitions around the world, as well as a featured sport in the Summer Olympics. Speed comes not only from the rowers' physical strength, but also from their harmony and cohesion as part of a team. To achieve optimal effectiveness, each of the eight rowers must pull on his or her oar in unison with the others, following the direction of the coxswain, who is seated in the stern. A similar synergy and integration between each of the 8Ps is required for success in any competitive service business (Figure 1.5). The cox—who steers the boat, sets

integrated service management: the coordinated planning and execution of those marketing, operations, and human resources activities that are essential to a service firm's success.

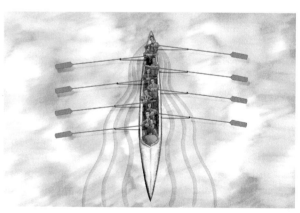

PRODUCT
ELEMENTS

PLACE,
CYBERSPACE,
AND TIME

PROMOTION
AND EDUCATION

PRICE AND
OTHER USER
OUTLAYS

PROCESS

PRODUCTIVITY
AND QUALITY

PEOPLE

PHYSICAL
EVIDENCE

FIGURE 1.5

The Eight Components of Integrated Service Management

the pace, motivates the crew, and keeps a close eye on competing boats in the race—is a metaphor for management.

product elements: all components of the service performance that create value for customers.

Product Elements   Managers must select the features of both the core product and the bundle of supplementary service elements surrounding it, with reference to the benefits desired by customers and how well competing products perform.

place, cyberspace, and time: management decisions about when, where, and how to deliver services to customers.

Place, Cyberspace, and Time   Delivering product elements to customers involves decisions on both the place and time of delivery and may involve physical or electronic distribution channels (or both), depending on the nature of the service being provided. Messaging services and the Internet allow information-based services to be delivered in cyberspace for retrieval by telephone or computer wherever and whenever it suits the customer. Firms may deliver service directly to their customers or through intermediary organizations like retail outlets owned by other companies, which receive a fee or percentage of the selling price to perform certain tasks associated with sales, service, and customer-contact. Customer expectations of speed and convenience are becoming important determinants in service delivery strategy.

process: a particular method of operations or series of actions, typically involving steps that need to occur in a defined sequence.

Process   Creating and delivering product elements to customers requires the design and implementation of effective processes. A process describes the method and sequence in which service operating systems work. Badly designed processes are likely to annoy customers because of slow, bureaucratic, and ineffective service delivery. Similarly, poor processes make it difficult for front-line staff to do their jobs well, result in low productivity, and increase the likelihood of service failures.

productivity: how efficiently service inputs are transformed into outputs that add value for customers.

quality: the degree to which a service satisfies customers by meeting their needs, wants, and expectations.

Productivity and Quality   These elements, often treated separately, should be seen as two sides of the same coin. No service firm can afford to address either element in isolation. Improved productivity is essential to keep costs under control but managers must beware of making inappropriate cuts in service levels that are resented by customers (and perhaps by employees, too). Service quality, as defined by customers, is essential for product differentiation and for building customer loyalty. However, investing in quality improvement without understanding the trade-off between incremental costs and incremental revenues may place the profitability of the firm at risk.

people: customers and employees who are involved in service production.

People   Many services depend on direct, personal interaction between customers and a firm's employees (like getting a haircut or eating at a restaurant). The nature of these interactions strongly influences the customer's perceptions of service quality.[14] Customers often judge the quality of the service they receive largely on their assessment of the people providing the service. Successful service firms devote significant effort to recruiting, training, and motivating their personnel, especially—but not exclusively—those who are in direct contact with customers.

promotion and education: all communication activities and incentives designed to build customer preference for a specific service or service provider.

Promotion and Education   No marketing program can succeed without an effective communication program. This component plays three vital roles: providing needed information and advice, persuading target customers of the merits of a specific product, and encouraging them to take action at specific times. In service marketing, much communication is educational in nature, especially for new customers. Companies may need to teach these customers about the benefits of the service, where and when to obtain it, and how to participate effectively in service processes. Communications can be delivered by individuals, such as salespeople and trainers, or through such media as TV, radio, newspapers, magazines, billboards, brochures, and Web sites.

Physical Evidence The appearance of buildings, landscaping, vehicles, interior furnishing, equipment, staff members, signs, printed materials, and other visible cues all provide tangible evidence of a firm's service style and quality. Service firms need to manage physical evidence carefully because it can have a profound impact on customers' impressions. In services with few tangible elements, such as insurance, advertising is often employed to create meaningful symbols. For instance, an umbrella may symbolize protection, and a fortress, security.

physical evidence: visual or other tangible clues that provide evidence of service quality.

Price and Other User Outlays This component addresses management of the *outlays* incurred by customers in obtaining benefits from the service product. Responsibilities are not limited to the traditional pricing tasks of establishing the selling *price* to customers, which typically include setting trade margins and establishing credit terms. Service managers also recognize and, where practical, seek to minimize other costs and burdens that customers may bear in purchasing and using a service, including additional financial expenditures, time, mental and physical effort, and negative sensory experiences.

price and other user outlays: expenditures of money, time, and effort that customers incur in purchasing and consuming services.

Linking Service Marketing, Operations, and Human Resources

As shown by the component elements of the 8Ps model, marketing cannot operate in isolation from other functional areas in a successful service organization. Operations specialists, who usually have responsibility for productivity improvements and quality control, manage the processes required to create and deliver the service product. Similarly, employees are recruited and trained by human resource managers. Even those who have customer-contact responsibilities often report to operations managers.

In future chapters, we will be raising the question of how marketers should relate to and involve their colleagues from other functional areas—especially operations and human resources—in planning and implementing marketing strategies. Firms whose managers succeed in developing integrated strategies will have a better chance of surviving and prospering. Those that fail to grasp these implications, by contrast, are likely to be outmaneuvered by competitors that are more adept at responding to the dramatic changes affecting the service economy.

You can expect to see the 8Ps framework used throughout this book. Although any given chapter is likely to emphasize just one (or a few) of the eight components, you should always keep in mind the importance of integrating the component(s) under discussion with each of the others when formulating an overall strategy. For a quick clue about the principal focus of each chapter, find the boat diagram on the opening page of the chapter. You'll see that each oar represents one of the 8Ps. Note which of the eight oars are highlighted for the chapter you are studying. Oars highlighted in dark blue indicate those components that will be covered extensively in a particular chapter, while a medium blue highlight identifies one that receives relatively brief coverage. If an oar remains white, it signals that this component is not featured in the chapter.

THE EVOLVING ENVIRONMENT OF SERVICES

We've already noted that the service sector is in an almost constant state of change. What are the forces that drive its growth, shape its composition, and determine the basis for competition? As shown in Figure 1.6, numerous factors are at work. They can be divided into five broad groups: government policies, social changes, business trends, advances in information technology, and internationalization and globalization.

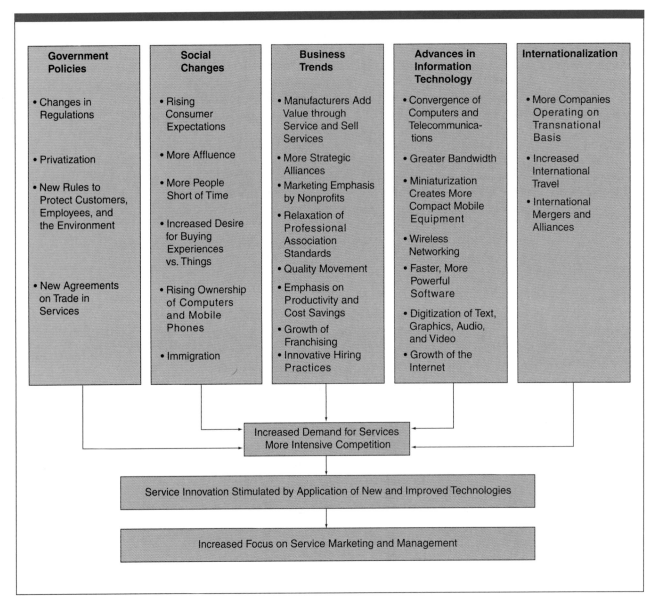

Government Policies	Social Changes	Business Trends	Advances in Information Technology	Internationalization
• Changes in Regulations	• Rising Consumer Expectations	• Manufacturers Add Value through Service and Sell Services	• Convergence of Computers and Telecommunications	• More Companies Operating on Transnational Basis
• Privatization	• More Affluence	• More Strategic Alliances	• Greater Bandwidth	• Increased International Travel
• New Rules to Protect Customers, Employees, and the Environment	• More People Short of Time	• Marketing Emphasis by Nonprofits	• Miniaturization Creates More Compact Mobile Equipment	• International Mergers and Alliances
	• Increased Desire for Buying Experiences vs. Things	• Relaxation of Professional Association Standards	• Wireless Networking	
• New Agreements on Trade in Services	• Rising Ownership of Computers and Mobile Phones	• Quality Movement	• Faster, More Powerful Software	
		• Emphasis on Productivity and Cost Savings	• Digitization of Text, Graphics, Audio, and Video	
	• Immigration	• Growth of Franchising	• Growth of the Internet	
		• Innovative Hiring Practices		

Increased Demand for Services More Intensive Competition

Service Innovation Stimulated by Application of New and Improved Technologies

Increased Focus on Service Marketing and Management

FIGURE 1.6

Factors Stimulating the Transformation of the Service Economy

Government Policies

Actions by governmental agencies at regional, national, and international levels continue to shape the structure of the service economy and the terms under which competition takes place. Traditionally, many service industries were highly regulated. Government agencies mandated price levels, placed geographic constraints on distribution strategies, and, in some instances, even defined the product attributes. Since the late 1970s, there has been a trend in the United States and Europe toward complete or partial deregulation in several major service industries. In Latin America, democratization and new political initiatives are creating economies that are much less regulated than in the past. Reduced government regulation has already eliminated or minimized many constraints on competitive activity in such industries as airfreight, airlines, railroads, trucking, banking, securities, insurance, and telecommunications. Barriers that had prevented new firms from entering the industry have been dropped in many instances: Geographic restrictions on service delivery have been reduced, there is more freedom to compete on price, and existing firms have been able to expand into new markets or new lines of business.

However, reduced regulation is a mixed blessing. Fears have been expressed that if successful firms become too large, through a combination of internal growth and acquisitions, there may eventually be a decline in the level of competition. Conversely, lifting restrictions on pricing benefits customers in the short run as competition lowers prices but leaves insufficient profits for needed future investments. For instance, fierce price competition among American domestic airlines led to huge financial losses within the industry during the early 1990s, bankrupting several airlines. This made it difficult for unprofitable carriers to invest in new aircraft and raised troublesome questions about service quality and safety.[15] Profitable foreign airlines, such as British Airways and Singapore Airlines, gained market share by offering better service on international routes instead of engaging in damaging price wars.

Another important action taken by many national governments has been privatization of what were once government-owned services. The term "privatization," first widely used in the United Kingdom, describes the policy of transforming government organizations into investor-owned companies. Privatization has been moving ahead rapidly in many European countries, as well as in Canada, Australia, New Zealand, and more recently in some Asian and Latin American nations. The transformation of operations like national airlines, telecommunication services, and utilities into private enterprise services has led to restructuring, cost cutting, and a more market-focused posture.

When privatization is combined with a relaxing of regulatory barriers to allow entry of new competitors, the marketing implications can be dramatic, with foreign competitors moving into markets that were previously closed to outside investment. Thus, French companies specializing in water treatment have purchased and modernized many of the privatized water utilities in Britain, while American companies have invested in a number of British regional electrical utilities. In turn, British Telecommunications has responded vigorously to new competition at home and made numerous investments around the world, including a strategic alliance with AT&T for delivery of global services to international companies.

Privatization can also apply to regional or local government departments. At the local level, for instance, services such as trash removal and recycling have been shifted from the public sector to private firms. Not everyone is convinced that such changes are beneficial to all segments of the population. When services are provided by public agencies, there are often cross subsidies, designed to achieve broader social goals. With privatization, there are fears that the search for efficiency and profits will lead to cuts in service and price increases. The result may be to deny less affluent segments the services they need at prices they can afford. Such fears fuel the arguments for continued regulation of prices and terms of service in key industries such as health care, telecommunications, water, electricity, and passenger rail transportation.

Not all regulatory changes represent a relaxation of government rules. In many countries, steps continue to be taken to strengthen consumer protection laws, safeguard employees, improve health and safety, and protect the environment. These new rules often require service firms to change their marketing strategies, their operational procedures, and their human resource policies.

Finally, national governments control trade in both goods and services. Negotiations at the World Trade Organization have led to a loosening of restrictions on trade in some services, but not all. Some countries are choosing to enter into free-trade agreements with their neighbors. Examples include the North American Free Trade Agreement (NAFTA) concluded between Canada, Mexico, and the United States;

Mercosur and Pacto Andino in South America; and, of course, the European Union, whose membership may soon be expanded beyond the current 15 countries.

Social Changes

The demand for consumer services—and the ways in which people use them—have been strongly influenced by a host of social changes. More people are living alone than before and there are more households containing two working adults (including telecommuters who work from in-home offices); as a result, more people find themselves short on time. They may be obliged to hire firms or individuals to perform tasks like childcare, housecleaning, laundry, and food preparation that were traditionally performed by a household member. Per capita income has risen significantly in real terms for many segments of the population (although not all have benefited from this trend). Increasing affluence gives people more disposable income and there has been an observed trend from purchasing new physical possessions to buying services and experiences. In fact, some pundits have begun speaking of the "experience economy."[16]

A combination of changing lifestyles, higher incomes, and declining prices for many high-technology products has meant that more and more people are buying computers, thus enabling them to use the Internet to send and receive e-mail and access Web sites from around the world. In the meantime, the rapid growth in the use of mobile phones and other wireless equipment means that customers are more "connected" than ever before and no longer out of touch once they leave their homes or offices.

Another important social trend has been increased immigration into countries such as the United States, Canada, and Australia. These countries are becoming much more multicultural, posing opportunities—and even requirements—for service features designed to meet the needs of non-traditional segments now living within the domestic market. For instance, many immigrants, even if they have learned to speak the language of their new country, prefer to do business in their native tongues and appreciate those service organizations that accommodate this preference by offering communications in multiple languages.

Business Trends

Over the past 25 years, significant changes have taken place in how business firms operate. For instance, service profit centers within manufacturing firms are transforming many well-known companies in fields such as computers, motor vehicles, and electrical and mechanical equipment. Supplementary services once designed to help sell equipment—including consultation, credit, transportation and delivery, installation, training, and maintenance—are now offered as profit-seeking services in their own right, even to customers who have chosen to purchase competing equipment. Several large manufacturers (including General Electric, Ford, and DaimlerChrysler) have become important players in the global financial services industry as a result of developing credit financing and leasing divisions. Similarly, many manufacturers now base much of their competitive appeal on the capabilities of their worldwide consultation, maintenance, repair, and problem-solving services. In fact, service profit centers contribute a substantial proportion of the revenues earned by such well-known "manufacturers" as IBM, Hewlett-Packard, and Xerox.

The financial pressures confronting public and nonprofit organizations have forced them to develop more efficient operations and to pay more attention to customer needs and competitive activities. In their search for new sources of income, many "non-business" organizations are developing a stronger marketing orientation that often involves rethinking their product lines; adding profit-seeking services such as shops, retail catalogs, restaurants, and consultancy; becoming more selective about the market segments they target; and adopting more realistic pricing policies.[17]

Government or legal pressures have forced many professional associations to remove or relax long-standing bans on advertising and promotional activities. Among the types of professionals affected by such rulings are accountants, architects, doctors, lawyers, and optometrists, whose practices now engage in much more vigorous competitive activity. The freedom to engage in advertising, promotion, and overt selling activities is essential in bringing innovative services, price cuts, and new delivery systems to the attention of prospective customers. However, some critics worry that advertising by lawyers, especially in the United States, simply encourages people to file more and more lawsuits, many of them frivolous.

With increasing competition, often price-based, has come greater pressure for firms to improve productivity. Demands by investors for better returns on their investments have also fueled the search for new ways to increase profits by reducing the costs of service delivery. Historically, the service sector has lagged behind the manufacturing sector in productivity improvement, but there are encouraging signs that some services are beginning to catch up. Using technology to replace labor (or to permit customer self-service) is one cost-cutting route that has been followed in many service industries. Reengineering of processes often results in speeding up operations by cutting out unnecessary steps. However, managers need to be aware that cost-cutting measures, driven by finance and operations personnel without regard for customer needs, may lead to a perceived deterioration in quality and convenience.

Recognizing that improving quality was good for business and necessary for effective competition has led to a radical change in thinking. Traditional definitions of quality (based on conformance to standards defined by operations managers) were replaced by the new imperative of letting quality be customer driven. This had enormous implications for the importance of service marketing and the role of customer research in both the service and manufacturing sectors.[18] Numerous firms have invested in research to determine what their customers want in every dimension of service, in quality improvement programs designed to deliver what customers want, and in ongoing measurement of how satisfied their customers are with the quality of service received. However, maintaining quality levels over time is difficult and customer dissatisfaction has risen in recent years.[19]

Franchising has become widespread in many service industries, not only for consumer services but also for business-to-business services. It involves the licensing of independent entrepreneurs to produce and sell a branded service according to tightly specified procedures. Because these entrepreneurs must invest their own capital, franchising has become a popular way to finance the expansion of multi-site service chains that deliver a consistent service concept. Large franchise chains are replacing (or absorbing) a wide array of small, independent service businesses in fields as diverse as bookkeeping, car hire, dry-cleaning, haircutting, photocopying, plumbing, quick service restaurants, and real estate brokerage services. Among the requirements for success are creation of mass media advertising campaigns to promote brand names nationwide (and even worldwide), standardization of service operations, formalized training programs, an ongoing search for new products, continued emphasis on improving efficiency, and dual marketing programs directed at both customers and franchisees.

Finally, changes have occurred in service firms' hiring practices. Traditionally, many service industries were very inbred. Managers tended to spend their entire careers working within a single industry, even within a single organization. Each industry was seen as unique and outsiders were suspect. Relatively few managers possessed graduate degrees in business although they might have held an industry-specific diploma in a field such as hotel management or health care administration. In recent years, however, competition and enlightened self-interest have led companies to recruit more highly educated managers who are willing to question traditional ways of doing business and able to bring new ideas from previous work experience in another industry. Some of the best service companies are known for being very selective in hiring employees, seeking individuals who will share the firm's strong service quality culture and be able to relate to customers well. Within many firms, intensive-training programs are now exposing employees, at all levels, to new tools and concepts.

Advances in Information Technology

New and improved technologies are radically altering the ways in which many service organizations do business with their customers, as well as altering what goes on behind the scenes. Many types of technology have important implications for service, including biotechnology, power and energy technology, methods technology (how people work and how processes are organized), materials technology, physical design technology, and information technology. In some cases, technology enables service firms to substitute automation for service personnel. But in other instances, as suggested in recent advertising for Singapore Airlines (Figure 1.7), traditional personal service and new technology may go hand in hand to create an enhanced experience for customers.

Perhaps the most powerful force for change in service businesses comes from information technology, reflecting the integration of computers and telecommunications. Digitization allows text, graphics, video, and audio to be manipulated, stored, and transmitted in the digital language of computers. Faster and more powerful software enables firms to create relational databases that combine information about customers with details of all their transactions and then to "mine" these databases for insights into new trends, new approaches to segmentation, and new marketing opportunities. Greater bandwidth, made possible by innovations such as fiber-optic cables, allows fast transmission of vast amounts of information so that customer-contact personnel can interact almost instantly with a central database, no matter where they are located. The creation of wireless networks and the miniaturization of electronic equipment—from cell

FIGURE 1.7

Singapore Airlines Promotes Both Its People and Its High-Tech Entertainment Technology

phones to laptops and scanners—allow sales and customer service personnel to keep in touch while on the move. Companies operating information-based services, such as financial service firms, have seen the nature and scope of their businesses totally transformed by the advent of global electronic delivery systems.

In recent years, the development of the Internet and its best-known component, the World Wide Web, have provided not only an important new medium of communication between service organizations and their customers, but also the potential for creating radically new business models for delivery of services. Properly designed and configured, such Internet-based services offer unprecedented speed and reach. For instance, by taking advantage of the Internet, Amazon.com became a global operation in just a few short years, marketing its huge array of books, music, and other items through its Web site and using modern business logistics to ship purchases quickly to customers all over the world.

However, for many "dot.com" companies, including Amazon, profitability has proved elusive and numerous start-up firms have failed. In some cases, the problem lies in development of inappropriate e-commerce business models that failed to generate sufficient revenues to cover expenses.[20] Greater competition than anticipated, failure to understand customer needs and expectations, poor execution, technology failures, insufficient working capital, and higher operating costs than predicted have all contributed to such failures. Underlying such failures is often a lack of understanding of some of the key principles of service marketing and management.

Technological change affects many other types of services, too, from airfreight to hotels to retail stores. Express package firms such as TNT, DHL, FedEx, and UPS recognize that the ability to provide real-time information about customers' packages has become as important to success as the physical movement of those packages. Technology does more than enable creation of new or improved services. It may also facilitate reengineering of such activities as delivery of information, order-taking and payment; enhance a firm's ability to maintain more consistent service standards; permit creation of centralized customer service departments; allow replacement of personnel by machines for repetitive tasks; and lead to greater involvement of customers in operations through self-service technology. All in all, technology is an important theme running through this book. It's covered in detail in Chapter 16.

Internationalization and Globalization

The internationalization of service companies is readily apparent to any tourist or business executive traveling abroad. More and more services are being delivered through national or global chains. Brand names such as Air Canada, Burger King, Body Shop, Hertz, Kinko's, and Mandarin Hotels have spread far from their original national roots. In some instances, such chains are entirely company owned. In other instances, the creator of the original concept has entered into partnership with outside investors. Airlines and airfreight companies that were formerly just domestic in scope now have extensive foreign route networks. Numerous financial service firms, advertising agencies, hotel chains, fast-food restaurants, car rental agencies, and accounting firms now operate on several continents. Some of this growth has been internally generated, but much has also come about through acquisitions of other companies.

A strategy of international expansion may be driven by a search for new markets or by the need to respond to existing customers who are traveling abroad in increasing numbers. A similar situation prevails in business-to-business services. When companies set up operations in other countries, they often prefer to deal with a few international suppliers rather than numerous local firms.

The net effect of such developments is to increase competition and to encourage the transfer of innovation in both products and processes from country to country. Developing a strategy for competing effectively across different countries is becoming a major marketing priority for many service firms. Franchising offers a way to enable a service concept developed in one nation to be delivered around the world through distribution systems owned by local investors. For example, FedEx and UPS have expanded into numerous countries by purchasing local courier firms.

Many well-known service companies around the world are American-owned; examples include Citicorp, McDonald's, and Accenture (Andersen Consulting). The upscale Four Seasons hotel chain is Canadian. North Americans are often surprised to learn that Dunkin' Donuts and Holiday Inn are both owned by British companies, while France's Groupe Accor owns Motel 6 and Red Roof Inns and the Hoyts chain of movie theaters is Australian owned. An alternative to mergers and takeovers is strategic alliances, where several firms working in the same or complementary industries in different countries join forces to expand their geographic reach and product scope. The airline and telecommunication industries are good examples.

Managing in a Continually Changing Environment

It has been said that the only person in the world who really appreciates a change is a wet baby. However, the willingness and ability of managers in service firms to respond to the dramatic changes affecting the service economy will determine whether their own organizations survive and prosper or are defeated by more agile and adaptive competitors. On the positive side, these changes are likely to increase the demand for many services, and the opening of the service economy means that there will be greater competition for that demand. In turn, more competition will stimulate innovation, notably through the application of new and improved technologies. Both singly and in combination, these developments will require managers of service organizations to focus more sharply on marketing strategy.

A STRUCTURE FOR MAKING SERVICE MANAGEMENT DECISIONS

As mentioned previously, this text has a strategic focus. The 8Ps of integrated service strategy are tools that service managers can use to develop effective strategies for marketing and managing many different types of services. The service decision framework reproduced in Figure 1.8 (and described in more depth in the introduction to Part I) outlines some of the key questions managers need to ask. Figure 1.8 also indicates which of the 8Ps are particularly relevant in each instance. Your challenge is to learn to ask the right questions and to learn to use the resulting answers to develop a viable strategy, employing different elements of the 8Ps as appropriate.

The framework begins with a question that lies at the heart of marketing and business strategy in general: ***What business are we in?*** Determining the nature of the business goes beyond just specifying the industry with which a specific service is usually associated. Astute managers recognize that competition may come from outside that industry as well as within it. Hence they ask: With what other goods and services do we compete?" The answers may show that there are several different ways for customers to satisfy their needs. The need for forward thinking in decision making requires that managers also ask themselves, "What forces for change do we face?" But perhaps the most valuable insights come from determining what *solutions* a service offers to customers. Only when service marketers understand what problems customers are trying to solve through use of their products can we truly say that they know what business they are in.

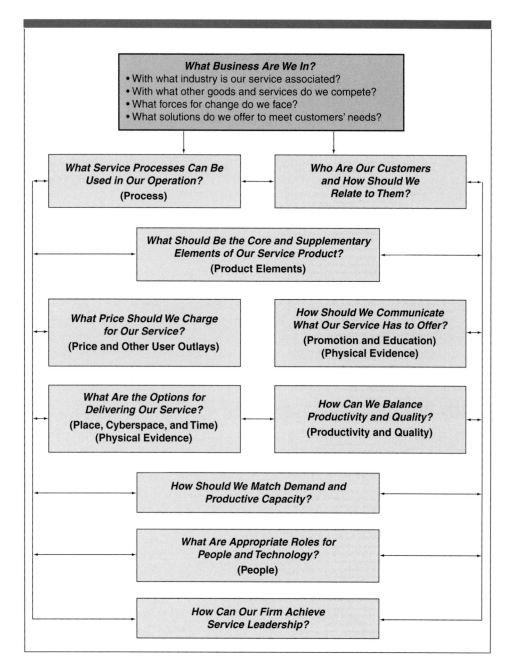

The question, ***Who are our customers and how should we relate to them?*** is also central to the study and practice of marketing. Recognizing that most readers of this book already have some familiarity with marketing, we try to build on this prior understanding rather than repeating the basics of introductory marketing theory and practice. Hence we leave detailed discussion of customers to Part II of the book and focus there on what is distinctive about service consumption.

One of the keys to strategy formulation in services, not normally addressed in goods marketing, is the question: ***What service processes can be used in our operation?*** As we show in this text, the importance of this question goes beyond operational issues. Marketers must understand how the processes used to create and deliver service affect their customers, influence the nature of the service product, and shape the options for delivering this service. Human resource managers must understand how the choice of processes influences skill requirements and job descriptions for employees, including the nature of their interactions with customers. We examine the issue of service processes in depth in Chapter 2.

Conclusion

Why study services? Modern economies are driven by service businesses, both large and small. Services are responsible for the creation of a substantial majority of new jobs, both skilled and unskilled, around the world. The service sector includes a tremendous variety of different industries, including many activities provided by public and nonprofit organizations. It accounts for over half the economy in most developing countries and for over 70 percent in many highly developed economies.

As we've shown in this chapter, services differ from manufacturing organizations in many important respects and require a distinctive approach to marketing and other management functions. As a result, managers who want their enterprises to succeed cannot continue to rely solely on tools and concepts developed in the manufacturing sector. In the remainder of this book, we'll discuss in more detail the unique challenges and opportunities faced by service businesses. It's our hope that you'll use the material from this text to enhance your future experiences not only as a service employee or manager, but also as a customer of many different types of service businesses!

Study Questions and Exercises

1. Business schools have traditionally placed more emphasis on manufacturing industries than on service industries in their courses. Why do you think this is so? Does it matter?

2. Why is time so important in services?

3. What are the implications of increased competition in service industries that have been deregulated?

4. Give examples of how computer and telecommunications technologies have changed services that you use in your professional or personal life.

5. Choose a service company you are familiar with and show how each of the eight elements (8Ps) of integrated service management applies to the company.

6. Is the risk of unethical business practices greater or lesser in service businesses than in manufacturing firms? Explain your answer.

7. Why do marketing, operations, and human resources have to be more closely linked in services than in manufacturing? Give examples.

8. Answer the four questions associated with "What business are we in?" from Figure 1.8 for Southwest Airlines, Charles Schwab, Aggreko, Intrawest, and eBay.

Endnotes

1. The gross domestic product (GDP) and gross national product (GNP) are both widely used measures of a nation's economic activity. They differ in their treatment of international transactions. For the United States, there is little difference between the two measures, since only a tiny percentage of Americans work abroad and the foreign earnings

of U.S. firms are broadly equal to the U.S. earnings of foreign firms. However, differences between GDP and GNP are substantial for countries where many nationals work abroad (e.g., Pakistan) or where foreign investment in the country greatly exceeds investment abroad by domestic firms (e.g., Canada).

2. James C. Cooper and Kathleen Madigan, "Fragile Markets Are Tying the Fed's Hands," *Business Week*, 4 November 1997, 33.

3. World Bank, *El Mundo del Trabajo en una Economia Integrada* (Washington D.C., 1995).

4. Javier Reynoso, "Progress and Prospects of Services Management in Latin America," *International Journal of Service Industry Management,* 10, no. 5 (1999), 401–408.

5. See, for example, the discussion of outsourcing information-based services in James Brian Quinn, *Intelligent Enterprise* (New York: The Free Press, 1992), chap. 3, 71–97.

6. Leonard L. Berry, "Services Marketing Is Different," *Business*, May-June 1980.

7. W. Earl Sasser, R. Paul Olsen, and D. Daryl Wyckoff, *Management of Service Operations: Text, Cases, and Readings* (Boston: Allyn & Bacon, 1978).

8. G. Lynn Shostack, "Breaking Free from Product Marketing," *Journal of Marketing* 41, no. 2 (April 1977).

9. Gary Knisely, "Greater Marketing Emphasis by Holiday Inns Breaks Mold," *Advertising Age,* 15 January 1979.

10. Curtis P. McLaughlin, "Why Variation Reduction Is Not Everything: A New Paradigm for Service Operations," *International Journal of Service Industry Management* 7, no. 3 (1996), 17–31.

11. This section is based on Valarie A. Zeithaml, "How Consumer Evaluation Processes Differ Between Goods and Services," in J. A. Donnelly and W. R. George, *Marketing of Services* (Chicago: American Marketing Association, 1981), 186–190.

12. The 4Ps classification of marketing decision variables was created by E. Jerome McCarthy, *Basic Marketing: A Managerial Approach* (Homewood, IL: Richard D. Irwin, Inc., 1960).

13. Since the late 1970s, many theorists have tried to go beyond the 4Ps to capture the complexity of service marketing in memorable fashion, emphasizing singly or in combination, such factors as processes, personnel, and peripheral clues. Our 8Ps model of service management has been derived and expanded from a framework that encompassed seven elements: the original 4Ps, plus Participants, Physical evidence and Process; it was proposed by Bernard H. Booms and Mary J. Bitner, "Marketing Strategies and Organization Structures for Service Firms," in J. H. Donnelly and W. R. George, *Marketing of Services* (Chicago: American Marketing Association, 1981), 47–51. Subsequently, Booms created a cartoon diagram showing seven little "pea people," two of them carrying oars, lifting a peapod-shaped boat. This gave us the idea for the metaphor of a racing "eight," comprising eight rowers (the eighth being labeled "productivity and quality") plus a coxswain to control the boat's speed and direction.

14. For a review of the literature on this topic, see Michael D. Hartline and O. C. Ferrell, "The Management of Customer Contact Service Employees," *Journal of Marketing* 60, no. 4 (October 1996): 52–70.

15. Timothy K. Smith, "Why Air Travel Doesn't Work," *Fortune*, 3 April 1995, 42–56; and Bill Saporito, "Going Nowhere Fast," *Fortune*, 3 April 1995, 58–59.

16. B. Joseph Pine II and James H. Gilmore, *The Experience Economy* (Boston: Harvard Business School Press, 1999).

17. See Christopher H. Lovelock and Charles B. Weinberg, *Public and Nonprofit Marketing*, 2/e (Redwood City, CA: The Scientific Press/Boyd and Davis, 1989); and Philip Kotler and Alan Andreasen, *Strategic Marketing for Nonprofit Organizations*, 5/e (Upper Saddle River, NJ: Prentice-Hall, 1996).

18. See Valarie A. Zeithaml, A. Parasuraman, and Leonard L. Berry, *Delivering Quality Service* (New York: The Free Press, 1990); and Sandra Vandermerwe, "The Market Power Is in the Services Because the Value Is in the Results," *European Management Journal* 8, no. 4 (1990).

19. Diane Brady, "Why Service Stinks," *Business Week*, 23 October 2000, 118–128.

20. See Marcia Vickers, "Models from Mars," *Business Week*, 4 September 2000, 106–107; and Jerry Useem and Eryn Brown, "Dot-Coms: What Have We Learned?" *Fortune*, 30 October 2000, 82–104.

chapter two

Understanding Service Processes

Susan Munro, Service Consumer

Susan Munro, a final-year business student, had breakfast and then clicked onto the Internet to check the local weather forecast. It predicted rain, so she grabbed an umbrella before leaving the apartment and walking to the bus stop for her daily ride to the university. On the way, she dropped a letter in a mailbox. The bus arrived on schedule. It was the usual driver, who recognized her and gave a cheerful greeting as she showed her commuter pass. The bus was quite full, carrying a mix of students and office workers, so she had to stand.

Arriving at her destination, Susan left the bus and walked to the College of Business. Joining a throng of other students, she took a seat in the large classroom where her finance class was held. The professor lectured in a near monotone for 75 minutes, occasionally projecting charts on a large screen to illustrate certain calculations. Susan reflected that it would be just as effective—and far more convenient—if the course were transmitted over the Web or recorded on videotapes that students could watch at their leisure. She much preferred the marketing course that followed because this professor was a very dynamic individual who believed in having an active dialog with the students. Susan made several contributions to the discussion and felt that she learned a lot from listening to others' analyses and opinions.

She and three friends ate lunch at the recently modernized Student Union. The old cafeteria, a gloomy place that served boring food at high prices, had been replaced by a well-lit and colorfully decorated new food court, featuring a variety of small kiosks. These included both local suppliers and brand-name fast-food chains, which offered choices of sandwiches, as well as health foods and a variety of desserts. Although she

had wanted a sandwich, the line of waiting customers at the sandwich shop was rather long, so Susan joined her friends at Burger King and then splurged on a caffe latte from the adjacent Hav-a-Java coffee stand. The food court was unusually crowded today, perhaps because of the rain now pouring down outside. When they finally found a table, they had to clear off the dirty trays. "Lazy slobs!" commented her friend Mark, referring to the previous customers.

After lunch, Susan stopped at the cash machine, inserted her bank card, and withdrew some money. Remembering that she had a job interview at the end of the week, she telephoned her hairdresser and counted herself lucky to be able to make an appointment for later in the day because of a cancellation by another client. Leaving the Student Union, she ran across the rain-soaked plaza to the Language Department. In preparation for her next class, Business Spanish, she spent an hour in the language lab, watching an engaging videotape of customers making purchases at different types of stores, then repeating key phrases and listening to her own recorded voice. "My accent's definitely getting better!" she said to herself.

With Spanish phrases filling her head, Susan headed off to visit the hairdresser. She liked the store, which had a bright, trendy decor and well-groomed, friendly staff. Unfortunately, the cutter was running late and Susan had to wait 20 minutes, which she used to review a chapter for tomorrow's human resources course. Some of the other waiting customers were reading magazines provided by the store. Eventually, it was time for a shampoo, after which the cutter proposed a slightly different cut. Susan agreed, although she drew the line at the

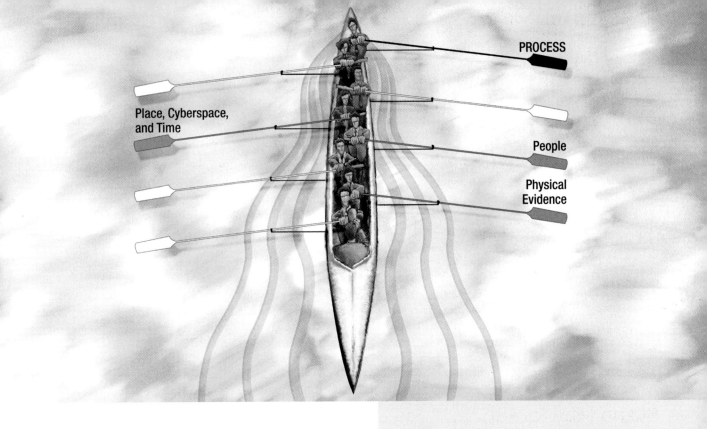

PROCESS

Place, Cyberspace, and Time

People

Physical Evidence

suggestion to lighten her hair color. She sat very still, watching the process in the mirror and turning her head when requested. She was pleased with the result and complimented the cutter on her work. Including the shampoo, the process had lasted about 40 minutes. She tipped the cutter and paid at the reception desk.

The rain had stopped and the sun was shining as Susan left the store, so she walked home, stopping on the way to pick up clothes from the cleaners. This store was rather gloomy, smelled of cleaning solvents, and badly needed repainting. She was annoyed to find that although her silk blouse was ready as promised, the suit she would need for her interview was not. The assistant, who had dirty fingernails, mumbled an apology in an insincere tone without making eye contact. Although the store was convenient and the quality of work quite good, Susan considered the employees unfriendly and not very helpful.

Back at her apartment building, she opened the mailbox in the lobby. Her mail included a bill from her insurance company, which required no action since payment was deducted automatically from her bank account. There was also a postcard from her optometrist, reminding her to schedule a new eye exam. Susan made a mental note to call for an appointment, anticipating that she might need a revised prescription for her contact lenses. She was about to discard the junk mail when she noticed a flyer promoting a new dry-cleaning store and including a coupon for a discount. She decided to try the new firm and pocketed the coupon.

Since it was her turn to cook dinner, she looked in the kitchen to see what food was available. Susan sighed—there wasn't much. Maybe she would make a salad and call for delivery of a large pizza.

⇒ Learning Objectives

After reading this chapter, you should be able to

⇒ appreciate the value of classification in services marketing

⇒ understand useful ways of classifying differences between various types of services

⇒ define a service process

⇒ describe four different types of service processes and their strategic implications

⇒ recognize that the nature of a customer's contact with a service varies according to the underlying process

HOW DO SERVICES DIFFER FROM ONE ANOTHER?

The service sector is amazingly varied, and the variety of transactions made by Susan Munro represents only a small sample of all the services directed at individual consumers. As a review of the listings in the Yellow Pages will show, there are also many business services directed at corporate purchasers. It's surprising how many managers in service businesses consider their industries to be unique—or at least distinctively different. Certainly, there are distinctions to be drawn, but it would be a mistake to assume that any one service used by Susan has nothing in common with any of the others she might use.

In Chapter 1, we looked at some of the ways in which services might differ from goods. In this chapter, our focus is on developing useful ways of grouping services into categories that share managerially relevant characteristics, especially as they relate to marketing strategy. In particular, we examine the nature of the *processes*—a key element among the 8Ps—by which services are created and delivered. We find that important insights can be gained by looking for similarities between "different" service industries. The more service managers can identify meaningful parallels to their own firms' situations, the better their chances of beating the competition by borrowing good ideas from other businesses. One hallmark of innovative service firms is that their managers have been willing to look outside their own industries for useful ideas that they can try in their own organizations. We start our search for useful categorization schemes by examining how goods have traditionally been classified.

The Value of Classification Schemes

Classification schemes are the primary means used by researchers to organize items into different classes or groups for the purpose of systematic investigation and theory development.[1] They are as useful in management research as in pure science. Marketing practitioners have long recognized the value of developing distinctive strategies for different types of goods. One of the most famous classification schemes divides goods into convenience, shopping, and specialty categories, according to how frequently consumers buy them and how much effort they are prepared to put into comparing alternatives and locating the right product to match their needs.[2] This scheme helps managers obtain a better understanding of consumer expectations and behavior and provides insights into the management of retail distribution systems. This same classification can also be applied to retail service institutions, from financial service providers to hair salons.

Another major classification is between durable and nondurable goods. Durability is closely associated with purchase frequency, which has important implications for the development of both distribution and communications strategies. Although service performances are intangible, the durability of benefits is relevant to repurchase frequency. For example, you probably purchase a haircut less often than you buy a caffe latte (at least if you are a typical student or a coffee connoisseur).

Yet another classification is consumer goods (those purchased for personal or household use) versus industrial goods (those purchased by companies and other organizations). This classification relates not only to the types of goods purchased—although there is some overlap—but also to methods for evaluating competing alternatives, purchasing procedures, size of purchase orders, and actual usage. Once again, this classification is transferable to services. For example, you may be the only one involved in a decision about whether to purchase America Online (AOL) or another Internet provider for your own computer, but a corporate decision about what online services to select for employees may involve managers and technical specialists from several departments. Business-to-business services, as the name suggests, include a large group of services targeted at corporate customers and may range from executive recruiting to security and from payroll management to sandblasting.

Although these goods-based classification schemes are helpful, they don't go far enough in highlighting the key strategic issues. We need to classify services into marketing-relevant groups, looking for points of similarity among different service industries. We can use the insights from these classifications to focus on marketing strategies that are relevant to specific service situations.

Core Products versus Supplementary Services

Many service products consist of a "bundle" that includes a variety of service elements and even some physical goods. It's important to distinguish between the *core product* that the customer buys and the set of *supplementary services* that often accompany that product. For instance, the core product of the lodging industry is a bed for the night, whether that bed is located in a youth hostel dorm or in a luxury room at a five-star hotel. Youth hostels don't offer many additional services beyond reservations, basic meals, and simple washing facilities. By contrast, as shown in Figure 2.1, a luxury hotel will offer many additional services to enhance its guests' visits. Some of these services will be offered free and others will carry a charge, but they are all secondary to the core service of overnight sleeping accommodation that defines the lodging industry.

When we speak of services in this chapter, we are referring to the core service that the customer is buying—such as taking an airline flight, attending a concert, hiring an accounting firm to prepare an audit of a company's accounts, or purchasing a homeowner's insurance policy. A cluster of supplementary services that are intended to add value to the core also accompanies most services. Examples include meals and baggage

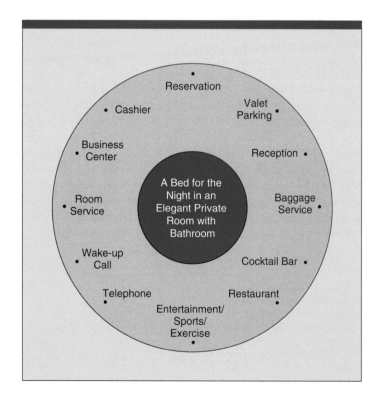

FIGURE 2.1

Core Product and Supplementary Services for a Luxury Hotel

service on an airline flight, refreshments at a concert, professional advice from an experienced auditor, or a helpful booklet from an insurance company with suggestions on how to protect your home.

How Might Services Be Classified?

The traditional way of grouping services is by industry. Service managers may say, "We're in the transportation business" (or hospitality, banking, telecommunications, or repair and maintenance). These groupings help us define the core products offered by the firm and understand both customer needs and competition. However, they may not capture the true nature of each business because service delivery can differ widely even within a single category (i.e., food can be provided to customers in settings that range from airport Taco Bells to four-star restaurants).

Various proposals have been made for classifying services.[3] Among the meaningful ways in which services can be grouped or classified are those listed in Table 2.1.

tangible: capable of being touched, held, or preserved in physical form over time.

intangibility: a distinctive characteristic of services that makes it impossible to touch or hold on to them in the same manner as physical goods.

Degree of Tangibility or Intangibility of Service Processes   Does the service do something physical and **tangible** (like food services or dry cleaning), or do its processes involve a greater amount of **intangibility** (like teaching or telephoning)? Different levels of intangibility in service processes shape the nature of the service delivery system and also affect the role of employees and the experience of customers. Susan's burger was a very tangible outcome of Burger King's service process. But the effects of Susan's experiences in her finance and marketing classes are highly intangible and thus much more difficult to evaluate.

Direct Recipient of the Service Process   Some services, like haircutting or public transportation, are directed at customers themselves. Customers also seek services (like dry cleaning) to restore or improve objects that belong to them, but they remain uninvolved in the process of service delivery and do not consume the benefits until later. The nature of the service encounter between service suppliers and their customers varies widely according to the extent to which customers themselves are integrally involved in the service process. Contrast Susan's extended interactions with the haircutter and her brief encounter with the mailbox on her way to school.

Place and Time of Service Delivery   When designing delivery systems, service marketers must ask themselves whether customers need to visit the service organization at its own sites (as Susan did with the university, the hair salon, and the cleaners) or whether service should come to the customer (like the Internet weather information service and the pizza delivery to her apartment). Or perhaps the interaction can occur through physical channels like mail (as with her insurance) or electronic channels (as with her ATM banking transaction). These managerial decisions involve consideration of the nature of the service itself, where customers are located (both home and workplace may be relevant), their preferences relating to time of purchase and use, the relative costs of different alternatives, and—in some instances—seasonal factors.

TABLE 2.1

Selected Ways of Classifying Services

- degree of tangibility or intangibility of service processes
- direct recipient of the service process
- place and time of service delivery
- customization versus standardization
- nature of the relationship with customers
- extent to which demand and supply are in balance
- extent to which facilities, equipment, and people are part of the service experience

Customization versus Standardization   Services can be classified according to the degree of **customization** or **standardization** involved in service delivery. An important marketing decision is whether all customers should receive the same service or whether service features (and the underlying processes) should be adapted to meet individual requirements. Susan's insurance policy is probably one of several standard options. The bus service is standardized, with a fixed route and schedule (unlike a taxi), but passengers can choose when to ride and where to get on and off. By encouraging student discussion and debate, Susan's marketing professor is offering a more customized course than her finance professor. Her haircut is customized (although other women may wear the same style), and although her future eye exam will follow standardized procedures, the optometrist's analysis of the results will result in a customized prescription for new contact lenses to correct her vision.

customization: tailoring service characteristics to meet each customer's specific needs and preferences.

standardization: reducing variation in service operations and delivery.

Nature of the Relationship with Customers   Some services involve a formal relationship, in which each customer is known to the organization and all transactions are individually recorded and attributed (like Susan's bank or optometrist). But in other services, unidentified customers undertake fleeting transactions and then disappear from the organization's sight (for instance, the phone company has no record of her call from the pay phone). Some services lend themselves naturally to a "membership" relationship, in which customers must apply to join the "club" and their subsequent performance is monitored over time (as in insurance or college enrollment). Other services, like buses, hair salons, dry cleaners, and restaurants, need to undertake proactive efforts to create an ongoing relationship. Although the bus company does not record Susan's rides, it could keep records of all monthly pass holders so that it can mail out passes every month, plus a newsletter describing service improvements or route and schedule changes. Sometimes companies create special club memberships or frequent user programs to reward loyal customers. For instance, both the hair salon and the dry cleaner could record customers' names and addresses and periodically make them special offers. Similarly, Internet sites can be designed to record visits from a specific user address.

To enjoy the services of a whitewater rafting company, you have to go to a suitable river at the right time of the year.

Extent to which Demand and Supply Are in Balance   Some service industries face steady demand for their services, whereas others encounter significant fluctuations. When the demand for service fluctuates widely over time, capacity must be adjusted to accommodate the level of demand or marketing strategies must be implemented to predict, manage, and smooth demand levels to bring them into balance with capacity. Some demand fluctuations are tied to events that marketers can't control. For example, more students eat lunch in the Student Union at Susan's university on a rainy day, resulting in a long line at the sandwich shop and a shortage of empty tables.

Extent to which Facilities, Equipment, and People Are Part of the Service Experience   Customers' service experiences are shaped, in part, by the extent to which they are exposed to tangible elements in the service delivery system. The bus that Susan rides is very tangible; so are her classrooms, the table and chairs in the food court, and the VCR in the language lab. In contrast, the physical evidence of her insurance company may be limited to occasional letters, and she may see little more of her bank than monthly statements and the ATM that she uses at the Student Union.

The cheerful bus driver humanizes Susan's bus ride. She appears to think better of her dynamic marketing professor than of her dull finance professor. She likes her trendy hair salon and the friendly cutter but not the smelly dry-cleaning store and its unfriendly employees, even though the quality of cleaning is good. When the cleaner fails to deliver her suit on time and, coincidentally, she receives a discount coupon in the mail from a competitor, she's ready to switch.

The service classification strategies we've just discussed can help managers address the following questions: What does our service operation actually do? What sorts of processes are involved in creating the core product that we offer to customers? And speaking of customers, where do they fit into our operation? The answers will differ, depending on the nature of the underlying service process required to create and deliver a particular service. So now we turn to the most fundamental of the 8Ps of integrated service management—the *processes* by which service products are created and delivered.

SERVICE AS A PROCESS

Marketers don't usually need to know the specifics of how physical goods are manufactured—that responsibility belongs to the people who run the factory. However, the situation is different in services. Because their customers are often involved in service production and may have preferences for certain methods of service delivery, marketers do need to understand the nature of the processes through which services are created and delivered. Furthermore, they should be involved in any decisions to change the nature of a given process if that change will affect customers.

A process is a particular method of operation or a series of actions, typically involving multiple steps that often need to take place in a defined sequence. Think about the steps that Susan went through at the hair salon: phoning in advance to make an appointment, arriving at the store, waiting, having a shampoo, discussing options with the cutter, having her hair cut and styled, tipping, paying, and finally leaving the store. Service processes range from relatively simple procedures involving only a few steps—such as filling a car's tank with fuel—to highly complex activities like transporting passengers on an international flight.

The characteristics of the processes that might be used in a particular service operation necessarily reflect the nature of the business. Within certain constraints, the choice

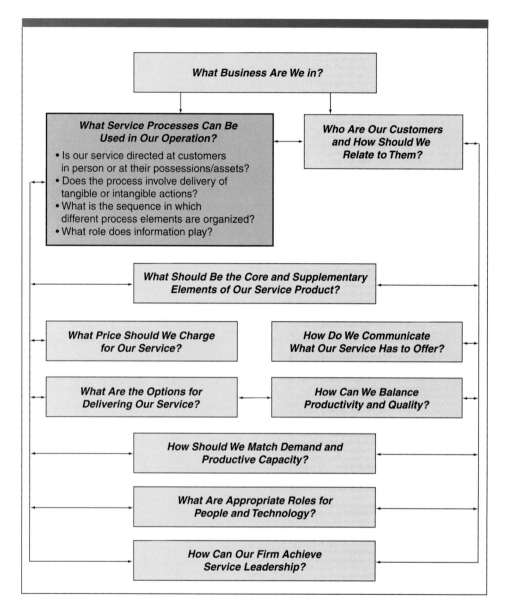

FIGURE 2.2

Service Decision Framework as It Relates to Processes

of processes may also be shaped by customer expectations and preferences. Looking at the processes *currently* used is only part of the story, since alternative processes may be available for exploration. As indicated by our service decision framework (Figure 2.2), it's important for marketers to understand: (1) whether the service is directed at customers themselves or at their possessions, (2) whether service entails delivery of tangible or intangible actions, (3) the sequence in which different elements of service delivery need to be organized, and (4) the role played by information.

The answers to be gained from such analysis can help managers to identify the service benefits offered by the service product, consider options for improving productivity and quality, clarify how customer involvement relates to design of service facilities, evaluate alternative channels for service delivery, and determine if there will be problems in balancing demand for the service against our organization's productive capacity. Finally, understanding these service processes helps managers to evaluate the strategic roles that might be played by people and technology.

Categorizing Service Processes

A process involves transforming input into output. But what is each service organization actually processing and how does it perform this task? Two broad categories are processed in services: people and objects. In many cases, ranging from passenger transportation to education, customers themselves are the principal input to the service process. In other instances, the key input is an object like a malfunctioning computer or a piece of financial data. In some services, as in all manufacturing, the process is physical and something tangible takes place. But in information-based services, the process can be almost entirely intangible.

By looking at services from a purely operational perspective, we see that they can be categorized into four broad groups. Table 2.2 shows a four-way classification scheme based on tangible actions either to people's bodies or to customers' physical possessions and intangible actions to people's minds or to their intangible assets.[4]

Each of these four categories involves fundamentally different forms of processes, with vital implications for marketing, operations, and human resource managers. We refer to the categories as people processing, possession processing, mental stimulus processing, and information processing. Although the industries within each category may appear at first sight to be very different, analysis will show that they do, in fact, share important process-related characteristics. As a result, managers in one industry may be able to obtain useful insights by studying another one and then creating valuable innovations for their own organization.

people processing: services that involve tangible actions to people's bodies.

1. **People processing** involves tangible actions to people's bodies. Examples of people-processing services include passenger transportation, haircutting, and dental work. Customers need to be physically present throughout service delivery to receive its desired benefits.

TABLE 2.2

Understanding the Nature of the Service Act

What Is the Nature of the Service Act?	Who or What Is the Direct Recipient of the Service?	
	People	Possessions
Tangible Actions	*(People Processing)* **Services directed at people's bodies:** Passenger transportation Health care Lodging Beauty salons Physical therapy Fitness centers Restaurants/bars Haircutting Funeral services	*(Possession Processing)* **Services directed at physical possessions:** Freight transportation Repair and maintenance Warehousing/storage Janitorial services Retail distribution Laundry and dry cleaning Refueling Landscaping/lawn care Disposal/recycling
Intangible Actions	*(Mental Stimulus Processing)* **Services directed at people's minds:** Advertising/PR Arts and entertainment Broadcasting/cable Management consulting Education Information services Music concerts Psychotherapy Religion Voice telephone	*(Information Processing)* **Services directed at intangible assets:** Accounting Banking Data processing Data transmission Insurance Legal services Programming Research Securities investment Software consulting

2. **Possession processing** includes tangible actions to goods and other physical possessions belonging to the customer. Examples of possession processing include airfreight, lawn mowing, and cleaning services. In these instances, the object requiring processing must be present, but the customer need not be.

3. **Mental stimulus processing** refers to intangible actions directed at people's minds. Services in this category include entertainment, spectator sports, theater performances, and education. In such instances, customers must be present mentally but can be located either in a specific service facility or in a remote location connected by broadcast signals or telecommunication linkages.

4. **Information processing** describes intangible actions directed at a customer's assets. Examples of information-processing services include insurance, banking, and consulting. In this category, little direct involvement with the customer may be needed once the request for service has been initiated.

Let's examine why these four different types of processes often have distinctive implications for marketing, operations, and human resource strategies.

possession processing: tangible actions to goods and other physical possessions belonging to customers.

mental stimulus processing: intangible actions directed at people's minds.

information processing: intangible actions directed at customers' assets.

People Processing

From ancient times, people have sought out services directed at themselves (e.g., being transported, fed, lodged, restored to health, or made more beautiful). To receive these types of services, customers must physically enter the service system. Because they are an integral part of the process, they cannot obtain the benefits they desire by dealing at arm's length with service suppliers. They must enter the **service factory**, which is a physical location where people or machines (or both) create and deliver service benefits to customers. Sometimes, of course, service providers are willing to come to customers, bringing the necessary tools of their trade to create the desired benefits in the customers' choice of locations.

If customers want the benefits that a people-processing service has to offer, they must be prepared to cooperate actively with the service operation. For example, Susan cooperates with her hair stylist by sitting still and turning her head as requested. She will also have to be part of the process when she visits the optometrist for her next eye exam. The level of involvement required of customers may entail anything from boarding a city bus for a five-minute ride to undergoing a lengthy course of unpleasant treatments at a hospital. In between these extremes are such activities as ordering and eating a meal; having one's hair washed, cut, and styled; and spending some nights in a hotel room. The output from these services (after a period of time that can vary from minutes to months) is a customer who has reached her destination or satisfied his hunger or is now sporting clean and stylishly cut hair or has had a good night's sleep away from home or is now in physically better health.

It's important for managers to think about process and output in terms of what happens to the customer (or the physical object being processed) because it helps them to identify what benefits are being created. Reflecting on the service process itself helps to identify some of the nonfinancial costs—such as time, mental and physical effort, and even fear and pain—that customers incur in obtaining these benefits.

service factory: the physical site where service operations take place.

Possession Processing

Often, customers ask a service organization to provide treatment for some physical possession—which could be anything from a house to a hedge, a car to a computer, or a dress to a dog. Many such activities are quasi-manufacturing operations and do not always involve simultaneous production and consumption. Examples include cleaning, maintaining, storing, improving, or repairing physical objects—both live and inanimate—that belong to the customer in order to extend their usefulness. Additional possession-processing services include transport and storage of goods; wholesale and retail distribution; and installation, removal, and disposal of equipment—in short, the entire value-adding chain of activities that may take place during the lifetime of the object in question.

Customers are less physically involved with this type of service than with people-processing services. Consider the difference between passenger and parcel transportation. In the former you have to go along for the ride to obtain the benefit of getting from one location to another. But with package service, you drop the package off at a mailbox or post office counter (or request a courier to collect it from your home or office) and wait for it to be delivered to the recipient. In most possession-processing services, the customer's involvement is usually limited to dropping off the item that needs treatment, requesting the service, explaining the problem, and later returning to pick up the item and pay the bill (like Susan's visit to the cleaners to pick up her blouse and suit). If the object to be processed is something that is difficult or impossible to move, like landscaping, installed software, heavy equipment, or part of a building, the service factory must come to the customer, with service personnel bringing the tools and materials necessary to complete the job on-site.

The service process could involve applying insecticide in a house to get rid of ants, trimming a hedge at an office park, repairing a car, installing software in a computer, cleaning a jacket, or giving an injection to the family dog. The output in each instance should be a satisfactory solution to the customer's problem or some tangible enhancement of the item in question. In Susan's case, the cleaners disappointed her because her suit wasn't ready when promised.

Mental Stimulus Processing

Services that interact with people's minds include education, news and information, professional advice, psychotherapy, entertainment, and certain religious activities. Anything touching people's minds has the power to shape attitudes and influence behavior. So, when customers are in a position of dependency or there is potential for manipulation, strong ethical standards and careful oversight are required.

Receiving these services requires an investment of time on the customer's part. However, recipients don't necessarily have to be physically present in a service factory—just mentally in communication with the information being presented. There's an interesting contrast here with people-processing services. Passengers can sleep through a flight and still arrive at their desired destination. But if Susan falls asleep in class or during an educational TV broadcast, she will not be any wiser at the end than at the beginning!

Services like entertainment and education are often created in one place and transmitted by television, radio, or the Internet to individual customers in distant locations. However, they can also be delivered to groups of customers at the originating location in a facility such as a theater or lecture hall. We need to recognize that watching a live concert on television in one's home is not the same experience as watching it in a concert hall in the company of hundreds or even thousands of other people. Managers of concert halls face many of the same challenges as their colleagues in people-processing services. Similarly, the experience of participating in a discussion-based class through interactive cable television lacks the intimacy of people debating one another in the same room.

Because the core content of all services in this category is information based (whether music, voice, or visual images), it can easily be converted to digital bits or analog signals; recorded for posterity; and transformed into a manufactured product, such as a compact disc, videotape, or audiocassette, which may then be packaged and marketed much like any other physical good. These services can thus be "inventoried" because they can be consumed at a later date than when they were produced. For instance, Susan's Spanish videotape can be used over and over again by students visiting the language lab.

Information Processing

Information processing, one of the buzzwords of our age, has been revolutionized by computers. But not all information is processed by machines. Professionals in a wide variety of fields also use their brains to perform information processing and packaging. Information is the most intangible form of service output, but it may be transformed into more enduring, tangible forms as letters, reports, books, tapes, or CDs. Among the services that are highly dependent on the effective collection and processing of information are financial services and professional services like accounting, law, marketing research, management consulting, and medical diagnosis.

The extent of customer involvement in both information and mental stimulus processing is often determined more by tradition and a personal desire to meet the supplier face to face than by the needs of the operational process. Strictly speaking, personal contact is quite unnecessary in industries like banking or insurance. Why subject your firm to all the complexities of managing a people-processing service when you could deliver the same core product at arm's length? As a customer, why go to the service factory when there's no compelling need to do so? Susan appears comfortable dealing at arm's length with both her bank and her insurance company, using a self-service ATM for her banking transactions and receiving mail communications from her insurance company.

Habit and tradition often lie at the root of existing service delivery systems and service usage patterns. Professionals and their clients may say they prefer to meet face to face because they feel that in this way they learn more about each other's needs, capabilities, and personalities. However, experience shows that successful personal relationships, built on trust, can be created and maintained purely through telephone or e-mail contact.

Customers don't need to be present while their cars are being serviced.

DIFFERENT PROCESSES POSE DISTINCTIVE MANAGEMENT CHALLENGES

The challenges and tasks facing managers who work in each of the four different service categories just described are likely to vary to some extent. The classification of processes displayed earlier is central in understanding these differences and developing effective service strategies. Not only does it offer insights into the nature of service benefits in each instance, but it also provides an understanding of the behavior that is required of customers. As suggested in Figure 2.2, there are also implications for designing the service delivery system, balancing demand and capacity, applying technology to service processes, and managing people as part of the service product.

Balancing Productivity and Quality Concerns

Managers need to recognize that operational processes, however important, are basically just a means to an end. The key is to understand the specific benefits that a service provides for its users. Many firms bundle together lots of different activities as part of their effort to provide good service. But innovation in service delivery requires constant attention to the processes underlying delivery of the core product—a bed for the night in the lodging industry, fast transportation of people in the airline industry, or cleaning and pressing clothes in the laundry industry.

New processes may allow service organizations to deliver the same (or improved) benefits to customers through distinctly different approaches. But firms need to be clear about their objectives and the implications for customers. Sometimes, adopting a new process improves productivity by cutting costs at the expense of service quality. In other instances, customers are delighted to encounter faster, simpler, and more convenient procedures. So, operations managers need to beware of imposing new processes, in the name of efficiency, on customers who prefer the existing approach (particularly when the new approach replaces personal service by employees with automated procedures that require customers to do much of the work themselves). By collaborating with marketing personnel, operations specialists will improve their chances of designing new processes that deliver the benefits desired by customers in user-friendly ways. Among other things, customers may need to be educated about the benefits of new procedures and how to use them.

How Customer Involvement Affects Design of the Service Factory

Every service has customers (or hopes to find some), but not every service interacts with them in the same way. Customer involvement in the core activity may vary sharply for each of the four categories of service process. Nothing can alter the fact that people-processing services require the customer to be physically present in the service factory. If you're currently in New York and want to be in London tomorrow, you simply can't avoid boarding an international flight and spending time in a jet high above the Atlantic. If you want your hair cut, you can't delegate this activity to somebody else's head—you have to sit in the haircutter's chair yourself. If you have the misfortune to break your leg, you will personally have to submit to the unpleasantness of having the bone X-rayed, reset by an orthopedic surgeon, and then encased in a protective cast for several weeks.

When customers visit a service factory, their satisfaction will be influenced by such factors as:

➤ encounters with service personnel,

➤ appearance and features of service facilities—both exterior and interior,

➤ interactions with self-service equipment, and

➤ characteristics and behavior of other customers.

If customers are required to be physically present throughout service delivery, the process must be designed around them from the moment they arrive at what we call the "service factory." The longer they remain at that site, the more likely they are to need other services, including hospitality basics like food, beverages, and toilets. Service delivery sites that customers visit must be located and designed with their convenience in mind. Furthermore, the nature of the facilities offers important physical evidence of the service itself. If the service factory is ugly, noisy, smelly, confusingly laid out, and in an inconvenient location, customers are likely to have negative impressions. Marketing managers need to work closely with their counterparts in operations to design facilities that are both pleasing to customers and efficient to operate. At Susan's college, the redesigned food court at the Student Union replaced a cafeteria that provided a less attractive experience (as well as worse food). The exterior of a building creates important first impressions, whereas the interior can be thought of as the "stage" on which the service performance is delivered. The interior of Susan's hair salon appeals to her but that of the dry cleaner does not.

Marketers need to work with human resource managers, too. Here the task is to ensure that those employees who are in contact with customers present an acceptable appearance and have both the personal and technical skills needed to perform well. The workers at the dry-cleaning store Susan uses appear to lack such skills. If service delivery requires customers to interact with employees, both parties may need some basic training or guidance on how to work together cooperatively to achieve the best results. If customers are expected to do some of the work themselves—as in self-service—facilities and equipment must be user-friendly.

Evaluating Alternative Channels for Service Delivery

Unlike the situation in people-processing services, managers responsible for possession processing, mental stimulus processing, and information processing need not oblige their customers to visit a service factory. Instead, they may be able to offer a choice of several alternative delivery channels: (1) letting customers come to a user-friendly factory, (2) limiting contact to a small retail office that is separate from the factory, (3) coming to the customer's home or office, and (4) conducting business at arm's length.

Let's consider the cleaning and pressing of clothes—a possession-processing service—as an example. One approach is to do your laundry at home. If you lack the necessary machines, you can pay to use a laundromat, which is essentially a self-service cleaning factory. If you prefer to leave the task of laundry and dry cleaning to professionals, as Susan chose to do with her best clothes, you can go to a retail store that serves as a drop-off location for dirty clothes and a pickup point for newly cleaned items. Sometimes, cleaning is conducted in a space behind the store; at other times, the clothing is transported to an industrial operation some distance away. Home pickup and delivery is available in some cities, but this service tends to be expensive because of the extra costs involved. Innovation in service delivery sometimes takes the form of changing the delivery location to offer customers greater convenience (see the box, "Entrepreneur Sells Mobile Oil Changes").

Both physical and electronic channels allow customers and suppliers to conduct service transactions at arm's length. For instance, instead of shopping at the mall, you can study a printed catalog and order by telephone for mail delivery; or you can shop on the Internet, entering your orders electronically after reviewing your choices at a Web site. Information-based items, like software, research reports, or real estate listings can be downloaded immediately to your own computer.

Entrepreneur Sells Mobile Oil Changes

His market is busy delivery fleets and people on the go

By MIKE KARATH
Staff Writer

HYANNIS—Andrew Todoroff discovered oil on Cape Cod.

For people who don't have time to take their car in for an oil change, Todoroff brings the auto shop to them.

About two years ago he opened Lube On Location, which services commercial fleets and personal autos across the Cape. It provides oil changes for $26.95; tire rotation for $21.15; wiper blades starting at $15 and air filter changes starting at $12, tax included.

In the next several months he will add a vacuum system to his van and offer complete interior cleanings for about $30.

Todoroff popped up from beneath a red Mazda recently after finishing an oil change in the parking lot of a Main Street Hyannis business. A drop of motor oil ran down his face as he wiped his hands.

"The woman who owns the car, her husband called and said she wasn't really taking care of it," Todoroff said. "I had been doing work on his truck, so he asked if I could do his wife's car while she was at work." He added, "People at the bank saw me doing her car, and I got more business from it."

Lube On Location specializes in fleets like courier companies. Todoroff services them early in the morning while the trucks are being loaded and in the late afternoon while they are being unloaded.

"He saves me a ton of money," said Edward Matz, fleet manager of Cape Allied Transit in West Yarmouth, a courier service. "Just in manpower alone he saves me a lot because I don't have to pay a guy to take the truck to a station, sit and wait for an oil change."

Matz said Todoroff is so "efficient and clean" with the company's 70 trucks that he hired him for the company's New Hampshire and Rhode Island terminals as well.

Todoroff is registered with the state Environmental Protection Agency to carry waste oil, which is burned at a Hyannis car dealership's waste oil furnace. He also has a general insurance policy that covers accidents or spills.

Todoroff, 27, a Poughkeepsie, N.Y., native is married and is the father of a one-year-old son and another on the way. In 1989 he moved to the Cape to be near his brother.

He had been working as a cook and a carpet cleaner when a friend suggested he start an auto maintenance business.

"I've always worked on my own cars," Todoroff said. "He got me thinking about it, and soon after that, I read about a guy in Entrepreneur magazine who manufactures equipment to do oil changes on location."

Todoroff sold his car to buy used equipment he saw in a trade magazine classified ad.

The business has about 600 clients, Todoroff said, but he would not disclose his yearly sales. He plans to hire his first employee in May as sales continue to climb.

Despite Todoroff's success, skeptics like John Paul, a spokesman for the American Automobile Association in Rockland, don't see on-location businesses as a hot new trend.

"I don't know if you're going to see it take off," Paul said. "The idea never really caught on in this part of the country because it is contingent on good weather. I'd also say that if it wasn't for places like Jiffy Lube, it would be a service whose time had come."

But Todoroff may have the edge over those businesses. Jiffy Lube in Hyannis charges $28 including tax for an individual oil change. That is $1.39 more than what Lube On Location charges.

"My target customer during the day is someone who doesn't want to waste a Saturday to get an oil change done," Todoroff said. "They have such busy work weeks that when the weekend comes, they'd rather go for a ride or spend their time doing something fun or interesting."

Service on the go

Lube On Location oil change includes:

Change oil and oil filter, lube all fittings; check and fill antifreeze, automatic transmission fluid, power steering fluid, brake fluid, windshield washer fluid; check battery, wipers, belts, radiator hoses, air pressure in tires, and headlights.
Price: $26.95 (including tax)

Jiffy Lube in Hyannis:

Change oil and oil filter, lube the chassis, check and top off all fluids except antifreeze, vacuum interior, check tires, and clean front and rear outside windows.
Price: $28.34 (including tax)

Source: Reprinted with permission from the *Cape Cod Times*, 28 March 1998, C-9.

Today's managers need to be creative, because information technology and modern package transportation services offer many opportunities to rethink the place and time of service delivery. Some manufacturers of small pieces of equipment allow customers to bypass retail dealers when a product needs repair. Instead, a courier will pick up the defective item, ship it to a repair site, and return it a few days later when it has been fixed. Electronic distribution channels offer even more convenience because transportation time can be eliminated. For instance, using telecommunication links, engineers in a central facility (which could even be on the other side of the world) may be able to diagnose problems in defective computers and software at distant customer locations and send signals to correct the defects. As we noted in Chapter 1, advances in telecommunications and in the design of user-friendly terminals have played an important role in creating new services and new delivery channels for existing services.

Rethinking service delivery procedures for all but people processing may allow a firm to get customers out of the factory and transform a high-contact service into a low-contact one. When the nature of the process makes it possible to deliver service at arm's length, the design and location of the factory can focus on purely operational priorities. For example, some industry observers predict that the traditional bank branch will eventually cease to exist and we will conduct most of our banking and credit union transactions through ATMs, telephones, or personal computers (PCs) and modems. The chances of success in such an endeavor will be enhanced when the new procedures are user-friendly and offer customers greater convenience.

Balancing Demand and Capacity

In general, services that process people and physical objects are more likely to face capacity limitations than those that are information based. Radio and television transmissions, for instance, can reach any number of homes within their receiving area or cable distribution network. In recent years, capacity in such industries has been vastly increased by greater computer power, digital switching, and the replacement of coaxial cables with broadband fiber-optic ones. Yet technology has not found similar ways to increase the capacity of those service operations that process people and their physical possessions without big jumps in cost. As a result, managing demand effectively is essential to improve productivity in services that involve tangible actions. Either customers must be given incentives to use the service outside peak periods or capacity must be allocated in advance through reservations. For example, a golf course may employ both of these strategies by discounting greens fees during off-peak hours and requiring reservations for the busier tee times.

Sharp fluctuations in demand pose a problem for many organizations, although manufacturing firms can inventory supplies of their product as a hedge against fluctuations in demand. This strategy enables manufacturers to enjoy the economies derived from operating factories at steady production levels. Few service businesses can easily do the same. For example, the potential income from an empty seat on an airliner is lost forever once that flight takes off. Hotel rooms are equally perishable, and the productive capacity of an auto repair shop is wasted if no cars come in for servicing on a day when the shop is open. Conversely, when demand for service exceeds supply, the excess business may be lost. If someone cannot get a seat on one flight, another carrier gets the business or the trip is canceled. In other situations, customers may be forced to wait in line until sufficient productive capacity is available to serve them.

Unfortunately, in people-processing services there are limits to how long customers will wait in line. They have other things to do and become bored, resentful, tired, and hungry. Susan was not willing to wait for a sandwich at the food court, so she chose a burger instead. One strategy for reducing or eliminating the need for waiting is to institute a reservations system, but the times offered should be realistic. (Note that Susan's hair salon offered appointments but was not running on schedule the day that she visited it.) In contrast, physical possessions rarely suffer if they have to wait (unless they are highly perishable). In this case, customers are most concerned with the cost and inconvenience associated with delays. For example, Susan worries about what she'll do if her only suit is not returned from the dry cleaner in time for her job interview!

Applying Technology to Service Processes

In Chapter 1, we mentioned six types of technologies that have important implications for services: biotechnology, power and energy technology, methods technology (how people work and how processes are organized), materials technology, physical design technology, and information technology. The extent to which any of these technologies can be applied to the core product of a specific service business depends on the process underlying the creation and delivery of that product.

People-Processing Services   Because customers interact directly with the physical organization, this category of service is particularly concerned with the physical design of front-stage facilities and supporting equipment, as well as with the materials employed to construct them and the power sources used to drive them. Customer satisfaction with these facilities may be as important as internal operational concerns. For instance, the new food court at Susan's university, featuring a variety of different food vendors, represents innovation in physical design and in food preparation and delivery methods for institutional food services. It not only looks more appealing but also offers more choice. As such, the food court probably attracts more customers than the old cafeteria. But improved physical features alone may not suffice for an organization to achieve its productivity and quality goals. The right choice of methods technologies plays a key role in determining how employees, customers, and physical elements interact on-site to create the desired service.

Many technologies have been refined to serve the needs of specific industries. All transportation industries are shaped by new developments in power technologies, since these affect speed, fuel consumption, and both noise and air pollution. Hospitals are the beneficiaries of advances in the physical design of new equipment needed to diagnose and treat patients, as well as biotechnology. Methods of treatment in health care are constantly evolving, too, requiring both human and technical skills that are often practiced in a team setting. Restaurants have improved their productivity by investing in new food-related technologies (such as preprocessed meals and improved strains of vegetables derived from biotechnology research) as well as in devices to simplify food preparation and cooking.

Possession-Processing Services   These services also emphasize power, design, materials, and methods technologies, since the core products tend to involve physical activities ranging from transport to storage, from installation to cleaning, and from fueling to repair. But there's a key difference between people and "things." Unlike human beings, whose size and shape are more or less a given, physical possessions can be redesigned to make them easier to service. In fact, the first and best service that manufacturers and architects can give their customers is to design *serviceability* into physical goods and facilities. Unfortunately, this goal is often ignored. There are many examples of equipment that is difficult to package and transport; machines that have to be totally disassembled by an expert to replace a simple part; electronic controls that only an 11-year-old video-game specialist understands how to operate; and buildings that are hard to clean and maintain.

Mental Stimulus-Processing Services   Strategic developments in this category are driven primarily by information technology (IT). Advances in telecommunications, from cellular phones to satellite links and addressable cable TV, have opened up significant new possibilities for the information, news, entertainment, and education industries. However, making the most of advances in IT often requires development of innovative equipment that is, in turn, dependent on advances in physical design and materials technologies. For instance, miniaturization of power sources (such as tiny batteries) facilitates creation of smaller and lighter devices like flat screens, lightweight modems, portable faxes, cellular telephones, and pocket-size hard disks. Combining portability with wireless networks frees users from the constraints of fixed-site installations and dramatically extends the usefulness of the Internet and World Wide Web. In turn, making use of new applications requires changes in methods technology for both employees and customers.

Information-Processing Services   As with services in the previous category, advances in information-processing services depend heavily on IT. For instance, IT-based telemedicine allows health care providers to transmit real-time patient information—including scans, X rays, and data from monitoring equipment—to a distant expert who can provide immediate consultation and advise local providers on what treatments to offer. Once again, these IT advances are closely allied to physical design, materials, and methods technologies.

Making the Most of Information Technology   It's clear that **information-based services** (a term that covers both mental stimulus processing and information processing) have the most to gain from advances in information technology, because they allow the operation to be physically separate from customers. Modern telecommunications and computer technologies enable customers to connect through a computer (or other input-output devices, such as an ATM) with the service provider's system in another location.[5] For example, customers of a brokerage firm, such as Charles Schwab or E-trade, can connect to the company through the Internet and then manage their own portfolios, keying in orders for buying and selling stocks on their own computers.

> **information-based services:** all services in which the principal value comes from the transmission of data to customers (includes both mental stimulus processing and information processing).

The Internet offers new ways to deliver service for a broad array of industries.[6] Many Web sites, however, offer an example of marketing goods through service rather than marketing a core service product. Consider Figure 2.3. In the case of Flooz.com, the core product—financial services—can be delivered directly via e-mail. In the case of Lands' End, by contrast, the site offers only supplementary services, including information about the goods sold by the company and the opportunity to order and pay for them online. Actual delivery of the clothing sold by Lands' End requires the use of physical channels.

Several of the services used by Susan Munro employ IT applications designed not only to link customers in one location with providers in another, but also to enable customers to perform self-service. For instance, she accessed an Internet site to get a weather forecast, and withdrew money from an ATM. In the case of her Business Spanish course, technology allowed Susan to learn from viewing videotapes that were probably recorded elsewhere several years earlier. The ability to offer customers self-service through automated equipment (such as ATMs), intelligent telephones, and the Internet is of growing importance for service marketing strategy.[7]

Radio and television provide many examples of how technology has transformed the nature of the core product and its delivery system. From studio symphony performances to electronic churches and call-in gardening advice programs, broadcasting—and now interactive cable—has created new ways to bring advice, entertainment, cul-

FIGURE 2.3

Web sites can deliver
Flooz.com's electronic gift
certificates directly but . . .

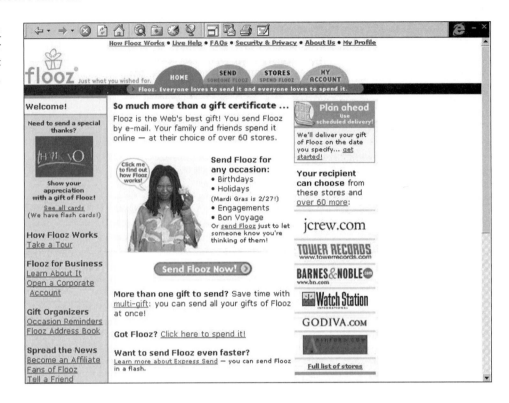

ture, and spiritual enlightenment to widely scattered audiences. In many countries, education is offered through electronic channels as an alternative to the traditional mode of face-to-face presentations in a physical classroom.

Entire virtual universities are springing up, such as the University of Phoenix in the United States. One of the oldest and most extensive efforts of this nature is the Open University (OU) in Great Britain. The OU has been offering degree programs to students nationwide through the electronic campus of the British Broadcasting Corporation (BBC) for over 30 years. Anyone can watch or hear the broadcast programs, of course, but students also receive printed course material and videotapes through the mail and communicate with tutors by mail, e-mail, or telephone. In a number of courses, real-time class discussions between instructors and students take place by telephone and a few even use videoconferencing. Yet these techniques still cannot provide all the features and benefits of education on a physical campus, where much of the learning takes place outside the classroom. So, to provide some of the advantages of traditional education, the OU encourages advanced students to participate in short residential programs, often held on a real college campus during vacation periods.

Thanks to advances in technology, distance education has become international in scope. It offers particular potential in Africa, where only 3 percent of 18 to 25 year olds enroll in college and few have any business experience. In 1997, the World Bank launched the African Virtual University, which enables students in 16 African countries to take courses and seminars taught by professors from universities around the world.[8] Instructors deliver lectures in front of cameras in their own classrooms and the video is routed via fiber optics, ISDN lines, or satellite to an uplink in Washington, D.C. From there it is transmitted by satellite to various locations in Africa, where a student in Ghana can talk with the instructor in real time via standard telephone lines while students in Kenya, Tanzania, and Zimbabwe listen to the dialog.

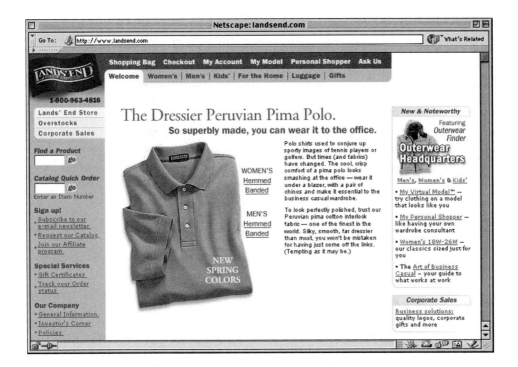

... Lands' End's clothing products require a physical channel to reach the customer.

Managing People as Part of the Service Product

The more involved customers become in the service delivery process, the more visible service personnel and other customers become (this is the *people* element of the 8Ps). In many people-processing services, customers meet lots of employees and often interact with them for extended periods of time. They are also more likely to run into other customers. After all, many service facilities achieve their operating economies by serving large numbers of customers simultaneously. When other people become a part of the service experience, they can enhance it or detract from it. Direct involvement in service production means that customers evaluate the quality of employees' appearance and social skills, as well as their technical skills—concerns that are important for human resource managers and front-line supervisors. And because people also make judgments about their fellow customers, managers find themselves trying to shape customer behavior, too.

Service businesses of this type tend to be harder to manage because of the human element. Susan enjoyed the comments made by other students in her marketing class. But at the food court, lazy customers had failed to clear their table. Even though they had already left, their behavior still detracted in a small way from the experience of Susan and her friends. The poor attitude and appearance of the employee at the dry cleaner compounded the problem of delays in cleaning Susan's suit and may lead to the loss of her business in the future. As a manager, how would you get customers to clear their tables after eating at the food court? How would you make the staff at the dry cleaner more friendly?

Conclusion

We've seen in this chapter that although not all services are the same, many do have important characteristics in common. Rather than focusing on broad distinctions between goods and services, it's more useful to identify different categories of services and to study the marketing, operations, and human resource challenges that they raise.

The four-way classification scheme in this chapter focuses on different types of service processes. Some services require direct physical contact with customers (haircutting and passenger transport); others center on contact with people's minds (education and entertainment). Some involve processing of physical objects (cleaning and freight transport); others process information (accounting and insurance). As you can now appreciate, the processes that underlie the creation and delivery of any service have a major impact on marketing and human resources. Process design (or redesign) is not just a task for the operations department. Both managers and employees must understand underlying processes (particularly those in which customers are actively involved) in order to run a service business that is both efficient and user-friendly. In a growing number of situations, those processes are being reshaped by advances in information technology.

Study Questions and Exercises

1. Identify each of the services used by Susan Munro.
   a. What needs is she attempting to satisfy in each instance?
   b. What alternative product or self-service could solve her need in each instance?
   c. What similarities and differences are there between the dry-cleaning store and the hair salon? What could each learn from the other?

2. Review Susan's day and identify which of the 8Ps are evident in her dealings with different services.

3. Make a list of all the services that you have used during the past week and categorize them by type of process.

4. List the different types of service factories that you visit in the course of a typical month and how many times you visit each one.

5. Review each of the different ways in which services can be classified. How would you explain the usefulness of these systems to the manager of a health and fitness center?

6. Identify the strategies used by your long-distance phone company or favorite restaurant to manage demand.

7. What do you see as the major ethical issues for those responsible for creating and delivering mental-stimulus-processing services?

8. How have other customers affected your service experiences either positively or negatively?

Endnotes

1. Shelby D. Hunt, *Marketing Theory: Conceptual Foundation of Research in Marketing* (Columbus, OH: Grid, Inc., 1976), 117–118.
2. Melvin T. Copeland, "The Relation of Consumers' Buying Habits to Marketing Methods," *Harvard Business Review*, 1 (April 1923): 282–289.
3. See, for example, Christopher H. Lovelock, "Classifying Services to Gain Strategic Marketing Insights," *Journal of Marketing* 47 (Summer 1983): 9–20; Christian Grönroos, *Service Management and Marketing* (Lexington MA: Lexington Books, 1990), 31–34; John Bowen, "Development of a Taxonomy of Services to Gain Strategic Marketing Insights," *Journal of the Academy of Marketing Science* 18 (Winter 1990): 43–49; Rhian Silvestro, Lyn Fitzgerald, Robert Johnston, and Christopher Voss, "Towards a Classification of Service Processes," *International Journal of Service Industry Management* 3, no. 3 (1992): 62–75; and

Hans Kasper, Wouter De Vries, and Piet Van Helsdingen, *Services Marketing Management: An International Perspective* (Chichester, UK: John Wiley & Sons, 1999), chap. 2, 43–70.

4. These classifications are derived from Lovelock (1983) and represent an extension and adaptation of a framework in T.P. Hill, "On Goods and Services," *Review of Income and Wealth* 23 (December 1977), 315–338.

5. For more detailed illustrations of the impact of information technology on services, see Frances Cairncross, *The Death of Distance* (Boston: Harvard Business School Press, 1997); and Philip Evans and Thomas S. Wurster, *Blown to Bits* (Boston: Harvard Business School Press, 2000).

6. Leyland Pitt, Pierre Berthoin, and Jean-Paul Berthon, "Changing Channels: The Impact of the Internet on Distribution Strategy," *Business Horizons* (March-April 1999): 19–28.

7. Pratibha A. Dabholkar, "Technology in Service Delivery: Implications for Self-Service and Service Support," in T. A. Schwartz and D. Iacobuci, *Handbook of Services Marketing and Management* (Thousand Oaks, CA: Sage Publications, 2000), 103–110.

8. David A. Light, "Pioneering Distance Education in Africa," *Harvard Business Review* (September-October 1999), 26.

part**two**

The Service Customer

All successful service firms are customer oriented. To the greatest possible extent, these companies try to build their operations around the customer rather than forcing customers to conform to a predefined operating model. They also recognize that not all customers have similar needs, that their firm's services will appeal more to certain types of customers than others, and that customers differ in terms of their potential value to the firm. The four chapters in Part II are built around increasing your understanding of the service customer. Figure II.1 emphasizes those elements of the service management decision framework that relate to the question: ***Who are our customers and how should we relate to them?***

Understanding the nature of the processes used to create and deliver services is the key to designing service encounters and creating appealing experiences for customers. Marketers need to work with their colleagues in operations to answer the question: *Where should customers fit in our service operation*? In people-processing services, customers themselves are an integral part of the process and must physically remain in the company's facilities (e.g., a hotel, an airliner, or a hospital) for the duration of service delivery. Other types of services may have the opportunity to select processes that will substantially reduce contact with customers. Before a firm chooses a particular process, marketers should address the question: *Do customers and prospects prefer high or low levels of contact with service personnel and facilities*? The answer to this question may help guide decisions on

whether to offer self-service options. We discuss these issues in Chapter 3.

Many marketing decisions—including those involving product elements, pricing, promotion and education, and service delivery—are related to the question: *How do customers evaluate, purchase, and use our services*? *And how satisfied are they*? We need to learn what alternatives customers consider, how they evaluate services, what criteria they use in making their decisions, where and when they make purchases, whether there are differences among customers in how they use a specific service, and what factors lead to satisfaction or dissatisfaction. The purchase decision process for services is one of the key topics addressed in Chapter 4, which also addresses how customer expectations are formed and introduces the technique of mapping the service experience from the customer's perspective.

Managers must understand their customers' behavior in order to design services that best fulfill identified needs. But they should also realize that not all customers are equally desirable to a firm. Some current customers are likely to offer greater value than others. And not all prospects are attractive either. Thus marketers should ask: *What are the key characteristics of the market segments that we target*? The more a firm knows about its existing customers, the better it will be able to answer the question: *Which customer relationships are worth developing and preserving*? Chapter 5 reviews the concept of market segmentation, introduces

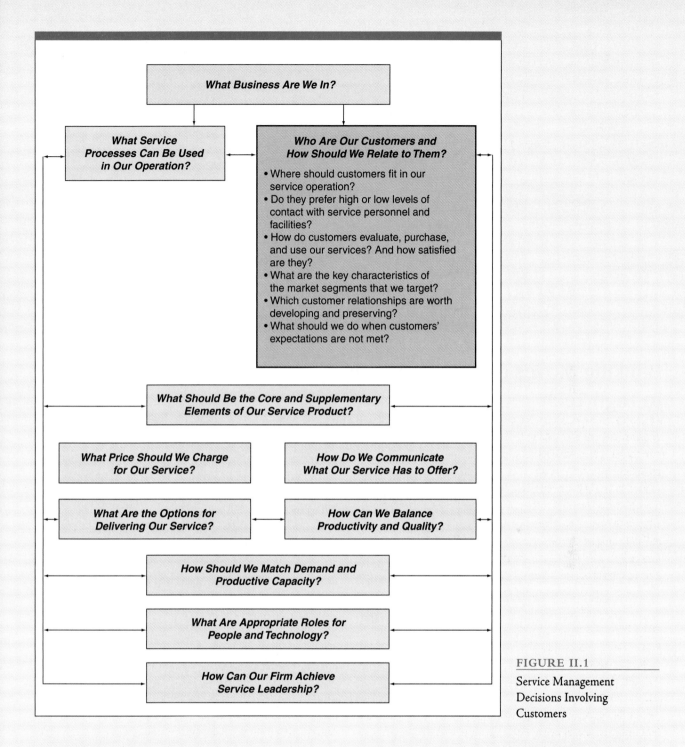

FIGURE II.1

Service Management Decisions Involving Customers

the concept of relationship marketing, and covers strategies for building customer loyalty.

Finally, managers need to recognize that service delivery does not always go perfectly from the customer's perspective. To develop an effective service recovery strategy—the topic of Chapter 6—they should be able to respond with specifics to the question: *What should we do when customers' expectations are not met?*

chapter three

Managing Service Encounters

Banking Moves from High Touch to High Tech

Developments in technology often offer radically new ways for a business to create and deliver its services, particularly those core and supplementary services that are information-based.[1] But it's not always easy to insert a new, technology-based model of service delivery into a traditional operation with an established culture and customers who are used to doing things in a certain way. Sometimes it may be easier to create an entirely new operation that is largely independent of the parent company. In an effort to attract new business and take advantage of cost-saving advances in Internet technology, First USA Bank created a separate Internet subsidiary with an unusual sounding name. WingspanBank.com was launched in mid-1999 with the slogan "If your bank could start over, this is what it would be." A similar strategy was used ten years earlier by Britain's Midland Bank (now HSBC Bank) when it launched First Direct, the world's first all-telephone bank. First Direct attracted worldwide attention within the financial service industry as the first bank to operate 24 hours a day, 7 days a week.[2]

Customers who undertake home banking by computer or by phone have a different type of relationship with their bank than those who continue to visit a traditional retail bank branch. The former benefit from place and time convenience, dealing with bank personnel at arm's length, using a computer or telephone (supplied by the customers or their employers), rather than entering a service factory. The only physical banking encounters these customers experience are with ATMs (automated teller machines), which can be found in numerous convenient locations and do not necessarily belong to the bank with which the user has an account. If there is a problem, a customer's first option is to send an e-mail or to telephone a 24-hour customer service center.

Customers' impressions of First Direct, therefore, reflect how fast the phone is answered (standards require 75 percent of all calls to be answered in 20 seconds or less), the courtesy and professionalism of the employee's voice, and the speed with which desired transactions can be completed. By contrast, customers' impressions of Wingspan are likely to be determined by the appearance and ease of use of the bank's Web site. To obtain assistance, Wingspan customers can send e-mails, use 24/7 free telephone service to reach Customer Care Advisors, or send a letter by regular mail. Industry experts have given Wingspan high marks. The company's site received a "Best of the Web" ranking from *Forbes* and a "Five-Star Rating for the Best Financial Supermarket" from *Kiplinger's Personal Finance*. And according to *Money* magazine, "WingspanBank.com is the best banking embodiment yet of the 'clicks and mortar' strategy."[3] Gómez.com, an Internet quality measurement firm that evaluates a wide array of online services against a variety of criteria, gave WingspanBank.com high ratings among virtual banks.[4]

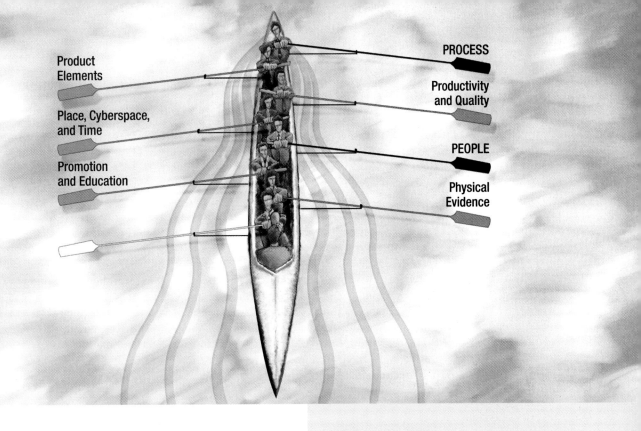

Product
Elements

Place, Cyberspace,
and Time

Promotion
and Education

PROCESS

Productivity
and Quality

PEOPLE

Physical
Evidence

⇒ Learning Objectives

**After reading this chapter, you should
be able to**

⇒ explain the different levels of
customer contact and their impact
on service design and delivery

⇒ discuss critical incidents and their
implications for customer
satisfaction

⇒ understand the elements of the total
service system

⇒ describe why service delivery can be
viewed as a form of theater

⇒ recognize the potential role of
customers as coproducers of services

⇒ appreciate how new technologies
may offer alternative ways of creating
and delivering services

WHERE DOES THE CUSTOMER FIT IN THE SERVICE OPERATION?

As we described in the opening vignette, different forms of banking operations involve customers in different ways. Compared to Web- or telephone-based service delivery, visiting a branch requires more personal and more time-consuming contacts. Customers can only visit a branch during certain hours and may have to travel some distance to get there. They are exposed to the exterior and interior of the building, may spend time waiting in a line with other customers, and deal face-to-face with an employee (who, in many banks, will be behind a security grill or glass screen).

Many people enjoy the social interaction of visiting a bank branch, especially if they don't trust machines and know the staff members who serve them. According to the U.S. banking industry, a third of all banking customers use only "high-contact" banking in a staffed branch, a third combine branch banking with remote banking by telephone and computer, and a third use predominantly the "low-contact" remote banking options.[5] The proportion of customers who prefer to bank electronically can be expected to grow as younger, more technology-oriented customers enter the market and at least some of the technophobes evolve, with education and experience, toward greater acceptance of new banking channels.

Contact with the Service Organization

An important theme in this chapter is that "high-contact" encounters between customers and service organizations differ sharply from "low-contact" ones. The four process-based service categories described in Chapter 2 prescribe the minimum level of customer contact needed to obtain service in each instance. However, many service organizations may provide far higher levels of contact than is necessary to deliver the service in question. Sometimes these high-contact levels reflect customer preferences for person-to-person service with **customer-contact personnel**. In many instances, though, they result from a management decision to continue relying on traditional approaches, instead of reengineering existing service processes to create innovative, lower-contact approaches.

Variability is a fact of life in situations where customers differ widely and service personnel interact with those customers on a one-on-one basis.[6] The longer and more actively that customers are involved in the process of service delivery, the greater the likelihood that each customer's experience will be somewhat different from that of other customers (and from previous experiences by the same customer). Not all variations are bad; in fact, many customers seek a tailored approach that recognizes them as individuals with distinctive needs. The challenge is for employees to be flexible, treating each person as an individual rather than as a clone.[7]

Many service problems revolve around unsatisfactory incidents between customers and service personnel. In an effort to simplify service delivery, improve productivity, and reduce some of the threats to service quality, a number of firms are using technology to minimize or even eliminate contact between customers and employees. Thus, face-to-face encounters are giving way to telephone and e-mail encounters. Meantime, personal service is being replaced by self-service, often through computers, kiosks, or easy-to-use machines.[8] Web sites are beginning to replace voice telephone contacts for some types of service transactions.[9]

This chapter builds on our earlier discussion of *processes* in Chapter 2 and introduces the concept of a spectrum of customer contact with the service organization that ranges from high to low. We'll show how the extent of customer contact affects the nature of the

customer-contact personnel: those service employees who interact directly with individual customers either in person or through mail and telecommunications.

service encounter as well as strategies for achieving *productivity* and *quality* improvements. As you review the contents of the chapter, including its examples, you should ask yourself how a strategy of reducing (or increasing) the level of customer contact might impact decisions relating to *product elements, place, cyberspace, and time, promotion and education, people,* and *physical evidence.* You should also recognize how the material in this chapter relates to the service decision framework (see Figure II.1 on page 49). By gaining a better understanding of where customers fit in different types of service operation and their preferences for high or low levels of contact with personnel and facilities, you'll begin to answer the broader question: ***Who are our customers and how should we relate to them?***

Service Encounters: Differing Levels of Customer Contact

A **service encounter** is a period of time during which customers interact directly with a service.[10] In some instances, the entire service experience can be reduced to a single encounter, involving ordering, payment, and execution of service delivery on the spot. In other cases, the customer's experience includes a sequence of encounters. This can mean an extended process that may be spread out over a period of time, involve a variety of employees, and even take place in different locations (think about flying on a passenger airline). Although some researchers use the term "encounter" simply to describe personal interactions between customers and employees,[11] realistically we also need to think about encounters involving interactions between customers and self-service equipment.[12]

As the level of customer contact with the service operation increases, there are likely to be more and longer service encounters. So in Figure 3.1, we've grouped services into three **levels of customer contact**, representing the extent of interaction with service person-

service encounter: a period of time during which customers interact directly with a service.

levels of customer contact: the extent to which customers interact directly with elements of the service organization.

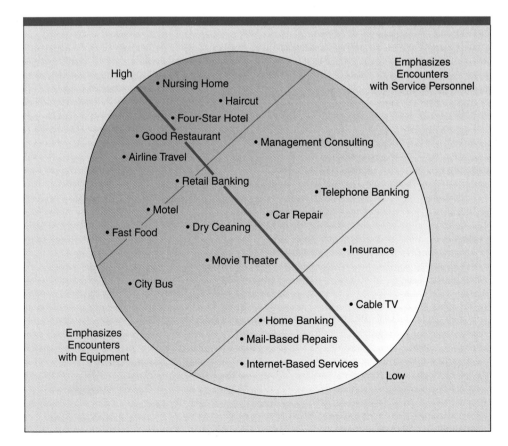

FIGURE 3.1

Levels of Customer Contact with Service Organizations

high-contact services: services that involve significant interaction among customers, service personnel, and equipment and facilities.

nel, physical service elements, or both. You'll notice that traditional retail banking, telephone banking, and home banking by Web site are all in different locations on the chart.

High-contact services tend to be those in which customers visit the service facility in person. Customers are actively involved with the service organization and its personnel throughout service delivery (e.g., hairdressing or medical services). All people-processing services (other than those delivered at home) are high contact. Services from the other three process-based categories may also involve high levels of customer contact when, for reasons of tradition, preference, or lack of other alternatives, customers go to the service site and remain there until service delivery is completed. Examples of services that have traditionally been high contact but can be low contact today because of technology include retail banking, purchase of retail goods, and higher education.

medium-contact services: services that involve only a limited amount of contact between customers and elements of the service organization.

Medium-contact services entail less interaction with service providers. They involve situations in which customers visit the service provider's facilities (or are visited at home or at a third-party location by the firm's employees) but either do not remain throughout service delivery or else have only modest contact with service personnel. The purpose of such contacts is often limited to: (1) establishing a relationship and defining a service need (e.g., management consulting, insurance, or personal financial advising, where clients make an initial visit to the firm's office but then have relatively limited interactions with the provider during service production), (2) dropping off and picking up a physical possession that is being serviced, or (3) trying to resolve a problem.

low-contact services: services that require minimal or no direct contact between customers and the service organization.

Low-contact services involve very little, if any, physical contact between customers and service providers. Instead, contact takes place at arm's length through the medium of electronic or physical distribution channels—a fast-growing trend in today's convenience-oriented society. Both mental stimulus-processing (e.g., radio, television) and information-processing services (e.g., insurance) fall naturally into this category. Also included are possession-processing services in which the item requiring service can

FIGURE 3.2

Unconventional Advertising for an Unconventional Bank

be shipped to the service site or subjected to "remote fixes" delivered electronically to the customers' premises from a distant location (increasingly common for resolving software problems). Finally, many high-contact and medium-contact services are being transformed into low-contact services as customers engage in home shopping, conduct their insurance and banking transactions by telephone, or research and purchase products through the World Wide Web.[13]

Advertising for low-contact, Web-based services often promotes speed and convenience. For instance, WingspanBank.com contrasts the old and new approaches: "In the 60 seconds it takes to find a parking spot at your old bank, you can get an answer on your loan application. . . . leave your car in the garage. Your new bank's in the den" (see Figure 3.2).

MANAGING SERVICE ENCOUNTERS

Many services (especially those classified as high contact) involve numerous encounters between customers and service employees, either in person or remotely by phone or e-mail. Service encounters may also take place between customers and physical facilities or equipment. In low-contact services, customers are having more and more encounters with automated machines that are designed to replace human personnel.

To highlight the risks and opportunities associated with service encounters, Richard Normann, a Paris-based Swedish consultant, borrowed the metaphor "**moment of truth**" from bullfighting. Normann writes:

> [W]e could say that the perceived quality is realized at the moment of truth, when the service provider and the service customer confront one another in the arena. At that moment they are very much on their own. . . . It is the skill, the motivation, and the tools employed by the firm's representative and the expectations and behavior of the client which together will create the service delivery process.[14]

moment of truth: a point in service delivery where customers interact with service employees or self-service equipment and the outcome may affect perceptions of service quality.

In bullfighting, what is at stake is the life of either the bull or the matador (or possibly both). The moment of truth is the instant at which the matador deftly slays the bull with his sword—hardly a very comfortable analogy for a service organization's intent on building long-term relationships with its customers! Normann's point, of course, is that it's the life of the relationship that is at stake. Contrary to bullfighting, the goal of relationship marketing—which we will explore in Chapter 5—is to prevent one unfortunate (mis)encounter from destroying what is already, or has the potential to become, a mutually valued, long-term relationship.

Jan Carlzon, the former chief executive of Scandinavian Airlines System, used the "moment-of-truth" metaphor as a reference point for transforming SAS from an operations-driven business into a customer-driven airline. Carlzon made the following comments about his airline:

> Last year, each of our 10 million customers came into contact with approximately five SAS employees, and this contact lasted an average of 15 seconds each time. Thus, SAS is "created" 50 million times a year, 15 seconds at a time. These 50 million "moments of truth" are the moments that ultimately determine whether SAS will succeed or fail as a company. They are the moments when we must prove to our customers that SAS is their best alternative.[15]

critical incident: a specific encounter between customer and service provider in which the outcome has proved especially satisfying or dissatisfying for one or both parties.

Critical Incidents in Service Encounters

Critical incidents are specific encounters between customers and service businesses that are especially satisfying or dissatisfying for one or both parties. The **critical incident technique (CIT)** is a methodology for collecting and categorizing such incidents in service encounters. Conducting such an analysis offers an opportunity to determine what incidents during service delivery are likely to be particularly significant in determining whether or not customers are satisfied. The types of encounters classified as critical incidents differ depending on whether the service is high or low contact in nature.

critical incident technique (CIT): a methodology for collecting, categorizing, and analyzing critical incidents that have occurred between customers and service providers.

Critical Incidents in High-Contact Services

In a study of critical incidents in the airline, hotel, and restaurant businesses, customers were instructed to think of a time when they had a particularly *satisfying (dissatisfying)* interaction with a service employee. They then answered the following questions:

➤ When did the incident happen?

➤ What specific circumstances led up to this situation?

➤ Exactly what did the employee say or do?

➤ What resulted that made you feel the interaction was *satisfying (dissatisfying)*?

A total of 699 incidents was recorded, split roughly equally between satisfying and unsatisfying incidents. They were then cat-egorized into three groups: (1) employee response to service fail-ures, (2) employee responses to requests for customized service, and (3) unprompted and unsolicited employee actions.

When employees responded to critical incidents involving a service failure, analysis showed that the outcomes were twice as likely to be dissatisfactory for customers as satisfactory. The reverse was true when customers asked employees to adapt the service in some way to meet a special need or request. In the third grouping, relating to unexpected events and employee behavior, satisfactory and unsatisfactory outcomes were equally matched. Figure 3.4 displays reports on specific incidents, as described in the customers' own words.

FIGURE 3.3

Customer Reports on Critical Incidents Involving Service Employees

GROUP 1 SAMPLE INCIDENTS: EMPLOYEE RESPONSE TO SERVICE DELIVERY FAILURES

Incident

Satisfactory	Dissatisfactory
A. Response to Unavailable Service	
They lost my room reservation but the manager gave me the V.I.P. suite for the same price.	We had made advance reservations at the hotel. When we arrived we found we had no room—no explanation, no apologies, and no assistance in finding another hotel.
B. Response to Unreasonably Slow Service	
Even though I didn't make any complaint about the hour and a half wait, the waitress kept apologizing and said that the bill was on the house.	The airline employees continually gave us erroneous information; a one-hour delay turned into a six-hour wait.
C. Response to Other Core Service Failures	
My shrimp cocktail was half frozen. The waitress apologized, and didn't charge me for any of my dinner.	One of my suitcases was all dented and looked as though it had been dropped from 30,000 feet. When I tried to make a claim for my damaged luggage, the employee insinuated that I was lying and trying to rip them off.

GROUP 2 SAMPLE INCIDENTS: EMPLOYEE RESPONSE TO CUSTOMER NEEDS AND REQUESTS

A. Response to "Special Needs" Customers	
The flight attendant helped me calm and care for my airsick child.	My young son, flying alone, was to be assisted by the stewardess from start to finish. At the Albany airport she left him alone in the airport with no one to escort him to his connecting flight.

Source: Mary Jo Bitner, Bernard H. Booms, and Mary Stanfield Tetreault, "The Service Encounter: Diagnosing Favorable and Unfavorable Incidents," *Journal of Marketing*, 54 (January 1990): 71–84.

Incident

Satisfactory	Dissatisfactory

B. Response to Customer Preferences

The front desk clerk called around and found me tickets to the Mariners' opening game.	The waitress refused to move me from a window table on a hot day, because there was nothing left in her section.
It was snowing outside—car broke down. I checked 10 hotels and there were no rooms. Finally, one understood my situation and offered to rent me a bed and set it up in one of their small banquet rooms.	The airline wouldn't let me bring my scuba gear on board coming back from Hawaii even though I brought it over as carry-on luggage.

C. Response to Admitted Customer Error

I lost my glasses on the plane; the stewardess found them and they were delivered to my hotel free of charge.	We missed our flight because of car trouble. The service clerk wouldn't help us find a flight on an alternative airline.

D. Response to Potentially Disruptive Others

The manager kept his eye on an obnoxious guy at the bar, to make sure that he didn't bother us.	The hotel staff wouldn't deal with the noisy people partying in the hall at 3 A.M.

GROUP 3 SAMPLE INCIDENTS: UNPROMPTED AND UNSOLICITED EMPLOYEE ACTIONS

A. Attention Paid to Customer

The waiter treated me like royalty. He really showed he cared about me.	The lady at the front desk acted as if we were bothering her. She was watching TV and paying more attention to the TV than the hotel guests.

B. Truly Out-of-the-Ordinary Employee Behavior

We always travel with our teddy bears. When we got back to our room at the hotel we saw that the maid had arranged our bears very comfortably in a chair. The bears were holding hands.	I needed a few more minutes to decide on a dinner. The waitress said, "If you would read the menu and not the road map, you would know what you want to order."

C. Employee Behaviors in the Context of Cultural Norms

The busboy ran after us to return a $50 bill my boyfriend had dropped under the table.	The waiter at this expensive restaurant treated us like dirt because we were only high school kids on a prom date.

D. Gestalt Evaluation

The whole experience was so pleasant … everything went smoothly and perfectly.	The flight was a nightmare. A one-hour layover went to three-and-one-half hours. The air conditioning didn't work. The pilots and stewardesses were fighting because of an impending flight attendant strike. The landing was extremely rough. To top it all off, when the plane stopped, the pilots and stewardesses were the first ones off.

E. Performance Under Adverse Circumstances

The counter agent was obviously under stress, but kept his cool and acted very professionally.	

CIT in High-Contact Environments   Most CIT research has focused on interpersonal interactions between customers and employees in high-contact service environments. In these situations, critical incidents tend to center around customer perceptions of employee attitudes and actions. For example, a lengthy wait for dinner in a restaurant would be classified as a critical incident because it represents a service delivery failure. But if an employee attempts to improve the situation by providing information about the cause of the wait and offering free drinks as compensation, customers may feel that the outcome was satisfactory even though the service delivery was problematic.

The findings reported in the boxed example come from a study of critical incidents described by customers who had particularly satisfying or dissatisfying experiences when using high-contact airline, hotel, or restaurant services. Note the 12 different

Critical Incidents in Low-Contact Services

A recent study used an online survey to examine critical incidents related to encounters with self-service technologies including ATMs, Internet shopping services, pay-at-the pump terminals, automated telephone services, package tracking, automated car rental pick-up and return, and online brokerage services. Study participants were instructed to think of a time when they had a particularly *satisfying (dissatisfying)* interaction with an SST. They then answered the following questions:

➤ Which self-service technology are you focusing on?

➤ Was this a satisfying or dissatisfying experience?

➤ Please describe what happened during the incident. What specific details do you recall that made this experience memorable to you?

A total of 823 incidents was recorded, with 56 percent classified as satisfactory encounters and 44 percent classified as dissatisfactory encounters. There were three categories of satisfying encounters: (1) solved an intensified need, (2) better than the alternative, and (3) did its job. Four types of dissatisfying encounters were identified: (1) technology failure, (2) process failure, (3) poor design, and (4) customer-driven failure. Figure 3.4 displays reports on specific incidents related to encounters with SSTs, as described in the customers' own words.

FIGURE 3.4

Satisfying and Dissatisfying Encounters with Self-Service Technologies

	SATISFYING INCIDENTS	
Group Number and Name	**Illustrative Quotes**	**Percentage of Total**
1. Solved intensified need	"My ride to work didn't show up, and I had no money in my pocket. I had 20 minutes to get to work. I went to the cash machine and got some cash for the cab ride.... I made it to work 10 minutes late instead of not at all."	11%
2. Better than the alternative		66%
2A. Easy to use	"The page's forms were clear and easy to use. I had no difficulty deciding on my purchase and going ahead with the order." (regarding purchasing roses through the 1-800-FLOWERS Internet page)	16%
2B. Avoid service personnel	"I like shopping on the Internet because there is no salesperson to bribe you."	3%
2C. Saved time	"I was on my way to a friend's house and was low on gas. I was in a huge hurry, so using the pay at the pump saved me a lot of time."	30%

Source: Matthew L. Meuter, Amy L. Ostrom, Robert I. Roundtree, and Mary Jo Bitner, "Understanding Customer Satisfaction with Technology-Based Service Encounters," *Journal of Marketing*, 64 (Summer 2000): 50–64.

types of incidents and examples of the language used by customers to describe both positive and negative interactions with service employees.

While customers' reactions are important, managers must also understand the employee's view of the situation. Thoughtless or poorly behaved customers can often cause needless problems for service personnel who are trying hard to serve them well. Dissatisfaction with a succession of negative incidents can even drive good employees to quit their jobs. A CIT study that examined hundreds of critical incidents from an employee perspective[16] showed that more than 20 percent of all incidents that employees found unsatisfactory could be attributed to problem customers, whose bad behavior included drunkenness, verbal and physical abuse, breaking laws or company policies, and failing to cooperate with service personnel. As you know if you've ever been

SATISFYING INCIDENTS

Group Number and Name	Illustrative Quotes	Percentage of Total
2D. When I want	"[I] was having a videotape of a house I was interested in putting an offer [on] and was very anxious to get the tape so I could make my decision. [It was] convenient to be able to check on [the] parcel's whereabouts any time of day or night."	8%
2E. Where I want	"I can check out [library] books by phone without having to drive all the way down to the library to renew them."	5%
2F. Saved money	"I called around to several car agencies and was unable to get a price that was within my range. I decided to try Alamo online. I entered the information and came up with a price that was $20 less per week than when I had called them."	6%
3. Did its job	"I needed gas... [, which involved] inserting the card, selecting credit, pumping the gas, and then asking for a receipt. I received the gas I needed and wanted, and got a receipt."	21%

DISSATISFYING INCIDENTS

Group Number and Name	Illustrative Quotes	Percentage of Total
4. Technology failure	"ATM broke down. It kept my card. I had to have the card reissued."	43%
5. Process failure	"After a month passed from placing my original order, I e-mailed the customer service center at Disney with my order confirmation number. They had lost my order. I reordered, only to be sent the incorrect merchandise twice."	17%
6. Poor design		36%
6A. Technology design problem	"I was trying to order books from a book club online. The system was confusing, and I ordered two of the same title without knowing it."	17%
6B. Service design problem	"I did not realize that some (ATM) machines put limits on how much you can get out. The machine did not tell me I went over my limit for the day. It just spit my card back out so I kept trying different amounts until I was able to get some cash out."	19%
7. Customer-driven failure	"I was attempting to get money from an ATM and couldn't remember my [personal identification] number. I was leaving in one hour before the bank opened for mainland Japan, and the machine took my card."	4%

service operations system: that part of the total service system where inputs are processed and the elements of the service product are created.

service delivery system: that part of the total service system where final "assembly" of the elements takes place and the product is delivered to the customer; it includes the visible elements of the service operation.

service marketing system: that part of the total service system where the firm has any form of contact with its customers, from advertising to billing; it includes contacts made at the point of delivery.

front stage: those aspects of service operations and delivery that are visible or otherwise apparent to customers.

backstage (or technical core): those aspects of service operations that are hidden from customers.

a front-line employee in a service business, it's simply not true that "the customer is always right."

CIT in Low-Contact Environments In low-contact services, encounters between customers and service businesses may not directly involve employees. Technology has provided new opportunities for self-service, where delivery takes place electronically through interactions with equipment rather than people. Examples of these self-service technologies (SSTs) include bank ATMs, automated package tracking, pay-at-the-pump terminals at gas stations, automated kiosks for airline tickets, and Internet investment transactions. In these types of encounters, employees are not present to compensate for problems or customize the service experience. A study of critical incidents in low-contact service environments highlights the necessity of educating customers about effective use of SSTs and training them to "self-recover" when a service failure has occurred. The boxed example on pages 58–59 describes service encounters that were identified as especially satisfying/dissatisfying incidents in low-contact, self-service environments.

SERVICE AS A SYSTEM

The types of relationships a service business has with its customers (and the kinds of misbehaviors that will be encountered during service delivery) depend to a great extent on the level of contact customers have with the firm. Whether a service is high, medium, or low contact becomes a major factor in defining the total service system, which includes the **service operations system** (where inputs are processed and the elements of the service product are created), the **service delivery system** (where final "assembly" of these elements takes place and the product is delivered to the customer), and the **service marketing system** (which embraces all points of contact with customers, including advertising, billing, and market research) (see Figure 3.5).

Parts of this system are visible (or otherwise apparent) to customers; other parts are hidden in what is sometimes referred to as the technical core, and the customer may not even know of their existence.[18] Some writers use the terms "front office" and "back office" in referring to the visible and invisible parts of the operation. Others talk about "**front stage**" and "**backstage**," using the analogy of theater to dramatize the notion that service is a performance.[19] We like this analogy—sometimes referred to as "dra-

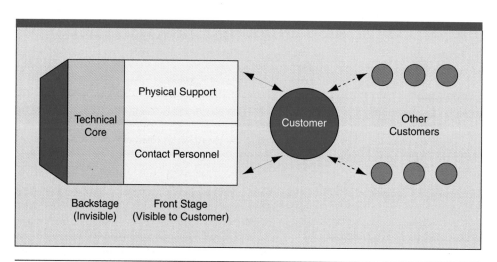

FIGURE 3.5

The Service Business as a System

Source: Adapted from Langeard et al.[17]

TABLE 3.1

Theatrical Considerations for Different Types of Services

Service Process Category	Level of Contact	Drama Implications
People processing	High contact	Because the actors and audience are in close contact, the setting and front stage performances affect customers' perceptions of service quality. Important theater aspects include design and ambience of the setting, appearance and behavior of the actors, props, costumes, and scripts. Other audience members (customers) can influence one another's service experience and the perceived quality of the service performance.
Mental stimulus processing	High contact	If actors and audience are in close physical proximity, then many of the drama implications for people-processing services may apply.
	Low contact	If the performance is conducted at arm's length, audience members do not typically interact with each other. The physical appearances of the actors and setting are less important. Scripts may still be useful in ensuring that actors and audience members play their parts correctly.
Possession processing	Medium contact	The performance can either take place at the service firm or at the audience members' home or business. Contact between actors and audience may be limited to the start and end of the service. (At these contact points, the drama elements described for people-processing services do apply but on a less substantial level.)
	Low contact	In some circumstances—for instance, lawn mowing and office janitorial services—the service performance may occur without the audience present. The outcomes of such services are usually tangible and may be used as a proxy for judging the quality of the service performance.
Information processing	Low contact	There is minimal contact between actors and audience members. Both the act and the recipient (intangible assets) are intangible, and the performance usually occurs in the absence of the customer. Because of these factors, only the outcomes can be assessed, not the process; however, even the outcome may be difficult for customers to evaluate.

Source: Adapted from Stephen J. Grove, Raymond P. Fisk, and Joby John, "Services as Theater: Guidelines and Implications," in Teresa A. Schwartz and Dawn Iacobucci, *Handbook of Service Marketing and Management* (Thousand Oaks, CA: Sage Publications, 2000), p. 31.

maturgy"—and will be using it throughout the book. The extent to which theatrical elements exist depends largely on the nature of the service process. Table 3.1 summarizes the drama implications for the four categories of service processes identified in Chapter 2.

Service Operations System

Like a play in a theater, the visible components of service operations can be divided into those relating to the actors (or service personnel) and those relating to the stage set (or physical facilities, equipment, and other tangibles). What goes on backstage is of little interest to customers. Like any audience, they evaluate the production on those elements they actually experience during service delivery and on the perceived service outcome. Naturally, if the backstage personnel and systems (e.g., billing, ordering, account keeping) fail to perform their support tasks properly in ways that affect the quality of front stage activities, customers will notice. For instance, restaurant patrons will be disappointed if they order fish from the menu but are told it is unavailable or find that their food is overcooked. Other examples of backstage failures include receiving an incorrect hotel bill due to a keying error, not receiving course grades because of a computer failure in the college registrar's office, or being delayed on a flight because the aircraft has been taken out of service for engine repairs.

The proportion of the overall service operation that is visible to customers varies according to the level of customer contact. Since high-contact services directly involve the physical person of the customer, customers must enter the service "factory" (although there may still be many backstage activities that they don't see) or service workers and their tools must leave the backstage and come to the customers' chosen location. Examples include roadside car repair by automobile clubs and physical fitness trainers who work with clients at their homes or offices. Medium-contact services, by contrast, require customers to be less substantially involved in service delivery. Consequently, the visible component of the service operations system is smaller.

Low-contact services usually strive to minimize customer contact with the service provider, so most of the service operations system is confined to a remotely located backstage (sometimes referred to as a technical core); front stage elements are normally limited to mail and telecommunications contacts. Think for a moment about the telephone company that you use. Do you have any idea where its exchange is located? If you have a credit card, it's likely that your transactions are processed far from where you live.

Service Delivery System

Service delivery is concerned with where, when, and how the service product is delivered to the customer. As shown earlier in Figure 3.5, this subsystem embraces not only the visible elements of the service operating system—buildings, equipment, and personnel—but may also involve exposure to other customers.

Service providers traditionally had direct interactions with their customers. But to achieve goals ranging from cost reduction and productivity improvement to greater customer convenience, many services that don't need the customers to be physically present in the factory now seek to reduce direct contact. Midland Bank's creation of First Direct is a prime example of this trend. As a result, the visible component of the service operations system is shrinking in many industries as electronic technology or redesigned physical flows are used to drive service delivery from higher to lower levels of contact.

Self-service delivery often offers customers greater convenience than face-to-face contact. Machines such as automated petrol pumps, ATMs, or coin-operated food and drink dispensers can be installed in numerous locations and made accessible 24 hours a day, 7 days a week. Electronic food retailing sites like wine.com and tabasco.com provide extensive product information and a greater selection of specialty items than most bricks and mortar outlets can offer.[20] Cafeteria service allows customers to see menu items before making their selection. Self-guided museum tours allow visitors to enjoy an exhibition at their own pace. Online college courses allow students to complete work at their own pace in an off-campus location.

But there are potential disadvantages to self-service delivery, too. The shift from personal service (sometimes referred to as "high touch") to self-service ("high tech") sometimes disturbs customers. So a strategy of replacing employees by machines or other self-service procedures may require an information campaign to educate customers and promote the benefits of the new approach. It also helps to design user-friendly equipment, including free telephone or e-mail access to an employee who can answer questions and solve problems. Of course, not all self-service is installed in remote locations. Cafeterias and self-guided museum tours are examples of customers taking on tasks that would otherwise have to be assigned to service personnel. Later in this chapter, we'll discuss the role of the customer as a coproducer of service in collaboration with the service provider.

Using the theatrical analogy, the distinction between high-contact and low-contact services can be likened to the differences between live theater on a stage and a drama created for television. That's because customers of low-contact services normally never see the "factory" where the work is performed; at most, they will talk with a service provider (or problem solver) by telephone. Without buildings and furnishings or even the appearance of employees to provide tangible clues, customers must make judgments about service quality based on ease of telephone access, followed by the voice and responsiveness of a telephone-based customer service representative.

When service is delivered through impersonal electronic channels, such as self-service machines, automated telephone calls to a central computer, or via the customer's own computer, there is very little traditional "theater" left to the performance. Some firms compensate for this by giving their machines names, playing recorded music, or installing moving color graphics on video screens, adding sounds, and creating computer-based interactive capabilities to give the experience a more human feeling. Another option is to design a retail Web site to resemble a display in a store window. Some virtual companies now offer real-time, interactive e-mail communications between shoppers and customer service personnel. Consider Flooz.com, a provider of electronic gift certificates that can be spent online at more than 60 stores (see page 44). If a customer logs onto the Flooz.com site and accesses the "Live Help" link at the top of the home page, there is an immediate response similar to the one quoted below:[21]

> *A Flooz.com Customer Care Representative will be with you momentarily!*
> *Please feel free to continue browsing below.*
> *JasonMa has arrived to help you!*
> *JasonMa says, "Thank you for accessing Live Chat. My name is Jason.*
> *May I please have your e-mail address so I can better assist you?"*

Responsibility for designing and managing service delivery systems has traditionally fallen to operations managers. But marketing needs to be involved, too, because

What Options Do You Use for Delivery of Bank Services?

Not everyone is comfortable with the trend toward low-contact services, which is why some firms give their customers a choice. For instance, many retail banks now offer an array of service delivery options. Consider this spectrum of alternatives. Which options do you currently use at your bank? Which would you like to use in the future? And which are currently available?

1. Visit the bank in person and conduct transactions with a bank clerk.
2. Use postal service to send deposits or request new checkbooks.
3. Use an ATM.
4. Conduct transactions by telephone with a customer service representative.
5. Use the keys on a telephone to interact with the bank in response to voice commands (or a telephone screen display).
6. Conduct home banking through your own computer, using a modem and special software.
7. Conduct transactions by computer through the World Wide Web.
8. Complete banking transactions by mobile phone or PDA (personal digital assistant).

In each instance, what factors explain your preference? Do they relate to the type of transactions you need to conduct or a situational element like the weather or time of day? Are you influenced by your feelings of liking (or disliking) human contact in a banking context? Or is there some other explanation? What advice would you give to your bank for how to serve you better?

understanding customer needs and concerns is important to ensure that the delivery system works well.

The Dramaturgy of Service Delivery

As we've pointed out earlier, the theater is a good metaphor for services because service delivery consists of a series of events that customers experience as a *performance*.[22] It's a particularly useful approach for high-contact service providers (e.g., physicians, educators, restaurants, and hotels) and for businesses that serve many people simultaneously rather than providing individualized service (e.g., professional sports, hospitals, and entertainment). Figure 3.6 shows the relative importance of theatrical dimensions for different types of service businesses. As you can see, watch repair services have very few front stage theatrical components compared to services like airlines and spectator sports.

Service facilities contain the stage on which the drama unfolds. Sometimes the setting changes from one act to another (e.g., when airline passengers move from the entrance to the terminal to the check-in stations and then on to the boarding lounge and finally step inside the aircraft). The stage may have minimal "props," as in a typical post office, or elaborate scenery, as in some modern resort hotels. Many service dramas are tightly scripted (as in the way that service is delivered in a formal restaurant setting), while others are improvisational in nature (like teaching a university class).

Some services are more ritualized than others. In highly structured environments like dental services, "blocking" may define how the actors (in this case, receptionists, dental hygienists, technicians, and dentists) should move relative to the stage (the dentist's office), items of scenery (furniture and equipment), and other actors.

Not all service providers require customers to attend performances at the company's "theater." In many instances, the customer's own facilities provide the stage where the service employees perform with their props. For example, outside accountants are often hired to provide specialized services at a client's site. (While this may be convenient for customers, it isn't always very appealing for the "visiting accountants," who

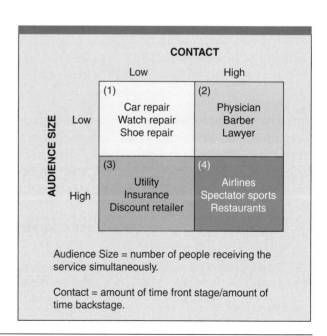

FIGURE 3.6

Relative Importance of Theatrical Dimensions

Source: Stephen J. Grove and Raymond P. Fisk, "The Dramaturgy of Service Exchange: An Analytical Framework for Services Marketing," in *Emerging Perspectives of Services Marketing*, L. L. Berry, I. L. Shostack, and G. D. Upah, eds. (Chicago: American Marketing Association, 1983), 45–49. Reprinted with Permission.

sometimes find themselves housed in rat-infested basements or inventorying frozen food for hours in a cold storage locker![23]) Telecommunication linkages offer an alternative performance environment, allowing customers to be involved in the drama from a remote location—a delivery option long awaited by those traveling accountants, who would probably much prefer to work for their clients from the comfort of their own offices via modems and computers.

Front stage personnel are members of a cast, playing roles as *actors* in a drama, and supported by a backstage production team. In some instances, they are expected to wear special costumes when on stage (like the protective clothing—traditionally white—worn by dental professionals, the fanciful uniforms often worn by hotel doormen, or the more basic brown ones worn by UPS drivers). When service employees wear distinctive apparel, they stand out from personnel at other firms. In this respect, uniform designs can be seen as a form of packaging that provides physical evidence of brand identity.[24] In many service companies, the choice of uniform design and colors is carefully integrated with other corporate design elements. Many front stage employees must conform to both a dress code and grooming standards (e.g., Disney's rule that employees can't wear beards).

Depending on the nature of their work, employees may be required to learn and repeat specific lines ranging from announcements in several languages to a singsong sales spiel (just think of the last telemarketer who called you!) to a parting salutation of "Have a nice day!" Just like the theater, companies often use scripting to define actors' behavior as well as their lines. Eye contact, smiles, and handshakes may be required in addition to a spoken greeting. McDonald's has an extensive handbook that prescribes employee behavior worldwide—even down to the width of the smile, according to some who've worked in the shadow of the golden arches. Other rules of conduct may include bans on smoking, eating and drinking, or gum chewing while on duty.

Role and Script Theories

Role and script theories offer some interesting insights for service providers. If we view service delivery as a theatrical experience, then both employees and customers act out their parts in the performance according to predetermined roles.

Roles   Grove and Fisk define a **role** as "a set of behavior patterns learned through experience and communication, to be performed by an individual in a certain social interaction in order to attain maximum effectiveness in goal accomplishment."[25] Roles have also been defined as combinations of social cues, or expectations of society, that guide behavior in a specific setting or context.[26] In service encounters, employees and customers each have roles to play. The satisfaction of both parties depends on **role congruence**, or the extent to which each person acts out his or her prescribed role during a service encounter. Employees must perform their roles to customer expectations or risk dissatisfying or losing customers all together. And customers, too, must "play by the rules," or they risk causing problems for the firm, its employees, and even other customers.

Scripts are sequences of behavior that both employees and customers are expected to learn and follow during service delivery. Scripts are learned through experience, education, and communication with others.[27] Much like a movie script, a service script provides detailed actions that customers and employees are expected to perform. The more experience a customer has with a service company, the more familiar the script becomes. Any deviations from this known script may frustrate both customers and employees and can lead to high levels of dissatisfaction. If a company decides to change a service script (e.g., by using technology to turn a high-contact service into a low-contact one), service personnel and customers should be educated about the new script and the benefits it provides.

Some scripts are highly structured and allow service employees to move through their duties quickly and efficiently (e.g., flight attendants' scripts for economy class). This

role: a combination of social cues that guides behavior in a specific setting or context.

role congruence: the extent to which both customers and employees act out their prescribed roles during a service encounter.

scripts: learned sequences of behaviors obtained through personal experience or communications with others.

approach helps to overcome two of the inherent challenges facing service firms—how to reduce variability and ensure uniform quality. The risk is that frequent repetition may lead to mindless service delivery that ignores customers' needs.

Not all services involve tightly scripted performances. For providers of highly customized services—like doctors, educators, hair stylists, or consultants—the service script is flexible and may vary by situation and by customer. When customers are new to a service, they may not know what to expect and may be fearful of behaving incorrectly. Organizations should be ready to educate new customers about their roles in service delivery, since inappropriate behaviors can disrupt service delivery and make customers feel embarrassed and uncomfortable.

A well-planned script should provide a full description of the service encounter and can help identify potential or existing problems in a specific service process. Figure

FIGURE 3.7

Script for Teeth Cleaning and Simple Dental Exam

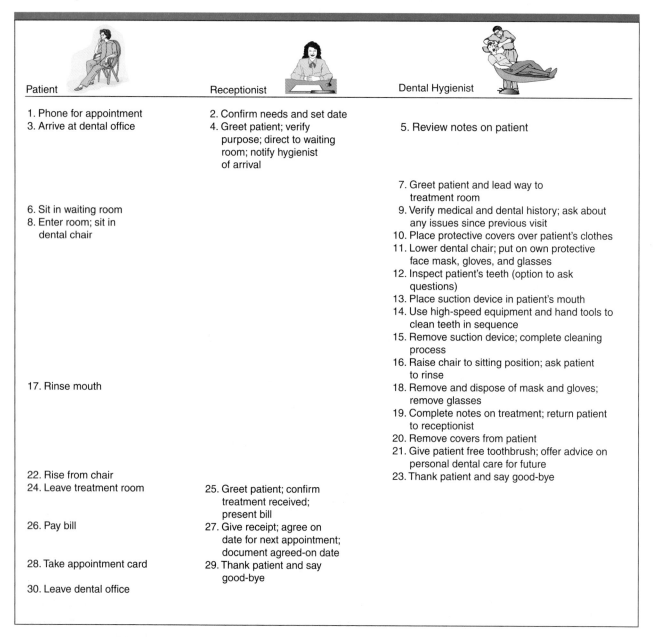

Patient	Receptionist	Dental Hygienist
1. Phone for appointment	2. Confirm needs and set date	
3. Arrive at dental office	4. Greet patient; verify purpose; direct to waiting room; notify hygienist of arrival	5. Review notes on patient
		7. Greet patient and lead way to treatment room
6. Sit in waiting room		9. Verify medical and dental history; ask about any issues since previous visit
8. Enter room; sit in dental chair		10. Place protective covers over patient's clothes
		11. Lower dental chair; put on own protective face mask, gloves, and glasses
		12. Inspect patient's teeth (option to ask questions)
		13. Place suction device in patient's mouth
		14. Use high-speed equipment and hand tools to clean teeth in sequence
		15. Remove suction device; complete cleaning process
		16. Raise chair to sitting position; ask patient to rinse
17. Rinse mouth		18. Remove and dispose of mask and gloves; remove glasses
		19. Complete notes on treatment; return patient to receptionist
		20. Remove covers from patient
		21. Give patient free toothbrush; offer advice on personal dental care for future
22. Rise from chair		23. Thank patient and say good-bye
24. Leave treatment room	25. Greet patient; confirm treatment received; present bill	
26. Pay bill	27. Give receipt; agree on date for next appointment; document agreed-on date	
28. Take appointment card	29. Thank patient and say good-bye	
30. Leave dental office		

3.7 shows a script for teeth cleaning and a simple dental examination, involving three players—the patient, the receptionist, and the dental hygienist. Each has a specific role to play. In this instance, the script is driven primarily by the need to execute a technical task both proficiently and safely (note the mask and gloves). The core service of examining and cleaning teeth can only be accomplished satisfactorily if the patient cooperates in an experience that is at best neutral and at worst uncomfortable or even painful.

Several script elements refer to information flows. Confirming appointments avoids delays for customers and ensures effective use of dental professionals' time. Obtaining patient histories and documenting analysis and treatment are vital for maintaining complete dental records and also for accurate billing. Payment on receipt of treatment improves cash flow and avoids the problem of bad debts. Adding greetings, statements of thanks, and good-byes displays friendly good manners and helps to humanize what most people see as a slightly unpleasant experience.

By examining existing scripts, service managers may discover ways to modify the nature of customer and employee roles to improve service delivery, increase productivity, and enhance the nature of the customer's experience. As service delivery procedures evolve in response to new technology or other factors, revised scripts may need to be developed.

Service Marketing System

In addition to the service delivery system described above, other elements also contribute to the customer's overall view of a service business. These include communication efforts by the advertising and sales departments, telephone calls and letters from service personnel, billings from the accounting department, random exposures to service personnel and facilities, news stories and editorials in the mass media, word-of-mouth comments from current or former customers, and even participation in market research studies.

Collectively, the components just cited—plus those in the service delivery system—add up to what we call the service marketing system. This represents all the different ways the customer may encounter or learn about the organization in question. Because services are experiential, each of these elements offers clues about the nature and quality of the service product. Inconsistency between different elements may weaken the organization's credibility in the customers' eyes. Figure 3.8 depicts the

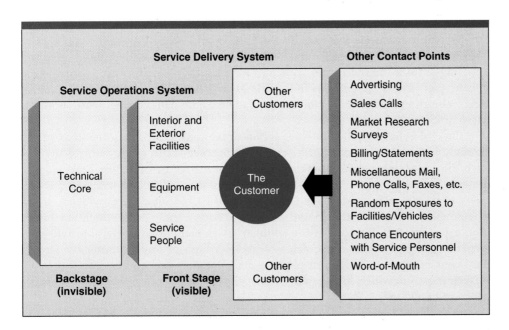

FIGURE 3.8

The Service Marketing System for a High-Contact Service

FIGURE 3.9

The Service Marketing
System for a Low-Contact
Service

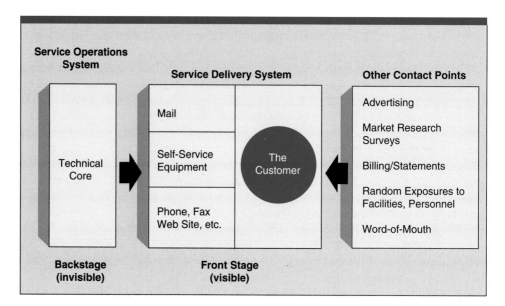

service marketing system for a high-contact service like a hotel, dental office, or full-service restaurant.

As you know from your own experience, the scope and structure of the service marketing system often vary sharply from one type of organization to another. Figure 3.9 shows how things change when we are dealing with a low-contact service, such as a credit card account. The significance of this approach to conceptualizing service creation and delivery is that it represents the customer's view, looking at the service business from the outside, as opposed to an internally focused operations perspective.

Physical Evidence

Many service performances are hard to evaluate. As a result, customers often look for tangible clues about the nature of the service. For instance, what impression is created in your mind if you see a damaged vehicle belonging to an express delivery service broken down by the side of the road? Or observe a poorly groomed flight attendant traveling to (or from) the airport wearing a frayed and dirty uniform? Or visit a friend in a hospital where the grounds and buildings are beautifully maintained, the interior decor cheerful rather than institutional, and the friendly staff wearing smart, spotlessly clean uniforms?

Physical evidence provides clues about service quality, and in some cases it will strongly influence how customers (especially inexperienced ones) evaluate the service. Thus managers need to think carefully about the nature of the physical evidence provided to customers by the service marketing system. We'll be addressing this element of the 8Ps in more depth in Chapters 8 and 10, but Table 3.2 provides an initial checklist of the main tangible and communication elements to which customers might be exposed. Of course, the number of elements that are visible will vary depending on whether service delivery involves high or low customer contact. In low-contact services, additional physical evidence may be communicated through advertising, using video footage on TV or printed illustrations in newspapers, magazines, or brochures.

1. **Service personnel.** Contacts with customers may be face-to-face, by telecommunications (telephone, fax, telegram, telex, electronic mail), or by mail and express delivery services.
   These personnel may include
   - Sales representatives
   - Customer service staff
   - Accounting/billing staff
   - Operations staff who do not normally provide direct service to customers (e.g., engineers, janitors)
   - Designated intermediaries whom customers perceive as directly representing the service firm
2. **Service facilities and equipment**
   - Building exteriors, parking areas, landscaping
   - Building interiors and furnishings
   - Vehicles
   - Self-service equipment operated by customers
   - Other equipment
3. **Nonpersonal communications**
   - Form letters
   - Brochures/catalogs/instruction manuals/Web sites
   - Advertising
   - Signage
   - News stories/editorials in the mass media
4. **Other people**
   - Fellow customers encountered during service delivery
   - Word-of-mouth comments from friends, acquaintances, or even strangers

TABLE 3.2

Tangible Elements and Communication Components in the Service Marketing System

THE CUSTOMER AS COPRODUCER

In some service environments, customers play a relatively passive role, waiting to be served. So long as they can state their needs clearly and pay promptly when billed, they play a minimal role in the *process* of service delivery (think about leaving clothes at a laundry). But sometimes customers are expected to actively participate in the production process—one of the distinctive features of service management that we noted in Chapter 1. Customer participation refers to the actions and resources supplied by customers during service production and/or delivery; it includes customers' mental, physical, and emotional inputs.[28] Table 3.3 illustrates the differing levels of participation required of customers across an array of service businesses.

Service Firms as Teachers

Although service providers attempt to design the ideal level of customer participation into the service delivery system, in reality it is customers' actions that determine the actual amount of participation. Underparticipation causes customers to experience a decrease in service benefits (a student learning less or a dieter losing less weight). If customers overparticipate, they may cause the firm to spend more resources customizing a service than was originally intended (a request for customization of a hamburger at a fast-food restaurant). Service businesses must teach their customers what roles to play to optimize participation levels during service production and consumption.

The more work that customers are expected to do, the greater their need for information about how to perform for best results. The necessary education can be provided in many different ways. Brochures and posted instructions are two widely used approaches. Automated machines often contain detailed operating instructions and diagrams (unfortunately, these are sometimes only intelligible to the engineers who wrote them). Thoughtful banks place a telephone beside their ATMs so that customers can call a real person for help and advice at any time if they are confused about the on-screen instructions. Advertising for new services often contains significant educational content.

Source: Adapted from Mary Jo Bitner, William T. Faranda, Amy R. Hubbert, and Valarie A. Zeithaml, "Customer Contributions and Roles in Service Delivery," *International Journal of Service Industry Management* 8, no. 3 (1997): 193–205.

TABLE 3.3

Levels of Customer Participation Across Different Services

Low (Customer Presence Required During Service Delivery)	Moderate (Customer Inputs Required for Service Creation)	High (Customer Coproduces the Service Product)
Products are standardized	Client inputs customize a standard service	Active client participation guides the customized service
Service is provided regardless of any individual purchase	Provision of service requires customer purchase	Service cannot be created apart from the customer's purchase and active participation
Payment may be the only required customer input	Customer inputs (information, materials) are necessary for an adequate outcome, but the service firm provides the service	Customer inputs are mandatory and coproduce the outcome
Examples:		
Consumer services		
Bus travel	Hair cut	Marriage counseling
Motel stay	Annual physical exam	Personal training
Movie theater	Full-service restaurant	Weight-reduction program
Business-to-business services		
Uniform cleaning service	Agency-created advertising campaign	Management consulting
Pest control	Payroll service	Executive management seminar
Interior greenery maintenance	Independent freight transportation	Install wide area network (WAN)

In many businesses, customers look to employees for advice and assistance and are frustrated if they can't obtain it. Service providers, ranging from sales assistants and customer service representatives to flight attendants and nurses, must be trained to help them improve their teaching skills. As a last resort, people may turn to other customers for help.

Schneider and Bowen suggest giving customers a realistic **service preview** in advance of service delivery to provide them with a clear picture of the role they will play in service coproduction.[29] For example, a company might show a video presentation to help customers understand their role in the service encounter. This technique is used by some dentists to help patients understand the surgical processes they are about to experience and indicate how they should cooperate to help make things go as smoothly as possible.

service preview: a demonstration of how a service works to educate customers about the roles they are expected to perform in service delivery.

Customers as Partial Employees

Some researchers argue that firms should view customers as "partial employees," who can influence the productivity and quality of service processes and outputs.[30] This perspective requires a change in management mindset, as Schneider and Bowen make clear:

If you think of customers as partial employees, you begin to think very differently about what you hope customers will bring to the service encounter. Now they must bring not only expectations and needs but also relevant service production competencies that will enable them to fill the role of partial employees. The service management challenge deepens accordingly.[31]

Schneider and Bowen suggest that customers who are offered an opportunity to participate at an active level are more likely to be satisfied—regardless of whether or not they actually choose the more active role—because they like to be offered a choice.

Managing customers as partial employees requires using the same human resource strategy as managing a firm's paid employees and should follow these four steps:

1. Conduct a "job analysis" of customers' present roles in the business and compare it against the roles that the firm would like them to play.

2. Determine if customers are aware of how they are expected to perform and have the skills needed to perform as required.

3. Motivate customers by ensuring that they will be rewarded for performing well (e.g., satisfaction from better quality and more customized output, enjoyment of participating in the actual *process*, a belief that their own productivity speeds the *process* and keeps costs down).

4. Regularly appraise customers' performance. If it is unsatisfactory, seek to change their roles and the procedures in which they are involved. Alternatively, consider "terminating" these customers (nicely, of course!) and look for new ones.

Effective human resource management starts with recruitment and selection. The same approach should hold true for "partial employees." So if coproduction requires specific skills, firms should target their marketing efforts to recruit new customers who have the competency to perform the necessary tasks.[32] After all, many colleges do just this in their student selection process!

Conclusion

Service encounters cover a spectrum from high contact to low contact. Their position on this spectrum is often determined by the nature of the operational processes used in service creation and delivery. With the growing trend to deliver information-based services through electronic channels, many service encounters are shifting to a lower-contact mode, with important implications for the nature of the customer experience.

In all types of services, understanding and managing service encounters between customers and service personnel are central to creating satisfied customers who are willing to enter into long-term relationships with the service provider. Critical incidents occur when some aspect of the service encounter is particularly satisfactory or unsatisfactory.

Service businesses can be divided into three overlapping systems. The operations system consists of the personnel, facilities, and equipment required to run the service operation and create the service product. Only part of this system, called "front stage," is visible to the customer. The delivery system incorporates the visible operations elements and the customers, who sometimes take an active role in helping to create the service product as opposed to being passively waited on. The higher the level of contact, the more we can apply theatrical analogies to the process of "staging" service delivery in which employees and customers play roles, often following well-defined scripts. In high-contact services, customers are exposed to many more tangible clues and experiences than they are in medium-contact and low-contact situations. Finally, the marketing system includes not only the delivery system, which is essentially composed of the product and distribution elements of the traditional marketing mix, but also additional components such as billing and payment systems, exposure to advertising and sales people, and word-of-mouth comments from other people.

In some instances, customers act as service coproducers, or "partial employees," whose performance will affect the productivity and quality of output. Under these circumstances, service managers must be sure to educate and train customers so that they have the skills needed to perform well during all types of service encounters.

Study Questions and Exercises

1. What actions could a senior bank executive take to encourage more customers to bank by phone, mail, Internet, or through ATMs rather than visiting a branch?

2. What are the backstage elements of (a) an insurance company, (b) a car repair facility, (c) a hotel, (d) an airline, (e) a university, (f) a funeral home, (g) a consulting firm, (h) a television station? Under what circumstances would it be appropriate to allow customers to see some of these backstage elements and how would you do it?

3. What roles are played by front stage service personnel in low-contact organizations? Are these roles more or less important to customer satisfaction than in high-contact services?

4. Use Figures 3.8 and 3.9, plus Table 3.2, to develop a profile of the service marketing system for a variety of services—hospital, airline, consulting engineer or legal service, college, hotel, dry cleaner, credit union, automobile service center, or post office. (You can base your profiles on your own experience or interview other customers.)

5. What is the difference between a moment of truth, a service encounter, and a critical incident?

6. Describe a critical incident that you have experienced with a self-service technology during service delivery. If your incident was dissatisfying, what could the service provider have done to improve the situation?

7. Review Figure 3.3. As a manager, how would you try to prevent future recurrence of the 12 unsatisfactory incidents? (Hint: Consider the underlying cause of the problem for each incident and possible reasons for the inappropriate response that upset the customer.)

8. Develop two different customer scripts, one for a standardized service and one for a customized service. What are the key differences between the two?

9. Define the term "partial employee" and describe three recent situations in which you were engaged in such a role.

Endnotes

1. Robert J. Peterson, Sridar Balasubramanian, and Bart J. Bronnenberg, "Exploring the Implications of the Internet for Consumer Marketing," *Journal of the Academy of Marketing Sciences* 25, no. 4 (1997): 329–346.
2. Saul Hansell, "500,000 Clients, No Branches," *New York Times*, 3 September 1995, sec. 3, 1.
3. WingspanBank.com Web site, www.WingspanBank.com, September 2000.
4. Gómez Web site, www.Gomez.com, January 2001.
5. Alex Frew McMillan, "Banking with a Mouse," CNNfn.com, 13 September 1999.
6. Curtis P. McLaughlin, "Why Variation Reduction Is Not Everything: A New Paradigm for Service Operations," *International Journal of Service Industry Management* 7, no. 3 (1996): 17–39.
7. Lance A. Bettencourt and Kevin Gwinner, "Customization of the Service Experience: The Role of the Frontline Employee," *International Journal of Service Industry Management* 7, no. 2 (1996): 2–21.
8. Richard Gibson, "Machine Takes Orders in Test by McDonald's," *Wall Street Journal*, 11 August 1999, B1. See also, Ann Merrill, "Rainbow's Version of Fast Food," *Star Tribune* (Minneapolis), 12 August 1999, D1; and Yukari Iwatani, "From Bars to Car Washes Internet Is Everywhere," *Yahoo! News*, 11 September 2000.
9. Matthew L. Meuter, Amy L. Ostrom, Robert I. Roundtree, and Mary Jo Bitner, "Understanding Customer Satisfaction with Technology-Based Service Encounters," *Journal of Marketing* 64 (Summer 2000): 50–64.
10. Lynn Shostack, "Planning the Service Encounter," in *The Service Encounter*, ed. J. A. Czepiel, M.R. Solomon, and C.F. Surprenant (Lexington, MA: Lexington Books, 1985), 243–254.
11. Carole F. Surprenant and Michael R. Solomon, "Predictability and Personalization in the Service Encounter," *Journal of Marketing* 51 (Winter 1987): 73–80.
12. Matthew L. Meuter and Mary Jo Bitner, "Self-Service Technologies: Extending Service Frameworks and Identifying Issues for Research," in *Marketing Theory and Applications*, ed.

Dhruv Grewal and Connie Pechman (Chicago, IL: The American Marketing Association, 1998), 12–19.

13. James G. Barnes, Peter A. Dunne, and William J. Glynn, "Self-Service and Technology: Unanticipated and Unintended Effects on Customer Relationships," in *Handbook of Service Marketing and Management*, ed. Teresa A. Schwartz and Dawn Iacobucci (Thousand Oaks, CA: Sage Publications, 2000), 89–102.

14. Normann first used the term "moments of truth" in a Swedish study in 1978; subsequently it appeared in English in Richard Normann, *Service Management: Strategy and Leadership in Service Businesses*, 2d ed. (Chichester, UK: John Wiley & Sons, 1991), 16–17.

15. Jan Carlzon *Moments of Truth* (Cambridge, MA: Ballinger Publishing Co., 1987), 3.

16. Mary Jo Bitner, Bernard Booms, and Lois A. Mohr, "Critical Service Encounters: The Employee's View," *Journal of Marketing* 58 (October 1994): 95–106.

17. Eric Langeard, John E. G. Bateson, Christopher H. Lovelock, and Pierre Eiglier, *Services Marketing: New Insights from Consumers and Managers* (Cambridge, MA: Marketing Science Institute, 1981).

18. Richard B. Chase, "Where Does the Customer Fit in a Service Organization?" *Harvard Business Review* 56 (November–December 1978), 137–142.

19. Stephen J. Grove, Raymond P. Fisk, and Mary Jo Bitner, "Dramatizing the Service Experience: A Managerial Approach," in *Advances in Services Marketing and Management, Vol. 1*, ed. T. A. Schwartz, D. E. Bowan, and S. W. Brown (Greenwich, CT: JAI Press, 1992), 91–122. See also, B. Joseph Pine II and James H. Gilmore, *The Experience Economy* (Boston: Harvard Business School Press, 1999).

20. Gregory R. Heim and Kingshu K. Sinha, "Design and Delivery of Electronic Services: Implications for Customer Value in Electronic Food Retailing," in *New Service Development: Creating Memorable Experiences*, ed. James A. Fitzsimmons and Mona Fitzsimmons (Thousand Oaks, CA: Sage Publications, 2000), 152–182.

21. Flooz.com Web site, www.Flooz.com, January 2001.

22. Stephen J. Grove, Raymond P. Fisk, and Joby John, "Services as Theater: Guidelines and Implications," in *Handbook of Service Marketing and Management*, ed. Teresa A. Schwartz and Dawn Iacobucci (Thousand Oaks, CA: Sage Publications, 2000), 21–36.

23. Elizabeth MacDonald, "Oh, the Horrors of Being a Visiting Accountant," *Wall Street Journal*, 10 March 1997, B1.

24. Michael R. Solomon, "Packaging the Service Provider," *The Service Industries Journal*, July 1986.

25. Stephen J. Grove and Raymond P. Fisk, "The Dramaturgy of Services Exchange: An Analytical Framework for Services Marketing," in *Emerging Perspectives on Services Marketing*, ed. L. L. Berry, G. L. Shostack, and G. D. Upah (Chicago, IL: The American Marketing Association, 1983), 45–49.

26. Michael R. Solomon, Carol Suprenant, John A. Czepiel, and Evelyn G. Gutman, "A Role Theory Perspective on Dyadic Interactions: The Service Encounter," *Journal of Marketing* 49 (Winter 1985): 99–111.

27. See R. P. Abelson, "Script Processing in Attitude Formation and Decision-Making," in *Cognitive and Social Behavior*, ed. J. S. Carrol and J. W. Payne (Hillsdale, NJ: Erlbaum, 1976), 33–45; and Ronald H. Humphrey and Blake E. Ashforth, "Cognitive Scripts and Prototypes in Service Encounters," in *Advances in Service Marketing and Management* (Greenwich, CT: JAI Press, 1994), 175–199.

28. Amy Risch Rodie and Susan Schultz Klein, "Customer Participation in Services Production and Delivery," in *Handbook of Service Marketing and Management*, ed. Teresa A. Schwartz and Dawn Iacobucci (Thousand Oaks, CA: Sage Publications, 2000), 111–125.

29. Benjamin Schneider and David E. Bowen, *Winning the Service Game* (Boston: Harvard Business School Press, 1995), 92.

30. David E. Bowen, "Managing Customers as Human Resources in Service Organizations," *Human Resources Management* 25, no. 3 (1986): 371–383.

31. Benjamin Schneider and David E. Bowen, *Winning the Service Game*, p. 85.

32. Bonnie Farber Canziani, "Leveraging Customer Competency in Service Firms," *International Journal of Service Industry Management* 8, no. 1(1997): 5–25.

chapter four

Customer Behavior in Service Environments

Understanding Technology Users— From Mouse Potatoes to Media Junkies

Delivering services through the Internet is an appealing strategy for many firms. However, not every prospective customer is enthusiastic about this concept.[1] As the consumer market for technology grows, companies selling products from cellular phones to Internet services are struggling to understand who their customers are and what motivates them to buy. The failure of some highly publicized high-tech goods and services, such as Kodak's PhotoCD and Web TV, has convinced many marketers that new approaches are needed to help us understand what makes technology users tick (or not tick, as the case may be). For instance, traditional consumer research may identify who bought a computer, but it won't specify which of four different household members use it and for what purposes.

Delivery of many information-based services depends not only upon customers having access to relevant equipment—such as computers, cell phones, and PDAs—but also on customers being willing and able to use it to access the services in question. Consequently, market researchers have been working to determine whether the purchase process is different for such goods and services and to examine how people actually use information technology in their home and work environments.

Forrester Research Inc., a technology consulting firm based in Cambridge, Massachusetts, has created a subscription research service called Technographics that processes continuous survey data from more than 375,000 online and off-line households in the United States, Canada, and Europe. Forrester asks consumers about their motivations, buying habits, and financial ability to buy technology-related goods and services. Many big-name service providers, like Sprint, Visa, and Bank of America, are willing to pay handsomely to receive the results of these surveys. "Technology is not just changing the way consumers spend time," says Technographics client Gil Fuchsberg. "It's also changing the way nearly every company is making, selling, and delivering products."

To help companies identify the right target customers, Forrester has defined 10 "technographical" categories ranging from the tech-crazy "Fast Forwards" to the disinterested "Sidelined Citizens."

To get an idea of how this segmentation scheme works, consider the Williams family. Cindy, age 46, is an administrative secretary in Tulsa, Oklahoma. She and her husband Gary, 44, have one computer they bought three years ago. They don't use this computer much themselves and are not connected to the Internet (which makes them unable to access online services). Their sons, ages 11 and 12, would like an upgraded PC that is better for the computer-based games they love, but their parents have no plans to get one. Because of the Williams' status and income—two traditional segmentation variables—many researchers might identify them as promising technology buyers.

But Forrester maintains such a conclusion would be misleading because it fails to take into account the family's priorities as revealed through their behavior. The firm believes that any high-tech firm attempting to market sophisticated products to a family such as the Williams would be wasting its money. Technographics classifies the Williams as "Traditionalists"—family-oriented buyers who could afford

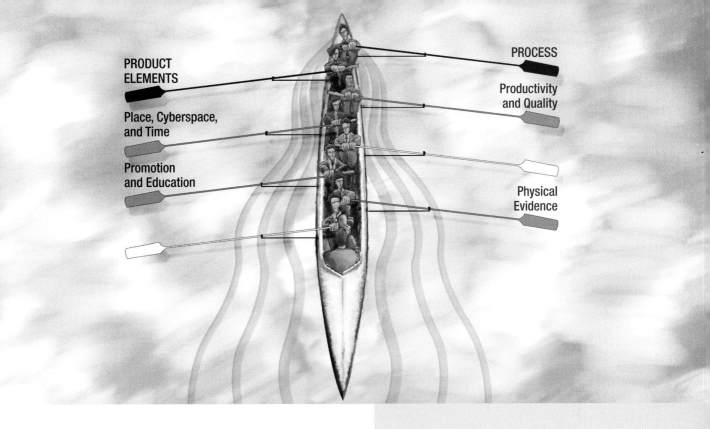

PRODUCT
ELEMENTS

Place, Cyberspace,
and Time

Promotion
and Education

PROCESS

Productivity
and Quality

Physical
Evidence

new technology-based products but are not convinced that they're worth buying. Why would the Williams be Traditionalists? The age of their computer (three years old is ancient by tech standards) and the lack of an Internet connection are two big clues. On the basis of this information, marketers of high-tech goods and services might decide to bypass the Williams in spite of their promising demographic profile.

⇒ Learning Objectives

After reading this chapter, you should be able to

⇒ recall the principles of segmentation, particularly as they relate to customer behavior

⇒ describe the three different types of attributes that consumers use to evaluate products and how they relate to service offerings

⇒ discuss why service characteristics like intangibility and quality control problems affect consumer evaluation processes

⇒ describe the relationship between customer expectations and customer satisfaction

⇒ explain the purchase process for services

⇒ construct a simple flowchart showing a service process from the customer's perspective

market segmentation: the process of dividing a market into different groups within which all customers share relevant characteristics that distinguish them from customers in other segments.

segment: a group of current or prospective customers who share common characteristics, needs, purchasing behavior, or consumption patterns.

FOCUSING ON THE RIGHT CUSTOMERS

In this chapter, we continue to address the question, *Who are our customers and how should we relate to them?* We start by building on our opening vignette with a further discussion of **market segmentation** (see Figure 4.1 for a depiction of Forrester Research's Technographics approach) and then look at how people evaluate, purchase, and use services.

More and more, firms are trying to decide which types of customers they can serve well and make loyal, rather than trying to be all things to all people. However, relatively few service businesses can survive by serving just a single **segment**, especially if, like hotels, airlines, and restaurants, they have a lot of capacity to fill, hour after hour and day after day during different seasons of the year. Managers facing this problem need to be creative and try to attract new segments that will fit well with the firm's capabilities.

	CAREER	**FAMILY**	**ENTERTAINMENT**
OPTIMISTS	**Fast Forwards** These consumers are the biggest spenders, and they're early adopters of new technology for home, office, and personal use.	**New Age Nurturers** Also big spenders but focused on technology for home uses, such as a family PC.	**Mouse Potatoes** They like the online world for entertainment and are willing to spend for the latest in technology.
	Techno-strivers Use technology from cell phones and pagers to online services primarily to gain a career edge.	**Digital Hopefuls** Families with a limited budget but still interested in new technology; good candidates for the under-$1,000 PC.	**Gadget Grabbers** They also favor online entertainment but have less cash to spend on it.
PESSIMISTS	**Hand-shakers** Older consumers—typically managers—who don't touch their computers at work; they leave that to younger assistants.	**Traditionalists** Willing to use technology, but slow to upgrade; not convinced upgrades and other add-ons are worth paying for.	**Media Junkies** Seek entertainment and can't find much of it online; prefer TV and other, older media.
Sidelined Citizens Not interested in technology.			

Data: Forrester Research Inc.

More Affluent   Less Affluent

FIGURE 4.1

Segmenting Customers Relative to Technology Use

Source: Paul C. Judge, "Are Tech Buyers Different? *Business Week,* 26 January 1998, 65.

We hear the term "mass marketing" less and less these days. Instead the talk is of "focus" or "targeting" or "**mass customization**." Underlying such terms is the notion of market segmentation, which calls for dividing any given market into distinctive groups or segments. Segmentation is a key concept in marketing, so if you have not previously taken a marketing course, please review the key aspects of segmentation in the box on pages 78–79.

As service providers explore innovative alternatives to creating and delivering services, especially those relating to the Internet and automated machines, they are discov-

mass customization: offering a service with some individualized product elements to a large number of customers at a relatively low price.

Attracting Older Passengers at Southwest Airlines

Like most airlines, Southwest Airlines can divide its passengers into two broad groups: business travelers and leisure travelers. Although business travelers fly far more frequently than most leisure travelers, the latter help fill the aircraft outside commuting hours and enable Southwest to offer more frequent service at lower prices. A significant target segment within the broad leisure group is older customers, who are growing in numbers as the population ages and has the time and inclination to travel—and can afford to do so at Southwest's very low fares.

However, many senior citizens are not experienced flyers. In fact, some have never flown before in their lives. To encourage these people to fly, Southwest has created a brochure titled "Travel Tips for Seniors" (see the reproduced cover), which is educational in nature rather than promotional. It begins by pointing out that the airline offers special fares to people aged 65 and older, then continues with bullet-pointed tips on Packing and Travel, Making Reservations, Checking In, and Travel Talk Language. The brochure concludes with a map of the United States, showing the cities that Southwest serves, plus the head office address, the airline's toll-free phone number, and its Web site address.

Through such efforts, the airline seeks to demystify air travel; help older people prepare for a journey by air; and explain each step in what is, for an inexperienced traveler, a relatively complex process. The brochure also explains the terms commonly used in airline travel, many of which (such as *preboard* or *gate agent*) are not often heard outside an airport. In this way, older travelers will know what to expect and—equally important—what is expected of them. Knowledge reduces anxiety, thus eliminating one of the barriers to trying something new. To the extent that readers of the brochure appreciate the advice, try a flight on Southwest, and enjoy it, the airline can expect to create loyal customers and stimulate positive word of mouth.

Dreaming of jetting away to explore the history and fun of these United States? Southwest Airlines would like to make getting away as easy and fun as possible for those **age 65 or over** by offering some travel tips to Seniors who are keen on life and life's adventures!

ering that not all customers are equally receptive to new technologies. This situation has led to development of segmentation schemes based on how willing and able customers are to use the latest technologies, as illustrated by our discussion of the Technographics framework developed by Forrester Research.

An individual's behavior often reflects personal attitudes and beliefs. Recent research by Parasuraman shows that certain personal characteristics are associated with customer readiness to accept new technologies. These attributes include innovativeness, a positive view of technology, and a belief that technology offers increased control, flexibility, and efficiency in people's lives.[2] Factors that are negatively associated with the adoption of technology include distrust, a perceived lack of control, feelings of being overwhelmed by technology, and skepticism about whether the technology will perform satisfactorily. Service providers must consider these factors before implementing new technologies that may negatively affect customers' evaluations of the service experience.

UNDERSTANDING CUSTOMER NEEDS AND EXPECTATIONS

needs: subconscious, deeply felt desires that often concern long-term existence and identity issues.

Customers buy goods and services to meet specific **needs**, and they evaluate the outcomes of their purchases based on what they expect to receive. Needs, which may represent a useful basis for segmentation, are often deeply rooted in people's unconscious minds and may concern long-term existence and identity issues. When people feel a need, they are motivated to take action to fulfill it. In many instances, purchase of a good or service may be seen as offering the best solution to meeting a particular need. Subsequently, consumers may compare what they received against what they expected, especially if it cost them money, time, or effort that could have been devoted to obtaining an alternative solution.

Review of Principles of Market Segmentation

Market segmentation is central to almost any professionally planned and executed marketing program. The concept of segmentation recognizes that customers and prospects within a market vary across a variety of dimensions and that not every segment constitutes a desirable target for the firm's marketing efforts.

Market segments. A segment is composed of a group of current and potential customers who share common characteristics, needs, purchasing behavior, or consumption patterns. Effective segmentation should group buyers into segments in ways that result in as much similarity as possible on the relevant characteristics *within* each segment but dissimilarity on those same characteristics *between* each segment. Two broad categories of variables are useful in describing the differences between segments. The first deals with user characteristics, the second with usage behavior.

User characteristics may vary from one person to another, reflecting demographic characteristics (e.g., age, income, and education), geographic location, and psychographics (the attitudes, values, lifestyles, and opinions of decision makers and users). Another important variable is the specific benefits that individuals and corporate purchasers seek from consuming a particular good or service.

Usage behavior relates to how a product is purchased and used. Among such variables are when and where purchase and consumption take place, the quantities consumed ("heavy users" are always of particular interest to marketers), frequency and purpose of use, the occasions under which consumption takes place (sometimes referred to as "occasion segmentation"), and sensitivity to such marketing variables as advertising, pricing, speed and other service features, and availability of alternative delivery systems.

Target segment. After evaluating different segments in the market, a firm should focus its marketing efforts by targeting one

Types of Needs

Abraham Maslow identified five categories of human needs—physiological, safety, love, esteem, and self-actualization—and proposed that basic needs like food and shelter must be met before others can be fulfilled.[3] Although poverty, malnutrition, and lack of housing remain pressing issues around the world, including North America, physiological needs have long ceased to be the sole issue for most residents of advanced industrialized countries like the United States and Canada.

Greater prosperity means that increasing numbers of individuals are seeking to satisfy social and self-actualization needs. These needs create demand for more sophisticated goods and services. For instance, travel and leisure services have been a major beneficiary of increased disposable income, leading many firms to develop a variety of enticing vacation packages. However, as customer needs and preferences continue to evolve, the leisure industry needs to adapt its offerings accordingly.

In North America, as in other highly developed regions of the world, there is evidence that many consumers are reaching the point where they have most of the physical goods they want and are now turning to services to fill new or still unmet needs. Increased spending on more elaborate vacations, sports, entertainment, restaurant meals, and other service experiences is assuming greater priority, even at the expense of spending slightly less on physical goods. According to Daniel Bethamy of American Express, consumers want "memorable experiences, not gadgets."[4] This shift in consumer behavior and attitudes provides opportunities for those service companies that understand and meet changing needs, continuing to adapt their offerings over time as needs evolve. For example, some astute service providers have capitalized on the increased interest in extreme sports by offering services like guided mountain climbs, paragliding, white water rafting trips, and mountain biking adventures. And new financial services (like online investment brokers) have been introduced to cash in on consumers' willingness to risk their financial futures by trading in the stock market.[5] The notion of service experiences also extends to business and industrial situations; con-

---

or more segments that fit well with the firm's capabilities and goals. Target segments are often defined on the basis of several variables. For instance, a hotel in a particular city might target prospective guests who shared such user characteristics as (1) traveling on business (demographic segmentation), (2) visiting clients within a defined area around the hotel (geographic segmentation), and (3) willing to pay a certain daily room rate (user response).

Issues for research. When studying the marketplace, service marketers should be looking for answers to such questions as:

➢ In what useful ways can the market for our firm's service be segmented?

➢ What are the needs of the specific segments that we have identified?

➢ Which of these segments best fits both our institutional mission and our current operational capabilities?

➢ What do customers in each segment see as our firm's competitive advantages and disadvantages? Are the latter correctable?

➢ In light of this analysis, which specific segment(s) should we target?

➢ How should we differentiate our marketing efforts from those of the competition to attract and retain the types of customers that we want?

➢ What is the long-term financial value to us of a loyal customer in each of the segments that we currently serve (and those that we would like to serve)?

➢ How should our firm build long-term relationships with customers from the target segments? And what strategies are needed to create long-term loyalty?

sider the example of modern trade shows where exhibitors, including manufacturers, set out to engage the customer's interest through interactive presentations and even entertainment.[6]

Expectations and How They Are Formed

expectations: internal standards that customers use to judge the quality of a service experience.

Customers' **expectations** about what constitutes good service vary from one business to another. For example, although accounting and veterinary surgery are both professional services, the experience of meeting an accountant to talk about your tax returns tends to be very different from visiting a vet to get treatment for your sick pet. Expectations are also likely to vary in relation to differently positioned service providers in the same industry. While travelers expect no-frills service for a short domestic flight

Club Med Responds to Changing Customer Needs

When Gilbert Trigano launched "Club Med" in the 1950s, the concept of holiday villages, offering limitless food and innumerable sporting activities in splendid natural surroundings at a single price, was unique. It also reflected a significant change in social behavior. Trigano recognized the emergence of a new, younger segment among French and other European consumers, who were influenced by growing affluence and American values rather than traditional formality. The Club Med concept provided an attractive form of escapism with its informality and friendly customer service from an enthusiastic staff. The atmosphere attracted a crowd that was primarily young, affluent, educated, and single. These people enjoyed sports, travel, and exotic locations. It was a burgeoning market.

By the late 1960s, Club Med, with its communal lifestyle—which included shared huts, group activities, and large dining tables designed to break down social barriers between guests—had captured the spirit of the times. In the 1970s and 1980s, as standards of living and status-seeking behavior continued to grow, leisure became a much more important part of people's lives. Club Med opened villages around the world and epitomized the ultimate leisure experience: a relatively expensive holiday, either at the beach or at winter ski villages in the mountains.

Yet 10 years later, problems began to emerge. The group's financial situation weakened and there was widespread criticism that the "Club concept" had become outdated. Critics claimed that younger people were now more individualistic and no longer valued the kinds of group activities for which Club Med was renowned. Finding new young customers was becoming harder and harder. Meantime, the Club's most loyal customers had grown older and had different interests and needs. Rather than seeking ways to

have fun as "swinging singles," these guests were concerned about what to do with their children on vacation. They were also interested in achieving a healthy lifestyle, including nutritious food, low-impact exercises, and other ways to restore physical and emotional well-being. By 1990, the conspicuous consumption of the 1980s was also giving way to more emphasis on value for money. The emergence of low-price, all-inclusive holiday package tours was eroding Club Med's traditional customer base, yet the Club had not lowered its own prices in response.

After huge losses in 1996, the Trigano family was ousted from the daily running of the company, and Philippe Bourguignon—who had turned Disneyland Paris around—was brought in to revive the Club. In his words, "Club Med has tried to be everything for everyone. But you have to make choices. . . ." His plan was to enhance value for money, attract a younger clientele, and extend the vacation season by providing services such as entertainment, sports, and cafés throughout the year rather than simply during an annual holiday. His approach was aimed at meeting the needs of two very different kinds of segments—the younger, value-conscious market that Club Med had not yet succeeded in winning over and the mature group of customers who had been the backbone of Club Med's past success but whose loyalty was now at risk.

To meet the needs of younger consumers, Bourguignon immediately closed several unprofitable villages and converted a number of others into lower-priced camps branded as "Club Aquarius." The traditional Club Med concept has been redesigned in order to be more responsive to the "creature comfort" requirements of older, existing customers. Many Club Med resorts now cater to families and have special activities to keep children occupied while parents enjoy a much-needed jog on the beach or a massage in the spa.

on a discount carrier, they would undoubtedly be very dissatisfied with that same level of service on a full-service airline flying from Los Angeles to Sydney, or from Toronto to Paris, even in economy class. Consequently, it's very important for marketers to understand customer expectations of their own firm's service offerings—especially as they relate to specific product elements.

When individual customers or corporate purchasing department employees evaluate the quality of a service, they may be judging it against some internal standard that existed prior to the service experience.[7] Perceived service quality results from customers comparing the service they perceive they have received against what they expected to receive. People's expectations about services tend to be strongly influenced by their own prior experience as customers—with a particular service provider, with competing services in the same industry, or with related services in different industries. If they have no relevant prior experience, customers may base their prepurchase expectations on factors like word-of-mouth comments, news stories, or the firm's marketing efforts.

Over time, certain norms develop for what to expect from service providers within a given industry. As we discussed in Chapter 3, roles and scripts help reinforce these expectations for both customers and service employees. Norms are also affected by customer experiences and supplier-controlled factors like advertising, pricing, and the physical appearance of the service facility and its employees. For example, Americans don't expect to be greeted by a doorman and a valet at a Motel 6, but they certainly do at a Ritz-Carlton hotel, where service levels are known to be much higher.

Customer expectations may also vary from one industry to another, reflecting industry reputations and past experience. In many countries, people have lower expectations of government service providers than they do of private companies. Expectations may even vary within different demographic groups (e.g., between men and women, older and younger consumers, or blue- versus white-collar workers). To make things more complicated, expectations also differ from country to country. For instance, while it may be acceptable and unsurprising for a train to arrive several hours late in some countries, rail schedules are so precise in Switzerland that the margin for error is measured in seconds.

The Components of Customer Expectations

Customer expectations embrace several different elements, including desired service, adequate service, predicted service, and a zone of tolerance that falls between the desired and adequate service levels.[8] The model shown in Figure 4.2 shows how expectations for desired service and adequate service are formed.

Desired and Adequate Service Levels   The type of service customers hope to receive is termed **desired service**. It is a "wished for" level—a combination of what customers believe can and should be delivered in the context of their personal needs. However, most customers are realistic and understand that companies can't always deliver the level of service they would prefer; hence, they also have a threshold level of expectations, termed **adequate service**, which is defined as the minimum level of service customers will accept without being dissatisfied. Among the factors that set this expectation are situational factors affecting service performance and the level of service that might be anticipated from alternative suppliers. The levels of both desired and adequate service expectations may reflect explicit and implicit promises by the provider, word-of-mouth comments, and the customer's past experience (if any) with this organization.[9]

desired service: the "wished for" level of service quality that a customer believes can and should be delivered.

adequate service: the minimum level of service that a customer will accept without being dissatisfied.

FIGURE 4.2

Factors That Influence
Customer Expectations of
Service

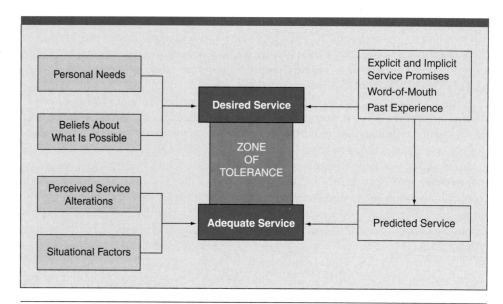

Source: Adapted from Valarie A. Zeithaml, Leonard A. Berry, and A. Parasuraman, "The Nature and Determinants of Customer Expectations of Service," *Journal of the Academy of Marketing Science* 21, no. 1 (1993): 1–12.

predicted service: the level of service quality a customer believes a firm will actually deliver.

Predicted Service Level   The level of service that customers actually anticipate receiving is known as **predicted service**, which directly affects how they define "adequate service" on that occasion. If good service is predicted, the adequate level will be higher than if poorer service is predicted. Customer predictions of service may be situation specific. For example, from past experience, customers visiting a museum on a summer day may expect to see larger crowds if the weather is poor than if the sun is shining. So a 10-minute wait to buy tickets on a cool, rainy day in summer might not fall below their adequate service level.

zone of tolerance: the range within which customers are willing to accept variations in service delivery.

Zone of Tolerance   The inherent nature of services makes consistent service delivery difficult across employees in the same company and even by the same service employee from one day to another. The extent to which customers are willing to accept this variation is called the **zone of tolerance** (shown in Figure 4.2). A performance that falls below the adequate service level will cause frustration and dissatisfaction, whereas one that exceeds the desired service level will both please and surprise customers, creating the "customer delight" that we discussed earlier in this chapter. Another way of looking at the zone of tolerance is to think of it as the range of service within which customers don't pay explicit attention to service performance.[10] When service falls outside this range, customers will react either positively or negatively.

The zone of tolerance can increase or decrease for individual customers depending on factors like competition, price, or importance of specific service attributes. These factors most often affect adequate service levels (which may move up or down in response to situational factors), while desired service levels tend to move up very slowly in response to accumulated customer experiences. Consider a small-business owner who needs some advice from her accountant. Her ideal level of professional service may be a thoughtful response by the next business day. But if she makes the request at the time of year when all accountants are busy preparing corporate and individual tax returns, she will probably know from experience not to expect a fast response. Although her ideal service level probably won't change, her zone of tolerance for response time may be much broader because she has a lower adequate service threshold.

HOW CUSTOMERS EVALUATE SERVICE PERFORMANCES

Service performances—especially those that contain few tangible clues—can be difficult for consumers to evaluate. As a result, there is a greater risk of making a purchase that proves to be disappointing. If a customer buys a physical good that proves unsatisfactory, the product can usually be returned or replaced—although this action may require extra effort on the customer's part. These options are not as readily available with services, although some services can be repeated. Consider the four process-based categories of service introduced in Chapter 2. In the case of *possession-processing services*, repeating the performance may be an acceptable option. For example, a cleaning service can reclean an office if a customer complains about the quality of the job. By contrast, *people-processing services* that are performed on people's bodies may be hard to reverse. A bad haircut must be grown out, and the consequences of a faulty surgical operation or a poorly done tattoo may last a lifetime.

Mental stimulus-processing services like education, live entertainment, or sporting events can also be difficult to "replace" if quality does not meet customers' expectations. Theatergoers cannot realistically ask for their money back if actors perform their roles poorly or the script is bad. Sports fans can't expect refunds if their favorite team plays badly. (But they do find ways of letting the players know of their dissatisfaction! One university recently prohibited people from booing in the football stadium when the home team was playing poorly.) Similarly, universities don't usually compensate students for poor quality classroom experiences. Even if a college let dissatisfied students repeat classes free of charge with a different instructor, those students would still incur significant extra time and psychological costs.

Finally, *information-based services* present risks for customers when service quality is unsatisfactory. Banking or accounting errors may not be noticed until later, by which time damage may have been done to a customer's reputation (e.g., a check was returned rather than paid, or a faulty tax return was filed). Customers who receive a questionable consulting recommendation or medical opinion have the option of seeking a second opinion, but that will involve extra money, time, and even psychological costs.

A Continuum of Product Attributes

As we've pointed out, one of the basic differences between goods and services is that services are harder for customers to evaluate. We also briefly mentioned that **product attributes** could be divided into search, experience, and credence properties.[11] We'll expand on the concept of these three categories here, since they provide a useful framework for understanding how consumers evaluate different types of market offerings. All products can be placed on a continuum ranging from "easy to evaluate" to "difficult to evaluate" depending on whether they are high in search attributes, experience attributes, or credence attributes. As shown in Figure 4.3, most physical goods are located toward the left of the spectrum, with services to the middle or right.

product attributes: all features (both tangible and intangible) of a good or service that can be evaluated by customers.

Search Attributes Physical goods tend to emphasize those attributes that allow customers to evaluate a product before purchasing it. Features like style, color, texture, taste, and sound allow prospective consumers to try out, taste test, or "test drive" the product prior to purchase. These tangible attributes help customers understand and evaluate what they will get in exchange for their money and reduce the sense of uncertainty or risk associated with the purchase occasion. Goods such as clothing, furniture, cars, electronic equipment, and foods are high in **search attributes**.

search attributes: product characteristics that consumers can readily evaluate prior to purchase.

FIGURE 4.3

How Product Attributes
Affect Ease of Evaluation

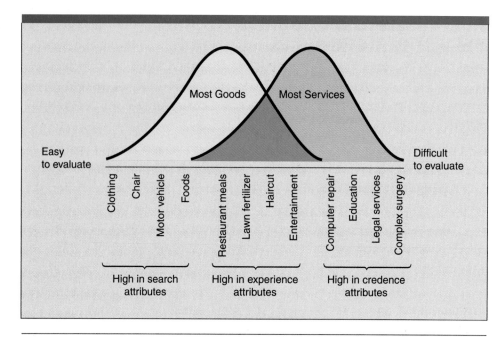

Source: Adapted from Valarie A. Zeithaml, "How Consumer Evaluation Processes Differ Between Goods and Services," in J. H. Donnelly and W. R. George, *Marketing of Services* (Chicago: American Marketing Association, 1981).

experience attributes:
product performance
features that customers can
only evaluate during service
delivery.

Experience Attributes   When attributes can't be evaluated prior to purchase, customers must "experience" the service to know what they are getting. Holidays, live entertainment performances, sporting events, and restaurants fall into the **experience attributes** category. Although people can examine brochures, scroll through Web sites describing the holiday destination, view travel films, or read reviews by travel experts, they can't really evaluate or feel the dramatic beauty associated with hiking in the Canadian Rockies or the magic of scuba diving in the Caribbean until they actually experience these activities. Nor can customers always rely on information from friends, family, or other personal sources when evaluating these and similar services, because different people may interpret or respond to the same stimuli in different ways. Think about your own experiences in following up on recommendations from friends to see a particular film. Although you probably walked into the theater with high expectations, you may have felt disappointed after viewing the film if you didn't like it as much as your friends did.

credence attributes:
product characteristics that
customers may not be able to
evaluate even after purchase
and consumption.

Credence Attributes   Product characteristics that customers find impossible to evaluate confidently even after purchase and consumption are known as **credence attributes**, because the customer is forced to trust that certain benefits have been delivered, even though it may be hard to document them. For example, relatively few people possess enough knowledge about financial markets to assess whether their stockbroker got the best possible returns on their invested funds. Patients can't usually evaluate how well their dentists have performed complex dental procedures. And most college students must simply have faith that their professors are providing them with a worthwhile educational experience!

Strategic Responses to Difficulties in Evaluating Services

Most goods fall to the left of the continuum in Figure 4.3, since they are high in search properties. Most services, however, tend to be located from the center to the right of the continuum. The reason for this relates to two of the basic differences between goods and services that we discussed in Chapter 1: intangibility of service performances and variability of inputs and outputs (which often leads to quality control problems). These characteristics present special challenges for service marketers, requiring them to find ways to reassure customers and reduce the perceived risks associated with buying and using services whose performance and value can't easily be predicted.

Intangibility of Service Performances   Marketers whose products are high in experience characteristics often try to provide more search attributes for their customers. One approach is to offer a free trial. Some providers of online computer services have adopted this strategy. For example, AOL offers potential users a free software diskette and the chance to try its services without charge for a certain number of hours. This reduces customers' concerns about entering into a paid contract without first being able to test the service. AOL hopes that consumers will be "hooked" on its Web services by the end of the free trial period.

Advertising is another way to help customers visualize service benefits. For instance, the only tangible thing credit card customers get directly from the company is a small plastic card, followed at monthly intervals by an account statement. But that's hardly the essence of the benefits provided by this low-contact service. Think about the credit card advertisements you've seen recently. Did they promote the card itself or did they feature exciting products you could purchase and exotic places to which you could travel by using your card? Such advertisements stimulate consumer interest by showing physical evidence of the benefits of credit card use.

Providers of services that are high in credence characteristics have an even greater challenge. Their benefits may be so intangible that customers can't evaluate the quality of what they've received even after the service has been purchased and consumed. In this case, marketers often try to provide tangible cues to customers about their services. Professionals like doctors, architects, and lawyers often display their degrees and other certifications for the same reason—they want customers to "see" the credentials that qualify them to provide expert service. Many professional firms have developed Web sites to inform prospective clients about their services, highlight their expertise, and even showpiece successful past engagements.

Variability and Quality Control Problems   The continuum of product attributes in Figure 4.3 also has implications for another distinguishing service characteristic—the degree of customer involvement in the production process. Products that are highest in search attributes are most often physical goods that are manufactured in a factory with no customer involvement, then purchased and consumed. Quality is much easier to control in this situation since the elements of production can be more closely monitored and failures spotted before the product reaches the customer. In fact, some manufacturers like Motorola claim to be able to guarantee product quality at the so-called six-sigma level— that is 99.999 percent! However, quality control for services that fall in the experience and credence ranges is complicated by customer involvement in production.

Evaluations of such services may be affected by customers' interactions with the physical setting of the business, employees, and even other customers. For example, your experience of a haircut may combine your impression of the hair salon, how well you can describe what you want to the stylist, the stylist's ability to understand and do what you've requested, and the appearance of the other customers and employees in the salon. Stylists note that it's difficult for them to do a good job if customers are uncooperative.

Many credence services have few tangible characteristics and rely on the expertise of a professional service provider to provide a quality offering. In this case, providers must be able to interact with customers effectively to produce a satisfactory product. Problems can occur when this interaction doesn't produce an outcome that meets customers' expectations, even though the service provider may not be at fault.

Service providers must also work hard to maintain consistent levels of quality. This is more difficult when production involves direct interaction with service employees, whose performances are likely to vary from one day to another. But customers don't want variations in quality, as Michael Flatley, the Irish founder, director, and lead dancer of *Lord of the Dance* knows. As he said once in a television interview, "The people who drive hundreds of miles to see this show . . . they don't want to know I'm almost 39 . . . they don't want to know my legs are sore . . . they don't want to know I go home and put my feet in ice. They just want to know that what they're seeing is the best show ever—tonight, not tomorrow night!"[12] Flatley's insistence on providing the best performance possible every time has produced results—his company achieves sold-out performances around the world, and audiences often show their appreciation by giving the dancers a standing ovation. He has recently moved from dancing to producing the shows, counting on the younger dancers to provide consistently thrilling performances.

Progressive Insurance Delights Its Customers

Progressive Insurance Corporation is one of the largest writers of private passenger auto insurance in the United States. The firm prides itself on providing extraordinary customer service—and its accomplishments in this area are impressive. Its industry-leading innovations have included Immediate Response, the first 24/7 claims service in the industry, and claims representatives traveling in Immediate Response Vehicles (introduced in 1994) that can come straight to the scene of an accident. Consider the following scenario.

➤ The crash site in Tampa, Florida, was chaotic and tense. Two cars were damaged and although the passengers weren't bleeding, they were shaken up and scared. Lance Edgy, a senior claim representative for Progressive, arrived on the scene just minutes after the collision, bearing a clipboard, a camera, and a cassette recorder. He calmed the victims and advised them on medical care, repair shops, police reports, and legal procedures. Edgy then invited William McAllister, Progressive's policyholder, into an air-conditioned van equipped with comfortable chairs, a desk, and two cellular phones. Even before the tow trucks cleared away the wreckage, Edgy had offered his client a settlement for the market value of his totaled 1988 Mercury Topaz. McAllister, who did not appear to have been at fault in this accident, stated in amazement: "This is great—someone coming right out here and taking charge. I didn't expect it at all."

Progressive Insurance continues to find new ways to delight its customers. Its Web site, progressive.com, recently won top honors for the second year in a row from Gómez.com (an Internet quality measurement firm). Progressive was cited for pleasantly surprising its customers with consumer-friendly innovations and extraordinary customer service.

William McAllister, the unfortunate auto accident victim in the scenario described above, experienced something unusual. He was actually delighted at the service provided by his insurance company! But what is delight? Is it more than just a very high level of satisfaction? One view is that achieving delight requires focusing on what is currently unknown or unexpected by the customer. In short, it's more than just avoiding problems—the "zero defects" strategy. Managers of companies like Progressive that are known for their commitment to quality believe that satisfaction is not enough, making comments such as "we must take quality beyond customer satisfaction to customer delight" and "sheer survival means companies have to deliver more than customer satisfaction."

The results of a research project done by Oliver, Rust, and Varki[13] suggest that delight is a function of three components: (1) unexpectedly high levels of performance, (2) arousal (e.g., surprise, excitement), and (3) positive affect (e.g., pleasure, joy, or happiness). Satisfaction is a function of positively disconfirmed expectations (better than expected) and positive affect. These researchers ask "If delight is a function of surprisingly unexpected pleasure, is it possible for delight to be manifest in truly mundane services and products, such as newspaper delivery or trash collecting?"

Source: Ronald Henkoff, "Service Is Everybody's Business," *Fortune,* June 27, 1994; Progressive Insurance Corporation Web site, www.progressive.com, January 2001.

How Perceived Quality Relates to Satisfaction

The terms "quality" and "satisfaction" are sometimes used interchangeably. But some researchers believe that perceived **service quality** is just one component of **customer satisfaction**, which also reflects price/quality trade-offs, and personal and situational factors.[14]

Satisfaction can be defined as an attitude-like judgment following a purchase act or a series of consumer product interactions.[15] Most studies are based on the theory that the confirmation/disconfirmation of preconsumption product standards is the essential determinant of satisfaction.[16] This means that customers have certain service standards in mind prior to consumption (their expectations), observe service performance and compare it to their standards, and then form satisfaction judgments based upon this comparison. The resulting judgment is labeled *negative disconfirmation* if the service is worse than expected, *positive disconfirmation* if better than expected, and simple *confirmation* if as expected.[17] When there is substantial positive disconfirmation, plus pleasure and an element of surprise, then customers are likely to be delighted. Having read the vignette about Progressive Insurance (see box), think about your own insurance provider—if you have one—and the kind of service you receive. Are you delighted with the service—or even satisfied? However, once customers have been delighted, their expectations are raised. They will be dissatisfied if service levels return to previous levels, and it will take more effort to "delight" them in the future.[18]

Why is satisfaction important to service managers? There's evidence of strategic links between the level of customer satisfaction and a firm's overall performance. Researchers from the University of Michigan found that on average, every 1 percent increase in customer satisfaction is associated with a 2.37 percent increase in a firm's Return on Investment (ROI).[19] Fournier and Mick state:

> Customer satisfaction is central to the marketing concept. . . . [I]t is now common to find mission statements designed around the satisfaction notion, marketing plans and incentive programs that target satisfaction as a goal, and consumer communications that trumpet awards for satisfaction achievements in the marketplace.[20]

Some marketers claim that the phrase "your satisfaction is guaranteed or your money back" has become a standard promise for many businesses. However, customer satisfaction is not an end in itself. Instead, it's the means to achieving key business goals. First, satisfaction is inextricably linked to customer loyalty and relationship commitment. Second, highly satisfied (delighted) customers spread positive word-of-mouth. They become walking, talking advertisements for an organization whose service has pleased them, thus lowering the cost of attracting new customers. First Direct, the all-telephone bank described in the opening story for Chapter 3, has gained huge numbers of new customers from recommendations by its existing account holders. Recommendations are particularly important for providers of services that are high in credence attributes, such as professional service firms. The quality of legal, accounting, consulting, and engineering services, for example, is hard to evaluate in advance of purchase, so positive comments by a satisfied client reduce the risk for a new purchaser.

Third, highly satisfied customers may be more forgiving. Someone who has enjoyed good service delivery many times in the past is more likely to believe that a service failure is a deviation from the norm. It may take more than one unsatisfactory incident for strongly loyal customers to change their perceptions and consider switching to an alternative supplier. In this respect, high levels of customer satisfaction act like an insurance policy against the impact of a single failure. Finally, delighted customers are less susceptible to competitive offerings than customers who are simply satisfied or are unhappy with their current service provider.

service quality: customers' long-term, cognitive evaluations of a firm's service delivery.

customer satisfaction: a short-term emotional reaction to a specific service performance.

THE PURCHASE PROCESS FOR SERVICES

purchase process: the stages a customer goes through in choosing, consuming, and evaluating a service.

When customers decide to buy a service to meet an unfilled need, they go through what is often a complex **purchase process**. This process has three separate stages: the prepurchase stage, the service encounter stage, and the postpurchase stage, each containing two or more steps (see Figure 4.4).

Prepurchase Stage

prepurchase stage: the first stage in the service purchase process, where customers identify alternatives, weigh benefits and risks, and make a purchase decision.

The decision to buy and use a service is made in the **prepurchase stage**. Individual needs and expectations are very important here because they influence what alternatives customers will consider. If the purchase is routine and relatively low risk, customers may move quickly to selecting and using a specific service provider. But when more is at stake or a service is about to be used for the first time, they may conduct an

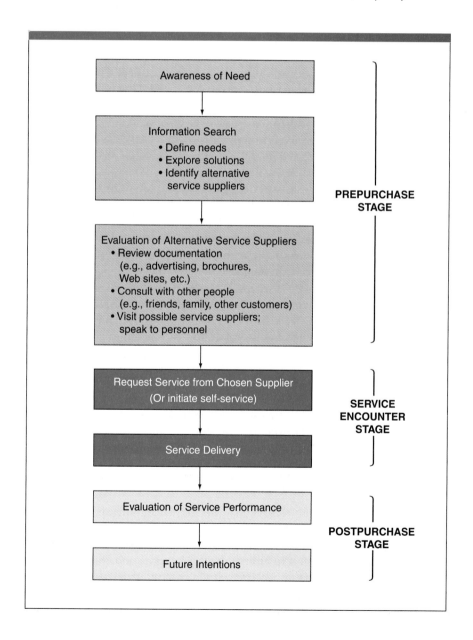

FIGURE 4.4

The Purchase Process: Customer Activities in Selecting, Using, and Evaluating Service intensive information search (contrast how you approached the process of applying to college versus buying a pizza or a hamburger!). The next step is to identify potential suppliers and then weigh the benefits and risks of each option before making a final decision.

This element of perceived risk is especially relevant for services that are high in experience or credence attributes and thus difficult to evaluate prior to purchase and consumption. First-time users are especially likely to face greater uncertainty. Risk perceptions reflect customers' judgments of the probability of a negative outcome. The worse the possible outcome and the more likely it is to occur, the higher the perception of risk. Different types of perceived risks are outlined in Table 4.1.

When customers feel uncomfortable with risks, they can use a variety of methods to reduce them during the prepurchase stage. In fact, you've probably tried some of the following risk-reduction strategies yourself before deciding to purchase a service:

➤ Seeking information from respected personal sources (family, friends, peers)

➤ Relying on a firm with a good reputation

➤ Looking for guarantees and warranties

➤ Visiting service facilities or trying aspects of the service before purchasing

➤ Asking knowledgeable employees about competing services

➤ Examining tangible cues or other physical evidence

➤ Using the Web to compare service offerings

Type of Risk	Examples of Customer Concerns
Functional risk (unsatisfactory performance outcomes)	■ Will this training course give me the skill I need to get a better job? ■ Will this credit card be accepted wherever and whenever I want to make a purchase? ■ Will the dry cleaner be able to remove the stains from this jacket?
Financial risk (monetary loss, unexpected costs)	■ Will I lose money if I make the investment recommended by my stockbroker? ■ Will I incur lots of unanticipated expenses if I go on this vacation? ■ Will repairing my car cost more than the original estimate?
Temporal risk (wasting time, consequences of delays)	■ Will I have to wait in line before entering the exhibition? ■ Will service at this restaurant be so slow that I will be late for my afternoon meeting? ■ Will the renovations to our bathroom be completed before our friends come to stay with us?
Physical risk (personal injury or damage to possessions)	■ Will I get hurt if I go skiing at this resort? ■ Will the contents of this package get damaged in the mail? ■ Will I fall sick if I travel abroad on vacation?
Psychological risk (personal fears and emotions)	■ How can I be sure this aircraft won't crash? ■ Will the consultant make me feel stupid? ■ Will the doctor's diagnosis upset me?
Social risk (how others think and react)	■ What will my friends think of me if they learn I stayed at this cheap motel? ■ Will my relatives approve of the restaurant I have chosen for the family reunion dinner? ■ Will my business colleagues disapprove of my selection of an unknown law firm?
Sensory risk (unwanted impacts on any of the five senses)	■ Will I get a view of the parking lot from my room, rather than the beach? ■ Will the bed be uncomfortable? ■ Will I be kept awake by noise from the guests in the room next door? ■ Will my room smell of stale cigarette smoke? ■ Will the coffee at breakfast taste disgusting?

TABLE 4.1

Perceived Risks in Purchasing and Using Services

One strategy to help reduce the risk perceived by customers is to educate them about the features of the service, describe the types of users who can most benefit from it, and offer advice on how to obtain the best results.

Service Encounter Stage

service encounter stage: the second stage in the service purchase process where the service delivery takes place through interactions between customers and the service provider.

After deciding to purchase a specific service, customers experience one or more contacts with their chosen service provider. The **service encounter stage** often begins with submitting an application, requesting a reservation, or placing an order. As we saw in Chapter 3, contacts may take the form of personal exchanges between customers and service employees, or impersonal interactions with machines or computers. In high-contact services, such as restaurants, health care, hotels, and public transportation, customers may become actively involved in one or more service processes. Often, they experience a variety of elements during service delivery, each of which may provide clues to service quality.

Service environments include all of the tangible characteristics to which customers are exposed. The appearance of building exteriors and interiors; the nature of furnishings and equipment; the presence or absence of dirt, odor, or noise; and the appearance and behavior of other customers can all serve to shape expectations and perceptions of service quality.

Service personnel are the most important factor in most high-contact service encounters, where they have direct, face-to-face interactions with customers. But they can also affect service delivery in low-contact situations like telephone-based service delivery. Knowledgeable customers often expect employees to follow specific scripts during the service encounter; excessive deviations from these scripts can lead to dissatisfaction. Handling service encounters effectively on the part of the employee usually combines learned skills with the right type of personality.

Support services are made up of the materials and equipment plus all of the backstage processes that allow front stage employees to do their work properly. This element is critical, because many customer-contact employees can't perform their jobs well without receiving internal services from support personnel. As an old service-firm axiom goes: "If you aren't servicing the customer, you are servicing someone who is."[21]

Other Customers When customers use people-processing or mental stimulus-processing services, they often find themselves in close proximity to other customers. Waiting rooms at a medical clinic may be filled with other patients; trains, buses, or aircraft are usually carrying many passengers at once, requiring travelers to sit next to strangers. Similarly, restaurants serve many patrons simultaneously, and a successful play or film will attract a large audience (in fact, the absence of an audience is a bad sign!). Unfortunately, some of these other customers occasionally behave badly, thus detracting from the service experience. Managers need to anticipate such incidents and have contingency plans in place for how to deal with the different types of problems that might occur.

Postpurchase Stage

postpurchase stage: the final stage in the service purchase process where customers evaluate service quality and their satisfaction/dissatisfaction with the service outcome.

During the **postpurchase stage**, customers continue a process they began in the service encounter stage—evaluating service quality and their satisfaction/dissatisfaction with the service experience. The outcome of this process will affect their future intentions, such as whether or not to remain loyal to the provider that delivered service and whether to pass on positive or negative recommendations to family members and other associates.

Customers evaluate service quality by comparing what they expected with what they perceive they received. If their expectations are met or exceeded, they believe they have received high-quality service. If the price/quality relationship is acceptable and other situational and personal factors are positive, then these customers are likely to be satisfied. As a result, they are more likely to make repeat purchases and become loyal customers. However, if the service experience does not meet customers' expectations, they may complain about poor service quality, suffer in silence, or switch providers in the future.[22]

MAPPING THE CUSTOMER'S SERVICE EXPERIENCE

In order to design a service that meets or exceeds the expectations of its customers, service providers not only need to know what customers want but also to understand the nature of their actual experiences, especially during the service encounter stage. In the high-contact service environments common to most people-processing services, customers usually arrive at a service site with certain expectations. Their subsequent behavior, however, may be shaped by the nature of the physical environment, the employees they encounter, the sequence in which different activities take place, and by the roles that they are expected to play. Recent research suggests that consumers' expectations are continuously updated during the course of a service encounter, with final evaluations of service quality reflecting these updated expectations, rather than the expectations held before the encounter began.[23]

Managers and service employees are often unaware of the full extent of customers' service experiences. An effective way to gain insights into customer behavior during service delivery is to create a description, in sequence, of the steps that both customers and employees go through in a given service environment. These steps can be shown visually using a tool called a **flowchart**. By identifying each contact between customers and a service provider, flowcharts can highlight problems and opportunities in the service delivery process as they affect customers during front stage activities. They may also suggest a need to examine backstage supporting processes.

flowchart: a visual representation of the steps involved in delivering service to customers.

Developing a Flowchart

Flowcharting can be usefully applied to any type of service and the technique is relevant to both high-contact and low-contact service environments. The objectives of the exercise are threefold:

1. Understand each step in the process that constitutes the customer's overall experience with the service;

2. Identify what encounters customers have with different service personnel, specific physical facilities, and equipment; and

3. Relate the customers' behavior and experience at each step to the backstage activities needed to create quality service in timely fashion front stage.[24]

Developing a flowchart begins by identifying each interaction that a particular type of customer has when using a specific service. Managers need to distinguish between the core product and the supplementary service elements we discussed in Chapter 2; in fact, flowcharting is a very useful way of figuring out what these supplementary elements actually are. Interactions should be depicted in the sequence in which they normally occur. Service delivery is like a river flowing through time: Some activities take place "upstream," others "downstream." At each step, management needs to ask: What do customers really want (perhaps they would like to speed up this step or even avoid it altogether)? What are their expectations? And where is the potential for failure at this step?

Let's illustrate flowcharting with a simplified model of a service to which most readers can relate fairly easily: a stay at a hotel (Figure 4.5). As with many services, the customer's first encounter with a hotel involves a supplementary service rather than the core product (which is basically rental of a bedroom for a night's sleep). The initial step, for most business travelers, is to make a reservation. This action may be taken some time before the visit actually takes place, typically by telephone or through the Internet.

On arrival, guests traveling by car will need to park the vehicle (perhaps a valet will do it for them). The next step is to check in at reception, after which an employee may offer to carry the bags and escort guests to their rooms. Hence, four service encounters occur before guests even reach their rooms! Before retiring for the night, a guest may choose to use several more services, such as dinner at one of the hotel restaurants or watching a pay-TV movie. After rising, guests may request that room service deliver breakfast. Then guests may make phone calls before checking out and asking a valet to retrieve their cars from the parking garage.

In this flowchart, the customer's experience is depicted, in simplified form, as a series of boxes in linear sequence. Note that the core product—a bed for the night—is surrounded by a variety of supplementary services. Some hotel guests might use more supplementary services than those shown in the flowchart, others fewer. A variety of activities is taking place backstage, too, behind the scenes, but these activities are not shown here. In fact, each step front stage is supported by a series of backstage activities, including assignment of staff, maintenance of facilities and equipment, and capture, storage, and transfer of information. As you review this flowchart, ask yourself: At what points might the poor performance by staff members or misbehavior by other customers spoil a guest's experience? And as the hotel manager, what strategy would you plan for anticipating and handling such problems?

The Value of Flowcharting

Marketers find flowcharting particularly useful for defining the point(s) in the process at which the customer uses the core service and identifying the different supplementary services that make up the overall service package.

Although some service encounters are very brief and consist of just a few discrete delivery steps—such as a taxi ride or a simple haircut—others may extend over a longer time frame and involve multiple steps. A leisurely restaurant meal might stretch over a couple of hours or more, while a visit to a theme park might last all day. From arrival to departure, the one-night hotel visit described above probably lasts at least 12 to 14 hours; and the first step, the reservation, may take place days or even weeks prior to arrival.

FIGURE 4.5

Flowcharting a Customer's
Visit to a Hotel

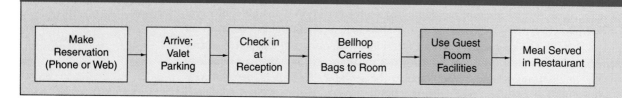

As customers interact with representatives of the service firm, impersonal delivery systems such as Web sites, the physical environment of the service encounter, and—in high-contact environments—other customers—they are exposed to information that can influence both their expectations and their evaluations of the service. In Chapter 3, we used the term "moments of truth" to highlight the importance of the impressions created by airline passengers' contacts with staff before, during, and after a flight. A key question for managers is whether customers' expectations change during the course of service delivery in light of the perceived quality of sequential steps in the process. (You might want to reflect on whether your own impressions and expectations change during the course of an extended service performance.) Ideally, service firms should try to provide consistently high performance at each step in service delivery. But in reality, many service performances are inconsistent.

It's difficult to improve service quality and productivity unless you fully understand the customer's involvement in a given service environment. Speeding up processes and weeding out unnecessary steps to avoid wasted time and effort are often important ways to improve the perceived value of a service. When we come to discuss design of new services in Chapter 8, we introduce a more structured version of the flowchart known as a service blueprint that includes what takes place backstage, out of the customer's sight.

Conclusion

Successful service firms are well informed about their customers and are selective about the prospects that they target. Underlying this focus is the concept of market segmentation, which groups both individual consumers and corporate buyers according to their expressed or implied needs, their observed or reported behavior, readiness to use technology, or other marketing-relevant variables.

Gaining a better understanding of how customers evaluate, select, use, and occasionally abuse services should lie at the heart of strategies for designing and delivering the service product. It also has implications for choice of service processes, presentation of physical evidence, and use of marketing communications—not least for educational purposes. Several of the distinctive characteristics of services (especially intangibility and quality control problems) result in customer evaluation procedures that differ from those involved in evaluating physical goods.

Because the consumer evaluation and purchase processes for many services are complex, service managers need to understand how customers view the service offering and to explore the factors that determine customer expectations and satisfaction. To understand service usage, it's helpful to employ flowcharting, which provides a visual picture of the service delivery process from the customer's perspective.

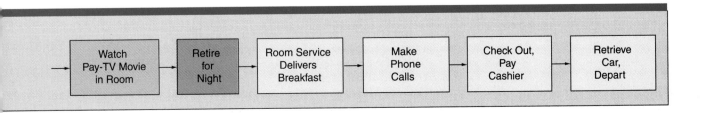

Study Questions and Exercises

1. Review Figure 4.1. Which technographical category are you in? What factors have influenced your consumption of high-tech goods and services?

2. Is it ethical for companies to target specific customer groups (like the elderly and children)? Explain your response.

3. Describe search, experience, and credence attributes and give examples of each.

4. Explain why services are harder than goods for customers to evaluate.

5. How are customers' expectations formed? Explain the difference between desired service and adequate service with reference to a service experience you've had recently.

6. What role do needs play in consumer purchase behavior?

7. Define the three stages in the purchase process for services.

8. Choose a service that you are familiar with and create a simple flowchart for it. Define the "front stage" and "backstage" activities.

Endnotes

1. Based on information in Paul C. Judge, "Are Tech Buyers Different?" *Business Week*, 26 January 1998, 64–68; Mary Modahl, *Now or Never* (New York: Harper Business, 2000).
2. A. Parasuraman, "Technology Readiness Index [TRI]: A Multiple-Item Scale to Measure Readiness to Embrace New Technologies," *Journal of Service Research*, 2 (2000).
3. Abraham H. Maslow, *Motivation and Personality* (New York, NY: Harper and Brothers, 1954).
4. Stephanie Anderson Forest, Katie Kerwin, and Susan Jackson, "Presents That Won't Fit Under the Christmas Tree," *Business Week*, 1 December 1997, 42.
5. Karl T. Greenfield, *Life on the Edge, Taking Sides: Clashing Views on Controversial Issues in Marketing* (Guilford, CT: McGraw-Hill/Dushkin, 2001), 220–225.
6. B. Joseph Pine and James H. Gilmore, "Welcome to the Experience Economy," *Harvard Business Review* 76 (July-August 1998): 97–108.
7. See Benjamin Schneider and David E. Bowen, *Winning the Service Game* (Boston: Harvard Business School Press, 1995); and Valarie A. Zeithaml, Leonard L. Berry, and A. Parasuraman, "The Nature and Determinants of Customer Expectations of Services," *Journal of the Academy of Marketing Science* 21 (1993).
8. Valarie A. Zeithaml, Leonard L. Berry, and A. Parasuraman, "The Behavioral Consequences of Service Quality," *Journal of Marketing* 60 (April 1996): 31–46.
9. Cathy Johnson and Brian P. Mathews, "The Influence of Experience on Service Expectations," *International Journal of Service Industry Management* 8, no. 4 (1997): 46–61.
10. Robert Johnston, "The Zone of Tolerance: Exploring the Relationship between Service Transactions and Satisfaction with the Overall Service," *International Journal of Service Industry Management* 6, no. 5 (1995): 46–61.
11. Valarie A. Zeithaml, "How Consumer Evaluation Processes Differ Between Goods and Services," in J. H. Donnelly and W. R. George, *Marketing of Services* (Chicago: American Marketing Association, 1981).
12. Quoted from a television interview with Michael Flatley on the news magazine *Dateline NBC*, 13 October 1997.
13. Richard L. Oliver, Roland T. Rust, and Sajeev Varki, "Customer Delight: Foundations, Findings, and Managerial Insights," *Journal of Retailing* 73 (Fall 1997): 311–336.
14. Valarie A. Zeithaml and Mary Jo Bitner, *Services Marketing: Integrating Customer Focus Across the Firm*, 2d ed (Burr Ridge, IL: Irwin-McGraw-Hill, 2000).
15. Youjae Yi, "A Critical Review of Customer Satisfaction," in *Review of Marketing 1990*, ed. V. A. Zeithaml (Chicago, American Marketing Association, 1990).

16. Richard L. Oliver, "Customer Satisfaction with Service," in Teresa A. Schwartz and Dawn Iacobucci, *Handbook of Service Marketing and Management* (Thousand Oaks, CA: Sage Publications, 2000), 247–254.

17. Richard L. Oliver, *Satisfaction: A Behavioral Perspective on the Consumer* (New York: McGraw-Hill, 1997).

18. Roland T. Rust and Richard L. Oliver, "Should We Delight the Customer?" *Journal of the Academy of Marketing Science* 28, no. 1 (2000): 86–94.

19. Eugene W. Anderson and Vikas Mittal, "Strengthening the Satisfaction-Profit Chain," *Journal of Service Research* 3, November 2000, 107–120.

20. Susan Fournier and David Glen Mick, "Rediscovering Satisfaction," *Journal of Marketing* 63 (October 1999): 5–23.

21. Bill Fromm and Len Schlesinger, *The Real Heroes of Business* (New York, NY: Currency Doubleday, 1993), 241.

22. Jaishankar Ganesh, Mark J. Arnold, and Kristy E. Reynolds, "Understanding the Customer Base of Service Providers: An Examination of the Differences Between Switchers and Stayers," *Journal of Marketing* 64, no. 3 (2000): 65–87.

23. Lawrence O. Hamer, Ben Shaw-Ching Liu, and D. Sudharshan, "The Effects of Intraencounter Changes in Expectations on Perceived Service Quality Models," *Journal of Service Research* 1 (February 1999): 275–289.

24. For more details of this technique see G. Lynn Shostack, "Understanding Services through Blueprinting," in T. A. Schwartz, D. E. Bowen, and S. W. Brown, *Advances in Services Marketing and Management, Vol. I* (Greenwich CT, JAI Press, 1992), 75–90. For alternative approaches, see Christian Grönroos' description of "The Customer Relationship Life Cycle," in *Service Management and Marketing* (Lexington, MA: Lexington Books, 1990), 129–133; and Sandra Vandermerwe, "Jumping into the Customer's Activity Cycle," in *From Tin Soldiers to Russian Dolls* (Oxford: Butterworth Heinemann, 1993), ch. 4, 48–71.

chapter five

Relationship Marketing and Customer Loyalty

Creating a Formula for Success in Ski Resorts

Located high in the Coast Mountain range of British Columbia, Whistler and Blackholm ski resorts receive an average of some 30 feet (9 meters) of snow each year and claim to offer the longest ski season and largest skiable terrain in North America. Vancouver-based Intrawest Corporation, whose other ski properties include Mammoth in California, Copper Mountain in Colorado, Stratton in Vermont, and Mont Tremblant in Quebec, owns the two resorts.[1]

Whistler and Blackholm, located 75 miles (120 km) northeast of Vancouver, offer the greatest vertical drop of any ski mountains in North America—one vertical mile (1600 m)! Day skiers from Vancouver and its suburbs were originally Whistler and Blackholm's only source of business—and the resort still courts their loyalty with big savings on season passes. But by creating a major destination resort, Intrawest has been able to appeal to vacationers from across the continent and even overseas. Whistler's appeal is evident from the fact that it has been named the number one ski resort on the North American continent by three different ski magazines. This recognition has boosted the ski resort's success, since skiers' vacation destination preferences tend to be shaped by the best facilities they have experienced, heard about from their friends, seen on TV, or read about in magazines.

Intrawest's management believes that it has created a formula for success. The strategy begins with enhancing the skiing experience on each mountain. The skiers' experiences on the slopes must be good if they are to remain loyal customers. This means that Intrawest must provide well-maintained trails that will satisfy skiers from beginners to experts, plus sufficient lift capacity to avoid lengthy delays.

Recent investments to improve facilities at Whistler and Blackholm have included replacing old chairlifts with new express "quads" to improve reliability, increase lift capacity, and reduce waiting times. Recognizing the growing popularity of snowboarding, the company also purchased a new Pipe Dragon, a unique machine used to shape and groom snowboard half-pipes. Meantime, a wide range of new trails was opened at Blackholm. New snow cats were purchased for trail grooming, and upgrades were made to snowmaking equipment to ensure good skiing conditions, even on days when Mother Nature is not cooperative. To appeal to summer visitors, Intrawest expanded the trail system for the Whistler Mountain Bike Park. New construction at the base includes improved guest services and a children's facility with one-stop check-in, a learning center, and a special kids' shuttle train to the gondola.

In addition to enhancing the ski facilities, Intrawest also wanted to provide an attractive and lively resort community so that people would choose to stay longer. After all, après-ski activities are part of the appeal of a ski vacation for many people! Satisfied skiers have started coming back more often and spending more money. They have also told their friends about their positive experiences. This has created a larger customer base of new and returning customers, who

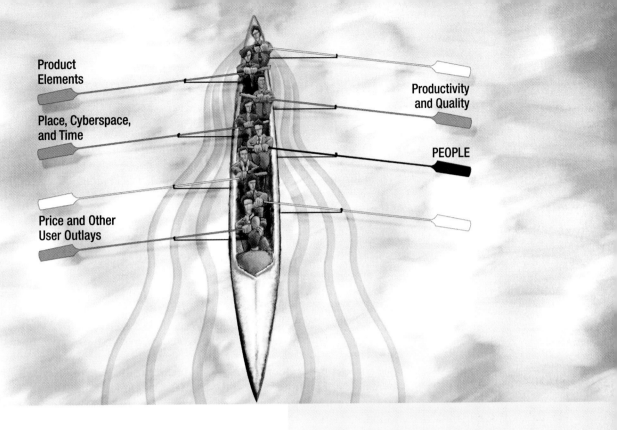

Product
Elements

Place, Cyberspace,
and Time

Price and Other
User Outlays

Productivity
and Quality

PEOPLE

have helped finance the construction of more lodging and additional attractions.

Intrawest is now drawing even more people to the resort by increasing its year-round activities to maximize the use of shops, hotels, convention facilities, and restaurants. The resort's goal is to expand its target market (and profitability) by including non-skiers in its customer base. Intrawest is also encouraging customers to purchase condominiums or chalets, since property owners tend to come back more often throughout the year. After all, the mountains are lovely in summer and fall as well as in winter and early spring when there is still snow on the upper slopes for skiing. And the resort operators can also manage properties on behalf of their owners, who can receive income by renting to other visitors.

Learning Objectives

After reading this chapter, you should be able to

⟹ set priorities for targeting specific customer segments

⟹ understand that not all customers are equally attractive to a firm

⟹ recognize the role of customer loyalty in determining financial success

⟹ calculate the value of a customer who remains loyal to a firm

⟹ provide examples of customer loyalty programs

⟹ identify different types of customer misbehaviors and strategies for handling them

TARGETING THE RIGHT CUSTOMERS

Intrawest targets customers who will enjoy the skiing experience that it offers, can afford this relatively expensive sport, and are also likely to purchase additional services at the resort. It also appeals to non-skiers looking for a mountain vacation. This company is not alone in recognizing the need for ongoing investments to keep current customers loyal and to appeal to prospective customers. Managers in innovative service firms constantly debate what new services or improvements in product elements they need to offer to attract and retain customers in attractive **target segments**. Whistler would not have grown to its present size if it had continued to rely on skiers from nearby Vancouver, which is close enough to allow residents to make an easy day trip to the slopes. Its carefully planned growth is designed to attract vacationers who will spend a week or more at the resort.

target segments: segments selected because their needs and other characteristics fit well with a specific firm's goals and capabilities.

In this chapter, we continue to examine the question, ***What customers should we serve and how should we relate to them?*** (see the service decision framework in Figure II.1, page 49). In particular, we emphasize the importance of asking: *Which customer relationships are worth developing and preserving?* A service business must take a focused approach to its markets, targeting prospects in the desired segments, while seeking to avoid those it cannot hope to serve profitably. In the case of nonprofit organizations, where financial profits are not the goal (except in fundraising), the objective should be to focus on attracting and serving those customers who are central to the organization's mission.

Acquiring the right customers is only the beginning. The real challenge lies in building a relationship with them, growing the volume of business they transact, and maintaining their loyalty over a long period of time. Even when customers fit the desired profile, a few may prove through undesirable behavior to be candidates for prompt termination rather than retention. Although some believe the saying "the customer is always right," that's not true in every instance. We address this issue in more depth later in the chapter when we discuss the different ways in which customers may misbehave.

Airborne skier at Whistler.

FROM TRANSACTIONS TO RELATIONSHIPS

Too many service firms still focus on the number of customers they serve without giving sufficient attention to the value of each customer. As David Maister emphasizes, marketing is about getting better business, not just more business.[2] Volume alone is not a good measure of excellence, sustainability, or profitability. Generally speaking, customers who buy more frequently and in larger volumes are more profitable than occasional users. Consider your own behavior. Do you have a favorite restaurant where you often eat with friends or family? Is there a movie theater that you patronize regularly? Are you a frequent customer at your local laundromat? If you answered yes to any of these questions, then you are probably a lot more valuable to the management of these different organizations than a one-time visitor who is just passing through town. The revenue stream from your purchases may amount to a considerable sum over the course of the year. (You would probably be quite surprised if you calculated the amount!)

Sometimes your value as a frequent user is openly recognized and appreciated. In these situations, you feel that the business is tailoring its service features, including schedules and prices, to foster a relationship with you and encourage your long-term loyalty. But at other times, you may feel that nobody in the organization knows or cares who you are. You may be a valuable customer, but you certainly don't feel valued. Thus you are not likely to remain loyal if an opportunity arises to switch to another service provider. Well-managed organizations work hard to develop relationships with desirable customers and to grow the volume of business that they conduct. That strategy is usually a wise use of marketing resources, since it may cost a firm five to six times as much to attract a new customer as it does to retain an existing one.[3]

Building relationships with desirable customers can be very profitable. But what constitutes a relationship? One **transaction**—or even a series of transactions—does not necessarily represent a relationship. Mutual recognition and knowledge between the parties is required for a relationship to exist. When each transaction between a customer and a service provider is essentially separate and anonymous, with no long-term record of a customer's purchasing history and little or no mutual recognition between the customer and the firm's employees, then no meaningful marketing relationship can be said to exist.

A word of caution is in order at this point. Not all customers *want* to have in-depth relationships with the firms whose services they buy. Some people prefer to patronize several suppliers, either because they enjoy variety or because they like to search for the best terms on any given purchase. Some dislike constant contact from a firm—by mail, telephone, or e-mail—informing them about new developments and selling them new services. Others are worried about privacy. They don't like the idea of a firm gathering detailed information about their background and product usage behavior, because they worry that this information might be sold or otherwise made available to other organizations without their permission. The advent of the Internet as an interactive marketing channel has increased these concerns.[4]

transaction: an event during which an exchange of value takes place between two parties.

The Nature of Service Relationships

Although some services involve discrete transactions, in other instances purchasers receive service on a continuing basis. But even when transactions are separate and independent, there may still be opportunities to create an ongoing relationship. The different nature of these situations offers an opportunity for categorizing services. First, we can ask: Does the supplier enter into a formal **membership relationship** with customers, as with telephone subscriptions, banking, and the family doctor? Or is there no defined relationship? And second: Is the service delivered on a continuous basis, as in insurance,

membership relationship: a formalized relationship between the firm and a specified customer that may offer special benefits to both parties.

TABLE 5.1

Relationships with
Customers

Nature of Service Delivery	Type of Relationship Between the Service Organization and Its Customers	
	"Membership" Relationship	No Formal Relationship
Continuous Delivery of Service	Insurance Cable TV subscription College enrollment Banking	Radio station Police protection Lighthouse Public highway
Discrete Transaction	Long-distance calls from subscriber phone Theater series subscription Travel on commuter ticket Repair under warranty Health treatment for HMO member	Car rental Mail service Toll highway Pay phone Movie theater Public transportation Restaurant

broadcasting, and police protection? Or is each transaction recorded and charged separately? Table 5.1 shows the resulting matrix, with examples in each category.

A membership relationship is a formalized relationship between the firm and an identifiable customer, who signs up in advance for service. Firms in the top left quadrant of Table 5.1 are natural "membership" organizations; customers must apply in advance before they can receive service. Such relationships have the potential to offer special benefits to both parties, because the potential exists for both sides to get to know each other better.

The advantage to the service organization of having membership relationships is that it knows who its current customers are, what they spend, and (usually) when, where, and how often they use the services offered. This information can be valuable for segmentation purposes if good records are kept and the data are readily accessible in a format that lends itself to computerized analysis. Knowing the identities and addresses of current customers enables the organization to make effective use of direct mail (including e-mail), telemarketing, and personal sales calls—all highly targeted methods of marketing communication. In turn, members can be given access to special numbers or even designated account managers to facilitate their communications with the firm.

Discrete transactions—when each usage involves a payment to the service supplier by an essentially "anonymous" consumer—are typical of services like transportation, restaurants, cinemas, and shoe repair shops. The problem for marketers of such services is that they are usually less informed about who their customers are and what use each customer makes of the service than their counterparts in membership-type organizations. But firms that sell their services on a transactional basis to anonymous customers can create relationships with frequent users by selling the service in bulk (for instance, a theater series subscription or a commuter ticket on public transport) and recording the customer's name and address. Another approach is to offer extra benefits to customers who agree to register with the firm so that their usage can be tracked (for example, loyalty programs for hotels, airlines, and car rental firms). In this way, an organization can shift at least part of its customer base from the bottom right quadrant of the matrix shown in Table 5.1 to the bottom left one.

In small businesses such as hair salons, frequent customers are (or should be) welcomed as "regulars" whose needs and preferences are remembered. Keeping formal records of customers' needs, preferences, and purchasing behavior is useful even in small firms. Accurate records eliminate the need for employees to ask repetitive questions during every service encounter. Customer data can also be used to personalize the service given to each customer. In large companies with substantial customer bases, transactions can be transformed into relationships by opening accounts, maintaining computerized customer records, and instituting account management programs that provide customers with a telephone number to call for assistance or a designated account representative. Long-term contracts between suppliers and their business customers take the nature of relationships to a higher level, transforming them into partnerships and strategic alliances.

The different types of service relationships shown in Table 5.1 have important implications for pricing. Whenever service is offered on an ongoing basis, there can be a single periodic charge covering all contracted services. Most insurance policies fall in this category, as do tuition and board fees at a residential college. The big advantage of this package approach is its simplicity. In other instances, the price paid by "members" is tied to the number and type of specific transactions and may also include a base subscription fee. While more complex to administer, such an approach recognizes variations in usage patterns and may discourage wasteful use of the service. In these cases, "members" may be offered advantages over casual users—for instance, discount rates (telephone subscribers pay less for long-distance calls made from their own phones than do pay phone users) or advance notification and priority reservations (such as theater subscriptions). Some services require no fee and are available to all. The final category in Table 5.1 represents continuously delivered services like broadcasting, police protection, lighthouse services, and public roads that are typically funded by advertising, donations, or tax revenues.

Micro-Segmentation at the Royal Bank of Canada

At least once a month, Toronto-based analysts at the Royal Bank of Canada (the country's largest bank) use data modeling to segment its base of 10 million customers. The segmentation variables include credit risk, current and projected profitability, life stage, likelihood of leaving the bank, channel preference (whether customers like to use a branch, the call center, or the Internet), product activation (how quickly customers actually use a product they have bought), and propensity to purchase another product. Says a senior vice president, "Gone are the days when we had mass buckets of customers that would receive the same treatment or same offer on a monthly basis. Our marketing strategy is [now] much more personalized. Of course, it's the technology that allows us to do that."

The main source of data is the marketing information file, which records what products customers hold with the bank, the channels they use, their responses to past campaigns, transactional data, and details of any restrictions on soliciting customers. Another source is the enterprise data warehouse, which stores billing records and information from every document that a new or existing customer fills out.

Royal Bank analysts run models based on complex algorithms that can slice the bank's massive customer database into tightly profiled micro-segments that are based on simultaneous use of several variables, including the probability that target customers will respond positively to a particular offer. Customized marketing programs can then be developed for each of these micro-segments, giving the appearance of a highly personalized offer. The data can also be used to improve the bank's performance on unprofitable accounts by identifying these customers and offering them incentives to use lower-cost channels.

An important goal of Royal Bank's segmentation analysis is to maintain and enhance profitable relationships. The bank has found that customers who hold packages of several services are more profitable than those who don't. These customers also stay with the bank an average of three years longer. As a result of the sophisticated segmentation practices at Royal Bank, the response rates to its direct marketing programs have jumped from an industry average of only 3 percent to as high as 30 percent.

Source: Meredith Levinson, "Slices of Lives," *CIO Magazine*, 15 August 2000.

Relationship Marketing

relationship marketing:
activities aimed at developing long-term, cost-effective links between an organization and its customers for the mutual benefit of both parties.

There's a fundamental distinction in marketing between strategies intended to bring about a single transaction and those designed to create extended relationships with customers. **Relationship marketing** involves activities aimed at developing long-term, cost-effective links between an organization and its customers for their mutual benefit. Among the approaches used by service firms to maintain and enhance relationships are such basics as treating customers fairly, offering service augmentations, and treating each customer as though he or she were a segment of one—the essence of mass customization.[5] Service "extras" often play a key role in building and sustaining relationships between vendors and purchasers of industrial goods.

Research by Coviello, Brodie, and Munro suggests that there are three distinct categories of relationship marketing: database marketing, interaction marketing, and network marketing.[6]

Database Marketing   In this type of marketing, the focus is on the market transaction but includes information exchange. Marketers rely on information technology—in the form of a database or the Internet—to form a relationship with targeted customers and retain their patronage over time. However, the nature of these relationships is often not a close one, with communication being driven and managed by the seller. Technology is used to (1) identify and build a database of current and potential customers, (2) deliver differentiated messages based on consumers' characteristics and preferences, and (3) track each relationship to monitor the cost of acquiring the consumer and the lifetime value of the resulting purchases.[7] Although technology can be used to personalize the relationship (as in word-processed letters that insert the customer's name), relations remain somewhat distant, as illustrated by utility services such as electricity, gas, and cable TV.

Interaction Marketing   A closer relationship exists in situations where there is direct interaction between customers and company representatives (in person or by telephone and e-mail). Although the service itself remains important, people and social processes also add value through interactions that may include negotiations and mutual sharing of information. This type of relationship has long existed in many local environments where buyer and seller know and trust each other, ranging from community banks to dentistry. It is also commonly found in many business-to-business services. Both the firm and the customer are prepared to invest resources to develop a mutually beneficial relationship. This investment may include time spent sharing and recording information. As service companies grow, they face the challenge of maintaining satisfying relationships with customers as new technologies encourage a shift from high- to low-contact service.

Network Marketing   We often say that someone is a "good networker" because he or she is able to put individuals in touch with others who have a mutual interest. This type of marketing occurs primarily in a business-to-business context, where firms commit resources to develop positions in a network of relationships with customers, distributors, suppliers, the media, consultants, trade associations, government agencies, competitors, and even the customers of their customers. Often a team of individuals within a supplier's firm must collaborate to provide effective service to a parallel team within the customer organization. However, the concept of networking is also relevant in consumer marketing environments where customers are encouraged to refer friends and acquaintances to the service provider.

CREATING AND MAINTAINING VALUED RELATIONSHIPS

For the service provider, a valued relationship is one that is financially profitable in the long run. In addition, the benefits of serving a customer may extend beyond revenues to include such intangibles as the knowledge and pleasure obtained from working with that customer over time. In a healthy and mutually profitable relationship, both parties have an incentive to ensure that it extends for many years. The seller, in particular, recognizes that it pays to take an investment perspective. The initial costs of acquiring new customers and learning about their needs—which may even make the account unprofitable in the short run—are justified by the expectation of future profits.

How do customers define a valued relationship? It's one in which the benefits received from service delivery significantly exceed the associated costs of obtaining them. Research suggests that relational benefits for individual consumers include greater confidence, social benefits, and special treatment (see the boxed discussion on "How Customers See Relational Benefits"). Valued relationships in business-to-business services are largely dependent on the quality of the interactions between individuals at each of the partnering firms. "As relationships strengthen over a period of time," Piyush Kumar observes, "the service provider's personnel often assume the role of outsourced departments and make critical decisions on behalf of their clients."[8]

How Customers See Relational Benefits

What benefits do customers gain from an extended relationship with a service firm? In personal interviews, respondents were asked to identify service providers that they used on an ongoing basis and discuss any benefits they received as a result of being a regular customer. Their comments included the following:

➤ "I like him [hair stylist]. . . . He's really funny and always has lots of good jokes. He's kind of like a friend now."

➤ "I know what I'm getting—I know that if I go to a restaurant that I regularly go to, rather than taking a chance on all of the new restaurants, the food will be good."

➤ "I often get price breaks. The little bakery that I go to in the morning, every once in a while, they'll give me a free muffin and say, 'You're a good customer, it's on us today.'"

➤ "You can get better service than drop-in customers . . . . We continue to go to the same automobile repair shop because we have gotten to know the owner on a kind of personal basis, and he . . . can always work us in."

➤ "Once people feel comfortable, they don't want to switch to another dentist. They don't want to train or break a new dentist in."

After evaluating and categorizing such comments, the researchers designed a second study. Subjects were told to select a specific service provider with which they had a strong, established relationship. They were then asked to indicate what benefits they received from this relationship and how important these benefits were to them. Analysis of the results showed that most of the benefits could be grouped into three clusters.

Confidence benefits—the most important group—included feelings by customers that in an established relationship there was less risk of something going wrong, more confidence in correct performance, greater ability to trust the provider, lowered anxiety when purchasing, better knowledge of what to expect, and an expectation of receiving the firm's highest level of service.

Social benefits involved mutual recognition between customers and employees, being known by name, friendship with the service provider, and enjoyment of certain social aspects of the relationship.

Special treatment benefits included better prices, discounts or special deals that were unavailable to most customers, extra services, higher priority when there was a wait, and faster service than most customers.

Source: Kevin P. Gwinner, Dwayne D. Gremler, and Mary Jo Bitner, "Relational Benefits in Services Industries: The Customer's Perspective," *Journal of the Academy of Marketing Science* 26, no. 2 (1998): 101–114.

The Loyalty Effect

loyalty: a customer's voluntary decision to continue patronizing a specific firm over an extended period of time.

Loyalty is an old-fashioned word, traditionally used to describe fidelity and enthusiastic devotion to a country, cause, or individual. More recently, in a business context, it has been used to describe a customer's willingness to continue patronizing a firm over the long term, purchasing and using its goods and services on a repeated and preferably exclusive basis, and voluntarily recommending it to friends and associates. "Few companies think of customers as annuities," says Frederick Reichheld, author of *The Loyalty Effect*, and a major researcher in this field.[9] And yet that is precisely what a loyal customer can mean to a firm: a consistent source of revenues over a period of many years. However, this loyalty cannot be taken for granted. It will only continue as long as the customer feels that he or she is receiving better value (including superior quality relative to price) than could be obtained by switching to another supplier.

There are many possible ways to disappoint customers through service quality failures. A major source of disappointment, especially in high-contact situations, is poor performance by service employees. Researchers believe that there is an explicit link between customers' satisfaction with service and employees' satisfaction with their jobs (Figure 5.1). To the extent that service workers are capable, enjoy their jobs, and perceive themselves as well treated by their employer, they will be motivated to remain loyal to that firm for an extended period of time rather than con-

FIGURE 5.1

The Links in the Service-Profit Chain

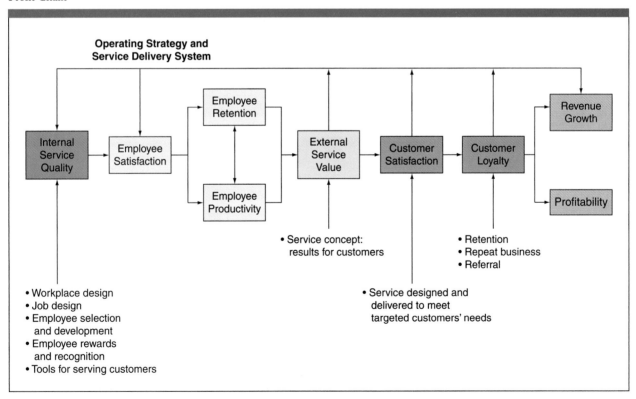

Source: James L. Heskett, Thomas O. Jones, Gary W. Loveman, W. Earl Sasser, Jr., and Leonard A. Schlesinger, "Putting the Service Profit Chain to Work," *Harvard Business Review,* March-April 1994. Copyright © 1994 by the President and Fellows of Harvard College.

stantly switching jobs. Competent and loyal workers tend to be more productive than new hires, to know their customers well, and to be better able to deliver high-quality service. In short, employee loyalty can contribute to customer loyalty through a series of links referred to as the "service profit chain."[11]

"Defector" was a nasty word during the Cold War in the mid-1900s. It described disloyal people who sold out their own side and went over to the enemy. Even when they defected to "our" side, rather than away from it, they were still suspect. Today, the term **defection** is being applied to customers who transfer their brand loyalty to another supplier. Reichheld and Sasser popularized the term "zero defections," which they describe as keeping every customer the company can profitably serve. (As we've already said, there are always some customers a firm is not sorry to lose.)[10] Not only does a rising defection rate indicate that something is wrong with quality—or that competitors offer better value—it may also signal the risk of a future decrease in revenues. Profitable customers don't necessarily disappear overnight; they may signal their mounting disaffection by steadily reducing their purchases. Observant firms record customer purchase trends carefully and are quick to respond with recovery strategies in the event of decreased purchases, customer complaints, or other indications of service failure.

defection: a customer's decision to transfer brand loyalty from a current service provider to a competitor.

Realizing the Full Profit Potential of a Customer Relationship

How much is a loyal customer worth in terms of profits? In a classic study, Reichheld and Sasser analyzed the profit per customer in many different industries, categorized by the number of years that a customer had been with the firm.[12] They found that the longer customers remained with a firm in each of these industries, the more profitable they became to the company. Annual profits per customer, which have been indexed over a five-year period for easier comparison, are summarized for four different service industries in Figure 5.2.

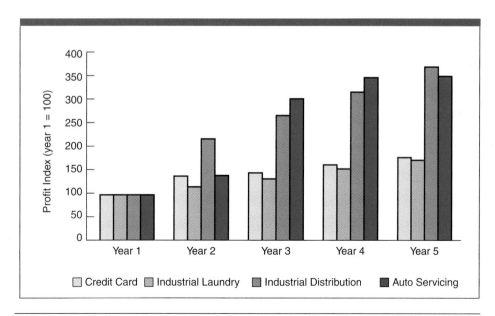

Source: Based on data in Frederick F. Reichheld and W. Earl Sasser, Jr., "Zero Defections: Quality Comes to Services," *Harvard Business Review,* October 1990.

FIGURE 5.2

How Much Profit a Customer Generates Over Time

According to Reichheld and Sasser, four factors work to the supplier's advantage in creating incremental profits over an extended period of time. In order of magnitude at the end of a seven-year period, these factors are:

1. *Profit derived from increased purchases* (or higher account balances in credit card or banking environments). Over time, business customers often grow larger and need to purchase in greater quantities. Individuals may purchase more as their families grow or as they become more affluent. Both types of customers may decide to consolidate their purchases with a single supplier who provides high-quality service.

2. *Profit from reduced operating costs.* As customers become more experienced, they make fewer demands on the supplier (for instance, less need for information and assistance). They may also make fewer mistakes when involved in operational processes, thus contributing to greater productivity.

3. *Profit from referrals to other customers.* Positive word-of-mouth recommendations are like free sales and advertising, saving the firm from having to invest as much money in these activities.

4. *Profit from price premium.* New customers often benefit from introductory promotional discounts whereas long-term customers are more likely to pay regular prices. Moreover, when customers trust a supplier they may be more willing to pay higher prices at peak periods or for express work.

Reichheld argues that the economic benefits of customer loyalty noted above often explain why one firm is more profitable than a competitor. Further, the upfront costs of attracting these buyers can be amortized over many years. For insights on how to calculate customer value in any given business, see the worksheet in Table 5.2.

It's important to note that not all loyal customers are necessarily profitable. Banks and telephone companies, for instance, have many small accounts whose revenues do not cover the costs of servicing them. Reinarz and Kumar suggest that the loyalty model works best in situations where customers enter into a formal membership relationship with the supplier.[13] When such a relationship is absent, then customers are free to shop around each time they need to make a transaction.

TABLE 5.2

Worksheet for Calculating Long-Term Customer Value

Acquisition		Ongoing Use	Year 1	Year 2	Year 3	Year *n*
Initial Revenue		**Annual revenues**				
Application fee[a]	_____	Annual account fee[a]	_____	_____	_____	_____
Initial purchase[a]	_____	Sales	_____	_____	_____	_____
		Service fees[a]	_____	_____	_____	_____
		Value of referrals[b]	_____	_____	_____	_____
Total Revenues	_____		_____	_____	_____	_____
Initial Costs		**Annual Costs**				
Marketing:	_____	Account Management	_____	_____	_____	_____
Credit check[a]	_____	Cost of sales	_____	_____	_____	_____
Account set up[a]	_____	Write-offs (e.g., bad debts)	_____	_____	_____	_____
Less Total Costs	_____		_____	_____	_____	_____
Net Profit (Loss)	_____		_____	_____	_____	_____

[a]If applicable.
[b]Anticipated profits from each new customer referred (could be limited to the first year or expressed as the net present value of the estimated future stream of profits through year *n*); this value could be negative if an unhappy customer starts to spread negative word of mouth that leads existing customers to defect.

For profit-seeking firms, the potential value of a customer should be a key driver in marketing strategy. Grant and Schlesinger state:

Achieving the full profit potential of each customer relationship should be the fundamental goal of every business. . . . Even using conservative estimates, the gap between most companies' current and full potential performance is enormous.[14]

They suggest analysis of three gaps between actual and potential performance:

> ➤ What percentage of its target customers does a firm currently have, and what percentage could it potentially obtain? (If there is a large gap between a firm's current share and its potential, then it may make sense to develop strategies to attract new customers.)

> ➤ What is the current purchasing behavior of customers in each target segment? What would the impact be on sales and profits if they exhibited the ideal behavior profile of (1) buying all services offered by the firm, (2) never purchasing from competitors, and (3) paying full price? (To get customers to buy more, firms should examine opportunities to cross-sell new services to existing customers. Frequent user programs that reward loyalty can help to strengthen relationships. But getting customers to pay higher prices than they are used to may be difficult unless competitors are also trying to reduce the availability of discount promotions.)

> ➤ How long, on average, do customers remain with the firm? What impact would it have if they remained customers for life? (As we showed earlier, the profitability of a customer often increases over time. If valued customers are defecting, it is important to identify the reasons why customers defect and then take corrective action.)

Many elements are involved in gaining market share, cross-selling other products and services to existing customers, and creating long-term loyalty. The process starts, as we suggested earlier, by identifying and targeting the right customers, then learning everything possible about their needs, including their preferences for different forms of service delivery. However, there's a dark side to the emphasis on identifying and catering to an organization's most profitable customers. Some companies are making very little effort to serve those customers who offer little or no financial value to the firm. According to a recent *Business Week* article,

The result could be a whole new stratification of consumer society. The top tier may enjoy an unprecedented level of personal attention, but customers who fall below a certain level of profitability for too long may find themselves bounced from the customer rolls altogether or facing fees that all but usher them out the door. . . . [M]arketers . . . are doing everything possible to push their customers—especially low-margin ones—toward self-service.[15]

Such strategies take segmentation analysis and database marketing to a new extreme in identifying which customers will be most profitable to a firm in the long run and actively courting them at the expense of less-profitable segments.

Loyalty Reward Programs

The big challenge for service marketers lies not only in giving prospective customers a reason to do business with their firms, but also in offering existing customers incentives to remain loyal and perhaps even increase their purchases. Among the best-known strategies for rewarding frequent users are the "frequent flyer" programs offered by passenger airlines (see box).

American Airlines was probably the first service firm to realize the value of its customer database for learning more about the travel behavior of its best customers. The company uses this data to create direct mail lists targeted at specific customers (such as travelers who fly regularly between a certain pair of cities). The airline was also quick to examine bookings for individual flights to see how many seats were filled by frequent flyers, most of whom were probably traveling on business and therefore less price sensitive than vacationers and pleasure travelers. This information helped American to counter competition from low-cost discount airlines, whose primary target segment was price-conscious pleasure travelers. Rather than reducing all fares on all flights between a pair of cities, American realized that it only needed to offer a limited number of discount fares. These fares were available primarily on those flights known to be carrying significant numbers of nonbusiness passengers. Even on such flights, the airline would limit availability of discount fares by such

Reinforcing Loyalty by Rewarding Frequent Flyers

American Airlines established the original "frequent flyer" program in 1983. Targeted at business travelers (the individuals who fly the most), this promotion enabled passengers to claim travel awards based on the accumulated distance they had traveled on the airline. "Miles" flown became the scoring system that entitled customers to claim from a menu of free tickets in different classes of service. American was taken by surprise at the enormous popularity of this program. Other major airlines soon felt obliged to follow and implemented similar schemes of their own. Each airline hoped that its own frequent flyer program, branded with a distinctive name such as "AAdvantage" (American) or "Mileage Plus" (United), would induce a traveler to remain brand loyal, even to the extent of some inconvenience in scheduling. However, many business travelers enrolled in several programs, thereby limiting the effectiveness of these promotions for individual carriers.

To make their programs more appealing, the airlines signed agreements with regional and international carriers, "partner" hotels, and rental car firms, allowing customers to be credited with mileage accrued through a variety of travel-related activities. What had begun as a one-year promotion by American Airlines was soon transformed into a permanent—and quite expensive—part of the industry's marketing structure. In due course, many international airlines felt obliged to introduce their own frequent flyer programs, offering miles (or kilometers) to compete with American carriers and with each other.

As time passed, airlines in the United States started to use double and triple mileage bonus awards as a tool for demand management, seeking to encourage travel on less-popular routes. A common strategy was to award bonus miles for flying during the low season when many empty seats were available or for changing flights at an intermediate hub rather than taking a nonstop flight. To avoid giving away too many free seats at peak time, some airlines offered more generous redemption terms during off-peak times. A few even created "blackout periods" during key vacation times like Christmas and New Year, in order to avoid cannibalizing seat sales to paying customers.

Competitive strategies often involved bonus miles, too, with "bonus wars" breaking out on certain routes. At the height of its mid-1980s battle with New York Air on the lucrative 230-mile (370 km) New York–Boston shuttle service, the PanAm Shuttle offered passengers 2,000 miles for a one-way trip and 5,000 miles for a round trip completed within a single day. Bonus miles were also awarded for travel in first or business class. And bonuses might also be used to encourage passengers to sample new services or to complete market research surveys.

To record the mileage of passengers enrolled in their frequent flyer programs, the airlines have had to install elaborate tracking systems that capture details of each flight. They have also created systems for recording and maintaining each member's current account status. United uses its extensive customer database to reward loyalty in a unique way. If a flight is canceled, passengers are placed on a waiting list for the next available flight according to how many miles they have accumulated. Thus more loyal customers are given preferential treatment in terms of service and convenience.

means as requiring an advance purchase or an extended stay in the destination city, making it difficult for business travelers to trade down from full fare to a discount ticket.

One problem with frequent flyer programs is that customers who travel extensively tend to belong to several different programs. To encourage loyalty to a single carrier, some airlines have added a points system, based upon the *value* of the customer's business in a given year, not just the mileage. For instance, at British Airways Executive Club, travel in business class and first class qualifies, respectively, for double and triple the number of points awarded in economy class, but discounted economy fares do not qualify for points at all. Longer flights, being more expensive, yield more points. Once club members have amassed a certain number of points, they receive silver or gold tier status, valid for 12 months. This points-based reward system offers a number of privileges, including automatic doubling of air miles for gold tier members and a 25 percent bonus for silver tier members. A number of other airlines now use similar approaches, but the tier system gives travelers an incentive to consolidate their flights with a single airline.

Service businesses in other industries have sought to copy the airlines with frequent user programs of their own. Hotels, car rental firms, telephone companies, retailers, and even credit card issuers have been among those that seek to identify and reward their best customers. For instance, the Safeway supermarket chain offers a Club Card that provides savings on its own merchandise and discounts on purchases of services from partner companies. Similarly, car rental firms offer vehicle upgrades and hotels offer free rooms in vacation resorts. Not all companies offer their own products as rewards; instead, many firms offer miles credited to an airline's frequent flyer program since air miles have become a valuable promotional currency in their own right.

Perhaps the most creative awards are those that even wealthy customers might find difficult to obtain on their own. For example, Merrill Lynch recently offered its premium clients an opportunity to use Visa card points to "purchase" top seats at an award-

By specializing in cutting children's hair and providing an appealing environment for them, this salon hopes to build a relationship with both the kids and their parents.

winning Broadway musical or a VIP package to attend the 2001 All-Star Hockey Game in Denver, including a champagne reception at which the legendary player, Gordie Howe, was scheduled to speak.

Despite the popularity of customer loyalty programs, researchers claim that these programs have proved "surprisingly ineffective" for many firms. To succeed in competitive markets, they suggest that loyalty programs must enhance the overall value of product or service and motivate loyal buyers to make their next purchase.[16] In some instances, like the airline's frequent flyer miles, the benefits are popular with customers and virtually all players in the industry have felt obliged to offer a loyalty program. Additional valued benefits for loyal airline customers often include priority reservation and check-in services, use of airport lounges, and upgrades. In other industries, however, the benefits are not perceived as valuable enough to encourage loyalty or justify a higher price than competitors. This may have been one reason why AT&T, facing fierce price competition in the telecommunications industry, ended its "True Rewards" loyalty program in 1998.

The bottom line is that rewards alone will not enable a firm to retain its most desirable customers. If these customers are not delighted with the quality of service they receive, or believe that they can obtain better value from a less-expensive service, they may quickly become disloyal. No service business can afford to lose sight of the broader goals of providing quality service and good value relative to the price and other costs of service that customers incur.

Ending Unprofitable Relationships

Although our focus so far has been on increasing customer loyalty, not all of a firm's existing customers may be worth keeping. Some customers no longer fit the firm's strategy, either because that strategy has changed or because the customer's behavior and needs have changed. Many relationships are no longer profitable for the firm, since they cost more to maintain than the revenues they generate. Just as investors need to dispose of poor investments and banks may have to write off bad loans, each service firm needs to regularly evaluate its customer portfolio and consider terminating unsuccessful relationships. (Legal and ethical considerations, of course, will help determine whether it is possible or proper to take such actions.)

Occasionally customers have to be terminated directly (although concern for due process is still important). Bank customers who bounce too many checks, students who are caught cheating on exams, or country club members who consistently abuse the facilities (or staff and other members) may be asked to leave or face expulsion. In other situations, termination may be less confrontational. Banks have been known to sell accounts that no longer fit with corporate priorities to other financial institutions; the "traded" customers typically receive a letter in the mail or a phone call from the new supplier informing them of the change. Professionals such as doctors or lawyers may suggest to difficult or dissatisfied clients that they should consider switching to another provider whose expertise or style is more suited to their needs and expectations.

THE PROBLEM OF CUSTOMER MISBEHAVIOR

Customers who act in uncooperative or abusive ways are a problem for any organization. But they have more potential for mischief in service businesses, particularly those in which the customer comes to the service factory. As you know from your own experience, the behavior of other customers can affect your enjoyment of a service. If you like classical music and attend symphony concerts, you expect audience members to keep quiet during the performance, rather than spoiling the music by talking or coughing loudly. By contrast, a silent audience would be deadly during a rock concert or team sports event, where active audience participation adds to the excitement. There is a fine line, however, between spectator enthusiasm and abusive behavior by supporters of rival sports teams. Firms that fail to deal effectively with customer misbehaviors risk damaging their relationships with all the other customers they would like to keep.

Addressing the Challenge of Jaycustomers

Visitors to North America from other English-speaking countries are often puzzled by the term "jaywalker," that distinctively American word used to describe people who cross streets at unauthorized places or in a dangerous manner. The prefix "jay" comes from a nineteenth-century slang term for a stupid person. We can create a whole vocabulary of derogatory terms by adding the prefix "jay" to existing nouns and verbs. How about "*jaycustomer*," for example, to denote someone who "jayuses" a service or "jayconsumes" a physical product (and then "jaydisposes" of it afterwards)? We define a **jaycustomer** as one who acts in a thoughtless or abusive way, causing problems for the firm, its employees, and other customers.[17]

Every service has its share of jaycustomers. But opinions on this topic seem to polarize around two opposing views of the situation. One is denial: "The customer is king and can do no wrong." The other view sees the marketplace of customers as positively overpopulated with nasty people who cannot be trusted to behave in ways that self-respecting service providers should expect and require. The first viewpoint has received wide publicity in gung-ho management books and in motivational presentations to captive groups of employees. But the second view often appears to be dominant among cynical managers and employees who have been burned at some point by customer misbehaviors. As with so many opposing viewpoints in life, there are important grains of truth in both perspectives. What is clear, however, is that no self-respecting firm would want to have an ongoing relationship with an abusive customer.

jaycustomer: a customer who acts in a thoughtless or abusive way, causing problems for the firm, its employees, and other customers.

Six Types of Jaycustomers

Jaycustomers are undesirable. At worst, a firm needs to control or prevent their abusive behavior. At best, it would like to avoid attracting them in the first place. Since defining the problem is the first step in resolving it, let's start by considering the different segments of jaycustomers who prey upon providers of both goods and services. We've identified six broad categories and given them generic names, but many customer-contact personnel have come up with their own special terms. As you reflect on these categories, you may be tempted to add a few more of your own.

The Thief   This jaycustomer has no intention of paying and sets out to steal goods and services (or to pay less than full price by switching price tickets or contesting bills on baseless grounds). Shoplifting is a major problem in retail stores. What retailers euphemistically call "shrinkage" is estimated to cost them huge sums of money in annual revenues. Many services lend themselves to clever schemes for avoiding payment. For those with technical skills, it's sometimes possible to bypass electricity meters, access telephone lines free of charge, or circumvent normal cable TV feeds. Riding free on public transportation, sneaking into movie theaters, or not paying for restaurant meals are also popular. And we mustn't forget the use of fraudulent forms of payment such as stolen credit cards or checks drawn on accounts without any funds. Finding out how people steal a service is the first step in preventing theft or catching thieves and, where appropriate, prosecuting them. But managers should try not to alienate honest customers by degrading their service experiences. And provision must be made for honest but absent-minded customers who forget to pay.

The Rulebreaker Just as highways need safety regulations (including "Don't Jaywalk"), many service businesses need to establish rules of behavior for employees and customers to guide them safely through the various steps of the service encounter. Some of these rules are imposed by government agencies for health and safety reasons. The sign found in many restaurants that states "No shirt, no shoes—no service" demonstrates a health-related regulation. And air travel provides one of the best of examples of rules designed to ensure safety—there are few other environments outside prison where healthy, mentally competent, adult customers are quite so constrained (albeit with good reason).

In addition to enforcing government regulations, suppliers often impose their own rules to facilitate smooth operations, avoid unreasonable demands on employees, prevent misuse of products and facilities, protect themselves legally, and discourage individual customers from misbehaving. Ski resorts, for instance, are getting tough on careless skiers who pose risks to both themselves and others.[18] Collisions can cause serious injury and even death. So ski patrol members must be safety oriented and sometimes take on a policing role. Just as dangerous drivers can lose their licenses, so dangerous skiers can lose their lift tickets.

At Vail and Beaver Creek in Colorado, ski patrollers once revoked nearly 400 lift tickets in just a single weekend. At Winter Park near Denver, skiers who lose their passes for dangerous behavior may have to attend a 45-minute safety class before they can get their passes back. Ski patrollers at Vermont's Okemo Mountain may issue warnings to reckless skiers by attaching a bright orange sticker to their lift tickets. If pulled over again for inappropriate behavior, such skiers may be escorted off the mountain and banned for a day or more. "We're not trying to be Gestapos on the slopes," says the resort's marketing director, "just trying to educate people."

How should a firm deal with rulebreakers? Much depends on which rules have been broken. In the case of legally enforceable ones—theft, bad debts, trying to take guns on aircraft—the courses of action need to be laid down explicitly to protect employees and to punish or discourage wrongdoing by customers. Company rules are a little more ambiguous. Are they really necessary in the first place? If not, the firm should get rid of them. Do they deal with health and safety? If so, educating customers about the rules should reduce the need for taking corrective action. The same is true for rules designed to protect the comfort and enjoyment of all customers. There are also unwritten social norms such as "thou shalt not jump the queue" (although this is a much stronger cultural expectation in the United States or Canada than in many countries, as any visitor to Paris Disneyland can attest!). Other customers can often be relied upon to help service personnel enforce rules that affect everybody else; they may even take the initiative in doing so.

There are risks attached to making lots of rules. They can make an organization appear bureaucratic and overbearing. And they can transform employees, whose orientation should be service to customers, into police officers who see (or are told to see) their most important task as enforcing all the rules. The fewer the rules, the more explicit the important ones can be.

The Belligerent You've probably seen him (or her) in a store, at the airport, in a hotel or restaurant—red in the face and shouting angrily, or perhaps icily calm and mouthing off insults, threats, and obscenities.[19] Things don't always work as they should:

Machines break down, service is clumsy, customers are ignored, a flight is delayed, an order is delivered incorrectly, staff are unhelpful, a promise is broken. Or perhaps the customer in question is expressing resentment at being told to abide by the rules. Service personnel are often abused, even when they are not to blame. If an employee lacks authority to resolve the problem, the belligerent may become madder still, even to the point of physical attack. Drunkenness and drug abuse add extra layers of complication (see the box "Air Rage"). Organizations that care about their employees go to great efforts to develop skills in dealing with these difficult situations. Training

Air Rage: Unruly Passengers a Growing Problem

Joining the term "road rage"—coined in 1988 to describe angry, aggressive drivers who threaten other road users—is the newer term, "air rage." Perpetrators of air rage are violent, unruly passengers who endanger flight attendants, pilots, and other passengers. Incidents of air rage are perpetrated by only a tiny fraction of all airline passengers—reportedly about 5,000 times a year—but each incident in the air may affect the comfort and safety of hundreds of other people.

Acts of violence may be committed against employees or the aircraft itself. On a flight from Orlando (Florida) to London, a drunken passenger smashed a video screen and began ramming a window, telling fellow passengers they were about to "get sucked out and die." The crew strapped him down and the aircraft made an unscheduled landing in Bangor (Maine), where U.S. marshals arrested him. Another unscheduled stop in Bangor involved a drug smuggler flying from Jamaica to the Netherlands. When a balloon filled with cocaine ruptured in his stomach, he went berserk, pounding a bathroom door to pieces and grabbing a female passenger by the throat.

On a flight from London to Spain, a passenger who was already drunk at the time of boarding became angry when a flight attendant told him not to smoke in the lavatory and refused to serve him another drink. Later, he smashed her over the head with a duty-free vodka bottle before being restrained by other passengers (she required 18 stitches to close the wound). Other dangerous incidents have included throwing hot coffee at flight attendants, head butting a copilot, invading the cockpit and disengaging the autopilot, throwing a flight attendant across three rows of seats, and attempting to open an emergency door in flight. In August 2000, a violent passenger was restrained and ultimately suffocated by other passengers after he kicked through the cockpit door of an airliner 20 minutes before it was scheduled to land in Salt Lake City.

In testimony before the U.S. Congress, an airline captain speaking for the Air Line Pilots Association declared, "Passenger interference is the most pervasive security problem facing airlines." A growing number of carriers are taking air rage perpetrators to court. Northwest Airlines permanently blacklisted three violent travelers from flying on its aircraft. British Airways gives out "warning cards" to any passenger getting dangerously out of control. Some airlines carry physical restraints to subdue out-of-control passengers until they can be handed over to airport authorities. In April 2000, the U.S. Congress increased the civil penalty for air rage from $1,100 to $25,000 in an attempt to discourage passengers from misbehaving. Criminal penalties—a $10,000 fine and up to 20 years in jail—can also be imposed for the most serious incidents. However, airlines have been reluctant to publicize this information for fear of appearing confrontational or intimidating.

What causes air rage? Researchers suggest that air travel has become increasingly stressful as a result of crowding and longer flights; the airlines themselves may have contributed to the problem by squeezing rows of seats more tightly together and failing to explain delays. Findings suggest that risk factors for air travel stress include anxiety and an anger-prone personality; they also show that traveling on unfamiliar routes is more stressful than on a familiar one. Another factor may be restrictions on smoking.

Airlines are training their employees to handle violent individuals and to spot problem passengers before they start causing serious problems. Some carriers offer travelers specific suggestions on how to relax during long flights. And a few European airlines are considering offering nicotine patches to passengers who are desperate for a smoke but are no longer allowed to light up.

Source: Daniel Eisenberg, "Acting Up in the Air," *Time*, 21 December 1998; Carol Smith, "Air Travel Stress Can Make Life Miserable," *Seattle Post Intelligencer*, syndicated article, August 1999; "Air Rage Capital: Bangor Becomes Nation's Flight Problem Drop Point," *The Baltimore Sun*, syndicated article, September, 1999; "Airlines Strangely Mum About New Fine," *The Omaha World-Herald*, syndicated article, 25 September 2000; and Melanie Trottman and Chip Cummins, "Passenger's Death Prompts Calls for Improved 'Air Rage' Procedures," *The Wall Street Journal*, 26 September 2000.

exercises that involve role-playing help employees develop the self-confidence and assertiveness that they need to deal with upset, belligerent customers (sometimes referred to as "irates"). Employees also need to learn how to defuse anger, calm anxiety, and comfort distress (particularly when there is good reason for the customer to be upset with the organization's performance).

What should an employee do when an aggressive customer brushes off attempts to defuse the situation? In a public environment, one priority should be to move the person away from other customers. Sometimes supervisors may have to arbitrate disputes between customers and staff members; at other times, they need to stand behind the employee's actions. If a customer has physically assaulted an employee, then it may be necessary to summon security officers or the police. Some firms try to conceal such events, fearing bad publicity. But others feel obliged to make a public stand on behalf of their employees, like the Body Shop manager who ordered an ill-tempered customer out of the store, telling her: "I won't stand for your rudeness to my staff."

Telephone rudeness poses a different challenge. Service personnel have been known to hang up on angry customers, but that action doesn't resolve the problem. Bank customers, for instance, tend to get upset when learning that checks have been returned because they are overdrawn (which means they've broken the rules) or that a request for a loan has been denied. One approach for handling customers who continue to berate a telephone-based employee is for the latter to say firmly: "This conversation isn't getting us anywhere. Why don't I call you back in a few minutes when you've had time to digest the information?" In many cases, a break for reflection is exactly what's needed.

The Family Feuders   People who get into arguments (or worse) with other customers—often members of their own family—make up a subcategory of belligerents we call family feuders. Employee intervention may calm the situation or actually make it worse. Some situations require detailed analysis and a carefully measured response. Others, like customers starting a food fight in a nice restaurant (yes, such things do happen!), require almost instantaneous response. Service managers in these situations need to be prepared to think on their feet and act fast.

The Vandal   The level of physical abuse to which service facilities and equipment can be subjected is truly astonishing. Soft drinks are poured into bank cash machines; graffiti are scrawled on both interior and exterior surfaces; burn holes from cigarettes scar carpets, tablecloths, and bedcovers; bus seats are slashed and hotel furniture broken; telephone handsets are torn off; customers' cars are vandalized; glass is smashed and fabrics are torn. The list is endless. Customers don't cause all of the damage, of course. Bored or drunk young people are the source of much exterior vandalism. And disgruntled employees have been known to commit sabotage. But much of the problem does originate with paying customers who choose to misbehave. Alcohol and drugs are sometimes the cause, psychological problems may contribute, and carelessness can play a role. There are also occasions when unhappy customers, feeling mistreated by the service provider, try to take revenge in some way.

The best cure for vandalism is prevention. Improved security discourages some vandals. Good lighting helps, as does open design of public areas. Companies can choose pleasing yet vandal-resistant surfaces, protective coverings for equipment, and rugged furnishings. Educating customers on how to use equipment properly (rather than fighting with it) and providing warnings about fragile objects can reduce the likelihood of abuse or careless handling. And there are economic sanctions: security deposits or signed agreements in which customers agree to pay for any damage that they cause.

What should managers do if prevention fails and damage is done? If the perpetrator is caught, they should first clarify whether there are any extenuating circumstances (because accidents do happen). Sanctions for deliberate damage can range from a warning to prosecution. As far as the physical damage itself is concerned, it's best to fix it fast (within any constraints imposed by legal or insurance considerations). The general manager of a bus company had the right idea when he said: "If one of our buses is vandalized, whether it's a broken window, a slashed seat, or graffiti on the ceiling, we take it out of service immediately, so nobody sees it. Otherwise you just give the same idea to five other characters who were too dumb to think of it in the first place!"

The Deadbeat   Leaving aside those individuals who never intended to pay in the first place (our term for them is "the thief"), there are many reasons why customers fail to pay for services they have received. Once again, preventive action is better than a cure. A growing number of firms insist on prepayment. Any form of ticket sale is a good example of this. Direct marketing organizations ask for your credit card number as they take your order, as do most hotels when you make a reservation. The next best thing is to present the customer with a bill immediately on completion of service. If the bill is to be sent by mail, the firm should send it fast, while the service is still fresh in the customer's mind.

Not every apparent delinquent is a hopeless deadbeat. Perhaps there's good reason for the delay and acceptable payment arrangements can be worked out. A key question is whether such a personalized approach can be cost-justified, relative to the results obtained by purchasing the services of a collection agency. There may be other considerations, too. If the client's problems are only temporary ones, what is the long-term value of maintaining the relationship? Will it create positive goodwill and word-of-mouth to help the customer work things out? These decisions are judgment calls, but if creating and maintaining long-term relationships is the firm's ultimate goal, they bear exploration.

Conclusion

All marketers need to be concerned about who their customers are, because some are more profitable (or more central to the organization's mission) than others. This concern takes on added dimensions for certain types of services. When customers have a high level of contact with the service organization and with one another, the customer mix helps to define the character of the organization, because customers themselves become a part of the product. So marketers must be selective in targeting the desired customer segments. Too diverse a portfolio of customers may result in an ill-defined image, especially if different customer segments are present at the same time. Avoiding inappropriate behavior is a related issue. Abusive customers—what we call "jaycustomers"—are a particular concern since they may spoil the experience for others and hurt profitability in other ways, too.

Marketers need to pay special attention to those customers who offer the firm the greatest value. Programs to reward frequent users—of which the most highly developed are the frequent flyer clubs created by the airlines—help identify and provide rewards for high-value customers and track their behavior in terms of where and when they use the service, what service classes or types of product they buy, and how much they spend. The most successful organizations give their best customers incentives to remain loyal, creating valued relationships that are nurtured over time.

Study Questions and Exercises

1. What criteria should a marketing manager use to decide which customer segments should be targeted by the firm?

2. Make a case both for and against the statement that "The customer is always right."

3. Identify some of the measures that can be used to encourage long-term relationships with customers.

4. Why should companies spend money to keep existing customers loyal?

5. Evaluate the strengths and weaknesses of frequent user programs in different types of service industries.

6. Select a people-processing service business. Then pick two types of jaycustomers and develop strategies designed (a) to discourage these customers from using your service, (b) to prevent them from causing distress to other customers and/or to employees, and (c) to minimize financial loss to your organization.

Endnotes

1. Based on information from the Intrawest Web site, www.intrawest.com, November 2000, and past annual reports of Intrawest Corporation, Vancouver, BC.
2. David H. Maister, *True Professionalism* (New York: The Free Press, 1997) (see especially ch. 20).
3. Paul S. Bender, *Design and Operation of Customer Service Systems* (New York: AMACOM, 1976), determined that, on average, a lost customer reduced profits by $118 compared with a $20 cost to keep a customer satisfied.
4. See "Special Report: Privacy in the Digital Age," *Yahoo Internet Life* 6 (October 2000), 98–115.
5. Leonard L. Berry and A. Parasuraman, *Marketing Services: Competing Through Quality* (New York: The Free Press, 1991). See especially ch. 8, 132–150.
6. Nicole E. Coviello, Roderick J. Brodie, and Hugh J. Munro, "Understanding Contemporary Marketing: Development of a Classification Scheme," *Journal of Marketing Management*, 13, no.6 (1995), 501–522.
7. J. R. Copulsky and M. J. Wolf, "Relationship Marketing: Positioning for the Future," *Journal of Business Strategy* 11, no. 4 (1990): 16–20.
8. Piyush Kumar, "The Impact of Long-Term Client Relationships on the Performance of Business Service Firms," *Journal of Service Research* 2 (August 1999): 4–18.
9. Frederick F. Reichheld, *The Loyalty Effect* (Boston: Harvard Business School Press, 1996).
10. Frederick F. Reichheld and W. Earl Sasser, Jr., "Zero Defections: Quality Comes to Services," *Harvard Business Review*, 68 October 1990.
11. James L. Heskett, W. Earl Sasser, Jr., and Leonard A. Schlesinger, *The Service Profit Chain* (New York: The Free Press, 1997).
12. Reichheld and Sasser, "Zero Defections."
13. Werner J. Reinarz and V. Kumar, "On the Profitability of Long-Life Customers in a Noncontractual Setting: An Empirical Investigation and Implications for Marketing," *Journal of Marketing* 64 (October 2000): 17–35.
14. Alan W. H. Grant and Leonard H. Schlesinger, "Realize Your Customer's Full Profit Potential," *Harvard Business Review* 73 (September-October, 1995): 59–75.
15. Diane Brady, "Why Service Stinks," *Business Week*, 23 October 2000, 118–128.
16. Gerald R. Dowling and Mark Uncles, "Do Customer Loyalty Programs Really Work?" *Sloan Management Review* (Summer 1997): 71–81.

17. This section is adapted from Christopher Lovelock, *Product Plus* (New York: McGraw-Hill, 1994), ch. 15.

18. Based on Rob Ortega and Emily Nelson, "Skiing Deaths May Fuel Calls for Helmets," *Wall Street Journal*, 7 January 1998, B1–B16.

19. For an amusing and explicit depiction of various types of belligerent customers, see Ron Zemke and Kristin Anderson, "The Customers from Hell," *Training* 26 (February 1990): 25–31 [reprinted in John E. G. Bateson and K. Douglas Hoffman, *Managing Services Marketing*, 4th ed. (Fort Worth, TX: The Dryden Press, 1999), 61–62.].

chapter six

Complaint Handling and Service Recovery

Why Did the Hotel Guests Pass Up a Free Breakfast?

An alert hostess at a Hampton Inn in California noticed that two guests from an Australian tour group were passing up her hotel's complimentary breakfast.[1] On the second morning, she asked if anything was wrong. "To be honest, the food is just not what we're used to at home," they replied, describing a typical Australian breakfast. When they came down the next morning, the hostess greeted them cheerfully. "I think we might be able to give you some breakfast this morning," she smiled, laying out items they had mentioned the previous day. She had made a quick trip to a nearby supermarket and added some items from her own kitchen at home. The guests were thrilled. "So this is what 100 percent satisfaction means?" they asked. "*We* get to define satisfaction?" They were so impressed that they arranged to have the other members of their tour group, who were staying at another hotel, move to the Hampton Inn. The two weeks of unexpected tour revenue from the group resulted in a more than adequate return on the extra time and money.

The 1,000-plus Hampton Inns offer their guests a valued promise: an *unconditional* guarantee of satisfaction. Guests define satisfaction on their own terms, and the hotel guarantees the customer-defined satisfaction—without negotiation. These two elements make the guarantee extraordinary and give Hampton Inn a competitive advantage in its lodging segment. Since its introduction, only a few competitors have imitated Hampton Inn's "100% Satisfaction Guarantee." More important, mere imitation has not produced the same results, because the imitators lack the supporting infrastructure, culture, and above all the necessary *attitude* to make the guarantee more than a slogan. Initially, the guarantee was viewed as a proactive approach to what Ray Schultz, later chairman of Hampton Inn's parent company, referred to as "the heartbreak of franchising," the all-too-familiar deterioration of a lodging chain that traditionally plagues the lodging industry. He recognized how easily quality and service standards could slip as properties aged. Investments in properties—either hard dollars for capital improvements or soft dollars for employee training, for example, were often compromised to support short-term earnings.

Furthermore, Schultz recognized the inherent difficulty of maintaining quality standards across a large and diverse multi-site franchise system, in which properties are owned by outside investors. He knew that the challenge would only intensify given the company's aggressive growth strategy. "We cannot compromise the quality of Hampton Inns as we grow, because ultimately that would constrain our growth," he asserted. "Deteriorating quality inevitably will result in declining guest satisfaction, lower guest loyalty, and negative word-of-mouth. That's a recipe for further deterioration in revenue and operating cash flow. It is easy to lower service standards, but once lowered, it is very difficult to raise them."

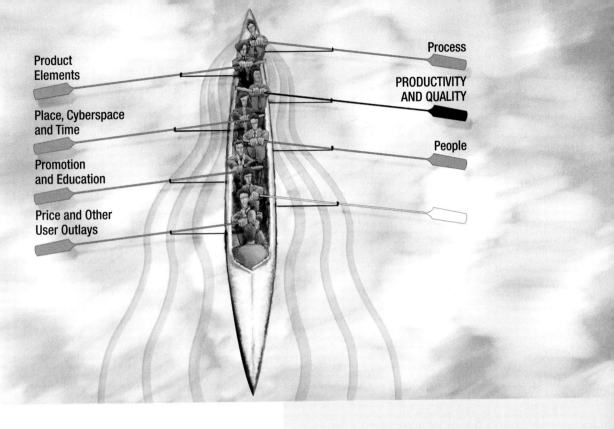

Product
Elements

Place, Cyberspace
and Time

Promotion
and Education

Price and Other
User Outlays

Process

PRODUCTIVITY
AND QUALITY

People

⇛ **Learning Objectives**

After reading this chapter, you should be able to

⇛ discuss the nature and extent of consumer complaints

⇛ outline the courses of action available to a dissatisfied consumer

⇛ explain the factors that influence consumer complaining behavior

⇛ identify the principles of an effective service recovery system

⇛ demonstrate the value of an effective service guarantee

CONSUMER COMPLAINING BEHAVIOR

"Thank Heavens for Complainers" was the provocative title of an article about customer complaining behavior. "The ones I worry about," declared one successful manager, "are the ones I never hear from."[2] Customers who do complain give a firm the chance to correct problems (including some the firm may not even know it has), restore relationships with the complainer, and improve future satisfaction for all.

Although the first law of service productivity and quality might be "Do it right the first time," we can't ignore the fact that failures continue to occur, sometimes for reasons outside the organization's control. You've probably noticed from your own experience that the various "moments of truth" in service encounters are especially vulnerable to breakdowns. Such distinctive service characteristics as real-time performance, customer involvement, people as part of the product, and difficulty of evaluation greatly increase the chance of perceived service failures. This chapter addresses the question: *What should we do when customers' expectations are not met*? How well a firm handles complaints and resolves problems may determine whether it builds customer loyalty or watches former customers take their business elsewhere.

The chances are that you're not entirely satisfied with the quality of at least some of the services that you use. Specific complaints can be related to any of the 8Ps. A common source of frustration results from inappropriate trade-offs between *productivity and quality*, when a firm tries to boost productivity without thinking about its impact on customers. Perhaps some of the *product elements* are poorly executed. Or maybe the service *processes* in which you are involved are badly organized. Shortcomings in delivery—*place, cyberspace, and time*—are common. For example, a service may be unavailable where and when you want it; or a Web site may not be functioning satisfactorily. Failings in physical evidence include ugly or poorly maintained facilities and dirty or poorly fitting staff uniforms.

Price and other user outlays are a major source of complaints. You can probably recall occasions when you felt you were overcharged, were kept waiting too long, or endured unnecessary hassles. Your disappointment with a service may also have resulted from *promotion and education* strategies that promised too much (thus raising your expectations too high), or failed to instruct you properly in how to use the service. And perhaps you were inconvenienced or annoyed at some point by the behavior of the *people* in a service environment—either customer-contact personnel or other customers.

complaint: a formal expression of dissatisfaction with any aspect of a service experience.

How do you respond when you have been disappointed? Do you complain informally to an employee, ask to speak to the manager, file a **complaint** with the head office of the firm that let you down, write to some regulatory authority, or telephone a consumer advocacy group? Or do you just grumble to your friends and family, mutter darkly to yourself, and take your business elsewhere next time you need that type of service?

If you don't normally tell a company (or outside agency) of your displeasure with unsatisfactory service or faulty goods, then you're not alone. Research around the world has exposed the sad fact that most people do not complain, especially if they don't think it will do any good. And even when they do communicate their dissatisfaction, managers may not hear about complaints made to customer-contact personnel.[3]

Customer Response to Service Failures

service failure: a perception by customers that one or more specific aspects of service delivery have not met their expectations.

What options are open to customers when they experience a **service failure**? Figure 6.1 depicts the courses of action available.

This model suggests at least four major courses of action:

➤ Do nothing

➤ Complain to the service firm

> Take action through a third party (consumer advocacy group, consumer affairs or regulatory agencies, civil or criminal courts)

> Switch suppliers and discourage other people from using the original service firm (through negative word-of-mouth)

It's possible to imagine a variety of outcomes to the actions listed in Figure 6.1 that might cause customers to feel a range of emotions from fury to delight. The risk of defection is high if customers are dissatisfied, especially when there is a variety of competing alternatives available. One study of customer switching behavior in service industries found that close to 60 percent of all respondents who reported changing suppliers did so because of a perceived failure: 25 percent cited failures in the core service, 19 percent reported an unsatisfactory encounter with an employee, 10 percent reported an unsatisfactory response to a prior service failure, and 4 percent described unethical behavior on the part of the provider.[4]

Managers need to be aware that the impact of a defection can go far beyond the loss of that customer's future business. Angry customers often tell many other people about their problems. The Web has made life more difficult for companies that provide poor service, because unhappy customers can now reach thousands of people by posting complaints on bulletin boards or setting up Web sites to publicize their bad experiences with specific organizations.[5] There are even Internet-based services like Ellen's Poison Pen (www.ellenspoisonpen.com) that, for a fee, will deluge CEOs of offending companies with letters, e-mails, and faxes until the disgruntled customer is compensated—or at least acknowledged. Companies who have been on the receiving end of correspondence from these new online consumer complaint services have charged that cyberspace is fast becoming "Whine Country."[6]

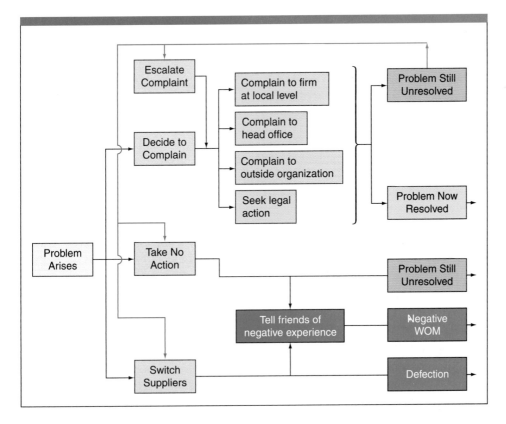

FIGURE 6.1

Courses of Action Open to a Dissatisfied Customer

The TARP Study of Consumer Complaint Handling

TARP, a leading customer satisfaction and loyalty measurement firm (now known as e-Satisfy), has studied consumer complaint handling in many countries. It published a landmark research study based on its own research and a detailed review of other studies from around the world.[7] The findings, which were widely publicized, prompted many managers to consider the impact of dissatisfied customers—especially those who never complained but simply defected to a competitor. Let's take a closer look at some specific findings, recognizing that some of the percentages reported may change for better or worse over time.

What Percentage of Problems Are Reported? From its own research and detailed literature studies, TARP found that when U.S. customers experienced problems concerning manufactured consumer products, only 25 percent to 30 percent of them actually complained. For grocery products or their packaging, the market research firm of A.C. Nielsen found a complaint rate of 30 percent. Even for problems with large-ticket durables, TARP determined that the complaint rate among dissatisfied customers was only 40 percent. Similar findings come from other countries. A Norwegian study found that the percentage of dissatisfied consumers who complained ranged from 9 percent for coffee to 68 percent for cars. A German study showed that only a small fraction of customers expressed dissatisfaction, but among this group the complaint rates ranged from 29 percent to 81 percent. And finally, a Japanese study found complaint rates of 17 percent among those experiencing a problem with services and 36 percent for those experiencing a problem with goods.

Where Do People Complain? Studies show that the majority of complaints are made at the place where the product was bought or the service received. Very few dissatisfied consumers complain directly to the manufacturers or to the head office. In fact, industry-specific studies conducted by TARP suggest that fewer than 5 percent of complaints about large-ticket durable goods or services ever reach corporate headquarters, presumably because retail intermediaries fail to pass them on.

Who Is Most Likely to Complain? In general, research findings suggest that consumers from high-income households are more likely to complain than those from lower income ones, and younger people are more likely to complain than older ones. People who complain also tend to be more knowledgeable about the products in question and the procedures for complaining. Other factors that increase the likelihood of a complaint include problem severity, importance of the product to the customer, and whether financial loss is involved. Customers are also more likely to complain if the problem involves a technology failure during a self-service interaction instead of an encounter with a service employee.[8]

Why Don't Unhappy Customers Complain? TARP found three primary reasons why dissatisfied customers don't complain. In order of frequency, customers stated that:

> ➤ they didn't think it was worth the time or effort,

> ➤ they decided no one would be concerned about their problem or resolving it, and

> ➤ they did not know where to go or what to do.

Unfortunately, this pessimism seems justified since a large percentage of people (40 percent to 60 percent in two studies) reported dissatisfaction with the outcome of their complaints. Another reason why people don't complain reflects culture or context. A study in Japan found that 21 percent of dissatisfied customers felt awkward or embarrassed about complaining. In some European countries, there is a strong guest-host relationship between service providers and customers (especially in the restaurant industry) and it's considered bad manners to tell customer-contact personnel that you are dissatisfied in any way with the service or the meal. Think about an occasion when you were dissatisfied but did not complain. What were the reasons?

Impact on Repurchase Intentions   When complaints are satisfactorily resolved, there's a much better chance that the customers involved will remain brand loyal and continue to repurchase the items in question. TARP found that intentions to repurchase different types of products ranged from 69 percent to 80 percent among those complainers who were completely satisfied with the outcome of the complaint. This figure dropped to 17 percent to 32 percent (depending on the type of product) for complainers who felt that their complaint had not been settled to their satisfaction.

Variations in Dissatisfaction by Industry

Although significant improvements in complaint handling practices occurred during the 1980s and early 1990s in some industries, many customers remain dissatisfied with the way in which their problems are resolved.

There are discouraging signs that the situation is deteriorating again. Data from Better Business Bureaus showed that consumer complaints more than doubled between 1995 and 1999. One reason may be that customer expectations are rising at the same time that companies are focusing their attention on their most loyal and profitable customers and paying less attention to the rest.[9] Firms have also been trying to save money by automating their complaint handling procedures, making it increasingly difficult for customers to speak with a real person.

A valuable measure of how well different industries in the United States are performing relative to the needs and expectations of the marketplace is provided by the American Customer Satisfaction Index (ACSI), which measures customers' evaluations of the total purchase and consumption experience, both actual and anticipated, on an annual basis.[10] ACSI results show that most manufactured products score higher than most services. Figure 6.2 shows the trend in annual satisfaction scores for several major service industries between 1995 and 2000. Most show a decline, with the airline indus-

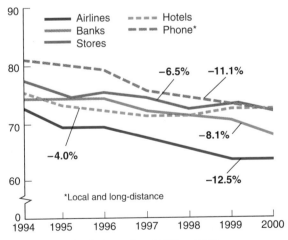

Based on annual poll of more than 50,000 customers, measuring overall satisfaction with products and services.
Scale: 1-10

Source: American Customer Service Index, University of Michigan Business School.

FIGURE 6.2

Declining Satisfaction Hits Major Service Industries in the USA, 1995–2000

try showing the sharpest deterioration in customer satisfaction. As these data suggest, many service industries are still a long way from meeting their customers' expectations on service. But some companies do better than others. Within each industry, there are often considerable variations in performance between different firms.

Findings from a large-scale study of consumer complaining behavior in Australia showed that, among the industries studied, a majority of customers who had a serious problem did make the effort to complain.[11] The results showed considerable disparity from one service industry to another in both the incidence of unsatisfactory service as well as in customers' likeliness to complain. For instance, more Australians were willing to complain about telephone service and other utilities than about restaurants and health services.

Other key findings from this study were the following:

➢ 57 percent of respondents had experienced at least one problem with products or services within the past 12 months.

➢ On average, 73 percent of those respondents who had a serious problem took some action to have it corrected.

➢ Only 34 percent who took action were satisfied with the way the problem was resolved.

➢ Among those who were not happy with their complaint outcome, 89 percent reported they would not deal with the same firm again.

➢ Complaining households made an average of 3.4 contacts each in an effort to have their most serious problems resolved.

➢ The further up the management hierarchy customers had to go to get the problem resolved, the more their satisfaction declined.

➢ On average, a dissatisfied customer told nine other people while a satisfied customer told only half as many.

What do people actually complain about? Inevitably, there are variations from one industry to another when it comes to problems with the core product, but certain aspects of customer service are common to numerous service industries. Figure 6.3 highlights the extent of different types of complaints about telephone service in the United States, as reported to the Federal Communications Commission. It's striking to note that 41 percent of all complaints concern inaccurate information. A substantial proportion of the

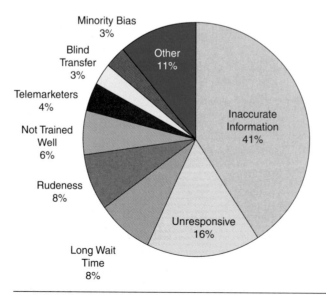

FIGURE 6.3

How U.S. Complaints About
Phone Service Break Down

Data: Federal Communications Commission.

remaining complaints revolve around failings on the part of service personnel, including unresponsiveness, rudeness, poor training, and a bias against minorities.

Factors Influencing Complaining Behavior

When consumers have an unsatisfactory service encounter, their initial (often unconscious) reaction is to assess what is at stake. In general, studies of consumer complaining behavior have identified two main purposes for complaining. First, consumers will complain to recover some economic loss, seeking either to get a refund or to have the service performed again (e.g., car repairs, dry-cleaning services). They may take legal action if the problem remains unresolved. A second reason for complaining is to rebuild self-esteem. When service employees are rude, aggressive, deliberately intimidating, or apparently uncaring (such as when a sales assistant is discussing his weekend social activities with colleagues and pointedly ignores waiting customers), the customers' self-esteem, self-worth, or sense of fairness may be negatively affected. They may feel that they should be treated with more respect and become angry or emotional.

There are *costs* associated with complaining. These may include the monetary cost of a stamp or phone call, time and effort in writing a detailed letter or making a verbal complaint, and the psychological burden of risking an unpleasant personal confrontation with a service provider—especially if this involves someone whom the customer knows and may have to deal with again). Such costs may well deter a dissatisfied customer from complaining. Often, it is simply less stressful to defect to a different service supplier—especially when the switching costs are low or nonexistent. If you are unhappy with the service you receive from your travel agent, for example, you may easily switch to a different agent next time. However, if you decide to switch doctors or dentists, you may have to ask to have all of your medical records transferred. This requires more effort and might make you feel uncomfortable.

Complaining represents a form of social interaction and therefore is likely to be influenced by role perceptions and social norms. One study found that for services where customers have "low power" (defined as the perceived ability to influence or control the transaction), they are less likely to voice complaints.[12] Professional service providers such as doctors, dentists, lawyers, professors, and architects are a good example. Social norms tend to discourage criticism by clients of such individuals, who are seen as "experts" about the service being offered. A clear implication is that professionals need to develop comfortable ways for their clients to express legitimate complaints.

What do customers expect after investing time and effort in making a complaint? In a very real sense, they are looking for justice and fairness. Based on a study of consumers' experiences with complaint resolution, Tax and Brown identified three types of fairness.[13] The first, *outcome fairness*, relates to customer expectations of outcomes or compensation that matches the level of dissatisfaction. Second, customers expect *procedural fairness*, in terms of clear, timely, and hassle-free procedures for handling complaints and resolving problems. Third, customers look for *interaction fairness*, which involves being treated politely, with care and honesty.

Complaints as Market Research Data

Responsive service organizations look at complaints as a stream of information that can be used to help monitor productivity and quality and highlight changes needed to improve service design and execution. Complaints about slow service or bureaucratic procedures, for instance, may provide useful documentation of inefficient and unproductive processes. Personal or telephone interviews offer much better opportunities than mail or in-store surveys to dig deeper and probe for what lies behind certain responses. A skilled interviewer can solicit valuable information by asking customers questions such as: "Can you tell me why you feel this way? Who (or what) caused this situation? How did customer-contact employees respond? What action would you like to see the firm take to prevent a recurrence of such a situation?"

For complaints to be useful as research input, they should be funneled into a central collection point, recorded, categorized, and analyzed. Compiling this documentation requires a system for capturing complaints wherever they are made—without hindering timely resolution of each specific problem—and transmitting them to a central location where they can be recorded in a company-wide **complaint log**. The most useful roles for centralized complaint logs are: (1) to provide a basis for following up on and tracking all complaints to see that they have in fact been resolved; (2) to serve as an early warning indicator of perceived deterioration in one or more aspects of service; and (3) to indicate topics and issues that may require more detailed research. However, creating and maintaining a company-wide log is not a simple matter because there are many different entry points for complaints, including the following:

> the firm's own employees at the front line, who may be in contact with customers face-to-face or by telecommunications;

> intermediary organizations acting on behalf of the original supplier;

> managers who normally work backstage but who are contacted by a customer seeking higher authority;

> suggestion or complaint cards mailed or placed in a special box; and

> complaints to third parties—consumer advocate groups, legislative agencies, trade organizations, and other customers.

complaint log: a detailed record of all customer complaints received by a service provider.

Making It Easier for Customers to Complain

How can managers make it easier for unhappy customers to complain about service failures? Many companies have improved their complaint collection procedures by adding special toll-free phone lines, prominently displayed customer comment cards, Web sites and e-mail addresses, and video or computer terminals for recording complaints. Some go even further, encouraging their staff to ask customers if everything is satisfactory and to intervene if a customer is obviously unhappy.[14] The hostess at Hampton Inn was clearly very observant. She noticed that the two Australian guests

When unhappy customers complain, it makes life stressful for service personnel like this pharmacist—especially if it's not the latter's fault.

passed up the opportunity for breakfast two mornings in a row and sensed—or perhaps overheard them express—their disappointment.

Of course, just collecting complaints doesn't necessarily help to resolve them. In fact, accepting complaints and then ignoring them may make matters worse! Although friendly sympathy from an employee is much better than an irritable shrug, companies need to have a well-designed service recovery strategy that empowers employees to resolve problems quickly and satisfactorily. For example, the Hampton Inn hostess asked the two guests what they would normally eat for breakfast at home and then took the initiative during her free time to obtain the preferred items and bring them to the hotel. Ritz-Carlton employees are empowered to spend up to $2,000 to find a solution for a customer complaint. They also have permission to break from their routine jobs for as long as necessary to make a guest happy.[15]

IMPACT OF SERVICE RECOVERY EFFORTS ON CUSTOMER LOYALTY

Complaint handling should be seen as a profit center, not a cost center. TARP has even created a formula to help companies relate the value of retaining a profitable customer to the overall costs of running an effective complaint handling unit. Plugging industry data into this formula yielded some impressive returns on investment: from 50 percent to 170 percent for banking, 20 percent to 150 percent for gas utilities, over 100 percent for automotive service, and from 35 percent to an astonishing 400 percent for retailing.[16]

Underlying these statistics is a simple fact. When a dissatisfied customer defects, the firm loses more than just the value of the next transaction. It may also lose a long-term stream of profits from that customer and from anyone else who switches suppliers because of negative comments from an unhappy friend. So it pays to invest in **service recovery** efforts designed to protect those long-term profits. Efforts to design service recovery procedures must take into account a firm's specific environment and the types of problems that customers are likely to encounter. Figure 6.4 displays the components of an effective service recovery system.

service recovery: systematic efforts by a firm after a service failure to correct a problem and retain a customer's goodwill.

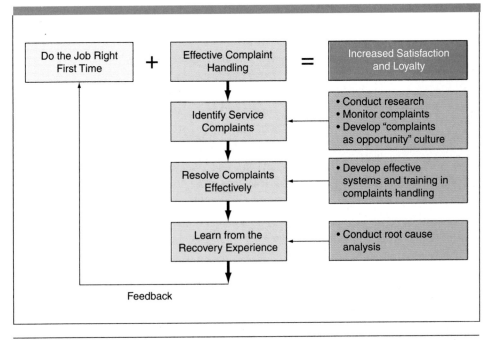

FIGURE 6.4

Components of an Effective Service Recovery System

Service Recovery Following Customer Complaints

Service recovery plays a crucial role in restoring customer satisfaction following a service failure and retaining a customer's goodwill. The true test of a firm's commitment to satisfaction and service quality isn't in the advertising promises or the decor and ambience of its offices, but in the way it responds when things go wrong for the customer. Recent research suggests that customers' satisfaction with the way in which complaints are handled has a direct impact on the trust they place in that supplier and on their future commitment to the firm.[17] Unfortunately, firms don't always react in ways that match their advertised promises. Effective service recovery requires thoughtful procedures for resolving problems and handling disgruntled customers, because even a single service problem can destroy a customer's confidence in a firm if the following conditions exist:[18]

> ➤ The failure is totally outrageous (e.g., blatant dishonesty on the part of the supplier).
> ➤ The problem fits a pattern of failure rather than being an isolated incident.
> ➤ The recovery efforts are weak, serving to compound the original problem rather than correct it.

Principles of Effective Problem Resolution

Recovering from service failures takes more than just pious expressions of determination to resolve any problems that may occur. It requires commitment, planning, and clear guidelines. Both managers and front-line employees must be prepared to deal with angry customers who are confrontational and sometimes behave in insulting ways toward service personnel who aren't at fault in any way. Service recovery efforts should be flexible, with employees being trained to handle complaints and empowered to develop solutions that will satisfy complaining customers.[19]

Guidelines for Effective Problem Resolution

1. *Act fast.* If the complaint is made during service delivery, then time is of the essence to achieve a full recovery. When complaints are made after the fact, many companies have established policies of responding within 24 hours, or sooner. Even when full resolution is likely to take longer, fast acknowledgment remains very important.

2. *Admit mistakes but don't be defensive.* Acting defensively may suggest that the organization has something to hide or is reluctant to fully explore the situation.

3. *Show that you understand the problem from each customer's point of view.* Seeing situations through the customers' eyes is the only way to understand what they think has gone wrong and why they are upset. Service personnel should avoid jumping to conclusions with their own interpretations.

4. *Don't argue with customers.* The goal should be to gather facts to reach a mutually acceptable solution, not to win a debate or prove that the customer is an idiot. Arguing gets in the way of listening and seldom diffuses anger.

5. *Acknowledge the customer's feelings,* either tacitly or explicitly (e.g., "I can understand why you're upset"). This action helps to build rapport, the first step in rebuilding a bruised relationship.

6. *Give customers the benefit of the doubt.* Not all customers are truthful and not all complaints justified. But customers should be treated as though they have a valid complaint until clear evidence to the contrary emerges. If a lot of money is at stake (as in insurance claims or potential lawsuits), careful investigation is warranted; if the amount involved is small, it may not be worth haggling over a

The material in the box on guidelines for effective problem resolution is based on discussions with executives in many different industries. Well-managed companies seek to act quickly and perform well on each of the 10 guidelines. Research suggests that the slower the resolution of a service problem, the greater the compensation (or "atonement") needed to make customers satisfied with the outcome of the service recovery process.[20] Treating complaints with suspicion is likely to alienate customers. The president of TARP (the company that undertook the studies of complaining behavior described earlier) notes:

> Our research has found premeditated rip-offs represent 1 to 2 percent of the customer base in most organizations. However, most organizations defend themselves against unscrupulous customers by . . . treating the 98 percent of honest customers like crooks to catch the 2 percent who are crooks.[21]

Taking care of customers requires that the firm also take care of its employees. Managers need to recognize that handling complaints about service failures and attempting service recovery can be stressful for employees, especially when they are treated abusively for problems over which they have no control. Compounding the stress are policies that impose inflexible, bureaucratic procedures rather than empowering customer-contact personnel to handle recovery situations as they see fit. Bowen and Johnston argue that service firms need to develop "internal service recovery strategies" designed to help employees recover from the negative feelings that they may incur from being the target of customer anger and dissatisfaction.[22]

Similarly, management must ensure that the firm employs a sufficient number of well-trained and motivated employees to be able to provide good service in the first place. Downsizing (a deliberate policy of reducing the number of employees to reduce costs) often involves a calculated gamble that replacing people by automated phone messages and Web sites will enable the firm to continue to respond satisfactorily to customers' problems. The telecommunications industry provides a cautionary tale of the risks of cutting back people-based service in favor of automated solutions, especially

---

refund or other compensation. But it's still a good idea to check records to see if there is a past history of dubious complaints by the same customer.

7. *Clarify the steps needed to solve the problem*. When instant solutions aren't possible, telling customers how the organization plans to proceed shows that corrective action is being taken. It also sets expectations about the time involved (so firms should be careful not to overpromise!).

8. *Keep customers informed of progress*. Nobody likes being left in the dark. Uncertainty breeds anxiety and stress. People tend to be more accepting of disruptions if they know what is going on and receive periodic progress reports.

9. *Consider compensation*. When customers don't receive the service outcomes promised or suffer serious inconvenience and/or loss of time and money because of service failures, either a monetary payment or an offer of equivalent service in kind is appropriate. This type of recovery strategy may also reduce the risk of legal action by an angry customer. Service guarantees often lay out in advance what such compensation will be, and the firm should ensure that all guarantees are met.

10. *Persevering to regain customer goodwill*. When customers have been disappointed, one of the biggest challenges is to restore their confidence and preserve the relationship for the future. Perseverance may be required to defuse customers' anger and to convince them that actions are being taken to avoid a recurrence of the problem. Truly exceptional recovery efforts can be extremely effective in building loyalty and referrals.

during a period of continuing mergers, acquisitions, and divestitures. Corporate customers, ranging from international airlines to the Chicago Board of Trade, are among those whose telephone or Internet operations have been paralyzed by service failures; these situations worsened dissatisfaction when customers were unable to find anyone who could promptly resolve their problems.[23]

service guarantee: a promise that if service delivery fails to meet predefined standards, the customer is entitled to one or more forms of compensation.

SERVICE GUARANTEES

A small but growing number of companies offer customers an unconditional guarantee of satisfaction. These guarantees promise that if service delivery fails to meet predefined standards, the customer is entitled to one or more forms of compensation—such as an easy-to-claim replacement, refund, or credit. Christopher Hart argues that **service guarantee** is a powerful tool for promoting and achieving service quality, citing the following reasons:

1. Guarantees force firms to focus on what their customers want and expect in each element of the service.

2. Guarantees set clear standards, telling customers and employees alike what the company stands for. Compensating customers for poor service causes managers

Four Service Guarantees

1. Excerpt from the "Quality Standard Guarantees" of an office services company

We guarantee six-hour turnaround on documents of two pages or less . . . (does not include client subsequent changes or equipment failures). We guarantee that there will be a receptionist to greet you and your visitors during normal business hours . . . (short breaks of less than five minutes are not subject to this guarantee). You will not be obligated to pay rent for any day on which there is not a manager onsite to assist you (lunch and reasonable breaks are expected and not subject to this guarantee).

Source: Reproduced in Eileen C. Shapiro, *Fad Surfing in the Boardroom* (Reading, MA: Addison-Wesley, 1995), 180.

2. U.S. Postal Service Express Mail Guarantee

Excludes all international shipments. Military shipments delayed due to Customs' inspections are also excluded. If this shipment is mailed at a designated USPS Express Mail facility on or before the specified time for overnight delivery to the addressee, it will be delivered to the addressee or agent before the guaranteed time the next delivery day. Signature of the addressee, addressee's agent, or delivery employee is required upon delivery. If it is not delivered by

the guaranteed time and the mailer makes a claim for a refund, the USPS will refund the postage unless: (1) delivery was attempted but could not be made, (2) this shipment was delayed by strike or work stoppage, or (3) detention was made for a law enforcement purpose.

Source: Printed on back of Express Mail receipt.

3. L.L. Bean's Guarantee

Our products are guaranteed to give 100 percent satisfaction in every way. Return anything purchased from us at any time if it proves otherwise. We will replace it, refund your purchase price, or credit your credit card. We do not want you to have anything from L.L. Bean that is not completely satisfactory.

Source: Printed in all L.L. Bean catalogs and on the company's Web site, www.llbean.com/customerservice/, *January 2000.*

4. Blockbuster Video's Guarantee

Get a Movie Rental FREE if you don't love *Keeping the Faith*. FREE movie rental given only on visit with return of paid rental of *Keeping the Faith*. Recipient responsible for applicable taxes and extended viewing fees. If recipient rents more than one movie, credit will be applied to lowest rental price. Offer valid at participating stores. Limit one (1) satisfaction guarantee coupon per featured title.

Source: Blockbuster Video monthly mailing to Rewards program members, October 2000.

to take guarantees seriously, because they highlight the financial costs of quality failures.

3. Guarantees require the development of systems for generating meaningful customer feedback and acting on it.

4. Guarantees force service organizations to understand why they fail and encourage them to identify and overcome potential fail points.

5. Guarantees build "marketing muscle" by reducing the risk of the purchase decision and building long-term loyalty.[24]

Many firms have enthusiastically leapt on the service guarantees bandwagon without carefully thinking through what is implied in making and keeping the promises of an unconditional service guarantee. Compare the four examples of service guarantees in the box on page 130 and ask yourself how much is covered by each guarantee, how much each contributes to reducing risk for the customer, and how much pressure each puts on its respective organization to maintain service standards.

Building Strategy Around a Hotel Service Guarantee

Hampton Inn's 100 percent Satisfaction Guarantee (see Figure 6.5) has proved to be a very successful business-building program.[25] The strategy of offering to refund the cost of the room for the day on which a guest expresses dissatisfaction has attracted new customers and also served as a powerful guest-retention device. People choose to stay at a Hampton Inn because they are confident they will be satisfied. At least as important, the guarantee has become a vital tool to help managers to identify new opportunities for quality improvement and to make those improvements happen. In this regard, the 100% Satisfaction Guarantee "turned up the pressure in the hose," as one manager put it, showing where "leaks" existed, and providing the incentive to plug

FIGURE 6.5

The Hampton Inn 100% Satisfaction Guarantee

them. As a result, the guarantee has had an important impact on product consistency and service delivery across the Hampton Inn chain, dramatically improving on financial performance.

However, fully implementing a 100 percent Satisfaction Guarantee is no easy task, as some competitors who have tried to imitate it can attest. Successful implementation of a 100 percent Satisfaction Guarantee requires that its underlying philosophy of guest satisfaction be embraced by every employee, from senior management to hourly workers. This has proved challenging even for Hampton Inn, where the guarantee has faced both resistance and skepticism from hotel managers in spite of its proven benefits. The box "How Unconditional Is Your Guarantee?" illustrates just how challenging it is for other hotels to imitate the concept of a truly unconditional guarantee.

Designing the Guarantee The first step in designing the guarantee at Hampton Inn was to answer a key question: "What would guests want in a guarantee?" Research revealed that they were most interested in the quality and cleanliness of their accommodations, friendly and efficient service, and a moderate price. They also wanted

How Unconditional Is Your Guarantee?

Christopher Hart tells this story of an incident at a hotel in a well-known chain. He and his two cousins, Jeff and Roxy Hart, were nearing the end of an extended holiday weekend and needed to find an inexpensive place to stay. It was late in the day and their flight left early the following morning. Jeff called Hampton Inn and found nothing available in the area. So he called (name deleted) Inn, which had rooms available and booked one for $62.

We found the hotel [said Chris], noticing a huge banner draped from the bottom of the sign, advertising, "Rooms for $55.95, including breakfast." We went inside. After giving the front-desk clerk the basic information, Jeff was told that his room would be $69. "But the reservation agent I just booked the room with quoted me $62. What's the story? And, by the way, what about the $55.95 price advertised on your sign? Can I get a room for that price?"

"Oh," replied the front-desk clerk. "That was a special promotion for the spring. It's over now." (It was late June.)

Jeff replied, "But you're still advertising the price. It's illegal to advertise one price and charge another one."

"Let me get my manager," came the nervous response. Out came the manager. In the middle of the conversation, in which Jeff was arguing the same points that he made with the front-desk clerk, Chris interjected, "By the way, I understand you offer a satisfaction guarantee. Right?"

"Not on the $55.95 rooms," came the reply from the manager.

"Well, what rooms is it on?"

"Only the good rooms."

"You mean you have bad rooms?"

"Well, we have some rooms that have not been renovated. Those are the ones we sell for $55.95. But we're sold out of them tonight."

Chris said, "Well, Jeff, you'd better get one of the more expensive rooms, because I'm not sure how satisfied you're going to be tomorrow."

The manager quickly added, "Did I mention that the guarantee doesn't apply on weekends?"

"No," barked Jeff, who had worked for 15 years conducting cost-benefit and compliance studies for the U.S. government, "and that's illegal too!"

"Wait just a minute," said the manager, getting a puzzled look as though something had just popped into his head. "Let me see something." He then buried his head into the computer, clicking away madly at the keyboard, creating the impression that he was working on our behalf. After an appropriate time, up popped his head, now with a big smile.

"One of the guests who originally reserved a $55.95 room, called and upgraded—but the upgrade wasn't recorded in the computer. I could let you have that room—but I can't guarantee your satisfaction."

"We'll take it," said an exhausted Roxy.

a guarantee that was simple and easy to invoke if necessary. In-depth guest interviews yielded 53 "moments of truth" critical to guests' satisfaction with their Hampton Inn stays. These moments of truth translated into concrete and controllable aspects of Hampton Inn's product and service delivery. Throughout the guarantee design process, an important new mindset was reinforced: Listen to the guests, who knew best what satisfied them.

According to the vice president of marketing for Hampton Inn, "Designing the guarantee made us understand what made guests satisfied, rather than what *we thought* made them satisfied." It became imperative that everyone, from front-line employees to general managers and personnel at corporate headquarters, should listen carefully to guests, anticipate their needs to the greatest extent possible, and remedy problems quickly so that guests were satisfied with the solution. Viewing a hotel's function in this customer-centric way had a profound impact on the way the parent company conducted business.

Even among those who fully supported the guarantee concept in principle, pressing concerns remained:

➤ "Will guests try to cheat and rip us off?"

➤ "Will our employees give the store away?"

➤ "What will be the return on our efforts to increase customer satisfaction?"

The Pilot Test   To prepare for the launch of the guarantee, a pilot test was conducted in 30 hotels that already had high customer satisfaction. Training was seen as critical. First, general managers were trained in the fundamentals of the guarantee—what it was and how it worked. Then the general managers trained their employees. Managers were taught to take a leadership role by actively demonstrating their support for the guarantee and helping their employees gain the confidence to handle guest concerns and problems. Finally, the guarantee was explained and promoted to guests.

After learning basic guarantee concepts and reviewing the Hampton Inn 100 percent Satisfaction Guarantee, general managers were asked to form groups of 10 to 12. Their charge was to list the positive and negative aspects of the guarantee on a flipchart. Few groups could come up with more than one or two pages of positives, but they had little difficulty creating lists of negatives; one such list was 26 pages long! Senior corporate managers went through each negative issue, addressing managers' concerns one by one. The concerns remained relatively consistent and centered on management control. There were also worries about guests abusing the guarantee and cheating (those nasty "jaycustomers" that were described in Chapter 5). For a discussion of how the company identifies such guests, see the box "Tracking Down Guests Who Cheat."

The pilot test produced some interesting results. Even at hotels that already had a high-satisfaction culture, corporate management found that front-line employees weren't always fully *empowered* to do whatever was needed to make a guest 100 percent satisfied. Further, employees did not always feel they had explicit responsibility for guest satisfaction. So they had to be taught that their job responsibilities now extended beyond the functional roles for which they were initially hired (i.e., property maintenance, breakfast staff, front desk).

Managers and employees discovered that the guarantee was not about giving money away—it was about making guests satisfied. They learned that satisfying guests by correcting problems had to be a priority. Employees were encouraged to creatively fix problems "on the spot," and rely on the guarantee as a "safety net" to catch guests who were still dissatisfied.

Ongoing Experience   Now that the 100 percent Satisfaction Guarantee has become standard practice at Hampton Inn, the company provides reports every quarter that show the top five reasons for guarantee payouts. Managers are encouraged to develop clear action plans for eliminating the sources of guarantee payouts at their hotels. Once the sources of problems are systematically eliminated, payouts become less frequent. Guest satisfaction has increased substantially at those hotels where the guarantee has been most strongly embraced. Hampton Inn has also implemented an employee-awards program for employees who have undertaken exceptional acts of customer service. When this "cycle of success" occurs at a specific hotel, its employees become "guarantee advocates" who spread word of their success throughout the chain.

Over time, hotel managers have recognized two things. First, the number of people invoking the guarantee represents only a small percentage of all guests. Second, the percentage of cheaters in this group amounts to a ridiculously small number. As one manager admitted, "It occurred to me that I was managing my entire operation to accommodate the half of one percent of guests who actually invoke the guarantee. And out of that number, maybe only 5 percent were cheating. Viewed this way, I was focused on managing my business to only 0.025 percent of total revenues."

Experience has shown that guests are not typically looking for a refund—they just want to be satisfied with what they pay for. And because the 100 percent Satisfaction Guarantee promises just that, it's a powerful vehicle for attracting and retaining guests. The guarantee was subsequently extended to several of Hampton Inn's sister brands, Hampton Inn and Suites, Embassy Suites, and Homewood Suites. A subsequent survey found that:

➤ Fifty-four percent of guests interviewed said they were more likely to consider Hampton Inn (or one of its sister brand hotels) because of the guarantee.

➤ Seventy-seven percent of guests interviewed said they would stay again at the same hotel.

➤ Ninety-three percent of guests interviewed said they would stay at another hotel in the same chain.

➤ Fifty-nine percent of guests interviewed have already returned.

Tracking Down Guests Who Cheat

As part of its guarantee tracking system, Hampton Inn has developed ways to identify guests who appeared to be cheating—using aliases or different satisfaction problems to invoke the guarantee repeatedly in order to get the cost of their room refunded. Guests who request frequent compensation receive personalized attention and follow-up from the company's Guest Assistance Team. Wherever possible, senior managers will telephone these guests to ask them about their recent stays. The conversation might go as follows: "Hello, Mr. Jones. I'm the director of guest assistance and I see that you've had some difficulty with the last four Hampton Inn properties you've visited. Since we take our guarantee very seriously, I thought I'd give you a call and find out what the problems were." The typical response is dead silence! Sometimes the silence is followed with questions of how headquarters could possibly know about their problems. These calls have their humorous moments as well. One individual, who had invoked the guarantee 17 times in what appeared to be a trip that took him across the United States and back, was asked, innocuously, "Where do you like to stay when you travel?" "Hampton Inn," came the enthusiastic response. "But," said the executive making the call, "our records show that the last 17 times you have stayed at a Hampton Inn, you have invoked the 100 percent Satisfaction Guarantee." "That's why I like them!" proclaimed the guest (who turned out to be a long-distance truck driver).

Among the reasons for the success of the Hampton Inn service guarantee are careful planning, listening to employee and manager concerns, an emphasis on training, and a willingness to delegate more authority to employees. The company has evaluated the possibility that customers would abuse its service guarantee—namely, making fraudulent claims to obtain a free night in a hotel—and has determined that the incidence of such fraud is confined to a tiny fraction of its customers. So customers are trusted when they register a complaint and a refund is cheerfully given on the spot. However, the firm's management is not naïve: There is careful tracking *after the fact* of all claims against the guarantee and any suspicious-looking pattern of repeated claims is followed up.

Developing Viable Guarantees

Guarantees need to be clear, so that customers and employees can understand them easily. Sometimes, this means relating the terms of the guarantee to satisfaction with a specific activity rather than overall performance. For instance, the Irish Electricity Supply Board (ESB) offers 12 clearly stated service guarantees in its "Customer Charter," relating to such elements as network repair, the main fuse, meter connection and accuracy, and scheduled appointments (when an employee visits the customer's premises). In each instance, the ESB has established a service standard, such as a promised speed of response, stating the payment that will be made to the customer if the company fails to meet the promised standard. The charter is written in simple language and tells customers what to do if they encounter a problem with any of the problems covered by the 12 guarantees. Compensation payments range from IR£20–100 ($23–115) depending on the nature of the problem and whether the customer is a household or a business.

Is it always a good idea for a service firm to offer a guarantee? The answer, according to Ostrom and Hart, is that managers should first think carefully about their firms' strengths and weaknesses in the context of the markets in which they compete.[26] Companies that already have a strong reputation for high-quality service may not need a guarantee; in fact, it might even be incongruent with their image to offer one. Firms whose service is currently poor must first work to improve quality to a level above that at which the guarantee might be invoked on a regular basis by most of their customers! Service organizations that suffer from high turnover, poor employee attitudes, and inability to recruit strong managers are also in no position to start offering guarantees. Similarly, firms whose service quality is truly uncontrollable (due to outside forces) would be foolish to consider guaranteeing any aspect of their service that was not amenable to improvement through internal strategies.

Service managers should ask themselves: Do the benefits outweigh the costs? Potential costs include compensating customers for failures covered by the guarantee and the cost of investments to improve operational effectiveness and staff performance. In evaluating benefits, managers need to look at the value of the extra business gained, the long-term potential for greater operational productivity, increased staff pride and motivation, and the firm's ability to recruit and retain the best employees.

In a market where customers see little financial, personal, or psychological risk associated with purchasing and using the service, it's questionable whether much value would be added by instituting a guarantee. However, where perceived risks do exist but there is little identifiable difference in service quality among competing offerings, the first company to institute a guarantee may be able to obtain a first-mover advantage and differentiate its services. But what should managers do if one or more competitors already have a guarantee in place? Doing nothing is a risk in that it may be seen as a de facto admission of inconsistent quality. There is also the possibility that the availability of a guarantee may eventually become a requirement in customers' purchase decision criteria. So the best response may be to attract customers' attention by launching a highly distinctive guarantee like Hampton Inn's that goes beyond what the competition offers and will also be difficult for them to match or exceed in the short run.

Conclusion

Collecting customer feedback via complaints, suggestions, and compliments provides a means of increasing customer satisfaction. It's a terrific opportunity to get into the hearts and minds of customers. In all but the worst instances, complaining customers are indicating that they want to continue their relationship with the service firm. But they are also signaling that all is not well, and that they expect the company to make things right.

Service firms need to develop effective strategies for recovering from service failures so that they can maintain customer goodwill. This is vital for the long-term success of the company. However, service personnel must also learn from their mistakes and try to ensure that problems are eliminated. After all, even the best recovery strategy isn't as good in the customer's eyes as being treated right the first time. Well-designed unconditional service guarantees have proved to be a powerful vehicle for identifying and justifying needed improvements, as well for creating a culture in which staff members take proactive steps to ensure that guests will be satisfied.

Study Questions and Exercises

1. Explain the courses of action available to a dissatisfied consumer.

2. Describe the factors that may prevent a dissatisfied consumer from complaining. How can service providers encourage dissatisfied customers to complain?

3. When was the last time you were truly satisfied with an organization's response to your complaint? Describe in detail what happened and what made you satisfied.

4. Think about the last time you experienced a less than satisfactory service experience. Did you complain? Why? If you did not complain, explain why not.

5. Apply the service recovery concepts presented in this chapter to a service organization with which you are familiar. Describe how this organization follows/does not follow these guidelines. What impact do you think this has on the firm's customers in terms of loyalty?

6. Evaluate the 100 percent Service Guarantee introduced by Hampton Inn. What are its main advantages and disadvantages?

Endnotes

1. Based on information in Christopher W. Hart with Elizabeth Long, *Extraordinary Guarantees* (New York: AMACOM, 1997).
2. Oren Harari, "Thank Heavens for Complainers," *Management Review* (March 1997): 25–29.
3. Technical Assistance Research Programs Institute (TARP), *Consumer Complaint Handling in America; An Update Study, Part II* (Washington DC: TARP and US Office of Consumer Affairs, April 1986).
4. Susan M. Keveaney, "Customer Switching Behavior in Service Industries: An Exploratory Study," *Journal of Marketing* 59 (April 1995): 71–82.

5. Bernd Stauss, "Global Word of Mouth," *Marketing Management* (Fall 1997): 28–30.

6. Sam McManis, "Whine Online: Web Sites Are Cropping Up to Do the Griping for You," *San Francisco Chronicle*, 14 September 1999.

7. TARP, *Consumer Complaint Handling in America*.

8. Matthew L. Meuter, Amy L. Ostrom, Robert I. Roundtree, and Mary Jo Bitner, "Understanding Customer Satisfaction with Technology-Based Service Encounters," *Journal of Marketing* 64 (Summer 2000): 50–64.

9. Diane Brady, "Why Service Stinks," *Business Week*, 23 October 2000, 118–128.

10. Eugene W. Anderson and Claes Fornell, "The Customer Satisfaction Index as a Leading Indicator," in Teresa A. Schwartz and Dawn Iacobucci, *Handbook of Service Marketing and Management* (Thousand Oaks, CA: Sage Publications, 2000), 255–270. See also Claes Fornell, Michael D. Johnson, Eugene W. Anderson, Jaesung Cha, and Barbara Everitt Bryant, "The American Customer Satisfaction Index: Nature, Purpose, and Findings," *Journal of Marketing* 60 (October 1996): 7–18.

11. Society of Consumer Affairs Professionals (SOCAP), *Study of Consumer Complaint Behaviour in Australia*, 1995.

12. Cathy Goodwin and B.J. Verhage, "Role perceptions of Services: A Cross-Cultural Comparison with Behavioral Implications," *Journal of Economic Psychology* 10 (1990): 543–558.

13. Stephen S. Tax and Stephen W. Brown, "Recovering and Learning from Service Failure," *Sloan Management Review* (Fall 1998): 75–88.

14. Christopher W.L. Hart, James L. Heskett, and W. Earl Sasser Jr., "The Profitable Art of Service Recovery," *Harvard Business Review* 68 (July-August, 1990): 148–156.

15. Rahul Jacob, "Why Some Customers Are More Equal than Others," *Fortune*, 9 September 1994, 224.

16. TARP, *Consumer Complaint Handling in America*.

17. Stephen S. Tax, Stephen W. Brown, and Murali Chandrashekaran, "Customer Evaluations of Service Complaint Exercises: Implications for Relationship Marketing," *Journal of Marketing* 62 (April 1998): 60–76.

18. Leonard L. Berry, *On Great Service: A Framework for Action* (New York: The Free Press, 1995).

19. Ko de Ruyter and Martin Wetzels, "Customer Equity Considerations in Service Recovery: A Cross Industry Perspective," *International Journal of Service Industry Management* 11, no. 1 (2000): 91–108.

20. Christo Boshoff, "An Experimental Study of Service Recovery Options," *International Journal of Service Industry Management* 8, no. 2 (1997): 1110–130.

21. John Goodman, quoted in "Improving Service Doesn't Always Require Big Investment," *The Service Edge* (July-August, 1990): 3.

22. David E. Bowen and Robert Johnston, "Internal Service Recovery: Developing a New Construct," *International Journal of Service Industry Management* 10, no. 2 (1999): 118–131.

23. Rebecca Blumenstein and Stephanie N. Mehta, "Lost in the Shuffle: As the Telecoms Merge and Cut Costs, Service Is Often a Casualty," *Wall Street Journal*, 19 January 2000, A1, A6.

24. Christopher W. L. Hart, "The Power of Unconditional Service Guarantees," *Harvard Business Review* 68 (July-August 1990): 54–62.

25. Information on the 100 percent Satisfaction Guarantee at Hampton Inn is drawn from Christopher W. Hart with Elizabeth Long, *Extraordinary Guarantees* (New York: AMACOM, 1997).

26. Amy L. Ostrom and Christopher Hart, "Service Guarantees: Research and Practice," in Teresa A. Schwartz and Dawn Iacobucci, *Handbook of Service Marketing and Management*, (Thousand Oaks, CA: Sage Publications, 2000), 299–316.

part**three**

Service Marketing Strategy

In Part III of the book, we focus on some key marketing components of the 8Ps—*product elements*, *price and other user outlays,* and *promotion and education.* Figure III.1 shows how these three elements relate to the service management decision framework.

We've already addressed service product issues in several previous chapters, where we (1) defined service as an act or performance that provides benefits for customers, (2) showed how the core product is surrounded by a group of supplementary service elements, and (3) specified how the nature of the underlying service process shapes the performance and thus the customer's experience. Chapter 7 raises the question: ***What should be the core and supplementary elements of our service product?*** Developing service product strategy requires managers to identify the characteristics of the core product, consider how it should be augmented and enhanced by supplementary services, and determine how best to design the overall service experience. These decisions are shaped by the nature of the market for the service, requiring consideration of what product benefits will create the most value for target customers.

The question ***What price should we charge for our service?*** is addressed in Chapter 8. Identifying the costs to be recovered tends to be a more challenging task for services than for manufactured goods. Service prices may vary by time of day, day of week, or season. And the price actually paid by customers may be a combination of several different pricing elements like a fixed monthly rate, a usage charge that offers volume discounts, and various supplementary charges. Service managers need to recognize that price is not the only cost incurred by customers. There may be out-of-pocket expenditures associated with purchasing and using the service. Customers may also incur significant nonfinancial outlays and burdens ranging from time costs to physical and mental effort.

Designing a good product and pricing it appropriately will not ensure its success if people are unaware of it. So service firms must address the question: ***How should we communicate what our service has to offer?*** Credibility is an important issue in marketing communication and may depend, in part, on the reputation of the organization, its capabilities, and its brand names. Managers must ask themselves what customers need to know about the service and its benefits. Communication must go beyond mere promotion. Many customers, especially new ones, will need to be educated about the service. Service businesses have to determine what communication methods and media will be most effective in reaching their target audiences. They also need to examine the role that physical evidence can play in creating desired impressions. These issues are discussed in Chapter 9.

Finally, service managers must decide how to differentiate their firm's offerings from those of the competition—which is the essence of positioning strategy. Chapter 10 examines issues

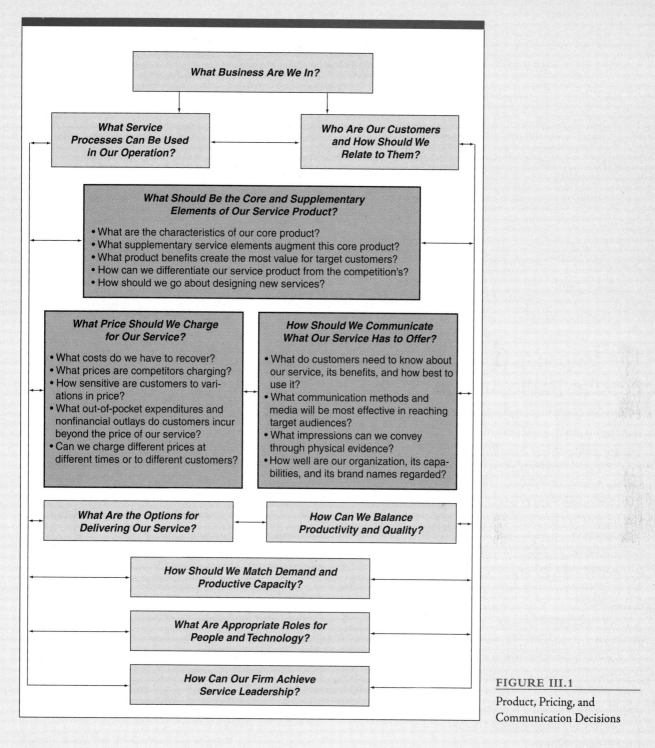

What Business Are We In?

What Service Processes Can Be Used in Our Operation?

Who Are Our Customers and How Should We Relate to Them?

What Should Be the Core and Supplementary Elements of Our Service Product?

- What are the characteristics of our core product?
- What supplementary service elements augment this core product?
- What product benefits create the most value for target customers?
- How can we differentiate our service product from the competition's?
- How should we go about designing new services?

What Price Should We Charge for Our Service?

- What costs do we have to recover?
- What prices are competitors charging?
- How sensitive are customers to variations in price?
- What out-of-pocket expenditures and nonfinancial outlays do customers incur beyond the price of our service?
- Can we charge different prices at different times or to different customers?

How Should We Communicate What Our Service Has to Offer?

- What do customers need to know about our service, its benefits, and how best to use it?
- What communication methods and media will be most effective in reaching target audiences?
- What impressions can we convey through physical evidence?
- How well are our organization, its capabilities, and its brand names regarded?

What Are the Options for Delivering Our Service?

How Can We Balance Productivity and Quality?

How Should We Match Demand and Productive Capacity?

What Are Appropriate Roles for People and Technology?

How Can Our Firm Achieve Service Leadership?

FIGURE III.1

Product, Pricing, and Communication Decisions

related to linking product, pricing, and communication in a strategic context. This chapter also emphasizes the need to (1) integrate different elements of the 8Ps so that they are mutually reinforcing, (2) ensure that key product attributes relate to the needs of specific target segments, and (3) create a service package that is differentiated from competitors' offerings in meaningful ways.

chapter seven

The Service Product

The Moose Is Loose at Germany's Most Popular Radio Station

SWF3 is Germany's most popular radio station, reaching more than two million listeners in southwestern Germany every day. Some say that it's more than radio—it's a lifestyle.[1] Perhaps SWF3's noteworthy feature is the never-ending production of its comic radio skits. For over 20 years the station has created characters and slogans that have become part of everyday conversation in Germany. These skits, plus investigative journalism and trend-setting music, reflect the station's philosophy and are essential keys to its success. SWF3's trademark, the moose, was chosen because the station is headquartered in Baden-Baden in the famous Black Forest. The animal has become a part of the station's lifestyle, to the extent that quality is referred to as "moose-proof."

Following deregulation of the German radio broadcasting market, hundreds of new local and national radio stations swamped the market. To compete more effectively and to build greater loyalty among its listeners, SWF3 established a club, now some 100,000 strong, that offers members a variety of financial and nonfinancial benefits with a high emotional and economic value. Holders of the SWF3 Club's gold Wildcard (which costs the equivalent of about $15) can obtain savings on a variety of purchases.

The Club's popular quarterly publication, *ON*, offers a mix of journalism, music, and humor written by the station's staff, including DJs, editors, and anchors. The members' newsletter, published every six weeks and called *ONFO*, contains details of Club events throughout the year, news from the station, and current ticket and merchandise offers. The Club is also featured on SWF3's Web site, www.swf3.de.

Of course, anyone can access the Web site, and fans living far outside SWF3's broadcast reception area—even on another continent—can still listen to the station live on Web radio. The user-friendly site features information on the station, its staff, and programming, as well as offering services ranging from weather forecasts to *Kinodatenbank* (a useful database of movie reviews). There is also a chat room and a library of pictures of real moose, cartoon moose, and stuffed toy moose in many amusing situations.

To serve listeners who want information about the station, club services, and related activities, the station has instituted the SWF3 Service Center (even using the English-language term as its name), which also handles ticket sales and merchandise orders. The SWF3 Club produces and coproduces about 120 events each year. Large open-air concerts and festivals can draw over 100,000 visitors, whereas the numerous smaller shows with newcomer bands attract just a few hundred. At all major events, a Club Lounge—open to members and event guests only—provides special catering. After the show, rock and pop stars show up for scheduled "unplugged" sessions and interviews. Club members can save up to $6 off the ticket prices to all major pop and rock concerts in Germany, including concerts of major artists such as the Rolling Stones, Simple Minds, R.E.M., and U2. In addition to tickets for the Club's own productions, members also get offers for preferential tickets to hundreds of events each year.

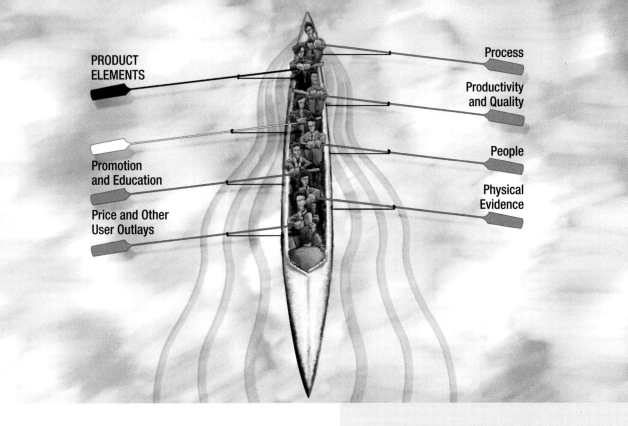

PRODUCT
ELEMENTS

Promotion
and Education

Price and Other
User Outlays

Process

Productivity
and Quality

People

Physical
Evidence

SWF3 believes that its club program and event sponsorship have helped the station to build high awareness, develop a strong relationship with its listeners, and increase its ratings. In short, the Club has proven to be absolutely "moose-proof."

Learning Objectives

After reading this chapter, you should be able to

⟹ discuss several frameworks for describing the augmented service product

⟹ define the eight petals of the Flower of Service

⟹ distinguish between facilitating and enhancing supplementary services

⟹ complete a service blueprint for different kinds of services

⟹ describe the types of information that service blueprints can provide

THE SERVICE OFFERING

In this chapter, we address the question, ***What should be the core and supplementary elements of our service product?*** The core addresses the customer's need for a basic benefit—such as transportation to a desired location, resolution of a specific health problem, or repair of malfunctioning equipment. Supplementary services facilitate and enhance use of the core service; they range from information, advice, and documentation to problem solving and acts of hospitality.

As an industry matures and competition increases, there's a risk that prospective customers may view competing core products as commodities that are indistinguishable from each other. For instance, many airlines fly the same types of aircraft, all credit cards perform the same basic function, and it's hard to distinguish one hotel bed from another within a given class of service. In these cases, the customer's natural tendency is to choose the option with the cheapest price. Hence, the search for competitive advantage in a mature industry often focuses on differentiating the product through better supplementary services. SWF3, the German radio station in the opening story, uses a mix of financial and nonfinancial benefits to offer a value-oriented package that attracts listeners in the highly competitive radio broadcasting market and keeps them loyal.

augmented product: the core product (a good or a service) plus all supplementary elements that add value for customers.

molecular model: a framework that uses a chemical analogy to describe the structure of service offerings.

The Augmented Product

Marketers use the term **augmented product** to describe the combination of a core product with a bundle of value-adding supplementary elements. Theorists have developed several frameworks to describe augmented products. Lynn Shostack created a **molecular model** (Figure 7.1) that can be applied to either goods or services. The

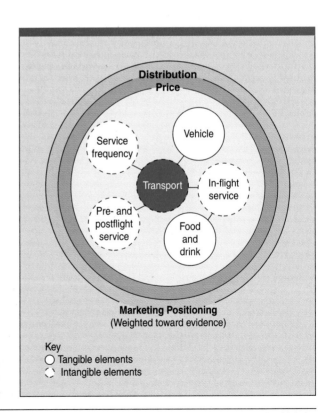

FIGURE 7.1

Shostack's Molecular Model: Passenger Airline Service

Source: G. Lynn Shostack, "Breaking Free from Product Marketing," *Journal of Marketing* (April 1977), published by the American Marketing Association. Reprinted with permission.

model uses a chemical analogy to help marketers visualize and manage what she termed a "total market entity."[2] At the center is the core benefit that addresses the basic customer need, with links to a series of other service characteristics. Surrounding the molecules is a series of bands representing price, distribution, and market positioning (communication messages). As in chemical formulations, a change in one element may completely alter the nature of the entity.

The molecular model helps identify the tangible and intangible elements involved in service delivery. By highlighting tangible elements, marketers can determine whether their services are tangible-dominant or intangible-dominant. In an airline, for example, the intangible elements include transportation itself, service frequency, and pre-flight, in-flight, and post-flight service. But the aircraft itself and the food and drinks that are served to passengers are all tangible. The more intangible elements exist, the more necessary it is to provide tangible clues about the features and quality of the service.

Eiglier and Langeard developed a different model to describe the augmented product. In their model, the core service is surrounded by a circle containing a series of supplementary services that are specific to that particular product.[3] Their approach, like Shostack's, emphasizes the interdependence of the various components. They distinguish between those elements needed to facilitate use of the core service (such as the reception desk at a hotel) and those that enhance the appeal of the core service (such as a fitness center and business services at a hotel). Eiglier and Langeard focus on two issues: (1) whether supplementary services are needed to facilitate use of the core service or simply to add extra appeal; and (2) whether customers should be charged separately for each service element or whether all elements should be bundled under a single price tag.

IDENTIFYING AND CLASSIFYING SUPPLEMENTARY SERVICES

The more we examine different types of core services, the more we find that most of them have many supplementary services in common. Although core products may differ widely, certain supplementary elements—like information, billing, and reservations or order taking—keep recurring.[4] There are dozens of different supplementary services,

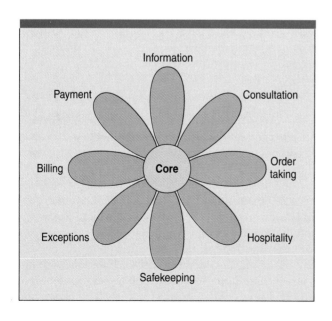

FIGURE 7.2

The Flower of Service: Core Product Surrounded by Clusters of Supplementary Services

TABLE 7.1

Examples of Information Elements

Directions to service site
Schedules/service hours
Prices
Instructions on using core product/supplementary services
Reminders
Warnings
Conditions of sale/service
Notification of changes
Documentation
Confirmation of reservations
Summaries of account activity
Receipts and tickets

facilitating supplementary services: supplementary services that aid in the use of the core product or are required for service delivery.

enhancing supplementary services: supplementary services that may add extra value for customers.

Flower of Service: a visual framework for understanding the supplementary service elements that surround and add value to the product core.

but almost all of them can be classified into one of the following eight clusters. We have listed them as either **facilitating supplementary services**, which aid in the use of the core product or are required for service delivery, or **enhancing supplementary services,** which add extra value for customers.

Facilitating Services	**Enhancing Services**
➤ Information	➤ Consultation
➤ Order Taking	➤ Hospitality
➤ Billing	➤ Safekeeping
➤ Payment	➤ Exceptions

In Figure 7.2, these eight clusters are displayed as petals surrounding the center of a flower—which we call the **Flower of Service**. We've shown them clockwise in the sequence in which they are often likely to be encountered by customers (although this sequence may vary—for instance, payment may have to be made before service is delivered rather than afterwards). In a well-run service organization, the petals and core are fresh and attractive. But a badly designed or poorly executed service is like a flower with missing, wilted, or discolored petals. Even if the core is perfect, the overall flower is unattractive. Think about your own experiences as a customer. When you were dissatisfied with a particular purchase, was it the core that was at fault or was there a problem with one or more of the supplementary service petals? Not every core product is surrounded by supplementary elements from all eight clusters. As we'll see, the nature of the product helps to determine which supplementary services must be offered and which might be added to enhance the value of the core service.

Information

To obtain full value from any service experience, customers need relevant information (Table 7.1). New customers and prospects are especially information hungry. Customer needs may include directions to the physical location where the product is sold (or details of how to order it by telephone or Web site), service hours, prices, and usage instructions. Further information, sometimes required by law, could include conditions of sale and use, warnings, reminders, and notification of changes. Finally, customers may want documentation of what has already taken place, such as confirmation of reservations, receipts and tickets, and monthly summaries of account activity.

Companies should make sure the information they provide is both timely and accurate; if it's not, customers may be annoyed or inconvenienced. Traditional ways of providing information to customers include using front-line employees (who are not always as well informed as customers might like), printed notices, brochures, and

TABLE 7.2

Examples of Order-Taking Elements

Applications
- Membership in clubs or programs
- Subscription services (e.g., utilities)
- Prerequisite-based services (e.g., financial credit, college enrollment)

Order Entry
- On-site order fulfillment
- Mail/telephone order placement
- E-mail/Web site order placement

Reservations and Check-in
- Seats
- Tables
- Rooms
- Vehicles or equipment rental
- Professional appointments
- Admission to restricted facilities (e.g., museums, aquariums)

instruction books. Other media include videotapes or software-driven tutorials, touch-screen video displays, and menu-driven recorded telephone messages. The most significant recent innovation has been corporate use of Web sites. Companies use the Internet for a wide range of useful applications including the provision of information about train and airline schedules, hotel availability and reservations, the location of specific retail outlets such as restaurants and stores, and service descriptions and prices. Many business logistics companies offer shippers the opportunity to track the movements of their packages—each of which has been assigned a unique identification number.

Order Taking

Once customers are ready to buy, companies must have effective supplementary service processes in place to handle applications, orders, and reservations (Table 7.2). The process of order taking should be polite, fast, and accurate so that customers do not waste time and endure unnecessary mental or physical effort.

Banks, insurance companies, and utilities require prospective customers to go through an application process designed to gather relevant information and to screen out those who do not meet basic enrollment criteria (like a bad credit record or serious health problems). Universities also require prospective students to apply for admission. Reservations (including appointments and check-in) represent a special type of order taking that entitles customers to a defined unit of service at a specific time and location—for example, an airline seat, a restaurant table, a hotel room, time with a qualified professional, or admission to a facility such as a theater or sports arena.

Ticketless systems, based upon telephone or online reservations, provide enormous cost savings for airlines. There is no travel agent commission since customers book directly, and the administrative effort is drastically reduced. A paper ticket at an airline may be handled 15 times while an electronic ticket requires just one step. But some customers are not comfortable with the paperless process.

Billing

Billing is common to almost all services (unless the service is provided free of charge). Inaccurate, illegible, or incomplete bills risk disappointing customers who may, up to that point, have been quite satisfied with their experience. Such failures add insult to injury if the customer is already dissatisfied. Billing procedures range from verbal statements to a machine-displayed price, and from handwritten invoices to elaborate monthly statements of account activity and fees (Table 7.3). Due to recent technological advances, many

TABLE 7.3

Examples of Billing Elements

- Periodic statements of account activity
- Invoices for individual transactions
- Verbal statements of amount due
- Machine display of amount due
- Self-billing (computed by customer)

forms of billing are computerized to capitalize on the potential for productivity improvements. But computerized billing can sometimes cause service failures, as when an innocent customer tries futilely to contest an inaccurate bill and is met by an escalating sequence of ever-larger bills (compounded interest and penalty charges) accompanied by increasingly threatening, computer-generated letters.

Customers usually expect bills to be clear and informative, and itemized in ways that make it clear how the total was computed. Unexplained or confusing charges do not create a favorable impression of the supplier. Nor does fuzzy printing or illegible handwriting. Laser printers, with their ability to switch fonts and typefaces, to box and to highlight, can produce statements that are not only more legible but also organize information in more useful ways.

Marketing research can help companies design user-friendly bills by identifying what information customers want and how they would like it to be organized. Sometimes billing information can even be used to provide extra value to customers. For example, American Express built its Corporate Card business by offering companies detailed documentation of the spending patterns of individual employees and departments on travel and entertainment. Its Corporate Purchasing Card is particularly useful

FIGURE 7.3

American Express Promotes the Benefits of Its Corporate Purchasing Card for firms making purchases through the Internet, allowing senior management to establish spending limits, designate preferred vendors, and track expenses (Figure 7.3). Intelligent thinking about customer needs led AmEx to realize that well-organized billing information and control of spending were valuable to its business customers, beyond just the basic requirement of knowing how much to pay.

Busy customers hate to be kept waiting for a bill. Some service providers offer express checkout options, taking customers' credit card details in advance and documenting charges later by mail. Many hotels push bills under guests' doors on the morning of departure showing charges to date; others offer customers the option of previewing their bills before checkout on the TV monitors in their rooms. Some car rental companies use an alternative express checkout procedure. An agent meets customers as they return their cars, checks the odometer and fuel gauge readings, and then prints a bill on the spot using a portable wireless terminal. Accuracy is essential with all of these billing methods. Since customers use the express checkouts to save time, they certainly don't want to waste time later seeking corrections and refunds.

Payment

In most cases, a bill requires the customer to take action on payment. Bank statements are an exception, since they detail charges that have already been deducted from the customer's account. Increasingly, customers expect ease and convenience of payment, including credit, wherever they make their purchases.

A variety of options exists to facilitate customer bill paying (Table 7.4). Self-service payment systems, for instance, require customers to insert coins, banknotes, tokens, or cards in machines. But equipment breakdowns destroy the whole purpose of such a system, so good maintenance and speedy trouble-shooting are essential. Much payment still takes place through hand-to-hand transfers of cash and checks, but credit and debit cards are growing in importance as more and more establishments accept them. Other alternatives include tokens, vouchers, coupons, or prepaid tickets. Firms benefit from prompt payment, since it reduces the amount of accounts receivable.

To ensure that people actually pay what they owe, some services employ control systems, such as ticket collection before entering a movie theater or boarding a train. However, inspectors and security officers must be trained to combine politeness with firmness in performing their jobs, so that honest customers do not feel harassed.

Self-service
• Exact change in machine
• Cash in machine with change returned
• Insert prepayment card
• Insert credit/charge/debit card
• Insert token
• Electronic funds transfer
• Mail a check
• Enter credit card number online
Direct to payee or intermediary
• Cash handling and change giving
• Check handling
• Credit/charge/debit card handling
• Coupon redemption
• Tokens, vouchers, etc.
Automatic deduction from financial deposits (e.g., bank charges)
Control and verification
• Automated systems (e.g., machine-readable tickets that operate entry gates)
• Human systems (e.g., toll collectors, ticket inspectors)

TABLE 7.4

Examples of Payment Elements

TABLE 7.5

Examples of Consultation Elements

- Advice
- Auditing
- Personal counseling
- Tutoring/training in product usage
- Management or technical consulting

Consultation

Consultation is an enhancing supplementary service that involves a dialog to identify customer requirements and develop a personalized solution. Table 7.5 provides examples of several supplementary services in the consultation category. At its simplest, consultation consists of immediate advice from a knowledgeable service person in response to the request: "What do you suggest?" (For example, you might ask the person who cuts your hair for advice on different hairstyles and products.) Effective consultation requires an understanding of each customer's current situation before suggesting a suitable course of action. Good customer records can be a great help in this respect, particularly if relevant data can be retrieved easily from a remote terminal.

Counseling represents a more subtle approach to consultation. It involves helping customers better understand their situations so that they can come up with their "own" solutions and action programs. This approach can be a particularly valuable supplement to services such as health treatment. Part of the challenge in this situation is to get customers to take a long-term view of their personal situation and to adopt more healthful behaviors, which often involve some initial sacrifice. Diet centers like Weight Watchers use counseling to help customers change their behaviors so that weight loss can be sustained after the initial diet is completed.

Finally, there are more formalized efforts to provide management and technical consulting for corporate customers, such as the "solution selling" associated with marketing expensive industrial equipment and services. The sales engineer researches the business customer's situation and then offers objective advice about what particular package of equipment and systems will yield the best results. Some consulting services are offered free of charge in the hope of making a sale. In other instances the service is "unbundled" and customers are expected to pay for it.

Hospitality

Hospitality-related services should ideally reflect pleasure at meeting new customers and greeting old ones when they return. Companies like Wal-Mart take this concept quite literally, designating a specific employee in each store to welcome customers as they enter. Well-managed businesses try to ensure that their employees treat customers as guests. Courtesy and consideration for customers' needs apply to both face-to-face encounters and telephone interactions (Table 7.6). Hospitality finds its full expression in face-to-face encounters. In some cases, it starts with an offer of transport to and from

TABLE 7.6

Examples of Hospitality Elements

Greeting
Food and beverages
Toilets and washrooms
Waiting facilities and amenities
- Lounges, waiting areas, seating
- Weather protection
- Magazines, entertainment, newspapers
Transport
Security

the service site, as with courtesy shuttle buses. If customers must wait outdoors before the service can be delivered, then a thoughtful service provider will offer weather protection. If the wait occurs indoors, then guests should have access to a waiting area with seating and entertainment (TV, newspapers, or magazines) to pass the time. Recruiting employees who are naturally warm, welcoming, and considerate for customer-contact jobs also helps to create a hospitable atmosphere.

The quality of a firm's hospitality services can increase or decrease satisfaction with the core product. This is especially true for people-processing services where customers cannot easily leave the service facility. Private hospitals often seek to enhance their hospitality by providing the level of room service—including meals—that might be expected in a good hotel.

Some air transportation companies (like Singapore Airlines) differentiate themselves from their competitors with better meals and more attentive cabin crew. While in-flight hospitality is important, an airline journey also includes passengers' pre- and post-flight experiences. Air travelers have come to expect departure lounges, but British Airways (BA) came up with the novel idea of an arrivals lounge for its terminals at London's Heathrow and Gatwick airports to serve passengers arriving early in the morning after a long, overnight flight from the Americas, Asia, Africa, and Australia. The airline allows holders of first- and business-class tickets or a BA Executive Club gold card (awarded to the airline's most frequent flyers) to use a special lounge where they can take a shower, change, have breakfast, and make phone calls or send faxes before continuing to their final destination. The arrivals lounge provided such a significant competitive advantage for British Airways that other airlines felt obliged to copy it.

Safekeeping

While visiting a service site, customers often want assistance with their personal possessions. In fact, unless certain safekeeping services are provided (like safe and convenient parking for their cars), some customers may not come at all. The list of potential on-site safekeeping services is long. It includes: provision of coatrooms; luggage transport, handling, and storage; safekeeping of valuables; and even child and pet care (Table 7.7).

Caring for possessions customers bring with them
• Childcare
• Pet care
• Parking facilities for vehicles
• Valet parking
• Coatrooms
• Luggage handling
• Storage space
• Safe deposit boxes
• Security personnel
Caring for goods purchased (or rented) by customers
• Packaging
• Pick-up
• Transportation
• Delivery
• Installation
• Inspection and diagnosis
• Cleaning
• Refueling
• Preventive maintenance
• Repairs and renovation
• Upgrade

TABLE 7.7

Examples of Safekeeping Elements

Additional safekeeping services are directed at physical products that customers buy or rent. They include packaging, pick-up and delivery, assembly, installation, cleaning, and inspection. Sometimes there's a charge for these services.

Exceptions

Exceptions involve supplementary services that fall outside the routine of normal service delivery (Table 7.8). Astute businesses anticipate exceptions and develop contingency plans and guidelines in advance. That way, employees will not appear helpless and surprised when customers ask for special assistance. Well-defined procedures make it easier for employees to respond promptly and effectively.

There are several different types of exceptions:

1. *Special requests.* There are many circumstances when a customer may request service that requires a departure from normal operating procedures. Advance requests often relate to personal needs, including childcare, dietary requirements, medical needs, religious observances, and personal disabilities. Such special requests are common in the travel and hospitality industries.

3. *Problem solving.* Situations arise when normal service delivery (or product performance) fails to run smoothly as a result of accidents, delays, equipment failures, or customers experiencing difficulty in using the product.

3. *Handling of complaints/suggestions/compliments.* This activity requires well-defined procedures. It should be easy for customers to express dissatisfaction, offer suggestions for improvement, or pass on compliments, and service providers should be able to make an appropriate response quickly.

4. *Restitution.* Many customers expect to be compensated for serious performance failures. Compensation may take the form of repairs under warranty, legal settlements, refunds, an offer of free service, or other forms of payment-in-kind.

A flexible approach to exceptions is generally a good idea because it reflects responsiveness to customer needs. On the other hand, too many exceptions may

---

TABLE 7.8

Examples of Exceptions Elements

Special requests in advance of service delivery
- Children's needs
- Dietary requirements
- Medical or disability needs
- Religious observances
- Deviations from standard operating procedures

Handling special communications
- Complaints
- Compliments
- Suggestions

Problem solving
- Warranties and guarantees against product malfunction
- Resolving difficulties that arise from using the product
- Resolving difficulties caused by accidents, service failures, and problems with staff or other customers
- Assisting customers who have suffered an accident or medical emergency

Restitution
- Refunds
- Compensation in kind for unsatisfactory goods and services
- Free repair of defective goods

compromise safety, negatively impact other customers, and overburden employees. Managers need to keep an eye on the level of exception requests. Large numbers of exceptions may indicate a need to reexamine standard service procedures. For instance, if a restaurant constantly receives requests for special vegetarian meals when there are none on the menu, then it may be time to revise the menu to include at least one meatless dish.

Managerial Implications of the Flower of Service

The eight categories of supplementary services that form the Flower of Service provide many options for enhancing the core service product. Most supplementary services do (or should) represent responses to customer needs. As noted earlier, some are facilitating services—like information and reservations—that enable customers to use the core product more effectively. Others are "extras" that enhance the core or even reduce its nonfinancial costs (for example, meals, magazines, and entertainment are hospitality elements that help pass the time). Some elements—notably billing and payment—are imposed by the service provider. But even if not actively desired by the customer, they still form part of the overall service experience. Any badly handled element may negatively affect customers' perceptions of service quality. The "information" and "consultation" petals emphasize the need for education as well as promotion in communicating with service customers.

A key insight from the Flower of Service concept is that different types of core products often share use of similar supplementary elements. As a result, customers may make comparisons across unrelated industries. For instance, "If my stockbroker can give me clear documentation of my account activity, why can't the department store where I shop?" Or "If my favorite airline can take reservations accurately, why can't the French restaurant up the street?" Questions like these suggest that managers should be studying businesses outside their own industries in a search for "best-in-class" performers on specific supplementary services.

Not every core product will be surrounded by a large number of supplementary services from all eight petals. People-processing services tend to be the most demanding in terms of supplementary elements like hospitality, since they involve close (and often extended) interactions with customers. When customers do not visit the service factory, the need for hospitality may be limited to simple courtesies in letters and telecommunications. Possession-processing services sometimes place heavy demands on safekeeping elements, but there may be no need for this particular petal in information-processing services where customers and suppliers deal entirely at arm's length. However, financial services that are provided electronically are an exception to this. Companies must ensure that their customers' intangible financial assets are carefully safeguarded in transactions that occur via phone or the Web.

Companies in the business-to-business sector face many decisions concerning what types of supplementary services to offer. A study of Japanese, American, and European firms found that most simply added layer upon layer of services to their core offerings without knowing what customers really valued.[5] Managers surveyed in the study indicated that they did not understand which services should be offered to customers as a standard package accompanying the core, and which should be offered as options for an extra charge.

There are no simple rules governing decisions about core products and supplementary services. But managers should continually review their firms' product offerings to make sure they are in line with both market practice and customer needs. A study of plastic surgeons' offices and procedures suggests that poor performance on supplementary services—notably, unwanted information and inhospitable waiting areas—creates unfavorable initial impressions that may lead patients to cancel surgery or even change doctors (see the box titled "Cosmetic Surgeons' Offices Disappoint Patients").

Customer needs and expectations often vary by segment. Consider the example of Asea Brown Boveri (ABB), a supplier of power plant equipment and maintenance services to utilities companies. ABB's Power Transformers business realized that not all customers needed or wanted the same levels of maintenance service; some utilities prefer to handle maintenance in-house, using their own employees and equipment. Instead of simply supplying a comprehensive maintenance service to all of its customers, ABB now offers different levels of service and prices as part of a negotiated service agreement. It no longer requires customers to have ABB service all aspects of their transformers. Instead, they can choose the combination of supplementary services that they prefer.[6]

Tables 7.1 through 7.8 can be used to identify value-added ways to augment existing core products and design new offerings. The lists provided in these eight tables do not claim to be all encompassing, since some products may require specialized supplementary elements. A company's marketing strategy helps to determine which supplementary services should be included. A strategy of adding benefits to increase customers' perceptions of quality will probably require more supplementary services (and also a higher level of performance on all such elements) than a strategy of competing on low prices. In general, a firm that competes on a low-cost, no-frills basis will require fewer supplementary elements than one that is marketing an expensive, high-value-added product. And firms that offer different grades of service—like first class, business class, and economy class in an airline context—often

Cosmetic Surgeons' Offices Disappoint Patients

It appears that plastic surgeons could use some service marketing training along with their other courses in medical school. That's the diagnosis of two experts, Kate Altork and Douglas Dedo, who did a study of patients' reactions to doctors' offices. They found that many patients will cancel a surgery, change doctors, or refuse to consider future elective surgery if they feel uneasy in the doctor's office. The study results suggested that patients won't usually "doctor-jump" because they don't like the doctor; they defect because they don't like the context of the service experience. The list of common patient dislikes includes: graphic posters of moles and skin cancers decorating office walls; uncomfortable plastic identification bracelets for patients; claustrophobic examining rooms with no windows or current reading material; bathrooms that aren't clearly marked; and not enough wastebaskets and water coolers in the waiting room.

What do patients want? Most requests are surprisingly simple and involve creature comforts like tissues, water coolers, telephones, plants, and bowls of candy in the waiting room and live flower arrangements in the lobby. Patients also want windows in the examining rooms and gowns that wrap around the entire body. They would like to sit on a real chair when they talk to a doctor instead of perching on a stool or examining table. Finally, preoperative patients prefer to be separated from postoperative patients, since they are disturbed by sitting next to someone in the waiting room whose head is enclosed in bandages.

These study results suggest that cosmetic surgery patients would rather visit an office that looks more like a health spa than a hospital ward. By thinking like service marketers, savvy surgeons could look outside their own industries to find ways of creating patient-friendly environments that will complement rather than counteract their technical expertise.

Source: Lisa Bannon, "Plastic Surgeons Are Told to Pay More Attention to Appearances," *Wall Street Journal*, 15 March 1997, B1.

differentiate them by adding extra supplementary services to a common core for each upgrade in service.

Regardless of which supplementary services a firm decides to offer, the elements in each petal should receive the care and attention needed to consistently meet defined service standards. That way the resulting Flower of Service will always have a fresh and appealing appearance rather than looking wilted or disfigured by neglect.

SERVICE DESIGN

Service design is a complex task that requires an understanding of how the core and supplementary services are combined to create a product offering that meets the needs of target customers. For physical objects like new buildings or ships, the design is usually captured on architectural drawings called blueprints (because reproductions have traditionally been printed on special paper where all the drawings and annotations appear in blue). These blueprints show what the product should look like and detail the specifications to which it should conform.

In contrast to the physical architecture of a building, ship, or piece of equipment, services have a largely intangible structure that makes them all the more difficult to plan and execute. However, it is possible to map service processes by defining the steps required to provide the core and supplementary product elements. To do this, we borrow process-mapping techniques from logistics, industrial engineering, decision theory, and computer systems analysis, each of which uses blueprint-like techniques to describe processes involving flows, sequences, relationships, and dependencies.[7]

Blueprinting can be used to document an existing service or design a new service concept. We introduced a simpler version of blueprinting known as flowcharting in Chapter 4. But in that case our focus was limited to front-stage service delivery from the customer's perspective. As you'll see, blueprinting provides more extensive documentation of the activities involved in producing a service.

To develop a blueprint, you need to be able to identify all of the key activities involved in service delivery and production, clarify the sequence, and to specify the linkages between these activities.[8] **Service blueprints** clarify the interactions between customers and employees and how these are supported by additional activities and systems backstage. As a result, they can facilitate the integration of marketing, operations, and human resource management within a firm. This can be beneficial, since operationally oriented businesses are sometimes so focused on managing backstage activities that they neglect to consider the customer's view of front-stage activities. Accounting firms, for instance, often have elaborately documented procedures and standards for how to conduct an audit properly, but may lack clear standards for when and how to host a client meeting or how to answer the telephone when clients call.

By analyzing blueprints, managers are often able to identify potential **fail points** in the service delivery process where there's a significant risk of problems that can hurt service quality. Knowledge of these fail points enables managers to design procedures to avoid their occurrence or implement effective recovery strategies if necessary. Blueprints can also pinpoint parts of the process where customers commonly have to wait. Standards can then be developed for these activities that include times for completion of a task, maximum wait times in between tasks, and scripts to guide interactions between staff members and customers.

Blueprints of existing services can suggest ideas for product improvements. Managers may spot opportunities to reconfigure delivery systems (perhaps through

service blueprint: a visual map of the sequence of activities required for service delivery that specifies front-stage and backstage elements and the linkages between them.

fail point: a point in a process where there is a significant risk of problems that can damage service quality.

use of new technologies), add or delete specific elements, or reposition the service to appeal to other segments. For example, Canadian Pacific Hotels (which operates hotels under Fairmont and Delta brand names) decided to redesign its hotel services. It had already been successful with conventions, meetings, and group travel but wanted to build greater brand loyalty among business travelers. The company blueprinted the entire "guest experience" from pulling up at the hotel to getting the car keys from the valet. For each encounter, Canadian Pacific defined an expected service level based on customer feedback and created systems to monitor service performance. It also redesigned some aspects of its service processes to provide business guests with more personalized service. The payoff for Canadian Pacific's redesign efforts was a 16-percent increase in its share of business travelers in a single year.

There's no single "best" way to prepare a service blueprint, but it's helpful to adopt a consistent approach within a single organization. In this chapter, we adapt and simplify an approach proposed by Jane Kingman-Brundage.[9] If desired, any aspect of a blueprint can subsequently be examined in greater detail.

Developing a Service Blueprint

To illustrate blueprinting, let's examine the process of dining at Chez Jean, an upscale restaurant that enhances its core food service with a variety of supplementary services. A typical rule of thumb in full-service restaurants is that the cost of purchasing the food ingredients represents about 20 to 30 percent of the price of the meal. The balance can be seen as the "fees" that the customer is willing to pay for supplementary benefits like renting a table and chairs in a pleasant setting, hiring the services of food preparation experts and their kitchen equipment, and having staff to wait on them both inside and outside the dining room.

Figure 7.4 (shown on pages 156–159) contains a blueprint of the Chez Jean restaurant experience. The key components of the blueprint (reading from top to bottom) are:

1. Definition of standards for each front-stage activity (only a few examples are actually specified here)
2. Physical and other evidence for front-stage activities (specified for all steps)
3. Principal customer actions (illustrated by pictures)
4. Line of interaction
5. Front-stage actions by customer-contact personnel
6. Line of visibility
7. Backstage actions by customer-contact personnel
8. Support processes involving other service personnel
9. Support processes involving information technology

Reading from left to right, the blueprint prescribes the sequence of actions over time. To emphasize the involvement of human actors in the service delivery process, our blueprint uses pictures to illustrate each of the 14 principal steps in which our two customers are involved. The process begins with making a reservation and concludes with departure from the restaurant after the meal. Like many high-contact services involving discrete transactions, the restaurant experience can be divided into three "acts," representing activities that take place before the core product is encountered, delivery of the core product (in this case, the meal), and subsequent activities while still involved with the service provider.

Act I: Starting the Service Experience

Act I begins with the customer making a reservation—an interaction conducted by telephone with an unseen employee. In theatrical terms, the telephone conversation might be likened to a radio drama, with impressions being created by the speed of response, tone of the respondent's voice, and style of the conversation. Once the customers arrive at the restaurant, the "stage" or servicescape includes both the exterior and interior of the restaurant. From this point on, front-stage actions take place in a very visual environment. Restaurants are often quite theatrical in their use of physical evidence like furnishings, décor, uniforms, lighting, and table settings; they may also employ background music to help create an environment that matches their market positioning.

By the time our customers reach their table in the dining room, they have been exposed to several supplementary services, including reservations, valet parking, coatroom, cocktails, and seating. They have also seen a sizeable cast of characters, including five or more contact personnel and many other customers. Standards that are based on a good understanding of guest expectations should be set for each of these service activities. Below the line of visibility, the blueprint identifies key actions that should take place to ensure that each front-stage step is performed in a manner that meets or exceeds customer expectations. These actions include recording reservations, handling customers' coats, delivery and preparation of food, maintenance of facilities and equipment, training and assignment of staff for each task, and use of information technology to access, input, store, and transfer relevant data.

Identifying the Fail Points   Running a good restaurant is a complex business and much can go wrong. The most serious fail points, marked by Ⓕ, are those that will result in failure to access or enjoy the core product. They involve the reservation (Could the customer get through by phone? Was a table available at the desired time and date? Was the reservation recorded accurately?) and seating (Was a table available when promised?). Since service delivery takes place over time, there is also the possibility of delays between specific actions that will cause customers to wait. Points at which there is a risk of such a wait are identified by a ⚠W Excessive waits at critical steps in delivery can be classified as fail points, because they will annoy customers and negatively impact perceived service quality.

Every step in the process has some potential for failures and delays. David Maister coined the term OTSU ("opportunity to screw up") to highlight the importance of thinking about all the things that might go wrong in delivering a particular type of service.[10] OTSUs can be very humorous if you're not personally involved. John Cleese made millions laugh with his portrayal of an inept hotel manager in the television series *Fawlty Towers*. Chevy Chase and Steve Martin have entertained movie audiences for years by playing customers tortured by inept, rude, or downright cruel service employees. However, customers don't always see the funny side when the joke is on them. That's why it is important for service managers to identify all the possible OTSUs associated with a particular task so they can put together a delivery system that is explicitly designed to avoid these problems.

Setting Service Standards   Through both formal research and on-the-job experience, service managers can learn the nature of customer expectations at each step in the process. As discussed in other chapters, customers' expectations range across a spectrum—referred to as the *zone of tolerance*—from desired service (an ideal) to a threshold level of merely adequate service. Service providers should design

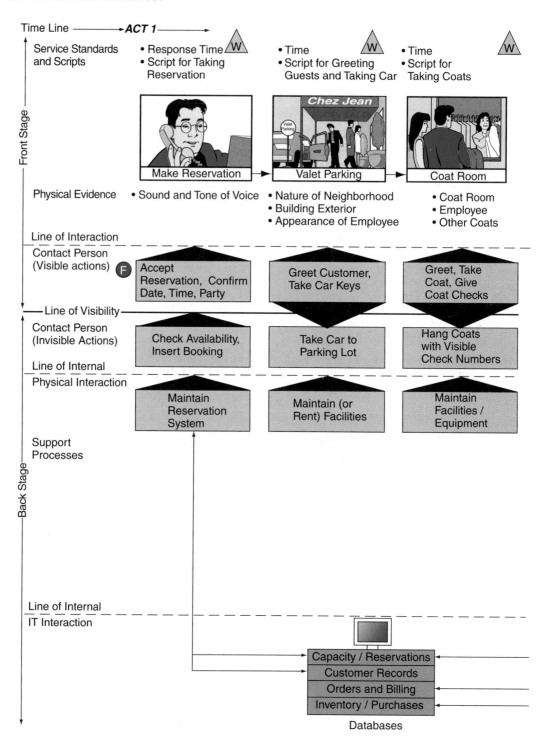

FIGURE 7.4

Blueprinting a Full-Service
Restaurant Experience

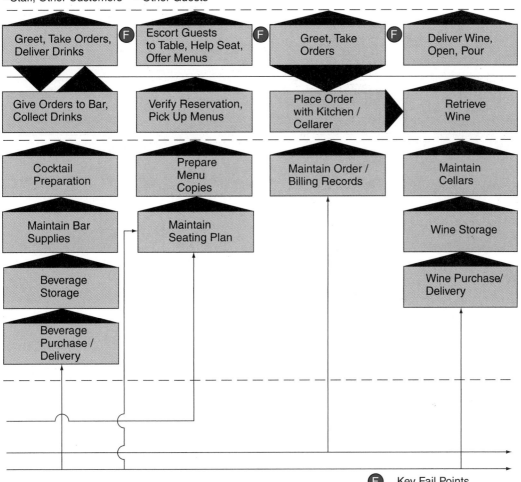

- Time
- Order Accuracy
- Script for Serving Drinks

- Punctuality vs. Reservation
- Script for Seating

ACT II ⟶

- Time
- Script for Greeting Guests, Taking Order

- Time
- Script for Wine Service

| Cocktails | Seating | Order Food and Wine | Wine Service |

- Cocktail Lounge Decor
- Furnishings
- Table Setting
- Staff, Other Customers

- Dining Room Decor
- Appearance / Demeanor of Staff
- Table Setting
- Other Guests

- Wine Quality

Greet, Take Orders, Deliver Drinks — F

Escort Guests to Table, Help Seat, Offer Menus — F

Greet, Take Orders — F

Deliver Wine, Open, Pour

Give Orders to Bar, Collect Drinks

Verify Reservation, Pick Up Menus

Place Order with Kitchen / Cellarer

Retrieve Wine

Cocktail Preparation

Prepare Menu Copies

Maintain Order / Billing Records

Maintain Cellars

Maintain Bar Supplies

Maintain Seating Plan

Wine Storage

Beverage Storage

Wine Purchase/ Delivery

Beverage Purchase / Delivery

F Key Fail Points

W Risk of Excessive Wait (Standard times should specify limits)

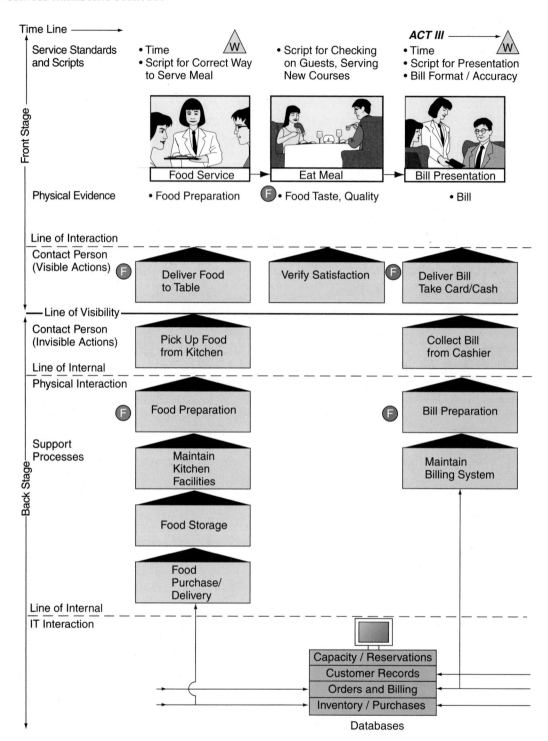

FIGURE 7.4

(continued)

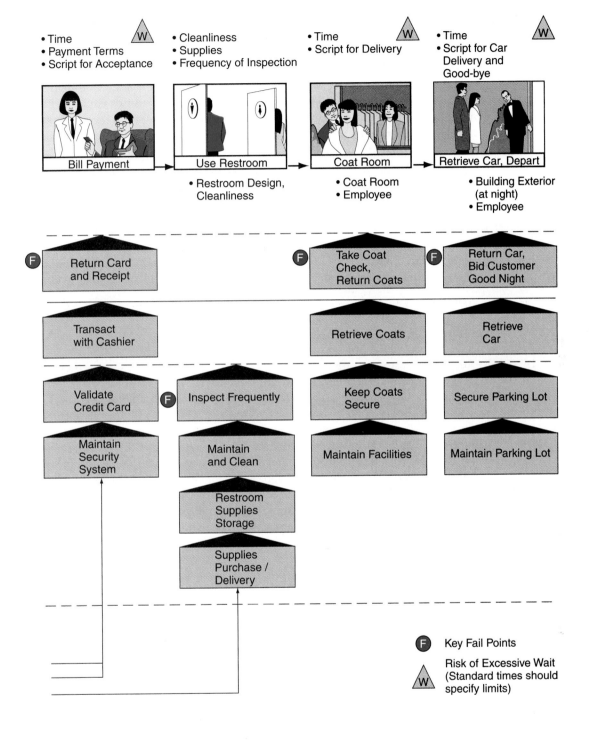

- Time
- Payment Terms
- Script for Acceptance

- Cleanliness
- Supplies
- Frequency of Inspection

- Time
- Script for Delivery

- Time
- Script for Car Delivery and Good-bye

Bill Payment

Use Restroom
- Restroom Design, Cleanliness

Coat Room
- Coat Room
- Employee

Retrieve Car, Depart
- Building Exterior (at night)
- Employee

Return Card and Receipt

Take Coat Check, Return Coats

Return Car, Bid Customer Good Night

Transact with Cashier

Retrieve Coats

Retrieve Car

Validate Credit Card

Inspect Frequently

Keep Coats Secure

Secure Parking Lot

Maintain Security System

Maintain and Clean

Maintain Facilities

Maintain Parking Lot

Restroom Supplies Storage

Supplies Purchase / Delivery

F Key Fail Points

W Risk of Excessive Wait (Standard times should specify limits)

standards for each step that are sufficiently high to satisfy and even delight customers. These standards may include time parameters for specific activities, the script for a technically correct performance, and prescriptions for appropriate employee style and demeanor.

The initial steps of service delivery are particularly important, since customers' first impressions can affect their evaluations of quality during later stages of service delivery. Perceptions of their service experiences tend to be cumulative.[11] If things go badly at the outset, customers may simply walk out. Even if they stay, they may be looking for other things that aren't quite right. On the other hand, if the first steps go well, their zones of tolerance may increase so that they are more willing to overlook minor mistakes later in the service performance.

Research by Marriott Hotels has found that four of the five top factors contributing to customer loyalty come into play during the first 10 minutes of service delivery.[12] While initial impressions are critical, performance standards should not be allowed to fall off toward the end of service delivery. Other research findings point to the importance of a strong finish. They suggest that a service encounter that starts poorly but then increases in quality will be better rated than one that starts well but declines to a poor conclusion.[13]

Act II: Delivery of the Core Product

In Act II, our customers are finally about to experience the core service they came for. We've condensed the meal into just four scenes for simplicity's sake. But reviewing the menu and placing the order are actually two separate activities and meal service typically proceeds on a course-by-course basis. Assuming all goes well, the two guests will have an excellent meal, nicely served in a pleasant atmosphere, and perhaps a fine wine to enhance it. But there is always the possibility that the restaurant won't satisfy customer expectations during Act II. The answers to the following questions can help managers identify potential fail points: Is the menu information complete? Is it intelligible? Is everything that's listed on the menu available this evening? Will employees provide explanations and advice in a friendly and noncondescending manner for guests who have questions about specific menu items or are unsure about which wine to order?

After our customers decide on their meals, they place their order with the server, who must then pass on the details to personnel in the kitchen, bar, and billing desk. Mistakes in transmitting information are a frequent cause of quality failures in many organizations. Bad handwriting or unclear verbal requests can lead to delivery of the wrong items altogether—or of the right items incorrectly prepared.

As Act II continues, our customers evaluate not only the quality of food and drink—the most important dimension of all—but also how promptly it is served and the style of service. A disinterested, ingratiating, or overly casual server can still spoil a technically correct performance.

Act III: Concluding the Service Performance

The meal may be over, but much activity is still taking place both front stage and backstage as the service process moves to its close. The core service has now been delivered, and we'll assume that our customers are happily digesting it. Act III should be short. The action in each of the remaining scenes should move smoothly, quickly, and pleasantly, with no shocking surprises at the end. In a North

American environment, most customers' expectations would probably include the following:

➤ An accurate, intelligible bill is presented promptly as soon as customers request it.

➤ Payment is handled politely and expeditiously (with all major credit cards accepted).

➤ Guests are thanked for their patronage and invited to come again.

➤ Customers visiting the restrooms find them clean and properly supplied.

➤ The right coats are promptly retrieved from the coat room.

➤ The customers' car is brought promptly to the door in the same condition as when it was left.

➤ The parking lot attendant thanks them again and bids them a good evening.

But how often do failures at the end of a service intervene to ruin the customers' experience and spoil their good humor? Can you remember situations in which the experience of a nice meal was completely spoiled by one or more failures in concluding the service delivery? Informal research among participants in dozens of executive programs has found that the most commonly cited source of dissatisfaction with restaurants is an inability to get the bill quickly when customers are ready to leave! This seemingly minor OTSU can sour the overall dining experience even if everything else has gone well. (For some suggestions on reducing customer waits, see the box, "In and Out Food Service.")

We chose a restaurant example to illustrate blueprinting because it is a high-contact, people-processing service that is familiar to most readers. However, many possession-processing services (like repair or maintenance) and information-processing services (like insurance or accounting) involve far less contact with customers since much of the action takes place backstage. In these situations, a

In and Out Food Service

When customers are on a tight time budget, making them wait unnecessarily at any point in the process is akin to stealing their time. *Restaurant Hospitality*, a trade magazine for the restaurant industry, offers the following 10 suggestions for serving customers quickly without making them feel like they've been pushed out of the door. As you'll see, some of these tactics involve front-stage processes while others take place backstage—but it is the interaction between front stage and backstage that creates the desired service delivery.

1. Distinguish between patrons who are in a hurry, and those who are not.

2. Design specials that are quick.

3. Guide hurried customers to those specials.

4. Place the quickest, highest-margin menu items either first or last on the menu.

5. Offer dishes that can be prepared ahead of time.

6. Warn customers when they order menu items that will take a lot of time to prepare.

7. Consider short-line buffets, roving carts, and more sandwiches.

8. Offer "wrap"-style sandwiches, which are a quickly prepared, filling meal.

9. Use equipment built for speed, like combination ovens.

10. Eliminate preparation steps that require cooks to stop cooking.

Adapted from Paul B. Hertneky, "Built for Speed," *Restaurant Hospitality*, January 1997, 58.

failure committed front stage is likely to represent a higher proportion of the customer's service encounters with a company. Thus it may be viewed even more seriously, because there are fewer subsequent opportunities to create a favorable impression.

REENGINEERING SERVICE PROCESSES

Blueprinting can provide valuable insights by suggesting opportunities to reengineer business processes, improve capacity planning, and better define employee roles. The design of business processes has important implications for the nature and quality of the customer's experience as well as the cost, speed, and productivity with which the desired outcome is achieved.

Improving productivity in services often requires speeding up the overall process, since the cost of creating a service is usually related to how long it takes to deliver each step in the process (plus any dead time between each step). When they are relaxing or being entertained, customers don't mind spending time. But when they are busy, they hate wasting time and often view time expenditures as something to be minimized. Even when customers aren't directly involved in the process, the elapsed time between ordering and receiving a service may be seen as burdensome (for example, waiting for repair of a broken machine, installation of a new computer system, receipt of legal advice, or delivery of a consulting report).

Reengineering involves analyzing and redesigning business processes to achieve faster and better performance. To reduce the overall time for a process, analysts must identify each step, measure how long it takes, look for opportunities to speed it up (or even eliminate it altogether), and cut out dead time. Running tasks in parallel rather than in sequence is a well-established approach to speed up processes (a simple household example would be to cook the vegetables for a meal while the main dish was in the oven, rather than waiting to cook them until after the main dish was removed).

Examination of business processes sometimes leads to creation of alternative delivery forms that are so radically different as to constitute entirely new service concepts. Options may include eliminating certain supplementary services, adding new ones, transforming personal service into self-service, or rethinking the location where service delivery takes place. Figure 7.5 illustrates this principle with simple flowcharts of four alternative ways to deliver meal service. Take a moment to compare and contrast what happens front stage at a fast-food restaurant, a drive-in restaurant, home delivery, and home catering. And now, for each alternative, think about the implications for backstage activities.

> **reengineering:** the analysis and redesign of business processes to create dramatic performance improvements in such areas as cost, quality, speed, and customers' service experiences.

Understanding Employee Roles

Many of the benefits of blueprinting come from the actual nature of the work required to create the charts—especially if employees themselves are directly involved in the task. Participation in mapping specific processes gives employees a clearer picture of their roles and responsibilities and makes them feel like part of a team that is responsible for implementing a shared service vision. Blueprints can also help managers and employees understand the service delivery process as customers experience it.

Blueprinting can also be used to show backstage personnel how their work relates to that of their front-stage colleagues. Backstage personnel provide a series of internal services (represented by each of the vertically stacked boxes in Figure 7.4) that support

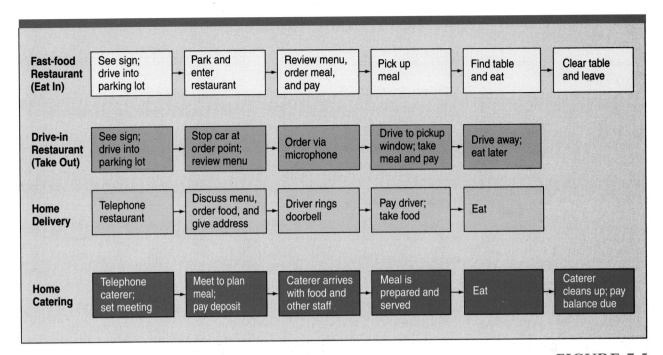

FIGURE 7.5

Flowcharts for Meal Delivery
Scenarios

front-stage activities. If they do their jobs poorly, the employees working backstage may create problems for their coworkers with customer-contact responsibilities. It's not always possible to give either external or internal customers exactly the service that they would like, but blueprinting can be a valuable tool for facilitating discussion about how to improve service processes.

Conclusion

In mature industries, the core service can become a commodity. The search for competitive advantage often centers on improvements to the supplementary services that surround this core. In this chapter, we grouped supplementary services into eight categories, circling the core like the petals of a flower. They are categorized as either facilitating or enhancing supplementary services. Facilitating supplementary services aid in the use of the core product or are required for service delivery, while enhancing supplementary services add extra value for customers.

Designing the overall service experience is a complex task that requires an understanding of how the core and supplementary services should be combined and sequenced to create a product offering that meets the needs of target customers. Blueprinting is a structured procedure for analyzing existing services and planning new ones. In particular, it enables us to define the different components of the augmented service, to examine the sequence in which they are delivered, and to identify potential fail points. We also gain insights into what is happening to the customer at each stage. Supporting each front-stage action are backstage activities involving people, supporting equipment and facilities, and information (often stored in a databank). As we discussed, a poorly organized backstage can lead to failures that are experienced by the customer.

Study Questions and Exercises

1. Define what is meant by the core product and supplementary services. Can they be applied to goods as well as services? Explain your answer.

2. What service failures have you encountered recently? Did they involve the core product or supplementary service elements? Identify possible causes and suggest how such failures might be prevented in the future.

3. Explain the distinction between enhancing and facilitating supplementary services. Give several examples of each for services that you have used recently.

4. Review the blueprint of the restaurant experience in this chapter (Figure 7.4). Identify and categorize each of the supplementary services described in the figure.

5. Prepare detailed blueprints for the following services:

   a. Repair of a damaged bicycle

   b. Applying to college or graduate school

   c. Renting a car

6. Describe the different types of information that service blueprints can provide.

Endnotes

1. Thomas Brinckwirth and Stephen A. Butscher, "Germany's Most Popular Radio Station Creates Loyal Listeners," *Colloquy* (the Frequency Marketing, Inc. quarterly newsletter) 6, no. 3 (1998); SWF3 Web site, www.swf3.de, January 2001.

2. G. Lynn Shostack, "Breaking Free from Product Marketing," *Journal of Marketing*, 44 (April 1977): 73–80.

3. Pierre Eiglier and Eric Langeard, "Services as Systems: Marketing Implications," in P. Eiglier, E. Langeard, C. H. Lovelock, J.E.G. Bateson, and R. F. Young, *Marketing Consumer Services: New Insights* (Cambridge, MA: Marketing Science Institute, 1977), 83–103. Note: An earlier version of this article was published in French in *Révue Française de Gestion*, March-April, 1977, 72–84.

4. The "Flower of Service" concept presented in this section was first introduced in Christopher H. Lovelock, "Cultivating the Flower of Service: New Ways of Looking at Core and Supplementary Services," in P. Eiglier and E. Langeard (eds.) *Marketing, Operations, and Human Resources: Insights into Services* (Aix-en-Provence, France: IAE, Université d'Aix-Marseille III, 1992), 296–316.

5. James C. Anderson and James A. Narus, "Capturing the Value of Supplementary Services," *Harvard Business Review*, 73 (January-February 1995): 75–83.

6. From James C. Anderson and James A. Narus, *Business Market Management* (Upper Saddle River, NJ: Prentice Hall, 1999), 180.

7. See G. Lynn Shostack, "Understanding Services through Blueprinting" in T. Schwartz et al., *Advances in Services Marketing and Management* (Greenwich, CT: JAI Press, 1992), 75–90.

8. G. Lynn Shostack, "Designing Services That Deliver," *Harvard Business Review* (January-February 1984): 133–139.

9. Jane Kingman-Brundage, "The ABCs of Service System Blueprinting," in M. J. Bitner and L. A. Crosby (eds.), *Designing a Winning Service Strategy* (Chicago, IL: American Marketing Association, 1989).

10. David Maister, now president of Maister Associates, coined the term OTSU while teaching at Harvard Business School in the 1980s.

11. See for example, Eric J. Arnould and Linda L. Price, "River Magic: Extraordinary Experience and the Extended Service Encounter," *Journal of Consumer Research* 20 (June 1993): 24–25; Nick Johns and Phil Tyas, "Customer Perceptions of Service Operations: Gestalt, Incident or Mythology?" *The Service Industries Journal* 17 (July 1997): 474–488.

12. "How Marriott Makes a Great First Impression," *The Service Edge* 6 (May 1993): 5.

13. David E. Hansen and Peter J. Danaher, "Inconsistent Performance during the Service Encounter: What's a Good Start Worth?" *Journal of Service Research* 1 (February 1999): 227–235.

chapter eight

Pricing Strategies for Services

"Name Your Own Price" with Priceline.com

Priceline.com was launched in 1998 to give customers some leverage in purchasing a variety of services.[1] Using the slogan, "Name Your Own Price," the Internet-based company invited price-conscious consumers to make offers for services such as airline tickets, hotel rooms, rental cars, long-distance phone service, and mortgages. In addition to helping customers save money, Priceline offered sellers an opportunity to generate incremental revenue without disrupting their existing distribution channels or retail pricing structures.

Priceline termed its approach a demand collection system. Through its Web site, the firm collected consumer demand (in the form of individual bids guaranteed by a credit card) for a particular service at prices set by those customers. It then communicated that demand directly to participating sellers or to their private databases. Customers agreed to hold their offers open for a specified period of time, during which Priceline sought to fulfill their offers from inventory provided by participating sellers. Users of the service had to be flexible with regard to brands, sellers, and/or product features. Once fulfilled, purchases normally couldn't be canceled.

The concept of giving customers the freedom to set their own prices initially attracted a lot of attention and enthusiasm. The firm's market value rose to $20 billion within a month after it went public in 1999. Founder (and then-CEO) Jay Walker expanded Priceline's offerings to include hotel rooms, rental cars, home mortgages, long-distance telephone services, and cars. He also added services like WebHouse Club that allowed customers to bid on groceries and gasoline. Promoted heavily through television advertising featuring actor William Shatner (best known for his role of Captain Kirk in *Star Trek*), Priceline soon became one of the most widely recognized brand names in e-commerce.

But in spite of Priceline's promising start, things began to go wrong in 2000. Instead of taking a markup on the inventory that it held and resold, Priceline sometimes found itself selling rooms, tickets, and even gasoline at prices below its own cost. There was a growing number of complaints, ranging from hidden airline charges to shabby hotel facilities; consumer dissatisfaction was compounded by poor customer service, eventually leading to an investigation by the attorney general in the company's home state of Connecticut and expulsion from the local Better Business Bureau. The company's business model had worked best in the air travel market, where Priceline accounted for about 4 percent of all ticket sales in the United States. However, new competition emerged in October 2000 when a number of airlines got together to create their own Internet service to dispose of unsold tickets at discounts of up to 40 percent. Named Hotwire, this service differed from Priceline in that users specified their travel needs (but no price) and received an almost immediate fare offer; however, as with Priceline, customers didn't learn the carrier name or precise schedule until after they had purchased the ticket.

WebHouse Club service had to be discontinued in late 2000 when it became clear that suppliers weren't eager to provide groceries or gasoline at cut-rate prices in response to consumer bids. And consumers themselves got frustrated at the conditions that sellers often

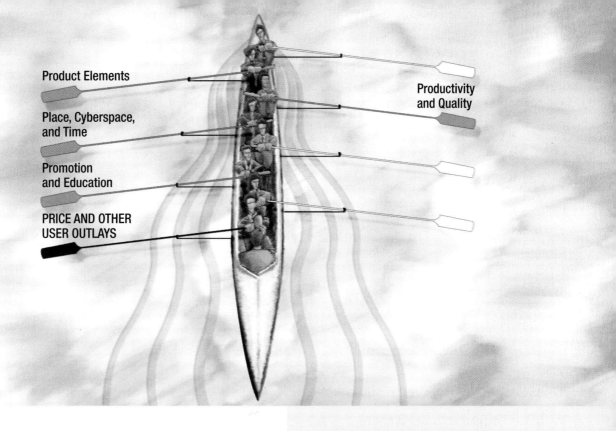

Product Elements

Place, Cyberspace, and Time

Promotion and Education

PRICE AND OTHER USER OUTLAYS

Productivity and Quality

attached to sales, such as a requirement to sign up for trial magazine subscriptions.

In response to investigations into consumer complaints, the firm added more customer service reps, improved its training procedures, and instituted more consistent guidelines on problem resolution. Misleading procedures on the Web site were corrected. In particular, the full amount that customers would have to pay for an airline ticket, including all taxes and fuel charges, was disclosed on a single page; previously, the extras were noted on separate screens. Finally, an important phrasing change, from "Submitting my offer now" to "Buy my ticket now" clarified that customers were committing themselves to a purchase if their offer was accepted.

Seeking to sharpen its focus, Priceline announced that it was restructuring its operations, cutting staff, and canceling plans to add cell phone services and insurance. But Hotwire disclosed that it was expanding service to include hotel rooms and international air travel. Further bad news for Priceline came from the departure of key executives and a plummeting stock price.

All in all, the future looked very uncertain for Priceline as it entered 2001, with promises of profits still unfulfilled and news that the company's market valuation on Wall Street had sunk to an all-time low of only $200 million—down more than 99 percent from its peak.

Learning Objectives

After reading this chapter, you should be able to

⇒ explain how the differences between goods and services affect pricing strategy

⇒ appreciate ethical concerns in pricing policy

⇒ identify the different outlays customers incur in purchasing and using a service

⇒ discuss the relationship between pricing and demand

⇒ understand yield management and how it relates to price elasticity

⇒ describe the key issues in designing and implementing pricing strategies

PAYING FOR SERVICE: THE CUSTOMER'S PERSPECTIVE

Have you ever noticed what a wide variety of terms service organizations use to describe the prices they set? Universities talk about *tuition*, professional firms collect *fees*, and banks charge *interest* on loans or add *service charges*. Some bridges and highways impose *tolls*, transport operators collect *fares*, clubs charge *subscriptions*, utilities set *tariffs*, insurance companies establish *premiums*, and hotels establish *room rates*. These diverse terms are a signal that service industries have historically taken a different approach to pricing than manufacturers.

Answering the question, ***What price should we charge for our service?*** is a task that can't be left solely to financial managers. The challenges of service pricing require active participation from marketers who understand customer needs and behavior and from operations managers who recognize the importance of matching demand to available capacity. The discussion that follows in this chapter assumes a basic understanding of the economic costs—fixed, semivariable, and variable—incurred by companies, as well as the concepts of contribution and break-even analysis. If you haven't previously been exposed to this material or feel you could benefit from a refresher, you may want to review the information in the box titled "Understanding Costs, Contribution, and Break-Even Analysis" on page 169.

What Makes Service Pricing Different?

Let's consider how some of the differences between goods and services marketing that we discussed in Chapter 1 may affect pricing strategy.

No Ownership of Services　It's usually harder for managers to calculate the financial costs involved in creating an intangible performance for a customer than it is to identify the labor, materials, machine time, storage, and shipping costs associated with producing a physical good. Yet without a good understanding of costs, how can managers hope to price at levels sufficient to achieve a desired profit margin?

Higher Ratio of Fixed Costs to Variable Costs　Because of the labor and infrastructure needed to create performances, many service organizations have a much higher ratio of fixed costs to variable costs than is found in manufacturing firms.[2] Service businesses with high fixed costs include those with an expensive physical facility (e.g., a hotel, a hospital, a university, or a theater), or a fleet of vehicles (e.g., an airline, a bus company, or a trucking company), or a network dependent on company-owned infrastructure (e.g., a telecommunications company, an Internet provider, a railroad, or a gas pipeline). While the fixed costs may be high for such businesses, the variable costs for serving one extra customer may be minimal.

Variability of Both Inputs and Outputs.　It's not always easy to define a unit of service, raising questions as to what should be the basis for service pricing. And seemingly similar units of service may not cost the same to produce, nor may they be of equal value to all customers. The potential for variability in service performances (especially those that involve interactions with employees and other customers) means that customers may pay the same price for a service but receive different levels of quality and value. Alternatively, they may be charged radically different prices for the same service offering, as often happens in the hotel industry. Advertising by Travelscape.com, the do-it-yourself travel site, emphasizes its ability to help customers quickly find the cheapest price for a hotel room (see Figure 8.1).

Many Services Are Hard to Evaluate The intangibility of service performances and the invisibility of the backstage facilities and labor make it harder for customers to know what they are getting for their money than when they purchase a physical good.

Consider the homeowners who call an electrical firm, seeking repairs to a defective circuit. A few days later (if they are lucky) an electrician arrives with a small bag of tools. Within 20 minutes, the problem is located and a new circuit breaker installed. Presto, everything works! Subsequently, the owners are horrified to receive a bill for $65, most of it for labor charges. But they're overlooking all the fixed costs that the firm needs to recover, such as the office, telephone, vehicles, tools, fuel, and support staff. The variable costs of the visit are also higher than they appear. Fifteen minutes of driving back and forth plus 5 minutes to unload (and later reload) needed tools and supplies from the van on arrival at the house must be added to the 20 minutes spent at the customers' house. These activities effectively double the labor time devoted to this call. Finally, the firm

Understanding Costs, Contribution, and Break-Even Analysis

Fixed costs—sometimes referred to as overheads—are those economic costs that a supplier would continue to incur (at least in the short run) even if no services were sold. These costs may include rent, depreciation, utilities, taxes, insurance, salaries and wages for managers and long-term employees, security, and interest payments.

Variable costs refer to the economic costs associated with serving an additional customer, such as making another bank transaction, selling an additional seat in a train or theater, serving an extra hotel guest for the night in a hotel, or completing one more repair job. For many services, such costs are very low. There is, for instance, very little labor or fuel cost involved in transporting an extra bus passenger. Selling a hotel room for the night has slightly higher variable costs, since the room will need to be cleaned and the linens sent to the laundry after a guest leaves. More significant variable costs are associated with activities like serving food and beverages or installing a new part when making repairs, since they include the provision of costly physical products in addition to labor. Just because a firm has sold a service at a price that exceeds its variable costs does not mean that the firm is now profitable. There are still fixed and semivariable costs to be covered.

Semivariable costs fall in between fixed and variable costs. They represent expenses that rise or fall in stepwise fashion as the volume of business increases/decreases. Examples include adding an extra flight to meet increased demand on a specific air route, or hiring a part-time employee to work in a restaurant on busy weekends.

Contribution is the difference between the variable cost of selling an extra unit of service and the money received for that service. It goes to cover fixed and semivariable costs before creating profits.

Determining and allocating economic costs can be a challenging task in some service operations. For example, it's difficult to decide how to assign fixed costs in a multi-service facility like a hospital. There are certain fixed costs associated with running the emergency unit. Beyond that there are fixed costs for running the entire hospital. How much of the hospital's fixed costs should be allocated to the emergency unit? A hospital manager might use one of several approaches to calculate the unit's share of overheads. These could include (1) the percentage of total floor space that it occupies, (2) the percentage of employee hours or payroll that it accounts for, or (3) the percentage of total patient contact hours involved. Each method is likely to yield a totally different fixed-cost allocation. One method might indicate that the emergency unit is very profitable, another might make it seem like a break-even operation, and a third might suggest that the unit is losing money.

Break-even analysis. Managers need to know at what sales volume a service will become profitable. This is called the break-even point. The necessary analysis involves dividing the total fixed and semivariable costs by the contribution obtained on each unit of service. For instance, if a 100-room hotel needs to cover fixed and semivariable costs of $2 million a year and the average contribution per room-night is $100, then the hotel will need to sell 20,000 room-nights per year out of a total annual capacity of 36,500. If prices are cut by an average of $20 per room night (*or* variable costs rise by $20), then the contribution will drop to $80 and the hotel's break-even volume will rise to 25,000 room nights.

FIGURE 8.1

Travelscape.com Helps Customers
Find the Cheapest Price for a
Hotel Room

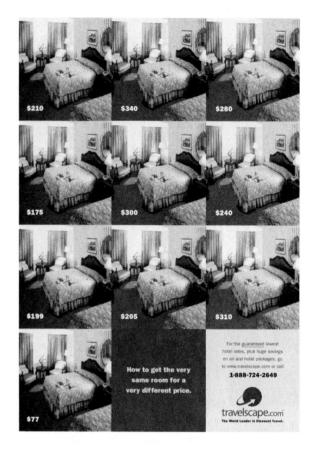

has to add a margin to the bill in order to make a profit for the owner. However, these intrinsic costs are not readily visible to the customers, who are making their comparisons of price versus value based solely on visible service attributes.

Importance of the Time Factor   Time often drives value. In many instances, customers are willing to pay more for a service delivered at a preferred time than for a service offered at a less convenient time. They may also choose to pay more for faster delivery of some services—compare the cost of express mail against that of regular mail. Sometimes greater speed increases operating costs for the service provider, reflecting the need to pay overtime wages or use more expensive equipment. In other instances, achieving faster turnaround is simply a matter of giving priority to one customer over another. For instance, clothes requiring express dry-cleaning take the same amount of time to clean. The firm saves time for these customers by moving their jobs to the head of the line.

Availability of Both Electronic and Physical Distribution Channels   The use of different channels to deliver the same service can affect costs and perceived value. Electronic banking transactions are much cheaper for a bank than face-to-face contact in a branch. While some people like the convenience of impersonal but efficient electronic transactions, others prefer to deal with a real bank teller. Thus, a service delivered through a particular channel may have value for one person but not for another. Companies must balance customer needs and preferences against the desire to reduce production costs, because in some cases customers may be willing to accept a price increase in order to have access to a physical distribution channel.

Ethical Concerns

Services often invite performance and pricing abuses. The problem is especially acute for services that are high in credence attributes, whose quality and benefits are hard to evaluate even after delivery.[3]

Exploiting Customer Ignorance   When customers don't know what they are getting from a service supplier, are not present when the work is being performed, and lack the technical skills to know if a good job has been done, they are vulnerable to paying for work that wasn't done, wasn't necessary, or was poorly executed. Although price can serve as a surrogate for quality, it's sometimes hard to be sure if the extra value is really there. This is an important issue, since customers may rely more heavily on price cues as an indication of service value when perceived risks (e.g., functional, financial, psychological, or social) are high.[4]

Web sites sometimes take advantage of customer ignorance, particularly where airline tickets are concerned. Although there are many Internet travel sites, finding the cheapest fare isn't easy. Priceline initially confused customers by not clarifying that airport taxes and fuel surcharges had to be added to ticket prices.

Complexity and Unfairness   Pricing schedules for services are often quite complex. Changing circumstances sometimes result in complicated pricing schedules that are difficult for consumers to interpret. Consider the credit card industry. Traditionally, the banks that issue these cards received revenues from two sources: a small percentage of the value of each transaction (paid by the merchant), and high interest charges on credit balances. As credit cards became more popular, costs started to rise for the banks on two fronts. First, more customers defaulted on their balances, leading to a big increase in bad debts. Second, as competition increased between banks, marketing expenses rose and gold and platinum cards started offering more affluent customers features like free travel insurance, emergency card replacement, and points redeemable for air miles. But as marketing expenses were rising, more customers started to pay off their monthly balances in full and competition led to lower interest rates, resulting in lower revenues. So the banks increased other charges and imposed new fees that were often confusing to customers. Details of charges by one major bank for its platinum card are shown in the box entitled "Charges, Fees, and Terms for a Platinum Visa Card."

Another industry that has gained notoriety for its complex and sometimes misleading pricing schedules is cellular telephone service. *Consumer Reports* has warned its readers about such practices as rounding up calling time to the nearest minute, misrepresentation of "free" service elements that turn out not to be so, and huge cancellation fees ($150 to $200) for terminating a one-year contract before it expires.[5]

Complexity makes it easier—and perhaps more tempting—for firms to engage in unethical behavior. The car rental industry has attracted some notoriety for advertising bargain rental prices and then telling customers on arrival that other fees like collision insurance and personal insurance are compulsory. And employees sometimes fail to clarify certain "small print" contract terms such as a high per mile charge that is added once the car exceeds a very low threshold of free miles. The "hidden extras" phenomenon for car rentals in some Florida resort towns got so bad at one point that people were joking: "the car is free, the keys are extra!" A not uncommon practice is to charge fees for refueling a partially empty tank that far exceed what the driver would pay at the pump.

When customers know that they are vulnerable to potential abuse, they become suspicious of both the firm and its employees. Assuming that a firm has honest management, the best approach is a proactive one, spelling out all fees and expenses clearly in advance so that there are no surprises. A related approach is to develop a simple fee structure so that customers can easily understand the financial implications of a specific usage situation.

Identifying User Outlays

From a customer's standpoint, the monetary price charged by a supplier is not the only cost or outlay associated with purchase and delivery of a service. Let's take a look at what's involved (see Figure 8.2). As we do so, please consider your own experiences in different service contexts.

financial outlays: all monetary expenditures incurred by customers in purchasing and consuming a service.

Price and Other Financial Expenses   Customers often spend additional amounts over and above the purchase price. Necessary incidental expenses may include travel to the service site, parking, and purchase of other facilitating goods or services ranging from meals to babysitting. We call the total of all these expenses (including the price of the service itself) the **financial outlays** associated with purchasing and consuming a service.

Charges, Fees, and Terms for a Platinum Visa Card

Annual fee	First year free; thereafter $65
Finance charges on unpaid balances	
Purchases	9.99% (min. charge $0.50)*
Cash advances	19.99% (min. charge $0.50)
After failure to make two monthly payments within 6 months (applies to all balances)	22.99%
Transaction charges for purchase of money order, wire transfer, or use of "convenience checks"	3% of transaction value (min. $5)
Cash advance (use card to obtain money from an ATM or bank)	2% of cash advance value (min. $10)
Other charges	
Late fee	$29
Returned check fee (payment)	$29
Overlimit fee	$29
Payment terms	Due by 10 A.M. on payment due date specified on monthly statement. Failure to enclose coupon, pay by check or money order, or use envelope provided may result in up to a 5-day delay in posting.

*Minimum annual percentage rates (or prime rate + 0.99%, whichever is higher)
Source: First USA Bank (data taken from card member agreement, amended May 2000).

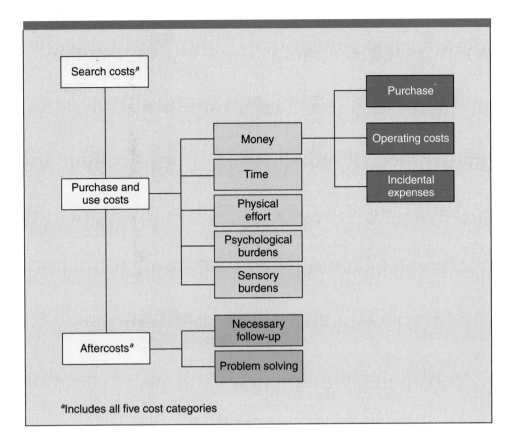

FIGURE 8.2

Determining the Total Costs of a Service: More Than Meets the Eye?

Nonfinancial Outlays   Customers may incur a variety of **nonfinancial outlays**, representing the time, effort, and discomfort associated with searching for, purchasing, and using a service. We can group nonfinancial outlays into four distinct categories.

> **Time expenditures** are inherent in the service delivery process. Time may also be wasted simply waiting for service. There's an opportunity cost involved because customers could spend that time in other ways.

> **Physical effort** (including fatigue, discomfort, and occasionally even injury) may be incurred during visits to the service factory or while using a company's self-service equipment.

> **Psychological burdens** like mental effort, feelings of inadequacy, or fear may accompany the tasks of evaluating service alternatives, making a selection, and then using the chosen service. Services that are high in experience and credence attributes may create psychological burdens like anxiety since service outcomes are more difficult to evaluate.

> **Sensory burdens** relate to unpleasant sensations affecting any of the five senses. They may include putting up with noise, unpleasant smells, drafts, excessive heat or cold, uncomfortable seating or lighting, visually unappealing environments, and even unpleasant tastes.

The total costs of purchasing and using a service also include those associated with search activities. When you were looking at colleges, how much money, time, and effort did you spend before deciding where to apply? And how much effort would you put into comparing alternative haircutters if your existing one was no longer available? There may even be further outlays after service delivery is completed. A doctor may

nonfinancial outlays: the time expenditures, physical and mental effort, and unwanted sensory experiences associated with searching for, buying, and using a service.

time expenditures: time spent by customers during all aspects of the service delivery process.

physical effort: undesired consequences to a customer's body that occur during the service delivery process.

psychological burdens: undesired mental or emotional states experienced by customers as a result of the service delivery process.

sensory burdens: negative sensations experienced through a customer's five senses during the service delivery process.

FIGURE 8.3

Net Value = Benefits − Outlays

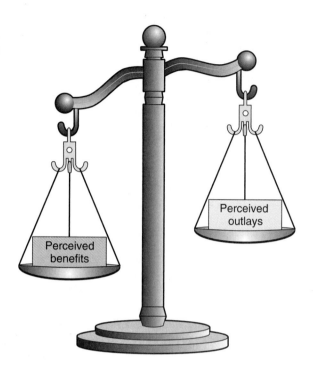

diagnose a medical problem for a patient and then prescribe a course of physical therapy and drugs to be continued over several months. Obtaining refunds after service failures may force customers to waste time, money, and effort in trying to resolve the problem.

Understanding Net Value

When customers evaluate a service, they consider the benefits it offers relative to the financial and nonfinancial outlays they will incur in purchasing and using it. Although there are several ways to describe value, we have chosen to define value as "what I get for what I give."[6] **Net value** is defined as the sum of all the perceived benefits (gross value) minus the sum of all the perceived outlays for the customer. The greater the positive difference between the two, the greater the net value. If the perceived costs and other outlays are greater than the perceived benefits, then the service in question will possess negative net value.

Perceptions of net value may vary widely between customers, and even for the same customer depending on the situation. How customers feel about the net value of a service may be sharply different post-use and pre-use, reflecting the experiential qualities of many services. When customers use a service and find that it has cost more and delivered fewer benefits than expected, they are unlikely to repurchase it and may complain about "poor value."

You can think of the value calculations that customers make in their minds as being similar to weighing materials on an old-fashioned pair of scales, with product benefits in one tray and the outlays associated with obtaining those benefits in the other (see Figure 8.3). When customers evaluate competing services, they are basically comparing the relative net values.

Increasing Net Value by Reducing Nonfinancial Outlays

Although our focus in this chapter is mainly on the monetary aspects of pricing, you've probably noticed that people often pay a premium to save time, minimize unwanted effort, and obtain greater comfort. In other words, they are willing to pay higher prices to reduce

net value: the sum of all perceived benefits (gross value) minus the sum of all perceived outlays.

their nonfinancial outlays. Marketers can increase the net value of a service by adding benefits to the core product, enhancing supplementary services, or reducing the financial costs and other outlays associated with purchase and use of the product. People who fly first class versus coach class are paying for more spacious seating, better food, and more personalized attention from flight attendants in return for a more expensive fare. Other types of service companies have also recognized the different trade-offs that customers are willing to make and have created multiple levels of service. For example, Capital One Financial provides thousands of credit card options with varying benefits and interest rates. The company uses its sophisticated database technology to segment the market based on spending patterns and other consumer characteristics. It is then able to offer personally customized bundles of benefits that add value for customers while reducing risk for Capital One.[7]

In many cases, service firms can improve value by minimizing unwanted nonfinancial outlays for customers. Reducing such outlays may even cause firms to increase the monetary price for their services while still offering what customers perceive as "good value." Strategies for reducing nonfinancial outlays include:

➤ Reducing the time involved in service purchase, delivery, and consumption—especially time wasted in waiting for service delivery

➤ Minimizing unwanted psychological burdens during all stages of service consumption

➤ Eliminating unwanted physical effort, especially during the search and delivery processes

➤ Decreasing unpleasant sensory burdens by creating more attractive visual environments, reducing noise, installing more comfortable furniture and equipment, curtailing offensive smells, and ensuring that foods, drinks, or medicines taste appealing

FOUNDATIONS OF PRICING STRATEGY

The foundations underlying pricing strategy can be described as a tripod, with costs to the provider, competition, and value to the customer as the three legs (see Figure 8.4). The costs that a firm needs to recover usually impose a minimum or floor price for a specific service offering. The perceived value of the offering to customers sets a maximum, or ceiling. The price charged by competitors for similar services typically deter-

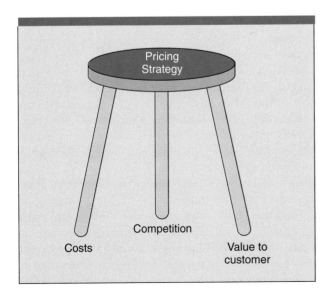

Costs

Competition

Value to customer

FIGURE 8.4

The Pricing Tripod

mines where, within the floor-to-ceiling range, the price should actually be set. Let's look at each leg of the pricing tripod in more detail.

Cost-Based Pricing

cost-based pricing: the practice of relating the price to be charged to the costs associated with producing, delivering, and marketing a product.

Cost-based pricing involves setting prices relative to financial costs. Companies seeking to make a profit must set a price sufficient to recover the full costs—variable, semi-variable, and fixed—of producing and marketing a service. A sufficient margin must also be added to provide the desired level of profit at the predicted sales volume. When fixed costs are high and the variable costs of serving an additional customer are very low, managers may feel that they have tremendous pricing flexibility and be tempted to price low in order to make an extra sale. However, there can be no profit at the end of the year unless all relevant costs have been recovered. Firms that compete on the basis of low prices need to analyze their cost structure and identify the sales volume needed to break even at particular prices.

Regulatory Pressures   Not all service firms are free to charge whatever price they choose. Most local utilities—like telephone, water, cable TV, electricity, and gas—have been regulated historically by government agencies that control all changes in prices and terms of service. Industry regulators or politicians, responding to complaints about excessively high prices, sometimes put pressure on these types of businesses to clarify and account for service costs.

Sometimes companies lack the necessary information to calculate the costs associated with serving different types of users. In this case, managers may simply determine the total costs incurred during a certain period, divide them by actual unit sales, calculate an average cost per unit of service (e.g., kilowatt-hours or monthly phone line rental fees), and add a certain percentage for profit. However, more sophisticated costing analysis in the telecommunications industry has shown that this is not always the most effective pricing strategy. The results of this analysis indicated that business users had been subsidizing household subscribers who were, in fact, much more expensive to serve. The net result was a shift in regulatory policy to allow relatively larger price increases for households than for business users.

activity-based costing: an approach to costing based on identifying the activities being performed and then determining the resources that each consumes.

Activity-Based Costing   It's a mistake to look at costs from just an accounting perspective. Progressive managers view them as an integral part of their company's efforts to create value for customers.[8] Unfortunately for the accountants, costs have nothing to do with value, which is market driven.[9] Customers aren't interested in what it costs the firm to produce a service; instead, they focus on the relationship between price and value. **Activity-based costing** (ABC) provides a structured way of thinking about activities and the resources that they consume.

Many firms have developed ABC systems that link resource expenses to the variety and complexity of products produced, not just to physical volume. Instead of focusing on expense categories, such as labor or fuel, ABC analysis zeroes in on the activities that are performed and then determines the cost of each activity as it relates to each expense category. As activities are segregated, a cost hierarchy emerges, reflecting the level at which the cost is incurred. For instance, unit-level activities need to be performed for each unit of service (such as rotating the tires on a customer's car at a service garage), whereas batch-level activities relate to each batch or set-up of work performed (for instance, periodically maintaining the tire rotation equipment).

Cooper and Kaplan note "ABC analysis enables managers to slice into the business in many different ways—by product or group of similar products, by individual customer or client group, or by distribution channel."[10] Thus ABC analysis can pinpoint differences in the costs of serving individual customers, while traditional cost analysis tends to result in loading the same overhead costs on all customers. This can lead to the assumption that large customers are more profitable. But a large customer who makes extensive demands on a supplier may, in fact, be less profitable than a small and undemanding customer.

Controlling costs by cutting back certain activities often leads to reduced value for customers because a curtailed activity may be crucial to providing a certain level and quality of service. Many telecommunications firms created marketing problems for themselves when they dismissed customer service staff to save money. This strategy resulted in a sharp decline in service responsiveness that led discontented customers to take their business elsewhere.

Competition-Based Pricing

If customers see little or no difference between the services offered in the marketplace, they may just choose the cheapest alternative. Under conditions of **competition-based pricing**, the firm with the lowest cost per unit of service enjoys an enviable marketing advantage. It has the option of either competing on price at levels that higher-cost competitors cannot afford to match, or charging the going market rate and earning larger profits than competing firms.

competition-based pricing: the practice of setting prices relative to those charged by competitors.

Price Leadership   In some industries, one firm may act as the **price leader**, with others taking their cue from this company. You can see this phenomenon at the local level when several gas stations compete within a short distance of one another, or on opposite corners of a crossroads. As soon as one station raises or lowers its prices, each of the others will follow promptly. During boom times in competitive industries such as airlines, hotels, and rental cars, firms are often willing to go along with the leader since prices tend to be set at a level that allows good profits. However, during an economic downturn, these industries quickly find themselves with surplus productive capacity. To attract more customers, one firm (often not the original leader) may cut prices. Since pricing is the easiest and fastest marketing variable to change, a price war may result overnight as competitors rush to match the competition's bargain prices.

price leader: a firm that takes the initiative on price changes in its market area and is copied by others.

Price Bids and Negotiations   Industrial buyers sometimes request bids from competing service suppliers. Companies who outsource contracts to provide food service or facilities maintenance often use this approach to pricing. Under these conditions, each bidder needs to review costs and think about what the buyer might be willing to pay in addition to estimating the level of bid that competitors are likely to submit. The more tightly specified the buyer's requirements, the less opportunity there is to differentiate one bidder's offer from another. The terms of the bid will specify whether the bids are to be sealed or not, and whether the buyer is obligated to take the lowest bid. If the buyer feels that the bids are too high, it may change the specifications and invite a new round of bidding.

An alternative to bidding is negotiation. The firm may request proposals from several suppliers and then negotiate with a short list of those firms that seem the most qualified and have offered the most relevant or innovative approaches. Large consulting projects, accounting audits, and engineering studies are often initiated through requests for proposals. In this type of situation, the buyer may conduct several rounds of negotiations, giving participating suppliers at least some information about competing offers as an incentive to lower their prices, conduct the work faster, or offer more features.

Value-Based Pricing

Service pricing strategies are often unsuccessful because they lack any clear association between price and value.[11] In discussing **value-based pricing**, Berry and Yadav propose three strategies for capturing and communicating the value of a service: uncertainty reduction, relationship enhancement, and cost leadership.

value-based pricing: the practice of setting prices with reference to what customers are willing to pay for the value they believe they will receive.

benefit-driven pricing:
the strategy of relating the
price to that aspect of the
service that directly creates
benefits for customers.

flat-rate pricing: the
strategy of quoting a fixed
price for a service in advance
of delivery.

Pricing Strategies to Reduce Uncertainty   If customers are unsure about how much value they will receive from a particular service, they may remain with a known supplier or not purchase at all. **Benefit-driven pricing** helps reduce uncertainty by focusing on that aspect of the service that directly benefits customers (requiring marketers to research what aspects of the service the customers do and do not value). This strategy requires firms to communicate service benefits clearly so that customers can see the relationship between value and costs. **Flat-rate pricing** involves quoting a fixed price in advance of service delivery so that there are no surprises. This approach transfers the risk from the customer to the supplier in the event that service production costs more than anticipated. Flat-rate pricing can be an effective differentiation tool in industries where service prices are unpredictable and suppliers are poor at controlling their costs.

Relationship Enhancement   In general, discounting to win new business is not the best way to attract customers who will remain loyal over time, since those who are attracted by cut-rate pricing are easily enticed away by competing offers.[12] However, offering discounts when customers purchase two or more services together may be a viable relationship-building strategy. The greater the number of different services a customer purchases from a single supplier, the closer the relationship is likely to be. Both parties get to know each other better, and it's more inconvenient for such customers to take their business elsewhere.

Cost Leadership   This strategy is based on achieving the lowest costs in an industry. Low-priced services have particular appeal to customers who are on a tight financial budget. They may also lead purchasers to buy in larger volumes. One challenge when pricing low is to convince customers that they shouldn't equate price with quality—they

Southwest Airlines: Low-Price Leader with a Low-Cost Culture

The most consistently profitable airline in North America is Southwest Airlines, which emphasizes relatively short-haul, point-to-point routes within the United States and has no international service.[13] Southwest's strategy is to price low enough to compete with surface travel by car, bus, or train, rather than pricing to compete against other airlines. Whenever it enters a new market, demand increases substantially as people shift from other modes of transportation, start to travel more frequently, or make trips they would not previously have made before.

Supporting Southwest's low-price marketing efforts is a low-cost operational strategy and a culture among the airline's dedicated employees of doing everything possible to keep costs low, including working very productively. "Thanks to the Culture at Southwest Airlines," observed a recent annual report, "we do not have to motivate our Employees with programs to reduce costs; rather it is their goal each and every day."

By minimizing the amount of time aircraft spend at the gate, Southwest keeps them in the air more hours per day. Using only one aircraft type, the Boeing 737, in its fleet of some 350 aircraft simplifies the airline's operation and saves further costs. Southwest offers a very basic core service (transportation), with few of the supplementary elements found in full-service carriers. But it manages customer expectations so that travelers are not surprised to find no reserved seats, no meals, and no baggage transfer to other airlines. The absence of these supplementary services contributes to Southwest's record as having the lowest costs per seat-mile of any major American carrier. Southwest creates value by saving its customers time and money and by doing a superb job of delivering basic air transportation safely, reliably, and consistently, with friendly employees providing a human touch.

Source: Southwest Airlines Annual Reports (Dallas, 1996–1999).

must feel they are also getting good value. A second challenge is to ensure that economic costs are kept low enough to enable the firm to make a profit. Some service businesses have built their entire strategy around being the **cost leader**, which enables them to remain profitable despite rock bottom prices. Southwest Airlines provides a classic case of a focused low-cost pricing strategy that continues to be highly successful. The airline's approach is based on a low-cost culture that competitors find difficult to imitate (see the boxed story "Southwest Airlines: Low-Price Leader with a Low-Cost Culture").

cost leader: a firm that bases its pricing strategy on achieving the lowest costs in its industry.

PRICING AND DEMAND

In most services, there's an inverse relationship between price levels and demand levels. Demand tends to fall as price rises. This phenomenon has implications for revenue planning and also for filling capacity in businesses that experience wide swings in demand over time.

Price Elasticity

The concept of elasticity describes how sensitive demand is to changes in price. When **price elasticity** is at "unity," sales of a service rise (or fall) by the same percentage that prices fall (or rise). When a small price change has a big impact on sales, demand for that product is said to be *price elastic*. But when a change in price has little effect, demand is described as *price inelastic*. One advantage of Internet-based marketing is that it gives firms the opportunity to test prices continuously to determine customers' responses to price variations.[14]

price elasticity: the extent to which a change in price leads to a corresponding change in demand in the opposite direction. (Demand is described as "price inelastic" when changes in price have little or no impact on demand.)

Demand can often be segmented according to customers' sensitivity to price or service features. For example, few theaters, concert halls, and stadiums have a single, fixed admission price for performances. Instead, prices vary according to (1) seat locations, (2) performance times, (3) projected staging costs, and (4) the anticipated appeal of the performance. In establishing prices for different blocks of seats and deciding how many seats to offer within each price block (known as scaling the house), theater managers need to estimate the demand within each price category. A poor pricing decision may result in many empty seats in some price categories and immediate sell-outs (and disappointed customers) in other categories.

Management also needs to know theatergoers' preferences for scheduling of performances, such as matinees versus evenings, weekends versus weekdays, and even seasonal variations. In each instance, the goal is to manage demand over time to maximize attendance, revenues, or a combination of the two (e.g., maximizing revenues, subject to a minimum attendance goal of 70 percent of all seats sold at each performance). A good reason for seeking to achieve sell-outs is that they encourage people to book and pay in advance (thus committing themselves) instead of waiting until the last minute when they might change their minds.

What if the mission statement includes the goal of attracting less-affluent segments, such as students and senior citizens? In such cases, management may wish to set aside some seats at a discount for people in those target segments. In a theater context, this social goal is sometimes addressed by offering unsold tickets at deeply discounted prices on the day of the performance.

Yield Management

Service organizations often use the percentage of capacity sold as a measure of operational efficiency. By themselves, however, these percentage figures tell us little about the relative profitability of the customer base. High utilization rates may be obtained at the expense of heavy discounting, or even outright give-aways.

yield management: a pricing strategy based on charging different prices to different users in order to maximize the revenue yield that can be derived from a firm's available capacity at any specific point in time.

Yield management pricing strategies are based on maximizing the revenue yield that can be derived from available capacity at any given time. Effective yield management models can significantly improve a company's profitability. Airlines, hotels, and car rental firms, in particular, have become adept at varying their prices in response to the price sensitivity of different market segments at different times of the day, week, or season. The challenge is to capture sufficient customers to fill the organization's perishable capacity without selling at lower prices to those customers who would have been willing to pay more.

How does a firm know what level of demand to expect at different prices in a market environment where the factors influencing demand are constantly changing? Many markets are very dynamic. For instance, the demand for both business and pleasure travel changes in response to competition and economic conditions. Although business travelers may be less sensitive to price changes, tourists and other pleasure travelers may be so price sensitive that special promotions involving discounted airfares and hotel room rates can encourage them to undertake trips that they wouldn't otherwise have made.

Advances in software and computing power have made it possible for managers to use sophisticated mathematical models to address complicated yield management issues. In the case of an airline, for example, these models integrate massive historical databases on past passenger travel with real-time information on current bookings. The output helps analysts predict how many passengers would want to travel between two cities at a particular fare on a flight leaving at a specified time and date. Airlines use yield management analysis to allocate seats at different fares (known as **price buckets**) for a specific flight with the objective of improving its yield.

price bucket: an allocation of service capacity (for instance, seats) for sale at a particular price.

The use of price buckets illustrates the concept of price customization—that is, charging different customers different prices for what is, in effect, the same product. The basic idea is simple: have people pay prices based on the value they put on the product. As Simon and Dolan point out, "Obviously you can't just hang out a sign saying 'Pay me what it's worth to you' or 'It's $80 if you value it that much but only $40 if you don't.' You have to find a way to segment customers by their valuations. In a sense, you have to 'build a fence' between high-value customers and low-value customers so the 'high' buyers can't take advantage of the low price."[15] Successful yield management strategies require an understanding of the shape of the demand curve and an ability to relate the size and price levels of the different "buckets" to different value segments (see Figure 8.5).

rate fences: techniques for separating customers so that segments for whom the service offers high value are unable to take advantage of lower-priced offers.

Fencing Mechanisms   Firms need to be able to separate or "fence off" different value segments so that customers for whom the service offers high value are unable to purchase it cheaply. **Rate fences** can be either physical or nonphysical and involve setting qualifications that must be met in order to receive a certain level of discount from the full price.[16] Physical fences include observable characteristics of the customer (like child versus adult) and service characteristics such as class of travel, type of hotel room, or inclusion of certain amenities with a higher price (free breakfast at a hotel, free golf cart at a golf course). Nonphysical fences include penalties for canceling or changing an inexpensive reservation, requirements for advance purchase, group membership or affiliation, and time of use (e.g., happy hours in bars before 8:00 P.M., travelers must stay over a Saturday night to obtain a cheap airline booking).

Customer-Led Pricing: Auctions and Bids

auction: a selling procedure managed by a specialist intermediary in which the price is set by allowing prospective purchasers to bid against each other for a product offered by a seller.

One method of pricing that has attracted a lot of attention with the advent of the Internet is inviting customers to bid the price that they are prepared to pay. The Internet provides a good medium for **auctions** because of its ability to aggregate buyers from all around the world. DoveBid, a long-established auctioneer of capital assets, now

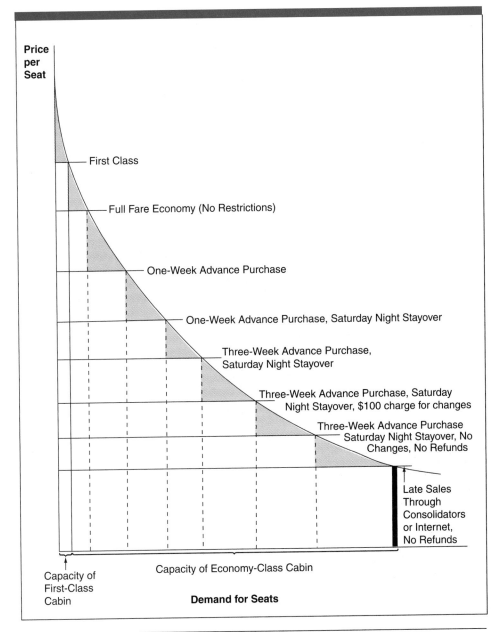

Note: Shaded areas denote amount of consumer surplus (goal of segmented pricing is to minimize this).

conducts Webcast business auctions worldwide (Figure 8.6). DoveBid's Webcast auctions are open-outcry auctions broadcast live via the Internet, allowing remote buyers around the globe to bid real-time against bidders who are on-location at plant auctions. This type of auction increases the number of auction bidders as well as creating price premiums. Auctions employing the speed and reach of the Internet are particularly useful for corporate purchasers seeking to identify sellers of such time-sensitive service products as energy, telecommunications capacity, and advertising space, and then bid competitively for the amount and type that they need.[17]

The Web also offers many opportunities for consumers to bid on prices for goods and services. eBay.com (which describes itself as "the world's online marketplace")

FIGURE 8.6

In Auctions, the Highest Bidder
Usually Sets the Selling Price

dominates the U.S. market and has plans to expand worldwide. Its unique approach to helping individual customers sell to each other is reflected in the following statement from its home page:

> Welcome! eBay is the world's first, biggest and best person-to-person online trading community. It's your place to find the stuff you want, to sell the stuff you have and to make a few friends while you're at it.[18]

Some financial services are sold through auctions. Rather than approaching individual financial institutions for a mortgage or other loan, borrowers can enter their requirements and personal situations at a Web site that solicits bids for the required loans. And online market makers let buyers decide how much they are willing to offer for many other types of services. uBid.com recently held an auction for an eight-day Hawaiian vacation on its site. The highest accepted bid was $519, but most successful bidders ended up paying only $99![19]

PUTTING PRICING STRATEGIES INTO PRACTICE

Although the main decision in pricing is usually seen as how much to charge, there are other important decisions to be made. Table 8.1 summarizes the questions that service marketers need to ask themselves as they design and implement a pricing strategy.

How Much to Charge?

Realistic decisions on pricing are critical for financial solvency. The pricing tripod model (Figure 8.4) provides a useful departure point. The task begins with determining the relevant financial costs, which set the relevant "floor" price. The second step is to establish a "ceiling" price for specific market segments. This involves assessing market sensitivity to different prices, which reflects both the overall value of the service to prospective customers and their ability to pay. Competitive prices provide a third input. The greater the number of similar alternatives, the greater the pressure to keep prices at or below those of the competition. The situation is particularly challenging when some competitors choose to compete on the basis of low price and couple this with an operating strategy designed to achieve low costs, as does Southwest Airlines.

The wider the gap between the floor and ceiling prices, the more room there is for maneuvering. If a ceiling price is below the floor price, the manager has several choices. One alternative is to recognize that the service is noncompetitive, in which case it should be discontinued. The other is to modify it in ways that differentiate it from the competition and add value for prospective customers. This makes it competitive at a higher price.[20]

Finally, a specific figure must be set for the price that customers will be asked to pay. Should the firm price in round numbers or try to create the impression that prices are

---

TABLE 8.1
Some Pricing Issues

1. How much should be charged for this service?
   a. What costs is the organization attempting to recover? Is the organization trying to achieve a specific profit margin or return on investment by selling this service?
   b. How sensitive are customers to different prices?
   c. What prices are charged by competitors?
   d. What discount(s) should be offered from basic prices?
   e. Are psychological pricing points (e.g., $4.95 versus $5.00) customarily used?
2. What should be the basis of pricing?
   a. Execution of a specific task
   b. Admission to a service facility
   c. Units of time (hour, week, month, year)
   d. Percentage commission on the value of the transaction
   e. Physical resources consumed
   f. Geographic distance covered
   g. Weight or size of object serviced
   h. Should each service element be billed independently?
   i. Should a single price be charged for a bundled package?
3. Who should collect payment?
   a. The organization that provides the service
   b. A specialist intermediary (travel or ticket agent, bank, retailer, etc.)
   c. How should the intermediary be compensated for this work—flat fee or percentage commission?
4. Where should payment be made?
   a. The location at which the service is delivered
   b. A convenient retail outlet or financial intermediary (e.g., bank)
   c. The purchaser's home (by mail or phone)
5. When should payment be made?
   a. Before or after delivery of the service
   b. At which times of day
   c. On which days of the week
6. How should payment be made?
   a. Cash (exact change or not?)
   b. Token (where can these be purchased?)
   c. Stored value card
   d. Check (how to verify?)
   e. Electronic funds transfer
   f. Charge card (credit or debit)
   g. Credit account with service provider
   h. Vouchers
   i. Third-party payment (e.g., insurance company or government agency)?
7. How should prices be communicated to the target market?
   a. Through what communication medium? (advertising, signage, electronic display, sales people, customer service personnel)
   b. What message content (how much emphasis should be placed on price?)

slightly lower than they really are? If competitors set prices like $4.95 or $19.95, then charging $5.00 or $20.00 may make the firm appear uncompetitive. However, most services (aside from car rental firms and hotels) tend to avoid odd pricing—perhaps because this pricing strategy is often associated with a discount or low-quality image.[21]

An ethical issue concerns the practice of promoting a price that excludes tax, service charges, and other extras. This approach is misleading if customers expect the quoted price to be inclusive. Managers also need to recognize that changes in pricing policy sometimes result in consumer opposition. For instance, new ATM surcharges have generated numerous complaints about "price gouging" (see box titled "Consumers Protest ATM Surcharges").

What Should Be the Basis for Pricing?

To set a price, managers must define the unit of service consumption. Should it be based on completing a specific service task, such as repairing a piece of equipment, cleaning a jacket, or cutting a customer's hair? Should it be based on admission to a service performance, such as an educational program, film, concert, or sports event? Should it be time based, as in using an hour of a lawyer's time, occupying a hotel room for a night, or renting a car for a week? Should it be tied to value, as when an insurance company scales its premiums to reflect the amount of coverage provided or a realtor takes a percentage commission on the selling price of a house?

Some service prices are tied to consumption of physical resources like food, water, or natural gas. Rather than charging customers an hourly rate for occupying a table and

Consumers Protest ATM Surcharges

Most banks charge their customers an extra fee when they use a "foreign" ATM (that is, one belonging to another bank). This surcharge is on top of any service charges for account activity, which might be as much as $1.25 per transaction if the balance falls below a certain level. The surcharge, initially $1.00, was first implemented in 1996 after heavy lobbying by banks to convince the two largest ATM networks—Visa's "Plus" and MasterCard's "Cirrus"—to withdraw their ban on additional surcharges. The banks argued successfully that permitting surcharges would encourage placement of ATMs in useful, but out-of-the-way places where volume would be lower. By 1999, 90 percent of all banks were surcharging at an average rate of $1.35; in addition, all independently owned ATMs imposed charges, averaging $1.59 per transaction. The result was accusations by consumer groups of price gouging, leading to growing political pressure in the United States to limit or even ban surcharges. Banks responded with claims that making ATMs available to noncustomers was a service that offered value and that people were clearly prepared to pay for this convenience. However, data showed ATM usage peaking in late 1999 as more people used their debit cards to obtain cash when making purchases at grocery stores, which don't typically charge fees.

The big winners from surcharges appear to be several dozen small companies that install inexpensive ATMs and connect them to a national network. These nonbank ATMs impose a double surcharge: first the $1+ fee for use of a "foreign" ATM *plus* an additional charge that may be as high as $3 for a simple cash withdrawal. To make matters worse, nonbank ATMs often fail to disclose the extra surcharge. The first that users know about it is when they find it billed to their bank accounts.

Despite these drawbacks, many small business owners approve of the nonbanks' approach to doing business. When the owner of a minimart was unable to persuade a bank to put an ATM in his store, he leased a machine from a company for about $300 a month. Users pay an extra $1.50 surcharge for each transaction, of which $0.80 goes to the minimart owner. He claims that, thanks to the machine, his store attracts more customers and sells more merchandise, netting him a profit of up to $50 a month after paying the leasing fee.

Sources: D. Foust, S. Browden, and G. Smith, "Mad as Hell at the Cash Machine," *Business Week*, 15 September 1997, 124; "High ATM Fees, Low Profiles," *Wall Street Journal*, 4 December 1997, B1; Mike McNamee, "Why ATM Outrage Is So Misplaced," *Business Week*, 29 November 1999.

chairs, restaurants put a sizeable mark-up on the food and drink items consumed. Long-distance phone call pricing reflects a combination of distance and time rates. Transportation firms have traditionally charged by distance, with freight companies using a combination of weight or cubic volume and distance to set their rates. Another straightforward pricing strategy involves charging a flat rate, like postal charges for domestic letters below a certain weight or a zone rate for packages that groups geographic distances into broad clusters. These policies have the virtue of consistency, but they ignore relative market strength on different routes.

Price Bundling   Many services unite a core product with various supplementary services, such as a cruise ship where the tariff includes meals and bar service. Should such service packages be priced as a whole (referred to as a "bundle"), or should each element be priced separately? If people prefer to avoid making many small payments, **price bundling** may be preferable—and it's certainly simpler to administer. However, if customers dislike being charged for product elements they don't use, itemized pricing may be better. Bundled prices offer a guaranteed revenue from each customer, while giving users a clear idea in advance of how much the bill will be. By contrast, unbundled pricing provides customers with flexibility. Some firms offer an array of choices. Mobile phone subscribers, for instance, can select from among several service options. One choice involves paying a small monthly fee for a basic service and then extra for each call. Another alternative is to pay a higher flat rate in return for several hundred minutes of calling time. At the top of the pricing scale is the option that provides business users with unlimited access to long-distance calls over a prescribed area.

price bundling: the practice of charging a base price for a core service plus additional fees for optional supplementary elements.

Discounting   To attract the attention of prospective buyers or to boost sales during a period of low demand, firms may discount their prices, often publicizing this price cut with coupons or an advertising campaign. Marketers of subscription services, such as cable television, Internet service, cellular telephone service, or credit cards, often employ a strategy of offering the service at a discount—or even free of charge—for an introductory period. There are risks to a **discounting** strategy. It dilutes the contribution from each sale, may attract customers whose only loyalty is to the firm that can offer the lowest price on the next transaction, and may give a bargain to customers who would have been willing to pay more. Nevertheless, selective price discounting targeted at specific market segments can help to fill capacity that would otherwise go unused. Volume discounts are sometimes used to cement the loyalty of large corporate customers, who might be inclined to spread their purchases among several different suppliers. Rewarding smaller customers by occasionally offering them a discount off their next purchase may also build loyalty.

discounting: a strategy of reducing the price of an item below the normal level.

Who Should Collect Payment?

Sometimes firms choose to delegate provision of supplementary services like billing to an intermediary. Although the original supplier pays a commission, using a third party may still be cheaper and more efficient than performing those tasks itself. Commonly used intermediaries include travel agents who make hotel and transportation bookings; ticket agents who sell seats for theaters, concert halls, and sports stadiums; and retailers who sell services ranging from prepaid phone cards to home and equipment repair.

Where Should Payment Be Made?

Payment for many services is collected at the service facility just before or immediately following service delivery. When consumers purchase a service well in advance of using it, there are obvious benefits to using intermediaries that are more conveniently located, or allowing payment by mail. (Airports, theaters, and stadiums, for instance, are often situated some distance from where potential customers live or work.) A growing number of service providers now accept credit cards for telephone bookings and sales over the Internet.

The simplicity and speed with which payment is made may influence the customer's perceptions of overall service quality. Thus service firms should pay special attention to providing payment collection procedures that are both efficient and effective from both the customers' and the companies' perspectives. Poorly designed payment methods may encourage "jaycustomer" behaviors like delayed payments—or worse yet—no payment at all. For example, one driver told a journalist that he refuses to pay tolls at New Jersey's automated tollbooths "on principle, because the toll plazas are badly designed and irritating—the state set up a system so bad, you have to abuse it."[22]

When Should Payment Be Made?

Two basic options are to ask customers to pay in advance (e.g., an admission charge, airline ticket, or postage stamps), or to bill them on completion of service delivery (e.g., restaurant bills and repair charges). Occasionally a service provider may ask for an initial payment in advance of service delivery, with the balance being due later (e.g., management consulting). This approach is also quite common with expensive repair and maintenance jobs, especially when the firm—often a small business with limited working capital—must buy materials up front. Asking customers to pay in advance means that the buyer is paying before the benefits are received. But prepayments may be advantageous to the customer as well as to the provider. Advance payment saves time and effort, especially with frequently purchased services.

How Should Payment Be Made?

Service businesses must decide on the types of payments they will accept. Although cash is a simple payment method, it raises security problems and is not always convenient for customers (especially for large purchases). Checks are convenient for customers, but sellers need to develop controls to discourage invalid payment. A $15 to $20 charge for returned checks is not uncommon at retail stores.

Credit cards are convenient and have the advantage of being accepted worldwide, regardless of currency. Businesses that refuse to accept such cards increasingly find themselves at a competitive disadvantage. Prepayment cards simplify the process of paying for services like road and bridge tolls or telephone calls. Internet service provider World Online has introduced a new type of prepayment card in the United Kingdom that operates on the prepaid model popular in the mobile phone industry. British consumers buy the cards from local retailers and then use a PIN number located on a scratch-off panel on the back of the card to open an account with World Online. These cards are mainly aimed at teenagers, but they are also marketed to the 50 percent of British adults who don't have credit cards. World Online plans to roll out the service across the rest of Europe.[23]

Smart cards store value in a microchip embedded within the card. To accept payment in this form, however, service firms must first install card readers. This sophisticated payment option requires partnerships between banks, retailers, and telephone companies. Working together, these partners can provide a smart card that serves as an "electronic wallet," enabling customers to download digital money to their cards from their bank accounts from an ATM or by telephone, using a special card reader. The latest innovation is card readers that can be attached to an account holder's computer. As a student, you may have personal experience with this form of payment, since many universities provide students with personalized smart cards that can be used to buy drinks from vending machines, make photocopies, pay fines for late return of library books, and many other purposes.

Other payment procedures include directing the bill to a third party for payment and using vouchers as supplements to (or instead of) cash. Insurance companies often designate approved garages to inspect and repair customers' vehicles when they are involved in accidents. To make life easier for the customer, the garage bills the insurance company directly for the work performed. This saves the customer the effort of paying personally, filing a claim, and waiting for reimbursement. Vouchers are sometimes provided by social service agencies to elderly or low-income people. Such a policy achieves the same benefits as discounting but avoids the need to publicize different prices or require cashiers to check eligibility.

In the business-to-business environment, most suppliers offer credit accounts, payable monthly, which generate membership relationships with customers. Online payments are often made through third-party firms like Clareon that specialize in managing electronic transactions between customers and vendors (Figure 8.7).

Communicating Prices to the Target Markets

The final task is to decide how the organization's pricing policies can best be communicated to its target markets. People need to know the price for some product offerings well in advance of purchase. They may also need to know how, where, and when that price is payable. This information must be presented in ways that are intelligible and unambiguous, so that customers will not feel misled. Managers must decide whether or not to include information on pricing in advertisements for the service or on the company's Web site. Advertising sometimes relates the price to those of competing products or to alternative ways of spending one's money. Customers expect salespeople and service representatives to be able to give prompt, accurate responses to queries about pricing, payment, and credit. Good signage at retail points of sale saves staff members from having to answer basic questions on prices.

Finally, when the price is presented in the form of an itemized bill, marketers should ensure that it is both accurate and intelligible. Hospital bills, which may run to several pages and contain dozens of items, have been much criticized for inaccuracy.[24] Telephone bills, too, used to be confusing. They were often printed on small sheets of

FIGURE 8.7

Clareon Offers Internet-Based B2B Payment Services

paper, crammed with technical jargon and it was hard to determine how the total charge due was computed. But many firms have worked to develop new and clearer formats that are easier for consumers to interpret.

Conclusion

Customers pay more to use a service than just the purchase price specified by the supplier. Additional outlays may include related financial costs (such as travel to the service site), time expenditures, psychological and sensory burdens, and physical effort. Customers are often willing to pay a higher price when the nonfinancial outlays are minimized, since the value of a service reflects the benefits that it delivers to the customer minus all the associated costs.

Pricing strategy must address the central issue of what price to charge for a given unit of service at a particular point in time, no matter how that unit may be defined. It's essential that the monetary price charged should reflect knowledge of the service provider's fixed and variable costs, competitor's pricing policies, and the value of the service to the customer.

Study Questions and Exercises

1. Is pricing strategy more difficult to implement in some service industries than in others? If so, why? Be specific and give examples.

2. Of the various nonfinancial outlays incurred by customers, which are likely to be the most significant in situations involving: (a) traditional retail banking; (b) home banking; (c) going to the movies; (d) taking a taxi in an unfamiliar city; (e) surgery?

3. Why is cost-based pricing (as it relates to financial costs) particularly problematic in service industries?

4. In what ways does competition-based pricing work in favor of many service providers? In what circumstances does it not?

5. Explain the concept of yield management in a service setting. How might it be applied to (a) a professional firm (e.g., consulting); (b) a restaurant; (c) a golf course?

6. Identify three aspects of pricing strategy that might raise ethical considerations. In each instance, how should such abuses be prevented?

7. From a customer perspective, what defines value in the following services: (a) a nightclub; (b) a hairdressing salon; (c) a legal firm specializing in business and tax law?

8. Choose a service organization and investigate its pricing policies and methods. In what respects are they similar to, or different from, what has been discussed in this chapter?

9. Review recent bills that you have received from service businesses. Evaluate each one against the following criteria: (a) general appearance and clarity of presentation; (b) easily understood terms of payment; (c) avoidance of confusing terms and definitions; (d) appropriate level of detail; (e) unanticipated ("hidden") charges; (f) accuracy; (g) ease of access to customer service in case of problems or disputes.

Endnotes

1. Thomas Eisenmann and Jon K. Rust, "Priceline WebHouse Club," *Journal of Interactive Marketing* 14, no. 4 (Autumn 2000): 47–72; Jeff Fischer, "Priceline as Rule Breaker," www.fool.com, 26 September 2000; Pamela L. Moore, "Will Priceline Need a Lifeline?" *Business Week*, 24 October 2000; "Priceline Says Fixing Customer Service Problems," Reuters News Service (reuters.com), 20 December 2000; and the priceline.com and *marketingguide.com* Web sites, December 2000.

2. Paul J. Kraus, "Pricing the Service Offering," in Teresa A. Schwartz and Dawn Iacobucci, *Handbook of Service Marketing and Management* (Thousand Oaks, CA: Sage Publications, 2000), 191–200.

3. Leonard L. Berry and Manjit S. Yadav, "Capture and Communicate Value in the Pricing of Services," *Sloan Management Review* 37 (Summer 1996): 41–51.

4. Richard W. Olshavsky, Andrew B. Aylesworth and DeAnna S. Kempf, "The Price-Choice Relationship: A Contingent Processing Approach," *Journal of Business Research* 33(1995): 207–218.

5. "Cellular without the Static," *Consumer Reports*, February 2001, 12–18.

6. Valarie A. Zeithaml, "Consumer Perceptions of Price, Quality, and Value: A Means-End Model and Synthesis of Evidence," *Journal of Marketing* 52 (July 1988): 2–21.

7. Adrian Slywotzky and David Morrison, "Off the Grid," *The Industry Standard*, 23 October 2000, 204–209. See also Jane Tanner, "Everyday Plastic Spun into Gold," nytimes.com, 17 September 2000.

8. H. T. Johnson and Robert S. Kaplan, *Relevance Lost: The Rise and Fall of Management Accounting* (Boston, MA: Harvard Business School Press, 1987).

9. Antonella Carù and Antonella Cugini, "Profitability and Customer Satisfaction in Services: An Integrated Perspective between Marketing and Cost Management Analysis," *International Journal of Service Industry Management* 10, no. 2 (1999): 132–156.

10. Robin Cooper and Robert S. Kaplan, "Profit Priorities from Activity-Based Costing," *Harvard Business Review*, May-June 1991.

11. Hermann Simon, "Pricing Opportunities and How to Exploit Them," *Sloan Management Review* 33 (Winter 1992): 71–84.

12. Frederick F. Reichheld, *The Loyalty Effect* (Boston: Harvard Business School Press, 1996), 82–84.

13. Christopher Lovelock, *Product Plus* (New York: McGraw-Hill, 1994), Chapter 6; Southwest Airlines, *1995 Annual Report* (Dallas, Texas, 1996), 8.

14. Walter Baker, Mike Marn, and Craig Zawada, "Price Smarter on the Net," *Harvard Business Review*, 79, February 2001, 122–127.

15. Hermann Simon and Robert J. Dolan, "Price Customization," *Marketing Management* (Fall 1998): 11–17.

16. Sheryl E. Kimes and Richard B. Chase, "The Strategic Levers of Yield Management," *Journal of Service Research* 1, no. 2 (November 1998): 156–166.

17. Amy E. Cortese and Marcia Stepanek, "Good-bye to Fixed Pricing?" *Business Week*, 4 May 1999, 71–84.

18. From the eBay Web site, www.eBay.com, December 2000.

19. From the uBid Web site, www.uBid.com, December 2000.

20. Cristopher C. Eugster, Jatin N. Kakkar, and Eric V. Roegner, "Bringing Discipline to Pricing," *The McKinsey Quarterly* no. 1 (2000): 132–139.

21. K. Douglas Hoffman, Lou W. Turley, and Scott W. Kelley, "Pricing Retail Services," *Journal of Business Research*, forthcoming 2001.

22. "The Cheater Principle," *The Wall Street Journal*, 25 August 2000, W1.

23. Wendy McAuliffe, "Pre-paid 'Credit' Card for the Web," from the zdnet.co.uk/news/2000 site, 4 September 2000.

24. See, for example, Anita Sharpe, "The Operation Was a Success; The Bill Was Quite a Mess," *Wall Street Journal*, 17 September 1997, 1.

chapter nine

Promotion and Education

Enterprise Rent-a-Car Courts Insurance Companies as Well as Consumers

Although most people probably think of vacation travel when Enterprise Rent-a-Car comes to mind, the company's roots are in the business-to-business arena.[1] Founder Jack Taylor started Enterprise as an auto-leasing service in 1957 out of the Cadillac shop where he worked. But business didn't really take off until the early 1980s when he switched his primary focus from the highly competitive consumer market into the less-crowded replacement rental market, taking advantage of new legislation requiring insurance companies to provide their customers with rental cars while their own vehicles were being repaired or replaced following accidents or theft. With this focus, Enterprise grew quickly and the company now holds a majority share of the U.S. replacement market. But it also targets customers in the business and leisure travel markets and is expanding abroad. Ninety percent of its 4,400 offices and its fleet of half a million cars are based in the United States, with the balance in Canada, Britain, Ireland, and Germany. Enterprise is now one of the world's largest car rental companies.

In addition to exploiting the replacement niche, what else makes Enterprise so successful? One reason is the company's location strategy, which emphasizes convenient access from people's homes and workplaces, placing 90 percent of the American population within 15 minutes of an Enterprise office. Its largest offices are limited to a maximum of 300 vehicles—in sharp contrast to some of its competitors, which may locate several thousand cars at a major airport.

Enterprise enjoys many advantages not found in the traditional model of car rental firms. They include avoiding the heavy expenses associated with airport space rental, not replacing its fleet as often, renting cars for longer periods of time, and experiencing more stability in demand (in contrast to fluctuations in business and pleasure travel, car accidents and breakdowns happen more consistently). And, as Jon LeSage, editor of *Auto Rental News*, observed, "repairs always take longer than they are supposed to."

The company is devoted to effective salesmanship and good customer service. In particular, it employs direct-marketing strategies to court the insurance companies that provide their policyholders with replacement vehicles when their own are stolen, under repair, or damaged beyond repair. Professionally trained telemarketers contact insurance agents to persuade them to set up accounts with Enterprise. They offer discounted rates and a direct billing option so that the insurance companies' customers will never have to pay personally for their Enterprise car rentals. The direct billing option makes it easier for the companies to handle financial transactions. Thanks to these attractive benefits and the skills of the highly trained telemarketers, Enterprise continues to capture a large percentage of the replacement market. Once an account is established, the company maintains the relationship by sending employees to make weekly sales calls and deliver gifts like food and plants to help foster goodwill and ensure that the insurance provider remains a loyal Enterprise customer.

The company also reaches out directly to individual customers who need to rent a car for business or pleasure. Its mass media advertising in 2000 was designed to draw attention to a distinctive aspect of

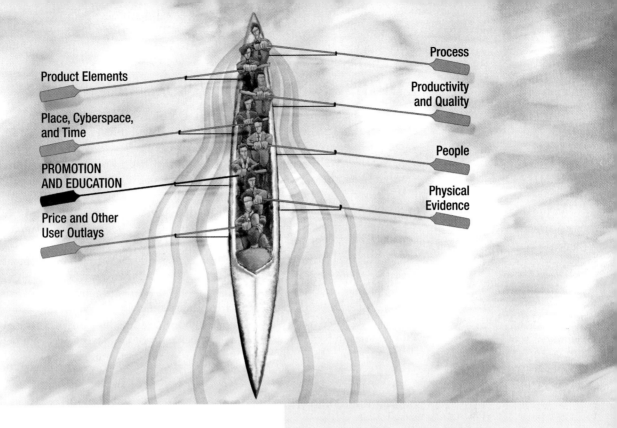

Product Elements

Place, Cyberspace, and Time

PROMOTION AND EDUCATION

Price and Other User Outlays

Process

Productivity and Quality

People

Physical Evidence

its service—picking people up at their homes or place of employment. The ads featured a car wrapped like a package speeding along the road with the name Enterprise emblazoned on the side (an advertising icon for almost a decade) and promoted the slogan: "Pick Enterprise. We'll Pick You Up." Complementing other marketing communications is the company's Web site, www.enterprise.com, which provides additional information about Enterprise (including job opportunities), and enables customers to search online for the nearest location, check prices, and then make a booking.

Learning Objectives

After reading this chapter, you should be able to

⇒ explain what is distinctive about marketing communications strategy for services

⇒ understand how the level of customer contact affects communication strategy

⇒ list common educational and promotional objectives for services

⇒ describe the marketing communications mix for services

⇒ discuss potential uses of the Internet as a communication channel

THE ROLE OF MARKETING COMMUNICATION

Marketing communications, in one form or another, are essential to a company's success. Enterprise Rent-a-Car could not have built its business without personal selling and advertising. Without effective communications, few prospects would ever have learned of Enterprise's existence, what it had to offer them, and how to use its services. In the absence of follow-up sales calls, a user-friendly Web site, and good signage, customers might be more easily lured away by competitors and competitive offerings, and there would be no proactive management and control of the firm's identity. So managers need to debate the question: ***How should we communicate what our service has to offer?***

Much confusion surrounds the scope of marketing communication. Some people still define it narrowly as the use of paid media advertising, public relations, and professional salespeople. But this view doesn't recognize the many other ways that a firm can communicate with its customers. The location and atmosphere of a service delivery facility, corporate design features like the consistent use of colors and graphic elements, the appearance and behavior of employees, Web site design—all of these factors contribute to an impression in the customer's mind.

Communicating with Customers

Communication efforts serve not only to attract new users but also to maintain contact with an organization's existing customers and build relationships with them. As we emphasized in Chapter 5, reinforcing loyalty and securing repeat sales are usually central to a firm's long-term profitability. Nurturing customer relationships depends on a comprehensive and up-to-date customer database, and the ability to make use of this in a personalized way.

Techniques for keeping in touch with customers and building their loyalty include direct mail and contacts by telephone or other forms of telecommunication, including

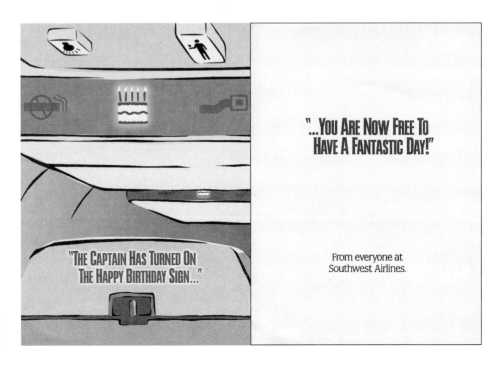

FIGURE 9.1

A Birthday Card from
Southwest Airlines

faxes, e-mail, and Web sites. Doctors, dentists, and household maintenance services often post annual checkup reminders to their customers. Some businesses even send birthday and anniversary cards to valued customers (Figure 9.1). Banks and utility companies often include a brief newsletter with their account statements or print customized information on each statement in an effort to cross-sell additional services.

Internal Communications

Marketing communications can be used to communicate with service employees as well as with external customers. **Internal communications** from senior managers to their employees play a vital role in maintaining and nurturing a corporate culture founded on specific service values. Well-planned internal marketing efforts are especially necessary in large service businesses that operate in widely dispersed sites, sometimes around the world. Even when employees are working far from the head office in the home country, they still need to be kept informed of new policies, changes in service features, and new quality initiatives. Communications may also be needed to nurture team spirit and support common corporate goals. Consider the challenge of maintaining a unified sense of purpose at the overseas offices of companies such as Citibank, Air Canada, Marriott, or McDonalds, where people from different cultures who speak different languages must work together to create consistent levels of service.

> **internal communications:** all forms of communication from management to employees in a service organization.

Effective internal communications can help ensure efficient and satisfactory service delivery, achieve productive and harmonious working relationships, and build employee trust, respect, and loyalty. Commonly used media include internal newsletters and magazines, videotapes, private corporate television networks like those owned by FedEx and Merrill Lynch, Intranets (private networks of Web sites and e-mail that are inaccessible to the general public), face-to-face briefings, and promotional campaigns using displays, prizes, and recognition programs.

COMMUNICATION STRATEGIES FOR SERVICES

Several of the differences distinguishing services from goods have important marketing communications implications. Thus communication strategies need to reflect the special characteristics of services.[2]

Intangible Nature of Service Performances

Since services are performances rather than objects, their benefits can be difficult to communicate to customers. Service providers should use tangible cues whenever possible in their advertising campaigns, especially for low-contact services that involve few tangible elements.[3] It is also helpful to include "vivid information" that will produce a strong, clear impression on the senses, especially for services that are complex and highly intangible.[4] For example, an ad by a large law firm showed a picture of empty jurors' chairs to draw attention to its trial lawyers' skills in presenting complex cases to juries, which must then withdraw from the courtroom to deliberate on the verdict (Figure 9.2). Similarly, MasterCard television and print advertisements emphasize the tangible things that can be purchased with its credit card—complete with a listing of the price of each item. In each ad, all of the items purchased with the card lead to a priceless experience (a clever and memorable reference to the concept of intangibility).

At a very basic level, some companies have succeeded in creating tangible, recognizable symbols to associate with their corporate brand names. Animal motifs are common physical symbols for services. Examples include the eagle of the U.S. Postal Service

FIGURE 9.2

Advertising by Robins, Kaplan, Miller & Ciresi in *The Wall Street Journal*, Fall 2000

(also used by AeroMexico and Eagle Star Insurance), the black horse of Norfolk Southern Railroad and Britain's Lloyd's Bank, Merrill Lynch's bull, the lion of Dreyfus Funds and Royal Bank of Canada, and the Chinese dragon of Hong Kong's Dragonair. Easily recognizable corporate symbols are especially important for international companies when services are offered in markets where the local language is not written in Roman script or where a significant proportion of the population is functionally illiterate.

Some companies have created metaphors that are tangible in nature to help communicate the benefits of their service offerings. Insurance companies often use this approach to market their highly intangible products. Thus Allstate advertises that "You're in Good Hands," Traveler's umbrella motif suggests protection, and Prudential uses the Rock of Gibraltar as a symbol of corporate strength.

When possible, advertising metaphors should also include some information about *how* service benefits are actually provided.[5] Consider Trend Micro's problem in advertising its new antivirus monitoring service for corporate Internets. Most advertisements for antivirus protection feature devils or evil-looking insects (remember the Millennium Bug used to highlight the Y2K problem?). That approach may capture the reader's interest, but it doesn't show how virus protection actually works or how devastating its effects might be. In a technical context like this, explaining the problem and its solution in ways that senior management will understand is not always possible. Trend Micro's clever solution was to use the easily grasped metaphor of airport security guarding against terrorism. A picture of an aircraft was captioned "this is your company," a briefcase containing a bomb was labeled "this is a virus," and two security officers checking that bag on an X-ray machine were captioned, "This is Trend Micro."

Prudential's marketing communications seek to educate as well as sell; its advertising encourages prospective clients to obtain a free guide to estate planning and to discuss their situations with a Prudential professional.

Customer Involvement in Production

In high-contact services, customers are often concerned about the risks associated with service delivery and consumption. Sometimes these risks are financial or psychological in nature, but there can also be physical risks—as in many outdoor sports and organized adventure activities like rock-climbing, skiing, and white-water rafting. The providers of such services have both a legal and a moral responsibility to educate their clients. The better informed customers are of potential dangers, and what to do in the event of, say, a raft tipping its occupants into a stretch of foaming rapids, the more likely they are to remain safe and have an enjoyable experience. Basic information on signs and in instructional brochures may need to be reinforced by personal briefings from employees.

When customers are actively involved in service production, they need training to help them perform well—just as employees do. Improving productivity often involves innovations in service delivery. But the desired benefits won't be achieved if customers resist new, technologically based systems or avoid self-service alternatives. So, service marketers need to become educators. One approach recommended by advertising experts is to show service delivery in action.[6] Television is a good medium, because of its ability to engage the viewer as it displays a seamless sequence of events in visual form. Some dentists show their patients videos of surgical procedures before the surgery takes place. This educational technique helps patients prepare mentally for the experience and shows them what role they should play during service delivery.

Advertising and publicity can make customers aware of changes in service features and delivery systems. Marketers often use sales promotions to motivate customers, offering them incentives to make the necessary changes in their behavior. Publicizing price discounts is one way to encourage self-service on an ongoing basis. At self-service gas pumps, for instance, the price difference from full-service is often substantial. Other incentives to change include promotions that offer a chance to win a reward. And if necessary, well-trained customer-contact personnel can provide one-to-one tutoring to help customers adapt to new procedures.

Evaluating Service Offerings

Even if you understand what a service is supposed to do, you may have difficulty distinguishing one firm from another and knowing what level of performance to expect from a particular supplier. What can a service business do to attract your attention and your patronage? Possible solutions include: providing tangible clues related to service performance; highlighting the quality of equipment and facilities; and emphasizing employee characteristics such as their qualifications, experience, commitment, and professionalism.

Some performance attributes lend themselves better to advertising than others. When an airline wants to boast about its punctuality, reporting favorable statistics collected by a government agency offers credible support for this claim. However, airlines don't like to talk overtly about safety, because even the admission that things might go wrong makes many passengers nervous. Instead, they approach this ongoing customer concern indirectly, advertising the expertise of their pilots, the newness of their aircraft, and the skills and training of their mechanics.

In low-contact services where much of the firm's expertise is hidden, firms may need to illustrate equipment, procedures, and employee activities that are taking place backstage. For instance, how do prospective buyers know if they are getting the best value from insurance services? One approach is to show how the firm is trying to reduce losses due to accidents or to cut costs. Liberty Mutual has run ads using attention-getting headlines like

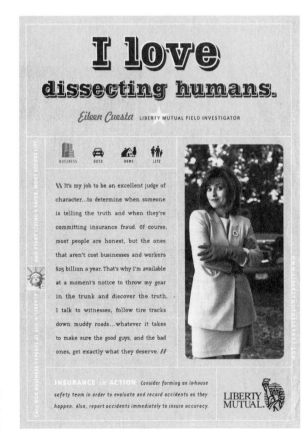

FIGURE 9.3

Liberty Mutual Advertising
Promotes the Firm's Efforts to
Counter Insurance Fraud

"Wake up, you're dead," which shows a grim-looking auto safety expert with a Ph.D. who is researching how to prevent highway accidents caused by driver fatigue. The company's "I love dissecting humans" ad includes an amusing photo of one of the company's field investigators, who describes her work in detecting and preventing insurance fraud (Figure 9.3). The fraud prevention ad shows just how serious the problem of jaycustomers is for the insurance industry, where fraudulent claims amount to an estimated $25 billion a year!

Supply-and-Demand Management

Many live service performances—like a seat at the Metropolitan Opera for Friday evening's performance of *Carmen*, a room at the Marriott on Monday, or a haircut at Supercuts on Tuesday morning—are time-specific and can't be stored for resale at a later date. Advertising and sales promotions can help to change the timing of customer use and thus help to match demand with the capacity available at a given time. Demand management strategies include reducing usage during peak demand periods and stimulating it during off-peak periods. Low demand outside peak periods poses a serious problem for service industries with high fixed costs, like hotels. One strategy is to run promotions that offer extra value—such as a room upgrade and a free breakfast, in an attempt to stimulate demand without decreasing price. When demand increases, the number of promotions can be reduced or eliminated.

Importance of Contact Personnel

In high-contact services, service personnel are central to service delivery. Their presence makes the service more tangible and, in many cases, more personalized. An ad that shows employees at work helps prospective customers understand the nature of the service encounter and implies a promise of the personalized attention that they can expect to receive (Figure 9.4). Advertisers must be realistic, since these messages help set cus-

FIGURE 9.4

A Uniformed Hotel Employee Leads a Guest Through the Check-in Script; Her Warmth Humanizes the Experience for Him

tomers' expectations. If a firm's brochures and ads show friendly, smiling workers but, in reality, most employees turn out to be glum, frazzled, or rude, customers will most certainly be disappointed. Advertising can also be effective in showing employees what customers are being promised. At a minimum, service personnel should be informed about the content of new advertising campaigns or brochures.

Reduced Role for Intermediaries

Intermediaries like retailers often play a key role in promoting products and teaching customers about their characteristics. Services are less likely than goods to be sold through channel intermediaries. Many service providers (such as universities, lawn care specialists, banks, restaurants, health clubs, and professional firms) sell directly to customers. But some service providers do rely on intermediaries for help in selling their products. Firms in the travel and insurance industries, which make extensive use of independent agents and brokers, must compete with other brands not only for physical display space but also for "top-of-mind" recall if they are to obtain adequate push from intermediaries in the distribution channels. Internal communication, personal selling, motivational promotions, and effective public relations can be critical in maintaining successful working relationships between intermediaries and service firms.

Setting Communication Objectives

When planning a campaign, marketers need to formulate specific communications objectives and select the most appropriate messages and tools to achieve them (see Table 9.1 for a list of common educational and promotional objectives for service businesses). To illustrate this point, let's assume that a rental car agency has defined the need to increase repeat purchase rates among business travelers as one of its key strategic objectives. In pursuit of this objective, the firm decides to implement an automatic upgrade program and an express delivery and drop-off system. For this plan to succeed, customers must be informed about these new features and educated on how to take advantage of them.

A specific set of communications objectives might be: (1) to create awareness of the new offering among all existing customers; (2) to attract the attention of prospective customers in the business traveler segment, inform them of the new features, and teach them how to use the new procedures effectively; (3) to stimulate inquiries and increase pre-bookings; and (4) to generate an increase in repeat patronage of 20 percent after six months.

Planning a marketing communications campaign should reflect a good understanding of the service product and the ability of prospective buyers to evaluate its characteristics in advance of purchase. It's also essential to understand target market segments and their exposure to different media, as well as consumer awareness of the product and attitudes toward it. Decisions include determining the content, structure, and style of the message

TABLE 9.1 Common Educational and Promotional Objectives in Service Settings	• Create memorable images of specific companies and their brands • Build awareness of and interest in an unfamiliar service or brand • Build preference by communicating the strengths and benefits of a specific brand • Compare a service with competitors' offerings and counter competitive claims • Reposition a service relative to competing offerings • Stimulate demand in low-demand periods and discourage demand during peak periods • Encourage trial by offering promotional incentives • Reduce uncertainty and perceived risk by providing useful information and advice • Provide reassurance (e.g., by promoting service guarantees) • Familiarize customers with service processes in advance of use • Teach customers how to use a service to their own best advantage • Recognize and reward valued customers and employees

to be communicated, its manner of presentation, and the media most suited to reaching the intended audience. Additional considerations include: the budget available for execution; time frames (as defined by such factors as seasonality, market opportunities, and anticipated competitive activities); and methods of measuring and evaluating performance.

THE MARKETING COMMUNICATIONS MIX

Most service marketers have access to numerous forms of communication, referred to collectively as the **marketing communications mix**. Different communication elements have distinctive capabilities relative to the types of messages that they can convey and the market segments most likely to be exposed to them. As shown in Figure 9.5, the mix includes personal contact, advertising, publicity and public relations, sales promotion, instructional materials, and corporate design.

How should service marketers approach the task of selecting communication elements to convey the desired messages efficiently and effectively to the target audience? In well-planned campaigns, several different communication elements may be used in ways that mutually reinforce each other. Effective sequencing of communications is important, since one element often paves the way for others. For example, advertising may encourage prospects to visit a Web site, request further information by mail, or shop in a specific store where they will be exposed to **retail displays** and can interact directly with a salesperson.

Communication experts draw a broad division between **personal communications**, involving personalized messages that move in both directions between two parties, and **impersonal communications**, in which messages move in only one direction and are generally targeted at a large group of customers and prospects rather than at a single individual. However, technology has created a gray area between the two. It's now very easy for a firm to combine word-processing technology with information from a database to create an impression of personalization. Think about the direct mail and e-mail messages that you have received, containing a personal salutation and perhaps some reference to your specific situation or past use of a particular product.

marketing communications mix: the full set of communication tools (both paid and unpaid) available to marketers.

retail displays: presentations in store windows and other locations of merchandise, service experiences, and benefits.

personal communications: direct communications between marketers and individual customers that involve two-way dialog (including face-to-face conversations, phone calls, and e-mail).

impersonal communications: one-way communications directed at target audiences who are not in personal contact with the message source (including advertising, promotions, and public relations).

FIGURE 9.5

The Marketing Communications Mix for Services

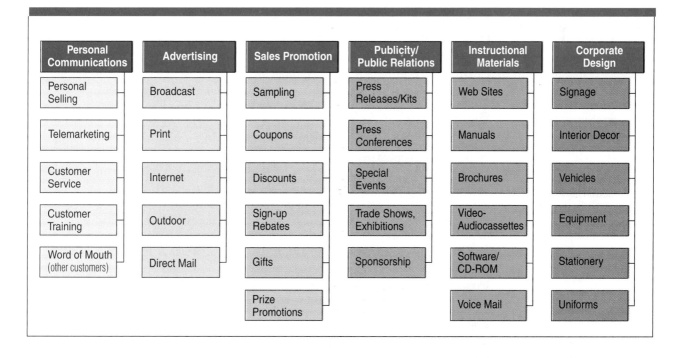

Personal Communications	Advertising	Sales Promotion	Publicity/ Public Relations	Instructional Materials	Corporate Design
Personal Selling	Broadcast	Sampling	Press Releases/Kits	Web Sites	Signage
Telemarketing	Print	Coupons	Press Conferences	Manuals	Interior Decor
Customer Service	Internet	Discounts	Special Events	Brochures	Vehicles
Customer Training	Outdoor	Sign-up Rebates	Trade Shows, Exhibitions	Video-Audiocassettes	Equipment
Word of Mouth (other customers)	Direct Mail	Gifts	Sponsorship	Software/ CD-ROM	Stationery
		Prize Promotions		Voice Mail	Uniforms

Personal Communications

As shown in Figure 9.5, personal communications include personal selling, telemarketing, customer training, customer service, and word of mouth.

personal selling: two-way communications between service employees and customers designed to directly influence the purchase process.

telemarketing: personal selling to prospective customers through the medium of the telephone.

Personal Selling   Interpersonal encounters in which efforts are made to educate customers and promote preference for a particular brand or product are referred to as personal selling. For infrequently purchased services like property, insurance, and funeral services, the firm's representative may act as a consultant to help buyers make their selections. Because face-to-face selling is usually expensive, it's most often used in business-to-business markets. A lower-cost alternative is **telemarketing**, involving use of the telephone to reach prospective customers. It's used by about 75 percent of all industrial companies.[7]

Relationship marketing strategies are often based on account management programs, where customers are assigned a designated account manager who acts as an interface between the customer and the supplier. Account management is most commonly practiced in industrial and professional firms that sell relatively complex services, resulting in an ongoing need for advice, education, and consultation. Examples of account management for individual consumers can be found in insurance, investment management, and medical services.

customer service: the provision of supplementary service elements by employees who are not specifically engaged in selling activities.

Customer Service   Employees in customer service positions are often responsible for delivery of a variety of supplementary services, including providing information, taking reservations, receiving payments, and problem solving. New customers, in particular, often rely on customer service personnel for assistance in learning how to use a service effectively and how to resolve problems.

When several different products are available from the same supplier, firms encourage their customer service staff to cross-sell additional services. However, this approach is likely to fail if strategies are not properly planned and executed.[8] In the banking industry, for example, a highly competitive marketplace and new technologies have forced banks to add more services in an attempt to increase their profitability. In many banks, tellers who traditionally provided customer service are now expected to promote new services to their customers as well. Despite training, many employees feel uncomfortable in this role and don't perform effectively as salespeople.

customer training: formal training courses offered by service firms to teach customers about complex service products.

Customer Training   Some companies, especially those selling complex business-to-business services, offer formal training courses to familiarize their customers with the service product and teach them how to use it to their best advantage.

word of mouth: positive or negative comments about a service made by one individual (usually a current or former customer) to another.

Word of Mouth   Recommendations from other customers can have a powerful influence on people's decisions to use a service, but word of mouth is a difficult form of communication for firms to control. Some advertisers try to encourage positive comments from customers who have already used a service since positive word of mouth can act as a powerful and highly credible selling agent.[9] In an effort to extend the reach of word of mouth, advertising and brochures sometimes feature comments from satisfied customers.

Research in the United States and Sweden shows that the extent and content of word of mouth is related to satisfaction levels. Customers holding strong views are likely to tell more people about their experiences than those with milder views. And extremely dissatisfied customers tell more people than those who are highly satisfied.[10]

Advertising

As the most dominant form of communication in consumer marketing, **advertising** is often the first point of contact between service marketers and their customers, serving to build awareness, inform, persuade, and remind. It plays a vital role in providing factual information about services and educating customers about product features and capabilities. To demonstrate this point, Grove, Pickett, and Laband carried out a study comparing newspaper and television advertising for goods and services[11]. Based on a review of 11,543 television advertisements over a 10-month period and of 30,940 newspaper display advertisements that appeared over a 12-month period, they found that ads for services were significantly more likely than those for goods to contain factual information on price; guarantees/warranties; documentation of performance; and availability (where, when, and how to acquire products).

One of the challenges facing advertisers is how to get their messages noticed. Television and radio broadcasts are cluttered with commercials, while newspapers and magazines sometimes seem to contain more ads than news and features. How can a firm hope to stand out from the crowd? Longer, louder commercials and bigger format ads are not necessarily the answer. Some advertisers stand out by using a sharply different format. For its ads in *Business Week*, where most advertising includes color photography and occupies one or two full pages, Williams Communications employs black-and-white cartoons occupying approximately half a page (Figure 9.6).

A broad array of paid advertising media is available, including broadcast (TV and radio), print (magazines and newspapers), movie theaters, and many types of outdoor

advertising: any form of nonpersonal communication by a marketer to inform, educate, or persuade members of target audiences.

"He absolutely hates stories about anachronistic networks, Ray. Try changing the subject to Williams Communications. He likes happy endings."

We're network top dog. Williams is local-to-global connectivity over the most-sophisticated next-generation network around. What's more, our big-time communications solutions always guarantee happy end-to-endings for your business.

Williams COMMUNICATIONS.

1-800-WILLIAMS • WWW.WILLIAMSCOMMUNICATIONS.COM • NYSE: WMB & WCG

FIGURE 9.6

Advertising by Williams Communications Uses Black-and-White Cartoons to Catch the Reader's Attention

media (posters, billboards, electronic message boards, and the exteriors of buses or bicycles). Some media are more focused than others, targeting specific geographic areas or audiences with a particular interest. Advertising messages delivered through mass media are often reinforced by direct marketing tools like mailings, telemarketing, faxes, or e-mail. Direct marketing, which offers the potential to send personalized messages to highly targeted micro-segments, is most likely to be successful when marketers possess a detailed database of information about customers and prospects.

Sales Promotion

sales promotion: a short-term incentive offered to customers and intermediaries to stimulate product purchase.

A few years ago, SAS International Hotels devised an interesting **sales promotion** targeted at older customers. If a hotel had vacant rooms, guests over 65 years of age could get a discount equivalent to their years (e.g., a 75-year-old could save 75 percent of the normal room price). All went well until a Swedish guest checked into one of the SAS chain's hotels in Vienna, announced his age as 102, and asked to be paid 2 percent of the room rate in return for staying the night. This request was granted, whereupon the spry centenarian challenged the general manager to a game of tennis—and got that, too. (The results of the game, however, were not disclosed!) Events like these are the stuff of dreams for PR people. In this case, a clever promotion led to a humorous, widely reported story that placed the hotel chain in a favorable light.

A useful way of looking at sales promotions is as a communication attached to an incentive. Sales promotions are usually specific to a time period, price, or customer group—sometimes all three, as in the SAS example. Typically, the objective is to accelerate the purchasing decision or motivate customers to use a specific service sooner, in greater volume with each purchase, or more frequently. Sales promotions for service firms may take such forms as samples, coupons and other discounts, gifts, and competitions with prizes. Used in these forms, sales promotions add value, provide a competitive edge, boost sales during periods when demand would otherwise be weak, speed the introduction and acceptance of new services, and generally get customers to act faster than they would in the absence of any promotional incentive.[12] The Cleanrite coupon

FIGURE 9.7

Cleanrite Coupon Encourages Repeat Usage

shown in Figure 9.7 is a simple example of a sales promotion designed to encourage past customers to become repeat customers.

Some promotional campaigns are very creative in their appeals to customers. For example, some international airlines provide passengers in first and business classes with free gifts including toiletries, pens, stationery, and playing cards. Gifts are sometimes offered simply to amuse customers and create a friendly environment. The Conrad Hotel in Hong Kong places a small teddy bear on each guest's bed and a yellow rubber duck in the bathroom; it reports that many guests take these items home with them.

Publicity and Public Relations

Public relations (PR) involves efforts to stimulate positive interest in an organization and its products by sending out news releases, holding press conferences, staging special events, and sponsoring newsworthy activities put on by third parties. A basic element in public relations strategy is the preparation and distribution of press releases (including photos and/or videos) that feature stories about the company, its products, and its employees. PR executives also arrange press conferences and distribute press kits when they feel a story is especially newsworthy. A key task performed by corporate PR specialists is to teach senior managers how to present themselves well at news conferences or in radio and television interviews.

Other widely used PR techniques include recognition and reward programs, obtaining testimonials from public figures, community involvement and support, fundraising, and obtaining favorable publicity for the organization through special events and *pro bono* work. These tools can help a service organization build its reputation and credibility; form strong relationships with its employees, customers, and the community; and secure an image conducive to business success.

Firms can also win wide exposure through sponsorship of sporting events and other high-profile activities where banners, decals, and other visual displays provide continuing repetition of the corporate name and symbol. For example, the U.S. Postal Service (USPS) was a major sponsor of the U.S. cycling team in the 2000 Tour de France. This provided many PR and advertising opportunities for the Postal Service including stamps, print articles, television news clips, and photos of the team members with "U.S. Postal Service" prominently displayed on their jerseys. USPS gained worldwide attention when team member Lance Armstrong won the Tour de France after a near-fatal battle with cancer.

Unusual activities can present an opportunity to promote a company's expertise. FedEx gained significant favorable publicity in December 2000 when it safely transported two giant pandas from Chengdu, China, to the National Zoo in Washington, D.C. The pandas flew in specially designed containers aboard an MD 11 aircraft renamed "FedEx PandaOne." In addition to press releases, the company also featured information about the unusual shipment on a special page in its Web site (Figure 9.8).

In the business-to-business marketplace, trade shows are a popular form of publicity.[13] They are not usually open to the public, and there is no entry fee. In many industries, trade shows are a great opportunity for business customers to find out about the latest products in their fields. Service vendors provide physical evidence in the form of exhibits, samples and demonstrations, and brochures to educate and impress these potential customers. For example, cosmetic surgeons from around the world attended trade shows to learn about advances in technology and equipment that will allow them to perform highly effective nonsurgical treatments with mysterious names like "botox," "vein sclerotherapy," and "collagen replacement therapy."

Trade shows can be very profitable promotional tools. Fifty percent of the sales leads generated at these shows can be closed with just one sales call—a much higher

public relations: efforts to stimulate positive interest in a company and its products by sending out news releases, holding press conferences, staging special events, and sponsoring newsworthy activities put on by third parties.

FIGURE 9.8

"Absolutely, Positively ... Pandas!" FedEx Promotes Its Role in an Unusual Shipment (*FedEx service marks used by permission.*)

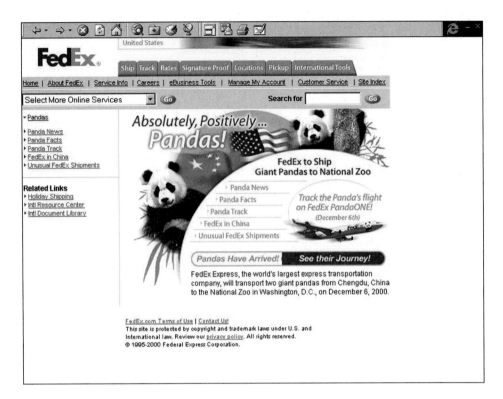

percentage than for leads generated in any other way. And a sales representative who usually reaches four to five prospective clients per day can average five qualified leads per *hour* at a show.

Instructional Materials

Promotion and education often go hand in hand. There's little point in promoting a new service (or service feature) if people are unsure of the benefits or don't know how to proceed. Service personnel are often called upon to play teaching roles, but they are not always available to help in the locations where customers need them. To remedy this problem, some firms offer free telephone calls to expert personnel or provide printed materials, video or audio instructions, or informative Web sites. Newspaper advertising by the CVS pharmacy chain encourages customers to use their telephones to access recorded information about prescription medications for a variety of different diseases.

Nowadays, many instructional media are technology based. Supermarkets and department stores sometimes feature a touch-screen store directory. Airlines show films to illustrate aircraft safety procedures and make customers aware of government regulations. Some banks install computerized displays that customers can use to learn about new financial products. Through access to Web sites, customers can access needed information from their homes or offices.

Corporate Design and Physical Evidence

corporate design: the consistent application of distinctive colors, symbols, and lettering to give a firm an easily recognizable identity.

Many service firms employ a unified and distinctive visual appearance for all tangible elements to facilitate recognition and reinforce a desired image. **Corporate design** strategies are usually created by external consulting firms and include such features as stationery and promotional literature, retail signage, uniforms, and color schemes for painting vehicles, equipment, and building interiors. The objective is to provide a unifying and recognizable theme linking all of the firm's operations in a branded service experience through the strategic use of *physical evidence*. The American Automobile Association has made good use of corporate design in solidifying its brand identity. The bright red AAA logo is recognized worldwide as a reliable source of travel information and assistance.

Corporate design is particularly important for companies operating in competitive markets where it's necessary to stand out from the crowd and to be instantly recognizable in different locations. For example, gasoline retailing provides striking contrasts in corporate designs, from BP's bright green and yellow service stations to Texaco's red, black, and white, and Sunoco's blue, maroon, and yellow.

Companies in the highly competitive express delivery industry tend to use their names as a central element in their corporate designs. When Federal Express changed its trading name to the snappier and more multilingual "FedEx," it also changed its logo to feature the new name in a distinctive typeface. Consistent applications of this design were developed for use in settings ranging from business cards to boxes and from employee caps to aircraft exteriors.

Some companies use a trademarked symbol, rather than a name, as their primary logo.[14] Shell makes a pun of its English name by displaying a yellow scallop shell on a red background, which has the advantage of making its vehicles and service stations instantly recognizable even in parts of the world that do not use the Roman alphabet. McDonald's "Golden Arches" is said to be the most widely recognized corporate symbol in the world. (However, international companies operating in many countries need to select their designs carefully to avoid conveying a culturally inappropriate message through unfortunate choices of names, colors, or images.)

Merrill Lynch, the global financial services company, used its famous slogan, "We're Bullish on America" as the basis for its corporate symbol—a bull. A recent advertising campaign by the company developed some intriguing variations of this highly recognizable symbol (an example is shown in Figure 9.9).

FIGURE 9.9

Corporate Advertising by Merrill Lynch

servicescape: the design of any physical location where customers come to place orders and obtain service delivery.

Servicescape Dimensions   The term **servicescape** describes the design of any physical location where customers come to place orders and obtain service delivery.[15] It consists of four dimensions: the physical facility; the location; ambient conditions (like temperature or lighting); and personnel. Each of these elements is a critical form of physical evidence, since the appearance of a firm's service facilities and personnel affects customers' perceptions of service quality. Corporate design consultants are sometimes asked to advise on servicescape design, to coordinate the visual elements of both interiors and exteriors—such as signage, décor, carpeting, furnishings, and uniforms—so that they may complement and reinforce the other design elements. We can think of the servicescape concept in terms of the design of the stage on which the service drama is enacted. A good set and costumes can't save a bad play but they can greatly enhance the audience's enjoyment of a good one. Conversely, a bad stage set can create a poor initial impression. Physical evidence and servicescape design are discussed in greater detail in Chapter 11.

Ethical Issues in Communication

Few aspects of marketing lend themselves so easily to misuse (and even abuse) as advertising, selling, and sales promotion. The fact that customers often find it hard to evaluate services makes them more dependent on marketing communication for information and advice. Communication messages often include promises about the benefits that customers will receive and the quality of service delivery. When promises are made and then broken, customers are disappointed because their expectations have not been met.[16] Their disappointment and even anger will be even greater if they have wasted money, time, and effort and have no benefits to show in return or have actually suffered a negative impact. Employees, too, may feel disappointed and frustrated as they listen to customers' complaints about unfulfilled expectations.

Some unrealistic service promises result from poor internal communications between operations and marketing personnel concerning the level of service performance that customers can reasonably expect. In other instances, unethical advertisers and salespeople deliberately make exaggerated promises about the benefits that customers can hope to receive. Finally, there are deceptive promotions that lead people to think that they have a much higher chance of winning prizes or awards than is really the case. Fortunately, there are many consumer watchdogs on the lookout for these deceptive marketing practices. They include consumer protection agencies, trade associations

Can You Recognize a Service Company from These Clues?

How easy to recognize are the facilities, vehicles, and personnel of your own bank, favorite fast-food restaurant, taxi service, and local public transport system? Try the quiz below to see how many internationally used symbols and design elements you recognize.

1. With which rental car companies are the colors yellow, red, and green associated?

2. Which international airline has a flying kangaroo for its symbol? Which one uses a maple leaf?

3. Which stockbroker displays a ram's head as its corporate symbol?

4. How many companies can you name that use a globelike symbol?

5. Which international financial services company uses a symbol of three crossed keys?

Note: The answers to this quiz can be found at the end of the chapter, before the Endnotes.

within specific industries, and journalists who investigate customer complaints and seek to expose fraud and misrepresentation.

A different type of ethical issue concerns unwanted intrusion into people's personal lives—including, perhaps, your own. You can, of course, simply turn the page if you don't want to look at an advertisement in a newspaper or magazine. Perhaps you ignore television advertising by pressing the mute button on your remote and by talking to friends or family members while the commercials are on. However, the increase in tele-marketing and direct mail is frustrating for those who receive unwanted sales communications. How do you feel if your evening meal at home is interrupted by a telephone call from a stranger trying to interest you in buying services in which you have no interest? Even if you are interested, you may feel, as many do, that your privacy has been violated and see the call as an unwanted intrusion. Trade associations like the Direct Marketing Association offer ways for consumers to remove their names from telemarketing and direct-mail lists in an attempt to address the growing hostility toward these types of direct-marketing techniques.

MARKETING COMMUNICATIONS AND THE INTERNET

The Internet is playing an increasingly important role in marketing communication. Few companies of any size are now without a Web site and a substantial industry has sprung up to support the design and implementation of Internet-based marketing activities. Perhaps the most remarkable aspect of the Internet is its ubiquity: A Web site hosted in one country can be accessed from almost anywhere in the world, offering the simplest form of international market entry available—in fact, as Christian Grönroos points out, "the firm cannot avoid creating interest in its offerings outside its local or national market."[17] However, creating international access and developing an international strategy are two very different things!

Internet Applications

Marketers use the Internet for a variety of communications tasks. These include promoting consumer awareness and interest, providing information and consultation, facilitating two-way communications with customers through e-mail and chat rooms, stimulating product trial, enabling customers to place orders, and measuring the effectiveness of specific advertising or promotional campaigns.[18] Firms can market through their own Web sites and place advertising on other sites. Advertising on the Web allows companies to supplement conventional communications channels at a reasonable cost. But like any of the elements of the marketing communications mix, Internet advertising should be part of an integrated, well-designed communications strategy.

Many early Web sites were little more than electronic brochures, featuring attractive graphics that took too long to download. By contrast, interactive Web sites allow customers to engage in dialog with a database and come up with customized information. Transportation firms like airlines and railroads offer interactive sites that allow travelers to evaluate alternative routes and schedules for specific dates, download printed information, and make reservations online. Some sites offer discounts on hotels and airfare if reservations are made over the Internet—a tactic designed to draw customers away from intermediaries like travel agents.

The interactive nature of the Internet has the potential to increase customer involvement dramatically, since it enables "self-service" marketing in which individual customers control the nature and extent of their contact with the Web sites they visit. Many banks allow customers to pay bills electronically, apply for loans over the Internet, and check their account balances online. Whistler/Blackholm ski resort in British Columbia uses its Web site to promote advance online purchase of lift tickets at a discount. The site also offers instructions on how the online ticket window works, describes where to pick up the tickets, and provides responses to frequently asked questions.

Enabling marketers to communicate and establish a rapport with individual customers is one of the Web's greatest strengths. These characteristics lend themselves to a new communication strategy called "**permission marketing**,"[19] which is based on the idea that traditional advertising doesn't work as well any more because it fights for attention by interrupting people. For example, a 30-second television spot interrupts a viewer's favorite program, a telemarketing call interrupts a meal, and a print ad interrupts the flow of a magazine or newspaper article.

In the permission marketing model, the goal is to persuade consumers to *volunteer* their attention. In essence, customers are encouraged to "raise their hands" and agree to learn more about a company and its products in anticipation of receiving something of value to them. This means that customers self-select into the target segment. Consider the approach used by the Health Communication Research Institute, which issues pre-paid phone cards to patients in doctors' offices or hospitals as a way to measure patient satisfaction. To activate the card, the patient uses it to call an automated service that records responses to questions about the individual's recent experience with medical care. As a reward, the caller gets 30 minutes of free long-distance calling.[20] For an illustration of how H&R Block used a promotional contest to get customers to volunteer to learn about a new tax preparation service, see the boxed story "Permission Marketing at H&R Block."

> **permission marketing:** a marketing communication strategy that encourages customers to voluntarily learn more about a company's products because they anticipate receiving information or something else of value in return.

Permission Marketing at H&R Block

When H&R Block wanted to introduce a new service called Premium Tax, aimed at upper-income customers, it hired a firm called Yoyodyne to create a contest. This promotional event was announced using banner ads on selected Web sites that said, "H&R Block: We'll pay your taxes sweepstakes." Through the action of clicking on these banners, more than 50,000 people voluntarily provided their e-mail addresses and said "tell me more about this promotion."

In return for the chance to have their taxes paid by somebody else, these people became players in a contest. Every week for 10 weeks, they received three e-mails, inviting them to answer trivia questions about taxes, H&R Block, and other relevant topics. They were given fun facts about the history of taxes or sent to H&R Block's Web site to find answers to questions. Each e-mail also included a promotional message about Premium Tax. Not everyone responded to every message—on average, about 40 percent did so. But over the life of the promotion, 97 percent of those people who entered the game stayed in.

At the end of 10 weeks, surveys were conducted of: (1) those who had participated actively in the game; (2) those who had participated, but less actively; and (3) a control group of nonparticipants. Among nonparticipants, knowledge of Premium Tax was essentially nonexistent. Among less-active participants, 34 percent had a good understanding of Premium Tax, and for active participants, the figure was 54 percent. By creatively applying the concept of permission marketing, H&R Block acquired a database of prospects that had already received some information and education about its new service offering.

Source: William C. Taylor, "Permission Marketing" (interview with Seth Godin), *Fast Company*, April-May 1998, 198–212.

Web Site Design Considerations

From a communication standpoint, a Web site should contain information that a company's target customers will find useful and interesting.[21] Internet users expect speedy access, easy navigation, and content that is both relevant and up-to-date.

Service firms should set explicit communication goals for their Web sites. Is the site to be a promotional channel; a self-service option that diverts customers away from contact with service personnel; an automated news room that disseminates information about the company and its products, as well as offering an archive of past press releases; or even all of these? Some firms choose to emphasize promotional content, seeking to present the firm and its products in a favorable light and to stimulate purchase; others view their sites as educational and encourage visitors to search for needed information, even providing links to related sites.

Innovative companies are continually looking for ways to improve the appeal and usefulness of their sites. The appropriate communication content varies widely from one type of service to another. A b2b site may offer visitors access to a library of technical information; by contrast, a resort hotel may include attractive photographs featuring the location, the buildings and the guest rooms, and even short videos depicting recreational options. Meantime, a radio station may display profiles and photos of key staff members, schedules of its broadcasts, background information about its programs, and access to its broadcasts via Web radio.

Marketers must also address other attributes, like downloading speed, that affect Web site "**stickiness**."[22] A sticky site is one that encourages repeat visits and purchases by keeping its audience engaged with interactive communication presented in an appealing fashion. Online service providers like EasyAsk have exploited a profitable niche in helping other companies design sticky Web sites that make information searches and site navigation easy for their customers.

stickiness: a Web site's ability to encourage repeat visits and purchases by keeping its audience engaged with interactive communication presented in an appealing fashion.

PSI Net's print advertising reinforces its television campaign, which shows individuals in different global settings knocking on a window to gain the audience's attention.

A memorable Web address helps to attract visitors to a site. Unlike phone or fax numbers, it's often possible to guess a firm's Web address, especially if it's a simple one that relates to the firm's name or business. However, firms that come late to the Internet often find that their preferred name has already been taken. For instance, many industries include a company called Delta, but there can only be one delta.com. This site name belongs to Delta Financial Corporation (the U.S. airline had to use the longer address, deltaairlines.com). Web addresses must be actively promoted if they are to play an integral role in the firm's overall communication and service delivery strategy. This means displaying the address prominently on business cards, letterhead stationery, catalogs, advertising, promotional materials, and even vehicles.

Internet Advertising

The Internet has become a new advertising medium. Many firms pay to place advertising banners and buttons on portals like Yahoo or Netscape, as well as on other firms' Web sites. The usual goal is to draw online traffic to the advertiser's own site. In many instances, Web sites include advertising messages from other marketers with related but noncompeting services. Yahoo's stock quotes page, for example, features a sequence of advertisements for various financial service providers. Similarly, many Web pages devoted to a specific topic feature a small message from Amazon.com, inviting the reader to identify books on these same topics by clicking the accompanying hyperlink button to the Internet retailer's book site. In such instances, it's easy for the advertiser to measure how many visits to its own site are generated by click-throughs.

However, the Internet has not proved to be as effective an advertising medium as many marketers originally anticipated. Experience shows that simply obtaining a large number of exposures ("eyeballs") to a banner ad or button doesn't necessarily lead to increases in awareness, preference, or sales for the advertiser. One consequence is that the practice of paying a flat monthly rate for banner advertising is falling out of favor. Even when visitors click through to the advertiser's site, this action doesn't necessarily result in sales. Consequently, there's now more emphasis on advertising contracts that tie fees to marketing-relevant behavior by these visitors, such as providing the advertiser with some information about themselves or making a purchase.

reciprocal marketing: a marketing communication tactic in which an online retailer allows its paying customers to receive promotions for another online retailer and vice-versa, at no upfront cost to either party.

Some companies use **reciprocal marketing**, where an online retailer allows its paying customers to receive promotions for another online retailer and vice-versa, at no upfront cost to either party.[23] For example, RedEnvelope.com customers received an online coupon offer from Starbucks when they logged onto the RedEnvelope site. In exchange, RedEnvelope had a promotional link on Starbucks.com, enabling both companies to capture a percentage of the other site's customer base.

Conclusion

The marketing communication strategy for services requires a somewhat different emphasis from that used to market goods. The communication tasks facing service marketers include emphasizing tangible clues for services that are difficult to evaluate, clarifying the nature and sequence of the service performance, highlighting the performance of customer-contact personnel, and educating the customer about how to effectively participate in service delivery.

Many different communication elements are available to help companies create a distinctive position in the market and reach prospective customers. The options in the marketing communication mix include personal communications like personal selling and customer service, as well as impersonal communications like advertising, sales promotions, public relations, corporate design, and the physical evidence offered by the servicescape of the service delivery site. Instructional materials, from brochures to Web sites, often play an important role in educating customers on how to make good choices and obtain the best use from the services they have purchased. Developments in technology, especially the Internet, are changing the face of marketing communications. We will explore the strategic implications of technology for service marketers in greater detail in Chapter 16.

Answers to Symbol Quiz on Page 206

1. Hertz (yellow), Avis (red), National or Enterprise (both green)

2. Qantas (kangaroo), Air Canada (maple leaf). Note: Some regional Canadian airlines also display a maple leaf.

3. T. Rowe Price (ram)

4. AT&T and Cable & Wireless are both quite well known; aircraft of Continental Airlines have a partial golden globe on their tailfins, while those of the now-defunct airline Pan Am featured a complete blue and white globe; UPS paints a golden globe on all its trucks to emphasize its worldwide delivery capabilities.

5. UBS and subsidiaries, e.g., UBS PaineWebber (three crossed keys).

Study Questions and Exercises

1. Describe four common educational and promotional objectives in service settings and provide a specific example for each of the objectives you list.

2. Which elements of the marketing communications mix would you use for each of the following scenarios? Explain your answers.
   - A newly established hair salon in a suburban shopping center
   - An established restaurant facing declining patronage because of new competitors
   - A large, single-office accounting firm in a major city that serves primarily business clients

3. What roles do personal selling, advertising, and public relations play in (a) attracting new customers to a service business and (b) retaining existing customers?

4. Describe the role of personal selling in service communications. Give examples of three different situations where you have encountered this approach.

5. Find examples of service promotional efforts in your local area and evaluate their strengths and weaknesses as effective communication tools.

6. Provide several current examples of public relations efforts made by service companies.

7. Discuss the relative effectiveness of brochures and Web sites for promoting (a) a ski resort, (b) a hotel, (c) a fitness center, and (d) a bank.

8. Explore the Web sites of an airline, a bank, and an Internet retailer. Critique them for ease of navigation, content, and visual design. What, if anything, would you change about each site?

Endnotes

1. Enterprise Rent-a-Car Web site, enterprise.com, February 2001 and research by Karen Sunblad.
2. For a useful review of research on this topic, see Kathleen Mortimer and Brian P. Mathews, "The Advertising of Services: Consumer Views v. Normative Dimensions," *The Service Industries Journal* 18 (July 1998): 14–19.
3. William R. George and Leonard L. Berry, "Guidelines for the Advertising of Services," *Business Horizons*, July-August 1981.
4. Donna Legg and Julie Baker, "Advertising Strategies for Service Firms," in C. Surprenant (ed.), *Add Value to Your Service* (Chicago, IL: American Marketing Association, 1987), 163–168.
5. Banwari Mittal, "The Advertising of Services: Meeting the Challenge of Intangibility," *Journal of Service Research* 2 (August 1999): 98–116.
6. Legg and Baker, "Advertising Strategies"; D. J. Hill and N. Gandhi, "Services Advertising: A Framework for Effectiveness," *Journal of Services Marketing* 6 (Fall 1992): 63–76.
7. Victor L. Hunter and David Tietyen, *Business to Business Marketing: Creating a Community of Customers* (Lincolnwood, IL: NTC Business Books, 1997).
8. David H. Maister, "Why Cross Selling Hasn't Worked," *True Professionalism* (New York: The Free Press, 1997), 178–184.
9. K. M. Haywood, "Managing Word of Mouth Communications," *Journal of Services Marketing* 3 (Spring 1989): 55–67.
10. Eugene W. Anderson, "Customer Satisfaction and Word of Mouth," *Journal of Service Research* 1 (August 1998): 5–17; Magnus Soderlund, "Customer Satisfaction and Its Consequences on Customer Behaviour Revisited: The Impact of Different Levels of Satisfaction on Word of Mouth, Feedback to the Supplier, and Loyalty," *International Journal of Service Industry Management* 9, no. 2 (1998): 169–188.
11. Stephen J. Grove, Gregory M. Pickett, and David N. Laband, "An Empirical Examination of Factual Information Content among Service Advertisements," *The Service Industries Journal* 15 (April 1995): 216–233.
12. Ken Peattie and Sue Peattie, "Sales Promotion—a Missed Opportunity for Service Marketers," *International Journal of Service Industry Management* 5, no. 1 (1995): 6–21. See also Paul W. Farris and John A. Quelch, "In Defense of Price Promotion," *Sloan Management Review* (Fall 1987): 63–69.
13. Dana James, "Move Cautiously in Trade Show Launch," *Marketing News*, 20 November 2000, 4 & 6; Elizabeth Light, "Tradeshows and Expos—Putting Your Business on Show," *Her Business*, March-April 1998, 14–18; and Susan Greco, "Trade Shows versus Face-to-Face Selling," *Inc.* (May 1992): 142.
14. Abbie Griffith, "Product Decisions and Marketing's Role in New Product Development," in *Marketing Best Practices* (Orlando, FL: The Dryden Press, 2000), 253.
15. Mary Jo Bitner, "Servicescapes: The Impact of Physical Surroundings on Customers and Employees," *Journal of Marketing* 56 (April 1992): 57–71.
16. Louis Fabien, "Making Promises: The Power of Engagement," *Journal of Services Marketing* 11, no.3 (1997): 206–214.
17. Christian Grönroos, "Internalization Strategies for Services," *The Journal of Services Marketing* 13, no. 4/5 (1999): 290–297.
18. J. William Gurley, "How the Web Will Warp Advertising," *Fortune*, 9 November 1998, 119–120.
19. Seth Godin and Don Peppers, *Permission Marketing: Turning Strangers into Friends and Friends into Customers* (New York: Simon & Schuster, 1999).

20. Kathleen V. Schmidt, "Prepaid Phone Cards Present More Info at Much Less Cost," *Marketing News*, 14 February 2000, 4.
21. Donald Emerick, Kim Round, and Susan Joyce, *Web Marketing and Project Management* (Upper Saddle River, NJ: Prentice Hall, 2000), 27–54.
22. Gary A. Poole, "The Riddle of the Abandoned Shopping Cart," *grok*, December 2000-January 2001, 76–82. See also Donald Emerick, Kim Round, and Susan Joyce, *Web Marketing and Project Management* (Upper Saddle River, NJ: Prentice Hall, 2000), 212–213.
23. Dana James, "Don't Wait—Reciprocate," *Marketing News*, 20 November 2000, 13 & 17.

chapter ten

Service Positioning and Design

Desperately Seeking Service Strategies

The basics of a travel agency's business have traditionally been quite straightforward. Customers call for flight, train, hotel, or cruise reservations.[1] The agent finds out what's available, maybe provides a bit of advice, books the transaction, and delivers the tickets. For decades, commissions on airline tickets provided about 60 percent of a typical agency's revenues. But that situation changed when Delta Airlines announced that it would no longer pay a 10-percent commission on every ticket sold. Regardless of the purchase price, there would be caps of $25 one-way and $50 round-trip for all domestic tickets. Other major airlines soon followed suit.

These commission caps were only the start of trouble for the travel agent industry. Other marketplace changes began to impact the roles that travel agents filled as information brokers and distributors of other companies' services. Travel agents are like stockbrokers, real estate agents, or consultants—their value is in what they know and what they can find out for customers. But access to information is being completely reshaped these days by computers and Web-based technologies. Customers can access travel information directly on the Internet at any time, and can handle their own bookings, too—either through a carrier's own Web site or through such Internet-based services as Travelocity or Priceline.

So what's a travel agent to do in this challenging new world? Many have closed, others are trying to survive by cutting costs or seeking to add value by doing the same things better. But a few moved quickly to create totally new service strategies. Here are three service revolutionaries—see what you think of their innovative approaches to establishing a secure competitive position!

THE MERCHANDISER

Company: *Travelfest*

Service Strategy: *Revamp the way travel is sold*

Gary Hoover likes to call his Austin, Texas-based travel agency the Home Depot of the travel industry. His goal was to "yank travel out of the retail Stone Age" by designing a travel superstore where customers could shop for tickets and travel-related products in an entertaining and educational environment. Fourteen monitors play travel videos simultaneously in Travelfest stores, and backlit walls show slides from around the world. Customers can browse for travel information in the Europe room, the Africa room, the Asia room, and kids have their own special room to explore. Visa and passport applications are available, and customers can check out the Hotel and Travel Index (a resource used by most travel agents but rarely available to their clients). There are also 10,000 travel-related items for sale, including books, videos, maps, luggage and clothing, water purifiers, and language guides. Oh yes—the store is also open from 9 A.M. to 11 P.M. seven days a week, and it accepts mail, Internet, and telephone orders.

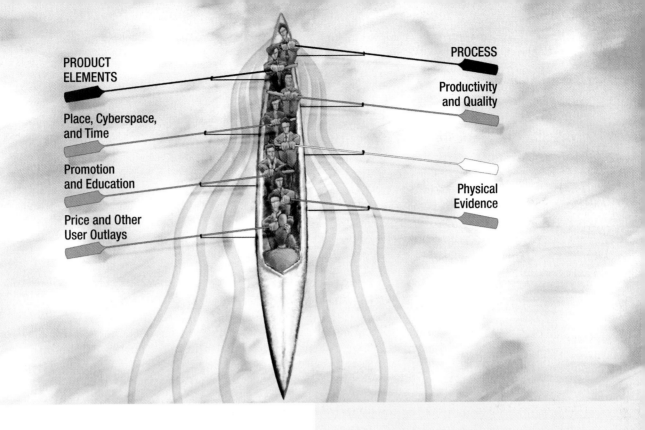

Labels on the diagram (clockwise from top-left):
- PRODUCT ELEMENTS
- Place, Cyberspace, and Time
- Promotion and Education
- Price and Other User Outlays
- PROCESS
- Productivity and Quality
- Physical Evidence

THE CONTRACTOR

Company: *Capital Prestige Travel*

Service Strategy: *Change the service-delivery model*

Derek Messenger, owner of Capital Prestige Travel, spends $1 million a year on statewide travel ads and infomercials about discount cruise sailings. His biggest challenge is having enough trained people to take all those calls his advertising generates. Messenger has solved this problem creatively by using independent contractors who work out of their homes and pay for the privilege of affiliating with a well-known travel agency, which routes calls to them. Each home-based contractor pays $7800 to Capital Prestige. In return, contractors get a computer, software that connects them to Sabre (a national computerized reservations system), a hookup to Capital Prestige phone lines, and eight days of training. They also get paid 35 to 70 percent of the agency's ticket commissions. Capital Prestige takes care of all of the marketing and backup services like handling tickets, collecting money, and providing a help line for home agents who run into problems. With its innovative home-agent system, the company has turned fixed costs into variable costs— which saves enough money to generate more business by doing large-scale promotions and advertising.

(continues)

➡ Learning Objectives

After reading this chapter, you should be able to

⇒ describe the four different focus approaches

⇒ explain the elements of competitive positioning strategy

⇒ discuss how perceptual maps help identify competitors' positions in a specific market

⇒ understand how branding relates to individual offerings within a product line

⇒ define the different types of service innovation

THE NICHE PLAYER

Company: *Aspen Travel*

Service Strategy: *Specialize in one service-intensive market niche*

Aspen Travel started out as a traditional travel agency. Its customer base was largely limited to Jackson Hole, Wyoming, whose isolated mountain location seemed an unlikely spot for building a large corporate clientele. Then a film production company from Los Angeles shot a movie in Jackson Hole, and Aspen did such a great job of handling its travel that the company retained Aspen's services for trips to other locations. Owners Randle Feagin and Andy Spiegel had discovered the perfect niche—and today they do 85 percent of their business with production companies from Los Angeles, New York, and Miami. Word of mouth in the tightly knit film production industry takes care of Aspen's marketing, while faxes, e-mail, and remote ticket printers allow the agency to operate from Jackson Hole. Aspen's specialized knowledge helps it outperform would-be competitors. After all, how many travel agents know how to get an AT&T phone booth to a film site in Belize or transport penguins to the deserts of Moab, Utah, without having them collapse from heatstroke?

THE NEED FOR FOCUS

If you ask a group of managers from different service businesses how they compete, many will simply say, "on service." Press them a little further, and they may add "value for money," "convenience," or "our people are the key." Some may even respond to the question "What makes your service different?" by saying "Truthfully, nothing. We're all pretty much the same." But no two services are ever exactly alike. It would be impossible for companies to be identical in the design of their servicescapes, the employees they attract, the personalities of their leaders, or the cultures they create. As competition intensifies for many businesses in the service sector, cultivating and communicating *meaningful* differences is becoming increasingly important for long-term profitability.[2]

In this chapter, we show how to find answers to the questions: *How can we differentiate our service product from the competition's?* and *How should we go about designing new services?*

Four Focus Strategies

It's not usually realistic for a firm to try to appeal to all actual or potential buyers in a market, because customers are too numerous, too widely scattered, and too varied in their needs, purchasing behavior, and consumption patterns. Firms themselves vary widely in their abilities to serve different types of customers. So rather than attempting to compete in an entire market, each company needs to focus its efforts on those customers it can serve best. In marketing terms, **focus** means providing a relatively narrow product mix for a particular market segment—a group of customers who share common characteristics, needs, purchasing behavior, or consumption patterns. Successful implementation of this concept requires firms to identify the strategically important elements in their service operations and concentrate their resources on these factors.[3]

focus: the provision of a relatively narrow product mix for a particular market segment.

market focus: the extent to which a firm serves few or many markets.

service focus: the extent to which a firm offers few or many services.

The extent of a company's focus can be described on two different dimensions—market focus and service focus. **Market focus** is the extent to which a firm serves few or many markets, while **service focus** describes the extent to which a firm offers few or many services. These dimensions define the four basic focus strategies shown in Figure 10.1.

A *fully focused* organization provides a very limited range of services (perhaps just a single core product) to a narrow and specific market segment. For example, Aspen Travel serves the specific needs of the film production industry. A *market-focused* company concentrates on a narrow market segment but has a wide range of services. Each Travelfest store serves a limited geographic market, appealing to families and individuals planning vacation trips rather than to business travelers, but offers a broad array of services. *Service-focused* firms offer a narrow range of services to a fairly broad market. Thus, Capital Prestige Travel specializes in the narrow field of discount cruise sailings, but reaches customers across a broad geographic market through a telephone-based delivery

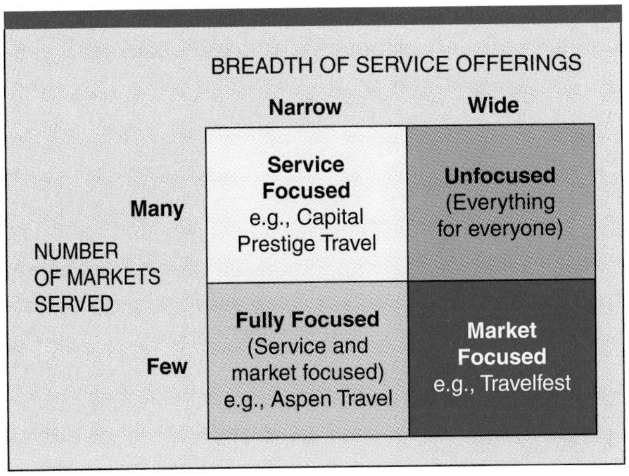

FIGURE 10.1

Basic Focus Strategies for Service Organizations

BREADTH OF SERVICE OFFERINGS

	Narrow	Wide
Many	**Service Focused** e.g., Capital Prestige Travel	**Unfocused** (Everything for everyone)
Few	**Fully Focused** (Service and market focused) e.g., Aspen Travel	**Market Focused** e.g., Travelfest

NUMBER OF MARKETS SERVED

Source: Adapted from Robert Johnston, "Achieving Focus in Service Organizations," *The Service Industries Journal* 16 (January 1996): 10–20.

system. Finally, many service providers fall into the *unfocused* category because they try to serve broad markets and provide a wide range of services.[4]

As you can see from Figure 10.1, focusing requires a company to identify the market segments that it can serve best with the services it offers. Effective market segmentation should group customers in ways that result in similarity *within* each segment and dissimilarity *between* each segment on relevant characteristics.

CREATING A DISTINCTIVE SERVICE STRATEGY

Once a company has decided which market segment(s) to target, the next task is to establish an overall strategic direction—a service strategy—in order to achieve and maintain a distinctive competitive position. Leonard Berry emphasizes the importance of these service strategies:

> All great service companies have a clear, compelling service strategy. They have a "reason for being" that energizes the organization and defines the word "service." A service strategy captures what gives the service value to customers. To forge a path to great service, a company's leaders must define correctly that which makes the service compelling. They must set in motion and sustain a vision of service excellence, a set of guideposts that point to the future and show the way.[5]

A company's service strategy can usually be expressed in a few sentences or words that guide and energize its employees. The best service strategies address basic human needs that don't change much over time. For example, Taco Bell's service strategy is to offer the best value fast meal whenever and wherever customers are hungry. While this statement sounds simple enough, it actually symbolizes a major change in the way the company defines itself and its operations. Club Med's basic service concept could be described as "a fully paid vacation package where you make your arrangements and pay the bill in advance in return for a well-managed program in which you don't need to worry much about money, transportation, food, activities or clothes."[6]

Dial-a-Mattress appeals to its target market's need for both convenience and risk reduction by selling brand-name bedding like Sealy, Serta, or Simmons over the telephone 24 hours a day, 7 days a week. Orders are delivered as soon as the customer wants them, and old mattresses are removed at no extra cost. The company's core service strategy makes buying a mattress so simple that new customers are often amazed. Founder and CEO Napoleon Barragan explains, "Buying a mattress is not a pleasurable experience; it's a chore. If you can make it easy for the customers, if you give them what they want, the way they want it, and when they want it, you can do business."[7]

Creating a Sustainable Competitive Advantage

The first step in establishing a service strategy is to focus on customers' needs. Important service needs that are not being met by competitors provide opportunities for a company to move into an "open" position in the marketplace. Two questions should be asked about the needs and expectations of a target market relative to a specific service offering: What attributes are absolutely essential to this group of customers? And what attributes will delight them? The service strategy can then be designed to include both the essential attributes and those features that have the potential to exceed customer expectations.

sustainable competitive advantage: a position in the marketplace that can't be taken away or minimized by competitors in the short run.

The best service strategies provide organizations with a **sustainable competitive advantage**—a way of meeting customer needs in a specific market segment better than other competitors. (By *sustainable*, we mean a position in the marketplace that can't be taken away or minimized by competitors in the short run.) Obtaining and keeping such an advantage presents a significant challenge, because it's hard for a firm to protect innovations legally and competitors can quickly copy many service attributes. Consider how Amtrak positions its high-speed rail service in the Boston–Washington corridor against competing air service.

Transporting Business Travelers Into the Twenty-First Century

Amtrak, America's national passenger railroad, illustrates a service strategy based on customers' needs related to travel in the 500 mile (800 km) Northeast Corridor that links Boston, Providence, New York, Newark, Philadelphia, Baltimore, and Washington, D.C. Over the years, air shuttles departing at 30-minute intervals on the Boston–New York and New York–Washington routes, as well as commuter flights serving other airports, had severely eroded the railroad's position in the business traveler segment of the market. The problem was particularly challenging between Boston and New York, where rail service was slow and not very reliable. But Amtrak's market research showed that in addition to speed, business travelers wanted both convenience *and* comfort at levels not currently available on most flights.

To address these unmet needs, Amtrak obtained funds to upgrade the track on the Northeast Corridor and electrify the line all the way to Boston. In December 2000, it introduced a new, high-speed rail service, named Acela Express. Acela—a new brand name that suggests both acceleration and excellence—promises fast, comfortable, reliable, and safe transportation. Amtrak's futuristic-looking, Canadian-built electric trains can transport passengers at speeds of up to 150 miles per hour (240 km/h), making travel times between city centers competitive with the airlines, once ground travel from airport to city center is included.

While seeking to match the airlines on essential attributes like convenience, reliability, and travel time, Amtrak plans to beat them on such features as customer service, spaciousness, and comfort. The company has extended its definition of the "Amtrak travel experience" beyond the core product of transportation to include elements that have the potential to delight its customers—including the service provided by on-board staff, the reservations and ticketing processes, and the train station environment. While waiting at the station, first-class passengers are entitled to use of a special lounge.

The trains' interior decor reflects customer preferences for attractive modern design, appealing colors, and more space than the cramped conditions found on air shuttles. The windows of the cars are large and the seats in first and business class are bigger and more comfortable than those on short-haul aircraft. There's plenty of space for stowing baggage and even the toilets are large and attractively designed. Lighting is bright enough to work by but still soft and unobtrusive. Acela Express also offers passengers the chance to stretch their legs and obtain food and drink in a new, upscale "bistro" car; those traveling in first class can dine at their seats, enjoying meals served on chinaware.

Source: Based on Ian P. Murphy, "Amtrak Enlists Customers' Help to Bring Service Up to Speed," *Marketing News*, 27 October 1997, 14; information from the Amtrak corporate Web site, www.amtrak.com, February 2001, and news reports.

SERVICE POSITIONING

After a service strategy has been identified, a company must decide how to position its product most effectively. The concept of **positioning** involves establishing a distinctive place in the minds of target customers relative to competing products. In *The New Positioning: The Latest on the World's #1 Business Strategy*, Jack Trout distills the essence of positioning into the following four principles:[8]

1. A company must establish a position in the minds of its targeted customers.

2. The position should be singular, providing one simple and consistent message.

3. The position must set a company apart from its competitors.

4. A company cannot be all things to all people—it must focus its efforts.

Cirque du Soleil is an example of a company that has taken these four principles to heart. Most Americans can't even pronounce the name (which is French for "circus of the sun"), and fewer than one in five know what Cirque offers. But the goal of the Quebec-based founders is to become a worldwide brand—a Circus Without Boundaries. Cirque provides a mystical mixture of stunningly choreographed dance, original music, exotic costumes, and amazing acrobatics that is more art than traditional circus entertainment. And the atmosphere is intimate, since the audience for most performances is limited to a few thousand people compared to crowds of ten thousand or more at typical circus events. Cirque's extravagant shows—with ticket prices of $60 to $100 per seat—are produced at multimillion dollar theaters on three different continents. The company is extremely profitable, and its long-term strategy is to become a megabrand targeted at the wealthy. Cirque has already cashed in on its brand equity with a licensed wallpaper line (a top seller in the United States), a Cirque du Soleil watch marketed by Swatch, and a $12 million IMAX film about the company that recently debuted in Berlin.[9]

> **positioning:** establishing a distinctive place in the minds of customers relative to competing products.

Positioning and Marketing Strategy

Companies use positioning strategies to distinguish their services from competitors and to design communications that convey their desired position to customers and prospects in the chosen market segments. There are a number of different dimensions around which positioning strategies can be developed, including:

1. *Product attributes*—America Online's e-mail service is "so easy to use, no wonder it's #1" (see Figure 10.2)

2. *Price/quality relationship*—Supercuts sells good haircuts at a "reasonable" price

3. *Reference to competitors*—"You'd better take your Visa card, because they don't take American Express"

4. *Usage occasions*—Ski resorts offer downhill and cross-country skiing in the winter; hiking and mountain biking in the summer

5. *User characteristics*—CheapTicket's online ticketing service is for travelers who are comfortable with both Internet usage and self-service

6. *Product class*—Blue Cross provides a variety of different health insurance packages for its corporate customers to choose from in putting together their employee benefit plans

Marketers often use a combination of these positioning approaches. Whatever strategy a firm chooses, the primary goal is to differentiate itself from competitors by emphasizing the distinctive advantages of its service offerings. If the core benefits are similar to those of the competition, the company may decide to stress different advan-

FIGURE 10.2

AOL E-Mail Emphasizes Ease of Use and Its Market Leadership

TABLE 10.1

Principal Uses of Positioning in Marketing Management

1. Provide a useful diagnostic tool for defining and understanding the relationships between products and markets:
   a. How does the product compare with competitive offerings on specific attributes?
   b. How well does product performance meet consumer needs and expectations on specific performance criteria?
   c. What is the predicted consumption level for a product with a given set of performance characteristics offered at a given price?
2. Identify market opportunities:
   a. *Introduce new products*
      - What segments should be targeted?
      - What attributes should be offered relative to the competition?
   b. *Redesign (reposition) existing products*
      - Should we appeal to the same segments or to new ones?
      - What attributes should be added, dropped, or changed?
      - What attributes should be emphasized in advertising?
   c. *Eliminate products that*
      - Do not satisfy consumer needs
      - Face excessive competition
3. Make other marketing mix decisions to preempt or respond to competitive moves:
   a. *Distribution strategies*
      - Where should the product be offered (locations and types of outlet)?
      - When should the product be available?
   b. *Pricing strategies*
      - How much should be charged?
      - What billing and payment procedures should be used?
   c. *Communication strategies*
      - What target audience(s) are most easily convinced that the product offers a competitive advantage on attributes that are important to them?
      - What message and attributes should be emphasized and which competitors, if any, should be mentioned as the basis for comparison on those attributes?
      - Which communication channels should be used, personal selling or different advertising media (selected not only for their ability to convey the chosen message to the target audience but also for their ability to reinforce the desired image of the product)?

tages in its promotional efforts. For example, at one point Sprint was stressing the price and value of its long-distance services, while AT&T emphasized reliability and expertise. Table 10.1 summarizes how positioning strategies relate to critical marketing issues like service development and delivery, pricing, and communications.

Service Repositioning

Market positions are rarely permanent. Competitive activity, new technologies, and internal changes may cause a company to reposition itself and its services. **Repositioning** involves changing the position a firm holds in a consumer's mind relative to competing services. This may be necessary to counter competitive attacks, remain attractive and appealing to current customers, or target new and additional segments. Repositioning can involve adding new services or abandoning certain offerings and withdrawing completely from some markets. In response to major changes in its business environment, Andersen Consulting recently repositioned itself and changed its name to Accenture to reflect its "accent on the future" (see the boxed story "Repositioning a Consulting Firm").

repositioning: changing the position a firm holds in a consumer's mind relative to competing services.

PERCEPTUAL MAPS AS POSITIONING TOOLS

Many companies use perceptual mapping to help finalize their positioning strategies. **Perceptual maps**—also called positioning maps—help managers identify the most critical attributes of their own and competing services, as viewed by customers. These maps provide a visual picture of a service's distinctive characteristics, identify the nature of competitive threats and opportunities, and highlight gaps between customer and management perceptions about competing services (as the Palace Hotel example in the next section illustrates).

perceptual map: a visual illustration of how customers perceive competing services.

Repositioning a Consulting Firm

Andersen Consulting, a management consulting firm whose clients include more than 5,000 companies worldwide, recently repositioned itself to reflect a new business strategy with an emphasis on cutting-edge technologies. On January 1, 2001, the company was officially "Renamed. Redefined. Reborn as Accenture." The company's name change reflects the new brand identity and repositioning strategy that it had been working on since early in 2000. According to Dave Seibel, the Canadian Managing Partner for Accenture:

> We are repositioning our firm in the marketplace to better reflect our new vision and strategy for becoming part of the fabric of the new economy and our strategy for getting there. We are creating new businesses through joint ven-

tures that will help us provide our traditional consulting clients and the market with the latest technological innovations. We are also investing in emerging technology providers with applications that will benefit our clients. We are moving beyond a traditional consulting firm, delivering innovations that improve the way the world lives and works.

To create awareness of its new name and its extended capabilities, Accenture implemented an integrated marketing communications program in 48 different countries at an estimated cost of $175 million. The campaign included four 30-second Super Bowl spots in addition to 6,000 other television commercials, print ads in newspapers and business journals, and extensive online advertising.

Source: Scotty Fletcher, "Accenture Buys Four Super Bowl Spots," localbusiness.com, 20 November 2000; Larry Greenemeier, "Andersen Consulting Changing Name to Accenture," informationweek.com, 26 October 2000; the company's Web sites www.ac.com and www.ac.ca, December 2000 and www.accenture.com, January 2001; and conversations with Accenture consultants.

To create a perceptual map, researchers first identify attributes that are important to customers and then measure how the firm and its competitors are performing on each attribute. The results can then be plotted on a chart, using the horizontal axis for measures of one attribute and the vertical axis for a second. Since charts are two-dimensional, perceptual maps are usually limited to two attributes. Sometimes, three-dimensional models are built so that a third dimension can be included. When marketers need to feature more than three dimensions to describe service positioning, they can create a series of two-dimensional maps or use computerized models to handle numerous attributes simultaneously. Some commonly used attributes include:

➤ Convenience
➤ Industry-specific characteristics that offer a unique benefit
➤ Level of personal service
➤ Price
➤ Quality of physical elements
➤ Reliability
➤ Speed
➤ Trustworthiness

In most cases, an attribute can be delivered at several different levels. Some of these variations are easy to measure. For instance, travel times can be faster or slower and prices can be higher or lower. Reliability—a key element in service quality—can be measured by how often a service fails to perform against predefined standards (for instance, errors in posting banking deposits or late arrival of flights). Evaluation of other attributes may be more subjective. For instance, researchers may ask customers to evaluate the level of convenience, comfort, or quality of personal service they encounter in a specific context.

A perceptual map is only as good as the quality of the information used in constructing it. Dynamic markets require that research be repeated periodically and perceptual maps redrawn to reflect significant changes in the competitive environment. New market entrants and repositioning of existing competitors may result in the disappearance of a formerly distinctive positioning advantage. Separate maps will have to be drawn for different market segments if research shows that there are sharp variations between segments. In the case of airlines, for instance, vacationers and business travelers may have different service priorities and vary in their willingness to pay extra for higher classes of service.

Using Perceptual Maps to Evaluate Positioning Strategies

To demonstrate the value of perceptual mapping, let's look at how the Palace—a successful four-star hotel in a large city that we'll call Belleville—used perceptual maps to develop a better understanding of potential threats to their established market position. The Palace was an elegant old hotel located on the edge of Belleville's booming financial district. Its competitors included 8 four-star establishments and the Grand Hotel, which had a five-star rating. The Palace had been very profitable for its owners in recent years and boasted an above-average occupancy rate. It was sold out on weekdays most of the year, reflecting its strong appeal to business travelers (who were very attractive customers because of their willingness to pay higher room rates than vacationers or convention participants). But the general manager and his staff saw problems on the horizon. Permission had recently been granted for four large new hotels in the city, and the Grand Hotel had just started a major renovation and expansion project.

To better understand these competitive threats, the hotel's management team worked with a consultant to prepare perceptual maps that displayed the Palace's position in the business traveler market both before and after the arrival of new competition. Four attributes were selected: room price; level of physical luxury; level of personal service; and location. Information on competing hotels was not difficult to obtain. The locations were known, the physical structures were relatively easy to visit and evaluate, and the sales staff kept informed on competitors' pricing policies and discounts. The ratio of rooms per employee was a convenient surrogate measure for service level; this was easily calculated from the published number of rooms and employment data filed with city authorities. Data from travel agents provided additional insights about the quality of personal service at each of the competing hotels.

The Palace's management team created scales for each attribute. Price was simple, since the average price charged to business travelers for a standard single room at each hotel was already known. The rooms per employee ratio formed the basis for a service-level scale, with low ratios indicating high service. This scale was then modified slightly to reflect what was known about the level of service actually delivered by each major competitor. The level of physical luxury was more subjective. The management team identified the Grand Hotel as the most luxurious hotel and decided that the Airport Plaza was the four-star hotel with the least luxurious physical facilities. The other four-star hotels were then rated relative to these two benchmarks.

The location scale was based on each hotel's distance from the stock exchange (which was in the heart of the financial district), since past research had shown that a majority of the Palace's business guests were visiting destinations in this vicinity. The set of 10 hotels lay within an area that extended from the stock exchange through the city's principal retail area (where the convention center was also located) to the inner suburbs and the nearby metropolitan airport.

Two positioning maps were created to portray the existing competitive situation. The first (Figure 10.3) showed the hotels on the dimensions of price and service level; the second (Figure 10.4) displayed them on location and degree of physical luxury.

A quick glance at Figure 10.3 shows a clear correlation between price and service. That's no surprise: Hotels offering higher levels of service can command higher prices. The shaded bar running from the upper left to the lower right highlights this relationship, and we would expect it to continue diagonally downward for three-star and lesser-rated establishments. Further analysis indicates that there appear to be three clusters of hotels within what is already an upscale market category. At the top end, the four-star Regency is close to the five-star Grand. In the middle, the Palace is clustered with four other hotels. Another set of three hotels is positioned at the lower end. One surprising insight from this map is that the Palace appears to be charging significantly more (on a relative basis) than its service level seems to justify. But since its occupancy rate is very high, guests are evidently willing to pay the present rate. What's the secret of its success?

In Figure 10.4, we see how the Palace is positioned relative to the competition on location and physical luxury. We would not expect these two variables to be directly related and they don't appear to be so. A key insight here is that the Palace occupies a relatively empty portion of the map. It's the only hotel located in the financial district— a fact that probably explains its ability to charge more than its service level (or degree of physical luxury) would normally command. There are two clusters of hotels in the vicinity of the shopping district and convention center: a relatively luxurious group of three, and a second group of two offering a moderate level of luxury.

After mapping the current situation, the Palace's management team turned to the future. Their next task was to predict the positions of the four new hotels being constructed in Belleville, as well as the probable repositioning of the Grand (see Figures 10.5 and 10.6). The construction sites were already known. Two would be in the

FIGURE 10.3

Belleville's Principal Business
Hotels: Positioning Map of
Service Level Versus Price
Level

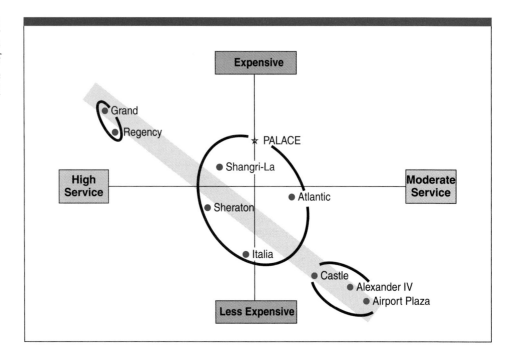

financial district and the other two in the vicinity of the convention center. Predicting the positions of the four new hotels was not difficult since preliminary details had already been released. The owners of two of the hotels intended to aim for five-star status, although they admitted that this goal might take a few years to achieve. Three of the newcomers would be affiliated with international chains. Their strategies could be guessed by examining hotels these same chains had opened recently in other cities. Press releases distributed by the Grand had already declared

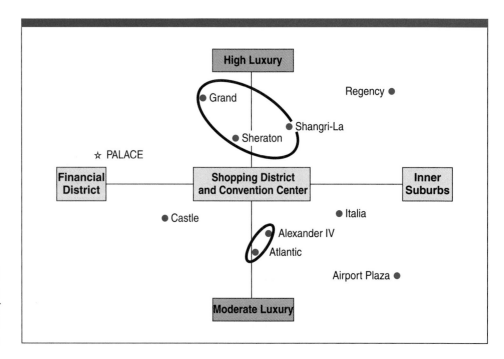

FIGURE 10.4

Belleville's Principal Business
Hotels: Positioning Map of
Location Versus Physical
Luxury

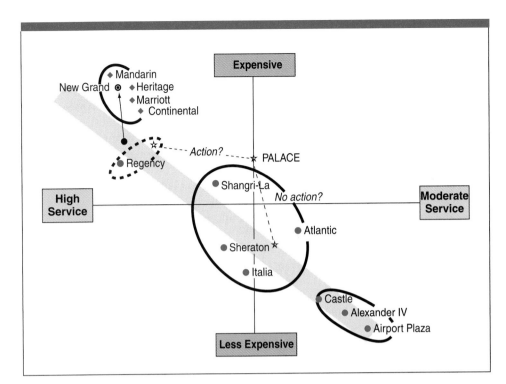

FIGURE 10.5

Belleville's Principal Business
Hotels, Following New
Construction: Positioning
Map of Service Level Versus
Price Level

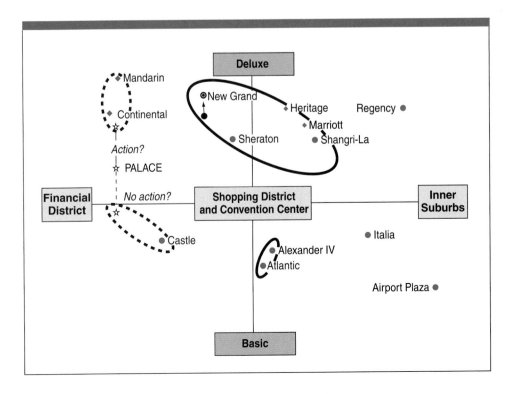

FIGURE 10.6

Belleville's Principal Business
Hotels after New
Construction: Positioning
Map of Location Versus
Physical Luxury

that the "New Grand" would be larger and even more luxurious, and its management planned to add new service features.

Pricing was easy to project because new hotels use a formula for setting posted room prices (the prices typically charged to individuals staying on a weekday in high season). This price is linked to the average construction cost per room at the rate of $1 per night for every $1000 of construction costs. Thus, a 500-room hotel that costs $100 million to build (including land costs) would have an average room cost of $200,000 and would need to set a price of $200 per room night. Using this formula, Palace managers concluded that the four new hotels would have to charge significantly more than the Grand or the Regency. This would have the effect of establishing what marketers call a "price umbrella" above existing price levels and would give other competitors the option of raising their prices. To justify the high prices, the new hotels would have to offer customers very high standards of service and luxury. At the same time, the New Grand would need to increase its prices to recover the costs of renovations, new construction, and enhanced service offerings.

Assuming that no changes were made by either the Palace or the other existing hotels, the impact of the new competition clearly posed a significant threat to the Palace. It would lose its unique locational advantage and become one of three hotels in the immediate vicinity of the financial district (see Figure 10.6). The sales staff believed that many of the Palace's existing business customers would be attracted to the Continental and the Mandarin and would be willing to pay higher rates in order to obtain superior benefits. The other two newcomers were seen as more of a threat to the Shangri-La, Sheraton, and New Grand in the shopping district/convention center cluster. The New Grand and the other entrants would create a high price/high service and luxury cluster at the top end of the market, leaving the Regency in what might prove to be a distinctive—and therefore defensible—space of its own.

What action should the Palace take under these circumstances? One option would be to do nothing in terms of service enhancements or physical improvements. But the loss of its locational advantage would probably destroy the hotel's ability to charge a price premium, leading to lower prices and profits. Some of the best staff might be enticed away by the new hotels, leading to a decline in service quality. And without renovations, there would be a gradual decline in physical luxury, too. The net result over time might be to shift the Palace into a new cluster with the Castle, serving guests who want to visit destinations in the financial district but are unable (or unwilling) to pay the high prices charged at the Mandarin and Continental. As you can see, doing nothing would have significant strategic implications! If other existing hotels decided to upgrade and the Palace did nothing, it would eventually slide even further down the scales on luxury and service, risking reclassification as a three-star hotel.

An alternative strategy would be to implement renovations, service improvements, and programs to reinforce the loyalty of current guests before the new hotels are completed. The price umbrella these hotels create would allow the Palace to raise its rates to cover the additional costs. The hotel might then move to a new position where it is clustered with the Regency on the dimensions of price and service. On the dimensions of luxury and location, it would be clustered with the Mandarin and Continental but with slightly lower prices than either competitor.

So what did the Palace actually do? Management selected the second option, concluding that the future profitability of the hotel lay in competing against the Continental (and to a lesser extent against the Mandarin) for the growing number of business travelers visiting Belleville's financial district. The Palace also tried to retain the loyalty of frequent guests by recording their preferences and special needs on the hotel database so that staff could provide more personalized service. Advertising and selling efforts promoted these improvements, and frequent guests were sent personalized direct mailings from the general manager. Despite the entrance of new and formidable competition, the Palace's occupancy levels and profits have held up very well.

CREATING AND PROMOTING COMPETITIVE ADVANTAGE

Creating a competitive advantage presents special challenges for service providers, who are often forced to compete with goods and customers' self-service options in addition to other service providers. Since customers seek to satisfy specific needs, they often evaluate reasonable alternatives that offer broadly similar benefits. For example, if your lawn desperately needs mowing, you could buy a lawn mower and do it yourself—or you could hire a lawn maintenance service to take care of the chore for you.

Customers may make choices between competing alternatives based on their skill levels or physical capabilities and their time availability, as well as on factors like cost comparisons between purchase and use, storage space for purchased products, and anticipated frequency of need. As you can see, direct competition between goods and services is often inevitable in situations where they can provide the same basic benefits. This concept is illustrated in Figure 10.7, which shows four possible delivery alternatives for both car travel and word processing. These alternatives are based on choices between ownership or rental of physical goods and self-service or hiring other people to perform the tasks.

Of course, many businesses rely on a mixture of both goods and services to satisfy customer needs. "Quasi-manufacturing" operations like fast-food restaurants sell goods supplemented by value-added service. At each site, customers can view a menu describing the restaurant's products, which are highly tangible and easily distinguishable from those of competitors. The service comes from speedy delivery of freshly prepared food items, the ability to order and pick up food from a drive-in location without leaving the car, and the opportunity to sit down and eat a meal at a table in a clean environment.

Providers of less tangible services also offer a "menu" of products, representing a bundle of carefully selected elements built around a core benefit. For instance, universities provide many types of undergraduate education, ranging from two-year certification programs to the completion of bachelors' degrees, and from full-time residency to evening extension programs. Most also offer graduate studies and nondegree continuing education classes. The supplementary service elements include advising, library and computer resources, entertainment opportunities like theater and sports events, food and health care services, and a safe, pleasant campus environment.

	Own a Physical Good	Rent the Use of a Physical Good
Perform the Work Oneself	• Drive own car • Type on own word processor	• Rent a car and drive it • Rent a word processor and type on it
Hire Someone to Do the Work	• Hire a chauffeur to drive car • Hire a typist to use word processor	• Hire a taxi or limousine • Send work out to a secretarial service

FIGURE 10.7

Services as Substitutes for Owning and/or Using Goods

The Power of Service Brands

Because of the difficult competitive challenges faced by service providers, especially the problem of differentiating an intangible performance, branding plays a special role in defining and positioning a company's service offerings. As Leonard Berry states:

> *Strong brands enable customers to better visualize and understand intangible products. They reduce customers' perceived monetary, social or safety risk in buying services, which are difficult to evaluate prior to purchase. Strong brands are the surrogate when the company offers no fabric to touch, no trousers to try on, no watermelons or apples to scrutinize, no automobile to test-drive.*[10]

brand: a name, phrase, design, symbol, or some combination of these elements that identifies a company's services and differentiates it from competitors.

While the product is the primary brand for packaged goods, the company itself serves as the brand for services. But what *is* a brand? Harry Beckwith argues in his book *Selling the Invisible* that for a service, a **brand** is more than a name or a symbol. It is an implicit promise that a service provider will perform consistently up to customer

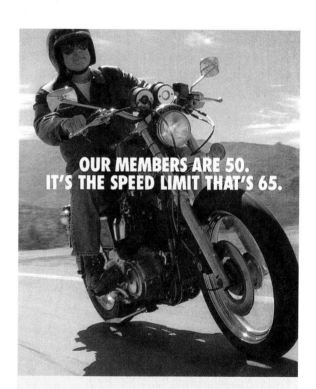

AARP members are definitely not riding off into the sunset. They're fit, fun and ready for more. Why not join them? For just $10 you and your spouse can get information on everything from finance to fitness. You'll have access to travel discounts and insurance programs. AARP can be your advocate in Washington and help you get involved in local AARP projects. There's also a great magazine, timely *AARP Bulletins* and lots of discounts.

If you're 50 or over, join AARP today!

Simply fill out and mail the attached card. If the card is missing, send your $10 dues payment to:

AARP
P.O. Box 199
Long Beach, CA 90801

www.aarp.org

96 MODERN MATURITY NOVEMBER–DECEMBER 2000

FIGURE 10.8

AARP Promotes a Fit, Fun Image to Attract New Members in Their Fifties

expectations over time. Brands are very important to service customers, because few services have warranties—in part because they are typically difficult to guarantee. For example, how do you guarantee that a doctor's diagnosis will be accurate? That a professor's class will be educational? That a tax accountant will find every legal deduction? Customers can't experience service quality in advance of purchase, so most of the time they have to rely on the service provider's brand image as a promise of future satisfaction.

Ritz-Carlton promises a particular type of luxury hotel experience; Motel 6 stands for something simpler and more affordable. Similarly, Southwest Airlines and Singapore Airlines, both respected as leaders in their industry, offer very different air travel experiences. Brands that offer good value on a consistent basis gain the trust and respect of their customers. In fact, when traveling on business or vacation, people who value consistency often seek out the same service providers that they patronize at home. Perhaps you're among them.

Advertising and other marketing communications play an important role in creating a positive brand image and establishing expectations. Even nonprofit organizations like AARP have developed brand image campaigns. Figure 10.8 shows an advertisement from a campaign designed, in part, to dispel misperceptions that the AARP (formerly the American Association of Retired Persons) consisted only of inactive, elderly individuals—in fact, membership is open to anyone over the age of 50. And the Chicago Symphony Orchestra experienced a 10-percent increase in donations following a communications program that introduced a modernized logo and sought to create a consistent, upbeat image for the orchestra.[11]

To maintain a well-defined brand identity, a firm must reinforce key brand attributes in all of its communications—from service encounters to television advertising. Marketing messages may vary by target audience, but there should be a consistent theme. This includes Web sites, which can be powerful communication links with customers if managed effectively. Companies like FedEx, UPS, Kinko's, and Sir Speedy use the Internet to provide online information and delivery options for their customers. These value-added services help to enhance customers' overall brand experiences.

The "Branded Customer Experience"

Customer satisfaction—the deep kind of satisfaction that builds loyalty—doesn't result from any one thing. A customer's decision to stay with a particular supplier or defect to another is often the result of many small encounters. Successful firms recognize this and design distinctive service strategies to ensure that ordinary events will be perceived as extraordinary. The Forum Corp., a consulting and training group in Boston, calls this creating a "branded customer experience."[12] According to the Forum, the promise of the service brand should be reinforced at every point of contact between a company and its customers. Forum senior vice president Scott Timmins says: "The question is, what is our brand of customer delight—what are we known for, what do customers expect us to deliver reliably, where's our wow?"

Southwest Airlines has mastered the branded service experience—with a twist. Its brand stands for the opposite of extravagant treatment, but passengers are not expecting that. Instead, the airline delights its customers by making and keeping a promise to provide simple, convenient, inexpensive service, with a little humor on the side. Southwest's positioning strategy is designed to reinforce its image as the "No Frills" carrier. This theme is emphasized in its clever advertising campaigns, the reusable plastic boarding passes, and the casual appearance and demeanor of its flight attendants.

Changing Brand Perceptions

halo effect: the tendency for consumer ratings of one prominent product characteristic to influence ratings for many other attributes of that same product.

Customers' perceptions about specific brands often reflect the cumulative impact of different service encounters. These experiences can result in a **halo effect**—either positive or negative—that makes it difficult for customers to assess the specific strengths and weaknesses of competing services.[13] For instance, reported customer dissatisfaction with one attribute of a particular service may be real (and thus need corrective action) or could be the result of a negative halo effect caused by a high dissatisfaction with a second attribute or even by a high overall dissatisfaction with the brand.

One problem in consumer satisfaction research is that respondents often complete survey questionnaires quickly, without carefully considering each of the different dimensions on which they are rating a service firm's performance. If they are unhappy with a service in general, they may rate all attributes poorly rather than identifying those that are actually dissatisfying. In-depth personal interviews usually offer a more reliable way to probe customers' evaluations and obtain more carefully considered responses. However, this type of research is time consuming and more expensive to administer.

Improving negative brand perceptions may require extensive redesign of the core product and/or supplementary services. However, weaknesses are sometimes perceptual rather than real. Ries and Trout describe the case of Long Island Trust, historically the leading bank serving this large suburban area to the east of New York City.[14]

After laws were passed to permit unrestricted branch banking throughout New York State, many of the big banks from neighboring Manhattan began invading Long Island. Research showed that Long Island Trust was rated below banks like Chase Manhattan and Citibank on such key selection criteria as branch availability, full range of services offered, service quality, and capital resources. However, Long Island Trust ranked first on helping Long Island residents and the Long Island economy.

The bank's advertising agency developed a campaign promoting the "Long Island position," playing to its perceived strengths rather than seeking to improve perceptions on attributes where it was perceived less favorably. The tenor of the campaign can be gauged from the following extract from a print ad:

> *Why send your money to the city if you live on the Island? It makes sense to keep your money close to home. Not at a city bank but at Long Island Trust. Where it can work for Long Island. After all, we concentrate on developing Long Island. Not Manhattan Island or some island off Kuwait—*

Other advertisements in the campaign promoted similar themes, such as, "The city is a great place to visit, but would you want to bank there?"

When identical research was repeated 15 months later, Long Island Trust's position had improved on every attribute. The campaign had succeeded in reframing its brand image by changing its customers' frame of reference from a global to a local perspective. Although the firm had not changed any of its core or supplementary services, the perceived strength of being a Long Island bank for Long Islanders now had a strongly positive halo effect on all other attributes.

NEW SERVICE DEVELOPMENT

Competitive intensity and customer expectations are increasing in nearly all service industries. Thus success lies not only in providing existing services well, but also in creating new approaches to service. Because the outcome and process aspects of a service often combine to create the experience and benefits obtained by customers, both aspects must be addressed in new service development.

A Hierarchy of Service Innovation

The word "new" is popular in marketing because it's a good way to attract people's attention. However, there are different degrees of "newness" in new service development. In fact, we can identify seven categories of new services, ranging from major innovations to simple style changes.

1. *Major service innovations* are new core products for markets that have not been previously defined. They usually include both new service characteristics and radical new processes. Examples include FedEx's introduction of overnight, nationwide, express package delivery in 1971, the advent of global news service from CNN, and eBay's launch of online auction services.

2. *Major process innovations* consist of using new processes to deliver existing core products in new ways with additional benefits. For example, the University of Phoenix competes with other universities by delivering undergraduate and graduate degree programs in a nontraditional way. It has no permanent campus; instead its courses are offered online or at night in rented facilities. Its students get most of the core benefits of a college degree in half the time and at a much lower price than other universities.[15] The existence of the Internet has led to the creation of many start-up businesses employing new retailing models that exclude the use of traditional stores, saving customers time and travel costs. Often, these models add new, information-based benefits such as greater customization, the opportunity to visit chat rooms with fellow customers, and suggestions for additional products that complement what has already been purchased.

3. *Product line extensions* are additions to current product lines by existing firms. The first company in a market to offer such a product may be seen as an innovator, but the others are merely followers who are often acting defensively. These new services may be targeted at existing customers to serve a broader array of needs, designed to attract new customers with different needs, or both. Starbucks, known for its coffee shops, has extended its offerings to include light lunches (Figure 10.9).

   Major computer manufacturers like Compaq, Hewlett-Packard, and IBM are going beyond their traditional business definitions to offer integrated "e-solutions" based on consulting and customized service.[16] Telephone companies have introduced numerous value-added services such as caller ID, call waiting, and call forwarding. Cable television providers are starting to offer broadband Internet access. Many banks sell insurance products in the hope of increasing the number of profitable relationships with existing customers. American Express, too, offers a full range of insurance products, including auto, home, and umbrella policies. And at least one insurance company—State Farm Insurance—has gone into the banking business, relying on its well-established brand name to help draw customers.

4. *Process line extensions* are less innovative than process innovations. But they do often represent distinctive new ways of delivering existing products, either with the intent of offering more convenience and a different experience for existing customers or of attracting new customers who find the traditional approach unappealing. Most commonly, they involve adding a lower-contact distribution channel to an existing high-contact channel, as when a financial service firm develops telephone-based or Internet-based services or a bricks-and-mortar retailer adds catalog sales or a Web site. For example, Barnes and Noble, the leading bookstore chain in the United States, added a new Internet subsidiary,

FIGURE 10.9
Starbucks Promotes Its Expanded
Service Offering

BarnesandNoble.com, to help it compete against Amazon.com. Creating self-service options for customers to complement delivery by service employees is another form of process line extension.

5. *Supplementary service innovations* involve adding new facilitating or enhancing service elements to an existing core service, or significantly improving an existing supplementary service. Low-tech innovations for an existing service can be as simple as adding parking at a retail site or agreeing to accept credit cards for payment. Multiple improvements may have the effect of creating what customers perceive as an altogether new experience, even though it is built around the same core. Theme restaurants like the Rainforest Café are examples of enhancing the core with new experiences. The cafés are designed to keep customers entertained with aquariums, live parrots, waterfalls, fiberglass monkeys, talking trees that spout environmentally related information, and regularly timed thunderstorms, complete with lightning.[17]

6. *Service improvements* are the most common type of innovation. They involve modest changes in the performance of current products, including improvements to either the core product or to existing supplementary services. For instance, a movie theater might renovate its interior, adding ergonomically designed seats with built-in cup holders to increase both comfort and convenience for customers during the show or an airline might add power sockets for laptops in its business-class cabins.

7. *Style changes* represent the simplest type of innovation, typically involving no changes in either processes or performance. However they are often highly visible, create excitement, and may serve to motivate employees. Examples include

repainting retail branches and vehicles in new color schemes, outfitting service employees in new uniforms, introducing a new bank check design, or making minor changes in service scripts for employees.

As you can see, service innovation can occur at many different levels. It's important to recognize that not every type of innovation has an impact on the characteristics of the core product or results in a significant change in the customer's experience.

Creating a New Service to Fill an Empty Market Position

As we noted earlier, positioning research sometimes reveals new opportunities in the marketplace. Perceptual maps can highlight positions where there is expressed or latent demand for a certain type of service but none of the existing offerings have attributes that closely meet potential customers' requirements. When a firm uncovers such an opportunity, the only way to take advantage of it is to develop a new service with the desired characteristics.

Service design is not typically a simple task. Most new services involve compromises, because there are usually limits to what most prospective customers are willing to pay. And service providers must be careful not to lose control of their costs in coming up with superior performance levels on the product characteristics that customers desire. So how can product planners determine what features and price will create the best value for target customers? It's hard to know without asking prospective users—hence the need for research. Let's examine how the Marriott Corporation employed market research to help develop a new service concept in the lodging industry.

Marriott had identified a niche in the business travel market between full-service hotels and inexpensive motels. The opportunities were seen as especially attractive in locations where demand was not high enough to justify a large full-service hotel. Having confirmed the presence of a niche where there was unmet market demand, Marriott executives set out to develop a product to fill that gap. As a first step, the company hired marketing research experts to help establish an optimal design concept.[18] Since there are limits to how much service and how many amenities can be offered at any given price, Marriott needed to know how customers would make trade-offs in order to arrive at the most satisfactory compromise in terms of value for money. The intent of the research was to get respondents to trade off different hotel service features to see which ones they valued most.

A sample of 601 consumers (who were part of the business travel market) from four metropolitan areas participated in the study. Researchers used a sophisticated technique known as conjoint analysis that asks survey respondents to make trade-offs between different groupings of attributes. The objective is to determine which mix of attributes at specific prices offers the highest degree of utility. The 50 attributes in the Marriott study were divided into the following seven factors (or sets of attributes), each containing a variety of different features based on detailed studies of competing offerings:

1. *External factors*—building shape, landscaping, pool type and location, hotel size
2. *Room features*—room size and decor, climate control, location and type of bathroom, entertainment systems, other amenities
3. *Food-related services*—type and location of restaurants, menus, room service, vending machines, guest shop, in-room kitchen
4. *Lounge facilities*—location, atmosphere, type of guests
5. *Services*—reservations, registration, check-out, airport limo, bell desk, message center, secretarial services, car rental, laundry, valet

FIGURE 10.10

Sample Description of a
Hotel Offering

ROOM PRICE PER NIGHT IS $44.85

BUILDING SIZE, BAR/LOUNGE
Large (600 rooms), 12-story hotel with:
- Quiet bar/lounge
- Enclosed central corridors and elevators
- All rooms have very large windows

LANDSCAPING/COURT
Building forms a spacious outdoor courtyard
- View from rooms of moderately landscaped courtyard with:
  —many trees and shrubs
  —the swimming pool plus a fountain
  —terraced areas for sunning, sitting, eating

FOOD
Small, moderately priced lounge and restaurant for hotel guests/friends
- Limited breakfast with juices, fruit, Danish, cereal, bacon and eggs
- Lunch—soup and sandwiches only
- Evening meal—salad, soup, sandwiches, six hot entrees including steak

HOTEL/MOTEL ROOM QUALITY
Quality of room furnishings, carpet, etc. is similar to:
- Hyatt Regency Hotels
- Westin "Plaza" Hotels

ROOM SIZE AND FUNCTION
Room one foot longer than typical hotel/motel room
- Space for comfortable sofa-bed and 2 chairs
- Large desk
- Coffee table
- Coffee maker and small refrigerator

SERVICE STANDARDS
Full service including:
- Rapid check in/check out systems
- Reliable message service
- Valet (laundry pick up/deliver)
- Bellman
- Someone (concierge) arranges reservations, tickets, and generally at no cost
- Cleanliness, upkeep, management similar to:
  —Hyatts
  —Marriotts

LEISURE
- Combination indoor-outdoor pool
- Enclosed whirlpool (Jacuzzi)
- Well-equipped playroom/playground for kids

SECURITY
- Night guard on duty 7 P.M. to 7 A.M.
- Fire/water sprinklers throughout hotel

"X" the ONE box below which best describes how likely you are to stay in this hotel/motel at this price:

Would stay there almost all the time	Would stay there on a regular basis	Would stay there now and then	Would rarely stay there	Would not stay there
☐	☐	☐	☐	☐

Source: Jerry Wind et al., "Courtyard by Marriott: Designing a Hotel Facility with Customer-Based Marketing Models," *Interfaces*, January/February 1989, 25–47.

6. *Leisure facilities*—sauna, whirlpool, exercise room, racquetball and tennis courts, game room, children's playground

7. *Security*—guards, smoke detectors, 24-hour video camera

For each of these seven factors, respondents were presented with a series of stimulus cards displaying different levels of performance for each attribute. For instance, the "Rooms" stimulus card displayed nine attributes, each of which had three to five different levels. Thus, *amenities* ranged from "small bar of soap" to "large soap, shampoo packet, shoeshine mitt" to "large soap, bath gel, shower cap, sewing kit, shampoo, special soap" and then to the highest level, "large soap, bath gel, shower cap, sewing kit, special soap, toothpaste, etc."

In the second phase of the analysis, respondents were shown cards depicting a number of alternative hotel profiles, each featuring different levels of performance on the various attributes contained in the seven factors. They were asked to indicate on a five-point scale how likely they would be to stay at a hotel with these features, given a specific room price per night. Figure 10.10 shows one of the 50 cards that were developed for this research. Each respondent received five cards.

The research yielded detailed guidelines for the selection of almost 200 features and service elements, representing those attributes that provided customers in the target segment with the highest utility for the prices they were willing to pay. An important aspect of the study was that it focused not only on what travelers wanted, but also identified what they liked but weren't prepared to pay for. (There's a difference, after all, between wanting something and being willing to pay for it!) Using these inputs, the design team was able to meet the specified price while retaining the features most desired by the study participants, who represented the desired business traveler market.

Marriott was sufficiently encouraged by the findings to build three prototype hotels that were given the brand name, "Courtyard by Marriott." After testing the concept under real-world conditions and making some refinements, the company developed a large chain whose advertising slogan became "Courtyard by Marriott—the hotel designed by business travelers." The new hotel concept filled a gap in the market with a product that represented the best balance between the price customers were prepared to pay and the physical and service features they most desired. The success of this project subsequently led Marriott to develop additional customer-driven products—Fairfield Inn and Marriott Suites—using the same research methodology.

Conclusion

Service companies must find ways to create meaningful competitive advantages for their products by responding to specific customer needs and developing a distinctive service strategy that responds to those needs better than any competing product. Successful positioning strategies are based on relating the opportunities (and threats) uncovered by market and competitive analysis to the firm's own strengths and weaknesses.

In this chapter, we introduced perceptual mapping, an important tool that companies can use to help define their competitive positions. Perceptual maps present a visual display of how competing firms perform relative to each other on key service attributes. This technique can be used to analyze opportunities for developing new services or repositioning existing ones so that companies can establish and maintain a sustainable competitive advantage by effectively addressing the needs and expectations of their target markets.

Because of the difficult challenge faced by service providers in differentiating intangible performances, branding plays a special role in defining and positioning a company's service offerings. Creating a distinctive branded service experience for customers requires consistency at all stages of the service delivery process. In designing services, managers should be aware of the importance of selecting the right mix of supplementary service elements—no more and no less than needed—and creating synergy to ensure that they contribute to a consistent, positive brand image.

Study Questions and Exercises

1. Give examples of companies in other industries that are facing challenges similar to those of the travel agents in the opening story. Describe what service strategies these companies might use to compete effectively.

2. Why should service firms focus their efforts? What options do they have for doing so?

3. In a sentence or two, describe Amtrak's service strategy for its new Acela Express service (refer to the boxed example on page 218).

4. Describe what is meant by the term "positioning." Choose an industry you are familiar with (like fast-food restaurants or movie theaters) and create a perceptual map showing the competitive positions of different companies in the industry.

5. Explain why branding is particularly important for services. Which service brands are you familiar with? What do they tell you about the companies they are associated with?

6. Discuss how a company's product attributes (including the core and supplementary services), price, and marketing communications all work together to create a branded customer experience. Provide an example of a service firm that you think has integrated these elements particularly well.

7. Define the seven categories of new services. Provide your own example for each category.

Endnotes

1. From J. Case and J. Useem, "Six Characters in Search of a Strategy," *Inc. Magazine*, March 1996, 46–55.
2. George S. Day, *Market Driven Strategy* (New York: The Free Press, 1990), 164.
3. See R. H. Hayes and S. C. Wheelwright, *Restoring Our Competitive Edge* (New York: Wiley and Sons, 1984); J. L. Heskett, *Managing in the Service Economy* (Boston, MA: Harvard Business School Press, 1986); and J. L. Heskett, W. E. Sasser, and C. W. L. Hart, *Service Breakthroughs: Changing the Rules of the Game* (New York: The Free Press, 1990).
4. Robert Johnston, "Achieving Focus in Service Organizations," *The Service Industries Journal* 16 (January 1996): 10–20.
5. Leonard L. Berry, *On Great Service* (New York: The Free Press, 1995), 62–63.
6. Graham Clark, Robert Johnston, and Michael Shulver, "Exploiting the Service Concept for Service Design and Development," in *New Service Development: Creating Memorable Experiences* (Thousand Oaks, CA: Sage Publications, 2000), 71–91.
7. Leonard L. Berry, "Cultivating Service Brand Equity," *Journal of the Academy of Marketing Science* 28, no. 1 (2000): 132.
8. Jack Trout, *The New Positioning: The Latest on the World's #1 Business Strategy* (New York: McGraw-Hill, 1997). See also Al Ries and Jack Trout, *Positioning: The Battle for Your Mind*, reissue ed. (New York: Warner Books, 1993).
9. Information from William G. Zikmund and Michael d'Amico, *Marketing: Creating and Keeping Customers in an E-Commerce World* (Cincinnati, OH: South-Western College

Publishing, 2001), 275–276; and Bruce Horovitz, "Dreaming Big Top: Cirque de Soleil Aims to Be Worldwide Brand," *USA Today*, 18 March 1999.

10. Berry, "Cultivating Service Brand Equity," p. 128.

11. Laura Koss Feder, "Branding Culture: Nonprofits Turn to Marketing to Improve Image and Bring in the Bucks," *Marketing News*, 1 January 1998, 1.

12. Thomas A. Stewart, "A Satisfied Customer Isn't Enough," *Fortune*, 21 July 1997, 112–113.

13. Jochen Wirtz and John E. G. Bateson, "An Experimental Investigation of Halo Effects in Satisfaction Measures of Service Attributes," *International Journal of Service Industry Management* 6, no. 3 (1995): 84–102.

14. Al Ries and Jack Trout, *Positioning: The Battle for Your Mind*, 1st ed., rev. (New York: Warner Books, 1986).

15. See James Traub, "Drive-Thru U.," *The New Yorker*, 20 and 27 October 1997; and Joshua Macht, "Virtual You," *Inc. Magazine*, January 1998, 84–87.

16. Mark Boslet and Elinor Abreu, "The New HP Way," *The Industry Standard*, 25 September 2000, 58–61.

17. Chad Rubel, "New Menu for Restaurants: Talking Trees and Blackjack, *Marketing News*, 29 July 1996, 1.

18. Jerry Wind, Paul E. Green, Douglas Shifflet, and Marsha Scarbrough, "Courtyard by Marriott: Designing a Hotel Facility with Consumer-Based Marketing Models," *Interfaces* (January-February 1989); 25–47.

part**four**

Service Delivery Issues

In Part IV, we address the task of how to deliver service products to the customer. As shown in Figure IV.1, managers face three key questions: ***What are the options for delivering our service? How can we balance productivity and quality concerns? How should we match demand and productive capacity?*** Service delivery issues have been dominated traditionally by operations. But progressive service organizations also include their marketing and human resource managers in these types of decisions.

Before they can make decisions on service delivery (the topic of Chapter 11), managers need to ask, *What physical and electronic channels can we use?* Service delivery is closely linked to the choice of service process—whether the service involves the physical person of the customer, a tangible possession, or some form of information. In high-contact services customers encounter employees and physical evidence of facilities. Even when physical channels are necessary to deliver the core service, information-based supplementary services may be delivered electronically. It's possible to deliver some information-based services entirely through automated, low-contact systems. *Is it feasible to shift from high-contact to low-contact delivery?* If so, *Should we offer customers a choice?* Abandoning existing high-contact delivery options is not necessarily a viable strategy. Some customers may not like the low-contact delivery alternatives, others may prefer having access to both physical and electronic delivery channels.

Another key service delivery consideration is: *When and where should our service be available?* Success in services increasingly depends on offering customers convenience. Electronic delivery through the Internet has the advantage of being accessible 24 hours a day, 7 days a week, from a location of the customer's choosing. Finally, managers need to address the issue of *What options exist for using third-party intermediaries?* Often a case can be made for subcontracting some aspects of service delivery to intermediaries who possess special expertise and may have better access to customers.

The challenge of balancing productivity and quality presents an ongoing headache for businesses. It can lead to conflict between marketers—who are advocates of customer satisfaction—and operations managers, who are concerned with efficiency and cost control. As we note in earlier chapters, customers' perceptions of service quality tend to be linked to their expectations of the service, raising the questions: *What quality improvements are needed to meet or exceed customer expectations? How can we reduce operating costs without spoiling the appeal of our service?* We address these and other quality and productivity issues in Chapter 12.

Making optimal use of available capacity is one way to improve productivity. However, many service businesses face wide swings in demand that result in wasted capacity when demand is low and lost business when it's too high. Chapter 13 addresses the question, *What strategies can we employ to match demand and capacity?* To

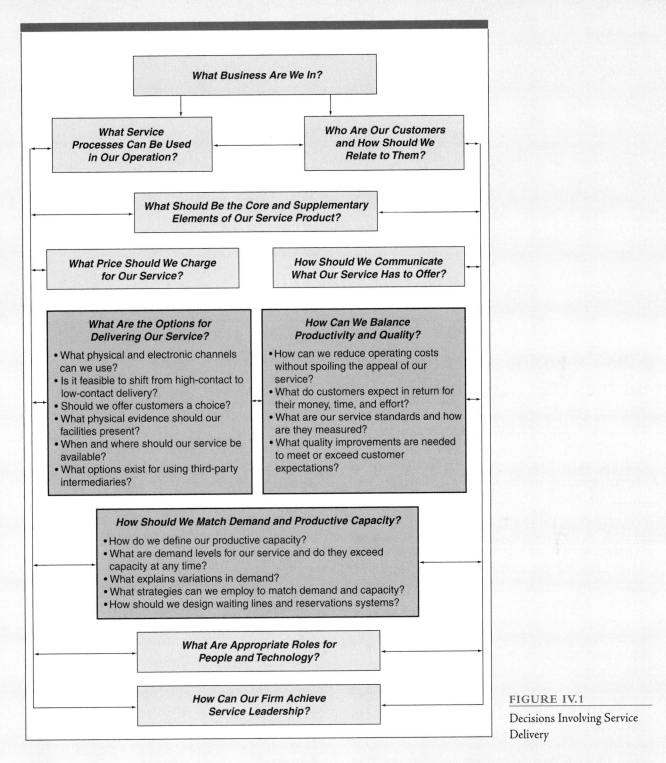

FIGURE IV.1

Decisions Involving Service Delivery

resolve this challenge, strategists need to understand both the nature of productive capacity and the factors that underlie periodic variations in demand. Both marketing and operational strategies can be employed. Issues relating to waiting lines and reservations are discussed in Chapter 14. Reservations systems provide one way of balancing demand against available capacity, since they allow customers to obtain a commitment for service delivery at a specific time in the future. Another approach is to develop a strategy for managing waiting lines, designing them with reference to the anticipated volume of business and the customer mix.

chapter eleven

Creating Delivery Systems in Place, Cyberspace, and Time

Kinko's: From Local Copyshop to Global Business Service Provider

In 1970, 22-year-old Paul Orfalea, just out of college, borrowed enough money to open a photocopy shop in Isla Vista, near the campus of the University of California at Santa Barbara.[1] Covering just 100 square feet (less than 10 square meters), the tiny store contained one copy machine and also sold film processing and felt-tip highlighter pens. Orfalea, the son of Lebanese immigrants, called the store Kinko's after the nickname given to him by his college buddies because of his curly reddish hair. Thirty years later, Kinko's boasted a chain of almost one thousand printing and copying stores, operating 24 hours a day from coast to coast in the United States, plus branches in Canada, Britain, the Netherlands, Australia, United Arab Emirates, and three Asian countries.

Kinko's offers ways to change companies' existing working procedures through services that include productivity consultation and outsourcing of document management. It also appeals to business travelers who may need to develop and deliver presentations, reports, and proposals far from their home offices. (A few years ago, Kinko's even ran a national advertising campaign positioning the firm as "Your Branch Office.")

Technological innovations in IT and printing have revolutionized Kinko's business model and created new methods of working for both the company and its customers. At its stores, Kinko's customers can print in color in almost any size, bind their documents in many different ways, send faxes, and work on in-house computers. Many locations also offer videoconferencing technology. The company provides an array of other services and products, including rentals of conference rooms, notary public service, and sale of office supplies.

Kinko's now describes itself as "the world's leading provider of visual communications services and document copying." The firm has created a global online network, employing broadband technology to link all its locations. Using Kinkonet, the firm's online service, customers can order supplies or submit files for printing. Thanks to digital file transmission, customers can compose reports in, say, Minneapolis and transmit them electronically to, say, Montreal where they can be printed and bound for a meeting. This procedure is an alternative to the traditional approach of first creating documents and graphics, then printing and binding them, and finally, shipping them physically to another location. Through a partnership with FedEx, couriers can deliver reports to local addresses in some 55 markets within only four hours. Recognizing that not all customers are in a position to transfer document files by modem and that printed materials may need to be delivered physically to their final destination, Kinko's has worked with FedEx to install "World Service Centers" at selected branches. These centers offer a full complement of express shipping solutions and provide access to late pickups.

In 2000, the firm announced creation of a separate company, Kinkos.com, combining its existing Internet-based activities with newly acquired e-business expertise, online design tools, and proprietary technology. Kinkos.com aimed to become a leading online resource for the small office/home office (SOHO) market, offering

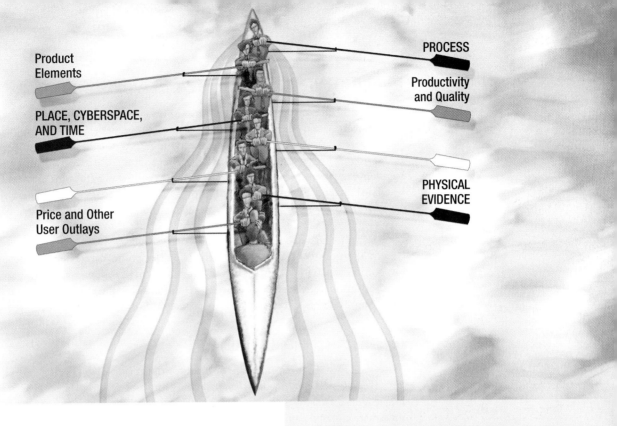

Product
Elements

PLACE, CYBERSPACE,
AND TIME

Price and Other
User Outlays

PROCESS

Productivity
and Quality

PHYSICAL
EVIDENCE

customers 24/7 access to expert advice, powerful online tools, and the worldwide Kinkos' network—all from their own desktops. Kinkos.com has a clicks-and-mortar relationship with the store-based company, using the latter's physical locations for in-store marketing, customer acquisition, and physical distribution.

⇒ Learning Objectives

After reading this chapter, you should be able to

⇒ distinguish between physical and electronic channels of delivery

⇒ recognize that delivery systems must address issues of where, when, and how service is to be delivered to customers

⇒ define the three different types of service delivery channels

⇒ understand the role of physical evidence and servicescapes in service delivery

⇒ explain the role of technology in enhancing the speed, convenience, and productivity of service delivery systems

⇒ describe the role of intermediaries in service delivery

EVALUATING ALTERNATIVE DELIVERY CHANNELS

This is both an exciting and challenging time for managers who are responsible for service delivery. Customers are demanding more convenience, and they expect services to be delivered where and when they want them.[2] As the Kinko's example shows, new technologies allow information-based services (and informational processes related to supplementary services) to be delivered almost anywhere through electronic channels.

This chapter explores a key question in service management: *What are the options for delivering our service?* In many cases, customers are no longer obliged to visit service factories as the concept of going to a physical place for service delivery gives way to delivery in cyberspace for information-based services.

In addition to moving from factory- to electronic-based delivery, progressive firms are coming up with different formats for face-to-face delivery in new locations. Such innovations include services like massage clinics on airport concourses and Wells Fargo's tiny bank branches occupying booths at the end of supermarket aisles.

Physical versus Electronic Delivery

As service managers consider the options for delivering their services, two key questions are, *What physical and electronic channels can we use?* and *Is it feasible to switch from high-contact to low-contact delivery?* While goods require physical distribution, those services that are information based can be delivered through either electronic or physical channels. Many of the supplementary services surrounding both intangible and tangible core products can now be delivered electronically. Even service businesses that involve physical core products—like retailing and repair—are shifting delivery of many supplementary services to the Web, closing some of their physical branches, and moving to low-contact strategies for interacting with customers. As you can see in Figure 11.1, five of the eight petals of

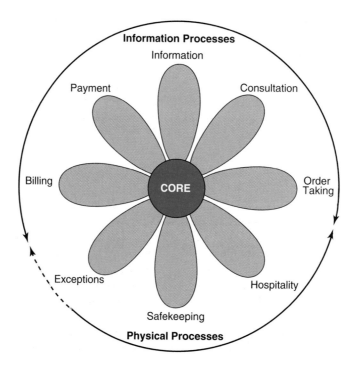

FIGURE 11.1

Information and Physical Processes Within the Augmented Service Product the augmented service product are information-based processes that can be delivered either physically or electronically. Consultation, order taking, billing, payment, and information can all be transmitted in the digital code of computers.

The growth of electronic channels is creating a fundamental change in the nature of marketing. Customers are moving from face-to-face contacts with suppliers in fixed locations that only operate during fixed hours to remote contacts in **cyberspace**, "anywhere, anytime."

> **cyberspace:** a term used to describe the absence of a definable physical location where electronic transactions or communications occur.

More and more services now fall into the category of arm's length relationships rather than face-to-face interactions. As Rayport and Sviokla note:

> *The traditional* marketplace *interaction between physical seller and physical buyer has been eliminated. In fact, everything about this new type of transaction—what we call a* marketspace *transaction—is different from what happens in the marketplace.*[3]

The Marketplace   Companies doing business in the **marketplace** need a physical environment in which customers can get together with suppliers to inspect merchandise or conduct service-related business. We can't get rid of the marketplace for people-processing services, because these services require customers to enter the physical environment of a service factory. In some instances, customers don't want to get rid of the marketplace because it is the physical and social environment that attracts them, like in destination resorts.

> **marketplace:** a physical location where suppliers and customers meet to do business.

The Marketspace   Companies doing business in the **marketspace** may be able to replace contact with physical objects with information about those objects (as in a paper or electronic catalog). For information-based services the context in which the transaction occurs is also different, with on-screen (or on-telephone) contact replacing physical contact; customers may also have the option to replace service from contact personnel by self-service through intelligent interactive systems.

> **marketspace:** a virtual location in cyberspace, made possible by telephone and Internet linkages, where customers and suppliers conduct business electronically.

A desire to save time has been one of the driving forces behind these trends, reflecting customer preferences for ever faster and more convenient service. A second factor has been interest on the part of some customers in obtaining easily accessible information about the goods and services that they buy. Ironically, electronic contacts may bring customers "closer" to manufacturers and service suppliers. Managers are beginning to realize that the opportunity to develop increased knowledge of customers may be as important a reason for doing business in the marketspace as seeking cost savings by eliminating physical contact. Conducting dialog with customers about their needs and preferences (information that can be stored in databases for future reference) can lead to delivery of better and more customized service—which may create greater value and therefore command higher prices.

Designing the Service Delivery Process

The nature of the service both influences and is shaped by distribution strategy. In high-contact services, the design of the physical environment and the way in which customer-contact personnel perform their tasks help create a distinctive identity for a service firm, shape the nature of customers' experiences, and enhance both productivity and quality. However, low-contact services are often designed specifically with improved productivity in mind. More and more frequently, customers deliver these services themselves through self-service technologies rather than interacting directly with service employees.

The design of service delivery systems should start with the core product and then be expanded to include the delivery of each of the supplementary services. Managers responsible for developing service delivery strategy will need to address the following marketing and operations issues:

➤ *What should be the nature of contact between the service provider and its customers?* Should customers come to the provider or the other way around? Or should the two parties deal at arm's length, using mail and telecommunications (ranging from telephone to the Web)?

➤ *What should be the sequencing of the various steps in the service delivery process?* Both operational and customer preferences need to be taken into account in making this decision. The blueprinting methods we discussed in Chapter 7 can be used in exploring alternative delivery sequences.

➤ *Where (location) and when (scheduling) should these steps take place?* The choice today is not only between different physical locations but also between physical space and cyberspace.

➤ *What should be the nature of customer involvement at each step?* If customers are required to be present, should they be served in batches or individually? Alternatively, should they serve themselves?

➤ *What imagery and atmosphere should the service delivery environment (or servicescape) try to create?* For a high-contact service, this concerns decisions on: facility design and layout; staff uniforms, appearance, and attitudes; the type of furnishings and equipment installed; and the use of music, lighting, and decor.

➤ *Should a service firm take responsibility for the entire delivery process or delegate some steps to intermediaries?* Some supplementary services, like information and reservations, can be handled very efficiently and cost-effectively by intermediaries.

➤ *What should be the serving protocol?* Should the firm operate a reservations system or work on a first-come, first-served basis, using queuing when necessary? Or should a priority system be established for certain types of customers (like many firms do for their larger industrial accounts or airlines do for their gold card frequent flyers)?

OPTIONS FOR SERVICE DELIVERY

Delivering a service to customers involves answering the questions "where?" "when?" and "how?" Service marketing strategy must address place and time, paying at least as much attention to speed, scheduling, and the potential for electronic access in cyberspace issues as to the more traditional notion of physical location. The nature of the delivery system has a powerful impact on the customer's experience with the service product.

Service delivery strategy is shaped by several factors, including the nature of the business, the service processes employed, the types of customers targeted, and productivity and quality concerns. A key question is whether the nature of the service or the firm's positioning strategy requires customers to be in direct physical contact with its personnel, equipment, and facilities. If so, do customers need to visit the service organization's facilities or should personnel and equipment be sent to the customer's site? Alternatively, can transactions between provider and customer be completed at arm's length through either telecommunications or modern physical channels of distribution? A second issue concerns the firm's strategy in terms of distribution sites. Should it maintain just a single outlet or serve customers through multiple outlets at different locations? The possible options, combining both type of contact and number of sites, can be seen in Table 11.1.

TABLE 11.1

Method of Service Delivery

Nature of Interaction Between Customer and Service Organization	Availability of Service Outlets	
	Single site	**Multiple Sites**
Customer goes to service organization	Theater Barbershop	Bus service Fast-food chain
Service organization comes to customer	House painting Mobile car wash	Mail delivery Auto club road service
Customer and service organization transact at arm's length (mail or electronic communications)	Credit card company Local TV station	Broadcast network Telephone company

Should we offer customers a choice? Just because a service can be delivered through low-contact channels doesn't necessarily mean it should be. Astute marketers recognize that preferences may vary from one customer to another and even from one situation to another for the same customer. Like Kinko's, many companies offer their customers a choice of **delivery channels**. Depending on the nature of the service, options may include serving a customer at a firm's own retail sites, delegating service delivery to an intermediary or franchisee, coming to the customer's house or place of business, and (in certain types of services) serving the customer at a distance through physical or electronic channels.

delivery channels: the means by which a service firm (sometimes assisted by intermediaries) delivers one or more product elements to its customers.

Customers Visit the Service Site

The convenience of service factory locations and operational schedules becomes an important marketing issue when customers are required to be physically present throughout service delivery—or even just to initiate and terminate the transaction. **Retail gravity models** and other elaborate statistical techniques are sometimes used to help decide how to locate businesses relative to where prospective customers live or work.[4] Traffic and pedestrian counts are used to establish how many prospective customers pass certain locations each day. Construction of a new highway or the introduction of new rail or bus service may have a significant effect on travel patterns and, in turn, determine which sites are now more desirable and which, less so.

retail gravity model: a mathematical approach to retail site selection that involves calculating the geographic center of gravity for the target population and then locating a facility to optimize customers' ease of access.

Providers Come to the Customer

For some types of services, the supplier visits the customer. This is, of course, essential when the target of the service is some immovable physical object like a building that needs cleaning, a large machine that needs repair, a house that requires pest-control treatment, or a garden that needs landscaping. Since it's more expensive and time consuming for service personnel and their equipment to travel to the customer than vice versa, the trend has been away from this approach where possible (few doctors make house calls nowadays!).

There may still be a profitable niche in serving customers who are willing to pay a premium price for the convenience of receiving personal visits from service providers. One young veterinarian has built her business around house calls to sick pets. She found that customers were glad to pay extra for a service that not only saves them time but is also less stressful for the pet than waiting in a crowded veterinary clinic, full of other animals and their worried owners. In remote areas such as Alaska or Canada's Northwest Territory, service providers may have to fly to their customers.

Australia is famous for its Royal Flying Doctor Service, in which physicians fly to make house calls at remote farms and stations. Other more recently established services that travel to the customer include mobile car washing and windshield repair, office and in-home catering, and made-to-measure tailoring services for business people. Some Web-based businesses were developed around the concept of home delivery of retail goods in markets where this type of service delivery had not previously been a viable option.[5]

Aggreko: A Different Kind of Rental Company

You probably think of electricity as coming from a distant power station and of air conditioning and heating as fixed installations. So how would you deal with the following challenges? Luciano Pavarotti is giving an open-air concert in Münster, Germany, and the organizers require an uninterruptible source of electrical power for the duration of the concert, independent of the local electricity supply. A tropical cyclone has devastated the small mining town of Pannawonica in Western Australia, destroying everything in its path, including power lines, and it's urgent that electrical power be restored as soon as possible so that the town and its infrastructure can be rebuilt. In Amsterdam, organizers of the World Championship Indoor Windsurfing competition need power for 27 wind turbines to create strong winds across a huge indoor pool. A U.S. Navy submarine needs a shore-based source of power when it spends time in a remote Norwegian port. Sri Lanka faces an acute shortage of electricity-generating capability when water levels fall dangerously low at the country's major hydroelectric dams due to insufficient monsoon rains two years in a row. A large, power-generating plant in Oklahoma urgently seeks temporary capacity to replace one of its cooling towers, destroyed yesterday in a tornado. And the organizers of the 2002 Winter Olympics outside Salt Lake City need a temporary, portable electricity generating and distribution system with a capacity equivalent to that required to power a city of two million people.

These are all challenges faced and met by a company called Aggreko, which describes itself as "The World Leader in Utility Rental Solutions." Aggreko operates from more than 110 depots in 20 countries around the world. It rents a "fleet" of mobile electricity generators, oil-free air compressors, and temperature control devices ranging from water chillers and industrial air conditioners to giant heaters and dehumidifiers.

Aggreko's customer base is dominated by large companies and government agencies. Although a lot of its business comes from needs that are foreseen far in advance—such as the Olympics and other major events, backup operations during factory maintenance, or a package of services during the filming of a James Bond movie—the firm is also poised to resolve problems arising unexpectedly from emergencies.

Much of the firm's rental equipment is contained in sound-proofed, boxlike structures that can be shipped anywhere in the world and coupled together to create the specific type and level of electrical power output or climate-control capability required by the client. Consultation, installation, and ongoing technical support add value to the core service. Says a company brochure "Emphasis is placed on solving customer problems rather than just renting equipment." Some customers have a clear idea in advance of their needs, others require advice on how to develop innovative, cost-effective solutions to what may be unique problems, and still others are desperate to restore power that has been lost due to an emergency. In the last-mentioned instance, speed is of the essence since downtime can be extremely expensive and in some cases lives may depend on the promptness of Aggreko's response.

Delivering service requires that Aggreko ship its equipment to the customer's site, so that the needed power or temperature control can be available at the right place and time. Following the Pannawonica cyclone, Aggreko's Western Australia team swung into action, rapidly organizing the dispatch of some 30 generators ranging in size from 60 to 750 kVA, plus cabling, refueling tankers, and other equipment. The generators were transported by means of four "road trains," each comprising a giant tractor unit hauling three 40-foot (13m) trailers. A full infrastructure team of technicians and additional equipment were flown in on two Hercules aircraft. The Aggreko technicians remained on site for six weeks, providing 24-hour service while the town was being rebuilt.

Source: Aggreko's "International Magazine," 1997, Web site www.aggreko.com, January 2001.

Service providers are more likely to visit corporate customers at their premises than individuals in their homes, reflecting the greater volume of business purchased and the trend toward outsourcing of activities such as cleaning and security. Many organizations need short-term rentals of equipment and labor for special purposes or to boost productive capacity during busy periods. Aggreko, an international company that rents generating and cooling equipment, is prepared to go anywhere in the world—and often at very short notice (see the box, "Aggreko: A Different Kind of Rental Company").

Arm's Length Transactions

Dealing with a service organization through **arm's length transactions** may mean that a customer never sees the service facilities or meets service personnel. As a result, service encounters tend to be fewer in number and involve telephone, mail, fax, Web sites, or e-mail.[6] The outcome of using the service remains very important to the customer, but much of the service delivery process is hidden. Credit cards and insurance are examples of services that can be requested and delivered by mail or telecommunications. Small equipment repair can often be handled by shipping the item to a maintenance facility. Companies like Stamps.com sell software, and Web-based services enable business customers to send first-class, priority, and express mail right from their office computers. Mailing and shipping histories can be tracked online.

Any information-based product can be delivered almost instantaneously through telecommunication channels to any point in the globe where a suitable reception terminal exists. As a result, physical logistics services, such as FedEx, UPS, and national postal services, now find themselves competing with telecommunications services. When we were writing this book, for instance, we had a choice of mail or courier services for physical shipments of the chapters in either paper or disk form. We could also fax the materials, feeding in the pages one sheet at a time. But by using e-mail, we were able to transmit chapters electronically from one computer to another, with the option of printing them out at the receiving end. In fact, we used all three methods, depending on the nature of the page (hand-drawn images and ads were faxed or mailed), time pressures, and the need for backup in the form of files saved on disks.

> **arm's length transactions:** interactions between customers and service suppliers in which mail or telecommunications minimize the need to meet face-to-face.

PHYSICAL EVIDENCE AND THE SERVICESCAPE

When customers visit a service facility, they expect it to be user friendly—easy to find, simple to use, and staffed by helpful personnel. Operations specialists tend to focus on the functional aspects of facility design, with an emphasis on productive use of resources and safe, efficient delivery of services. But marketers also care about the impression that service facilities and personnel make on customers and how they contribute to the overall service experience. In many instances, it's the nature of that experience that differentiates one service provider from its competitors. So marketers must address the question: *What physical evidence should our facilities present?* When you go to a service factory and interact directly with employees, you're exposed to more compelling evidence than when service is delivered at your home (or work locations) or through electronic channels.

Physical evidence—one of the 8Ps of integrated service management—refers, first, to the tangible elements encountered by customers in the service delivery environment and, second, to the tangible metaphors used in symbols, slogans, or advertising messages. For example, the clean streets, colorful signage, and costumed employees of theme parks like Disneyland and Legoland contribute to the sense of fun and excitement that visitors encounter on arrival and throughout the service experience. Alternatively, consider the office of a successful professional business—an investment bank or a law firm—where wood-paneled walls, leather-bound books, and antique furnishings are used to create an elegant and impressive atmosphere. Marketers use strategically managed physical evidence in three ways:

1. As an attention-creating medium, differentiating their company's services from those of competitors and attracting customers from target segments

2. As a message-creating medium, using symbolic cues to communicate with the intended audience about the distinctive nature and quality of the service experience

3. As an effect-creating medium, employing colors, textures, sounds, scents, and spatial design to create or heighten an appetite for certain goods, services, or experiences

FIGURE 11.2

Distinctive Servicescapes, from Table Settings to Furniture and Room Design, Create Different Customer Expectations of These Two Restaurants

Antique stores provide a nice example of how carefully crafted physical evidence can become an important effect-creating medium. As Philip Kotler noted:

> *Many antique dealers also make use of "organizational chaos" as an atmospheric principle for selling their wares. The buyer enters the store and sees a few nice pieces and a considerable amount of junk. The nice pieces are randomly scattered in different parts of the store. The dealer gives the impression, through his prices and his talk, that he doesn't really know values. The buyer therefore browses quite systematically, hoping to spot an undiscovered Old Master hidden among the dusty canvases of third-rate artists. He ends up buying something that he regards as value. Little does he know that the whole atmosphere has been arranged to create a sense of hidden treasures.[7]*

Take a look at Figure 11.2, which shows the interiors of two restaurants. Imagine that you have just entered one of these two dining rooms and examine the physical evidence each picture provides. How is each establishment positioning itself within the restaurant industry? What sort of meal experience can you expect? Which clues do you use in making your judgments?

Resort hotels provide another illustration of how physical evidence can be used as both an attention-creating and an effect-creating medium. Club Med's villages, designed to create a totally carefree atmosphere, may have provided the original inspiration for "get-away" holiday environments. The new destination resorts are not only far more luxurious than Club Med but also draw inspiration from theme park approaches to creating fantasy environments both inside and outside. Perhaps the most extreme examples come from Las Vegas. Facing competition from numerous casinos in other locations, Las Vegas has been trying to reposition itself from a purely adult destination, once described in a London newspaper as "the electric Sodom and Gomorrah," to a somewhat more wholesome resort appealing to families and convention organizers as well. The gambling is still there, of course, but many of the recently built (or rebuilt) hotels have been transformed into visually striking entertainment centers that feature such attractions as erupting "volcanoes," mock sea battles, and even reproductions of Venice and its canals.

Servicescape Design

The term *servicescape* describes the style and appearance of the physical surroundings where customers and service providers interact.[8] Since servicescapes can create powerful positive or negative impressions, it is important to manage them effectively (especially in high-contact environments). Consider these examples:

➤ Airlines employ corporate design consultants to help them differentiate the appearance of their aircraft and employees from those of competitors. Although the flight attendants from many airlines look interchangeable in their black or navy blue outfits, some have distinctive uniforms that identify them as employees of uniquely positioned carriers like Singapore Airlines or Southwest Airlines. And most airlines have specific color combinations and logos that appear consistently in the interior décor of the plane, the napkins, the snack food packaging, etc.

➤ Restaurants often seem to pay more attention to design than to the food they offer. Furnishings, pictures, real or fake antiques, carpeting, lighting, and choice of live or background music all seek to reinforce a desired look and style that may or may not be related to the cuisine. Some restaurants follow themes in both décor and food service. For example, the menus for the Outback

Steakhouse chain list hearty foods and beverages with distinctive names, and the settings are designed to make guests feel like they have just taken a journey "down under" to Australia for a meal.

➤ Many expensive hotels have become architectural statements. Some occupy classic buildings, lovingly restored at huge expense to a far higher level of luxury than ever known in the past, and using antique furnishings and rugs to reinforce their "old world" style. Modern hotels sometimes feature dramatic atriums in which wall-mounted elevators splash down in fountains. Resort hotels invest enormous sums to plant and maintain exotic gardens on their grounds.

As in a theater, servicescape elements like scenery, lighting, music and other sounds, special effects, and the appearance of the actors (employees) and audience members (customers) all serve to create an atmosphere in which the service performance takes place. In certain types of businesses, servicescapes are enhanced by judicious use of sounds, smells, and the textures of physical surfaces. Where food and drink are served, of course, taste is also highly relevant.

For first-time customers in particular, the servicescape plays an important role in helping frame expectations about both the style and quality of service to be provided. Because it's hard to evaluate many service performances in advance (or even after service delivery), customers seek pre-purchase clues about service quality. Hence, first impressions are important. But as customers move beyond the initial contact point, con-

Let's Go Shopping (Maybe at Your Store)

5 CART [RATING]:

- 🛒 Personnel
- 🛒 Store Services
- 🛒 Creativity
- 🛒 Selection/Inventory
- 🛒 Overall Store Atmosphere

"Let's Go Shopping" is a regular feature filed by "mystery shoppers" who visit grocery stores across the country to report on how stores measure up in terms of personnel, services, merchandise, selection, and overall store atmosphere.

Loblaws, #029
650 Dupont St. & Christie, Toronto

This chain-operated store's entrance was filled with tantalizing aromas from Movenpick: one of the many kiosks lining the store. The store's most unique asset is its one-stop, "under one roof"

shopping experience. The Internet, in-store pharmacy, cleaners, wine store, bank machine, etc. prove to be successful additions to the store's business. Everything is done on a larger scale. This is evident in the large aisles and large signage throughout the store and increased SKUs. To enhance the mood of the environment; music, lighting, and odors circulate to create customer comfort.

There were 14 cash registers in front of the store, five of which were open. The registers were completely computerized visual systems with scanning. Cashiers provide a choice between paper and plastic bags for those customers who are concerned with recycling. Shopping carts are clean and accessible at the store front with a dollar deposit. There were sufficient cart locations outside the store to attain/dispose of carts.

The pricing on the shelf after a random audit was accurate and highly visible. The overall impression of the shelves was that they were well stocked and faced with a large variety of SKUs. President's Choice, the store's private label products, are aggressively promoted with signage at shelf and throughout the store.

Source: Reprinted from *Canadian Grocer*, November 1997, 38.

tinued exposure and experiences combine to create a more detailed impression. Consider the impressions recorded by a mystery shopper appraising a Toronto supermarket for a grocery trade magazine—see the boxed story "Let's Go Shopping (Maybe at Your Store)."

Many servicescapes are purely functional. Firms that seek to convey the impression of cut-price service do so by locating in inexpensive neighborhoods, occupying buildings with a simple (even warehouse-like) appearance, minimizing wasteful use of space, and dressing their employees in practical, inexpensive uniforms like the bright red aprons worn at Home Depot. However, servicescapes don't always shape customer perceptions and behavior in ways intended by their creators, because customers often make creative use of physical spaces and objects to suit their own purposes.[9] For instance, business people (or college students) may appropriate a restaurant table for use as a temporary desk, with papers spread around and even a laptop computer and mobile phone competing for space with food and beverages. Smart designers keep an eye open for such trends, which often underlie creation of a new service concept like the cyber café.

PLACE, CYBERSPACE, AND TIME DECISIONS

How should service managers make decisions in response to the question: *When and where should our service be available?* The answer is likely to reflect customer needs and expectations, competitive activity, and the nature of the service operation. Some distribution strategies may be more appropriate for supplementary service elements than for the

---

In-Store Marketing

The promotional weekly flyers, store signs, and in-store features were promoted with large signage throughout the store. There was no loyalty card program or coupon clipping here, but there are store coupons available on the shelf. Similar to most stores they did accept manufacturers coupons. The primary displays included a variety of feature/advertised items, which are promoted on well-stocked displays throughout the store. The incremental displays were attractively done and promoted impulse purchases while the aisles are still clear and shoppable. While taking advantage of some good displays to cross promote, there were some obvious missed opportunities. The store has special racking for promoting some products, especially in the seasonal aisle. Overall the impression of in-store promotion was strong.

Staff

Customer service is definitely not a thing of the past in this store. The staff was extremely customer-focused and seemed to enjoy the work environment. They were well groomed with clean/pressed uniforms. The knowledge of store staff when asked about an item was good. The shopper was directed to the appropriate location but was not taken directly over.

Full of color, the produce section was clean and well maintained. The deli section was also clean and the meat/salads were well stocked. The seafood section filled with the catch of the day looked fresh and inviting. The meat/butcher counter was acceptable. The staff was knowledgeable and helpful in all departments.

General Impressions

The store's biggest strength is its one-stop shopping benefits. For a taste of international flair one must definitely shop the aisles. The one disappointment of the store was the meat department. The labels indicating specific meats were stained and the overall appearance of the department was unclean.

This store's overall ranking is outstanding. Shopping should be an excellent experience thus endorsing future loyalty to a store. OVERALL (RATING): 🛒 🛒 🛒 🛒

core product itself. Perhaps you're willing to go to a particular location at a specific time to attend a sporting or entertainment event. But you probably want greater flexibility and convenience when making an advance reservation. If so, you may expect the reservations service to be open for extended hours, to offer booking and credit card payment by phone, and to deliver tickets by mail, fax, or e-mail.

Locational Issues in Service Delivery

Although customer convenience is important, operational requirements set tight constraints for some services. Airports, for instance, are often inconveniently located relative to travelers' homes, offices, or destinations. Because of noise and environmental factors, finding suitable sites for new airports is a very difficult task. (A governor of Massachusetts was once asked what would be an acceptable location for construction of a second airport to serve Boston. He thought for a moment and then responded: "Nebraska!") As a result, airport sites are often far from the city centers to which many passengers wish to travel, and the only way to make them less inconvenient is to install high-speed rail links like the rail service to Hong Kong's new airport. A different type of location constraint is imposed by other geographic factors like terrain and climate. Obviously, ski resorts are limited to mountain environments while ocean beach resorts must be on the coast.

The need for economies of scale may also restrict choice of locations. Major hospitals consolidate many different health-care services—even a medical school—at a single, very large facility. Customers requiring complex, in-patient treatment must come to this service factory rather than being treated at home—although an ambulance (or even a helicopter) can be sent to pick them up if they are seriously ill or injured.

Some multi-site service firms have the option of creating service factories on a very small scale at locations that are close to where prospective customers live or work. For example, Taco Bell has become famous for its innovative K-Minus strategy, which involves creating restaurants without kitchens. All food preparation is done in a central commissary, with prepared meals then being shipped to restaurants and mobile food carts, where they are reheated prior to serving.[10]

Self-service electronic kiosks can deliver a variety of information-based services from many different locations (see box). The number of Internet kiosks is projected to increase from 151,000 worldwide in 2001 to 446,000 by 2006; over the same period, sales through kiosks are forecast to rise from $200 million to $6.5 billion.[11]

Another service delivery trend involves locating retail and other services close to gas stations and public transportation stops or in bus, rail, and air terminals. Major oil companies are developing chains of retail stores to complement the fuel pumps at their service stations, thus offering customers the convenience of one-stop shopping for fuel, auto supplies, food, and household products. Truck stops on intercity highways include laundromats, bathrooms, ATMs, fax machines, Internet access, and restaurants in addition to a variety of vehicle maintenance and repair services.

In one of the most interesting new retailing developments, airport terminals are being transformed from nondescript ticketing and waiting areas into vibrant shopping malls. Two pioneers of this trend were London's Heathrow and Gatwick airports. Seeking to capitalize on its expertise, the airport operator, a company called BAA (which operates seven British airports), established a U.S. subsidiary and won a 15-year master-developer contract to design, build, lease, and manage the Pittsburgh Airmall, the nation's first custom-built airport retail complex. Pittsburgh is U.S. Airways' major hub and most of its passengers are domestic travelers. Goods and services available at the Airmall range from tasty take-out sandwiches for passengers who don't expect a meal on their flight to $15 massages for tired travelers with aching backs. Sales per passenger at Pittsburgh increased from $2.40 in 1992 to $8.10 in

2000; sales per square foot of retailing space are now four to five times those of typical U.S. regional shopping centers.[12] BAA also has operating contracts at Harrisburg, Indianapolis, Newark, and Boston, as well as at Mauritius, Naples (Italy), and two Australian airports.

The underlying theme of modern service delivery is one of offering customers more choices in terms of where service is delivered. Some people want face-to-face contact, others like telephone contact with a human being, and still others prefer the greater anonymity and control offered by more impersonal options like self-service equipment and the Internet. Many customers also want the ability to switch between delivery alternatives depending on the specific situation at hand.

Electronic Kiosks Deliver Both Commercial and Government Services

The Internet is everywhere when it comes to service delivery. Electronic kiosks are turning up in such locations as amusement parks, campgrounds, bars, car washes, shopping centers, universities, libraries, and health clubs—all offering self-service options to new users and technology-savvy customers alike. Consider the following examples:

1. Simple health checks can be administered through self-service equipment. In the United States, Web-enabled kiosks that measure blood pressure, heart rate, weight, and body mass have been installed in Kmart stores across the country. They can also provide useful health information. And in Britain, the National Health Service has purchased 153 interactive touchscreen kiosks and monitoring services for installation in pharmacies, supermarkets, post offices, shopping malls, and holiday resorts.

2. Electronic kiosks offering Internet access are becoming common in airports, shopping malls, and other public locations. Some provide a combination of services, including an ATM for banking services, a pre-paid phone card dispenser, and access to the Web. Some communication technology vendors believe that Internet terminals will eventually become as ubiquitous as conventional ATM machines are now.

3. Several countries have installed kiosks as a way to ensure that the Internet is more widely accessible to their citizens. For example, Jamaica has installed Internet kiosks in post offices and other public locations in an attempt to provide affordable access and encourage Web usage in a nation where computer ownership remains far lower than in affluent, industrialized countries.

4. Government agencies see electronic kiosks as a way to cut administrative budgets and provide 24-hour service in convenient locations. From using kiosks to dispense information about public services, tourist attractions, and transit routes and schedules, some public agencies are now moving to automate a variety of transactions that previously required intervention by a public employee. Consumers touch the screen to choose from a menu of services, which can be programmed in multiple languages. They can pay parking tickets, speeding fines, and property taxes, obtain dog licenses and copies of birth certificates, and order license plates for their cars. In Utah, five "Quickcourt" kiosks assist people in filling out paperwork for no-fault divorces—a process that takes about 45 minutes, requires no lawyer, and costs only $10. Quickcourt also computes child support payments. In San Antonio, Texas, kiosks sell permits to hold garage sales and print out information on property taxes and city job openings. Users can also view pictures of animals available for adoption at the city pound. In New York, customers can look up certain kinds of records (like landlords' histories of building code violations) and swipe their credit cards through a slot to pay municipal taxes, license fees, or speeding fines.

Source: "Lifeclinic Announces Rollout of Web-Enabled Blood Pressure Kiosks to Kmart Stores Across the Country," www.spacelabs.com, 13 November 2000; "Action MultiMedia Secures NHS Direct Contract," www.kiosks.org, 1 November 2000; Yukari Iwatani, "From Bars to Car Washes Internet is Everywhere," *Yahoo!News*, 11 September 2000; "Internet Kiosks to be Placed in Post Offices and Other Public Areas Throughout Jamaica," www.atcominfo.com, 17 May 2000; "Kiosks Could Make Public Access Common," www.usatoday.com, 28 February 1999; and Carol Jouzaitis, "Step Right Up and Pay Your Taxes and Tickets," *USA Today*, 2 October 1997, 4A.

Delivering Services in Cyberspace

Technological developments during the last 20 years have had a remarkable impact on the methods by which services are produced and delivered. Advances in telecommunications and computer technology in particular continue to result in service delivery innovations. For example, personal computers and the Internet are changing the way people shop for both goods and services. In addition to placing catalog orders by mail or telephone, many people now also shop in cyberspace. The Internet's 24-hour service is particularly appealing to customers whose busy lives leave them short of time. Forrester Research says that customers are attracted to virtual stores by four factors in the following order of importance: convenience, ease of research (obtaining information and searching for desired items or services), better prices, and broad selection.[13]

Web sites have become an important competitive tool for service marketers. While some firms only view them as an alternative to paper brochures, others use them in more creative ways ranging from order-taking channels to electronic delivery systems. Delivery through the Internet is an option for any information-based product. Information-based services now delivered through commercial Web sites include software, news, research reports, music, and other forms of entertainment. Firms can also deliver information-based services to their customers as e-mail attachments or through corporate "extranets"—secure, private networks linking a company to its major suppliers and designated customers. Charles Schwab, the brokerage firm, offers investors wireless Internet access through its PocketBroker service.

Traditional retailers have been forced to respond to stiffer competition from Internet and telephone-based catalog retailing. One company, software and computer retailer Egghead Inc., decided to get out of physical retailing altogether. It closed its 80 stores across the United States, laid off 800 of its 1,000 workers, shifted its sales entirely to the Internet, and renamed itself Egghead.com. Other retailers, like the giant bookstore chain Barnes and Noble, have developed a strong Internet presence to complement their full-service bookstores in an effort to counter competition from "cyberspace retailers" such as Amazon.com (which has no retail outlets).[14]

Other store-based retailers are responding to this competitive challenge by trying to make the shopping experience more interesting and enjoyable for customers. Malls have become larger, more colorful, and more elaborate. Within the mall, individual stores try to create their own atmosphere, but tenancy agreements often specify certain design criteria to ensure that each store fits comfortably into the overall mall servicescape. The presence of "food courts" and other gathering places encourages social interaction among shoppers. Theatrical touches include live entertainment, special lighting effects, fountains, waterfalls, and eye-catching interior landscaping ranging from banks of flowers to surprisingly large trees. Individual stores try to add value by offering product demonstrations and such services as customized advice, gift-wrapping, free delivery, installation, and warranty services.

Service Schedules

In the past, most retail and professional services in industrialized countries followed a traditional and rather restricted schedule that limited service availability to 40 to 50 hours a week. This routine reflected social norms (and even legal requirements or union agreements) as to what were appropriate hours for people to work and for enterprises to sell things. The situation caused a lot of inconvenience for working people who either had to shop during their lunch break (if the stores themselves didn't close for lunch) or on Saturdays (if management chose to remain open a sixth day). The idea of doing business on a Sunday was strongly discouraged in most Christian cultures and often prohibited by law, reflecting long-standing traditions based on religious practice. Among commercial services, only those devoted to entertainment and relaxation, like movie theaters, bars, restaurants, and sporting facilities, geared their schedules toward weekends and evening hours when their customers had leisure time. Even so, they often faced restrictions on hours of operation, especially on Sundays.

Today, things are changing fast in terms of business operating hours. For some highly responsive service operations, the standard has become **24/7 service**—24 hours a day, 7 days a week, around the world. Some services like telecommunications and international airlines are 24-hour operations, every day of the year. Other examples include services that respond to emergencies, such as fire, police, and ambulance, or repairs to vital equipment. Hospitals and first-class hotels provide 24-hour care or room service. Ships and long-distance trains keep going through the night, too.

> **24/7 service:** service that is available 24 hours a day, 7 days a week.

Factors That Encourage Extended Operating Hours

At least five factors are driving the move toward extended operating hours and seven-day operations. The trend has been most noticeable in the United States and Canada, but it's spreading elsewhere.

➤ *Economic pressure from consumers.* The growing number of two-income families and single wage-earners who live alone need time outside normal working hours to shop and use other services, since they have nobody else to do these things for them. Once one store or firm in any given area extends its hours to meet the needs of these market segments, competitors often feel obliged to follow. Retail chains have often led the way in this respect.

➤ *Changes in legislation.* A second factor has been the decline in support for the traditional religious view that a specific day (typically Sunday in predominantly Christian cultures) should be legislated as a day of rest for everyone, regardless of religious affiliation. In a multicultural society, of course, it's difficult to establish just what day should be designated as special—for observant Jews and Seventh Day Adventists, Saturday is the Sabbath; and for Muslims, Friday is the holy day. There has been a gradual erosion of legislation related to this issue in Western nations in recent years, although it's still firmly in place in some countries and locations. In Switzerland, for example, most retail activities still close down on Sundays—except for bakeries, where people like to buy freshly baked bread on Sunday mornings.

➤ *Economic incentives to improve asset utilization.* Even if the number of extra customers served is minimal, there are both operational and marketing advantages to remaining open 24 hours. The incremental cost of extending hours is often relatively small (especially when part-timers can be hired without paying them overtime or benefits). If extending hours reduces crowding and increases revenues, then it's economically attractive. There are also costs involved in shutting down and reopening a facility like a supermarket. Climate control and some lighting must be left running all night, and security personnel must be paid to keep an eye on the place.

➤ *Availability of employees to work during "unsocial" hours.* Changing lifestyles and a desire for part-time employment have combined to create a growing labor pool

Modern ATMs not only offer 24-hour banking services but may also dispense tickets, stamps, and abbreviated bank statements.

of people who are willing to work evenings and nights. Some of these workers are students looking for part-time work outside their classroom hours or parents juggling child-care responsibilities. Others are "moonlighting," holding a full-time job by day and earning additional income by night. Some people simply prefer to work at night and relax or sleep during the day, while others are glad to obtain any paid employment, regardless of hours.

➤ *Automated self-service facilities.* Self-service equipment has become increasingly reliable and user friendly. Many machines now accept card-based payments in addition to coins and banknotes. Installing unattended machines may be economically feasible in places that couldn't support a staffed facility. Unless a machine requires frequent servicing or is particularly vulnerable to vandalism, the incremental cost of going from limited hours to 24-hour operation is minimal. In fact, it may be much simpler to leave machines running all the time than to turn them on and off, especially if they are placed in widely scattered locations.

Responding to Customers' Need for Convenience

American and Canadian retailers have led the way toward meeting customer needs for greater convenience, but many other countries are now beginning to follow suit. The changes initially began with early-morning to late-evening service in pharmacies and "7–11" convenience stores that were open from 7 a.m. to 11 p.m. (In continental Europe, which employs the 24-hour system for keeping time, such stores are sometimes referred to as "7–23" stores—for obvious reasons!) The trend has now extended to 24-hour service in a variety of retail outlets from service stations to restaurants to supermarkets.

The customer's search for convenience has not been confined to convenient times and places, nor to just the purchase of core products. People want easy access to supplementary services, too—especially information, reservations, and problem solving. As one credit card executive observed,

> *There are a lot of two-income families. Our customers are busy with their personal lives, and they don't have a lot of time to handle their personal business. They expect us to be available to them when it's convenient for them, not when it's convenient for us, so they expect extended hours. And most of all, they expect one contact to solve their problem.*

In many service industries, information and problem-solving needs were originally met by telephoning a specific store or facility during its regular operating hours. But led by airlines and hotel chains, separate customer service centers have evolved, reached by calling a single toll-free number. Service providers operate some of these centers themselves, while others, such as hotel chains, often subcontract functions such as reservations to specialist intermediaries. Once a firm departs from locally staffed phones and installs a centralized system, it can create more consistent service and offer greater expertise, but risks losing the local touch.

Moving to 24/7 Service

Providing extended-hours customer service is almost mandatory for any organization with a nationwide clientele in countries (or service regions) that cover multiple time zones. Consider a company that serves customers on both the Atlantic and Pacific coasts of North America. Between New York and Los Angeles, for example, there is a three-hour time difference. If the switchboard closes at 5:00 P.M. Eastern Time, then customers on the west coast are denied access to the number after 2:00 P.M. Pacific Time. The situation is even worse for those on Alaska-Hawaii time, where it's only 12 noon. Things are reversed when the supplier is located on the West Coast. Imagine a Canadian firm in Vancouver B.C. whose office opens at 8:30 A.M. Pacific Time. By then it's already 12:30 P.M. Atlantic Time in Halifax, Nova Scotia, and 1:00 P.M. in St. John's, Newfoundland (which has its own time zone).

When a North American business redefines its goal as offering continent-wide service on a daily basis—from first thing in the morning in Newfoundland to mid-evening in Alaska or Hawaii—managers don't need a fancy calculator to figure out that customer service lines will have to be open at least 18 hours a day. At this point, the firm may want to consider going to 24-hour operations. The desirability of this move depends on the firm's priorities, the costs involved, and the value that customers place on total accessibility. One alternative to operating the service factory around the clock is to use automated call centers or Web sites that can handle many kinds of transactions and queries without human backup.

Servicing Manufactured Products

Most manufactured products create a need for accompanying services, ranging from financing and training to transportation and maintenance. The competitiveness of a manufacturer's products in both domestic and global markets is often as much a function of the availability and quality of relevant services as the quality of the core product.

Both manufacturing and service companies now rely on computer-based systems to provide many of the supplementary services that customers need and expect. In turn, there is a huge market for servicing these computer systems. Powerful computers and peripherals—and the software to run them—have been sold to users all over the world. Although there are many niche players, large computer systems are supplied by a handful of international firms, dominated by American and Japanese companies. The systems that they sell can be found in operation in locations ranging from big city banks to chemical plants near rural towns. They are also present in such exotic locations as remote mining sites in Australia, oil rigs above the Arctic Circle, airports on Pacific islands, hydroelectric projects in the Andes, and on ships sailing the seven seas.

As powerful as these computers are, they are only of value when up and running. System failures can have disastrous consequences for both their users and the users' own customers. When a firm is dependent on a system 24 hours a day, downtime can be very disruptive: The consequences can range from personal inconvenience to the shutdown of a major facility. Some emergencies can be handled by a duty person, reached by a pager or cellular phone, who drives to the site of the problem, makes a physical inspection, and undertakes whatever repairs are necessary. Maintaining and repairing computers was historically a task that had to be performed on site. But, engineers at companies like IBM or Hewlett-Packard are now able to monitor customers' installations from a support center in a distant location—even on another continent—then diagnose and fix many hardware and software problems without ever leaving their own offices.

THE ROLE OF INTERMEDIARIES

Cost-conscious operations managers should consider: *What options exist for using third-party intermediaries?* Delegating specialized delivery tasks is often a cost-effective strategy, especially for supplementary service elements. It may also be an effective marketing strategy, enabling a firm to reach more customers—and offer them more supplementary services—than the firm could economically do on its own.

Delegating Specific Service Elements

Travel agents and theater ticket agents handle customer interactions like giving out information, taking reservations, accepting payment, and ticketing. Brokers sell and service insurance policies. Distributors representing manufacturers take responsibility not only for sales but also for such supplementary services as information, advice, order taking, delivery, installation, billing and payment, and some problem solving; in some cases, they may also handle repairs and upgrades. In Figure 11.3 we use the Flower of Service framework to illustrate how the original supplier may work in partnership with one or more intermediaries to deliver a complete service package to customers. In this example, the core product is still delivered by the originating supplier, together with certain supplementary elements in the information, consultation, and exceptions categories. The remaining supplementary services have been added by an intermediary to com-

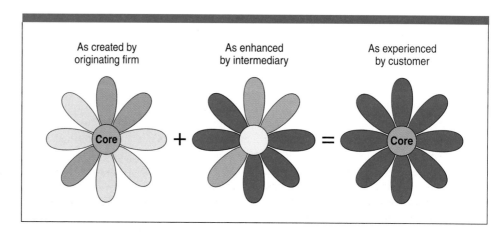

As created by originating firm + As enhanced by intermediary = As experienced by customer

FIGURE 11.3

Splitting Responsibilities for Supplementary Service Elements

plete the offering as experienced by the customer. In other instances, several specialist outsourcers might be involved as intermediaries for specific elements. The original service provider must act as the guardian of the overall process, ensuring that each element offered by intermediaries fits the overall service concept to create a consistent and seamless branded service experience.

Franchising

Even delivery of the core service product can be outsourced to an intermediary. This is the essence of franchising, a common strategy for expanding delivery of a proven service concept to multiple sites, without the level of investment capital required for rapid expansion of company-owned and managed sites. Franchisors recruit entrepreneurs who are willing to invest their own time and equity to manage a business based on a previously developed service concept. In return, the franchisor provides training in operations and marketing, sells necessary supplies, and provides promotional support at a national or regional level to augment local marketing activities (which are paid for by the franchisee but must adhere to copy and media guidelines prescribed by the franchisor).

A disadvantage of franchising is that it entails some loss of control over the delivery system and how customers experience the actual service. Franchisors usually attempt to exercise control over all aspects of the service performance through a contract that specifies adherence to tightly defined service standards, procedures, scripts, and physical presentation. There is ongoing monitoring of productivity and quality standards relating not only to output specifications, but also to the appearance of the physical facilities, employee performance, and hours of operation. As franchisees gain experience, they sometimes start to resent the various fees they pay the franchisor and believe that they can operate the business better without the constraints imposed by the agreement. The resulting disputes often lead to legal fights between the two parties.

Licensing and Distribution Agreements

An alternative to franchising is licensing another supplier to act on the original supplier's behalf to deliver the core product. Universities sometimes license another educational institution to deliver courses designed by the former. Trucking companies regularly use independent agents instead of locating company-owned branches in each of the different cities they serve. Many choose to contract with independent "owner-operators," who drive their own trucks, rather than buying trucks and employing full-time drivers.

Financial services also engage in service distribution agreements. Banks seeking to move into investment services will often act as the distributor for mutual fund products created by an investment firm that lacks extensive distribution channels of its own. Many banks also sell insurance products underwritten by an insurance company. They collect a commission on the sale but are not normally involved in handling claims.

Conclusion

Responses to the questions "Where? When? and How?" provide the foundation of service delivery strategy. The customer's overall service experience is a function of both service performance and delivery characteristics. "Where?" relates, of course, to the places where customers can obtain service delivery. In this chapter, we presented a categorization scheme for thinking about alternative place-related strategies, including remote delivery from virtual locations.

"When?" involves decisions about the scheduling of service delivery. Customer demands for greater convenience are now leading many firms to extend their hours and days of service. "How?" addresses channels and procedures for delivering the core and supplementary service elements to customers. Advances in technology continue to have a major impact on the alternatives available and on the economics of those alternatives.

Study Questions and Exercises

1. Review the story about Kinko's at the beginning of this chapter. What do you see as the key changes in (a) product strategy and (b) distribution strategy?

2. What are the key decisions managers must consider in designing a service delivery system? What are some of the trade-offs that must be made?

3. Identify a service whose delivery strategy fits each of the categories in Table 11.1. What are the implications for management in each case?

4. Describe the servicescapes of two different service businesses. To what extent are their roles strategic in design (differentiating one firm from its competitors) versus functional (adding value for customers and employees)? Give specific examples to support your answers.

5. Visit the Amazon.com and BarnesandNoble.com Web sites. Compare their design, structure, and ease of use. As a potential customer, which do you prefer and why? What enhancements would you suggest?

6. Select a service organization with which you are reasonably familiar, and construct a simple flowchart of service delivery. Identify the critical points within the service delivery process that are likely to have a significant bearing on the customer's experience. Clarify why these points in the process are particularly important and how you would manage them.

7. Identify five situations in which you use a self-service delivery option. In each case, explain your motivation for using this approach to delivery rather than having service personnel do it for you.

8. Using the same five situations you chose for Question 7, comment on the user-friendliness of the equipment, the mental and physical effort required, the time involved, and any negative sensory experiences. Are there any perceived risks for customers who use these self-service options? What recommendations for improvements would you offer to management?

9. What marketing and management challenges might result from the use of intermediaries in a service setting?

Endnotes

1. From Ann Marsh, "Kinko's Grows Up—Almost," *Forbes*, 1 December 1997, 270–272; and www.kinkos.com, January 2001.
2. See, for example, Regis McKenna, "Real-Time Marketing," *Harvard Business Review*, July-August 1995, 87–98; Jeffrey F. Rayport and John J. Sviokla, "Exploiting the Virtual Value Chain," *Harvard Business Review*, November-December 1995; and Regis McKenna, *Real Time* (Boston, MA: Harvard Business School Press, 1997).
3. Jeffrey F. Rayport and John J. Sviokla, "Managing in the Marketspace," *Harvard Business Review*, November-December 1994, 141–150.

4. For an empirical study of location decisions for established versus new services, see Roger W. Schmenner, "The Location Decisions of New Services," in James A. Fitzsimmons and Mona J. Fitzsimmons, *New Service Development* (Thousand Oaks, CA: Sage Publications, 2000), 216–238.

5. Mary Modahl, "Will E-Commerce Eliminate Traditional Intermediaries?" in *Taking Sides: Clashing Views on Controversial Issues in Marketing* (Guilford, CT: McGraw-Hill/Dushkin, 2001), 146–161.

6. Mary Jo Bitner, Stephen W. Brown, and Matthew L. Meuter, "Technology Infusion in Service Encounters," *Journal of the Academy of Marketing Science* 28, no. 1 (2000): 138–149.

7. Philip Kotler, "Atmospherics as a Marketing Tool," *Journal of Retailing*, 49, no. 4 (1973): 48–64.

8. Mary Jo Bitner, "Servicescapes: The Impact of Physical Surroundings on Customers and Employees," *Journal of Marketing* 56 (April 1992): 57–71.

9. Véronique Aubert-Gamet, "Twisting Servicescapes: Diversion of the Physical Environment in a Reappropriation Process," *International Journal of Service Industry Management* 8, no. 1 (1997): 26–41.

10. James L. Heskett, W. Earl Sasser Jr., and Leonard A. Schlesinger, *The Service Profit Chain* (New York: The Free Press, 1997), 218–220.

11. Stephanie Miles, "Netkey Transforms Kiosks into 'E-salespeople,'" WSJ.com, 17 May 2001.

12. Based on information at BAA plc's Web site, www.baa.co.uk, January 2001.

13. Information obtained from Forrester Research: www.forester.com 1998.

14. David D. Kirkpatrick, "Barnes and Noble to Coordinate Online Sales," www.nytimes.com, 27 October 2000.

chapter twelve

Creating Value Through Productivity and Quality

Cisco Systems Leads the Way in e-Productivity

Cisco Systems is the world's leader in electronic commerce, with over $5 billion in sales coming from its Web site alone in 2000.[1] The company supplies networking solutions that connect people, computing devices, and computer networks, allowing individuals and companies to access and transfer information without regard to differences in time, place, or type of computer system. In 2000, it held close to 80 percent of the market for products that keep the Internet functioning, such as routers, switching devices, relays, and Internet software.

Cisco's highly technical products require large amounts of customer support, which is seen as critical to maintaining service quality. But the company soon realized that it wouldn't be able to hire enough engineers to service its rapidly growing customer base. Doug Allred, Cisco's vice president for Consumer Advocacy, decided to implement a call-tracking system so that the company could monitor each technical support call that came in, find an answer to the customer's question in Cisco's own database of known problems and solutions, and track the call to completion. What was unusual about Cisco's approach at the time of implementation was that the system was designed to function as both a telephone-based call center and a virtual call center via the Web. Customers could have their problems posted in a section of the Cisco Web site that was accessible to other customers of the firm.

When someone posted problems or questions, Cisco's technical support staff started working on solutions—and much to the company's amazement, so did other customers! Whoever came up with an answer first posted it on the Web site, and there were often other helpful suggestions relating to the problem. As soon as information flowed into the database, the customer who had posed the original question received an e-mail notification.

In short, Allred had found a workable solution to the firm's technical support engineer shortage by letting its customers (all of whom had been trained and certified by Cisco) help each other out. The company has also created a knowledge base of frequently asked questions (FAQs) that enables customers to find answers to the most common problems without talking to anyone in the company. Cisco's customers are happy to help themselves and others on the Web site, and the sense of community that is created online enhances the perceived quality of the technical support service.

As a result of these productivity initiatives, Cisco found that it didn't need to expand its call center staffing, even though business was growing rapidly. In fact, the company actually documented a 70 percent reduction in calls received, resulting in a savings of $10 million a month (computed at an average of $200 a call). The number of technical support staff assigned to answering calls dropped from 1,000 to 700. Details of each new call and its solution now go to a technical writer to be edited and entered into the Cisco Knowledge Base, thus helping to minimize the number of future calls.

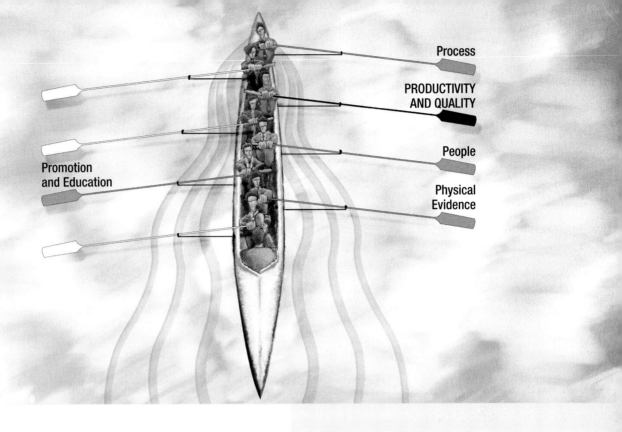

Process

PRODUCTIVITY
AND QUALITY

People

Physical
Evidence

Promotion
and Education

Learning Objectives

After reading this chapter, you should be able to

⇒ define what is meant by productivity and quality in a service context

⇒ understand the relationship between customer expectations, service quality, and customer satisfaction

⇒ explain the gaps model of service quality

⇒ describe the techniques for identifying the root cause of specific service quality problems

⇒ identify the components of a service quality information system

⇒ discuss productivity and quality measurement techniques

MINDING THE SERVICE Ps AND Qs

As you may have already noticed, productivity and quality are treated jointly in this book as one of the 8Ps of integrated service management. This reflects our belief—and that of others—that they are often two sides of the same coin. In fact, FedEx has even employed an internal slogan, $Q = P$.[2] If the two issues are totally divorced, companies risk introducing productivity efforts that will annoy customers or embarking on quality initiatives that will result in higher costs without increasing revenues. As you can see from our discussion of Cisco Systems, the strategic integration of both dimensions can provide greater value for customers and service providers. In fact, a focus on productivity and quality as perceived by customers is critical to a firm's long-term financial success.[3]

In this chapter, we address a particularly challenging question from our service decision framework, ***How can we balance productivity and quality***? This leads us to examine such issues as determining how to reduce operating costs without spoiling the appeal of a service; identifying what customers expect in return for their money, time, and effort; specifying appropriate measures of service quality and productivity; and clarifying what quality improvements are needed to meet or exceed customer expectations.

Creating Value for Customers

What is the fundamental role of marketing? Many theorists argue that it is to create customer value.[4] The search for value often begins with market research, seeking to identify the benefits sought by customers or prospects for a given product category and the costs that they are willing to incur to obtain these benefits. Perceived value is highly personal and may vary widely from one customer to another.[5] In fact, variations in desired benefits often form the basis for segmentation.

Productivity and quality were historically seen as issues for operations managers. Thus, companies focused internally on making process "improvements" that were not necessarily linked to customers' service priorities. However, continuing efforts to understand and improve quality led back to the customer—and to the recognition that quality should be customer defined. Quality enhancements that add no value for customers are a poor allocation of corporate resources.

A key theme running through this book is that marketing cannot operate in isolation from other functional areas in a service environment. Tasks that might be assigned only to operations in a goods-producing company need to include marketers in a service organization, because of customer exposure to service processes. Making these processes more efficient doesn't necessarily result in a better quality experience or improved benefits for customers. Getting service employees to work faster may sometimes be welcomed by customers, but at other times it may make them feel rushed and unwanted. So marketing, operations, and human resources managers all need to work together on designing front-stage jobs and processes. Similarly, service marketing strategies designed to improve customer satisfaction should be carefully reviewed with operations and human resources managers to minimize the risk that such strategies will prove costly and internally disruptive.

Marketing and Quality

Marketing's interest in service quality is obvious when you think about it: Poor quality places a firm at a competitive disadvantage. If customers perceive quality as unsatisfactory, they may be quick to take their business elsewhere. From a marketing standpoint, a key issue is whether or not customers notice differences in quality between competing suppliers. Brad Gale puts it succinctly when he says "value is simply quality, however the *customer* defines it, offered at the right price."[6] Improving quality from the customer's perspective pays off: Data from the PIMS (Profit Impact of Market Strategy) show that a perceived quality advantage leads to higher corporate profits.[7]

Service quality issues are not confined to traditional service industries. It has become increasingly difficult for industrial companies to establish a competitive advantage by offering higher quality products. Many manufacturing firms are working to improve the quality of the supplementary services that support their products—like consultation, financing, shipping and delivery, installation, training of operators, repair and maintenance, trouble-shooting, and billing—in order to keep or gain profitable positions within their industries.[8]

Marketing and Productivity

Why is improving productivity important to marketers? One reason is that it helps keep costs down. Lower costs mean either higher profits or the ability to hold down prices. The company with the lowest costs in an industry has the option to position itself as the low-price leader—usually a significant advantage among price-sensitive market segments. Firms with lower costs than their competitors also generate higher margins, giving them the option of spending more on marketing and customer service activities. They may also be able to offer higher margins to attract and reward the best distributors and intermediaries. These companies are also better able to invest in new service technologies. A second reason that productivity improvements are important to marketers is that they are often associated with faster operating procedures. To the extent that speed of service is valued by customers, it becomes a competitive advantage.

Efforts to improve productivity often affect customers. It's the marketer's responsibility to ensure that negative impacts are avoided or minimized and that new procedures are carefully presented to customers. When the impact is a positive one, the improvements can be promoted as a new advantage. Finally, as we'll see, there are opportunities for marketers themselves to help improve productivity by involving customers actively in service production and delivery.

UNDERSTANDING SERVICE QUALITY

As described in Chapter 4, after making a purchase, customers compare the service they expected to get with what they actually receive. They decide how satisfied they are with service delivery and outcomes, and they also make judgments about quality. Although service quality and customer satisfaction are related concepts, they are not exactly the same thing. Many researchers believe that customers' perceptions about quality are based on long-term, cognitive evaluations of a firm's service delivery, whereas customer satisfaction is a short-term emotional reaction to a specific service experience.[9]

Following a service encounter, customers may evaluate their levels of satisfaction or dissatisfaction and may use this information to update their perceptions of service quality. They must, of course, experience a service before they can be satisfied or dissatisfied with the outcome. But beliefs about quality don't necessarily reflect personal experience. People often make quality judgments about services they have never consumed, basing these evaluations on comments by acquaintances or on advertising messages. Figure 12.1 shows the relationship between expectations, customer satisfaction, and service quality.

Managing a business to optimize customer satisfaction is a strategic imperative at many firms, since the cost of mediocre service quality may be as high as 40 percent of revenues in some service industries.[10] Most companies realize that by improving per-

FIGURE 12.1

The Relationship Among
Expectations, Customer
Satisfaction, and Perceived
Service Quality

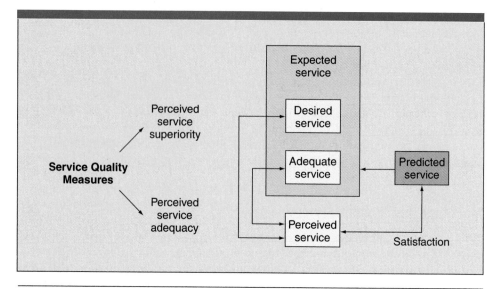

Source: Adapted from Valarie A. Zeithaml, Leonard L. Berry, and A. Parasuraman, "The Nature and Determinants of Customer Expectations of Service," *Journal of the Academy of Marketing Science* 21, no. 1 (1993): 1–12.

formance on service attributes, customer satisfaction should increase. This should, in turn, lead to greater customer retention and improved profitability. For example, the relative similarity of the products offered by different banks has led to an increased emphasis on service quality in the highly competitive retail banking sector. A large telephone survey of bank customers identified poor customer service quality as the most frequent reason for account closures. Analysis of the study results and bank branch profits indicated that customer service quality was a major determinant of how well individual branches performed.[11]

The relationship between service quality and profitability is typically not easy to track for a variety of reasons. Service quality benefits accumulate over time rather than being experienced in the short term. This makes them difficult to measure using traditional market research techniques. Another complicating factor is that many variables contribute to corporate profits (including pricing, distribution, advertising, and competition); it's hard to isolate the effects these individual factors have on the bottom line. And finally, just spending money on service quality initiatives doesn't necessarily lead to increased profits. Service companies must identify the right quality initiatives and execute them effectively.[12]

satisfaction-profit chain:
a strategic framework that
links performance on service
attributes to customer
satisfaction, then to customer
retention, and finally to
profits.

A strategic framework known as the **satisfaction–profit chain** can help managers identify the links between attribute performance, customer satisfaction, customer retention, and profits. However, the relationships between the different links in the chain are not necessarily linear. Sophisticated analysis may be needed to pinpoint the priorities for improvements; for instance, investments designed to avoid negative outcomes on specific attributes may be as important as actions to increase positive performance on others.[13]

Dimensions of Service Quality

Research has identified five broad dimensions of service quality:[14]

> *Reliability*: Is the company dependable in providing service as promised, over time?

> *Tangibles*: What do the service provider's physical facilities, Web site, equipment, personnel, and communication materials look like?

> ➤ *Responsiveness*: Are the firm's employees helpful and able to provide prompt service?

> ➤ *Assurance*: Are service employees knowledgeable, polite, competent, and trustworthy?

> ➤ *Empathy*: Does the service firm provide caring, personalized attention?

Of these five dimensions, reliability has consistently proven to be the most important factor in customers' judgments of service quality.[15] Reliability improvements lie at the heart of service quality enhancement efforts because unreliable service implies broken promises on the attributes that customers care about. If the core service is not performed reliably, customers may assume that the company is incompetent and may switch to another service provider. For a perspective on the dimensions of service quality in online environments, see the box "Service Quality Goes Online."

It isn't easy for many types of service businesses to maintain high levels of reliability day-in and day-out. When customers enter a service factory and are involved in service production, they experience mistakes directly—often before a firm has an opportunity to correct them. In labor-intensive services, employees add a large degree of variability to the service production process. It's difficult for service providers to control such variations, since each employee is somewhat different from the others in personality, skills, and attitudes. Moreover, the same employee can provide radically different service from one customer to the next—or the same customer over time—depending on situational factors like customer behavior, task complexity, and the employee's physical and mental state.

Service Quality Goes Online

Do customers use the same dimensions to evaluate service quality in electronic transactions as they do during more traditional service experiences? A recent study, based on data collected from focus group interviews, explored the criteria customers use to assess electronic service quality (e-SQ). The results indicate that some of the quality dimensions discussed earlier (reliability, responsiveness, and assurance) are important in both online and offline settings. However, some other dimensions are unique to customers' evaluations of e-SQ, including ease of navigation, flexibility, efficiency, site aesthetics, and price knowledge. All of these are technology related except price knowledge, which reflects customers' desire for information about what their total online shopping charges are before they hit the "submit" button to complete their purchases.

Why is e-SQ so important? While many marketers believe that price is the biggest concern for Internet customers, survey results indicate that poor service quality is the reason that most people leave Web sites. Specific failings include the lack of an easy-to-use search engine to help with site navigation; memory-intensive graphics that take too long to download; slow and confusing online ordering processes (especially when advertising promises that it will be easy); and hidden charges.

A good way to understand user requirements in e-commerce is to establish continuous processes (like Web surveys or chat rooms) to monitor customers' responses to their sites. If research shows that customer preferences vary by target market and the type of products being sold, the supplier may want to offer alternative sites for different segments. But in general, Web pages should be designed to load quickly while still conveying rich information. To close communication gaps, companies must plan realistically for adequate site functionality, promise only what their sites can deliver, and ensure that all aspects of fulfillment meet promised levels of performance.

Source: Mary B. Young, "What Customers Want Online," *Insights from MSI* (Cambridge, MA: Marketing Science Institute, Fall 2000), 5–6; Valarie A. Zeithaml, A. Parasuraman, and Arvind Malhotra, "A Conceptual Framework for Understanding e-Service Quality: Implications for Future Research and Managerial Practice" (Cambridge MA: Marketing Science Institute, 2001).

Although mistakes occur in every organization, many companies strive to minimize errors to provide greater service reliability for their customers. Leonard Berry describes how the Hard Rock Café Orlando addresses service reliability:

> *Performing the service right the first time is a bedrock value at Hard Rock Café Orlando, the immensely successful restaurant chain and merchandise retailer. Hard Rock Café emphasizes "double checking" to minimize errors. The message of double checking is: Perform the service carefully to avoid mistakes. If a mistake does occur, correct it before it reaches the customer. Hard Rock Café implements double checking through two "extra" people in the kitchen. One is stationed inside the kitchen and the other at the kitchen counter. The inside person reviews everything that is going on, looking for signs of undercooked or overcooked meals, wilting lettuce, or any below-standard product or performance. The counter person, or "expediter," checks each prepared plate against the order ticket before the food is delivered to the table.*[16]

Reliability is an outcome measure because customers judge it *after* the service experience: Either the service was delivered as promised or it wasn't. The other four dimensions of quality—tangibles (physical evidence), responsiveness, assurance, and empathy—are process dimensions because they can be evaluated by customers *during* service delivery. These dimensions provide companies with the opportunity to delight customers by exceeding their expectations during interactions with employees and the service environment. As shown in Figure 12.1, exceeding customers' desired levels of expectations leads to positive perceptions of service quality.

Quality Gaps

A service performance that surprises and delights customers by falling above their desired service levels will be seen as superior in quality. If service delivery falls within their zone of tolerance, they will feel that it's adequate. But if perceived quality falls below the adequate service level expected by customers, a discrepancy—or quality gap—has occurred between the service provider's performance and customer expectations.[17]

Why do quality failures occur? Gaps can occur at seven different points in the design, production, and delivery of services, as shown in Figure 12.2.[18] The service gap is the most critical, because it involves the customer's overall assessment of the service, comparing what was expected against perceptions of what was received. The ultimate goal in improving service quality is to narrow this gap as much as possible. To do so, service providers may have to reduce or close the six other gaps. The seven potential gaps in service quality are:

1. **The knowledge gap**—the difference between what service providers believe customers expect and customers' actual needs and expectations
2. **The standards gap**—the difference between management's perceptions of customer expectations and the quality standards established for service delivery
3. **The delivery gap**—the difference between specified delivery standards and the service provider's actual performance
4. **The internal communications gap**—the difference between what the company's advertising and sales personnel think are the product's features, performance, and service quality level and what the company is actually able to deliver
5. **The perceptions gap**—the difference between what is actually delivered and what customers perceive they have received (because they are unable to accurately evaluate service quality)
6. **The interpretation gap**—the difference between what a service provider's communication efforts actually promise and what a customer thinks was promised by these communications
7. **The service gap**—the difference between what customers expect to receive and their perceptions of the service that is actually delivered

FIGURE 12.2

Seven Quality Gaps Leading
to Customer Dissatisfaction

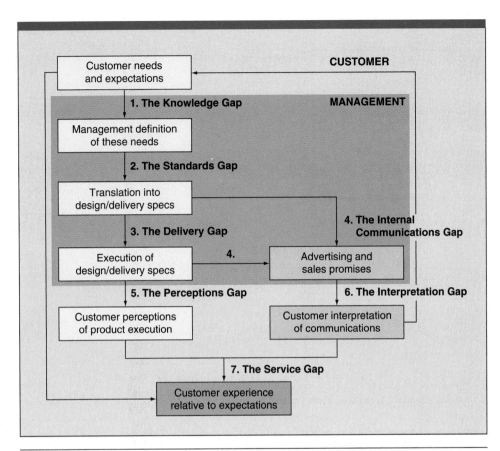

Source: Adapted from Christopher Lovelock, *Product Plus* (New York: McGraw-Hill, 1994), 112.

The presence of any one of these seven quality gaps can lead to a disappointing outcome that damages relationships with customers. Avoiding service gaps in every service encounter will help a firm improve its reputation for quality service. Although careful planning and monitoring will help reduce the likelihood that one of these gaps will occur, when customers indicate that service outcomes are disappointing, it's important to identify and eliminate the gap(s) that lead to this result.

A major problem in some firms is that *service standards* are defined by operations managers who have no knowledge of customer needs and expectations. Hence, it's vital that marketers be involved in the task of designing service standards and measuring performance against them.

Learning from Service Failures

Although every firm should have contingency plans for service recovery, there's no substitute for doing it right the first time. Recovery procedures shouldn't be seen as a substitute for improved service reliability.[19] When a problem is caused by controllable, internal forces, there's no excuse for allowing it to happen again. Recurring service failures lower service quality and reduce productivity as time and money are wasted on correcting mistakes.

With prevention in mind, let's look briefly at some simple but powerful tools for monitoring quality and determining the root causes of service failures. Among the many tools available to quality improvement specialists, the following ones are particularly helpful for managers in identifying service failures and designing effective recovery strategies.

FIGURE 12.3

Control Chart of Departure
Delays Showing Percentage of
Flights Departing Within 15
Minutes of Schedule

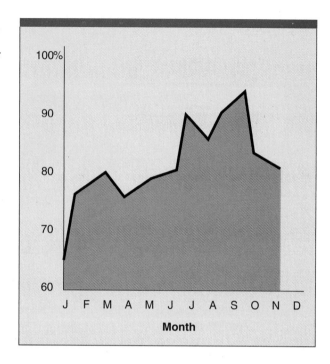

Flowcharts and Service Blueprints Flowcharts (see Chapter 3) and their more formalized derivative, service blueprints (see Chapter 7), are useful tools for thoroughly examining service delivery processes. Once managers understand these processes, it's easier for them to identify potential failure points, which are weak links in the chain. Knowing what can go wrong, and where, is an important first step in improving productivity and preventing service quality problems.

control charts: charts that graph quantitative changes in service performance on a specific variable relative to a predefined standard.

Control Charts It's frequently said that "you cannot manage what you do not measure." **Control charts** offer a simple method for graphing performance over time against specific quality criteria. Because the charts are visual, trends are easily identified. Figure 12.3 shows an airline's performance on the important criterion of on-time departures. The results in this example suggest that management would do well to investigate the situation, because aircraft departure performance is erratic and unsatisfactory.

fishbone diagram: a chart-based technique that relates specific service problems to different categories of underlying causes (also known as a cause-and-effect chart).

Cause-and-Effect Charts The Japanese quality expert Kaoru Ishikawa created the **fishbone diagram** for use in manufacturing firms. To produce a fishbone diagram (also known as a cause-and-effect chart), groups of managers and employees brainstorm factors that might be creating a specific problem. In a traditional version of this diagram, the resulting factors are then categorized into one of five groupings—equipment, people, materials, procedures, and other. It's important to recognize that failures are often sequential, with one problem leading to another in a different category. Figure 12.4 displays no less than 27 possible reasons for late departures of a passenger aircraft!

Notice that the fishbone diagram shown in Figure 12.4 includes eight groupings rather than just the five mentioned above. The extra categories are designed to provide additional information for service firms. For example, the People category has been changed to Front-Stage Personnel and Backstage Personnel. This highlights the fact that

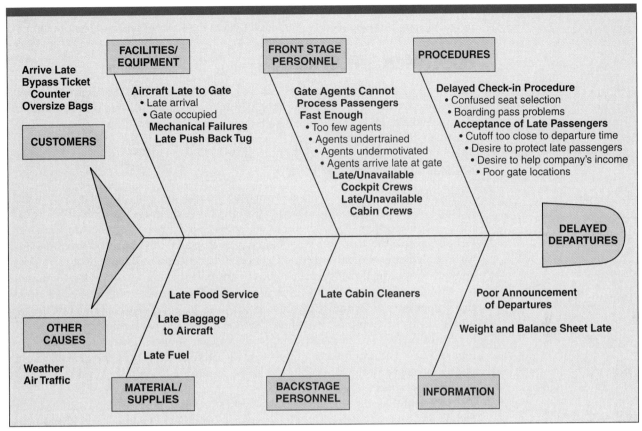

Source: Christopher Lovelock, *Product Plus* (New York: McGraw-Hill, 1994), 218.

FIGURE 12.4

Cause-and-Effect Chart for Airline Departure Delays

front-stage service problems are often experienced directly by customers, whereas back-stage failures tend to show up more indirectly. Information has been split from Procedures because many service problems result from information-related failures. For example, inadequate information about flight departures may lead passengers to arrive late at the gate.

The expanded fishbone diagram also includes a new category—Customers—to acknowledge their increased involvement in service production and delivery, because customers can also be the cause of problems for a service business. As we've discussed before, customers of high-contact services are often heavily involved in front-stage operations. If they don't play their roles correctly, they may reduce service productivity and cause quality problems for themselves and other customers. For instance, an aircraft that seats hundreds of passengers can be delayed if a single traveler tries to board at the last minute with an oversized bag, which then has to be loaded into the cargo hold.

Pareto Analysis The technique known as **Pareto analysis** (named after the Italian economist who first developed it) is useful in identifying the principal causes of observed outcomes. Application of this technique often highlights a phenomenon known as the "80/20 rule," showing that approximately 80 percent of the value of one variable (in this instance, the number of service failures) is accounted for by only 20 percent of the causal variables (i.e., the number of possible causes). In the airline example above, 88 percent of the company's late-departing flights were caused by only four (15 percent) of all the possible causes—late passengers, late push back tug, late fuel,

Pareto analysis: an analytical procedure to identify what proportion of problem events is caused by each of several different factors.

and late weight and balance sheet. So, focus on these four factors rather than tackling all potential causes simultaneously—especially when time and other resources are limited.

CUSTOMER SATISFACTION

Customers experience various levels of satisfaction or dissatisfaction after each service experience according to the extent to which their expectations were met or exceeded. Because satisfaction is an emotional state, their postpurchase reactions can involve anger, dissatisfaction, irritation, neutrality, pleasure, or delight.

Satisfaction, Delight, and Loyalty

Obviously, angry or dissatisfied customers are troublesome because they may switch to another company and spread negative word of mouth. But is it sufficient just to satisfy a customer? After all, a firm might reason that products and services are rarely perfect and people are hard to please. Companies that take this approach may be asking for trouble because there is a lot of evidence that merely satisfying customers is not enough.[20] Marginally satisfied or neutral customers can be lured away by competitors. A delighted customer, however, is more likely to remain loyal in spite of attractive competitive offerings. Customer satisfaction plays an especially critical role in highly competitive industries, where there is a tremendous difference between the loyalty of merely satisfied and completely satisfied—or delighted—customers (see Figure 12.5). For example, a study of retail banking customers showed that completely satisfied customers were nearly 42 percent more likely to be loyal than merely satisfied customers.

To improve its customer satisfaction levels, a company must first find out how satisfied or dissatisfied its current customers actually are. One common way of measuring satisfaction is to ask customers first to identify what factors are important in satisfying

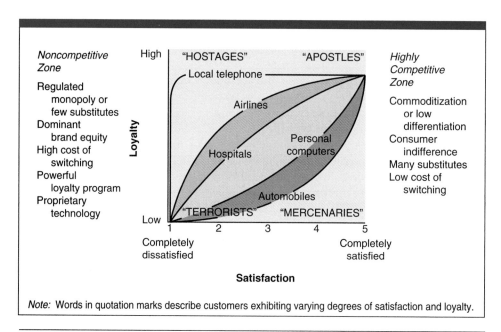

Note: Words in quotation marks describe customers exhibiting varying degrees of satisfaction and loyalty.

FIGURE 12.5

How the Competitive Environment Affects the Satisfaction-Loyalty Relationship them and then to evaluate the performance of a service provider and its competitors on these factors. Many firms use a five-point scale to measure customer satisfaction, with the following format:

1 = very dissatisfied

2 = somewhat dissatisfied

3 = neutral

4 = somewhat satisfied

5 = very satisfied

The results of these satisfaction surveys can be used to estimate the number of loyal customers a firm has, as well as how many are at risk of defecting.

As shown in Figure 12.6, research indicates that customers with satisfaction ratings of 0 to 3 are very likely to defect, whereas customers who rated themselves somewhat satisfied (4) can be lured away by a competing service. Only customers with a satisfaction rating of 5 are absolutely loyal. At the extremes of the scale are two customer groups with particular significance to service providers: "terrorists" and "apostles." Terrorists are every company's nightmare. They don't just defect—they make sure that everyone else shares their anger and frustration, too. Often these customers had a bad experience that was never corrected by the company; as a result, they are dedicated to spreading as much negative word of mouth as possible. In contrast, the apostle is the kind of customer of whom every service provider dreams; they are so satisfied with their service experiences that they want to share their enthusiasm with others. They are extremely loyal, and their obvious delight helps attract other customers. Creating apostles and eliminating terrorists should be a key goal for every service provider.[21]

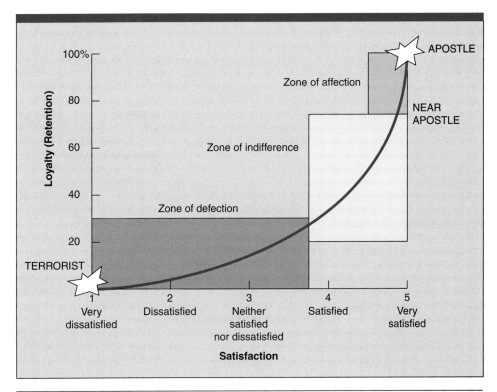

Source: James L. Heskett, W. Earl Sasser, Jr., and Leonard A. Schlesinger, *The Service Profit Chain* (New York: Free Press, 1997), 87.

FIGURE 12.6

"Apostles" and "Terrorists" on the Satisfaction-Loyalty Curve

Using Customer Satisfaction Information

Once a company has gathered satisfaction data from its customers, the next step is to decide on the most appropriate strategies for increasing satisfaction levels. If most of the satisfaction ratings fall in the 2–3 range, there is probably a problem with the firm's delivery of the core service—the basic package of benefits that customers expect every business in an industry to be able to provide. We can describe them as the "do-or-die" elements of service. However, they may change as customer expectations increase, competitive offerings improve, or new competitors enter the market. The solution for problems here is to make sure that a firm's basic product meets customer-defined industry standards.

Neutral or satisfied customers (the 3s and 4s) are probably happy with the core service but would like to have a consistent set of supplementary services that make the basic product more effective or easier to use. Service providers with a high proportion of neutral and satisfied customers need to increase their range of supporting services and provide responsive service recovery processes so that customers don't slide into the dissatisfied category when problems do occur. Formalized service recovery programs can help supplement the bundle of benefits provided by the core product and decrease the liklihood that customers will defect to competitors' services.[22]

Completely satisfied customers believe that a company thoroughly understands and addresses their own personal preferences, needs, expectations, and problems. Service providers whose customer satisfaction ratings are 5s have obviously listened carefully to their customers and, as a result, have been able to incorporate a significant number of innovative elements into their core offerings. In time, competitors may copy the innovator, so a firm that wishes to remain a leader must continually listen to customers and find new ways to delight them.

Benefits of Customer Satisfaction Management

Although every successful marketer wants to provide a service that satisfies customers, this isn't the only goal. Companies can't lose sight of other basic business goals such as achieving a competitive advantage or making a profit. As Figure 12.7 shows, customer

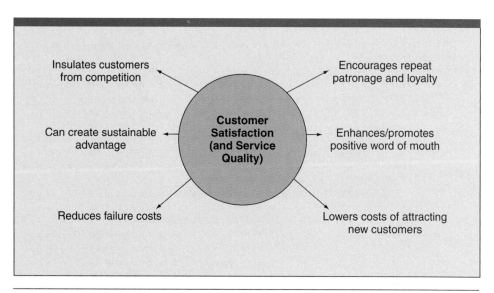

FIGURE 12.7

Benefits of Customer Satisfaction and Service Quality

Source: C. H. Lovelock, P. G. Patterson, and R. H. Walker, *Services Marketing: Australia and New Zealand* (Sydney: Prentice Hall, 1998), 119.

satisfaction provides many benefits for a firm, and higher levels of customer satisfaction lead to greater customer loyalty. In the long run, it is more profitable to keep good customers than to constantly attract and develop new customers to replace the ones who leave. Highly satisfied customers spread positive word of mouth and in effect become a walking, talking advertisement for a firm, which lowers the cost of attracting new customers. This is particularly important for professional service providers (like dentists, lawyers, engineers, or accountants), because reputation and word of mouth are key information sources for new clients.[23]

High levels of customer satisfaction are an insurance policy against something going wrong. Long-term customers tend to be more forgiving in these situations, because an occasional bad experience will be offset by previous positive ones, and satisfied customers are less susceptible to competitors' offerings. It's no wonder that many companies place so much emphasis on customer satisfaction, given its positive relationship to customer retention, market share, and profits.

Return on Quality

Many strategies to improve customer satisfaction are costly to design and implement. Thoughtful managers ask: Which quality improvement efforts will provide the greatest financial returns? This investment-oriented approach is called **return on quality** (ROQ).[24] A company's research and complaint data may show that some quality defects are much more important to customers than others, and some defects cost more money to fix. Moreover, not all quality improvement efforts will necessarily pay for themselves. An ROQ approach can help a firm set priorities based on investing resources to fix those defects that will subsequently yield the best financial returns. The objective should be to undertake a systematic method for rank-ordering quality improvement efforts according to their anticipated financial return.

return on quality: the financial return obtained from investing in service quality improvements.

Building a Quality Information System

Organizations that are known for providing excellent service quality are good at listening to both their customers and their front-line employees. To do this effectively, companies need to create an ongoing service research process that provides managers with useful, timely data. Information from service quality surveys—including how a firm compares with its competitors—can help managers understand the effects of changes in service quality and/or price on the firm's market share.[25] As Leonard Berry says in *On Great Service*, "Companies need to build a **service quality information system**, not just do a study. Conducting a service quality study is analogous to taking a snapshot. Deeper insight and an understanding of the pattern of change come from an ongoing series of snapshots taken of various subject matter from many angles."[26]

service quality information system: an ongoing service research process that provides timely, useful data to managers about customer satisfaction, expectations, and perceptions of quality.

Berry recommends that ongoing research should be conducted through a portfolio of research techniques that make up a firm's service quality information system. Possible approaches include:

➢ Post-transaction surveys

➢ Total market surveys

➢ Mystery shopping

➢ New, declining, and former customer surveys

➢ Focus groups

➢ Employee field reporting

post-transaction surveys: techniques to measure customer satisfaction and perceptions of service quality while a specific service experience is still fresh in the customer's mind.

Post-Transaction Surveys   This approach is useful when the goal is to measure customer satisfaction and perceptions about service experiences while they are still fresh in the customer's mind. **Post-transaction surveys** are conducted right after a service encounter or within a few days.[27] (See the boxed story about Toys"R"Us.) Many service businesses, including hotels and restaurants, invite customers to complete questionnaires on site (or to mail them back later). Some companies even offer incentives. For example, the Olive Garden restaurant sometimes gives customers a discount on their next meal if they complete the customer satisfaction survey that is provided with every bill. Data of this nature may also be collected electronically. For instance, customers at Einstein's Bagels can use a touch-activated screen that is located at the entrance to record their impressions of service quality.

total market surveys: periodic measurements of customers' overall evaluations of service quality based on accumulated experience over a period of time.

Total Market Surveys   The purpose of **total market surveys** is to measure customers' overall evaluations of service quality. Because such evaluations reflect customers' accumulated experience over time (and because this type of data collection is costly), these surveys are administered less frequently than transactional surveys. The information collected should include customers' service expectations and perceptions, the relative importance of different service dimensions, and customers' intentions about repurchasing and making positive recommendations to others. Companies can also use total market surveys to measure competitors' service quality. But they need to sample both customers and noncustomers to get an accurate picture of their competitive position.

Toys"R"Us Finds Out Why Customers Aren't Playing There Anymore

For most of the 1990s, Toys"R"Us was the undisputed leader among retailers of traditional toys. But in 1998, Wal-Mart surpassed Toys"R"Us in market share in this competitive market. Worried Toys"R"Us executives quickly implemented a new strategy—labeled "C3"—aimed at increasing sales, profits, and "most importantly, winning back mom." C3 (which stands for "customer friendly, cost effective, and concept for a long-term position") is based on ongoing post-transaction surveys that poll customers within 48 hours after they have completed a Toys"R"Us transaction.

Using household information compiled from the national daily transaction data stored in its centralized data warehouse, the company identifies approximately 60,000 customers a year who are then contacted by telephone to discuss their shopping experiences at Toys"R"Us. These customers are also asked about any recent service encounters thay have had with competitors like Wal-Mart, K-Mart, and Target. Data are collected in two different formats: numerical ratings in response to specific questions, and qualititative responses that are recorded verbatim.

Responses to the initial post-transaction surveys highlighted some of the reasons that customers were defecting to competitors' stores. Many respondents rated their customer satisfaction levels as "poor," stating that Toys"R"Us sales clerks were rude and unhelpful. Another complaint was that many popular toys were frequently out-of-stock. The survey data also allowed Toys"R"Us to analyze the relationship between customer satisfaction and profitability. Not surprisingly, customers who were delighted with their shopping experiences were significantly more profitable over time than those who were merely satisfied.

Armed with these results, Toys"R"Us has implemented an aggressive campaign to make all of its stores more customer-friendly. The number of out-of-stock incidents has been significantly reduced. Customer satisfaction is measured at each store every month through post-transaction surveys and mystery shopping. Toys"R"Us stores that rank highly receive incentives, while those that don't get additional customer service training.

Source: Seth Mendleson, "Fixing a Broken Toy," *Discount Merchandiser*, February 1999; Ellen Simon, "Toys'R'Us Talking Up New Concept: Friendly Help is Key to Chain's Effort to Regain No. 1 Status," *Newark Star Ledger*, 16 June, 1999; Ellen Simon, "Toys'R'Us Tries to Make Shopping a 'Magic' Moment," *Newark Star Ledger*, 22 June, 1999; and information presented by Timothy Keiningham at the 9th Annual Frontiers in Services Conference, Nashville, TN, September 2000.

Some marketers use a tool called **SERVQUAL** to gather this type of information (see the box, "The SERVQUAL Scale").[28] Customers are asked to complete a series of scales that measure their expectations of a particular company on a wide array of specific service characteristics, including aspects of the five quality dimensions. They then record their perceptions of actual service performance on these same characteristics. When perceived performance ratings are lower than expectations, it is a sign of poor quality; the reverse indicates good quality.

SERVQUAL: a standardized scale that measures expectations and perceptions about critical quality dimensions.

The SERVQUAL Scale

The SERVQUAL scale includes five dimensions: tangibles, reliability, responsiveness, assurance, and empathy. Within each dimension are several items measured on a seven-point scale from strongly agree to strongly disagree, for a total of 21 items.

SERVQUAL Questions

Note: For actual survey respondents, instructions are also included and each statement is accompanied by a seven-point scale ranging from "strongly agree = 7" to "strongly disagree = 1." Only the end points of the scale are labeled—there are no words above the numbers 2 through 6.

TANGIBLES

➤ Excellent banks [refer to cable TV companies, hospitals, or the appropriate service business throughout the questionnaire] will have modern-looking equipment.

➤ The physical facilities at excellent banks will be visually appealing.

➤ Employees at excellent banks will be neat in appearance.

➤ Materials associated with the service (like brochures or statements) will be visually appealing in an excellent bank.

RELIABILITY

➤ When excellent banks promise to do something by a certain time, they will do so.

➤ When customers have a problem, excellent banks will show a sincere interest in solving it.

➤ Excellent banks will perform the service right the first time.

➤ Excellent banks will provide their services at the time they promise to do so.

➤ Excellent banks will insist on error-free records.

RESPONSIVENESS

➤ Employees of excellent banks will tell customers exactly when service will be performed.

➤ Employees of excellent banks will give prompt service to customers.

➤ Employees of excellent banks will always be willing to help customers.

➤ Employees of excellent banks will never be too busy to respond to customer requests.

ASSURANCE

➤ The behavior of employees of excellent banks will instill confidence in customers.

➤ Customers of excellent banks will feel safe in their transactions.

➤ Employees of excellent banks will be consistently courteous with customers.

➤ Employees of excellent banks will have the knowledge to answer customer questions.

EMPATHY

➤ Excellent banks will give customers individual attention.

➤ Excellent banks will have operating hours convenient to all their customers.

➤ Excellent banks will have employees who give customers personal attention.

➤ The employees of excellent banks will understand the specific needs of their customers.

Mystery Shopping   Companies sometimes hire individuals to pose as ordinary customers and provide feedback about their service experiences. During their unannounced visits to service sites, these "mystery shoppers" observe both the physical environment and the interactions between customers and employees. One advantage of **mystery shopping** is that it provides feedback on the performance of individual service employees. This information can be used to reward exceptional performance, as well as to identify employees who could benefit from additional training or coaching. Companies like Wells Fargo Bank, Au Bon Pain, and Safeway use mystery shopping regularly to improve their customer service.

mystery shopping: a research technique that employs individuals posing as ordinary customers in order to obtain feedback on the service environment and customer-employee interactions.

Service providers should be sensitive to employees' feelings when using this approach, because employees often feel that mystery shoppers are spying on them. Tips for making mystery shopping successful include letting employees know what criteria they are being judged on and evaluating service quality over a series of visits rather than by a single encounter. For example, Au Bon Pain posts its criteria for service quality in each store, along with a list of employees who have received outstanding scores from mystery shoppers.

New, Declining, and Former Customer Surveys   New customers can provide information about what attracted them to a specific service provider, including the impact of the firm's reputation and its marketing efforts. Surveys that monitor declining patronage can identify the reasons and may predict future customer defections. Asking former customers why they left can provide helpful—if sobering—information about areas where a firm's service quality is deficient. Surveys of new, declining, or former customers are easiest to do in businesses where customers use the service on a fairly regular basis and sales transactions are recorded at the individual customer level. For instance, Safeway supermarkets conduct this type of research by using their Safeway Club "membership" cards to track each customer's purchases electronically over time. Since customer-contact data are collected when customers apply for the card, Safeway can easily contact new, declining, or former customers. The company also uses the membership card to reward loyal customers with special discounts and cash rebates.

Focus Groups   This research approach involves interviewing a group of representative customers about a specific topic or issue. The discussions, which typically last a couple of hours, are led by trained moderators who keep the participants— typically six to ten in number—on task. Convening a **focus group** is a useful way to get in-depth information about service problems and identify possible solutions. This procedure can also be used to determine what criteria customers use to evaluate service quality, to obtain feedback on a new service concept or a proposed marketing program, or to find out how customers actually use different types of services. However, the resulting information should not be projected onto an entire market segment without additional quantitative research.

focus groups: groups of customers sharing certain common characteristics who are convened by researchers for in-depth, moderator-led discussions on specific topics.

While most focus group research involves face-to-face conversations with participants, a few companies have gone high-tech. For example, the cable network Nickelodeon conducts online focus groups with 8- to 12-year-old viewers to gather their reactions to its programming and marketing. The company says the electronic focus groups provide faster, cheaper data than traditional methods but warns that other market research techniques should also be used.[29]

Employee Field Reporting   Whereas most service quality data are collected from customers, a firm's employees can also be a valuable source of qualitative information. Employee field reporting is a systematic method for finding out what employees learn from their interactions with customers and their direct observations of customer behavior. Data can be collected from employees through written surveys, telephone interviews, or focus groups. Employees can also record critical incidents that occur during service encounters. For example, employees in a dentist's office can be asked to record patients' reactions to all aspects of the service, including the physical environment, new equipment, or personal interactions.

PRODUCTIVITY ISSUES FOR SERVICE FIRMS

As we mentioned at the beginning of this chapter, improving service quality for customers in cost-effective ways is a key challenge for any service business. Companies must try to increase productivity in ways that won't have a negative impact on customer satisfaction or perceived quality. But what is productivity? Simply defined, productivity measures how efficiently a company can transform **inputs** into **outputs**. Inputs vary according to the nature of the business but may include labor (both physical and intellectual), materials, energy, and capital (land, buildings, equipment, information systems, and financial assets). Service outputs are the final outcomes of the service delivery process as perceived and valued by customers. Improving productivity requires increasing the ratio of outputs to inputs.

inputs: all resources (labor, materials, energy, and capital) required to create service offerings.

outputs: the final outcomes of the service delivery process as perceived and valued by customers.

Measuring Service Productivity

The intangible nature of service performances often makes it difficult to measure the productivity of service industries. The measurement task is perhaps the most straightforward in possession-processing services because many are quasi-manufacturing organizations, performing routine tasks with easily measurable inputs and outputs that often include physical elements. Examples include quick-service garages, which change a car's oil and rotate its tires, or fast-food restaurants, which offer limited and simple menus. But the task is more complicated when the customer's vehicle has an engine problem, or when the restaurant in question is famous for its varied and exotic cuisine.

In a people-processing service like a hospital, we can look at the number of patients treated in the course of a year and at the hospital's census, or average bed occupancy. But how do we account for the different types of procedures performed—removal of cancerous tumors, treatment of diabetes, or setting of broken bones—and the almost inevitable variability between one patient and another? And how do we evaluate the difference in service outcomes? Some patients get better, some develop complications, and some never recover. There are relatively few standardized procedures in medicine that offer highly predictable outcomes.

Information-based services also pose measurement issues. How should we define the output of a bank or a consulting firm? And how does an architect's output compare to a lawyer's? Some lawyers like to boast about their billable hours. But what were they actually doing during those hours, and how do we measure their output as opposed to their fees? It's alleged that some lawyers strive to bill for more than 24 hours of work per day, but is that really an accurate indication of productivity?

Finally, measuring productivity is a challenge for mental stimulus services like education. Many universities are under pressure to document outputs, and they have been struggling with how to measure the hours professors spend preparing for class, interacting with students, providing service to the university and the community, and contributing to their professional fields. And how do colleges (or their graduates) quantify the value of a college degree? Or the value of a good professor versus a mediocre one?

Variability is a major problem in measuring service productivity. Unfortunately, traditional measures of service output tend to ignore variations in the quality of service delivered and its perceived value to customers. In freight transportation, for instance, a

ton-mile of output for freight that is delivered late is treated the same for productivity purposes as a similar shipment delivered on time.[30] Another approach, counting the number of customers served per unit of time, suffers from the same shortcoming. What happens when an increase in the speed with which customers are served is achieved at the expense of perceived quality? Suppose a hair stylist serves three customers per hour and finds she can increase her output to four by giving what is technically just as good a haircut but using a faster but noisier hair dryer, eliminating all conversation, and rushing through the process. Even if the haircut is identical in quality, her customers may rate the overall service experience less positively because it did not meet their expectations of an adequate (or desired) level of service on multiple dimensions.

Efficiency and Effectiveness in Service Productivity

Some researchers argue that productivity measures in a service context must incorporate both efficiency and effectiveness.[31] Efficiency describes the degree to which an activity generates a given quantity of outputs with a minimum consumption of inputs (or the largest possible outputs from a given level of inputs). It relates the output to the resources (input) used and is about doing things the right way. Effectiveness, by contrast, is concerned with a firm's ability to attain a goal or purpose. The implication for service managers is that they must measure the characteristics of service output with reference to the goals set by the organization, since effectiveness is about doing the right things.

From this perspective, we can say that service productivity measures the ability of a service organization to use its inputs for providing services with quality matching the expectations of customers and can be presented as follows:

$$\text{Service productivity} = \frac{\text{quantity and quality of output}}{\text{quantity and quality of input}}$$

Using quantitative measures of the volume of inputs and outputs (e.g., labor hours, number of hours service is available, number of customers or transactions, etc.) is complicated when there is a lot of variability in inputs and outputs. An alternative is to use monetary measures, such as turnover relative to the total monetary value of inputs. In order to link productivity to profitability, the monetary values of both input and output must be determined, thus emphasizing the value added of the service process.

Productivity and Customer Satisfaction

The "productive" hair stylist described earlier illustrates an important issue for service providers.[32] Although many companies would like to increase both productivity (defined in volume terms) and quality (defined in satisfaction terms), the two are not always compatible. Managers may have to make trade-offs between quantity and quality, especially when customer satisfaction and willingness to pay depend on customized service provided directly by employees. High levels of productivity and customer satisfaction are most profitable—and most possible—for companies like mail-order firms, clothing stores, and fast-food restaurants that provide a mixture of goods and services to customers in a fairly standardized way. For example, the Taco Bell restaurant chain has been very successful in making productivity improvements that both added to customer satisfaction and had an extremely positive impact on profitability.

However, for companies whose outputs are more intangible—like airlines, banks, and charter travel agencies—the greatest profits are associated with higher customer satisfaction and a relatively lower volume of output per employee. A study of the hotel industry showed that the value added (output revenues less input costs) rose significantly with an increasing number of employees.[33] It's readily apparent that four-star and five-star hotels offer a much higher ratio of employees to customers than lower-rated hotels and are able to command much higher prices for their rooms. Thus, for more customized services, the primary focus should be on increasing customer satisfaction. Firms should make efficiency-based productivity improvements only if they are sure that the changes will not negatively affect customers' perceptions of service quality.

Many attempts to improve service productivity tend to center on efforts to eliminate waste and reduce labor costs. Cutbacks in front-stage staffing can mean either that the remaining employees have to work harder and faster or that there are insufficient personnel to serve customers promptly at busy times. Although employees may be able to work faster for a brief period of time, few can maintain a rapid pace for extended periods. They become exhausted, make mistakes, and treat customers in a disinterested way. Workers who are trying to do two or three things at once (e.g., serving a customer face to face while simultaneously answering the telephone and sorting papers) may do a poor job on each task. Excessive pressure to improve productivity breeds discontent and frustration among all employees. But it is especially difficult for customer-contact personnel, who are caught between trying to meet customer needs and attempting to achieve management's productivity goals.

Even successful firms like United Parcel Service (UPS) have experienced customer service declines because of the implementation of internal productivity improvement strategies that were not directly linked to customer priorities.

For example, UPS made an assumption that on-time delivery was the most important service quality feature for its customers. The company did time-and-motion studies to see how delivery processes could be made more efficient and pushed its workers to meet demanding delivery schedules. Much to its surprise, UPS discovered from its customer satisfaction surveys that customers actually wanted more interaction time with its drivers. After performing a return-on-quality analysis, the company designed a program to allow drivers to spend more time with customers by relaxing delivery schedules and hiring more drivers. Drivers received a small bonus for any sales leads they generated. Cost estimates for the first year were $4.2 million, which was quickly offset by over $10 million in additional revenues.[34]

Sometimes companies can use technology to streamline service processes in a way that reduces costs and satisfies customers. For example, cost cutting was a very important issue for Taco Bell because its strategy relied on providing customers with high-quality, low-priced fast food. The company's "value menu" pricing meant that profit margins were reduced. Cost reductions were mandatory, but what should be cut? Because improved customer service was an important part of the new strategy, Taco Bell could not easily improve productivity by decreasing its labor costs. Instead, it embarked on an approach called "K-minus" (K stands for kitchen). By using technology to reduce the labor intensity of food preparation, outsourcing some of the most time-intensive chores, and turning restaurant kitchens into strictly food assembly areas, Taco Bell was able to shrink the average kitchen size by 40 percent. Its restaurants moved from 70 percent kitchen and 30 percent dining to 70 percent dining and 30 percent kitchen, freeing both space and employees to serve customers. These dramatic changes significantly reduced operating costs, and customer waiting time decreased more than 70 percent.

Self-service pumps have increased gas station productivity.

Customer-Driven Approaches to Improving Productivity

In situations where customers are deeply involved in the service production process (most typical in people-processing services), operations managers should examine how customers' inputs can be made more productive. Marketing managers should be thinking about what marketing strategies can be employed to influence customers to behave in more productive ways. Two strategies, in particular, may be helpful: changing the timing of customer demand and involving customers more actively in the production process.[35]

Changing the Timing of Customer Demand   Managing demand in capacity-constrained service businesses is a recurring theme in this book. Customers often complain about crowding and congestion, reflecting time-of-day, seasonal, or other cyclical peaks in demand. During the off-peak periods in those same cycles, managers often worry that there are too few customers and that their facilities and staff are not fully productive. By shifting demand away from peaks, managers can make better use of their productive assets and provide better service.

However, some demand cannot easily be shifted without the cooperation of third parties like employers and schools, who control working hours and holiday schedules. To fill idle capacity during off-peak hours, marketers may need to target new market segments with different needs and schedules, rather than focusing exclusively on current segments. If the peaks and valleys of demand can be smoothed, using the tools and strategies we've discussed in earlier chapters, productivity will improve.

Involving Customers More in Production   Customers who assume a more active role in service production and delivery can take over some labor tasks from the service organization. Benefits for both parties may result when customers perform self-service. Some technological innovations are designed to enable customers to perform tasks previously undertaken by service employees. For instance, many companies are trying to encourage customers to use a corporate Web site to obtain information and place orders, rather than telephoning customer service staff directly. For such changes to succeed, Web sites must be made user-friendly and easy to "navigate" and customers must be convinced that it is safe to provide credit card information over the Internet. Some companies have offered promotional incentives (like a credit of air miles to a frequent flyer program or a discount on merchandise) to encourage customers to make an initial reservation or place an order on the Web.

Restaurants, which have traditionally had a high labor component and relatively low productivity, represent another service in which customers have been asked to do more of the work. We've become accustomed to self-service salad bars and buffets. Despite the reduction in personal service, this innovation has been positioned as a benefit that lets customers select the foods they want, without delay, in the quantities they desire.

Quality and productivity improvements often depend on customers' willingness to learn new procedures, follow instructions, and interact cooperatively with employees and other people. Customers who arrive at the service encounter with a set of preexisting norms, values, and role definitions may resist change. In fact, research results suggest that some customers may be more willing than others to serve themselves.

A large-scale study presented respondents with the choice of a do-it-yourself option versus traditional delivery systems at gas stations, banks, restaurants, hotels, airports, and travel services.[36] A particular scenario was outlined for each service, since earlier interviews had determined that decisions to choose self-service options were very situation specific, depending on such factors as time of day, weather conditions, presence or absence of others in the party, and the perceived time and cost involved. The results showed that in each instance a sizable proportion of respondents would select the self-service option—even in the absence of time or monetary savings. When these inducements were added, the proportions choosing self-service increased. Further analysis showed an overlap for some respondents in terms of their self-service behaviors across different services. If respondents didn't pump their own fuel, for instance, they were less likely to use an ATM and more likely to prefer being served by a bank clerk.

Conclusion

Service providers can't afford to consider productivity separately from quality. If the two issues are totally divorced, operations managers may launch productivity efforts that will degrade the service received by customers, and marketing managers may introduce service quality programs that complicate operations, raise costs, and hurt profits. Successful firms base their efforts to improve quality on an understanding of customers' expectations relative to different quality dimensions and analysis of service quality gaps that can lead to dissatisfaction. When things go wrong, they seek the underlying causes and try to prevent a recurrence. Their efforts to innovate often center on new approaches that will enhance productivity and quality simultaneously.

Firms that succeed in providing high-quality service are good at listening to both their customers and their employees, especially those in direct contact with customers. They build information systems that use a variety of research techniques to measure customer satisfaction and the quality of service delivered. However, measuring productivity can be difficult because of the intangible nature of service performances. Unfortunately, many traditional measures of service outputs ignore variations in the quality of service delivered and its perceived value to customers.

Study Questions and Exercises

1. Define customer expectations and describe where they come from.

2. Discuss the three different levels of expectations. How are they related to a customer's zone of tolerance?

3. Explain the difference between service quality and customer satisfaction.

4. Identify the seven gaps that can occur in service quality. What do you think service marketers can do to prevent each of these gaps?

5. What are the five dimensions customers use in evaluating service quality?

6. Explain the elements of a service quality information system and give examples of each element.

7. How can firms learn from service failures?

8. Define productivity. Why is it hard to measure in services?

9. Why is productivity a more difficult issue for services than for many manufactured goods? Explain the relationship between productivity and quality.

Endnotes

1. From Patricia B. Seybold, customers.com (New York, NY: Times Books/Random House, 1998); Philip Kotler, *Marketing Management, Millenium Edition* (Upper Saddle River, NJ: Prentice-Hall, Inc., 2000); and the Cisco Systems Web site, www.cisco.com, January 2001.

2. Christopher H. Lovelock, "Federal Express: Quality Improvement Program," Lausanne: IMD case, 1990 (distributed by European Case Clearing House).

3. James Brian Quinn, *Intelligent Enterprise* (New York: The Free Press, 1992), 325.

4. See, for example, the classic article, Philip Kotler, "A Generic Concept of Marketing," *Journal of Marketing*, 36 (April 1972): 46–54.

5. Morris Holbrook, "The Nature of Customer Value: An Anthology of Services in the Consumption Experience," in R. T. Rust and R. L. Oliver, *Service Quality: New Directions in Theory and Practice* (Thousand Oaks, CA: Sage Publications, 1994): 21–71.

6. Bradley T. Gale, *Managing Customer Value* (New York: The Free Press, 1994).

7. Robert D. Buzzell and Bradley T. Gale, *The PIMS Principles—Linking Strategy to Performance* (New York: The Free Press, 1987).

8. Christian Homburg and Bernd Garbe, "Towards an Improved Understanding of Industrial Services: Quality Dimensions and Their Impact on Buyer-Seller Relationships," *Journal of Business-to-Business Marketing*, 6, no. 2 (1999): 39–71.

9. See Roland T. Rust, Anthony J. Zahorik, and Timothy L. Keiningham, *Service Marketing* (New York: HarperCollins, 1996): 229; J. Joseph Cronin and Steven A. Taylor, "Measuring Service Quality: A Reexamination and Extension," *Journal of Marketing* 56 (1992): 55–68; and Richard L. Oliver, "A Conceptual Model of Service Quality and Service Satisfaction: Compatible Goals, Different Concepts," in *Advances in Services Marketing and Management: Research and Practice*, Teresa A. Swartz, David E. Bowen, and Stephen W. Brown, eds. (Greenwich, CT: JAI Press, 1993), vol. 2.

10. G. LeBlanc and N. Nguyen, "Customers' Perceptions of Service Quality in Financial Institutions," *International Journal of Bank Marketing* 6, no. 4 (1988): 7–18.

11. Necmi Kemal Avkiran, "Developing an Instrument to Measure Customer Service Quality in Banking," *International Journal of Bank Marketing*, 12, no. 6 (1996): 10–18.

12. Valarie A. Zeithaml, "Service Quality, Profitability and the Economic Worth of Customers: What We Know and What We Need to Learn," *Journal of the Academy of Marketing Science,* 28, no. 1 (2000): 67–85.

13. Eugene W. Anderson and Vikas Mittal, "Strengthening the Satisfaction-Profit Chain," *Journal of Service Research* 3 (November 2000): 107–120.

14. Valarie A. Zeithaml, A. Parasuraman, and Leonard L. Berry, *Delivering Quality Service: Balancing Customer Perceptions and Expectations* (New York: The Free Press, 1990).

15. A. Parasuraman, Valarie A. Zeithaml, and Leonard L. Berry, "SERVQUAL: A Multiple-Item Scale for Measuring Consumer Perceptions of Service Quality," *Journal of Retailing* 64 (1988): 12–40.

16. Leonard L. Berry, *On Great Service* (New York: The Free Press, 1995): 84.

17. Valarie A. Zeithaml, Leonard L. Berry, and A. Parasuraman, "Communication and Control Processes in the Delivery of Service Processes," *Journal of Marketing* 52 (1988): 36–58.

18. Adapted from Christopher Lovelock, *Product Plus* (New York: McGraw-Hill, 1994), 112–113; and K. Douglas Hoffman and John E. G. Bateson, *Essentials of Services Marketing* (Fort Worth, TX: Dryden Press, 1997), 300–301.

19. Steven W. Brown, Deborah L. Cowles, and Tracy L. Tuten, "Service Recovery: Its Value and Limitations as a Retail Strategy," *International Journal of Service Industry Management* 7, no. 5 (1996): 32–47.

20. See, for example, Thomas O. Jones and W. Earl Sasser, "Why Satisfied Customers Defect," *Harvard Business Review* (November-December 1995): 88–99.

21. Jones and Sasser, "Why Satisfied Customers Defect," 96.

22. Philip Kotler, *Marketing Management*, 9th ed. (Upper Saddle River, NJ: Prentice Hall, 1997).

23. Philip L. Dawes, Grahame R. Dowling, and Paul G. Patterson, "Criteria Used to Select Management Consultants," *Industrial Marketing Management* 21 (1992): 187–193.

24. Roland T. Rust, Anthony J. Zahorik, and Timothy L. Keiningham, "Return on Quality (ROQ): Making Service Quality Financially Accountable," *Journal of Marketing* 59 (1995): 58–70.

25. Roland T. Rust, Peter J. Danaher, and Sajeev Varki, "Using Service Quality Data for Competitive Marketing Decisions," *International Journal of Service Industry Management* 11, no. 5 (2000): 438–469.

26. Berry, *On Great Service*, 33.

27. Emil Becker, "Service Quality Requires Strategy and Tactics," *Marketing News*, 29 January 1996, 4.

28. Parasuraman, Zeithaml, and Berry, "SERVQUAL: A Multiple-Item Scale for Measuring Consumer Perceptions of Service Quality." 12–40.

29. Tibbett Speer, "Nickelodeon Puts Kids Online," *American Demographics* (January 1994): 16–17.

30. James L. Heskett, *Managing in the Service Economy* (New York: The Free Press, 1986).

31. Ismo Vuorinen, Raija Järvinen, and Uolevi Lehtinen, "Content and Measurement of Productivity in the Service Sector: A Conceptual Analysis with an Illustrative Case from the Insurance Business," *International Journal of Service Industry Management* 9, no. 4 (1998): 377–396.

32. This section is based on material from Eugene W. Anderson, Claes Fornell, and Roland T. Rust, "Customer Satisfaction, Productivity, and Profitability: Differences Between Goods and Services," *Marketing Science* 16 (1997): 131; Eugene W. Anderson, Claes Fornell, and Donald R. Lehmann, "Customer Satisfaction, Market Share and Profitability," *Journal of Marketing* 56 (1994): 53–66; and Lenard Huff, Claes Fornell, and Eugene W. Anderson, "Quality and Productivity: Contradictory and Complimentary," *Quality Management Journal* 4 (1996): 22–39.

33. James R. Brown and Chekitan S. Day, "Improving Productivity in a Service Business: Evidence from the Hotel Industry," *Journal of Service Research* 2, no. 4 (May 2000): 339–354.

34. David L. Kurtz and Kenneth E. Clow, *Services Marketing* (New York: Wiley), 122.

35. This discussion is based, in part, on Christopher H. Lovelock and Robert F. Young: "Look to Consumers to Increase Productivity," *Harvard Business Review* (May-June 1979): 168–178.

36. Eric Langeard, John E. G. Bateson, Christopher H. Lovelock, and Pierre Eiglier, *Services Marketing: New Insights from Consumers and Managers* (Cambridge, MA: Marketing Science Institute, 1981), especially Chapter 2. A good summary of this research is provided in J. E. G. Bateson, "Self-Service Consumer: An Exploratory Study," *Journal of Retailing* 51 (Fall 1985): 49–76.

chapter thirteen

Balancing Demand and Capacity

Cape Cod: A Seasonal Tourist Destination

Cape Cod is a remarkable peninsula of narrow land, jutting out into the Atlantic off the Massachusetts coast like a long arm, bent at the elbow. Native Americans have lived there for thousands of years. The Pilgrims landed there in 1619 but continued across Cape Cod Bay to found Plymouth. Not long afterwards, more immigrants from England settled on the Cape itself. Fishing, whaling, agriculture, and salt works were among the principal industries in the nineteenth century. By the mid-twentieth century, all but fishing had virtually disappeared and tourism was beginning to assume some significance. Events in the early 1960s put the Cape firmly in the public eye. John F. Kennedy became president of the United States and was regularly photographed at his family's vacation home in Hyannisport. While in office he signed legislation that created the Cape Cod National Seashore, preserving large areas of the Outer Cape as a national park. And the song, "Old Cape Cod," commissioned by tourism promoters and sung by popular vocalist, Patti Page, unexpectedly climbed to the top of the charts and was heard around the world. With its beaches and salt marshes, sand dunes and fishing harbors, picturesque towns and lobster dinners, the Cape rapidly became a destination resort, drawing millions of visitors each year from New England, the Mid-Atlantic states, Eastern Canada, and beyond. In season, that is. . . .

In summer, the Cape is a busy place. Colorful umbrellas sprout like giant flowers along the miles of sandy beaches. The parking lots are full. There are lines outside most restaurants and managers complain about the difficulty of hiring and retaining sufficient serving staff.

Thousands of students take summer jobs on the Cape (many come from Europe) and some employers recruit seasonal workers from Caribbean countries such as Jamaica. Stores and movie theaters are busy (especially when it rains). The Mid-Cape Highway is clogged. Hotels and motels sport "no vacancy" signs. Fishing trips have to be booked well in advance. Vacation cottages are rented, it's hard to get a car reservation on the ferries to the islands of Nantucket or Martha's Vineyard, and the visitor centers at the National Seashore are crowded with tourists.

But return for a weekend in mid-winter, and what do you find? A few walkers brave the chill winds on the otherwise empty beaches. You can park in almost any legal space you wish. Many restaurants have closed (their owners are wintering in Florida) and only the most popular of the remaining establishments even bother to suggest reservations. Student workers have gone back to college and employers have laid off their seasonal workers.

It's rare in winter to be unable to see the movie of your choice at your preferred time. The main problem on the Mid-Cape Highway is being stopped for speeding. If a motel displays a "no vacancy" sign, that means it's closed for the season; the open ones typically offer bargain rates. Recreational fishing? You must be crazy—there may even be ice on Cape Cod Bay! Owners of vacation cottages have drained their water systems and boarded up the windows. You can probably drive your vehicle straight onto one of the car ferries to the islands (although the sailing schedules are more limited), and the

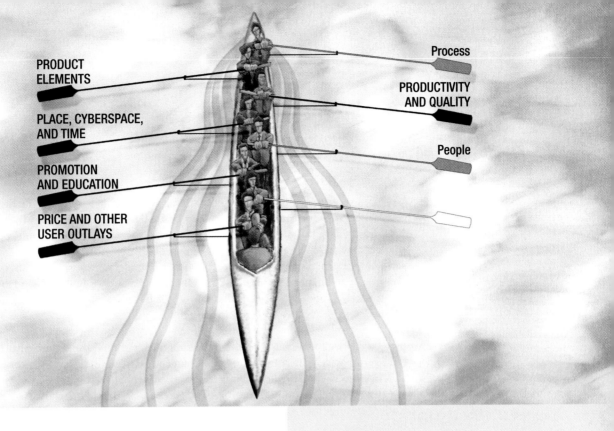

PRODUCT
ELEMENTS

PLACE, CYBERSPACE,
AND TIME

PROMOTION
AND EDUCATION

PRICE AND OTHER
USER OUTLAYS

Process

PRODUCTIVITY
AND QUALITY

People

rangers at the visitor centers are happy to talk with the few visitors who drop by during the shortened opening hours.

Faced with such a sharply peaked season, economic development agencies are working to extend the Cape's tourism season beyond the peak months of July and August, seeking to build demand during the spring and fall months. Among their targets are tourists from Europe, who appreciate the old-world charm of the Cape and tend to spend more money than visitors from Boston or New York.

Learning Objectives

After reading this chapter, you should be able to

⇒ describe the forms that productive capacity can take in a service organization

⇒ explain how to use capacity management techniques to address variations in demand

⇒ understand the concept of demand cycles

⇒ recognize different patterns of demand and their underlying causes

⇒ formulate demand management strategies appropriate to specific situations

THE UPS AND DOWNS OF DEMAND

Fluctuating demand for service, like that experienced by the retailers, movie theaters, motels, restaurants, ferries, and other establishments on Cape Cod, is not just found in vacation resorts. It's a problem for a huge cross-section of businesses serving both individual and corporate customers. These demand fluctuations—which may be as long as a season of the year or as short as an hourly cycle—play havoc with efficient use of productive assets.

> **inventory:** for *manufacturing*, physical output stockpiled after production for sale at a later date; for *services*, future output that has not yet been reserved in advance, such as the number of hotel rooms still available for sale on a given day.

Unlike manufacturing, service operations create a perishable **inventory** that cannot be stockpiled for sale at a later date. That's a problem for any capacity-constrained service that faces wide swings in demand. The problem is most commonly found among services that process people or physical possessions, like transportation, lodging, food service, repair and maintenance, entertainment, and health care. It also affects labor-intensive information-processing services that face cyclical shifts in demand. University education and accounting and tax preparation are cases in point.

This chapter—and the one that follows—address the question, *How should we match demand and productive capacity?* The task starts with defining the nature of the firm's productive capacity, which may vary significantly from one industry to another. Managers also need to document how demand levels vary, what factors explain those variations, and under what circumstances demand exceeds available capacity. Armed with this understanding, they should then be in a position to develop strategies for matching demand and capacity.

From Excess Demand to Excess Capacity

At any given moment, a fixed-capacity service may face one of four conditions (see Figure 13.1):

> **excess demand:** demand for a service at a given time exceeds the firm's ability to meet customer needs.

> ➤ **Excess demand**—the level of demand exceeds maximum available capacity, with the result that some customers are denied service and business is lost.

> ➤ *Demand exceeds optimum capacity*—no one is actually turned away, but conditions are crowded and all customers are likely to perceive a decline in service quality.

> ➤ *Demand and supply are well balanced at the level of optimum capacity*—staff and facilities are busy without being overtaxed, and customers receive good service without delays.

> **excess capacity:** a firm's capacity to create service output is not fully utilized.

> ➤ **Excess capacity**—demand is below optimum capacity and productive resources are underutilized, resulting in low productivity. In some instances, this poses a risk that customers may find the experience disappointing or have doubts about the viability of the service.

> **maximum capacity:** the upper limit to a firm's ability to meet customer demand at a particular time.

You'll notice that we've drawn a distinction between **maximum capacity** and **optimum capacity**. When demand exceeds the maximum available capacity, some potential customers may be turned away and their business could be lost forever. When the demand level is between optimum and maximum capacity, all customers can be served but there's a risk that they may receive inferior service and thus become dissatisfied.

> **optimum capacity:** the point beyond which a firm's efforts to serve additional customers will lead to a perceived decline in service quality.

Sometimes optimum and maximum capacities are one and the same. At a live theater or sports performance, a full house is very desirable since it stimulates the players and creates a sense of excitement and audience participation. The net result is a more satisfying experience for all. But with most other services, you probably feel that you get better service if the facility is not operating at full capacity. The quality of restaurant service, for instance, often deteriorates when every table is occupied. The employees are rushed and there's a greater likelihood of errors or delays. And if you're traveling by air you tend to feel more comfortable if the seat next to you is empty.

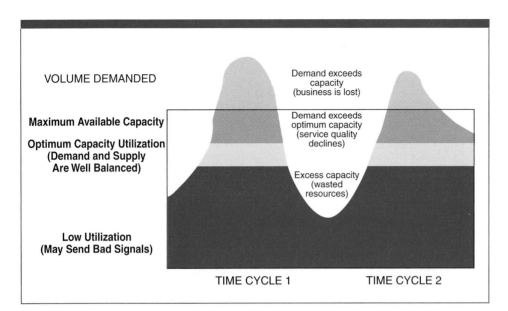

FIGURE 13.1

Implications of Variations in
Demand Relative to Capacity

There are two basic solutions to the problem of fluctuating demand. One is to adjust the level of capacity to meet variations in demand. This approach, which involves cooperation between operations and human resource management, requires an understanding of what constitutes productive capacity and how it may be increased or decreased on an incremental basis. The second approach is to manage the level of demand, using marketing strategies to smooth out the peaks and fill in the valleys to generate a more consistent flow of requests for service. Astute firms employ a mix of both strategies, which requires close collaboration between operations and marketing.[1]

MEASURING AND MANAGING CAPACITY

Many service organizations are capacity constrained. There's an upper limit to their capacity to serve additional customers at a particular point in time. They may also be constrained in terms of being unable to reduce their productive capacity during periods of low demand. In general, organizations that engage in physical processes like people processing and possession processing are more likely to face capacity constraints than those that engage in information-based processes. A radio station, for instance, may be constrained in its geographic reach by the strength of its signal. But within that radius, any number of listeners can tune in to a broadcast.

Defining Productive Capacity

What do we mean by **productive capacity**? The term refers to the resources or assets that a firm can use to create goods and services. In a service context, productive capacity can take at least five potential forms.

1. *Physical facilities designed to contain customers* that are used for delivering people-processing or mental stimulus-processing services. Examples include medical clinics, hotels, passenger aircraft, buses, restaurants, swimming pools, movie theaters, concert halls, executive education facilities, and college classrooms. In these situations, the primary capacity constraint is likely to be defined in terms of furnishings like beds, rooms, seats, tables, or desks. In some cases, local regulations may set an upper limit in the interest of health or fire safety.

productive capacity: the extent of the facilities, equipment, labor, infrastructure, and other assets available to a firm to create output for its customers.

2. *Physical facilities designed for storing or processing goods* that either belong to customers or are being offered to them for sale. Examples include supermarket shelves, pipelines, warehouses, parking lots, freight containers, or railroad freight wagons.

3. *Physical equipment used to process people, possessions, or information* may embrace a huge range of items and be very situation specific—machinery, telephones, hair dryers, computers, diagnostic equipment, airport security detectors, toll gates, cooking ovens, bank ATMs, repair tools, and cash registers are among the many items whose absence in sufficient numbers for a given level of demand can bring service to a crawl (or a complete stop).

4. *Labor* is a key element of productive capacity in all high-contact services and many low-contact ones. It may be used for both physical and mental work. Staffing levels for customer-contact personnel, from restaurant servers to nurses to telephone customer service personnel, need to be sufficient to meet anticipated demand—otherwise customers are kept waiting or service is rushed. Human beings tend to be far more variable than equipment in their ability to sustain consistent levels of output over time. One tired or poorly trained employee staffing a single station in an assembly-line service operation like a cafeteria restaurant or a motor vehicle license bureau can slow the entire service to a crawl. Professional services are especially dependent on highly skilled staff to create high value-added, information-based output. Abraham Lincoln captured it well when he remarked, "A lawyer's time and expertise are his stock in trade."

5. *Access to sufficient capacity in the public or private infrastructure* is critical in order for many organizations to deliver quality service to their own customers. Capacity problems related to infrastructure may include busy telephone circuits, electrical power failures (or "brown outs" caused by reduced voltage), congested airways that lead to air traffic restrictions on flights, and traffic jams on major highways.

Stretching and Shrinking the Level of Capacity

Measures of capacity utilization include the number of hours (or percentage of total available time) that facilities, labor, and equipment are productively employed in revenue operation, and the percentage of available space (e.g., seats, cubic freight capacity, telecommunications bandwidth) that is actually utilized in revenue operations. Some capacity is elastic in its ability to absorb extra demand. A subway car, for instance, may offer 40 seats and allow standing room for another 60 passengers with adequate handrail and floor space for all. Yet at rush hours, when there have been delays on the line, perhaps 200 standees can be accommodated under sardine-like conditions. Service personnel may be able to work at high levels of efficiency during these short periods of time, but they would tire quickly and begin providing inferior service if required to work that fast all day long.

Even where capacity appears fixed, as when it's based on the number of seats, there may still be opportunities to accept extra business at busy times. Some airlines, for example, increase the capacity of their aircraft by slightly reducing legroom throughout the cabin and cramming in another couple of rows. A restaurant may add extra tables and chairs. Upper limits to such practices are often set by safety standards or by the capacity of supporting services, such as the kitchen.

Another strategy for stretching capacity within a given time frame is to utilize the facilities for longer periods. Examples of this include restaurants that are open for early dinners and late meals, universities that offer evening classes and summer semester programs, and airlines that extend their schedules from 14 to 20 hours a day. Alternatively, the average amount of time that customers (or their possessions) spend in the process may be reduced. Sometimes this is achieved by minimizing slack time, as when the bill is presented promptly to a group of diners relaxing at the table after a meal. In other instances, it may be achieved by cutting back the level of service—like offering a simpler menu at busy times of day.

Chasing Demand

Another set of options involves tailoring the overall level of capacity to match variations in demand. This strategy is known as **chase demand**. There are several actions that managers can take to adjust capacity as needed:[2]

> *Schedule downtime during periods of low demand.* To ensure that 100 percent of capacity is available during peak periods, repairs and renovations should be conducted when demand is expected to be low. Employee holidays should also be taken during such periods (e.g., Cape Cod restaurant owners vacation in Florida during the quiet winter months).

> *Use part-time employees.* Many organizations hire extra workers during their busiest periods. Examples include postal workers and retail store clerks during the pre-Christmas season, extra staff in tax preparation firms at the end of the financial year, and additional hotel employees during holiday periods and major conventions.

> *Rent or share extra facilities and equipment.* To limit investment in fixed assets, a service business may be able to rent extra space or machines at peak times. Firms with complementary demand patterns may enter into formal sharing agreements.

> *Cross-train employees.* Even when the service delivery system appears to be operating at full capacity, certain physical elements—and their attendant employees—may be under-utilized. If employees can be cross-trained to perform a variety of tasks, they can be shifted to bottleneck points as needed to help increase total system capacity. In supermarkets, for instance, the manager may call on stockers to operate cash registers when checkout queues start to get too long. During slow periods, the cashiers may be asked to help stock shelves.

chase demand strategy: adjusting the level of capacity to meet the level of demand at any given time.

Creating Flexible Capacity

Sometimes the problem is not in the overall capacity but in the mix that's available to serve the needs of different market segments. For example, on a given flight, an airline may have too few seats in economy even though there are empty places in the business-class cabin. A hotel may find itself short of suites when there are standard rooms still available. One solution to this problem is to design physical facilities to be flexible. Some hotels build rooms with connecting doors. With the door between two rooms locked, the hotel can sell two bedrooms. With the door unlocked and one of the bedrooms converted into a sitting room, the hotel can now offer a suite.

The Boeing Co. received what were described, tongue-in-cheek, as "outrageous demands" from prospective customers in terms of flexible capacity when it was designing its new 777 airliner. The airlines wanted an aircraft in which galleys and lavatories could be relocated, plumbing and all, almost anywhere in the cabin within a matter of hours. Boeing gulped but solved this challenging problem (it was facing stiff competition from Airbus Industrie at the time). Airlines can rearrange the passenger cabin of the "Triple Seven" within hours, reconfiguring it with varying numbers of seats allocated among one, two, or three classes.

Another good example of highly flexible capacity comes from an eco-tourism operator in the South Island of New Zealand. During the spring, summer, and early autumn months the firm provides guided walks and treks, and during the snow season it offers cross-country skiing lessons and trips. Bookings all year round are processed through a contracted telephone-answering service. Guides and instructors are employed on a part-time basis as required. The firm has negotiated agreements to use national parks, huts, and cabins, and it has an exclusive arrangement with a local sports goods store that allows clients to purchase or rent equipment at reduced rates. As needed, the company can arrange charter bus service for groups. The firm has the capacity to provide a wide range of services, yet the owners' capital investment in the business is remarkably low.

Not all unsold productive capacity is wasted. Many firms take a strategic approach to disposition of anticipated surplus capacity, allocating it in advance to build relationships with customers, suppliers, employees, and intermediaries.[3] Possible applications include free trials for prospective customers and for intermediaries who sell to end users, customer or employee rewards, and bartering with the firm's own suppliers. Among the most widely traded services are advertising space or airtime, airline seats, and hotel rooms.

UNDERSTANDING THE PATTERNS AND DETERMINANTS OF DEMAND

Now that we've covered capacity-related issues, let's look at the other side of the equation. To control variations in demand for a particular service, managers need to determine the answers to a series of important questions about the patterns of demand and their underlying causes.[4]

As you think about some of the seemingly "random" causes of fluctuations in demand, consider how rain and cold affect the use of indoor and outdoor recreational or entertainment services. Then reflect on how heart attacks and births affect the demand for hospital services. Imagine what it's like to be a police officer, firefighter, or

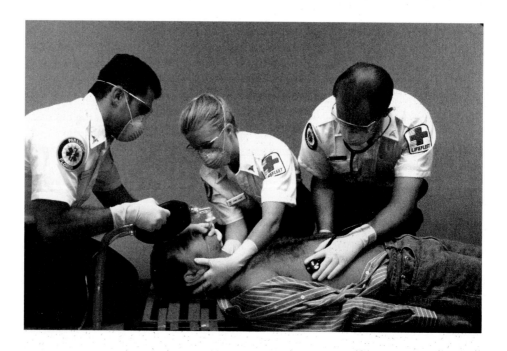

Emergency medical technicians never know when their services will next be needed.

ambulance driver—you never know exactly where your next call will come from or what the nature of the emergency will be. Finally, think about the impact of natural disasters like earthquakes, tornadoes, and hurricanes, not only on emergency services but also for disaster recovery specialists and insurance firms.

Random fluctuations are usually caused by factors beyond management's control. Where relevant, it's useful to record weather conditions and other special factors (a strike, an accident, a big convention in town, a price change, launch of a competing service, etc.) that might have influenced demand. Detailed market analysis may sometimes reveal that a predictable **demand cycle** is concealed within a broader, seemingly random pattern. For example, while a convenience store might experience wide swings in daily patronage, research may indicate that a core group of customers visits every weekday to buy staple items such as newspapers, candy, and lottery tickets.

A repair and maintenance shop servicing industrial electrical equipment may already know that a certain proportion of its work consists of regularly scheduled contracts to perform preventive maintenance. The balance may come from "walk-in" business and emergency repairs. While it might seem hard to predict or control the timing and volume of such work, further analysis could show that walk-in business was more prevalent on some days of the week than others and that emergency repairs were frequently requested following damage sustained during thunderstorms (which tend to be seasonal in nature and can often be forecast a day or two in advance).

> **demand cycle:** a period of time during which the level of demand for a service will increase and decrease in a somewhat predictable way before repeating itself.

Questions About the Patterns of Demand and Their Underlying Causes

1. Do demand levels follow a predictable cycle?

If so, is the duration of the demand cycle:

➢ one *day* (varies by hour)

➢ one *week* (varies by day)

➢ one *month* (varies by day or by week)

➢ one *year* (varies by month or by season; or reflects annual public holidays)

➢ some other period

2. What are the underlying causes of these cyclical variations?

➢ employment schedules

➢ billing and tax payment/refund cycles

➢ wage and salary payment dates

➢ school hours and vacations

➢ seasonal changes in climate

➢ occurrence of public or religious holidays

➢ natural cycles, such as coastal tides

3. Do demand levels seem to change randomly?

If so, could the underlying causes be:

➢ day-to-day changes in the weather

➢ health events whose occurrence cannot be pinpointed exactly

➢ accidents, fires, and certain criminal activities

➢ natural disasters, from earthquakes to storms to mudslides and volcanic eruptions

4. Can demand for a particular service over time be disaggregated by market segment?

If so, do demand patterns reflect:

➢ use patterns by a particular type of customer or for a particular purpose?

➢ variations in the net profitability of each completed transaction?

Analyzing Demand by Market Segment

No strategy for smoothing demand is likely to succeed unless it's based on an understanding of why customers from a specific market segment choose to use the service when they do. For example, it's difficult for hotels to convince business travelers to remain on Saturday nights since few executives do business away from home over the weekend. Instead, many hotels promote weekend use of their facilities for conferences or pleasure travel. Attempts to get commuters to shift their travel to off-peak periods will probably fail too, since such travel is determined by people's employment hours. Instead, efforts should be directed at employers to persuade them to adopt flextime or staggered working hours. Resort areas like Cape Cod may have good opportunities to build business during the "shoulder seasons" of spring and fall (which some consider the most attractive times to visit the Cape) by adapting the mix and focus of services to appeal to new target segments. For example, different attractions could be promoted—like hiking, bird watching, visiting museums, and looking for bargains in antique stores.

Discouraging Demand for Nonemergency Calls

Have you ever wondered what it's like to be a dispatcher for an emergency service such as 911 in the United States or 999 in Britain? Imagine yourself in the huge communications room at police headquarters in New York City. A gray-haired sergeant is talking patiently by phone to a woman who has dialed 911 because her cat has run up a tree and she's afraid it's stuck there. "Ma'am, have you ever seen a cat skeleton in a tree?" the sergeant asks her. "All those cats get down somehow, don't they?" After the woman has hung up, the sergeant turns to a visitor and shrugs. "These kinds of calls keep pouring in," he says. "What can you do?" The trouble is, when people call the emergency number with complaints about noisy parties next door, pleas to rescue cats, or requests to turn off leaking fire hydrants, there may be slower response times to fires, heart attacks, or violent crimes.

At one point, the situation in New York City got so bad that officials were forced to develop a marketing campaign to discourage people from making inappropriate requests for emergency assistance through the 911 telephone number. The problem was that what might seem like an emergency to the caller was not a life- (or property-) threatening situation of the type that the city's emergency services were designed to resolve. So a communications campaign, using a variety of media, was developed to urge people not to call 911 unless they were reporting a *dangerous emergency*. For help in resolving other problems, they were asked to call their local police station or other city agencies. The ad shown here appeared on New York buses and subways.

SAVE 911 for the real thing

CALL YOUR PRECINCT OR CITY AGENCY WHEN IT'S NOT A <u>DANGEROUS</u> EMERGENCY (noisy party, open hydrant, abandoned car, etc.)

911 NEW YORK CITY'S DANGEROUS EMERGENCY NUMBER

Keeping good records of customer transactions helps when it comes to analyzing demand by market segment. Computer-based services can track customer consumption patterns by date and time of day automatically and enter them into a company's database. For example, Harrah's recently installed magnetic card readers at its slot machines and gaming tables to track casino customers' gambling behavior. Customers are issued Total Gold cards that they swipe through the magnetic readers before gambling to earn reward points that are redeemable at any Harrah's location. This allows the company to collect accurate information about when customers visit its casinos and how much they spend by day, by week, and by trip.[5]

If each customer transaction is recorded separately and backed up by detailed notes (as in a medical or dental visit, or an accountant's audit), then the task of analyzing demand by market segment is greatly simplified. In subscription and charge account services, when each customer's identity is known and itemized monthly bills are sent, managers can gain immediate insights into usage patterns. Some services, such as telephone and electrical, even have the ability to track subscriber consumption patterns by time of day. Although this data may not always yield specific information on the purpose for which the service is being used, it is often possible to make informed judgments about the volume of sales generated by different user groups.

Sometimes it is in a firm's best interest to discourage demand from certain types of customers—or at least to encourage these customers to use the services at nonpeak times. Some requests for service are inappropriate and make it difficult for the organization to respond to the legitimate needs of its target segments. Discouraging **undesirable demand** through marketing campaigns or screening procedures may help keep peak demand levels within the service capacity of the organization.

undesirable demand: requests for service that conflict with the organization's mission, priorities, or capabilities.

Multiple Influences on Demand

Periodic cycles influencing demand for a particular service can vary in length from one day to one year. In many instances, multiple cycles may operate simultaneously. For example, demand levels for public transportation may differ by time of day (highest during commute hours), day of week (less travel to work on weekends but more leisure travel), and season of year (more travel by tourists in summer). The demand for service during the peak period on a Monday in summer may be different from the level during the peak period on a Saturday in winter, reflecting day-of-week and seasonal variations jointly.

Figure 13.2 shows how the combination of four time-of-day periods (morning peak, midday, afternoon peak, evening/night), two day-of-week periods (weekday, weekend), and three seasonal periods (peak, shoulder, off-peak) can be combined to create 24 different demand periods. In theory, each of these might have its own distinct

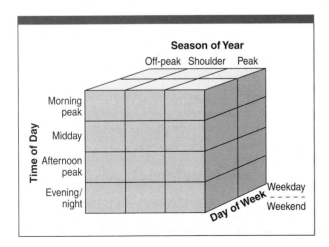

FIGURE 13.2

Identifying Variations in Demand by Time Period

demand level (at a given price) and customer profiles (with resulting differences in needs and expectations). But in practice, analysis might show close similarities between many of the periods. This would make it possible to collapse the framework into a total of three to six cells, each requiring a distinct marketing treatment to optimize the use of available capacity and obtain the most desirable customer mix.

STRATEGIES FOR MANAGING DEMAND

Many services, such as health care or repair and maintenance, involve multiple actions delivered sequentially. What this means is that a service organization's capacity to satisfy demand is constrained by one or more elements of its productive capacity—its physical facilities, equipment, personnel, or the number and sequence of services provided. Consequently, financial success in capacity-constrained businesses is, in large measure, a function of management's ability to use productive capacity as efficiently and as profitably as possible. Services involving tangible actions to customers or their possessions are more likely to be subject to capacity constraints than are information-based services. In the latter instance, however, similar capacity problems may occur when customers are obliged to come to a service site for delivery, as in live entertainment or traditional retail banking.

In a well-designed, well-managed service operation, the capacity of the facility, supporting equipment, and service personnel will be in balance. Sequential operations will be designed to minimize the risk of bottlenecks at any point in the process. This ideal, however, may prove difficult to achieve. The level of demand may vary, often randomly, and the time and effort required to process each person or thing may vary widely at any point in the process. In general, processing times for people are more variable than for objects or things, reflecting varying levels of customer preparedness ("I've lost my credit card"), argumentative versus cooperative personalities ("If you won't give me a table with a view, I'll have to ask for your supervisor"), and so forth. But information-processing and possession-processing service tasks are not necessarily homogeneous either. For both professional services and repair jobs, service delivery times vary according to the nature of the customers' needs.

Managing Demand Under Different Conditions

There are five basic approaches to managing demand. The first, which has the virtue of simplicity but little else, involves *taking no action and leaving demand to find its own levels*. Eventually customers learn from experience or word-of-mouth when they can expect to stand in line to use the service and when it will be available without delay. The problem is that they may also learn about a competitor who is more responsive.

More strategic approaches attempt to influence the level of demand at any given time by taking active steps to *reduce demand in peak periods* and *increase demand when there is excess capacity*. Two additional strategies involve *inventorying demand until capacity becomes available*. A firm can accomplish this either by introducing a *reservations system* that promises customers access to capacity at specified times, or by *creating formalized queuing systems* (or by a combination of the two).

Table 13.1 links these five approaches to the two problem situations of excess demand and excess capacity and provides a brief strategic commentary on each. Many service businesses face both situations at different points in their demand cycles and should consider using one or more of the strategies described above.

Using Marketing Strategies to Shape Demand Patterns

Four of the 8Ps play a part in stimulating demand during periods of excess capacity and decreasing it during periods of insufficient capacity. Price is often the first variable companies use to bring demand and supply into balance, but changes in product, distribu-

Approach Used to Manage Demand	Capacity Situation Relative to Demand	
	Insufficient Capacity (Excess Demand)	Excess Capacity (Insufficient Demand)
Take no action	Unorganized queuing results (may irritate customers and discourage future use)	Capacity is wasted (customers may have a disappointing experience for services like theater)
Reduce demand	Higher prices will increase profits; communication can encourage usage in other time slots (can this effort be focused on less profitable and desirable segments?)	Take no action (but see above)
Increase demand	Take no action, unless opportunities exist to stimulate (and give priority to) more profitable segments	Lower prices selectively (try to avoid cannibalizing existing business; ensure all relevant costs are covered); use communications and variation in products and distribution (but recognize extra costs, if any, and make sure appropriate trade-offs are made between profitability and usage levels)
Inventory demand by reservation system	Consider priority system for most desirable segments; make other customers shift to outside peak period or to future peak	Clarify that space is available and that no reservations are needed
Inventory demand by formalized queuing	Consider override for most desirable segments; try to keep waiting customers occupied and comfortable; try to predict wait period accurately	Not applicable

tion strategy, and communication efforts can also play an important role. Although we discuss each element separately here, effective demand management efforts often require changes in two or more elements simultaneously.

Price and Other User Outlays   One of the most direct ways of reducing excess demand at peak periods is to charge customers more money to use the service during those times. Increases in nonfinancial outlays may have a similar effect. For instance, if customers learn that they are likely to spend more time and physical effort during peak periods, this information may lead those who dislike waiting in crowded and unpleasant conditions to try later (or to use an arm's length delivery alternative like the Internet or self-service machines). Similarly, the lure of cheaper prices and an expectation of no waiting may encourage at least some people to change the timing of their consumption behavior.

For the monetary price of a service to be effective as a demand management tool, managers must have some sense of the shape and slope of a product's demand curve—that is, how the quantity of service demanded responds to increases or decreases in the price per unit at a particular point in time (Figure 13.3 shows a sample demand curve). It's important to determine whether the demand curve for a specific service varies sharply from one time period to another. (For example, will the same person be willing

FIGURE 13.3

Differing Demand Curves for
Business Travelers and Tourists
in High and Low Seasons
(Hypothetical Hotel Example)

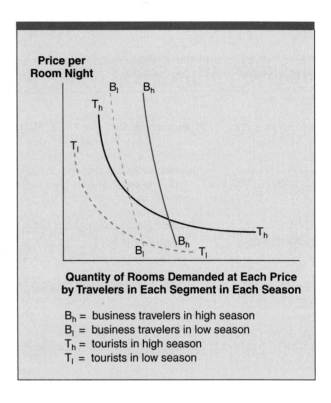

Price per Room Night

B_l B_h

T_h

T_l

B_l B_h T_l T_h

Quantity of Rooms Demanded at Each Price by Travelers in Each Segment in Each Season

B_h = business travelers in high season
B_l = business travelers in low season
T_h = tourists in high season
T_l = tourists in low season

to pay more for a weekend stay in a hotel on Cape Cod in summer than in winter? The answer is probably "yes.") If so, significantly different pricing schemes may be needed to fill capacity in each time period. To complicate matters further, there may be separate demand curves for different segments within each time period (for instance, business travelers are typically less price sensitive than vacationers).

One of the most difficult tasks facing service marketers is to determine the nature of all these different demand curves. Research, trial and error, and analysis of parallel situations in other locations or in comparable services are all ways of obtaining an understanding of the situation. Many service businesses explicitly recognize the existence of different demand curves by establishing distinct classes of service, each priced at levels appropriate to the demand curve of a particular segment. In essence, each segment receives a variation of the basic product, with value being added to the core service through supplementary services to appeal to higher-paying segments. For instance, first-class service on airlines offers travelers larger seats, free drinks, and better food. In computer and printing service firms, product enhancement takes the form of faster turnaround and more specialized services; and in hotels, a distinction is made between rooms of different size and amenities, and different types of views. The Outrigger Hotel on the Big Island of Hawaii charges premium prices for its ocean view suites and rooms. Rooms overlooking the hotel gardens and golf course are in the middle of the hotel's pricing tier, while parking lot views command the lowest prices.

When capacity is constrained, the goal in a profit-seeking business should be to ensure that as much capacity as possible is utilized by the most profitable segments available at any given time. Airlines, for instance, hold a certain number of seats for business passengers paying full fare and place restrictive conditions on excursion fares for tourists (such as requiring advance purchase and a Saturday night stay) in order to prevent business travelers from taking advantage of cheap fares designed to attract tourists who can help fill the aircraft.

Changing Product Elements   Although pricing is often a commonly advocated method of balancing supply and demand, it is not quite as universally feasible for services as for goods. A rather obvious example is provided by the respective demand problems of a ski manufacturer and a ski slope operator. The manufacturer can either produce for inventory or try to sell skis in the spring and summer at a discount. If the skis are sufficiently discounted, some customers will buy early in order to save money. However, in the absence of skiing opportunities, no skiers would buy lift tickets for use on a midsummer day at any price. So, to encourage summer use of the lifts, the operator has to change the service offering.

Similar thinking prevails in a variety of other businesses that undergo significant modifications according to the season. For example, tax preparation firms like H&R Block offer bookkeeping and consulting services to small businesses in slack months. Educational institutions offer weekend and summer programs for adults and senior citizens. Small pleasure boats offer cruises in the summer and a dockside venue for private functions in winter months. And resort hotels sharply alter the mix and focus of their peripheral services like dining, entertainment, and sports to reflect customer preferences in different seasons. All of these firms recognize that no amount of price discounting is likely to develop business out of season.

Summer on the Ski Slopes

Ski resorts traditionally shut down once the snow melted and the slopes became unskiable. The chairlifts stopped operating, the restaurants closed, and the lodges were locked and shuttered until winter approached and the snows fell again. However, some ski operators recognized that mountains offer summer pleasures, too, and started keeping lodging and restaurants open for hikers and picnickers. Some even built Alpine Slides—curving tracks in which wheeled toboggans could run from the summit to the base—to create demand for tickets on the ski lifts. With the construction of new condominiums, demand increased for warm-weather activities as the owners flocked to the mountains in summer and early fall.

The arrival of the mountain biking craze in the 1980s created opportunities for equipment rentals as well as chairlift rides. Killington Resort in Vermont has long encouraged summer visitors to ride to the summit, see the view, and eat at the mountaintop restaurant. But now it also enjoys a booming business in renting mountain bikes and related equipment (such as helmets). Beside the base lodge, where in winter skiers would find rack after rack of skis for rent, the summer visitor can now choose from rows of mountain bikes. Bikers transport their vehicles up to the summit on specially equipped lift-chairs, and then ride them down designated trails. Serious hikers reverse the process by climbing to the summit via trails that seek to avoid descending bikes. They get refreshments at the restaurant, and then take the chairlift back down to the base. Once in a while, a biker will actually choose to ride up the mountain, but such gluttons for punishment are few and far between.

Most large ski resorts look for a variety of additional ways to attract guests to their hotels and rental homes during the summer. While hikers and mountain bikers come to ride the lifts up the mountain at Mont Tremblant, Quebec, others come to enjoy swimming and water sports on the attractive lake beside the resort. Additional attractions include a championship golf course, tennis, roller-blading, and a children's day camp.

Riding the chairlift up Mont Tremblant to hike and bike rather than ski.

There can be variations in the product offering even during the course of a 24-hour period. Some restaurants provide a good example of this, marking the passage of the hours by changing menus and levels of service, variations in lighting and decor, opening and closing the bar, and the presence or absence of entertainment. The intent is to appeal to different needs within the same group of customers, to reach out to different customer segments, or to do both, according to the time of day.

Modifying the Place and Time of Delivery   Some firms attempt to modify demand for a service by changing the time and place of delivery by choosing one of two basic options. The first strategy involves *varying the times when the service is available* to reflect changes in customer preference by day of week, by season, and so forth. Theaters and cinema complexes often offer matinees on weekends when people have more leisure time. During the summer, cafes and restaurants may stay open later because of daylight savings time and the general inclination of people to enjoy the longer, warmer evenings outdoors. Retail shops may extend their hours in the pre-Christmas season or during school holiday periods.

A second strategy involves *offering the service to customers at a new location*. One approach is to operate mobile units that take the service to customers rather than requiring them to visit fixed-site service locations. Examples include traveling libraries, mobile car wash and windshield repair services, in-office tailoring services, home-delivered meals and catering services, and vans equipped with primary care medical facilities. A cleaning and repair firm that wishes to generate business during low-demand periods might offer free pickup and delivery during these times for portable items that need servicing. Alternatively, service firms whose productive assets are mobile may choose to follow the market when that, too, is mobile. For instance, some car rental firms establish seasonal branch offices in resort communities. In these locations, they will tailor the schedule of service hours (as well as certain product features) to meet local needs and preferences.

Customers using information-based services can be offered a cyberspace option, in the form of Internet or telephone-based delivery from a remote server or core center. Networked systems allow firms to transfer demand across time zones to locations where capacity is readily available.

Promotion and Education   Communication efforts alone may be able to help smooth demand even if the other variables of the marketing mix remain unchanged. Signage, advertising, publicity, and sales messages can be used to educate customers about the timing of peak periods and encourage them to use the service at off-peak times when there will be fewer delays. Examples include requests and incentives to "Mail Early for Christmas," public transportation messages urging noncommuters like shoppers or tourists to avoid the overcrowded conditions of the commute hours, and communications from sales reps for industrial maintenance firms advising customers of time periods when preventive maintenance work can be done quickly. Management can ask service personnel (or intermediaries such as travel agents) to encourage customers with discretionary schedules to favor off-peak periods. Short-term promotions, combining both pricing and communication elements as well as other incentives, may also provide customers with attractive incentives to shift the timing of service usage.

Conclusion

Several of the 8Ps of integrated service management underlie the discussion in this chapter. The first is *productivity*. Since many capacity-constrained service organizations have heavy fixed costs, even modest improvements in capacity utilization can have a significant effect on the bottom line. In this chapter we have explored how managers can transform fixed costs into variable costs through such strategies as using rented facilities or part-time labor. Creating a more flexible approach to productive capacity allows a firm to adopt a "chase demand" strategy, thereby improving productivity.

Decisions about *place, cyberspace, and time* are closely associated with balancing demand and capacity. Demand is often a function of where the service is located and when it is offered. As we saw with the opening example of Cape Cod, the appeal of many destinations varies seasonally. Marketing strategies involving the use of *price and other user outlays, product elements*, and *promotion and education* are often useful in managing the level of demand for a service at a particular place and time.

Study Questions and Exercises

1. Review each of the services described in the opening story about Cape Cod. Are there any that might attract increased business in nonpeak seasons by changing some part of their marketing mix? If so, what strategies would you suggest to increase off-season demand?

2. Why is capacity management particularly important in a service setting?

3. What does "inventory" mean for service firms and why is it perishable?

4. What is the difference between maximum capacity and optimal capacity? Provide examples of (a) a situation where the two might be the same, and (b) a situation where they might be different.

5. Select a specific service provider and discuss variations in demand that it experiences relative capacity with reference to Figure 13.1. What is the nature of this service organization's approach to capacity and demand management? What changes would you recommend in relation to its management of capacity and demand and why?

6. What does the term "chasing demand" mean? Describe the actions that firms can take in pursuing a chase demand strategy.

7. Choose a service organization and describe its demand cycles based on the questions about the patterns of demand and their underlying causes described in the boxed material on page 293.

8. Provide examples of service providers in your community (or region) that encourage business during what would otherwise be periods of low demand by (a) changing their pricing, (b) changing product elements, (c) modifying the place and time of service delivery, and (d) using promotional and educational tools.

Endnotes

1. Kenneth J. Klassen and Thomas R. Rohlader, "Combining Operations and Marketing to Manage Capacity and Demand in Services," *The Services Industries Journal* 21 (April 2001): 3–30

2. Based on material in James A. Fitzsimmons and M. J. Fitzsimmons, *Service Management: Operations, Strategy, and Information Technology,* 2nd ed. (New York: Irwin McGraw-Hill, 1998); and W. Earl Sasser, Jr., "Match Supply and Demand in Service Industries," *Harvard Business Review* (November-December 1976).

3. Irene C. L. Ng, Jochen Wirtz, and Khai Sheang Lee, "The Strategic Role of Unused Service Capacity," *International Journal of Service Industry Management* 10, no. 2 (1999): 211–238.

4. Christopher H. Lovelock, "Strategies for Managing Capacity-Constrained Service Organisations," *Service Industries Journal* (November 1984).

5. "Harrah's Takes a Chance on Its Best Customers," *Colloquy* 6, no. 3 (1998): 4–6.

chapter fourteen

Managing Customer Waiting Lines and Reservations

Cutting the Wait for Customers in Retail Banking

How should a big retail bank respond to increased competition from new financial service providers? A large bank in Chicago decided that enhancing service to its customers would be an important element in its strategy.[1] One opportunity for improvement was to reduce the amount of time that customers spent waiting in line for service in the bank's retail branches—a frequent source of complaints. Recognizing that no single action could resolve the problem satisfactorily, the bank adopted a three-pronged approach.

First, technological improvements were made to the service operation, starting with introduction of an electronic queuing system that not only routed customers to the next available teller station but also provided supervisors with online information to help match staffing to customer demand. Meantime, computer enhancements provided tellers with more information about their customers, enabling them to handle more requests without leaving their stations. And new cash machines for tellers saved them from selecting bills and counting them twice (yielding a time savings of 30 seconds for each cash withdrawal transaction).

Second, changes were made to human resource strategies. The bank adopted a new job description for teller managers that made them responsible for customer queuing times and expediting transactions. It created an officer-of-the-day program, where a designated officer was equipped with a beeper and assigned to help

staff with complicated transactions that might otherwise slow them down. A new job category of peak-time teller was introduced, paying premium wages for 12 to 18 hours of work a week. Existing full-time tellers were given cash incentives and recognition to reward improved productivity on predicted high-volume days. Management also reorganized meal arrangements. On busy days, lunch breaks were reduced to half-hour periods and staff received catered meals; in addition, the bank cafeteria was opened earlier to serve peak-time tellers.

A third set of changes centered on customer-oriented improvements to the delivery system. Quick-drop desks were established on busy days to handle deposits and simple requests, while newly created express teller stations were reserved for deposits and check cashing. Lobby hours were expanded from 38 to 56 hours a week, including Sundays. A customer brochure, *How to Lose Wait*, alerted customers to busy periods and suggested ways of avoiding delays.

Subsequently, internal measures and customer surveys showed that the improvements had not only reduced customer wait times but also increased customer perceptions that this bank was "the best" bank in the region for minimal waits in teller lines. Studies also showed that extended lobby hours had transferred some of the "noon rush" customers to before-work and after-work time periods.

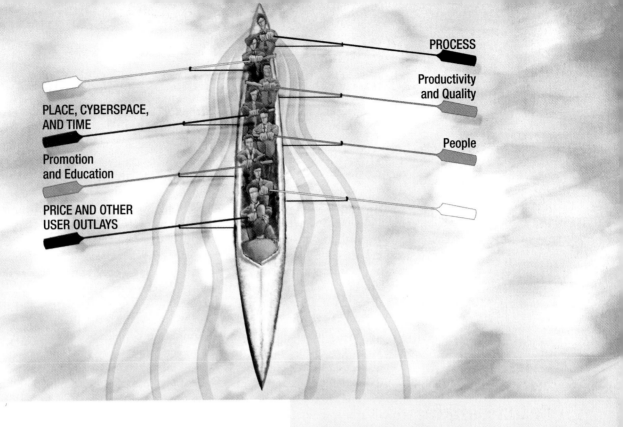

PROCESS

Productivity
and Quality

People

PLACE, CYBERSPACE,
AND TIME

Promotion
and Education

PRICE AND OTHER
USER OUTLAYS

⇒ Learning Objectives

After reading this chapter, you should be able to

⇒ recognize the different queue designs

⇒ understand the psychology of waiting lines

⇒ calculate expected waiting times under defined conditions

⇒ know the basics of designing an effective reservation system

⇒ discuss the principles of yield management and the use of segmented reservations strategies to improve profitability

WAITING TO GET PROCESSED

It's estimated that Americans spend 37 billion hours a year (an average of almost 150 hours per person) waiting in lines, "during which time they fret, fidget, and scowl," according to *The Washington Post*.[2] Similar (or worse) situations seem to prevail around the world. Richard Larson suggests that, when everything is added up, the average person may spend as much as half-an-hour per day waiting in line, which would translate to 20 months of waiting in an 80-year lifetime![3]

Nobody likes to be kept waiting. It's boring, wastes time, and is sometimes physically uncomfortable. And yet waiting for a service process is an almost universal phenomenon. Like the bank in our opening vignette, virtually every organization faces the problem of waiting lines somewhere in its operation. People are kept waiting on the phone, they line up with their supermarket carts to check out their grocery purchases, and they wait for their bills after a restaurant meal. They sit in their cars waiting for traffic lights to change, to enter drive-in car washes, and to pay at tollbooths.

Physical and inanimate objects wait for processing, too. E-mails pile up in an executive's in-box, equipment sits on racks waiting to be fixed at a repair shop, checks wait to be cleared at a bank, an incoming phone call waits to be switched to a customer service rep. In each case, a customer is waiting for the outcome of that work.

As the previous examples suggest, not all queues take the form of a physical waiting line in a single location. Some queues are geographically dispersed. For example, travelers wait at many different locations for the taxis they have ordered by phone to arrive and pick them up. And some queues are virtual rather than physical. When customers deal with a service supplier at arm's length, as in information-processing services, they interact from home, office, or college using telecommunication channels like voice telephone or the Internet. Calls are typically answered in the order received, often requiring customers to wait their turn in a virtual line. The advent of sophisticated Web sites has created additional opportunities for virtual waits. Although companies often promote the time savings that can be obtained, accessing the Web can sometimes be slow due to the virtual queuing that occurs when too many customers try to log on to a company's site or use the same server to go online simultaneously.

In an ideal world, nobody would ever have to wait to conduct a transaction at a service organization. But since services are performances, they can't typically be stored for later use during periods of excess demand. For example, a bank teller cannot prepackage a check-cashing transaction for the following day—it must be done in real time. This results in delays in service delivery when too many people want the same service at the same time.

As we discussed in Chapter 13, there are a number of ways to balance supply and demand. But what should a manager do when the possibilities for shaping demand and adjusting capacity have been exhausted, and supply and demand are still out of balance? Leaving customers to sort things out themselves is no recipe for service quality or customer satisfaction. Rather than allowing matters to degenerate into a random free-for-all, customer-oriented firms implement strategies for ensuring order, predictability, and fairness in their service delivery processes. In businesses where demand regularly exceeds supply, managers often try to manage demand in one of two ways: (1) by asking customers to wait in line (queuing), usually on a first-come, first-served basis; or (2) by offering them the opportunity to reserve or book space in advance.

The Nature of Queues

queue: a line of people, vehicles, other physical objects, or intangible items waiting their turn to be served or processed.

Waiting lines—known to operations researchers (and also the British) as "**queues**"[4]— occur whenever the number of arrivals at a facility exceeds the capacity of the system to process them. Queues are basically a symptom of unresolved capacity management

TABLE 14.1

Elements of a Queuing System

1. The *customer population*—the population from which demands for service originate (sometimes known to operations researchers as the "calling population")
2. The *arrival process*—the times and volumes of customer requests for service
3. *Balking*—a decision by an arriving customer not to join a queue
4. *Queue configuration*—the design of a system in terms of the number, location, and arrangement of waiting lines
5. *Reneging*—a decision by a customer already in a queue who has not yet been served to leave the line rather than wait any longer
6. *Customer selection policies*—formal or ad hoc policies about whom to serve next (also known as queue discipline)
7. The *service process*—the physical design of the service delivery system, the roles assigned to customers and service personnel, and the flexibility to vary system capacity

problems. The analysis and modeling of waiting lines is a well-established branch of operations management. Queuing theory has been traced back to 1917, when a Danish telephone engineer was given the responsibility of determining how large the switching unit in a telephone system had to be to keep the number of busy signals within reason.[5]

Queuing systems can be divided into seven elements, as shown in Table 14.1. Let's take a look at each, recognizing that strategies for managing waiting lines can exercise more control over some elements than others.

Customer Population   When planning queuing systems, operations managers need to know who their customers are and something about their needs and expectations. There is a big difference between a badly injured patient arriving at a hospital emergency unit and a sports fan arriving at a stadium ticket office—obviously, the hospital needs to be more geared for speed than the stadium. Based upon customer research, the population can often be divided into several distinct market segments, each with differing needs and priorities.

Arrival Process   The rate at which customers arrive over time relative to the capacity of the serving process, and the extent to which they arrive individually or in clusters, will determine whether or not a queue starts to form. We need to draw a distinction between the *average* arrival rate (e.g., 60 customers per hour = one customer every minute) and the *distribution* of those arrivals during any given minute of that hour. In some instances, arrival times are largely random (for instance, individuals entering a store in a shopping mall). At other times, some degree of clustering can be predicted, such as arrivals of students in a cafeteria within a few minutes of classes ending. Managers who anticipate surges of activity at specific times can plan their staff allocations around such events (for instance, opening an additional checkout line).

Balking   If you're like most people, you tend to be put off by a long line at a service facility and may decide to come back later (or go somewhere else) rather than waiting. Sometimes "**balking**" is a mistake, as the line may actually be moving faster than you think. Managers can disguise the length of lines by having them wind around corners, as often happens at theme parks like Disneyland. Alternatively, they may indicate the expected wait time from specific locations in the queuing area by installing information signs.

> **balking:** a decision by a customer not to join a queue because the wait appears too long.

Queue Configuration   There are a variety of different types of queues. Here are some common **queue configurations** that you may have experienced yourself in people-processing services (see Figure 14.1 for diagrams of each type).

> **queue configuration:** the way in which a waiting line is organized.

➤ *Single line, single stage.* Customers wait to conduct a single service transaction. Waiting for a bus is an example of this type of queuing system.

➤ *Single line, sequential stages.* Customers proceed through several serving operations, as in a cafeteria line. In such systems, bottlenecks will occur at any stage where the process takes longer to execute than at previous stages. Many cafeterias often have lines at the cash register because the cashier takes longer to calculate how much you owe and to make change than the servers take to put food on your plate (or you take to serve yourself).

➤ *Parallel lines to multiple servers (single or sequential stages).* This system offers more than one serving station, allowing customers to select one of several lines in which to wait. Fast-food restaurants usually have several serving lines in operation at busy times of day, with each offering the full menu. A parallel system can have either a single stage or multiple stages. The disadvantage of this design is that lines may not move at equal speed. How many times have you chosen what looked like the shortest line only to watch in frustration as the lines on either side of you move at twice the speed because someone in your line has a complicated transaction?

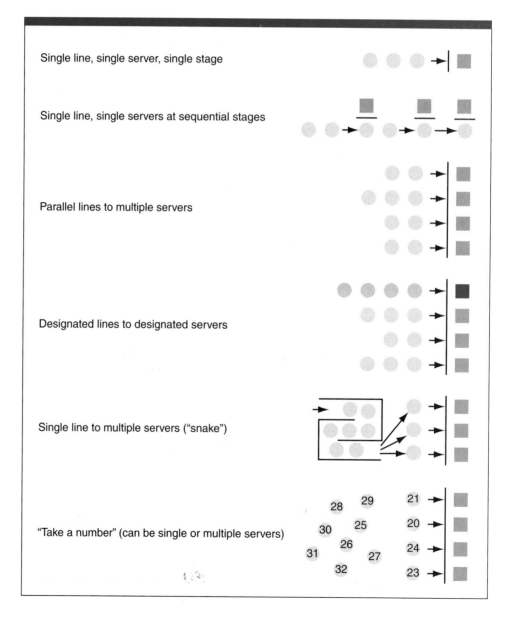

FIGURE 14.1

Alternative Queuing Configurations

➤ *Designated lines.* Different lines can be assigned to specific categories of customer. Examples include express lines (six items or less) and regular lines at supermarket checkouts, and different check-in lines for first-class, business-class, and economy-class airline passengers.

➤ *Single line to multiple servers ("snake").* Customers wait in a single line, often winding back and forth between rope barriers (hence the name). As each person reaches the head of the queue, he or she is directed to the next available serving position. This approach is encountered frequently in bank lobbies, post offices, and at airport check-ins. Its big advantages are fairness and reduced anxiety. The presence of ropes or other barriers makes it difficult for inconsiderate people to break into line. It may also discourage customers from leaving the line before being served.

➤ *Take a number.* In this variation of the single line, arriving customers take a number and are then called in sequence, thus eliminating the need to stand in a queue. This procedure allows them to sit down and relax (if seating is available) or to guess how long the wait will be and do something else in the meantime—but risk losing their place. Users of this approach include ice cream parlors like Baskin-Robbins, large travel agents, or supermarket departments, such as the butcher or baker. Some restaurants use a high-tech version of this queuing strategy. For example, customers who are waiting for tables at the Olive Garden or Outback Steakhouse are given electronic pagers that are numbered by order of arrival. This provides them with more freedom in occupying themselves (e.g., window shopping if the restaurant is located in a mall with other stores) until their pagers vibrate, signaling that their tables are ready.

Hybrid approaches to queue configuration also exist. For instance, a cafeteria with a single serving line might offer two cash register stations at the final stage. Similarly, patients at a small medical clinic might visit a single receptionist for registration, proceed sequentially through multiple channels for testing, diagnosis, and treatment, and conclude by returning to a single line for payment at the receptionist's desk.

Reneging   You know the situation—perhaps all too well! The line is not that long, but it's moving at a snail's pace. The person at the front of the queue has been there for at least five minutes and his problem seems nowhere near resolved. There are two other people ahead of you and you have an uneasy feeling that their transactions are not going to be brief either. You look at your watch for the third time and realize that you only have a few minutes left before your next appointment. Frustrated, you leave the line. In the language of queue management, you have reneged. It's important for service providers to determine how long a wait has to be before customers are likely to start **reneging**, because the consequences may include irritated customers who return later as well as business that is permanently lost.

reneging: a decision by a customer to leave a queue before reaching its end because the wait is longer or more burdensome than originally anticipated.

Customer Selection Policies   Most waiting lines work on the principle of first come, first served. Customers tend to expect this—it's only fair, after all. In many cultures (but not all), people get very resentful if they see later arrivals being served ahead of them for no obvious reason. But not all queuing systems are organized on a first-come, first-served basis. Market segmentation is sometimes used to design queuing strategies that set different priorities for different types of customers. Allocation to separate queuing areas may be based on the following:

➤ *Urgency of the job*—at many hospital emergency units, a triage nurse is assigned to greet incoming patients and decide which ones require priority medical treatment and which can safely be asked to register and then sit down while they wait their turn. Airline personnel will allow passengers whose flights are due to leave soon to check in ahead of passengers taking later flights.

> *Duration of service transaction*—banks, supermarkets, and other retail services often provide "express lanes" for shorter, less-complicated tasks.

> *Payment of a premium price*—airlines usually offer separate check-in lines for first-class and economy-class passengers, with a higher ratio of personnel to passengers in the first-class line (which results in reduced waits for those who have paid more for their tickets).

> *Importance of the customer*—special processes may be reserved for members of frequent user clubs. National Car Rental provides express pickup and drop-off procedures for its Emerald Club members and promises these customers "no waiting, no paperwork, no hassles."[6]

Service Process Poorly designed service processes can lead to waits that are longer and more burdensome than necessary. The root cause is sometimes one or more backstage delays, resulting in customer-contact employees that are kept waiting for a necessary action to occur somewhere else in the system. Flowcharts, employee interviews, and analysis of past service failures can help pinpoint where such problems might occur. The physical design of the front-stage service delivery system also plays a key role in effective queue management. Important design issues include:

> How customers are served (batch processes serve customers in groups, while flow processes serve them individually).

> Whether personnel, self-service equipment, or a combination of the two will serve customers.

> How fast service transactions can be executed, thus determining capacity.

> Whether service comes to customers or whether they must come to the service site and move from one step to another.

> The quality of the serving and waiting experiences, including personal comfort and design issues such as impression created by the servicescape.

MINIMIZING THE PERCEIVED LENGTH OF THE WAIT

As we've discussed in earlier chapters, customers may view the time and effort spent on consuming services as a burden. People don't like wasting their time on unproductive activities any more than they like wasting money. They also prefer to avoid unwanted mental or physical effort, including anxiety or discomfort. Research shows that people often think they have waited longer for a service than they actually did. Studies of public transportation use, for instance, have shown that travelers perceive time spent waiting for a bus or train as passing one and a half to seven times more slowly than the time actually spent traveling in the vehicle.[7]

The Psychology of Waiting Time

The noted philosopher William James observed: "Boredom results from being attentive to the passage of time itself." Based on this observation, David Maister formulated eight principles about waiting time.[8] Adding two additional principles gives us a total of ten, summarized in Table 14.2.

1. Unoccupied time feels longer than occupied time.
2. **Pre-process** and **post-process** waits feel longer than **in-process** waits.
3. Anxiety makes waits seem longer.
4. Uncertain waits are longer than known, finite waits.
5. Unexplained waits are longer than explained waits.
6. Unfair waits are longer than equitable waits.
7. The more valuable the service, the longer people will wait.
8. Solo waits feel longer than group waits.
9. Physically uncomfortable waits feel longer than comfortable waits.[9]
10. Waits seem longer to new or occasional users than to frequent users.[10]

TABLE 14.2

Ten Propositions on the Psychology of Waiting Lines

Unoccupied Time Feels Longer Than Occupied Time   When you're sitting around with nothing to do, time seems to crawl. Thus many service organizations give customers something to do to distract them while waiting. Doctors and dentists stock their waiting rooms with piles of magazines for people to read while waiting. Car repair facilities may have a television for customers to watch. One tire dealer goes further, providing customers with free popcorn, soft drinks, coffee, and ice cream while they wait for their cars to be returned. Theme parks supply roving bands of entertainers to amuse customers waiting in line for the most popular attractions.

Pre- and Post-Process Waits Feel Longer Than In-Process Waits   There's a perceived difference between waiting to buy a ticket to enter a theme park and waiting to ride on a roller coaster once you're in the park. There's also a difference between waiting for coffee to arrive near the end of a restaurant meal and waiting for the server to bring you the check once you're ready to leave. Customers are typically more patient during the core service delivery process than before it starts or after it's completed.

Anxiety Makes Waits Seem Longer   Can you remember waiting for someone to show up to meet you and worrying about whether you had the time and/or the location correct? This makes the perceived waiting time longer, because you are worried about whether you (or the person you're meeting) might have made a mistake.

pre-process wait: a wait before service delivery begins.

in-process wait: a wait that occurs during service delivery.

post-process wait: a wait that occurs after service delivery has been completed.

Customers must wait in line even at fast-food restaurants, but they can pass the time studying the menu.

While waiting in unfamiliar locations, especially out-of-doors and after dark, people are often anxious about their personal safety.

Uncertain Waits Are Longer Than Known, Finite Waits   Although any wait may be frustrating, we can usually adjust mentally to a wait of known length. It's the unknown that keeps us on edge. Maybe you've had the experience of waiting for a delayed flight when you haven't been told how long the delay is going to be. This is unsettling, because you don't know whether you have time to get up and walk around the terminal or whether to stay at the gate in case the flight is called any minute. Airlines often try to appease their customers by giving them new take-off times for delayed flights (which are usually extended several times before the aircraft actually leaves the gate).

Unexplained Waits Are Longer Than Explained Waits   Have you ever been in a subway or an elevator that has stopped for no apparent reason? Not only is there uncertainty about the length of the wait, there's added worry about what is going to happen. Has there been an accident on the line? Will you have to exit the subway in the tunnel? Is the elevator broken? Will you be stuck for hours in close proximity with strangers?

Unfair Waits Are Longer Than Equitable Waits   Expectations about what is fair or unfair sometimes vary from one culture or country to another. In America, Canada, or Britain, for example, people expect everybody to wait their turn in line and are likely to get irritated if they see others jumping ahead or being given priority for no apparent good reason. In some other countries, it is acceptable to push or shove to the front of a line to receive faster service.

The More Valuable the Service, the Longer People Will Wait   People will queue overnight under uncomfortable conditions to get good seats at a major concert, movie opening, or sports event that is expected to sell out.

Solo Waits Feel Longer Than Group Waits   It's reassuring to wait with one or more people you know. Conversation with friends can help to pass the time, and some people are comfortable conversing with strangers while they wait in line.

Physically Uncomfortable Waits Feel Longer Than Comfortable Waits   "My feet are killing me!" is one of the most frequently heard comments when people are forced to stand in line for a long time. And whether sitting or standing, a wait seems more burdensome if the temperature is too hot or too cold, if it's drafty or windy, or if there is no protection from rain or snow.

Unfamiliar Waits Seem Longer Than Familiar Ones   Frequent users of a service know what to expect and are less likely to worry while waiting. But new or occasional users of a service are often nervous, wondering about the probable length of the wait and what happens next. They may also be more concerned about such issues as personal safety.

What are the implications of these propositions about the psychology of waiting? When increasing capacity is not feasible, managers should look for ways to make waiting more palatable for customers. An experiment at a large bank in Boston found that installing an electronic news display in the lobby didn't reduce the perceived time spent waiting for teller service but it did lead to greater customer satisfaction.[11] Some large hotels now provide these digital news displays in their elevators to make rides less boring (in addition to the common practice of putting mirrors near the elevators on each floor to shorten the perceived pre-process wait). And the doorman at a Marriott Hotel in Boston has taken it upon himself to bring a combination barometer/thermometer to work each day, hanging it on a pillar at the hotel entrance where guests waiting can spend a moment or two examining it while they wait for a taxi or for their car to be delivered from the valet parking.[12]

Heated shelters equipped with seats make it more pleasant to wait for a bus or a train in cold weather. Theme park operators cleverly design their waiting areas to make the wait look shorter than it really is, find ways to give customers in line the impression of constant progress, and make time seem to pass more quickly by keeping customers amused or diverted while they wait. Restaurants solve the waiting problem by inviting dinner guests to have a drink in the bar until their table is ready—an approach that makes money for the house as well as keeping customers occupied. In similar fashion, guests waiting in line for a show at a casino may find themselves queuing in a corridor lined with slot machines.

Giving Customers Information on Waits

Does it help to tell people how long they are likely to have to wait for service? Common sense would suggest that this is useful information for customers, since it allows them to make decisions about whether they should wait now or come back later. It also enables them to plan the use of their time while waiting. An experimental study in Canada looked at how students responded to waits while conducting transactions by computer—a situation similar to waiting on the telephone in that there are typically no visual clues as to the probable wait time.[13] The study examined dissatisfaction with waits of 5, 10, or 15 minutes under three conditions: (1) the student subjects were told nothing, (2) they were told how long the wait was likely to be, or (3) they were told what their place in line was. The results suggested that for 5-minute waits, it was not necessary to provide information to improve satisfaction. For waits of 10 or 15 minutes, offering information appeared to improve customers' evaluations of service. However, for longer waits, the researchers suggest that it may be more positive to let people know how their place in line is changing than to let them know how much time remains before they will be served.

One conclusion we might draw is that people prefer to see (or sense) that the line is moving, rather than to watch the clock. Some companies have adopted this approach to manage the waits that customers encounter when dialing customer service numbers. Recorded messages tell the caller how many people are ahead in the queue—these messages are updated continuously until a customer service representative becomes available.

CALCULATING WAIT TIMES

Queue management involves extensive data gathering. Questions of interest include the rate at which customers (or objects requiring service) arrive per unit of time and how long it takes to serve each one. A typical operations strategy is to plan on the basis of average throughput in order to optimize use of employees and equipment. So long as customers (or objects) continue to arrive at the average rate, there will be no delays. However, fluctuations in arrivals (sometimes random, sometimes predictable) will lead to delays at times as the line backs up following a "clump" of arrivals. Planners need to know how easily customers will just walk away when they spot a lengthy line (*balking*) and how long customers will wait for service before giving up and leaving (*reneging*).

To streamline its check-in service at Boston's Logan International Airport, a major airline turned to MIT Professor Richard Larson, who heads a consulting firm called QED.[14] Technicians from QED installed pressure-sensitive rubber mats on the floor in front of the ticket counters. Pressure from each customer's foot on approaching or leaving the counter recorded the exact time on an electronic device embedded in the mats. From this data, Larson was able to profile the waiting situation at the airline's counters, including average waiting times, how long each transaction took, how many customers waited longer than a given length of time (and at what hours on what days), and even how many bailed out of a long line. This information, which was collected over a long time period, helped the airline plan its staffing levels to more closely match the demand levels projected at different times.

Analyzing Simple Queuing Systems

Complex mathematical models enable planners and consultants to calculate a variety of statistics about queue behavior and thus make informed decisions about changes or improvements to existing queuing systems. For basic queuing situations, the formulas are quite simple and yield interesting insights (see the boxed material on "Using Formulas to Calculate Statistics for Simple Queues"). More complex environments may require powerful simulation models that are beyond the scope of this book. Given certain information about a particular queuing situation, you can use these formulas to calculate such statistics as: (1) average queue length, (2) average wait times for customers, (3) average total time for customers in the service system, (4) the impact of increasing the number of service channels, and (5) the impact of reducing average serving time. The math is easy but requires reference to a one-page statistical table, which we have reproduced as an appendix at the end of the chapter.

Using Formulas to Calculate Statistics for Simple Queues

By using the information provided below and the table in the appendix at the end of this chapter, you will be able to make simple calculations about queue waiting times and how many people are likely to be waiting in a given queue under specified conditions. The formulas are very simple—don't be put off by the use of Greek letters for the notation!

Terminology

Certain terms and notation are used in queue analysis:

M = number of serving channels

λ (lambda) = average number of customers actually arriving per unit of time (60 minutes)

μ (mu) = average number of customers per channel that can be served per unit of time (60 minutes)

ρ (rho) = λ/μ = flow intensity through serving channel (% utilization)

$U = \lambda/M\mu$ = capacity utilization of the overall facility

L_q = expected length of line (number of people or objects waiting)

$W_q = L_q/\lambda$ = expected waiting time before being served

You should note that unless the average number of customers served (μ) exceeds the average number of arrivals (λ), it would never be possible to serve all the customers desiring service.

Example

Let's take a simple example. Consider the case of a theater ticket office that has one agent (M) who, on average, can serve 25 customers per hour (μ). This implies an average serving time of 60/25 = 2.4 minutes per customer. Let's assume that customers arrive at an average rate of 20 per hour (λ) in the busy period, which means that $\rho = 20/25 = 0.80$. We can now use the table in the appendix to calculate:

➤ expected length of the line (L_q): Looking down the column for one serving line (M) to $\rho = 0.80$, we can see that the line length will average <u>3.2 persons</u>.

Information Needs

Service managers require the following types of information in order to develop effective demand management strategies:

> *Historical data* on the level and composition of demand over time, including responses to changes in price or other marketing variables.

> *Forecasts* of the level of demand for each major segment under specified conditions.

> *Segment-by-segment data* to help management evaluate the impact of periodic cycles and random demand fluctuations.

> *Sound cost data* to enable the organization to distinguish between fixed and variable costs and to determine the relative profitability of incremental unit sales to different segments and at different prices.

> *Identification of meaningful variations in the levels and composition of demand* on a site-by-site basis in multi-site organizations.

> *Customer attitudes* toward queuing under various conditions.

> *Customer opinions* about whether service quality varies with different levels of capacity utilization.

Where might all this information come from? Although some new studies may be required, much of the needed data are probably already being collected within the organization—although not necessarily by marketers. A stream of information comes into most service businesses from distilling the multitude of individual transactions recorded on sales receipts and other routine business documents. Most companies also collect detailed information for operational and accounting purposes. Unfortunately, the marketing value of this data is often overlooked, and it is not always stored in ways that permit easy retrieval and analysis for marketing purposes. But customer transaction data can

---

> expected waiting time (W_q): $3.2 \times 60/20 = $ <u>9.6 minutes</u>

> expected total time in system ($W_q + 60/\mu$): 9.6 minutes + 2.4 minutes = <u>12.0 minutes</u>

> average capacity utilization (U): $\lambda/M\mu = 20/(1 \times 25) = $ <u>80%</u>

(In other words, 20 percent of the time, the agent will be idle.)

Let's suppose that customers are complaining about this wait and management wants to speed up service. The choices are to add a second agent with a separate single line of customers so that $M = 2$, or to purchase new equipment that halves the time required to issue a ticket and receive payment. Here are the comparative results:

(1) Using the table in the appendix, when $M = 2$ (indicating the addition of a second agent) and $\rho = 0.80$:

> the expected line length (L_q) will be only 0.15 persons

> the expected wait (W_q) = $L_q/\lambda = 0.15 \times 60/20 = 0.45$ minutes, plus 2.40 minutes for service = 2.85 minutes (down from 12.0 minutes)

(2) However, if we halve the service process time from 2.4 to 1.2 minutes by adding new equipment, we can now serve a maximum of 50 customers per hour per channel and the following results occur:

> the expected line length, when $M = 1$ and $\rho = 20/50 = 0.4$ is 0.27 persons

> the expected wait is $0.27 \times 60/20 = 0.81$ minutes + 1.2 = 2.01 minutes total

Both approaches cut the time sharply, but halving the service process time yields slightly better time savings than doubling the number of channels. In this instance, the decision on which approach to adopt would probably depend on the relevant costs involved—the capital cost of adding a second channel plus the wages and benefits paid to a second employee, versus the capital costs of investing in new technology and training (assuming no increase in wages).

often be reformatted to provide marketers with some of the information they require, including how existing segments have responded to past changes in marketing variables.

RESERVATIONS

Ask someone what services come to mind when you talk about reservations and most likely they will list airlines, hotels, restaurants, car rentals, and theater seats. Suggest synonyms like "bookings" or "appointments" and they may add haircuts, visits to professionals like doctors and consultants, vacation rentals, and service calls to fix anything from a broken refrigerator to a neurotic computer.

Reservations are intended to guarantee that service will be available when the customer wants it. Systems vary from a simple appointment book using handwritten entries to a central, computerized data bank for a company's worldwide operations. Reservations systems enable demand to be controlled and smoothed out in a more manageable way. They can also help pre-sell services and provide opportunities to inform and educate customers. A well-organized reservations system allows an organization to deflect demand for service from a first-choice time to earlier or later times, from one class of service to another ("upgrades" and "downgrades"), and even from first-choice locations to alternative ones.

Reservations systems are necessary for possession-processing businesses in fields like repair and maintenance. By requiring reservations for routine maintenance, management can ensure that some time will be kept free for handling emergency jobs that generate much higher margins because they carry a premium price. Households with only one car, for example, or factories with a vital piece of equipment often cannot afford to be without such items for more than a day or two and are likely to be willing to pay more for faster service.

Reservation systems are also used by many people-processing services including restaurants, hotels, airlines, hair salons, doctors, and dentists. Customers who hold reservations should be able to count on avoiding a queue, since they have been guaranteed service at a specific time. However, problems arise when customers fail to show or when service firms over-book. Marketing strategies for dealing with these operational problems include requiring a deposit, canceling nonpaid bookings after a certain time, and providing compensation to victims of over-booking.

The challenge in designing reservation systems is to make them fast and user-friendly for both staff and customers. Whether customers talk with a reservations agent or make their own bookings through a company's Web site, they want quick answers to queries about service availability at a preferred time. They also appreciate it if the system is designed to provide further information about the type of service they are reserving. For instance, can a hotel's reservation system assign a certain type of room for a specific date? (For example, can it guarantee a nonsmoking room with a queen-sized bed and a view of the lake, rather than one with two twin beds and a view of the nearby power station?)

Using Reservations Systems to Manage Yield

Service organizations often use percentage of capacity sold as a measure of operational efficiency. Transport services talk of the "load factor" achieved, hotels of their "occupancy rate," and hospitals of their "census." Professional firms calculate what proportion of a partner's or an employee's time can be classified as billable hours, and repair shops can look at utilization of both equipment and labor. By themselves, however, these percentage figures tell us little of the relative profitability of the business attracted, since high utilization rates may be obtained at the expense of heavy discounting—or even outright giveaways.

Many service firms prefer to rely on measurements of their **yield**—that is, the average revenue received per unit of capacity. The goal is to maximize yield in order to improve profitability. As we noted in Chapter 8, pricing strategies designed to achieve this goal are

yield: the average revenue received per unit of capacity offered for sale.

Getting there is half the fun: Passengers wait to check in at the airport.

widely used in capacity-constrained businesses like passenger airlines, hotels, and car rental agencies. Formalized yield management programs based upon mathematical modeling provide the greatest value to service firms that find it expensive to modify their capacity but incur relatively low costs when they sell another unit of available capacity.[15] Other characteristics encouraging use of such programs include fluctuating demand levels, ability to segment markets by extent of price sensitivity, and sale of services well in advance of usage.

Yield analysis forces managers to recognize the **opportunity cost** of accepting business from one customer or market segment when another might subsequently yield a higher rate. Consider the following problems facing sales managers for different types of capacity-constrained service organizations:

opportunity cost: the potential value of the income or other benefits foregone as a result of choosing one course of action instead of other alternatives.

- ➤ Should a hotel accept an advance booking for 200 room nights from a tour group at $80 each when these same room nights might be sold later at short notice to business travelers at the full posted rate of $140?

- ➤ Should a railroad with 30 empty freight cars accept an immediate request for a shipment worth $900 per car or hold the cars idle for a few more days in the hope of getting a priority shipment that would be twice as profitable?

- ➤ How many seats on a particular flight should an airline sell in advance at special excursion fares or discounted rates?

- ➤ Should an industrial repair and maintenance shop reserve a certain proportion of productive capacity each day for emergency repair jobs that offer a high contribution margin and the potential to build long-term customer loyalty? Or should it simply make sure that there are sufficient jobs—involving mostly routine maintenance—to keep its employees fully occupied?

- ➤ Should a print shop process all jobs on a first-come, first-served basis, with a guaranteed delivery time for each job? Alternatively, should it charge a premium rate for "rush" work and tell customers with "standard" jobs to expect some variability in completion dates?

Managers who make these types of decisions on the basis of guesswork and "gut feel" are little better than gamblers who bet on rolls of the dice. They need a systematic way to figure out the chances of getting more profitable business if they wait. The decision to accept or reject business should be based on a realistic estimate of the probabilities of obtaining more profitable business in the future and the need to maintain established (and desirable) customer relationships.

Segmenting Capacity for Reservations Purposes

There has to be a clear plan, based on analysis of past performance and current market data, that indicates how much capacity should be allocated on particular dates to different types of customers at certain prices. Based on this plan, "selective sell" targets can be assigned to advertising and sales personnel, reflecting allocation of available capacity among different market segments on specific future dates. The last thing a firm wants its sales force to do is to encourage price-sensitive market segments to buy capacity on dates when sales projections predict that there will be strong demand from customers willing to pay full price. Unfortunately, in some industries the least-profitable customers often book the furthest ahead. Tour groups, which pay much lower room rates than individual travelers, frequently ask airlines and hotels to reserve space more than a year in advance.

Figure 14.2 illustrates capacity allocation based on systematic yield analysis in a hotel setting, where demand from different types of customers varies not only by day of the week but also by season. These allocation decisions by segment, captured in reservation databases that are accessible worldwide, tell reservations personnel when to stop accepting reservations at certain prices, even though many rooms may still remain unbooked. Charts similar to those presented in Figure 14.2 can be constructed for most capacity-constrained businesses.

Advances in software and computing power have made it possible for managers to use sophisticated mathematical models to address complicated yield management issues. In the case of an airline, for example, these models can integrate massive historical databases on past passenger travel with real-time information on current bookings. The output helps analysts predict how many passengers would want to travel between two cities at a partic-

Pricing Seats on Flight 2015

American Airlines 2015 is a popular flight from Chicago to Phoenix, departing daily from the "windy city" at 5:30 P.M. The 125 seats in coach (economy class) are divided into seven fare categories, referred to by yield management specialists as "buckets," with round-trip ticket prices ranging from $238 for a bargain excursion fare (with various restrictions and a cancellation penalty attached) to an unrestricted fare of $1404. Seats are also available at a higher price in the small first-class section. Scott McCartney tells how ongoing analysis changes the allocation of seats between each of the seven buckets in economy class:

In the weeks before each Chicago-Phoenix flight, American's yield management computers constantly adjust the number of seats in each bucket, taking into account tickets sold, historical ridership patterns, and connecting passengers likely to use the route as one leg of a longer trip. If advance bookings are slim, American adds seats to low-fare buckets. If business customers buy unrestricted fares earlier than expected, the yield management computer takes seats out of the discount buckets and preserves them for last-minute bookings that the database predicts will still show up.

With 69 of 125 coach seats already sold four weeks before one recent departure of Flight 2015, American's computer began to limit the number of seats in lower-priced buckets. A week later, it totally shut off sales for the bottom three buckets, priced $300 or less. To a Chicago customer looking for a cheap seat, the flight was "sold out."

One day before departure, with 130 passengers booked for the 125-seat flight, American still offered five seats at full fare because its computer database indicated 10 passengers were likely not to show up or take other flights. Flight 2015 departed full and no one was bumped.

Source: Scott McCartney, "Ticket Shock: Business Fares Increase Even as Leisure Travel Keeps Getting Cheaper," *Wall Street Journal*, 3 November, 1997, A1, A10.

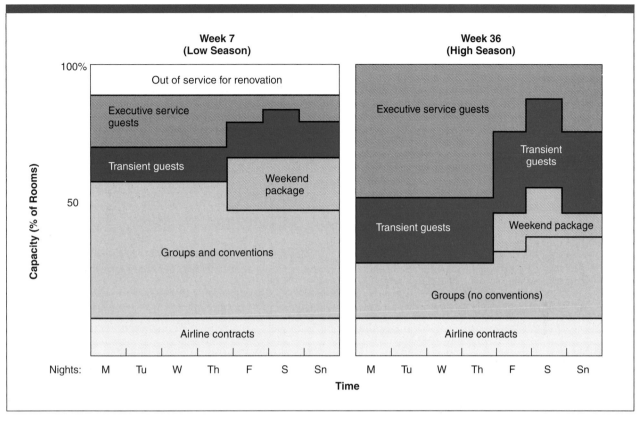

FIGURE 14.2

Setting Capacity Allocation
Sales Targets over Time

ular fare on a flight leaving at a specified time and date. The boxed example describes how American Airlines uses yield management analysis to set fares for a specific flight.

There's evidence that yield management programs can improve revenues significantly—many airlines report increases of 5 percent or more after starting such programs. But a word of warning is in order at this point. Yield management shouldn't mean blind pursuit of short-term yield maximization. Over-dependence on the output of computer models can easily lead to pricing strategies that are full of rules and regulations, cancellation penalties, and a cynical strategy of overbooking without thought for disappointed customers who believed they had a firm reservation. To maintain goodwill and build relationships, a company should take a long-term perspective. Managers need to build in pricing strategies for retaining valued customer relationships, even to the extent of not charging the maximum feasible amount on a given transaction. After all, customer perceptions of "price gouging" do not build trust. And as we mentioned in an earlier chapter, firms shouldn't make pricing policies too complex. Jokes abound about travel agents having nervous breakdowns because they get a different quote every time they call the airline for a fare, and because there are so many exclusions, conditions, and special offers. Finally, yield management strategies should include thoughtfully planned contingencies for victims of overbooking, with service recovery efforts designed to restore goodwill when customers have been disappointed.

Conclusion

The time-bound nature of services is a critical management issue today, especially since customers are becoming more conscious of their personal time constraints and availability. When demand exceeds capacity, not all customers can be served immediately.

Waiting lines and reservations are ways of inventorying demand until capacity is available. Advance reservations can shape the timing of arrivals, but sometimes queuing is inevitable. People-processing services are particularly likely to impose the burden of unwanted waiting on their customers, since the latter cannot avoid coming to the "factory" for service. Managers who can adopt strategies to save customers time (or at least make time in the queue pass more pleasantly) may be able to create a competitive advantage for their organizations. Both queuing and reservations systems can be designed to segment customers into different groups, according to the nature of their transaction or the desirability of their business. Yield management strategies, under which different customers pay different prices for effectively the same service, depend for their effectiveness on allocating units of capacity for reservations purposes to specific segments or price buckets, based on past experience and forecasts of future sales.

Study Questions and Exercises

1. Why should service marketers be concerned about the amount of time that customers spend in (a) pre-process waits and (b) in-process waits?

2. Based on your own experience, give examples of reservations systems that worked really well or really poorly for customers.

3. How might the principles of yield management be applied to rental car companies?

4. Review the 10 propositions on the psychology of waiting lines. Which are the most relevant in (a) a supermarket, (b) a city bus stop on a cold, dark evening, (c) check-in for a flight at the airport, (d) a doctor's office, (e) a ticket line for a football game that is expected to be a sell-out?

5. What are the seven elements of a queuing system? Which are under the control of the customer and which does the service provider control?

6. For an organization serving a large number of customers, what do you see as the advantages and disadvantages of the different types of queues shown in Figure 14.1?

7. Using the formulas on page 312 and the table in the appendix, calculate answers to the following problems:

    a. At Frank's office cafeteria, customers select their meals from different food stations and then go to the checkout station to pay. He knows that Maureen, the speedy cashier, can check out a customer every 20 seconds on average. With an arrival rate of 90 customers an hour during the 11 A.M. to 2 P.M. lunch period, what is the average length of the line that Frank can expect at the checkout? How many minutes will he have to wait?

    b. Maureen goes on maternity leave and is replaced by Willy, whom Frank times at one customer every 36 seconds. On average, how much longer will the line now be and how long will Frank have to wait?

    c. In response to complaints about delays at the checkout station, management assigns JoAnn to operate a second cash register during Maureen's absence. Like Willy, JoAnn can process the average customer in 36 seconds. How long, on average, will each line now be and how many minutes can Frank expect to wait (in either line)?

    d. Willy is off sick one day, so JoAnn must work alone. But she manages to improve her performance and to process one customer every 30 seconds. On average, how long is the line now? And how long is the wait?

8. What segmentation principles and variables are illustrated in the yield management example from American Airlines?

Endnotes

1. Based on an example in Leonard L. Berry and Linda R. Cooper, "Competing with Time-Saving Service," *Business* 40, no. 2, (1990): 3–7.
2. Malcolm Galdwell, "The Bottom Line for Lots of Time Spent in America," *The Washington Post* (syndicated article, February, 1993).
3. Dave Wielenga, "Not So Fine Lines," *Los Angeles Times*, 28 November, 1997, E1.
4. This section is based in part on James A. Fitzsimmons and Mona J. Fitzsimmons, *Service Management: Operations, Strategy and Information Technology* 2nd ed. (New York: Irwin McGraw-Hill, 1998): 515–537; and David H. Maister, "Note on the Management of Queues" 9-680-053, Harvard Business School Case Services, 1979, rev. 2/84.
5. Richard Saltus, "Lines, Lines, Lines, Lines . . . The Experts Are Trying to Ease the Wait," *The Boston Globe*, 5 October, 1992, 39, 42.
6. From the National Car Rental Web site, www.nationalcar.com, January 2001.
7. Jay R. Chernow, "Measuring the Values of Travel Time Savings, *Journal of Consumer Research* 7 (March 1981): 360–371. [Note: this entire issue was devoted to the consumption of time.]
8. David H. Maister, "The Psychology of Waiting Lines," in J. A. Czepiel, M. R. Solomon, and C. F. Surprenant, *The Service Encounter* (Lexington, MA: Lexington Books/D.C. Heath, 1986): 113–123.
9. M. M. Davis and J. Heineke, "Understanding the Roles of the Customer and the Operation for Better Queue Management," *International Journal of Operations & Production Management* 14, no. 5 (1994): 21–34.
10. Peter Jones and Emma Peppiatt, "Managing Perceptions of Waiting Times in Service Queues," *International Journal of Service Industry Management* 7, no. 5 (1996): 47–61.
11. Karen L. Katz, Blaire M. Larson, and Richard C. Larson, "Prescription for the Waiting-in-Line Blues: Entertain, Enlighten, and Engage," *Sloan Management Review* (Winter 1991): 44–53.
12. Bill Fromm and Len Schlesinger, *The Real Heroes of Business and Not a CEO Among Them* (New York: Currency Doubleday, 1994), 7.
13. Michael K. Hui and David K. Tse, "What to Tell Customers in Waits of Different Lengths: An Integrative Model of Service Evaluation," *Journal of Marketing* 80, no. 2 (April 1996): 81–90.
14. Malcolm Galdwell, "The Bottom Line for Lots of Time Spent in America.
15. Sheryl E. Kimes, "Yield Management: A Tool for Capacity-Constrained Service Firms," *Journal of Operations Management* 8, no. 4 (October 1989): 348–363; Sheryl E. Kimes and Richard B. Chase, "The Strategic Levers of Yield Management," *Journal of Service Research* 1 (November 1998): 156–166.

Appendix: Poisson Distribution Table

Calculating the Expected Number of People Waiting in Line for Various Values of M and ρ

Flow Intensity (ρ)	Number of Service Channels (M)			
	1	2	3	4
0.10	0.0111			
0.15	0.0264	0.0008		
0.20	0.0500	0.0020		
0.25	0.0833	0.0039		
0.30	0.1285	0.0069		
0.35	0.1884	0.0110		
0.40	0.2666	0.0166		
0.45	0.3681	0.0239	0.0019	
0.50	0.5000	0.0333	0.0030	
0.55	0.6722	0.0149	0.0043	
0.60	0.9000	0.0593	0.0061	
0.65	1.2071	0.0767	0.0084	
0.70	1.6333	0.0976	0.0112	
0.75	2.2500	0.1227	0.0147	
0.80	3.2000	0.1523	0.0189	
0.85	4.8166	0.1873	0.0239	0.0031
0.90	8.1000	0.2285	0.0300	0.0041
0.95	18.0500	0.2767	0.0371	0.0053
1.0		0.3333	0.0454	0.0067

Integrating Marketing, Operations, and Human Resources

Throughout this book, we have tried to strike a balance between marketing and two other key functions—operations and human resources. Senior managers need to make sure that these three functions are well integrated at all levels in the organization. The chapters in Part V address this issue by exploring the following questions (see Figure V.1): **What are appropriate roles for people and technology?** And **how can our firm achieve service leadership?**

Chapter 15 examines employee roles in service organizations. People—one of the 8Ps of integrated service management—play a distinctive role in service organizations. As discussed in earlier chapters, front-stage employees in high-contact organizations are responsible for delivering product elements. They also form part of the customer's overall experience. In these settings, employees are important to both marketing and operational strategies. As managers in high-contact services think about human resources strategy, they should be asking themselves: *How do employees' attitudes, appearances, and performances affect our success?* Understanding the roles that employees play, particularly in their encounters with customers, is a necessary prerequisite to addressing the question, *How should we select, train, and motivate customer contact employees?* In low-contact services, customers rarely encounter employees unless they have problems to resolve. In such organizations, marketing's interest lies with the small percentage of employees responsible for solving customer problems, whereas the operational focus is on the backstage aspects of service delivery.

Technology issues have been discussed in many previous chapters. Information technology, in particular, is shaping the way people work, leveraging the efforts of employees and managers, and enabling customers to serve themselves in a wide array of settings. In Chapter 16, we explore the role of technology in modern service businesses by raising the question: *Is technology a key strategic thrust in our business or just another operations tool?* Of particular concern is the impact of new technologies on both productivity and customer perceptions of service quality. Operations managers are often eager to replace personal service by automated alternatives. But before allowing this to happen, service marketers need to find answers to the question, *Do customers have the skills and desire to use self-service options?*

In Chapter 17, we use the theme of service leadership as a way to explore the mutually dependent responsibilities of marketing, operations, and human resources. Numerous firms aspire to be service leaders, but few attain it. Those that do achieve leadership status in their industry must work constantly to retain it. Many once-revered corporate names have declined in popularity or disappeared altogether.

The quest for service leadership begins with two questions: *Do we have a coherent vision for the future?* and, if so, *Is this vision defined and driven by a strong, effective leader?* Progress in achieving leadership can be measured, in part, by superior performance in the competitive marketplace, including perceptions of the

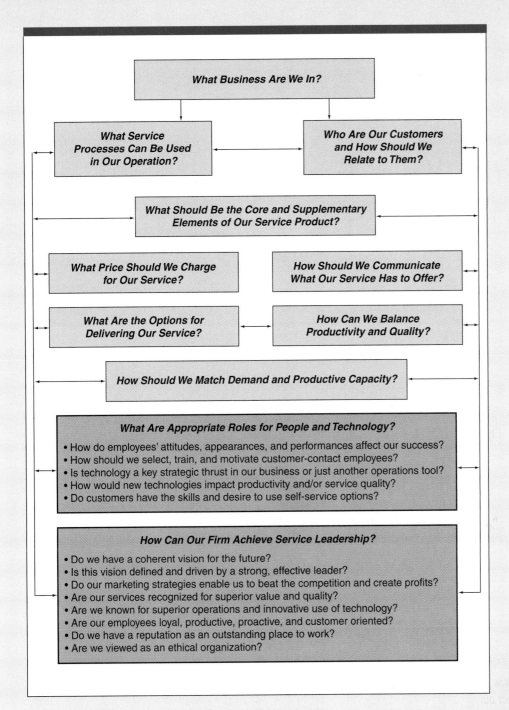

FIGURE V.1

Decisions Involving the Integration of Marketing, Operations, and Human Resources

value and quality of the firm's services and achievement of profits (or of broader social objectives in the case of nonprofit organizations). Leadership in marketing is often tied to superior operations and innovative use of technology. But the most difficult achievement for competitors to emulate is leadership in human resources management. Possessing a workforce that is loyal, productive, proactive, and customer-oriented can offer tremendous competitive advantages, both in retaining customers and in attracting

prospective employees. A firm that has a reputation as an outstanding place to work will find it that much easier to attract and retain the best candidates.

As you'll see, firms that successfully integrate marketing, operations, and human resources management are most likely to reach service leadership status. Achieving leadership is difficult, but sustaining it may be just as hard. A key ingredient is being perceived as an ethical organization.

chapter fifteen

Employee Roles in Service Organizations

USAA Treats Its Employees Right

USAA is an insurance and diversified financial services association that serves members of the U.S. military and their families.[1] With seven offices in the United States and two in Europe, it also offers access through mail, toll-free telephone numbers, and the Internet. It was founded in 1922 by 25 army officers who couldn't find adequate auto insurance because most insurers of that era considered military personnel to be poor insurance risks. During a meeting in a San Antonio, Texas, hotel room, the officers formed an association (which they called the United States Army Automobile Association) and pledged to share each other's financial risks. At that time, the group had little knowledge about auto insurance, no funding, and no office.

Today, USAA is made up of more than 85 subsidiaries and affiliates worldwide and owns more than $60 billion in assets. It ranks 217th among the largest U.S. corporations in terms of revenues, according to the 2000 *Fortune* 500 list. USAA's aggressive investment in technology, customer feedback systems, employee training, and quality of work life have all contributed to its reputation for outstanding service quality and a customer retention rate of about 97 percent.

The association is loyal to its employees, and in return it expects them to be loyal to their customers. Wilson Cooney, deputy CEO for USAA's Property and Casualty Insurance operations, calls this the "loyalty chain." He states, "If you don't take care of the employees, they can't take care of the customers. We give employees all they need to be happy and absolutely enthralled to be here. If they are not happy, we will not have satisfied customers in the long run. . . . We must have

a passion for customers. If we don't, we are in the wrong business." USAA has invested more in customer-oriented, state-of-the-art information systems than any other insurance company. These support systems are a vital element in enabling service representatives to deliver fast, accurate results to customers. The result is not only some of the highest customer satisfaction and loyalty levels in the industry but also high job satisfaction among employees.

USAA has been listed by *Fortune* as among the 100 best companies to work for in the United States. It attracts, motivates, and retains exceptional employees with an amazing selection of employee services and benefits. In addition to its retirement, investment, and insurance benefits, USAA also provides its workers with on-site laundry, dry-cleaning services, restaurants, and childcare. "Company stores" sell employees first-quality merchandise at discount prices. There are three fully equipped fitness centers complete with weight rooms, aerobics classes, and personal trainers. USAA has more than 100 company-owned vans to help employees get to work without the hassle and expense of commuting. And there are special events (like the employee art show, the spring fiesta and the Christmas party) that are free to employees throughout the year.

The association is also noted for its significant investment in job-related education. There are 75 classrooms and a curriculum of more than 200 courses at its corporate headquarters in San Antonio. The training for new account representatives lasts 10 weeks. The association also pays for its employees' college education. All full-time employees who

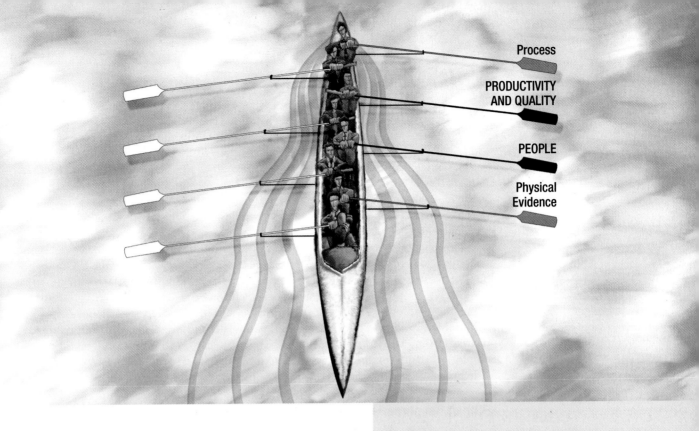

Process

PRODUCTIVITY
AND QUALITY

PEOPLE

Physical
Evidence

are on the job more than a year are eligible for full funding. USAA pays the tuition bills directly and will cover one undergraduate degree and one graduate degree per employee. Why is USAA willing to spend more than $2.6 million annually educating its employees? Karen Wolfshohl, manager of college studies, explains: "It has always been our culture that employees are our most important resource. They are the decisive factor in our competitiveness as a financial services provider. An educated work force is our only option given the force of change, especially technology change, in our business."

Learning Objectives

After reading this chapter, you should be able to

⟹ understand why human resources expenditures should be seen as an investment rather than a cost

⟹ recognize the strategic importance of recruitment, selection, training, motivation, and retention of employees

⟹ define what is meant by the "control" and "involvement" models of management

⟹ describe the benefits and implications of employee empowerment

⟹ discuss how the culture of a company impacts the service that customers receive

HUMAN RESOURCES: AN ASSET WORTH MANAGING

Many organizations have used the phrase, "People are our most important asset," yet all too few companies act as though top management really believes it. However, in successful service firms like USAA employees are seen as a resource to be nurtured, rather than a cost to be minimized. Hal Rosenbluth, owner of a chain of successful travel agencies, argues in his book, *The Customer Comes Second*, that a company's first focus should be on its employees: "Only when people know what it feels like to be first in someone else's eyes," he writes, "can they sincerely share that feeling with others."[2]

This chapter is the first of two addressing the question in our service decision framework, *What are appropriate roles for people and technology?* (see Figure V.1 on page 321). It focuses on a vital element of the 8Ps: *People*. The human factor in services involves two groups of players: employees and customers. Here we emphasize the task of managing employees, since we've already discussed the need to manage customer behavior in previous chapters. The field is potentially a vast one, since **human resource management** (**HRM**) includes recruitment, selection, training, and retention of employees. Both marketing and operations managers need to be aware of how employee attitudes, appearances, and performance affect the firm's success.

Human Resource Issues in High-Contact Environments

In Chapter 1, we introduced the notion of integrated service management, which suggests that marketing, operations, and human resource management should be seen as interdependent functions. Interactions between these three areas are most pronounced in the case of high-contact services, thus creating special challenges in job design, recruitment, and training.

In high-contact services, customers encounter service employees during service delivery. This contact creates a fundamental distinction between the jobs of front-stage service workers and those who work in the back offices of service firms or in manufacturing plants.[3] The backstage employees in a service organization support the efforts of their front-stage colleagues (called "**internal customers**"), who are serving end-customers directly.

Almost all of us can recount some horror story of a dreadful experience with a service business—and usually, we love to talk about it! If pressed, many of us can also recount a really good service experience. Service personnel usually feature prominently in such dramas—either in roles as uncaring, incompetent villains or as heroes who went out of their way to help, anticipating customer needs or resolving problems in a helpful and empathetic manner. Service people can play a vital role in lower-contact jobs where customers interact with the firm by telephone and an agent's voice is the only form of human contact. In high-contact service encounters, we tend to remember the role played by front-stage personnel better than any other aspect of the operation. In many respects, these employees *are* the service.

Customer-contact personnel must attend to both operational and marketing goals, since they are a part of both the delivery system and the product. On the one hand, they help "manufacture" the service output. At the same time, they may also be responsible for marketing it ("We've got some nice desserts to follow your main course" or "We could clean your machine at the same time that we repair the motor" or "Now would be a good time to open a separate account to save for your children's education").

In the eyes of their customers, service personnel may also be seen as an integral part of the service experience. Thus front-stage employees often perform a triple role as

---

human resource management (HRM): the coordination of tasks related to job design, employee recruitment, selection, training, and motivation; it also includes planning and administering other employee-related activities.

internal customers: employees who receive services from an internal supplier (another employee or department) as a necessary input to performing their own jobs.

Operational Issues	Typical Operations Goals	Common Marketing Concerns
Productivity improvement	Reduce unit cost of production	Strategies may cause decline in service quality
Make-versus-buy decisions (outsourcing)	Trade off control against comparative advantage and cost savings	"Make" decisions may result in lower quality and lack of market coverage; "buy" decisions may transfer control to unresponsive suppliers and hurt the firm's image
Facilities location	Reduce costs; provide convenient access for suppliers and employees	Customers may find location unattractive and inaccessible
Standardization	Keep costs low and quality consistent; simplify operations tasks; recruit low-cost employees	Consumers may seek variety, prefer customization to match segmented needs
Batch versus unit processing	Seek economies of scale, consistency, efficient use of capacity	Customers may be forced to wait, feel "one of a crowd," be turned off by other customers
Facilities layout and design	Control costs; improve efficiency by ensuring proximity of operationally related tasks; enhance safety and security	Customers may be confused, shunted around unnecessarily, find facility unattractive and inconvenient
Job design	Minimize error, waste, and fraud; make efficient use of technology; simplify tasks for standardization	Operationally oriented employees with narrow roles may be unresponsive to customer needs
Learning curves	Apply experience to reduce time and costs per unit of output	Faster service is not necessarily better service; cost saving may not be passed on as lower prices
Management of capacity	Keep costs down by avoiding wasteful underutilization of resources	Service may be unavailable when needed; quality may be compromised during high-demand periods
Quality control	Ensure that service execution conforms to predefined standards	Operational definitions of quality may not reflect customer needs, preferences
Management of queues	Optimize use of available capacity by planning for average throughput; maintain customer order, discipline	Customers may be bored and frustrated during wait, see firm as unresponsive

TABLE 15.1

Operations and Marketing Perspectives

Source: © 1989 by Christopher H. Lovelock. Reprinted from "Managing Interactions Between Operations and Marketing and Their Impact on Customers," Chapter 15 in Bowen et al. (eds.), *Service Management Effectiveness* (San Francisco: Jossey Bass, 1990), 362.

operations specialist, marketer, and part of the service product itself. They occupy **boundary spanning positions**—operating at the organization's boundary and providing a link between the external environment and internal operations. This multiplicity of roles may be difficult for employees, especially when they feel as physically and psychologically close to customers as they do to managers and other employees.[4] Table 15.1 highlights some of the conflicts between operations and marketing goals that may trap employees in the middle.

Because of the unique challenges that boundary-spanning situations create, employees in high-contact roles should be recruited and trained on the basis of specific characteristics like interpersonal skills, personal appearance and grooming, knowledge of the product and the operation, selling capabilities, and skills in coproduction (working jointly with customers to create the desired service). Additional attributes that are particularly valuable in selling situations include skills in monitoring nonverbal clues

boundary spanning positions: jobs that straddle the boundary between the external environment, where customers are encountered, the internal operation organization.

(such as the customer's body language), and adjusting one's behavior in the context of social situations. Both technical and interpersonal skills are *necessary* but neither alone is *sufficient* for optimal job performance.[5]

Emotional Labor

emotional labor: the act of expressing socially appropriate (but sometimes false) emotions toward customers during service transactions.

Service encounters entail more than just correct technical execution of a task. They also involve such human elements as personal demeanor, courtesy, and empathy. This brings us to the concept of **emotional labor** (or emotion work), which is the act of expressing socially appropriate (but sometimes false) emotions during service transactions.[6] Some jobs require service workers to act in a friendly fashion toward customers or to appear compassionate, sincere, or even self-effacing. Trying to conform to customer expectations on such dimensions can be a psychological burden for some service workers when they perceive themselves as having to act out emotions they do not feel.

Customer-contact employees comply with these "display rules" through both acting and the expression of spontaneous and genuine emotion.[7] Display rules generally reflect the norms imposed both by society—which may vary from one culture to another—and by specific occupations and organizations. For instance, customers' expectations for nurses are different from those for bill collectors. Expectations may also reflect the nature of a particular encounter (for example, what emotions would you expect a waiter to display if you discovered a fly in your soup?). Acting requires employees to simulate emotions that they do not actually feel, accomplished by careful presentation of verbal and nonverbal cues, such as facial expression, gestures, and voice tone. Some employees are natural actors, and those who are not can typically be coached to improve their acting skills. Under certain conditions, service providers may spontaneously experience the expected emotion without any need for acting—as when a firefighter feels sympathy for an injured child taken from a burning building.

Human resources (HR) managers need to be aware that performing emotional labor, day after day, can be stressful for employees as they strive to display feelings that may be false. From a marketing standpoint, however, failure to display the emotions that customers expect can be damaging and may lead to complaints that "employees don't seem to care." The challenge for HR managers is to determine what customers expect, recruit the most suitable employees, and train them well.

Dilbert encounters emotional labor at the bank.

JOB DESIGN AND RECRUITMENT

Many of the most demanding jobs in service businesses are boundary-spanning positions where employees are expected to be fast and efficient at executing operational tasks as well as courteous and helpful in dealing with customers. Service encounters are potentially "a three-cornered fight," with the customer (demanding attention and service quality) and the organization (demanding efficiency and productivity) at the two ends and frontline personnel caught in the middle. This creates tension as employees are torn between satisfying management and customers, and between meeting productivity and quality goals. If jobs are not designed carefully—or the wrong people are picked to fill them—there's a significant risk that employees may become stressed and eventually experience burnout, causing them to be unproductive.[8]

The nature of work varies enormously in the service sector. It may also differ between one company and another depending on the goals, culture, and values of each organization. Service jobs should be designed with reference to the skills required, the degree of discretion allowed to jobholders, the context within which individuals will be working—alone or with a team, for instance—and the extent of contact with customers. Job requirements often change as a company evolves, new technologies are implemented, and different ways of working are introduced. Job design is an ongoing task for HR specialists and line managers.

Recruiting the Right People for the Job

There's no such thing as a universally perfect employee. Some service jobs require prior qualifications, as opposed to giving employees the necessary training after they are hired. A nurse can apply for a job as a hotel receptionist, but the reverse is not true unless the applicant has nursing qualifications. Further, different positions—even within the same firm—are best filled by people with different styles and personalities. It helps to have an outgoing personality in many front-stage jobs, because employees are constantly meeting new customers. A shy, retiring person, by contrast, might be more comfortable working backstage with the same set of coworkers. Someone who loves to be physically active might do better as a restaurant server or courier than as a reservation agent or bank teller.

The Walt Disney Company, which is in the entertainment business, actually uses the theatrical term *casting* and assesses prospective employees in terms of their potential for on-stage or backstage work. On-stage workers, known as *cast members*, are assigned to those roles that best match their appearance, personalities, and skills. An individual's fit with organizational culture is also important. Robert Levering and Milton Moskowitz, authors of *The 100 Best Companies to Work for in America*, stress that, "No company is perfect for everyone. This may be especially true in good places to work since these firms tend to have real character . . . their own culture. Companies with distinctive personalities tend to attract—and repel—certain types of individuals."[9]

In trying to become more customer oriented, a number of service firms have put their front-stage employees through "charm schools," with the goal of creating warmer, friendlier staff members who can relate better to customers. But HR managers have discovered that while good manners and the need to smile and make eye contact can be taught, warmth cannot. In fact, a cool and insincere smile may be worse than no smile at all. The only realistic solution is to change the organization's recruitment criteria to favor candidates with naturally friendly personalities. As Jim Collins observes, "The old adage 'People are your most important asset' is wrong. The *right* people are your most important asset. The right people are those who would exhibit the desired behaviors anyway, as a natural extension of their character and attitude, regardless of any control and incentive system."[10]

What makes outstanding service performers so special? Often it's those characteristics that are intrinsic to individuals, qualities that they would bring to any employer. As one study of high performers concluded:

> *Energy . . . cannot be taught, it has to be hired. The same is true for charm, for detail orientation, for work ethic, for neatness. Some of these things can be enhanced with on-the-job training . . . or incentives. . . . But by and large, such qualities are instilled early on.*[11]

The logical conclusion is that service businesses that rely on the human qualities of their front-stage service personnel should devote great care to attracting and hiring the right candidates. As part of this strategy, managers should review the firm's recruitment advertising and ensure that it captures the human challenges of the work instead of just emphasizing the technical aspects and the glamour (if any).

Southwest Airlines, America's leading short-haul airline, believes that the selection process starts not with the candidate but with the individuals responsible for recruiting. In a sense, it is they who must ensure that new hiring decisions reflect and reinforce the company's distinctive culture. Everyone hired to work in the airline's People Department—Southwest doesn't use the terms "human resources" or "personnel"—comes from a marketing or customer-contact background. This marketing orientation is displayed in internal research on job descriptions and selection criteria, where each department is asked: "What are you looking for?" rather than told: "This is what we think you need!" Southwest invites supervisors and peers (with whom future candidates will be working) to participate in the in-depth interviewing and selection process. More unusually, it invites its own frequent flyers to participate in the initial interviews for flight attendants and to tell candidates what passengers value. The People Department admits to being amazed at the enthusiasm with which these busy customers have greeted this invitation and at their willingness to devote time to this task.

Technology and the Workplace

Rapid developments in information technology are enabling service businesses to make radical improvements in business processes and even completely reengineer their operations.[12] For example, technology innovations now allow both backstage and front-stage service jobs to be located around the world. American insurance companies, for instance, have recruited workers in Ireland to process claims. Barbados, Jamaica, Singapore, India, and the Philippines are emerging as other potential English-speaking locations for telecommunicated services, not only for backstage work but also for such front-stage supplementary services as airline reservations and technical help lines. The United States has also become a major exporter of management and technical assistance to overseas service providers. In 1999, the sale of data processing, market research, and legal services alone (provided by "knowledge workers" using telephones and desk-top computers from the comfort of their own offices or homes) totaled $18 billion, and this figure is expected to increase exponentially in the future as more U.S. firms expand overseas. Cendant (the franchisor for lodging chains like Days Inn, Howard Johnson, and Travelodge), McDonald's, Hertz, Kinko's, Ace Hardware, and ServiceMaster all rely on U.S.-based management consulting expertise in running their international operations.[13]

A growing number of customer-contact employees work by telephone, never meeting customers face to face. Customers may be unaware of where the service person they are talking to is located, and they typically don't care as long as they're dealing with people who have the necessary personal and technical skills—plus the enabling technological support—to provide high-quality service. As with other types of service work, these customer-contact jobs can be very rewarding or they can place employees in an electronic equivalent of the old-fashioned sweatshop. As discussed in the BT example (see box), recruiting people with the right skills and personalities, training them well, and giving them a decent working environment are some of the keys to success in this area.

Leveraging Employee Skills Through Training and Technology

One characteristic shared by many firms that provide outstanding service is their emphasis on building and leveraging employee skills. The opening vignette on USAA noted that organization's strong commitment to both internal training and external education for its employees. By combining careful selection and ongoing training, firms can grow talent internally and groom people for higher-level positions.

Some service companies use **expert systems** to leverage employees' skills to perform work that previously required higher qualifications, more extensive training, or years of on-the-job experience. Certain systems are designed to train novices by gradually enabling them to perform at higher levels. Other expert systems capture and make the scarce expertise of outstanding performers available to everyone. An expert system contains three elements: a knowledge base about a particular subject; an inference engine that mimics a human expert's reasoning in order to draw conclusions from facts and figures, solve problems, and answer questions; and a user interface that gathers information from—and gives it to—the person using the system. Like human experts, such systems can give customized advice and may accept and handle incomplete and uncertain data. American Express uses a well-known expert system called Authorizer's Assistant (originally called Laura's Brain, after a star authorizer), which contains the expertise of its best credit authorizers. It has improved the quality and

expert systems: interactive computer programs that mimic a human expert's reasoning to draw conclusions from data, solve problems, and give customized advice.

Recruiting Employees Who Work by Phone at BT

BT (formerly British Telecom) is a major supplier of telecommunication services. It also actively uses its own medium, the telephone, for managing relationships with its business accounts. Like a growing number of firms that do business by phone, its success is very dependent on recruiting and retaining employees who are good at telephone-based transactions with customers whom they never see. Executives responsible for BT's telephone account management (TAM) operation, serving small business customers, are highly selective in their recruitment efforts. They look for bright, self-confident people who can be trained to listen to customers' needs and use structured, probing questions to build a database of information on each of the 1,000 accounts for which an account manager is responsible.

BT begins its recruitment process with a telephone interview, to see if candidates have the poise, maturity, and good speaking voice to project themselves well and inspire trust in a telephone-based job. (Curiously, most recruiters of telephone-based employ-

ees leave this critical telephone test until much later in the process.) Those who pass this screen proceed to written tests and personal interviews.

Successful candidates receive intensive training. BT has built special training schools to create a consistent approach to customer care. Would-be account managers receive 13 weeks of training over a 12-month period, interspersed with live front-line experience at their home bases. They must develop in-depth knowledge of all the services and customer-premises equipment that BT sells, as well as the skills needed to build relationships with customers and to understand their business needs. Since modern telecommunications technology is changing so rapidly, customers need a trusted advisor to act as consultant and problem solver. And it is this role that BT's TAM program has succeeded in filling. For all the impressive supporting technology, the program would ultimately fail without good employees at the other end of the phone.

From driver to UPS Pacific Region Manager: UPS grows management talent internally.

speed of credit decisions dramatically and has contributed enormously to corporate profitability.[14]

Although information technology and methods technology offer the potential for significant improvements in both productivity and quality, these benefits will not materialize without employee support. ServiceMaster understands this requirement. Rated as the leading outsourcing company in the United States, the firm offers management services that provide equipment maintenance support and innovative solutions to streamline work processes. Using its 20 years of experience and a database of more than 17

Technology Solves a Skills Shortage

In the early 1990s, Singapore Airlines (SIA) was having trouble recruiting and retaining check-in agents for its home base at Changi Airport. It was getting harder to recruit people with the necessary skills at the wages SIA was willing to offer. And once they were on the job, many agents found it rather unchallenging. The predictable outcome: relatively high turnover and constant repetition of the expensive recruitment and training process. As part of a major program to update its departure control systems, SIA computer specialists created new software for check-in procedures, featuring screen formats with pull-down windows, menu-driven

commands, and other innovations on the video terminal displays— all designed to speed and simplify usage. The net result is that SIA has been able to lower the educational criteria for the check-in position. The job is now open to people who would not previously have qualified and who view the work and the wages as being fairly attractive. Employee satisfaction has increased, and turnover is down. Because the new system is so much easier to use, only one week's training is needed—resulting in significant savings for SIA. Finally, agents are able to process passengers faster, which has increased both productivity and customer satisfaction.

million equipment units, ServiceMaster can move immediately to lower its clients' costs by developing detailed models of exactly how each unit should perform, when to do preventive maintenance, and when replacement should occur.

However, when ServiceMaster is initially hired by a new client to manage certain internal services, it often finds the employees in a survival mode, stuck in seemingly dead-end jobs with no training and no opportunities for advancement. According to Senior Vice President Craig Frier, "Our technologies enable them to run things right. But we can't do anything or reach any of our goals for the facility until we can get rank-and-file maintenance, housekeeping or dietary employees to understand and believe in themselves, their futures, and their worth."[15]

ServiceMaster's first actions are focused on training the employees and making them feel more in control of their lives and their jobs, which results in an immediate improvement in morale. It then introduces the employees to a career development program that provides opportunities to obtain, say, an associate degree in plant engineering and work toward becoming a group or facilities manager for ServiceMaster and eventually even head a ServiceMaster unit.

EMPOWERMENT OF EMPLOYEES

Under the right conditions, providing employees with greater discretion (and training them to use their judgment) may enable them to provide superior service without referring to rulebooks or higher authority.[16] From a humanistic standpoint, the notion of encouraging employees to exercise initiative and discretion is an appealing one. **Empowerment** allows employees to find solutions to service problems and make appropriate decisions about customizing service delivery. It depends for its success on what is sometimes called **enablement**—giving workers the tools and resources they need to take on these responsibilities.

Is Empowerment Always Appropriate?

Advocates claim that the empowerment approach is more likely to yield motivated employees and satisfied customers than the "production line" alternative, in which management designs a relatively standardized system and expects workers to execute tasks within narrow guidelines. But is the choice between these two approaches really so obvious? The truth is that different situations may require different solutions. The payoffs from greater empowerment must be weighed against increased costs for selection and training, higher labor costs, slower service as customer-contact personnel devote more time to individual customers, and less consistency in service delivery. It's also important to avoid being seduced into too great a focus on recovery at the expense of service delivery reliability.

Heskett, Sasser, and Schlesinger argue that any employee needs to operate in a context of "latitude and limits."[17] Frontline employees want enough latitude to be able to deliver results to customers but also like to know the limits of their authority. There are two possible approaches, illustrated in Figure 15.1. The traditional approach sees latitude as a box within which the employee is free to operate. Actions that would exceed the limits of permitted behaviors require a supervisor's approval. In this instance, the extent of latitude is defined by the size of the box; companies adopting a policy of empowerment try to expand the box, within the constraints imposed by the nature of the business. The nontraditional approach is to define those behaviors that are required and then allow employees discretion on all other actions. In this instance, greater latitude is created by reducing the extent of required behaviors.

empowerment: authorizing employees to find solutions to service problems and make appropriate decisions about responding to customer concerns without having to ask a supervisor's approval.

enablement: providing employees with the skills, tools, and resources they need to use their own discretion confidently and effectively.

FIGURE 15.1

Two Approaches to Providing
Employee Latitude and
Limits

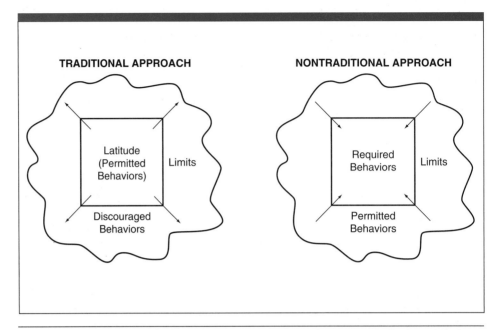

Source: James L. Heskett, W. Earl Sasser, Jr., Leonard A. Schlesinger, *The Service Profit Chain* (New York: The Free Press, 1997), 121.

Control versus Involvement

control model of management: an approach based on clearly defined roles, top-down control systems, a hierarchical organizational structure, and the assumption that management knows best.

The production line approach to managing people is based upon the well-established **"control" model of organization design and management**, with its clearly defined roles, top-down control systems, hierarchical pyramid structure, and assumption that management knows best. Empowerment, by contrast, is based upon the **"involvement" (or "commitment") model of management**. This approach is based on the assumption that most employees can make good decisions and produce good ideas for operating the business if they are properly socialized, trained, and informed. It also assumes that employees can be internally motivated to perform effectively and that they are capable of self-control and self-direction. Although broad use of the term "empowerment" is relatively new, the underlying philosophy of employee involvement is not.

In the control model, four key features are concentrated at the top of the organization, while in the involvement model, these features are pushed down through the organization:

involvement model of management: an approach based on the assumption that employees are capable of self-direction and, if properly trained, motivated, and informed—can make good decisions concerning service operations and delivery.

1. Information about organizational performance (e.g., operating results and measures of competitive performance)

2. Rewards based on organizational performance (e.g., profit-sharing and stock ownership)

3. Knowledge that enables employees to understand and contribute to organizational performance (e.g., problem-solving skills)

4. Power to make decisions that influence work procedures and organizational direction (e.g., through quality circles and self-managing teams)

The production line and empowerment approaches are at opposite ends of a spectrum that reflects increasing levels of employee involvement as additional knowledge, information, power, and rewards are pushed down to the front line. Empowerment can take place at several levels:

➤ *Suggestion Involvement* empowers employees to make recommendations through formalized programs, but their day-to-day work activities do not really change. McDonald's, often portrayed as an archetype of the production line approach,

TABLE 15.2

Factors Favoring a Strategy
of Employee Empowerment

- Business strategy is based on competitive differentiation and on offering personalized, customized service
- The approach to customers is based on extended relationships rather than on short-term transactions
- The organization uses technologies that are complex and nonroutine in nature
- The business environment is unpredictable and surprises are to be expected
- Existing managers are comfortable with letting employees work independently for the benefit of both the organization and its customers
- Employees have a strong need to grow and deepen their skills in the work environment, are interested in working with others, and have good interpersonal and group process skills

Source: Based on David E. Bowen and Edward E. Lawler III, "The Empowerment of Service Workers: What, Why, How, and When?" *Sloan Management Review*, Spring 1992, 32–39.

listens closely to its front line; innovations ranging from the Egg McMuffin to methods of wrapping burgers without leaving a thumbprint on the bun were invented by employees.

➤ *Job Involvement* represents a dramatic expansion of job content. Jobs are redesigned to allow employees to use a wider array of skills. In complex service organizations like airlines and hospitals, where individual employees cannot offer all facets of a service, job involvement is often accomplished through use of teams. To cope with the added demands accompanying this form of empowerment, employees require training and supervisors must be reoriented from directing the group to facilitating its performance in supportive ways.

➤ *High Involvement* gives even the lowest-level employees a sense of involvement in the total organization's performance. Information is shared. Employees develop skills in teamwork, problem solving, and business operations, and they participate in work-unit management decisions. There is profit sharing and employee ownership of stock in the business.

As shown in Table 15.2, a strategy of empowerment is most appropriate when certain factors are present within the organization and its environment. It's important to emphasize that not all employees are necessarily eager to be empowered. Many employees do not seek personal growth within their jobs and would prefer to be given specific directions rather than having to use their own initiative.

SERVICE JOBS AS RELATIONSHIPS

Marketing theory argues that successful relationships are built on mutually satisfying exchanges from which both customers and suppliers gain value. This same notion of value can be applied to any employee who has a choice of whether or not to work for a particular organization (and the best employees usually do have opportunities to move on, if dissatisfied). The net value of a job is the extent to which its benefits exceed its associated costs. When discussing such benefits, one thinks first of pay, health insurance, stock options, and pension funding. However, most jobs also generate other benefits. Some positions offer learning or experience-building opportunities; some provide deep satisfaction because they are inherently interesting or provide a sense of accomplishment; still others provide companionship, a valued chance to meet other people, feelings of dignity and self-worth, opportunities to travel, and the chance to make a social contribution.

But working in any job has its costs, too, beginning with the time spent on the job and traveling to and from work. Most jobs also entail some monetary costs, ranging from special clothes to commuting to childcare. Stress can be a psychological and physical cost in a demanding job. Unpleasant working conditions may involve exposure to noise, smells, hazardous chemicals, and temperature extremes. And, of course, some jobs require intense physical or mental effort.

Job design cannot be restricted to just ensuring that the firm gets its money's worth out of employees. Companies must also consider the design of the working environment, asking whether employees have the tools and facilities they need to deliver excellent service. To an increasing degree, health and safety legislation is requiring changes in the workplace to eliminate physical and even psychological hazards, but only management can create a positive working climate—and that takes a long time. Reducing the negative aspects of the job and improving its positive ones may make it easier for firms to hire and retain the best available employees, without having to pay premium salaries and load up on conventional "benefits." Employees who enjoy their work are more likely than unhappy ones to provide good service to customers.

Fortune's annual list of the "100 Best Companies To Work For" highlights corporate culture as the key dimension in employee retention.[18] But we shouldn't overlook the role of perks like daycare (offered by 26 percent of the best employers) and concierge services like dry-cleaning pickup (offered by 29 percent), which reduce stress for employees, save them time, and make them feel appreciated.

Employee Retention and Customer Retention

Researchers have found strong correlations between employees' attitudes and perceptions of service quality among customers of the same organization.[19] One retail banking study showed that when employees reported a strong service orientation imperative in the branch where they worked, customers reported that they received higher-quality service. A follow-up study determined that customer intentions to switch to a competitor could be predicted based on employee perceptions of the quality of service delivered. Employee turnover probabilities were also predictable, based on customer perceptions of service quality. Where customers reported high service quality, employees were less likely to leave. A reasonable inference is that it is not very rewarding to work in an environment where service is poor and customers are dissatisfied. For example, a study of a truck rental business found that higher levels of employee satisfaction were related to both lower turnover and lower worker's compensation claims.[20]

When jobs are low paid, boring, and repetitive, with minimal training, service is typically poor and employee turnover is high. Poor service generates high customer turnover, too, making the working environment even less rewarding. As a result, the firm

Loyal Agents Equal Loyal Customers at State Farm

One factor underlying the ongoing success of State Farm Insurance in the United States is the interactive effect of both customer and agent retention. According to industry studies, State Farm's customer retention rate exceeds 90 percent, consistently the best performance of all national insurers selling through agents. At the same time, more than 80 percent of newly appointed agents remain associated exclusively with State Farm through their fourth year, compared with only 20 to 40 percent for other companies in the industry. Further, the average State Farm agent has 18 years of tenure compared to between six and nine years for competitors, making them more experienced.

This underlying synergy at State Farm comes from the fact that agents who are committed to building a long-term relationship with the company are more likely to build lasting relationships with customers, too. In turn, it's easier for agents to work with (and sell to) loyal customers whose needs, lifestyles, and attitudes to risk they know well. The net result is that State Farm agents' productivity is 50 percent higher than industry norms.

Source: Frederick F. Reichheld, *The Loyalty Effect* (Boston, MA: Harvard Business School Press, 1996), Chapters 4 and 5.

spends all its resources trying to recruit both new customers and new employees. Loyal employees, by contrast, know the job and, in many cases, the customers too. To the extent that an organization's culture leads to long-term employees who are customer oriented, knowledgeable, and remain motivated, better service and higher customer retention should result. This is especially true for high-contact businesses that require customers to be on-site during service delivery.[21]

Researchers have been able to document the economic value of both customer retention and employee retention.[22] For example, Sears, Roebuck and Company, a major department store chain in the United States, spent more than three years rebuilding the company around its customers after experiencing the worst year of financial returns (in 1992) in its long and highly profitable history. In the course of refocusing the company's strategy, top executives at Sears developed a business model that tracked success from management behavior through employee attitudes to customer satisfaction, and ultimately to financial performance. Sears has been using its employee-customer-profit model to measure employee and customer satisfaction and the resulting impact on the bottom line since 1995. The results have been encouraging. In 1998, both employee and customer satisfaction increased by 4 percent, which translated into more than $4 million in additional revenues for the year.[23]

Cycles of Failure, Mediocrity, and Success

All too often, bad working environments translate into dreadful service, with employees treating customers the way their managers treat them. Businesses with high employee turnover are frequently stuck in what has been termed the "Cycle of Failure." Others, which offer job security but little scope for personal initiative, may suffer from an equally undesirable "Cycle of Mediocrity." However, there is potential for both vicious and virtuous cycles in service employment, with the latter being termed the "Cycle of Success."[24]

The Cycle of Failure   In many service industries the search for productivity is occurring with a vengeance. One solution takes the form of simplifying work routines and hiring workers as cheaply as possible to perform repetitive work tasks that require little or no training. The cycle of failure captures the implications of such a strategy, with its two concentric but interactive cycles: one involving failures with employees; the second, with customers (Figure 15.2).

The *employee cycle of failure* begins with narrowly designed jobs to accommodate low skill levels, emphasis on rules rather than service, and use of technology to control quality. A strategy of low wages is accompanied by minimal effort on selection or training. Consequences include bored employees who lack the ability to respond to customer problems, become dissatisfied, and develop a poor service attitude. Outcomes for the firm are low service quality and high employee turnover. Because of weak profit margins, the cycle repeats itself with hiring of more low-paid employees to work in this unrewarding atmosphere. Managers have offered a veritable litany of excuses and justifications for perpetuating this cycle:

> "You just can't get good people these days."

> "People just don't want to work today."

> "To get good people would cost too much and you can't pass on these cost increases to customers."

> "It's not worth training our front-line people when they leave you so quickly."

> "High turnover is simply an inevitable part of our business. You've got to learn to live with it."[25]

FIGURE 15.2

The Cycle of Failure

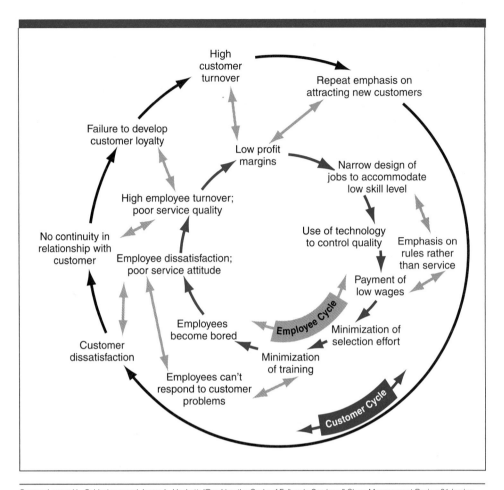

The *customer cycle of failure* begins with repeated emphasis on attracting new customers who become dissatisfied with employee performance and the lack of continuity implicit in continually changing faces. Customers fail to develop any loyalty to the sup-
~ and turn over as rapidly as the staff, thus requiring an ongoing search for new cus-
~in sales volume. This churn of discontented customers is especially
what we now know about the greater profitability of a loyal cus-
ncept of an enormous pool of nomadic service employees moving employer to the next, experiencing a stream of personal fail-
eeply disturbing for companies with a social conscience.
gers make shortsighted assumptions about the financial implica-
h-turnover human resources strategies. Part of the problem is fail-
elevant costs. Three key cost variables are often omitted: the cost of
hiring, and training (which is as much a time cost for managers as a
lower productivity of inexperienced new workers; and the costs of
ng new customers (requiring extensive advertising and promotional
evenue variables are also ignored: future revenue streams that might
or years but are lost when unhappy customers take their business else-
tial income from prospective customers who are turned away by neg-
outh. Finally, there are less easily quantifiable costs like disruptions to
job remains unfilled, and loss of the departing person's knowledge of the
s customers).

The Cycle of Mediocrity   Another vicious employment cycle is the "Cycle of Mediocrity" (Figure 15.3). It's most often found in large, bureaucratic organizations—typified by state monopolies, industrial cartels, or regulated oligopolies—where there is little incentive to improve performance and where fear of entrenched unions may discourage management from adopting more innovative labor practices.

In these environments, service delivery standards tend to be prescribed by rigid rulebooks that are oriented toward standardized service, operational efficiencies, and prevention of both employee fraud and favoritism toward specific customers. Employees may expect to spend their entire working lives with the organization. Job responsibilities tend to be narrowly and unimaginatively defined, tightly categorized by grade and scope of responsibilities, and further rigidified by union work rules. Salary increases and promotions are based on longevity, with successful performance in a job being measured by absence of mistakes, rather than by high productivity or outstanding customer service. What little training occurs is focused on teaching the rules and the technical aspects of the job, not on improving human interactions with customers and coworkers. Since there are minimal allowances for flexibility or employee initiative, jobs tend to be boring and repetitive. However, in contrast to cycle of failure jobs, most positions provide adequate pay and reasonable benefits combined with high security—thus making employees reluctant to leave. This lack of mobility is compounded by the absence of marketable skills that would be valued by other companies.

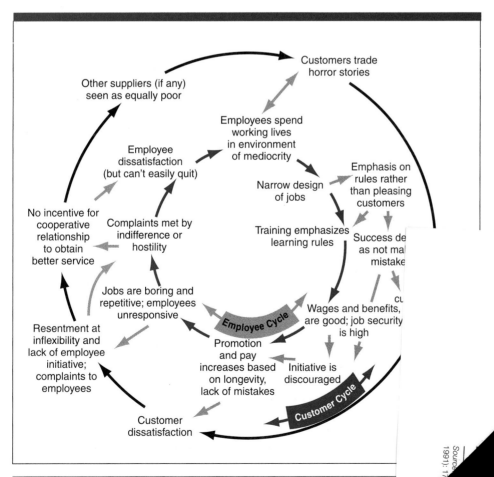

FIGURE 15.3

The Cycle of Mediocrity

Source: Christopher Lovelock, "Managing Services: The Human Factor" in *Understanding Service Management*, ed J.G. Barnes (Chichester: Wiley, 1995), 228.

Customers find such organizations frustrating to deal with. Faced with bureaucratic hassles, lack of service flexibility, and unwillingness of employees to make an effort to serve them better (often accompanied by the statement "That's not my job"), they may become resentful. What happens when there is nowhere else for customers to go—either because the service provider holds a monopoly, or because all other available players are perceived as being as bad or worse? We shouldn't be surprised if dissatisfied customers display hostility toward service employees who, feeling trapped in their jobs and powerless to improve the situation, protect themselves through such mechanisms as withdrawal into indifference, playing overtly by the rulebook, or countering rudeness with rudeness. The end result is a vicious cycle of mediocrity in which unhappy customers continually complain to sullen employees (and also to other customers) about poor service and bad attitudes, generating increased defensiveness and lack of caring on the part of the staff. Under such circumstances, there is little incentive for customers to cooperate with the organization to achieve better service.

The Cycle of Success   Some firms reject the assumptions underlying the cycles of failure and mediocrity. Instead, they take a long-term view of financial performance and invest in their people to create a "cycle of success" (Figure 15.4). As with failure or mediocrity, success applies to both employees and customers. Broadened job designs are accompanied by training and empowerment practices that allow front-stage personnel

FIGURE 15.4

The Cycle of Success

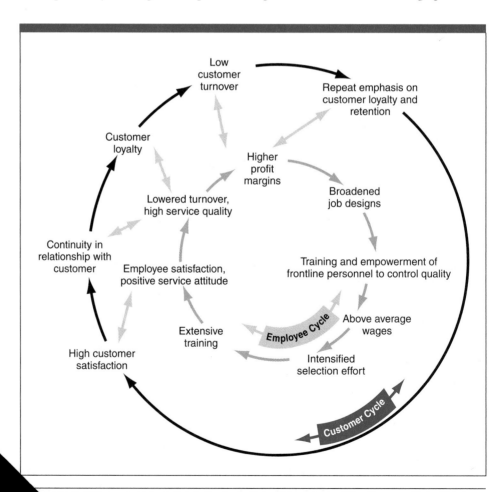

Leonard L. Schlesinger and James L. Heskett, "Breaking the Cycle of Failure in Services," *Sloan Management Review* 31 (spring 28.

to control quality. With more focused recruitment, more intensive training, and better wages, employees are likely to be happier in their work and to provide higher quality, customer-pleasing service. Regular customers also appreciate the continuity in service relationships resulting from lower turnover and are more likely to remain loyal. Profit margins tend to be higher, and the organization is free to focus its marketing efforts on reinforcing customer loyalty through customer retention strategies, which are usually much less costly to implement than strategies for attracting new customers. USAA, the company described in the opening story for this chapter, provides a good example of the long-term profitability that can result when investments in employees lead to a cycle of success.

The deregulation of many service industries and the privatization of government corporations have often been instrumental in extracting organizations from the cycle of mediocrity. For example, in both the United States and Canada formerly monopolistic regional telephone companies have been forced to adopt a more competitive stance. In many countries, public corporations have undergone radical culture changes in the wake of privatization and exposure to a more competitive environment. Unfortunately, however, pressures to increase shareholder value have sometimes led top management to focus on short-term profits, achieved through cost cutting and efficiency without regard to service quality or employee welfare. The risk is that such strategies will eventually take the firm in the direction of the cycle of failure rather than the cycle of success.

The Role of Unions

The power of organized labor is widely cited as an excuse for not adopting new approaches in both service and manufacturing businesses. "We'd never get it past the unions," managers say, wringing their hands and muttering darkly about restrictive work practices. Unions are often portrayed as the bad guys in the media, especially when high profile strikes in important service industries such as airlines, railroads, and postal service inconvenience millions. On the other hand, polls showed that customers and the general public were overwhelmingly sympathetic to union concerns of unfair treatment of part-time employees when the Teamsters Union struck United Parcel Service in 1997. Unions are not just limited to blue-collar workers; they may also embrace high-paid professionals such as airline pilots.

American managers have a reputation for being especially antagonistic toward unions. Professor Jeffrey Pfeffer has observed wryly that "the subject of unions and collective bargaining is . . . one that causes otherwise sensible people to lose their objectivity."[26] He urges a pragmatic approach to this issue, emphasizing, "the effects of unions depend very much on what *management* does." In reviewing numerous studies of the impact of unions (across many U.S. industries), he notes that unions do raise wage levels—especially for low-wage workers—as well as reducing turnover, improving working conditions, and leading to better resolution of grievances. They can also have a positive impact on productivity—but only in those companies where both management's and labor's leadership skills are strong. These improvements in productivity, he suggests, may reflect the greater selectivity in recruitment that is possible when jobs pay better and thus attract more candidates, together with the lower turnover often found in unionized firms and the resulting presence of a more experienced workforce.

In *The 100 Best Companies to Work for in America*, Levering and Moskowitz discuss many successful companies that are strongly unionized. The United States is a useful site for comparative research on the impact of unions, since firms in the same industry vary widely in the extent of unionization as well as in the impact of unionization on their success. For example, management-union confrontations have been damaging for airlines such as United and Northwest. In contrast, Southwest Airlines is more than 80 percent unionized yet boasts the lowest costs per mile, highest profits, best on-time performance, best baggage handling, and highest customer satisfaction of any American airline (as measured by fewest complaints to the U.S. Department of Transportation). The airline's unusually good labor-management relations are widely seen as a direct result of its chief executive's hands-on efforts. The one area on which management will not negotiate is work rules. It's also worth noting that Southwest employees collectively own 13 percent of the company's stock.

As you can see, the presence of unions in a service company is not an automatic barrier to high performance and innovation unless there is a long history of mistrust, acrimonious relationships, and confrontation. However, management cannot rule by fiat. Consultation and negotiation with union representatives are essential to ensure that employees will accept and implement new ideas.

HUMAN RESOURCE MANAGEMENT IN A MULTICULTURAL CONTEXT

The trend toward a global economy means that more and more service firms are operating across national frontiers. Two other important trends are increased tourism and business travel, plus substantial immigration of people from different cultural back-

Euro Disney and the Challenges of Multiculturalism

Few recent service ventures have attracted as much media comment and coverage as the operations of Walt Disney Co.'s theme park, Disneyland Paris. The cultural difficulties of creating and running an American-style theme park in the heart of Europe have been widely publicized. Since Disneyland Paris replicates three successful Disney theme parks, top management's objective has been to ensure that the park adapts itself to European conditions without losing the American feel that has always been seen as one of its main draws. For officials of the European operating company, Euro Disney, the park just outside Paris, opened in 1992, has proved even more of a challenge than Disney's first foreign theme park, Tokyo Disneyland, which opened in Japan 10 years earlier. Unlike the California, Florida, or Tokyo parks, no one nationality dominates the latest park. So handling languages and cultures has required careful planning, not least in terms of employee recruitment, training, and motivation.

Knowledge of two or more languages has been an important criterion in hiring "cast members" (front-line employees). Months before opening day, recruitment centers were set up in Paris, London, Amsterdam, and Frankfurt. During the park's first season, approximately two-thirds of those hired were French nationals; the balance came from 75 other nationalities, principally British, Dutch, German, and Irish. Some knowledge of French is required of all employees; in the park's opening year, about 75 percent of employees spoke this language fluently, another 75 percent spoke English, roughly 25 percent spoke Spanish, and 25 percent, German.

The reservations center caters to people of many tongues, with special phone lines for each of 12 different languages. Cast members speaking a broad cross section of tongues staff City Hall, the main information center in the park. Special procedures have been instituted at the park's medical center to handle medical emergencies involving speakers of less commonly encountered languages.

Source: Christopher Lovelock and Ivor Morgan, "Euro Disney: An American in Paris," case reprinted in Christopher Lovelock, *Services Marketing*, 4th ed. (Upper Saddle River, NJ: Prentice Hall, 2001), 602–614.

grounds into developed economies such as those of the United States, Canada, Australia, and many European countries. The result is pressure on service organizations to serve a more diverse array of customers—with different cultural expectations and speaking a variety of languages—and to recruit a more diverse workforce.

Striking a balance between diversity and conformity to common standards is not a simple task, because societal norms vary across cultures. When McDonald's opened a fast-food restaurant in Moscow, management trained staff members to smile at customers. However, this particular norm did not exist in Russia and some patrons concluded that staff members were making fun of them! The troubled early history of Euro Disney provides another example of how the application of American standards to European operations may be complicated by cultural conflicts (Euro Disney box).

Part of the HRM challenge as it relates to culture is to determine which performance standards are central and which should be treated more flexibly. For instance, some public service agencies in Britain (and elsewhere) that require employees to wear uniforms have been willing to allow Sikh employees to wear a matching colored turban with badge, whereas others have generated conflict by insisting on use of traditional uniform caps. Multiculturalism may also require new HRM procedures that respect the practices and traditions of diverse employee groups. The decision to be more responsive to employees whose first language is not English may require changes in recruiting criteria, use of role-playing exercises, and language training.[27]

With over 70 nationalities represented among its employees, there is a high probability that a cast member can be found somewhere on-site to interpret in such a situation. The company has noted the language capabilities of every employee, can access them by computer (e.g., "who do we have on duty who speaks Turkish?"), and can page them immediately by beeper or walkie-talkie.

However, Euro Disney has encountered many cultural problems in training and motivation. At the outset, the company announced that "a leading priority was to indoctrinate all employees in the Disney service philosophy, in addition to training them in operational policies and procedures." The apparent goal was to transform all employees, 60 percent of whom were French, into clean-cut, user-friendly, American-style service providers. Since the founding of Disneyland in 1958, Disney has been known for its strict professional guidelines. "The Look Book," for example, dictated that female employees should wear only clear nail polish, very little—if any—make-up, and, until recent years, only flesh-colored stockings. Men could not wear beards or mustaches (the latter are now permitted) and had to keep their hair short and tapered. Guests should be greeted within 60 seconds of entering a facility and helped as needed.

According to media reports, a key challenge has been to train French employees to adopt Disney standards. The park's manager of training and development for Disney University was quoted as saying: "The French are not known for their hospitality. But Disney is." During the first four months of operations, more than 1,000 employees left the park. According to management, half quit and the rest were asked to leave. Subsequently, the women's grooming guidelines were modified because "what is considered a classic beauty in Europe is not considered a classic beauty in America." Female cast members can now wear pink or red nail polish, red lipstick, and different colored stockings as long as they "complement [the] outfit and are in dark, subdued colors."

Another Disney trademark is to smile a lot. Yet as one observer commented, "If the French are asked to smile, they will answer 'I'll smile if I want to. Convince me.'" Although Disney stressed total customer satisfaction, in the eyes of some employees the company had imposed controls that had made that goal impossible to deliver. In the upshot, the training had to be adapted to suit the European workforce.

Conclusion

The caliber of a service firm's people is a major factor in its market performance. It's probably harder to duplicate high-performance human assets than any other corporate resource. The best firms invest heavily in recruitment and training of their employees. However, human resources managers recognize that certain human personality traits cannot be trained—they have to be hired. To the extent that employees understand and support the goals of an organization, have the skills needed to succeed in performing their jobs, work well together in teams, recognize the importance of ensuring customer satisfaction, and have the authority and self-confidence to use their own initiative in problem solving, the marketing and operational functions should actually be easier to manage.

Study Questions and Exercises

1. What is emotional labor? Explain how it might cause stress for employees, and illustrate your points with specific examples.

2. List five ways in which investment in hiring and selection, training, and ongoing motivation of employees will pay dividends in customer satisfaction for such organizations as (a) an airline, (b) a hospital, (c) a restaurant.

3. Define what is meant by the control and involvement models of management.

4. Identify the factors favoring a strategy of employee empowerment.

5. What is the difference between empowerment and enablement? Can you have one without the other?

6. Highlight specific ways in which technology—particularly information technology—is changing the nature of service jobs. Provide examples of situations in which use of IT is likely to (a) enhance and (b) detract from employee job satisfaction.

7. What can a marketing perspective bring to the practice of human resource management?

8. What important ethical issues do you see facing human resource managers in high-contact service organizations?

Endnotes

1. James L. Heskett, W. Earl Sasser Jr., and Leonard A. Schlesinger, *The Service Profit Chain.* (New York: The Free Press, 1997), 120–123; Leonard L. Berry, *Discovering the Soul of Service,* (New York, NY: The Free Press, 1999), pp. 9, 33, and 173; and the USAA corporate Web site, www.usaa.com, January, 2001.

2. Hal E. Rosenbluth, *The Customer Comes Second* (New York: William Morrow, 1992) 25.

3. Richard B. Chase and David A. Tansik, "The Customer Contact Model for Organizational Design," *Management Science* 29 (1983): 1037–1050.

4. David E. Bowen and Benjamin Schneider, "Boundary-Spanning Role Employees and the Service Encounter: Some Guidelines for Management and Research," in J. A. Czepiel, M. R. Solomon, and C. F. Surprenant, *The Service Encounter* (Lexington, MA: Lexington Books, 1985) 127–148.

5. David A. Tansik, "Managing Human Resource Issues for High Contact Service Personnel," in D. E. Bowen, R. B. Chase, T. G. Cummings, and Associates, *Service Management Effectiveness* (San Francisco: Jossey-Bass, 1990) 152–176.

6. Arlie R. Hochschild, *The Managed Heart: Commercialization of Human Feeling* (Berkeley, CA: University of California Press, 1983).

7. Blake E. Ashforth, and Ronald W. Humphrey, "Emotional Labor in Service Roles: The Influence of Identity," *Academy of Management Review* 18 no. 1 (1993): 88–115.

8. Jagdip Singh, "Performance Productivity and Quality of Frontline Employees in Service Organizations," *Marketing Science Institute Working Paper*, Report 99–127 (Cambridge, MA: Marketing Science Institute, 1999).

9. Robert Levering and Milton Moskowitz, *The 100 Best Companies to Work for in America* (New York: Currency/Doubleday, 1993).

10. Jim Collins, "Turning Goals into Results: The Power of Catalytic Mechanisms," *Harvard Business Review* (July-August 1999): 77.

11. Bill Fromm and Len Schlesinger, *The Real Heroes of Business* (New York: Currency Doubleday, 1994), 315–36.

12. Thomas H. Davenport, *Process Innovation: Reengineering Work through Information Technology* (Boston, MA: Harvard Business School Press, 1993).

13. Joel Millman, "Exporting Management Savvy," *Wall Street Journal*, 24 October, 2000, B1 and B18.

14. Rajendra Sisodia, "Expert Marketing with Expert Systems," *Marketing Management*, Spring 1992, 32–47.

15. James Brian Quinn, *Intelligent Enterprise* (New York: The Free Press, 1992), 322–323.

16. This section is closely based on David E. Bowen, and Edward E. Lawler, III, "The Empowerment of Service Workers: What, Why, How and When," *Sloan Management Review*, Spring 1992, 32–39.

17. James L. Heskett, W. Earl Sasser, Jr., and Leonard A. Schlesinger, *The Service Profit Chain*.

18. Robert Levering and Milton Moskowitz, "The 100 Best Companies to Work For," *Fortune*, 8 January, 2001, 148–168.

19. Benjamin Schneider and David E. Bowen, *Winning the Service Game* (Boston, MA: Harvard Business School Press, 1995).

20. Schneider, Benjamin, "HRM—A Service Perspective: Towards a Customer-focused HRM?" *International Journal of Service Industry Management* 5, no. 1 (1994): 64–76.

21. See David E. Bowen, Benjamin Schneider and Sandra S. Kim, "Shaping Service Cultures through Strategic Human Resource Management," in Teresa A. Schwartz and Dawn Iacobucci, *Handbook of Service Marketing and Management* (Thousand Oaks, CA: Sage Publications, 2000), 439–454, for a review of several research studies that document the relationship between employee and customer experiences and the effect of organizational climate and culture on customer satisfaction.

22. James L. Heskett, W. Earl Sasser, and Leonard A. Schlesinger, *The Service Profit Chain*.

23. Anthony J. Rucci, Steven P. Kirn, and Richard T. Quinn, "The Employee-Customer-Profit Chain at Sears," *Harvard Business Review*, January-February 1998, 83–97.

24. The terms "cycle of failure" and "cycle of success" were coined by Leonard A. Schlesinger and James L. Heskett, "Breaking the Cycle of Failure in Services," *Sloan Management Review*, Spring 1991, 17–28. The term, "cycle of mediocrity" comes from Christopher H. Lovelock, "Managing Services: The Human Factor," in W. J. Lynn and J. G. Barnes (eds.), *Understanding Services Management* (Chichester, UK: John Wiley & Sons, 1995), 228.

25. Schlesinger and Heskett, "Empowerment of Service Workers."

26. Jeffrey Pfeffer, *Competitive Advantage Through People* (Boston, MA: Harvard Business School Press, 1994), 160–163.

27. Christopher Lovelock, *Product Plus: How Product + Service = Competitive Advantage* (New York: McGraw-Hill, 1994), chapter 19.

chapter sixteen

The Impact of Technology on Services

eBay: A Virtual Community Where Almost Anything Can Be Auctioned

Auctions have been around since ancient times but have been geographically fragmented and time restricted, making it difficult for prospective buyers and sellers to meet. Pierre Omidyar, whose background was in computer science, was one of the first to recognize the Internet's potential for creating a more efficient auction marketplace. Working with Jeff Skoll, a Stanford MBA, he formed AuctionWeb in September 1995.[1]

The two partners had limited expectations of what Omidyar later described as their "little hobby-experiment" and thought it wise to keep their day jobs. Initially, the business operated out of Omidyar's small apartment. Its tools were a laptop computer, a filing cabinet, an old school desk, and a Web site at a local Internet service provider. In order to develop a critical mass of transactions, users were charged no fees. The site itself had a very basic appearance.

But AuctionWeb soon began to take on a life of its own, with growth driven by word-of-mouth recommendations. Within six months, the two entrepreneurs had to buy their own server and began charging a listing fee to cover their rising costs. Before long, the operation was moved to a separate office, the company incorporated, and its first employee hired. Growth was driven almost entirely by word-of-mouth recommendations. Customers found that the service was not only effective but also fun to use. With few limitations on what could be sold (exceptions now include firearms, drugs, alcohol, human body parts, and surveillance equipment), the number of categories expanded dramatically in response to market interest.

With thousands of listed items selling every day and the number of employees increasing, Omidyar and Skoll recognized the need for additional capital and management expertise. Heeding advice from a venture capital firm to establish a leadership position before competitors could overtake them, they changed the company's name to eBay in September 1997 and began to seek additional customers by advertising on other Web sites and in targeted publications. By year-end, eBay had expanded its employee headcount to 41 and could boast 850,000 registered users and annual transactions of $340 million.

The following year, the founders recruited an experienced manager as CEO. They offered the job to Meg Whitman, who had developed experience in building brands with a number of well-known consumer product companies. Two things impressed Whitman as she mulled the offer. First, she saw that eBay was doing something that could not be done effectively offline—unlike most dot-com companies, which were simply Internet versions of offline businesses. Second, she was struck by the emotional commitment of eBay users to the service.

Growth continued at an explosive rate. When the company went public in September 1998, both founders became billionaires. During 2000, the value of goods traded on the eBay site exceeded $5 billion and by early 2001 the number of registered users had reached 18.9 million, trading goods in some 4,700 categories around the world. Despite strong efforts from competitors (including Amazon and Yahoo),

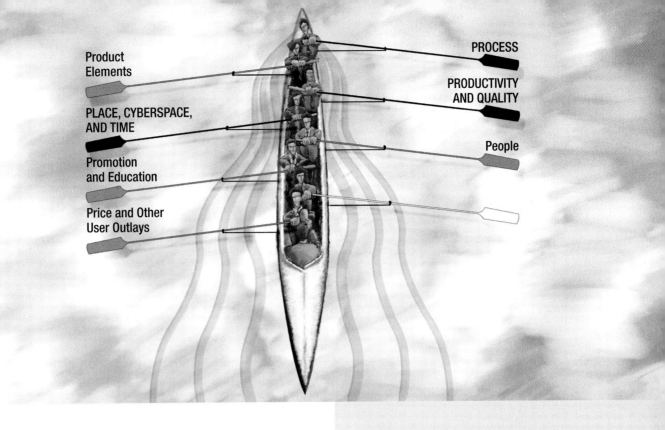

Product
Elements

PLACE, CYBERSPACE,
AND TIME

Promotion
and Education

Price and Other
User Outlays

PROCESS

PRODUCTIVITY
AND QUALITY

People

eBay remained not only the largest online auction site but also the highest rated by the Internet quality measurement firm, Gómez.com, which cited its ease of use, on-site resources, and wide range of listings.

Unlike many dot-com companies, eBay neither owns nor handles the merchandise that is sold through its site. Instead, it brings buyers and sellers together and then facilitates trading. Buyers pay sellers through Billpoint, an online bill-payment service operated for eBay by Wells Fargo Bank; a seller may also request use of a third-party escrow service to whom the buyer sends payment *before* receiving the purchased item.

eBay's revenue comes from a nonrefundable insertion fee for each item listed for auction, plus a sliding final value fee based on the amount of the winning bid. The company's average "toll" on site traffic is roughly 8 percent of the value of auctioned merchandise, so revenues are large and rising fast. However, costs have risen rapidly, too. They include continued investments in Web infrastructure—which must precede rather than follow transaction growth in order to prevent system breakdowns—as well as heavy expenditures on marketing to build the brand and enhance customer service. Further investments are being made on overseas expansion and acquisition of companies in related fields to broaden eBay's array of services and categories. General and administrative expenses are also rising, but more slowly.

(continued)

➡ Learning Objectives

After reading this chapter, you should be able to

⟹ explain the different types of technology applications in services

⟹ recognize the implications of technological innovation for customers and employees

⟹ describe the factors that have fueled the rapid growth of information technology

⟹ understand how the Internet is transforming service strategy

⟹ discuss guidelines for the effective use of technology in service organizations

What factors have spurred eBay's success? Its very size gives it an advantage over competitors in that sellers can expect to attract more buyers and, in turn, buyers find a broader array of items on which to bid. The easy-to-use Web site offers friendly advice and introduces newcomers to the eBay community. With growth has come a shift in the mix of sellers, with a growing number of small businesses now employing eBay as a major marketing channel; as a result, 20 percent of sellers account for 80 percent of sales.

Loyalty is reinforced by the real sense of community among users, who actively enjoy browsing, bidding, and chatting with other users at the "eBay Café." Recognizing the importance of protecting honest customers against fraud, eBay encourages users to post comments on their purchasing experiences, so that future bidders can review evaluations of individual sellers. In addition, the company offers a free program to insure every eligible transaction up to $250 (less a $25 deductible) in the case of actual fraud.

Underlying eBay's operations is a distinctive culture and some clearly expressed values. It has worked hard to develop customer trust, declaring that "eBay was founded with the belief that people are basically good. We believe that each of our customers, whether a buyer or a seller, is an individual who deserves to be treated with respect."

TECHNOLOGY IN SERVICE ENVIRONMENTS

Reflecting success stories like eBay, the Internet has attracted tremendous coverage in recent years. The rapid growth of the Internet demonstrates how the introduction and commercialization of new technologies can result in dramatic product innovations and lead to significant changes in how businesses operate and how people live and work. History is full of such examples. In the 19th century, the Industrial Revolution helped to usher in widespread use of such key technologies as water and steam power, railroads and electricity. People living in the 20th century found their lifestyles and opportunities shaped by innovations—such as personal automobiles, universal telephone service, global air travel, radio, television, computers, and satellites—that would have been unimaginable to earlier generations. As inhabitants of the 21st century, we can look forward to continuing new applications of technology in almost every area of our lives, giving us new options in fields such as financial services, education, medicine, entertainment, and transportation.

Each generation tends to use the word *technology* to describe, rather loosely, the practical application of cutting-edge tools and procedures. While many different types of technologies affect our lives, our focus in this chapter is on those that impact the way services are produced, delivered, and marketed. We begin with a brief look at different kinds of technology applications in services. Then we examine strategic issues related to the use of information technology in service delivery, with particular emphasis on the Internet and the World Wide Web. In the course of the chapter we explore whether companies should view technology as a strategic thrust in their business or just another operations tool, look at how new technologies impact productivity and service quality, and consider the potential for getting customers to use technology-based self-service options.

Different Types of Technology

At least six types of technology have implications for the service sector—power and energy, physical design, materials, methods, genetic biology, and information. The application of one type of technology in any service industry often requires assistance from some of the others.

Power and Energy Technology   The search is on for improved sources of power. One important development is more sophisticated approaches to renewable energy, such as solar and wind power. The equipment is often owned by entrepreneurs who act as small generating services, selling power to utility companies. There has also been huge progress in miniaturization of batteries; their bulk and weight have been reduced while battery life and strength have increased. Such batteries power small portable IT equipment like laptop computers, pagers, and cellular phones that are widely used by many service businesses. By facilitating mobile communications and service delivery in cyberspace, they enhance employee responsiveness and provide greater flexibility for customers.

Physical Design Technology   Creating smaller, lighter, faster, or more efficient equipment often requires new approaches to design. Laptops and cell phones look very different from desktop computers and conventional telephones. High-speed catamaran ferries are another example of innovative physical design. These ships, with their new hull designs and water jet propulsion systems (an alternative form of power technology), are revolutionizing marine transportation.

Materials Technology   New manufacturing techniques and materials have produced advanced plastics and metal alloys that make possible not only high-speed airfoils or miniaturized high-tech hardware, but also such mundane objects as energy-saving lighting to provide better security in shopping mall parking lots. Modern railroad cars make widespread use of materials technology, including metal composites for lightweight bodies, vandal-resistant plastics, artificial fibers for easy cleaning, and shatterproof insulating glass for good views without compromising climate control and safety.

Methods Technology   Here, attention is focused on developing new ways of working, including self-service by customers. It can be as simple as furnishing hotel bedrooms with box beds to simplify the cleaning task for housekeepers or installing beverage dispensers with automatic metering in a restaurant so that workers can perform other tasks while cups are filling.[2] Or it can be as complex as designing procedures for a hospital emergency room, an all-telephone bank, or an automated warehouse. Methods technology emphasizes that human involvement and success may depend on getting employees and customers to perform unfamiliar new tasks. To ensure that new methods are "user friendly," operations managers need to seek early and full participation of HR and marketing specialists in both design and implementation.

Biotechnology   "Biotech" includes research into the development and application of such procedures as gene splicing and gene therapy. Relevant service applications center around advances in medical treatments or development of genetically altered foods that might be served in restaurants. However, the long-term impact of these practices remains uncertain and their use—especially for broader public consumption—requires rigorous advance testing and thoughtful consideration of ethical criteria.

Information Technology   IT encompasses several key elements, beginning with the capture of data and its storage in memory systems. These systems may range in scope from a credit card's magnetic strip containing 200 bytes (equivalent to roughly three lines of typescript) to the terabytes of a super computer or data warehouse. IT is often identified with sophisticated hardware. But software is actually the key element in turning data into useful information (such as customer account profiles) or the intelligence found in expert systems that tell users—or even machines—what decisions to make. IT not only makes possible new service concepts such as Internet auctions, but potentially impacts almost every aspect of service.

Creating New Ways of Working

Before implementing new strategies to take advantage of emerging or improved technologies, managers have to ask how existing work patterns will need to change if an innovation is to fulfill its promise. There's an important link between IT and methods

Research via Internet: FieldSource can survey almost any demographic or lifestyle target group within its million-strong panel.

technology. Hammer and Champy make the point that companies often use IT simply to speed up existing processes. They claim that "the real power of technology is not that it can make the old processes work better, but that *it enables organizations to break old rules and create new ways of working*"[3] (emphasis added). In the case of IT, they argue that instead of "embedding outdated processes in silicon and software, we should be using the power of technology to radically redesign business procedures and dramatically improve their performance." (This assumes that firms are fully aware of what their existing processes are and emphasizes the value of blueprinting as a visual tool for process design or redesign.)

Service leaders employ technology as an active component of strategy. They seek to create and nurture a corporate culture that welcomes change and new methods of working. Many firms have their own technology units whose work is devoted to exploring how innovations might best be used to create value for customers and stockholders, higher quality, greater productivity, and a competitive advantage for the firm. The most desirable innovations are those that fulfill several—or even all—of these objectives simultaneously. Companies that want to be on the cutting edge of new technology applications often work closely with university researchers and innovative manufacturers to shape the development of emerging technologies.

Technology and Innovation

In previous chapters, we described some dramatic instances of how technology has stimulated and facilitated innovation in the service sector. But service managers need to be realistic about technology's potential to create profitable results for their firms. In his book, *Megamistakes: Forecasting and the Myth of Technological Change*, Steven Schnaars writes of what he calls a bias toward optimism. "Optimism," he says, "results from being enamored of technological wonder. It follows from focusing too intently on the underlying technology."[4] Much has been made of the Internet's potential for facilitating new business concepts and improving business productivity through savings in activities such as purchasing and delivery costs.[5] But rushing to adopt new technologies without thinking through the implications for employees, customers, and the overall operating system can be a recipe for disaster, as evidenced by the failure of many dot-com companies (see the box, "What Caused the Dot-Com Meltdown?"). Michael Porter, respected for his work on competitive strategy, argues persuasively that:

> We need to move away from the rhetoric about "Internet industries," "e-business strategies," and a "new economy" and see the Internet for what it is: an enabling technology— a powerful set of tools that can be used, wisely or unwisely, in almost any industry and as part of almost any strategy.[6]

What Caused the Dot-Com Meltdown?

Few business phenomena have caused quite such a stir in the past half-century as the rapid rise and fall of the companies popularly known as the "dot-coms." During the late 1990s, numerous businesses were created to take advantage of the possibilities offered by the Internet. Enthusiasm was contagious. Speakers on the lecture circuit proclaimed that "the Internet changes everything" and predicted dismal prospects for established firms without an Internet presence. Venture capitalists and investors poured money into dot-coms, many of which launched initial public offerings and for a while saw their stock prices rise at a dizzying rate, making their founders multimillionaires and even billionaires—at least on paper. Yet by mid-2000, most dot-coms were struggling and their once lofty stock prices had shriveled. A much-reported succession of failures began and continued into 2001. What went wrong?

A key problem was flawed business models, in particular how the company was expected to make money. In trying to attract customers through low prices, many Internet-based retailers found that their margins were too slim—if, indeed, there was any margin at all—to cover higher than anticipated costs. Heavy expenditures were required for construction and operation of automated warehouses, while delivery costs were sometimes higher than the shipping charges imposed on orders. Operating an effective Web site proved more complex than predicted. Additional funds were needed to improve customer service, handle complaints, and accept merchandise returns.

Content provider companies, whose product consisted of information about specialized topics, found that many people didn't like to pay for information—especially if most of it could be found free elsewhere. Generating original material proved costly, since

most dot-coms lacked the economies of scale and media affiliations enjoyed by portals such as Yahoo or AOL. Meantime, revenues received from advertising on their sites failed to match expectations.

Among other key problems faced by dot-coms were the high marketing costs of attracting visitors to their sites and intense competition from both traditional businesses and other online companies in the same field. Many "e-tailers" learned the hard way that running an Internet site isn't cheap, that when you don't carry your own inventory you lose control over pricing, that customers get angry when orders aren't filled promptly, and that what were anticipated as fixed administrative and infrastructure costs often turned out to be semi-variable, increasing stepwise with growth.

After studying 109 failed dot-coms, the Boston Consulting Group identified the following main reasons for failure (in some cases, there was more than one reason per company):

Poor revenue, cost, and profit model	59
No competitive advantage	55
Lack of benefit to consumers	34
Problems in organization and execution	15
Ineffective warehouse management and fulfillment	8
Firm's Web site conflicted with existing business partners	6

Marketing expenditures designed to build brand recognition and attract customers to company Web sites were often misdirected. No fewer than 17 dot-coms, representing a wide array of business activities, each spent $2.2 million for a 30-second TV spot during the 2000 Super Bowl. Observers concluded that many dot-coms had failed to understand that branding is not a strategy and that brand recognition alone doesn't necessarily lead to usage and brand loyalty.

Source: Marcia Vickers, "Models from Mars," *Business Week*, 4 September 2000, 106–107; Jerry Useem and Eryn Brown, "Dot-coms: What Have We Learned?" *Fortune*, 30 October 2000, 82–104; Matt Kranz, "What Detonated Dot-bombs?" *USA Today*, 4 December 2000, B1-B2; Paula Hjelt, "Collapse of the E-Universe," *Fortune*, 5 February 2001, 164–165.

Leading service firms treat technology as a critical component of their overall business strategy. These companies continuously explore ways to use technological innovations to create value for customers and stockholders, enhance quality and productivity, and provide a competitive advantage for the firm. Such innovations often present opportunities for—or even require—a change of strategy among existing firms. As we saw in Chapter 11, Kinko's has integrated the Internet into the firm's business model, using cyberspace to supplement existing, place-based delivery systems. Strategies of this nature are often referred to as **clicks and mortar** (also known as "clicks and bricks"). Other firms, like the software retailer Egghead (now Egghead.com), have abandoned physical space entirely in favor of the cyberspace alternative. Amazon.com, eBay, Webvan, and other "pure play" Internet firms have never had traditional retail outlets. From the customer's perspective, the goods they sell may be tangible but the companies themselves exist only in cyberspace.

clicks and mortar: a strategy of offering service through both physical stores and virtual storefronts via Web sites on the Internet.

IT AND THE AUGMENTED SERVICE PRODUCT

What do advances in IT mean for the augmented service product? As shown in Chapter 7, the supplementary services that surround the core, facilitating its use and enhancing its value, can be divided into eight categories: information, consultation, order taking, hospitality, safekeeping, exceptions, billing, and payment. We used the metaphor of a flower to depict the augmented service product as a core that is encircled by eight petals. In Chapter 11, we noted that a majority of the supplementary services represented by these petals are information dependent and can therefore be delivered electronically through such media as telephone, fax, electronic kiosks, or the Internet, rather than physically. When the core product itself is information based, then it, too, can be delivered through electronic channels.

As a result, there are many opportunities to employ IT when designing service strategy. And even though hospitality and safekeeping involve physical processes, there's still a need to record information about customer preferences and behavior relating to these supplementary elements. Figure 16.1 illustrates ways in which a Web site can be used to deliver or enhance service for each of the petals of the Flower of Service. In most instances, there's an opportunity to improve productivity by encouraging customers to perform self-service. Let's now examine in more detail some of the ways in which IT can be used to deliver different types of supplementary services.

Information and Consultation

Customers need information about the goods and services that they buy, including confirmation of orders and documentation of account activity. The Internet can enhance such service features. Well-designed sites provide the information that customers need about the firm and its services. Many sites include a section labeled FAQ (for "frequently asked questions") and an e-mail connection for additional follow-up to a customer service rep or specialist. Some even offer company-sponsored chat rooms where customers can talk with each other.

Employees can be transformed into instant experts by giving them easy access to relevant information. When a customer in Boston telephoned FedEx late one afternoon to request a pickup, the agent told him it was too late. However, there was still time, she added, to deposit his package in a FedEx drop box—would he like street directions to the nearest one? When he said yes, she gave him easily understood instructions on how to find the box, including references to local landmarks. The customer was impressed, complimented her on the clear directions, and said "You really know Boston well, you

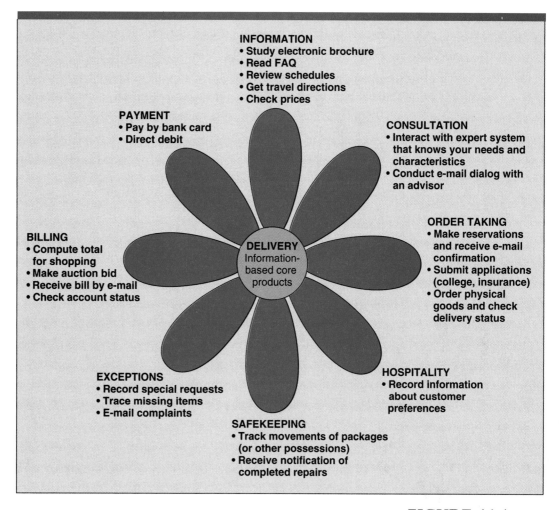

FIGURE 16.1

Applying the Power of the Internet to Core and Supplementary Services

must come from around here!" "No," she replied, "I work in the Chicago area and I've never even been to Massachusetts. I'm just reading this information off my computer screen!" FedEx had used the knowledge of local employees in Boston to create and record directions that any employee could subsequently access and provide with confidence. However, because even landmarks can change, such information needs to be periodically reviewed for accuracy.

Order Taking

How can technology make it easier for customers to place orders and for suppliers to take them? The key to improving productivity and quality in order-entry processes lies in minimizing the time and effort required of both parties, while also ensuring completeness and accuracy. Placing orders in person, by voice telephone, or by mail and fax are still widespread practices, but the Internet offers a cheaper option for such transactions.

Airlines, for example, encourage customers to check flight schedules on the Web and make their own reservations (Southwest Airlines notes that the cost per booking via Internet is about $1 as compared to $10 via a travel agent—and "somewhere in between" via a Southwest reservations agent[7]). Hotel chains enable customers to research different offerings in each city served, review maps of hotel locations, and then make room bookings. And, of course, there has been a tremendous growth in ordering merchandise from Web sites, with participation by traditional retailers such as Sears and Wal-Mart, catalog merchants such as Lands' End, and new Internet-only providers such as Amazon.com. Online ordering has also surged in business-to-business marketing and its sales volume greatly exceeds that of online consumer sales.

Large customers may be given access to customized and password-protected Web pages on restricted sites. There, corporate purchasers will find all the items that their firm normally orders at the prices previously negotiated, plus such useful information as ordering history and typical order quantities. The Web site may also prompt the buyer to consider additional products that complement those just ordered. Another customer's pages will probably contain a different mix of merchandise at somewhat different prices.

Whether customers order physical goods by mail, telephone, fax, Internet, or another medium, a vital challenge is to manage an effective order-entry process. Prompt execution of each order involves tasks such as order picking in the warehouse, packaging, and shipment. More and more firms are contracting out the shipping task to specialized intermediaries such as UPS, FedEx, and postal services.

McKesson, a San Francisco–based distributor of drugs, pioneered new methods of filling orders from retail druggists. Electronic orders are entered into the central computer at McKesson's warehouse. From there, each order is transmitted wirelessly to an order filler in the warehouse who wears a two-way radio and computer on the forearm and a laser scanner strapped to the back of the hand. The order is displayed on the three-square-inch computer screen, telling the worker where the items are and laying out the most efficient route through the 22,000-item warehouse to get them. As *Fortune* described this innovation when it first appeared:

> *Dick Tracy would gasp with astonishment. As the employee chooses each item, he points a finger, like some lethal space invader, at the bar-coded shelf label beneath it, shooting a laser beam that scans the label and confirms that he has picked the right product. When the order is complete, his arm-borne computer radios the warehouse's main computer, updating inventory numbers and the bill. The result: a 70% reduction in order errors and a hefty rise in the productivity of order takers.*[8]

The McKesson example illustrates the need to change work methods to take advantage of new IT developments. In this instance, employees were actively involved in a pretest of the new technology, offering suggestions for design refine-

Southwest Airlines promotes access to its Web site for checking frequent flyer "Rapid Rewards" status.

ments. Now, the way they work has changed and the machine prompts them on how best to proceed.

Hospitality, Safekeeping, and Exceptions

Hospitality and safekeeping elements, which usually involve tangible actions in physical settings, help to make customers' visits more pleasant by treating them as welcome guests and taking care of a variety of needs. The category known as exceptions includes both special requests (often presented at the time of reservation) and problem solving when things go wrong. Special requests, especially medical and dietary needs, are common in the travel and lodging industries. The basic challenge is to ensure that each request is passed on to those employees who will be responsible for fulfilling it. The role of IT consists of storing such requests, passing them on to the relevant department or person, and documenting execution.

Technology speeds problem solving, too. USAA, a Texas-based firm specializing in insurance for military families and their dependents around the world, scans all documents electronically and stores them on optical disks. It also digitizes recordings of telephone calls reporting accidents, and stores them with scans of photos and reports from lawyers, doctors, and appraisers concerning the same claim. The space required to store claim dossiers has already been enormously reduced (the company used to have a large warehouse), and the time wasted searching for missing dossiers—which were often on somebody's desk—has been eliminated.

Billing and Payment

Bills and account statements are important documents, whether displayed in paper or electronic form. Customers like them to be clear and informative, and itemized in ways that make plain how the total was computed. Forward-looking companies use market research to determine what customers expect from financial statements in terms of structure and detail, and then program their computers to organize and highlight the information in useful ways. When a Boston-based bank surveyed customers' preferences for bank statement formats, it found that people's opinions varied. Rather than trying to design a new statement that incorporated something for everybody but would have delighted nobody, the bank created three different formats offering varying degrees of detail and emphasis and let customers select the one they preferred.

Merrill Lynch continues to enhance the way it documents information on its award-winning monthly CMA (cash management account) statements, which have to integrate data on investment activity—including purchases, sales, dividend and interest receipts, and investment value—with details of checking and Visa card transactions. The first page provides boxed summaries, with comparative data for the previous month and year to date, plus charts showing asset distribution and trends in total account value during recent months. Clients can also review their account data on password-protected Web sites. At year-end, clients also receive an annual summary of checking and Visa card activity, organized by expense category, both monthly and for the year. Many clients find this information useful when preparing their taxes.

Wireless networks allow firms to take the checkout to the customer, rather than vice versa. At many rental car return lots, attendants take details of the fuel level, odometer reading, and driver's contract, then use a handheld device to print out a bill on the spot. In France, restaurant servers bring a wireless card reader to the table when it's time to pay. The amount is entered, the user's card is verified, and then the machine (about the size of a handheld video game) prints out the bill for the customer to sign. Machines such as these save time for customer and supplier alike, as well as reducing paperwork and minimizing the potential for errors that comes from manual transfer of data.

THE DIGITAL REVOLUTION

When computers were first developed for commercial purposes, they were used mainly for recordkeeping and backstage operations in large companies. Individual customers first noticed their application in fields such as bank statements in the late 1950s and airline reservations in the 1960s. By the 1970s, the technology of transmitting data by telecommunications had become sophisticated enough to permit creation of ATM networks in retail banking. The 1980s saw the advent of personal computers, modems, and fax machines, enabling customers and businesses to contact each other in new ways. In the mid-1990s, the technological focus shifted to the Internet.

The Power of Networks

Behind the Internet and many other IT innovations lies the merger of two separate technologies—computers and telecommunications. Underlying the global revolution that has resulted from this merger, which George Gilder described as a change that "leaves all previous technological history in its wake,"[9] are five key factors:

Moore's Law: a scientific theory that predicts a doubling of computing power for the same price every 18 months.

> An enormous and sustained increase in computing power, paralleled by a rapid fall in the cost of this power (**Moore's Law** predicts a doubling of computing power for the same price every 18 months).

> Digitization of all types of information—from the analog waves of radio, television, and telephone calls to the images of movies and graphics—so that they can be stored and manipulated in the binary language of computers.

> A huge increase in the capacity of telecommunications as new satellite and microwave linkages are installed and fiber-optic cable replaces conventional "twisted pair" and coaxial cables.

> A miniaturization of hardware and batteries that makes it possible to create a wide array of portable telecomputing devices.

> Advances in software, digital switching technology, and network architecture that enable high-quality voice, picture, and data transmissions to move seamlessly between different types of terminals located all over the world.

Collectively, these developments are fueling the rapid evolution of the Internet and its best-known component, the World Wide Web. The Internet is constructed of huge numbers of servers (large computers that control customers' e-mail and Web pages). As a global "network of networks" that links both individuals and businesses around the world, the Internet is open to all who can connect to it.

Metcalfe's Law: a scientific theory specifying that the utility of a network is the square of its number of users.

A fundamental characteristic of networks is that they increase in value dramatically with each additional node or user.[10] **Metcalfe's Law** (named for Robert Metcalfe, founder of 3Com Corporation) specifies that the utility of a network—whether of telephones, computers, or people—is the square of its number of users. Consider your telephone. It's useless if disconnected and would be of limited value if few of your friends, family members, or the organizations that you needed to contact could receive phone calls. The more people you can reach—and the more who can reach you—the more valuable the network. This fact helps explain the early emphasis placed by Web start-ups such as eBay and Amazon.com on growing their customer bases quickly instead of seeking immediate profits. Stimulating rapid growth requires both an attractive, well-executed service and heavy expenditures on marketing communication, thus necessitating substantial working capital.

E-Commerce: New Paradigms in Communication and Distribution

Regis McKenna, a consultant to high-technology companies, argues that marketing's traditional, research-based connections to customers are no longer sufficient in a real-time world:

> [M]ore continuous connections with customers can provide information that focus groups and surveys cannot. . . . The knowledge of individual customer needs that companies can capture through technology harkens back to the days when the butcher, baker, and candlestick maker knew their clientele personally. . . . In that setting, customer service relationships were built on face-to-face transactions. . . . Today's technology can recreate the conversation between the shopkeeper and the customer.[11]

As service firms grow larger and extend their operations across broader geographic areas, corporate managers may become far removed from the day-to-day operations of the business—and thus from intimate dialog with their customers. This development requires new efforts to understand and record customer needs so that representatives of the firm can reach out to each customer across time and geography. The interactive nature of the Web facilitates exchanges between customers and suppliers concerning customized information, advice, order entry, order status, and complaints. It shifts power from sellers to buyers by allowing conversations among customers through such mechanisms as chat-rooms and user groups. Independent virtual communities may evolve based on specific topics ranging from hobbies to health care. In a few instances, groups of discontented customers have even created negative Web sites (some bearing a variant of the corporate name plus the suffix "sucks") to air their complaints.[12]

The larger the number of households and businesses gaining access to the Internet (preferably through fast, broadband connections), the greater its potential. With no cost penalties to either suppliers or customers for accessing geographically distant sites, the size of the potential market for many products is greatly expanded. In turn, customers may be exposed to more choices and can more easily compare prices. Unlike traditional broadcast networks, the Internet is interactive. E-mails and the Web can be used as communication channels to supplement or replace traditional brochures, instruction manuals, press releases, sales promotion, and advertising.

However, managers need to recognize that creating and maintaining Web sites and their content can be expensive. Even such apparently simple tasks as composing and responding to e-mail messages costs money, and if a firm fails to respond promptly and effectively to customer e-mails, it may lose those customers and generate negative word-of-mouth. eBay's experience shows that major investments are needed in Web infrastructure and customer service as the firm grows in order to avoid system crashes and ensure prompt response to customer queries.

When physical goods are ordered through the Web, the cost of fulfillment, packaging, and shipping can be substantial. Provision must also be made for returns of unsatisfactory merchandise. The strategic issue for these types of companies is how to add more value through Internet-based relationships than they might through conventional distribution in the form of face-to-face contacts, telephone interactions, or mail order—and how to do so profitably (see the box "Webvan: Groceries from Cyberspace to Your Home or Office").

For many people, the term *e-commerce* conjures up images of purchasing from high-profile retail sites, making airline reservations, or conducting banking transactions online. In practice, however, use of the Net is more pervasive in business and industrial settings. In b2b (business-to-business) markets, where communities with common business interests lead to powerful networks of relationships, offline communities can readily be moved online. In the b2c (business-to-consumer) world, by contrast, communities must typically be formed and built from the ground up.[13]

Speed, choice, and cost savings have become key forces in business procurement.[14] Research suggests that b2b e-commerce has the potential to cut costs anywhere from 2 percent (in the coal industry) to as much as 29–39 percent (for electronic components). Most industries can expect savings in the range of 10–20 percent.[15] Companies are achieving these savings by reorganizing their procurement functions and reengineering traditional value chains. In their book *Blown to Bits*, Evans and Wurster describe how some existing supply chains are being completely dismantled and reformulated, in a process they call deconstruction.[16]

Forrester Research has forecast that intercompany trade in which the final order is placed over the Internet will amount to $2.7 trillion by 2004.[17] Although much e-commerce consists of companies marketing their products directly to customers, some entrepreneurs have created Web-based brokerages or "e-marketplaces," using the power of the network to bring buyers and sellers together in auctions, exchanges, and consolidated purchasing arrangements.[18] But this strategy has produced a competitive response from large industrial purchasers. Not wishing to lose control over their supplier relationships, some major buyers have created their own sites to facilitate interactions with suppliers.[19]

Webvan: Groceries from Cyberspace to Your Home or Office

Following its merger with HomeGrocer.com, Webvan.com was one of the few survivors among the many innovative "dot-com" firms created to offer home delivery of groceries and household products ordered by customers through the Internet. In early 2001, Webvan served ten major metropolitan areas. The company's target market included dual-income families and single professional workers who were too busy (or too exhausted!) to visit the supermarket themselves; parents with small children; and seniors or people with chronic illnesses who found city travel uncomfortable or impossible. The service depended on its couriers, who got 99 percent of grocery orders to their destinations within the 30-minute delivery window specified by customers.

Webvan also targeted the business market with a service called *Webvan@work*, which delivered drinks, snacks, prepared foods, and some office supplies to small- and medium-sized businesses. This service helped to increase productivity by keeping Webvan couriers more consistently occupied, since business delivereis were usually made during the workday, when the number of home deliveries was small.

Although most customers seemed very satisfied by Webvan's service, its future remained uncertain at the dawn of the 21st century. Its stock price had dropped dramatically during 2000, following the failure of several high-profile online grocers (including the industry pioneer, Peapod, which was purchased by the Dutch grocery giant Royal Ahold). Investors and analysts were wary about the long-term profitability of Webvan's business model, because making its customers happy had proved to be an expensive proposition; in fact, the company lost $241.6 million on sales of $57.5 million in 2000.

Yet another major challenge loomed large on Webvan's horizon. Some bricks-and-mortar grocers were currently exploring a similar delivery method as a supplement to their own retail stores. Safeway had invested $30 million for a 50 percent stake in GroceryWorks, a small online company destined to become the chain's Internet division. It planned to compete directly against virtual companies in urban areas where its grocery stores were already established. Hence, many observers wondered how long Webvan could survive as an independent company.

Source: Miguel Helft, "Webvan Goes Shopping," *The Industry Standard*, 10 July 2000, 65; Miguel Helft, "Going the Last Mile," *grok*, December 1999-January 2000, 84–92; and Webvan.com Web site, January 2001.

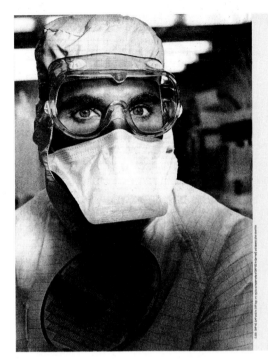

B2B e-commerce: There's more at stake with an order for 20,000 pounds (9 tonnes) of ammonia than one for just a couple of books.

The Internet, Intranets, and Extranets

To make the best use of Internet technology, marketers need to understand the difference between the Internet and the more restricted networks known as Intranets and Extranets. Figure 16.2 clarifies their different characteristics and how they relate to each other.

The **Internet** is a public network, accessible to all. It's an open, free-ranging array of millions of computer hosts, offering access to e-mail and all unrestricted Web activity that is available to any user around the world. As such, it provides countless sources of information on companies, government agencies, economic activities, vital statistics, the media, and academia. However, as experience has shown, it's vulnerable to attack from hackers.

Intranets are composed of e-mail and Web site networks that are internal to specific organizations and restricted to authorized personnel. For security reasons, some companies deliberately keep their Intranets disconnected from the outside world. Corporate Intranets link a firm's vital activities, facilitate access to important information—including that needed to serve customers better—and speed communication among different departments and geographically separated offices. In a sense, Intranets help a widely dispersed organization create a virtual corporation in cyberspace. Some companies have completely revitalized their operations by using in-house information networks to show employees how to work both better and smarter.[20]

Extranets form the core of most Internet business-to-business commerce and are generally open to suppliers, distributors, retailers, and other alliance partners, as well as large corporate customers. However, they can also be found in consumer settings, especially among businesses promoting sales to a group of known customers. Extranets are typically reached through a published Web address that contains a secured link to a restricted site, whose access is limited to authorized users. Access may require advance registration and use of a password. Extranets enable firms to engage in active conversations with known users and thus offer a high degree of personalization. They have become common in supply chains and are leading to a restructuring of these chains.

Internet: a public network that includes all e-mail and Web activity that is open and available to any user—around the world.

Intranets: e-mail and Web site networks that are internal to specific organizations, available only to authorized employees and other personnel, and protected from outside access.

Extranets: networks that are reached through a published Web address containing a secured link to a restricted site, whose access is limited by password to authorized users.

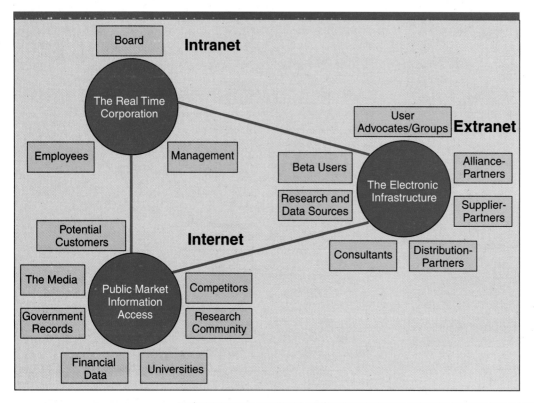

FIGURE 16.2

The Intranet, Extranet,
and Internet

Source: Regis McKenna, *Real Time*. Boston: Harvard Business School Press, 1997, p. 112. Copyright © 1997 by the President and Fellows of Harvard College. All rights reserved.

SERVICE STRATEGY AND THE INTERNET

Recent years have witnessed rapid growth in Internet commerce for both goods and services. The potential of the Internet (which includes both e-mail and the Web) extends to every element of service management.[21] It offers marketers exciting opportunities for service innovation, allowing marketers to create new service concepts—such as eBay's online auctions or Amazon's virtual bookstore—as well as adding new product elements and introducing new dynamics to communication, pricing, and distribution strategies in existing organizations. Although an intangible medium in itself, the Web's ability to integrate text, sound, and video creates interesting options to simulate physical evidence of services.

Many companies are attracted to the Internet by its potential for improving the productivity of service processes. At the same time, the Web's ability to combine centralized control with the responsiveness of speed and customization can, if properly implemented, lead to improvements in service quality, too. One way the Web can improve productivity is by enabling customers to perform more self-service tasks. As a result, the human factor plays a lesser role on the Web than in face-to-face or even telephone-based contact. But the people dimension still has a vital role to play in problem solving and service recovery. In fact, these two service dimensions will provide a key source of competitive advantage as Internet marketing matures.

Adaptive and Transformative Approaches to Strategy

Senior executives must decide to what extent the Web should become the driving force behind their firm's business strategy, as opposed to an enhancement of the existing, more traditional strategy. Alternative strategies can be divided into two broad groups—**adaptive applications** in which the Web supplements existing marketing arrangements and **transformative applications** in which the Internet becomes the major driver of the firm's strategy. For an example of shifting from an adaptive to a transformative strategy, consider the evolution of the brokerage firm, Charles Schwab (see box).

Unlike Schwab, many companies have chosen to hedge their bets by viewing the Internet as an additional medium for marketing communications, a supplement to telephone ordering procedures, or another way to deliver information-based services. Since Web sites can play a variety of tactical and strategic roles, service managers should choose the business model that is most appropriate at a particular point in time.

adaptive applications: situations in which the Web supplements a company's existing market arrangements.

transformative applications: situations in which the Internet becomes the major driver of a firm's strategy.

Technology and the Evolution of Charles Schwab

The Charles Schwab Corporation, which now describes itself as "a different kind of full-service broker," was founded as a discount securities broker to take advantage of the abolition of fixed commission rates in 1975. The company's initial service was very basic—accurate and timely execution of investment transactions for clients who conducted their own research and made their own investment decisions. By 1979–1980, Schwab's expanding customer base and transaction volumes enabled the firm to make significant investments in back-office technology and to offer new services like money market mutual funds and asset management accounts. By adding value through automation, Schwab altered its market position from one based on low-price transactions to one that promoted value-added service at a low price.

In 1995 Schwab introduced its "StreetSmart" software package, which allowed account holders to trade through their computers and to obtain online access to current investment information. But in 1996, a new and well-funded competitor, E*TRADE, offered online trading at a flat rate of $29.99 a trade. Schwab promptly launched Web-based online trading through a separate business unit called e-Schwab. Pricing soon became a sore point. Customers who telephoned their orders to a Charles Schwab call center still paid a commission, averaging $80 a trade; whereas the price at e-Schwab (originally $39) had been reduced to $29.95 in response to E*TRADE's cut to $19.95.

In 1998, the firm made a strategic shift, merging e-Schwab with Charles Schwab, adopting a single low-rate scale for all customers, and rebuilding its business model around the Internet. The firm's goal was to create a new segment in the brokerage business—the mid-tier broker—offering most of the service and advice provided by a full-service broker at a fraction of the cost. Thanks to rapid growth, the firm recovered from the revenue impact of this move in only 14 months.

To attract new customers, the firm changed its message from one emphasizing technology to one that demystified online investing and focused on the customer's whole experience with Schwab. It emphasized value, based on such innovations as online access to expert systems that help customers match their investment goals to, for example, specific mutual funds. Unlike other online brokers, Schwab's customers could choose between doing business online, by telephone, or in one of the firm's bricks-and-mortar stores. They could get advice by downloading articles, participating in online investment forums with experts and business leaders, sharing ideas with other Schwab investors, or—for a fee of several hundred dollars—meeting with a specialist for an in-depth portfolio analysis and consultation.

Schwab's success has forced traditional full-service brokers to reexamine their pricing policies and to consider offering online service too. In the meantime, however, Schwab has taken steps to strengthen its appeal to its long-time customers—around 175,000 out of a total of 6.6 million—who now have investable assets of more than $1 million and are at risk of defecting to high-service private banks. In January 2000, Charles Schwab announced the purchase of U.S. Trust Co., an asset management firm catering to the very wealthy.

Reflecting on the strategic role of the Internet at Schwab, the company's chief information officer, Dawn Lepore, remarked "to win in this new economy, the Internet must be integrated and imbedded into your company—not tacked on top of your existing business model."

Source: Kent Dorwin, "Repositioning a Leading Stockbroker," *Long Range Planning,* November–December 1988, 13–19; Jeffrey M. Laderman, "Remaking Charles Schwab," *Business Week,* 25 May 1998, 122–129; Mary Modahl, *Now or Never* (New York: Harper Business, 2000), 119–125; and Louise Lee and Mike McNamee, "Can Schwab Hang on to Its Heavy Hitters?" *Business Week,* 31 January 2000, 46; and www.aboutschwab.com, February 2001.

Customer Interactions with Web Sites

As we showed in Chapter 4, individuals can be segmented according to their willingness and ability to use technology.[22] A fundamental split exists between those with access to the Internet and those without. Users without home connections may still have access available at work, school, a library, or even an Internet café. Although computer ownership and Internet access are rising in all countries (60 percent of the U.S. population had access in early 2001), there is concern about individuals on the other side of the so-called "Digital Divide" who are isolated from the Internet economy due to lack of resources or poor education.

Understanding people's habits is also important. As shown in Table 16.1, not everyone with Internet access actually uses it to visit Web sites (many just use it for occasional e-mail). The average amount of time spent surfing per month varies from almost nine and a half hours for active users in the United States to less than half that amount in Ireland; but across six countries, the average amount of time per session is surprisingly consistent—about half an hour. Americans have more frequent sessions than Internet users in other countries and view more Web pages, but they actually visit fewer unique sites, suggesting more in-depth visits to a more limited array of sites. An open question is whether such behavior makes it harder for a new site to attract attention.

Web sites vary according to the level of customer interaction that they demand. Three different categories of Web site can be identified, offering different levels of capability.[23]

➢ *Publishing sites* are basically electronic brochures, catalogs, newspapers, magazines, or even encyclopedias that can be updated as frequently as the sponsor wishes. They offer the same information to all visitors and are best thought of as a broadcasting medium. They typically contain numerous pages organized around many different topics, which users can search and retrieve as they wish. Some also feature animated graphics and sound. However, interaction between a company and its Web site visitors is limited. In a simple publishing site, the only customer data available comes from counting clicks by visitors.

➢ *Databases and forms sites* combine publishing power with search engines that enable visitors to retrieve information in response to requests. Thus they offer interactivity and dialog. Much basic e-commerce is accomplished with capabilities that include the ability to get customized information, select products, and submit purchase orders. A user's interrogation of this type of site might include questions like: "Which Banana Republic store is closest to my home address and how do I get there?" or "What flights are available tomorrow between Houston and Mexico City?"

TABLE 16.1

Variations by Country in Average Internet Usage by Individuals

	Monthly data			Per session data			
	Percent with access actually surfing	No. sessions	Time online (hours)	Unique sites visited	Page views	Time online (minutes)	Page views
USA	63	19	9.5	11	671	30	36
Australia	50	12	7.2	15	468	35	38
Ireland	47	9	4.5	17	329	30	40
New Zealand	47	15	7.4	21	421	30	29
Singapore	23	13	6.9	20	506	32	40
UK	44	11	5.2	17	400	28	36

Source: Compiled from data by Nielsen//NetRatings, March 2000.

> *Personalization sites* offer the most sophisticated approach, because they are capable of dynamically creating a page catering to a specific individual. Moving beyond an "ask-respond" interaction into a dialog, they may anticipate user choices and suggest possible alternatives. Users must be prepared to reveal at least part of their identities and wants (by creating a customer profile) in order to benefit from such customization, and the site must be programmed to respond appropriately. eBay's auctions require personalization, since each item for sale requires separate treatment. Constructing, maintaining, and upgrading these sophisticated sites is an expensive proposition and the task is often outsourced.

Internet Revenue Models

Web sites are the public face of an organization's Internet operations. As any Internet surfer knows, not all Web sites are created equal. Apart from ease of navigation, quality of presentation, and volume of information, they also differ in terms of what they can do for customers. Some traditional organizations still employ Web sites as little more than electronic brochures, designed to supplement other elements in the marketing communication mix, without attempting to link exposure directly to sales. By contrast, pure Internet firms—the so-called dot-coms—seek to generate revenues from direct sales responses, partners, or advertisers. There are two basic kinds of revenue models: provider-based and user-based.

Provider-Based Revenue Models   This approach to doing business on the Web is based on obtaining fees from other companies who wish to reach visitors to a specific provider's site.

> *Content sponsorship* requires one or more sponsors to pay a fixed price for a defined period, based on the projected number of visitors, in return for having their names prominently displayed on the site, typically in some form of banner advertising. If the number of visitors changes in the future, so will the price—much as happens with newspaper circulation or TV viewership—since the goal is exposure to the advertiser's name. This approach is suitable for publishing sites, especially when the site owner does not expect to charge customers for access or downloading.

> *Retail alliances* involve exclusive or near-exclusive deals for a firm to be the preferred vendor in a specific product category (e.g., books, music, cars). Vendors pay substantial fees—often millions of dollars a year on popular sites—for the right to have a clickable link in a prominent spot on the site. Fees are determined by the anticipated volume of traffic and the extent of competitive exclusion.

> *Prospect fees* (also known as *click-through fees*) tie the payments for clickable links to the number of visitors who complete some action. At the simplest level, these fees are based on the number of visits to the advertiser's site. More sophisticated measures of performance include marketing-relevant behavior such as filling out a form or downloading software.

> *Syndicated selling* involves payment of sales commissions to affiliated sites when a customer clicks through from one site (an affiliate) to make a purchase on another, linked site. Online booksellers such as Barnes and Noble often enter into affiliate relationships with sites that can promote sales of books on particular topics.

From the standpoint of the site owner, fixed sponsorship fees offer the advantage of upfront payments that can help finance future improvements. However, many marketers have grown skeptical about the effectiveness of advertising on the Web and of site sponsorship. Moving to a pricing policy based on prospect fees or sales commissions is risky because the site's revenue becomes dependent on both traffic to the site and the advertiser's success in motivating behavior. If a Web site fails to attract many visitors and only a small percentage of them click through to the advertiser and buy something, then the revenue stream will be minimal.

User-Based Revenue Models The most widespread form of e-commerce (especially in the b2c domain) seeks revenues directly from customers, making it easy to evaluate effectiveness and profitability. Revenues from customer transactions may include direct sales of merchandise or services, subscription fees for the right of access to a restricted Web site with valued content, time-based pay-per-view fees, or pay-per-use transaction charges, such as accessing and downloading copies of articles from a publishing site. In the case of auction sites like eBay, revenues usually take the form of listing fees and commissions paid by sellers on the selling prices they obtain.

Competing on the Web

Throughout business history, the failure rate for new businesses (and new products) has always been high and dot-coms are proving no exception, with a majority of Internet start-ups predicted to disappear through bankruptcy, merger, or takeover. A number of traditional firms, especially channel intermediaries in b2b supply chains that no longer add value, will also disappear.

Although some established organizations have been very successful in reinventing their operations to take advantage of the Internet, others were left behind in the rush to add a Web presence and have been struggling to catch up. As service businesses become more experienced with online environments, they face a number of challenges in developing successful e-commerce marketing strategies and competing effectively on the Internet.[24]

- ➤ **Limited consumer exposure and buying**. Consumers tend do more browsing than buying, surfing from site to site. The average amount of time spent at any given Web site is surprisingly short, ranging from as little as 3 minutes for adult sites (which charge a high per-minute fee to view their often sexually explicit content) to 15 minutes for visits to finance, insurance, and investment sites (see Table 16.2). Overall, the average time spent per page on a site is less than a minute. The shorter the time, of course, the less opportunity there is to catch the visitor's attention with on-site advertising. In 2000, fewer than 20 percent of surfers used the Web regularly to purchase goods or services. In fact, the majority of online buyers are businesses rather than individuals.

- ➤ **Chaos and clutter**. The millions of Web sites on the Internet collectively provide a staggering amount of information. But many sites go unnoticed, and those that are visited must capture visitors' attention within a matter of seconds or risk losing them to another site.

- ➤ **Security**. Many consumers worry about making credit card payments online. Businesses are afraid that their computer systems might be invaded for espionage or sabotage purposes. Viruses are also a major concern. The Internet is becoming more secure, but there is an ongoing race between new security measures and new code-breaking tactics.

- ➤ **Ethical concerns**. Consumers are fearful that companies might collect information about them online and use it in unauthorized ways (like selling it to other firms who would then use it to create personal profiles or to e-mail unwanted advertising messages). An investigation of 674 commercial Web sites by the U.S. Federal Trade Commission in 1997 revealed that 92 percent collected personal information, but only 14 percent disclosed what they did with it. Since then, threats of government intervention have prompted many Web merchants to post privacy policies. (However, these policies did not stop some failed dot-com companies from selling their customer lists to help offset bankruptcy-

	Minutes
Adult	3.2
Health and fitness	5.0
Corporate information	5.7
Telecom/Internet services	6.6
Travel	7.2
Government/nonprofit	7.9
News and information	8.5
Sweepstakes/coupons	8.5
Search engines/portals	9.0
Sports	11.0
Entertainment	11.6
Online communities	13.0
Finance/insurance/investment	15.0

TABLE 16.2

Average Time Spent at a Web Site by Category of Site

Source: Nielsen//NetRatings, June 2000 (www.nielsen-netratings.com).

related costs.) A more recent survey indicated that 90 percent of the online marketers in their sample believed that their current Web site privacy self-regulation systems are adequately protecting consumers' rights.[25] But many consumers remain unconvinced.

➤ **Consumer backlash**. While the Web has shifted power to consumers by giving them more product information than ever before, it has also given them a more effective means for expressing their dissatisfaction. Rogue Web pages developed by irate consumers or former employees have taken on a range of big-name companies, including Wal-Mart, United Airlines, and Burger King.

The nature of doing business on the Web is continually evolving. Customers are becoming more demanding as the novelty of visiting Web sites and making electronic purchases wears off. As in conventional retailing, some firms seek to add value through service innovations, whereas others just compete on price. However, retail firms that seek to provide high levels of Internet service recognize that purchasers need to feel as comfortable making decisions online as they would in a store, where they can examine the merchandise and speak with a sales rep (see the box, "Lands' End Takes Its Business Online").

Few service businesses can be all-Internet operations. That option is available only to companies marketing information-based core products that can be delivered directly through the Web (like insurance, loans, and banking services) or whose service is to facilitate exchanges of information (such as auction sites and b2b exchanges). People-processing services like airlines and hotels must still serve their customers at physical locations. For them, the Internet is a way to build closer relationships with customers while minimizing the cost of taking reservations. The Internet plays a similar function for possession-processing services. Traditional retailers of physical goods will always need physical channels to get their merchandise to customers. The decision facing them is whether to continue operating retail stores or to focus (like Lands' End and other catalog/Internet retailers) on merchandise selection, marketing, and order taking, while contracting out many physical distribution aspects to a specialist logistics firm.

GUIDELINES FOR EFFECTIVE USE OF TECHNOLOGY

It's appropriate to conclude this chapter as we began it with a reminder that although technology will change the way many service firms interface with their customers in the future, not all new technical innovations will succeed. How should established service businesses—and especially retailers—approach the challenge of adapting to new technologies? Some guidelines for choosing and using technological innovations effectively are provided below.[26]

1. **Use technology to create an immediate, tangible benefit for customers**. If consumers don't see how it is going to help them, they often assume it's going to be used against them (hence their concern that data-gathering technologies are becoming too intrusive).

2. **Make the technology easy to use**. From the consumer's viewpoint, many technologies actually make shopping more difficult. For example, research shows that it takes customers 20 to 30 minutes to learn how to use most text-based Internet grocery shopping programs. By contrast, it takes them only 2 to 3 minutes to learn in a three-dimensional virtual store modeled after a bricks-and-mortar store, because the latter is more intuitive.

3. **Execution matters: prototype, test, and refine**. Many potentially viable concepts fail from poor execution. For instance, when customers tried to use a "meal solution" video kiosk at one supermarket, they became frustrated by their inability to print out a menu and the machine fell into disuse. The source of the problem? The printer was out of paper, but there was no screen message to communicate this fact!

4. **Recognize that customers' responses to technology vary**. Certain personal characteristics are associated with customer readiness to embrace new technologies. These attributes include innovativeness, a positive view of technology, and

Lands' End Takes Its Business Online

Lands' End, the direct sales clothing marketer, wants to change the way customers purchase its products. The firm has a strong motivation to move its customers from telephone use to Web use, since printing and mailing 250 million catalogs a year accounts for 43 percent of its total operating costs. Operating a 3,000-person call center is also expensive. One of the company's innovations has been to allow both male and female customers to evaluate clothes on its Web site by creating and saving an online profile called "Your Personal Model." By entering the relevant information, customers can build a three-dimensional model that matches their body shape, hair style and color, skin tone, and face shape. With a single click, they can dress this customized model in selected clothing items and view it from different perspectives.

Lands' End is also integrating its Web site and telephone call center, just as it earlier integrated toll-free telephone calling with its mail-order catalog. While online, customers can contact a call center agent by clicking on a callback button and entering a telephone number for the agent to call. Alternatively, they can click on an instant text-message button and chat online in a text dialog. In both instances, the customer's and agent's browsers are linked so that both can view the same Web page as they converse. As one researcher at the firm commented:

> We wanted a way to increase customer service. While some sites have taken the notion that the more they can reduce human interaction, the more cost effective their site would be, we've taken the exact opposite view. In the past few years, e-commerce was a novelty. But. . .now that people are used to the concept of shopping on line, they are starting to expect more. They want the same level of service they find when walking into a store or contacting a traditional call center. They want answers and access to knowledgeable agents.

In addition to selling to individual consumers, Lands' End makes substantial sales to corporations, often involving employee uniforms bearing a corporate logo. Purchasers can upload their logos to a special Lands' End site and then view how that logo would look on a particular item of clothing in various logo and color combinations. This option is very popular with customers, who not only save time and effort but also have greater confidence that they have made the right choice.

Source: "A Better Way to Get Clothes to Fit," *Newsweek*, 30 October 2000, 18; Rebecca Quick, "Getting the Right Fit—Hips and All, *Wall Street Journal*, 18 October 2000, B1; Mary Modahl, *Now or Never* (New York: HarperBusiness, 2000), 199–203; George V. Hulme, "Help! Companies Are Turning to Their Call Centers to Improve Customer Service on the Web," *Sales and Marketing Management*, February 2000, 78–82; Dana James, "Custom Goods Nice Means for Lands' End, *Marketing News*, 14 August 2000, 5–6.

the belief that it offers people increased control, flexibility, and efficiency in their lives. Factors that reduce customers' receptiveness to new technologies include distrust, a perceived lack of control, feelings of being overwhelmed by technology, and skepticism about its ability to work properly.[27] Research on technology anxiety has shown that customers may avoid using new technologies even if they understand the benefits. Educational efforts, including hands-on training, may be needed to minimize the impact of technology anxiety among both customers and employees. Providing alternative service delivery options allows customers to select the delivery method that best fits their needs.[28]

5. **Build systems that are compatible with the way customers make decisions**. Designers need to learn more about consumers' behaviors and observe them in action. One Internet start-up launched a grocery shopping system that grouped cold cereals by their main ingredients—rice, corn, wheat, etc. Unfortunately, many shoppers had trouble finding their favorite brands because they didn't know the ingredients!

6. **Study the effects of technology on what people buy and on how they shop**. Research in the United States shows that text-based home-shopping systems make consumers more price-sensitive than systems that display realistic images of the merchandise. In Sweden, a grocery store experimented with electronically adjusting prices according to the time of day. It found that a strategy of reducing prices in the evening increased sales by 40 percent during that time and doubled store traffic.

7. **Coordinate all technologies that touch the customer**. Whether a customer encounters a retailer via the Internet, a catalog, by telephone, or in the physical store, there should be some commonalities to the experience. Customers are often channel-blind. When they view a business as a single entity rather than a multi-channel operation, they expect a specific firm to offer the same merchandise at the same prices accompanied by the same knowledgeable and courteous service in all of its delivery channels, including the Internet.[29]

8. **Use technology to tailor marketing programs to individual customers' requirements**. Treating all customers alike puts traditional retailers at a disadvantage, since electronic retailers can use their databases to customize marketing programs instantly to match the needs of individual shoppers.

9. **Build systems that leverage existing competitive advantages**. Despite the role of cyberspace in electronic retailing, the constraints of time and space still exist. Consumers may not want to wait for a physical product to be shipped to them (assuming that it can be shipped at all). They may feel that a picture and specifications on a computer screen cannot fully compensate for not being able to see and touch the real thing. Bricks-and-mortar retailers should use technology in ways that magnify the positive differences separating them from their purely electronic competitors.

Conclusion

Technology in services goes beyond just information technology, central though that may be in modern life. Service managers also need to keep their eyes on developments in power and energy, biotechnology, physical design, methods of working, and materials. Changes in one technology often have a ripple effect, requiring leverage from other technologies to achieve their full potential. Every time technology changes, it creates threats to established ways of doing business and opportunities for new ways to offer service. Service leaders often seek to shape the evolution of technological applications to their own advantage. Forward-looking firms are restructuring their firms around the Internet, rather than treating it as an "add-on."

Although there has been a rapid increase in the volume of electronic commerce, we are still in the early stages of the "Internet Revolution." Experts continue to disagree on its ultimate impact. What is clear is that many customers are choosing to move away from face-to-face contacts with suppliers in fixed locations to remote contacts "anywhere, anytime." As more households acquire computers—especially those with high-speed Internet access—electronic commerce is likely to expand even further. However, this doesn't necessarily mean an end to physical retailing activities as we know them, since shopping for many types of goods and services will retain its appeal as a social experience.

Firms delivering information-based services are likely to see their industries transformed by the advent of the Internet. However, many customers prefer the present high-contact systems (as in retail banking) and see no reason to switch to technology-driven self-service options. So firms will have to find ways to offer greater value or lower prices. Ongoing monitoring of technographic segments will help managers plan effective strategies for smooth, but possibly extended, transitions to more Web-based delivery processes.

Study Questions and Exercises

1. Why should service marketers be concerned about new developments in technology?

2. Briefly describe the six different technologies that have implications for services. Identify several cases in which the successful application of one technology may be dependent on one or more of the other technologies described.

3. Create separate versions of the electronic flower of service for (a) retail banking, (b) hotels, (c) freight transportation, (d) car insurance. For each service, prepare a "flower" diagram that shows relevant activities for each "petal" of the augmented service product.

4. Discuss the differences between the Internet, Intranets, and Extranets.

5. What is the distinction between adaptive applications and transformative applications when an established firm incorporates the Internet into its business activities? Provide an example of a company that has used (a) an adaptive strategy, (b) a transformative strategy.

6. Describe the three different levels of business models for Web sites and identify sites that illustrate each of these levels.

7. Select a specific service industry with multiple competitors and visit the Web sites of four different firms in that industry. Compare the capabilities and the quality of execution of the four sites, including ease of navigation. Discuss your conclusions concerning the role that each company's site plays in its overall business strategy.

8. What ethical issues do companies need to consider when using electronic commerce strategies?

Endnotes

1. From David Bunnell with Richard Lueke, *The eBay Phenomenon* (New York: John Wiley & Sons, 2000); www.ebay.com/about ebay, February 2001; www. gomez.com, February 2001.

2. James L. Heskett, W. Earl Sasser Jr., and Christopher W. L. Hart, *Service Breakthroughs* (New York: The Free Press, 1990), 181.

3. Michael Hammer and James Champy, *Reengineering the Corporation* (New York: Harper Business, 1993), 90.

4. Steven Schnaars, *Megamistakes: Forecasting and the Myth of Rapid Technological Change* (New York: The Free Press, 1989).

5. Jennifer Reingold, Marcia Stepanik, and Diane Brady, "Why the Productivity Revolution Will Spread," *Business Week*, 14 February 2000, 112–118.

6. Michael E. Porter, "Strategy and the Internet" *Harvard Business Review*, 79, March 2001, 62–78.

7. Southwest Airlines Fact Sheet, www.southwest.com, February 2001.

8. Myron Magnet, "Who's Winning the Information Revolution?" *Fortune*, 30 November 1992, 78–82.

9. George Gilder, "Into the Telecosm," *Harvard Business Review*, March-April 1991, 150.

10. Larry Downes and Chunka Mui, *Unleashing the Killer App* (Boston, Harvard Business School Press, 1998), 5.

11. Regis McKenna, "Real-Time Marketing," *Harvard Business Review*, July-August 1995, 87–98.

12. Wendy Zellner, "A Site for Soreheads," *Business Week*, 12 April 1999, 86.

13. Mohanbir Sawhney and Steven Kaplan, "Let's Get Vertical," in *Internet Marketing* (New York: McGraw-Hill/Irwin, 2001), 263.

14. Jakki Mohr, *Marketing of High-Technology Products and Innovations* (Upper Saddle River, NJ: Prentice Hall, 2001), 321–327.

15. Laura Cohn, Diane Brady, and David Welch, "B2B: The Hottest Net Bet Yet?" *Business Week*, 17 January 2000, 36–37.

16. Philip Evans and Thomas S. Wurster, *Blown to Bits: How the New Economics of Information Transforms Strategy* (Boston: Harvard Business School Press, 2000).

17. "e-Marketplaces Will Lead U.S. Business eCommerce to $2.7 trillion in 2004, according to Forrester," Forrester Research press release, 7 February 2000.

18. Steven Kaplan and Mohanbir Sawhney, "E-Hubs: The New B2B Marketplaces," *Harvard Business Review* 78, (May-June 2000): 97–106.

19. Jerry Useem and Eryn Brown, "Dot-coms: What Have We Learned?" *Fortune*, 30 October 2000, 82–104.

20. Marcia Stepanek, "How an Intranet Opened Up the Door to Profits," *Business Week*, 26 July 1999, EB32–EB38.

21. Leyland Pitt, Pierre Berthon, and Richard T. Watson, "Cyberservice: Taming Service Marketing Problems with the World Wide Web," *Business Horizons*, January/February 1999, 11–18.

22. Mary Modahl, *Now or Never* (New York: Harper Business, 2000), 23–24; A. Parasuraman, "Technology Readiness Index [TRI]: A Multiple-Item Scale to Measure Readiness to Embrace New Technologies," *Journal of Service Research* 2, (May 2000).

23. Ward Hanson, *Principles of Internet Marketing* (Cincinnati, OH: South-Western College Publishing, 2000) (see especially 131–141).

24. Philip Kotler, *Marketing Management: The Millennium Edition* (Upper Saddle River, NJ: Prentice-Hall, Inc., 2000), 671–672.

25. "Companies Tell About Consumer Privacy," *Marketing News*, 4 December 2000, 3; and www.junkbusters.com, February 2001.

26. Based, in part, on observations and research by Raymond Burke featured in "Retailing: Confronting the Challenges that Face Bricks and Mortar Stores," (introduced by Regina Fazio Maruca), *Harvard Business Review*, 77 (July-August 1999): 159–170.

27. A. Parasuraman, "Technology Readiness Index [TRI]: A Multiple-Item Scale to Measure Readiness to Embrace New Technologies," *Journal of Service Research*, 2 (May 2000).

28. Matthew L. Meuter, Amy L. Ostrom, Mary Jo Bitner, and Robert Roundtree, "The Influence of Technology Anxiety on Consumer Use and Experiences with Self-Service Technologies," *Journal of Business Research,* forthcoming 2001.

29. "Lessons from the Online War for Customers," *Harvard Management Update*, December 2000.

chapter seventeen

Organizing for Service Leadership

Southwest Airlines: A Service Leader with a Common Touch

In the last 30 years, Southwest Airlines has gone from a feisty start-up to an industry leader, whose performance is closely studied by other airlines from around the world. The company has always been a maverick in the airline industry.[1] At the outset, what turned heads was Southwest's unconventional marketing strategies, with their zany promotions, outrageous stewardess uniforms, off-peak discount prices, creative advertising, and attention-getting public relations activities. But communications, however clever, only deliver a promise. The airline owes its long-term success to its continuing efforts to provide customers with better value than its competitors. It has been cited by *Fortune* as one of the most admired companies in the United States and consistently ranks near the top in the magazine's annual list of the 100 best companies to work for. Herbert D. Kelleher, Southwest's long-time chairman, has been recognized many times as one of the country's best managers.

Southwest launched its first flights in June 1971 amid a blaze of clever publicity. The airline featured numerous service innovations, a little fleet of four new Boeing 737s (later reduced to three), frequent and punctual service, easy check-in, friendly and highly motivated staff, and lower fares. Its cheeky slogan was "The somebody else up there who loves you." From that small beginning, Southwest has become one of the largest domestic air operations in the United States, serving almost 60 cities located from coast to coast. In 2000, it generated revenues of $5.6 billion and carried more than 60 million passengers. Southwest's recent advertising highlights its phenomenal growth with the phrase "You are now free to move about the country."

Over the years, the company has moved relentlessly into one new market after another, winning and keeping new customers and gaining a significant share of all short-haul passengers on the routes that it serves. (On any given day, about 80 percent of Southwest's passengers are repeat customers.) It has greatly expanded the market for air travel by bringing frequent, inexpensive airline service to communities and people for whom air travel was previously inaccessible. Attempts by competitors to counter its expansion have failed conspicuously.

Southwest's simple coherent philosophy has been a major factor in its continuing success. The company has consistently adhered to its low-cost priorities and low-fare, short-to-medium distance market niche. At the heart of its approach to operations is a search for simplicity that minimizes wasted time, lowers expenses, and creates the inexpensive, reliable service that its passengers desire. Lower costs allow Southwest to charge lower fares, making it the price leader in most of its markets. Lower fares attract more passengers. More passengers mean more frequent flights, which in turn attract more customers—especially business travelers who appreciate the convenience. More flights, more passengers, and lower costs have meant profits for Southwest even during recessions.

From an operational perspective, Southwest refuses to play by the rules of conventional airline wisdom (except, of course, those relating to safety, where it has an exceptional record). The company offers no assigned seating, so it has no need to store seat assignments in its reservations database, no need for equipment to print paper boarding passes, and no need to verify seating arrangements at check-in. The

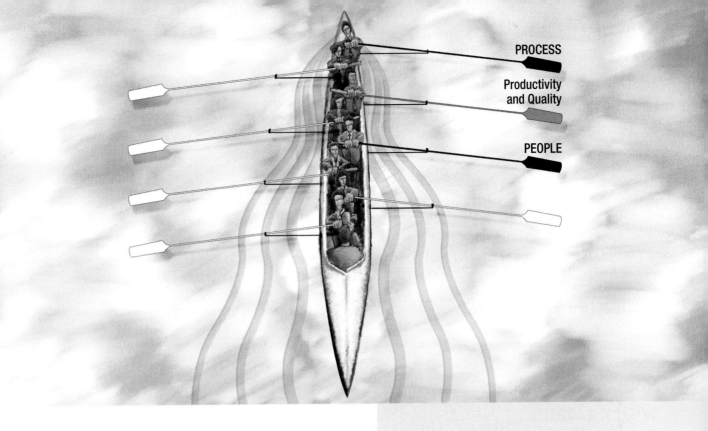

PROCESS

Productivity and Quality

PEOPLE

net result is more cost savings, simpler procedures for employees, faster service at the check-in desk, and faster boarding. It was also the first airline to offer a Web site and has actively encouraged customers to make their bookings on the Internet—the lowest-cost approach— instead of telephoning the airline or using travel agents.

Additional savings result from the airline's decision to provide only the most basic food service. Storing, heating, and serving traditional in-flight meals requires galley space, heavy food carts, and sometimes more cabin crew to serve it than the minimum number established by safety regulations. Provisioning at the start of the flight takes time, and there's more to unload at the destination. Since all these factors raise costs, Southwest just serves light snacks and encourages customers to bring their own food on board.

Southwest won't interline with other carriers (which means that it will not transfer passenger baggage to or from flights on other airlines), because its passengers would then be dependent on the on-time performance of another airline. Not having to transfer bags between its own flights and those of other airlines speeds up the turn-around time between arrival and departure—often as little as 15 minutes—and reduces the risk of lost bags. In addition, Southwest won't accept another carrier's ticket for a trip on the same route—a practice that greatly simplifies its accounting procedures.

There's more. Southwest's operations are not built around the large-scale hub-and-spoke designs that would allow it to offer a wide array of connecting flights from almost any airport in its system.

(continued)

⇒ Learning Objectives

After reading this chapter, you should be able to

⇒ explain the implications of the service-profit-chain for service management

⇒ discuss why marketing, operations, and human resource management functions should be coordinated in service businesses

⇒ identify the causes of interfunctional tensions and how they can be avoided

⇒ define the four levels of service performance

⇒ understand the role that service leaders play in fostering success within their organizations

Hub-and-spoke systems enable competing airlines to offer passengers a large number of city-pair destinations, with an intervening change at the hub. Aircraft descend in droves on a hub airport during a relatively brief period, passengers change flights, and then all the aircraft depart again in quick succession. The downside is that the amount of required ground-service capacity—airport gates, ground personnel, and ramp equipment—is determined by these peak periods of intense activity. The net result is that both equipment and personnel spend less time in productive activity. Moreover, one late-arriving flight can delay all departures.

The great majority of Southwest's routes are designed around short-haul point-to-point services, with an average trip length of about 500 miles (800 km). Passengers can change flights at intermediate points, but the schedules are not necessarily designed to facilitate tight connections. The advantage to Southwest is that its point-to-point flights can be spaced more evenly over the day (as long as departure times are convenient for passengers) and no one aircraft needs to be held for another. Southwest's fleet of some 350 aircraft consists only of Boeing 737s. Standardizing on one aircraft type simplifies maintenance, spares, flight operations, and training. Any pilot can fly any aircraft, any flight attendant is familiar with it, and any mechanic can maintain it. Long-distance flights would involve flying new types of aircraft with which Southwest has no experience.

In addition to its finely tuned operations strategy, Southwest also pays close attention to human resource issues. The company is known for its dedicated employees who remain loyal because they like their jobs and enjoy the working environment. In part, Southwest's positive work environment can be attributed to very selective recruitment. Another factor is stock ownership. Collectively, employees own 13 percent of the company's outstanding shares. Equally important is that, under Herb Kelleher's leadership, management has spent at least as much time courting its employees as it has the passengers the airline serves. As Kelleher says, "If you don't treat your employees right, they won't treat other people well."

THE SEARCH FOR SYNERGY IN SERVICE MANAGEMENT

As our Southwest Airlines example demonstrates, a firm must offer services that are known for superior value and quality to be recognized as a leader in its field. It must have marketing strategies that beat the competition, yet still be viewed as a trustworthy organization that does business in ethical ways. The company should be seen as a leader in operations, too—respected for its superior operational processes and innovative use of technology. Finally, it should be recognized as an outstanding place to work, leading its industry in human resource management practices and creating loyal, productive, and customer-oriented employees. Attaining service leadership requires a coherent vision of what it takes to succeed, defined and driven by a strong, effective leader. And implementation involves careful coordination between marketing (which includes customer service), operations (which includes management of technology), and human resources. As emphasized throughout this book, the marketing function in service businesses cannot easily be separated from other management activities.

Although there's a long tradition of functional specialization in business, such a narrow perspective tends to get in the way of effective service management. One of the challenges facing senior managers in any type of organization is to avoid creating what are sometimes referred to as "functional silos" in which each function exists in isolation from the others, jealously guarding its independence. Ideally, service firms should be organized in ways that enable the three functions of marketing, operations, and human resources to work closely together if a service organization is to be responsive to its different stakeholders.

service profit chain: a series of hypothesized links between profit; revenue growth; customer loyalty; customer satisfaction; value delivered to customers; and employee capability, satisfaction, loyalty, and productivity.

Integrating Marketing, Operations, and Human Resources

Using the concept of what they call the **service profit chain**, Heskett and colleagues lay out a series of hypothesized links in achieving success in service businesses. Figure 17.1 expands on a diagram presented earlier in Chapter 5.[2] The themes and relationships underlying the service profit chain illustrate the mutual dependency that exists between marketing, operations, and human resources. Although managers within each

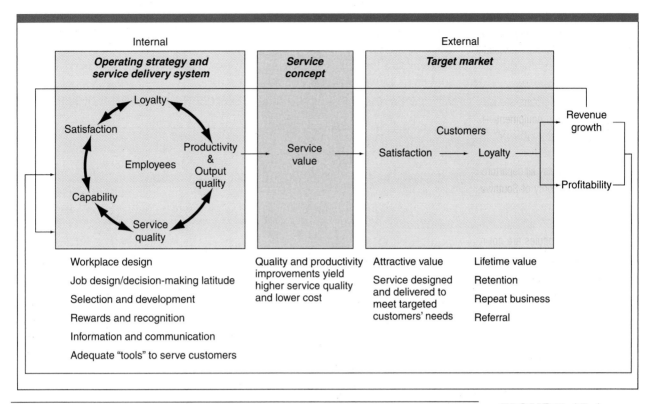

FIGURE 17.1

The Service Profit Chain

function may have specific responsibilities, effective coordination is the name of the game. They all must participate in strategic planning, and the execution of specific tasks must be well coordinated. Responsibility for the tasks assigned to each function may be present entirely within one firm or distributed between the originating service organization and its subcontractors, who must work in close partnership if the desired results are to be achieved. Other functions, such as accounting or finance, present less need for close integration because they're less involved in the ongoing processes of service creation and delivery.

The service profit chain highlights the behaviors required of service leaders in order to manage their organizations effectively (see Table 17.1). Links 1 and 2 focus on customers and include an emphasis on identifying and understanding customer needs,

1. Customer loyalty drives profitability and growth
2. Customer satisfaction drives customer loyalty
3. Value drives customer satisfaction
4. Employee productivity drives value
5. Employee loyalty drives productivity
6. Employee satisfaction drives loyalty
7. Internal quality drives employee satisfaction
8. Top management leadership underlies the chain's success

TABLE 17.1

Links in the Service Profit Chain

investments to ensure customer retention, and a commitment to adopting new performance measures that track such variables as satisfaction and loyalty among both customers and employees.[3] Link 3 focuses on the value for customers created by the service concept and highlights the need for investments to create higher service quality and productivity improvements to reduce costs.

Another set of service leadership behaviors (links 4–7) relates to employees and includes spending time on the front line, investing in the development of promising managers, and supporting the design of jobs that offer greater latitude for employees. Also included in this category is the concept that paying higher wages actually decreases labor costs after reduced turnover, higher productivity, and higher quality are taken into account. Underlying the chain's success (link 8) is top management leadership. Clearly, implementation of the service profit chain requires a thorough understanding of how marketing, operations, and human resources each relate to a company's broader strategic concerns.

The Marketing Function

As we've noted before, production and consumption are usually clearly separated in manufacturing firms. It's not normally necessary for production personnel to have direct involvement with customers where consumer goods are concerned. In such firms, marketing acts as a link between producers and consumers, providing the manufacturing division with guidelines for product specifications that reflect consumer needs, as well as projections of market demand, information on competitive activity, and feedback on performance in the marketplace. Marketing personnel also work with logistics and transportation specialists to develop distribution strategies.

In service firms, things are different. Many service operations—especially those involving people-processing services—are literally "factories in the field" that customers enter whenever they need the service in question. In a large chain (such as hotels, fast-food restaurants, or car rental agencies), the company's service delivery sites may be located across a country, a continent, or even the entire world. When, as a customer, you're actively involved in production and consume the service output as it is produced, direct contact with the operations function is mandatory. Even in services like repair and maintenance, where you don't usually get actively involved in production, you may still have contact with service employees at the beginning and end of the service delivery process. In some cases, of course, there's no contact with personnel since you are expected to serve yourself or communicate through more impersonal media like mail, fax, e-mail, or Web sites.

In manufacturing firms, marketers assume full responsibility for the product once it leaves the production line, often working closely with channel intermediaries such as retailers. In many services, by contrast, operations management is responsible for running service distribution systems, including retail outlets. Moreover, contact between operations personnel and customers is the rule rather than the exception—although the extent of this contact varies according to the nature of the service. Yet, as we have seen in the course of this book, there remains a need in service businesses for a strong, efficient marketing organization to perform the following tasks:

➤ Evaluate and select the market segments to serve.

➤ Research customer needs and preferences within each segment.

➤ Monitor competitive offerings, identifying their principal characteristics, quality levels, and the strategies used to bring them to market.

➤ Design the core product to meet the needs of the chosen market segments and ensure that they match or exceed those of competitive offerings.

Personal interviews can often obtain more insights about the nature of customer satisfaction and dissatisfaction than mail surveys.

➤ Select and establish service levels for supplementary elements needed to enhance the value and appeal of the core product or to facilitate its purchase and use.

➤ Collaborate with operations personnel in designing the entire service process to ensure that it is "user-friendly" and reflects customer needs and preferences.

➤ Set prices that reflect costs, competitive strategies, and consumer sensitivity to different price levels.

➤ Tailor location and scheduling of service availability to customers' needs and preferences.

➤ Develop appropriate communications strategies to transmit messages informing prospective customers about the service and promoting its advantages, without overpromising.

➤ Develop performance standards, based on customer needs and expectations, for establishing and measuring service quality levels.

➤ Ensure that all customer-contact personnel—whether they work for operations, marketing, or an intermediary—understand the firm's desired market position and customer expectations of their own performance.

➤ Create programs for rewarding and reinforcing customer loyalty.

➤ Conduct research to evaluate customer satisfaction following service delivery and identify any aspects requiring changes or improvements.

The net result of these requirements is that the services marketing function is closely interrelated with—and dependent on—the procedures, personnel, and facilities managed by the operations function, as well as on the quality of the service personnel recruited and trained by the human resources function. Although initially seen as a poor sister by many operations managers, marketing now possesses significant management clout in many service businesses, with important implications for strategy, organizational design, and assignment of responsibilities.

The Operations Function

Although marketing's importance has increased, the operations function still dominates line management in most service businesses. That's hardly surprising, because operations—typically the largest functional group—remains responsible for most of the processes involved in creating and delivering the service product. It must obtain the necessary resources, maintain operating equipment and facilities, manage the level of capacity over time, and transform inputs into outputs efficiently. When service delivery is halted for any reason, it's up to operations to restore service as quickly as possible.

Unlike marketing, the operations function is responsible for activities taking place both backstage and front stage. Operations managers—who may be divided among several subgroups—are usually responsible for maintaining buildings and equipment, including company-owned retail outlets and other customer facilities. In high-contact, labor-intensive services, operations managers may direct the work of large numbers of employees, including many who serve customers directly in widely dispersed locations. The ongoing push for cost savings and higher productivity in the service sector requires a continuing effort by all operations personnel to achieve greater efficiency in service delivery.

An increasingly important role—often assigned to a separate department—is management of the firm's information technology infrastructure. In technology-driven firms, operations managers with the appropriate technical skills work with research and development specialists to design and introduce innovative delivery systems, including use of the Internet. But it's essential that they understand the implications of such innovations for both employees and customers.

The Human Resources Function

Few service organizations are so technologically advanced that they can be operated without employees. Indeed, many service industries remain highly labor intensive, although the need for technical skills is increasing. People are required to perform operational tasks (either front stage or backstage), to execute a wide array of marketing tasks, and to provide administrative support.

Historically, responsibility for matters relating to employees was often divided among a number of different departments, such as personnel, compensation, industrial relations, and organization development (or training). But during the 1980s, human resources emerged as a separate management function. As defined by academic specialists, "Human resource management (HRM) involves all managerial decisions and actions that affect the nature of the relationship between the organization and its employees—its human resources."[4]

Just as some forward-looking service businesses have developed an expanded vision of marketing, viewing it from a strategic perspective rather than a narrow functional and tactical one, so is HRM coming to be seen as a key element in business strategy. People-related activities in a modern service corporation can be subsumed under four broad policy areas.[5]

1. *Human resource flow* is concerned with ensuring that the right number of people and mix of competencies are available to meet the firm's long-term strategic requirements. Issues include recruitment, training, career development, and promotions.

2. *Work systems* involve all tasks associated with arranging people, information, facilities, and technology to create (or support) the services produced by the organization.

3. *Reward systems* send powerful messages to all employees about what kind of organization the management seeks to create and maintain, especially regarding desired attitudes and behavior. Not all rewards are financial in nature; recognition may be a powerful motivator.

4. *Employee influence* relates to employee inputs concerning business goals, pay, working conditions, career progression, employment security, and the design and implementation of work tasks. The movement toward greater empowerment of employees represents a shift in the nature and extent of employee influence.[6]

In many service businesses, the caliber and commitment of the labor force have become a major source of competitive advantage. This is especially true in high-contact services where customers can discern differences between the employees of competing firms.[7] A strong commitment by top management to human resources (like that exhibited by Southwest Airlines's Herb Kelleher) is a feature of many successful service firms.[8] To the extent that employees understand and support the goals of their organization, have the skills and training needed to succeed in their jobs, and recognize the importance of creating and maintaining customer satisfaction, both marketing and operations activities should be easier to manage.

To adopt an increasingly strategic role, HR needs to shift its emphasis away from many of the routine, bureaucratic tasks like payroll and benefits administration that previously consumed much of management's time. Investments in technology can reduce some of the burden, but progressive firms are going even further, outsourcing many non-core administrative tasks. For HRM to succeed, argues Terri Kabachnick, "it must be a business-driven function with a thorough understanding of the organization's big picture. It must be viewed as a strategic consulting partner, providing innovative solutions and influencing key decisions and policies."[9] Among the tasks that she believes that HRM should perform are:

➤ Installing systems that measure an applicant's beliefs and values for comparison to the company's beliefs and values, in order to replace "gut instinct" hiring decisions that often result in rapid turnover.

➤ Studying similar industries and identifying what lessons can be learned from their HRM policies.

➤ Challenging corporate personnel policies if they no longer make sense in today's environment and describing how proposed changes (e.g., job sharing) will affect the bottom line.

➤ Demonstrating that HRM is in the business of developing and retaining productive workers rather than just being a training department.

Reducing Interfunctional Conflict

As service firms place more emphasis on developing a strong market orientation and serving customers well, there's increased potential for conflict among the three functions, especially between marketing and operations. How comfortably can the three functions coexist in a service business, and how are their relative roles perceived? Sandra Vandermerwe makes the point that high-value-creating enterprises should be thinking in term of *activities*, not functions.[10] Yet in many firms, we still find individuals from marketing and operations backgrounds at odds with one another. For instance, marketers may see their role as one of constantly adding value to the product offering in order to enhance its appeal to customers and thereby increase sales. Operations managers, by contrast, often take the view that their job is to pare back these elements to reflect the reality of service constraints—like staff and equipment—and the accompanying need for cost containment. Conflicts may also occur between human resources and the other two functions, especially where employees are in boundary spanning roles that require them to balance the seemingly conflicting goals imposed by marketing and operations.

Marketers who want to avoid conflicts with operations should familiarize themselves with the issues that typically provide the foundation for operations strategy. Changing traditional organizational perspectives doesn't come readily to managers who have been comfortable with established approaches. It's easy for them to become obsessed with their own functional tasks, forgetting that all areas of the company must pull together to create a customer-driven organization. As long as a service business continues to be organized along functional lines (and many are), achieving the necessary coordination and strategic synergy requires that top management establish clear imperatives for each function.

Each imperative should relate to customers and define how a specific function contributes to the overall mission. Part of the challenge of service management is to ensure that each of these three functional imperatives is compatible with the others and that all are mutually reinforcing. Although a firm will need to phrase each imperative in ways that are specific to its own business, we can express them generically as follows:

➤ **The Marketing Imperative**. To target specific types of customers whom the firm is well equipped to serve and create ongoing relationships with them by delivering a carefully defined service product package in return for a price that offers value to customers and the potential for profits to the firm. Customers will recognize this package as being one of consistent quality that delivers solutions to their needs and is superior to competing alternatives.

➤ **The Operations Imperative**. To create and deliver the specified service package to targeted customers, the firm will select those operational techniques that allow it to consistently meet customer-driven cost, schedule, and quality goals, and also enable the business to reduce its costs through continuing improvements in productivity. The chosen operational methods will match skills that employees and intermediaries or contractors currently possess or can be trained to develop. The firm will have the resources to support these operations with the necessary facilities, equipment, and technology while avoiding negative impacts on employees and the broader community.

➤ **The Human Resources Imperative**. To recruit, train, and motivate managers, supervisors, and employees who can work well together for a realistic compensation package to balance the twin goals of customer satisfaction and operational effectiveness. Employees will want to stay with the firm and to enhance their own skills because they value the working environment, appreciate the opportunities that it presents, and take pride in the services they help to create and deliver.

CREATING A LEADING SERVICE ORGANIZATION

In your own life as a consumer, you have probably encountered an assortment of service performances ranging from extremely satisfying to infuriatingly bad. There may be some organizations that you know you can always trust to deliver good service, whereas others are rather unpredictable—offering good service one day and indifferent the next. Perhaps you even know of a few businesses that consistently deliver bad service and mistreat their customers. Why would anybody remain a customer in these types of organizations? Sometimes there is no choice. Perhaps the company enjoys a monopoly position and there are no competitors to which unhappy customers can transfer their patronage. In fact, some of the worst service delivery takes place within larger organizations, where internal customers are held hostage to the dictates of an internal department whose services they are obliged to use.

From Losers to Leaders: Four Levels of Service Performance

Service leadership is not based on outstanding performance within a single dimension. Rather, it reflects excellence across multiple dimensions. In an effort to capture this performance spectrum, we need to evaluate the organization within each of the three functional areas described earlier—marketing, operations, and human resources. Table 17.2 modifies and extends an operations-oriented framework proposed by Chase and Hayes.[11] It categorizes service performers into four levels: loser, nonentity, professional, and leader. At each level, there is a brief description of a typical organization across 12 dimensions.

Under the marketing function, we look at the role of marketing, competitive appeal, customer profile, and service quality. Under the operations function, we consider the role of operations, service delivery (front stage), backstage operations, productivity, and introduction of new technology. Finally, under the human resources function, we consider the role of HRM, the workforce, and frontline management. Obviously, there are overlaps between these dimensions and across functions. Additionally, there may be variations in the relative importance of some dimensions between industries. However, the goal is to obtain some insights into what needs to be changed in organizations that are not performing as well as they might.

Service Losers   These are organizations at the bottom of the barrel from both customer and managerial perspectives. They get failing grades in marketing, operations, and human resource management alike. Customers patronize them for reasons other than performance; typically, because there is no viable alternative—which is one reason why service losers continue to survive. Such organizations see service delivery as a necessary evil. New technology is only introduced under duress, and the uncaring workforce is a negative constraint on performance. The cycles of failure and mediocrity presented in Chapter 15 (Figures 15.2 and 15.3) describe how such organizations behave and what the consequences are.

Service Nonentities   Although their performance still leaves much to be desired, nonentities have eliminated the worst features of losers. As shown in Table 17.2, they are dominated by a traditional operations mindset, typically based on achieving cost savings through standardization. They employ unsophisticated marketing strategies, and the roles of human resources and operations might be summed up, respectively, by the philosophies "adequate is good enough" and "if it isn't broken, don't fix it." Consumers neither seek out nor avoid such organizations. There are often several such firms competing in lackluster fashion within a given marketplace, and each one may be almost indistinguishable from the others. Periodic price discounts tend to be the primary means of trying to attract new customers.

Service Professionals   These organizations are in a different league from nonentities and have a clear market positioning strategy. Customers within the target segments seek out these firms based on their sustained reputation for meeting expectations. Marketing is more sophisticated, using targeted communications, and pricing strategies are likely to reflect the value of the service to the customer. Research is used to measure customer satisfaction and obtain ideas for service enhancement. Operations and marketing work together to introduce new delivery systems and recognize the trade-off between productivity and customer-defined quality. There are explicit links between backstage and front stage activities and a much more proactive, investment-oriented approach to human resource management than is found among nonentities.

TABLE 17.2

Four Levels of Service
Performance

Level	1. Loser	2. Nonentity
Marketing Function		
Role of marketing	Tactical role only; advertising and promotions lack focus; no involvement in product or pricing decision	Employs mix of selling and mass communication using simple segmentation strategy; makes selective use of price discounts and promotions; conducts and tabulates basic satisfaction surveys.
Competitive appeal	Customers patronize firm for reasons other than performance	Customers neither seek out nor avoid the firm
Customer profile	Unspecified; a mass market to be served at a minimum cost	One or more segments whose basic needs are understood
Service quality	Highly variable, usually unsatisfactory Subservient to operations priorities	Meets some customer expectations; consistent on one or two key dimensions
Operations Function		
Role of operations	Reactive, cost oriented	The principal line management function: Creates and delivers product, focuses on standardization as key to productivity, defines quality from internal perspective
Service delivery (frontstage)	A necessary evil. Locations and schedules are unrelated to preferences of customers, who are routinely ignored	Sticklers for tradition; "if it ain't broke, don't fix it;" tight rules for customers; each step in delivery run independently
Backstage operations	Divorced from frontstage; cogs in a machine	Contributes to individual frontstage delivery steps but organized separately; unfamiliar with customers
Productivity	Undefined; managers are punished for failing to stick within budget	Based on standardization; rewarded for keeping costs below budget
Introduction of new technology	Late adopter, under duress, when necessary for survival	Follows the crowd when justified by cost savings.
Human Resources Function		
Role of human resources	Supplies low-cost employees that meet minimum skill requirements for the job	Recruits and trains employees who can perform competently
Workforce	Negative constraint: poor performers, don't care, disloyal	Adequate resource, follows procedures but uninspired; turnover often high
Frontline management	Controls workers	Controls the process

Note: This framework was inspired by—and expands upon—work in service operations management by Richard Chase and Robert Hayes.

3. Professional	4. Leader

Marketing Function

Has clear positioning strategy against competition; employs focused communications with distinctive appeals to clarify promises and educate customers; pricing is based on value; monitors customer usage and operates loyalty programs; uses a variety of research techniques to measure customer satisfaction and obtain ideas for service enhancements; works with operations to introduce new delivery systems	Innovative leader in chosen segments, known for marketing skills; brands at product/process level; conducts sophisticated analysis of relational databases as inputs to one-to-one marketing and proactive account management; employs state-of-the art research techniques; uses concept testing, observation, and use of lead customers as inputs to new product development close to operations/HR
Customers seek out the firm based on its sustained reputation for meeting customer expectations	Company name is synonymous with service excellence; its ability to delight customers raises expectations to levels that competitors can't meet
Groups of individuals whose variation in needs and value to the firm are clearly understood	Individuals who are selected and retained based on their future value to the firm, including their potential for new service opportunities and their ability to stimulate innovation.
Consistently meets or exceeds customer expectations across multiple dimensions	Raises customer expectations to new levels; improves continuously

Operations Function

Plays a strategic role in competitive strategy; recognizes trade-off between productivity and customer-defined quality; willing to outsource; monitors competing operations for ideas, threats	Recognized for innovation, focus, and excellence; an equal partner with marketing and HR management; has in-house research capability and academic contacts; continually experimenting
Driven by customer satisfaction, not tradition; willing to customize, embrace new approaches; emphasis on speed, convenience, and comfort	Delivery is a seamless process organized around the customer; employees know who they are serving; focuses on continuous improvement
Process is explicitly linked to frontstage activities; sees role as serving "internal customers" who in turn serve external customers	Closely integrated with frontstage delivery, even when geographically far apart; understands how own role relates to overall process of serving external customers; continuing dialogue
Focuses on reengineering backstage processes; avoids productivity improvements that will degrade customers' service experience; continually refining processes for efficiency	Understands concept of return on quality; actively seeks customer involvement in productivity improvement; ongoing testing of new processes and technologies
An early adopter when it promises to enhance service for customers and provide a competitive edge	Works with technology leaders to develop new applications that create first-mover advantage; seeks to perform at levels competitors can't match

Human Resources Function

Invests in selective recruiting, ongoing training; keeps close to employees, promotes upward mobility; strives to enhance quality of working life	Sees quality of employees as strategic advantage; firm is recognized as outstanding place to work; HR helps top management to nurture culture
Motivated, hard-working, allowed some discretion in choice of procedures, offers suggestions	Innovative and empowered; very loyal, committed to firm's values and goals; creates procedures
Listens to customers; coaches and facilitates workers	Source of new ideas for top management; mentors workers to enhance career growth, value to firm

Service Leaders These organizations are the *crème de la crème* of their respective industries. While service professionals are good, service leaders are outstanding. Their company names are synonymous with service excellence and an ability to delight customers. They are recognized for their innovation in each functional area of management as well as for their excellent internal communications and coordination between these three functions—often the result of a relatively flat organizational structure and extensive use of teams. As a result, service delivery is a seamless process organized around the customer.

Marketing efforts by service leaders make extensive use of relational databases that offer strategic insights about customers, who are often addressed on a one-to-one basis. Concept testing, observation, and contacts with lead customers are employed in the development of new, breakthrough services that respond to previously unrecognized needs. Operations specialists work with technology leaders around the world to develop new applications that will create a first mover advantage and enable the firm to perform at levels that competitors cannot hope to reach for a long period of time. Senior executives see quality of employees as a strategic advantage. HRM works with them to develop and maintain a service-oriented culture and to create an outstanding working environment that simplifies the task of attracting and retaining the best people.[12] The employees themselves are committed to the firm's values and goals. Since they are empowered and quick to embrace change, they are an ongoing source of new ideas.

Moving to a Higher Level of Performance

Firms can move either up or down the performance ladder on any given dimension. Once-stellar performers can become complacent and sluggish. Organizations that are devoted to satisfying their current customers may miss important shifts in the marketplace and find themselves turning into has-beens. These businesses may continue to serve a loyal but dwindling band of conservative customers, but they are unable to attract demanding new consumers with different expectations. Companies whose original success was based on mastery of a specific technological process may find that, in defending their control of that process, they have encouraged competitors to find higher-performing alternatives. And organizations whose management has worked for years to build up a loyal workforce with a strong service ethic may find that such a culture can be quickly destroyed as a result of a merger or acquisition that brings in new leaders who emphasize short-term profits. Unfortunately, senior managers sometimes delude themselves into thinking that their company has achieved a superior level of performance when, in fact, the foundations of that success are actually crumbling.

In most markets, we can also find companies who are moving up the performance ladder through conscious efforts to coordinate their marketing, operations, and human resource management functions in order to establish more favorable competitive positions and better satisfy their customers. The box "Building Marketing Competence in a Ferry Company" describes how a Scandinavian firm successfully enhanced the performance level of a newly acquired subsidiary. As you read it, note the many different areas in which improvements had to be made.

IN SEARCH OF LEADERSHIP

Service leaders are those firms that stand out in their respective markets and industries. But it still requires human leaders to take them in the right direction, set the right strategic priorities, and ensure that the relevant strategies are implemented throughout the organization. Much of the literature on leadership is concerned with turnarounds and transformation. It is easy to see why poorly performing organizations may require a major transformation of their culture and operating procedures in order to make them more competitive; but in times of rapid change, even high-performing firms need to evolve on a continuing basis, transforming themselves in evolutionary fashion.

Leading a Service Organization

John Kotter, perhaps the best-known authority on leadership, argues that in most successful change management processes, people need to move through eight complicated and often time-consuming stages:[13]

> ➤ Creating a sense of urgency to develop the impetus for change
> ➤ Putting together a strong enough team to direct the process
> ➤ Creating an appropriate vision of where the organization needs to go
> ➤ Communicating that new vision broadly
> ➤ Empowering employees to act on that vision
> ➤ Producing sufficient short-term results to create credibility and counter cynicism
> ➤ Building momentum and using that to tackle the tougher change problems
> ➤ Anchoring the new behaviors in the organizational culture

Leadership versus Management   The primary force behind successful change is leadership, which is concerned with the development of vision and strategies, and the empowerment of people to overcome obstacles and make the vision happen. Management, by contrast, involves keeping the current situation operating through planning, budgeting, organizing, staffing, controlling, and problem solving. Bennis and Nanus distinguish between leaders who emphasize the emotional and even spiritual resources of an organization and managers who stress its physical resources, such as raw materials, technology, and capital.[14] Says Kotter:

> *Leadership works through people and culture. It's soft and hot. Management works through hierarchy and systems. It's harder and cooler. . . . The fundamental purpose of management is to keep the current system functioning. The fundamental purpose of leadership is to produce useful change, especially nonincremental change. It's possible to have too much or too little of either. Strong leadership with no management risks chaos; the organization might walk right off a cliff. Strong management with no leadership tends to entrench an organization in deadly bureaucracy.*[15]

However, leadership is an essential and growing aspect of managerial work because the rate of change has been increasing. Reflecting both competition and technological advances, new services or service features are being introduced at a faster rate and tend to have shorter lifecycles (if, indeed, they even survive the introductory phase). Meantime, the competitive environment shifts constantly as a result of international firms entering new geographic markets, mergers and acquisitions, and the exit of former competitors. The process of service delivery itself has speeded up, with customers demanding faster service and faster responses when things go wrong. As a result, declares Kotter, effective top executives may now spend up to 80 percent of their time leading, double the figure required not that long ago. Even those at the bottom of the management hierarchy may spend at least 20 percent of their time on leadership.

Setting Direction versus Planning   People often confuse these two activities. Planning, according to Kotter, is a management process, designed to produce orderly results, not change. Setting a direction, by contrast, is more inductive than deductive. Leaders look for patterns, relationships, and linkages that help to explain things and

Building Marketing Competence in a Ferry Company

When Stena Line purchased Sealink British Ferries (whose routes linked Britain to Ireland, France, Belgium, and Norway), the Scandinavian company more than doubled in size to become one of the world's largest car-ferry operators. Stena was known for its commitment to service quality and boasted a whole department dedicated to monitoring quality improvements. By contrast, this philosophy was described as "alien" to Sealink's culture, which reflected a top-down, military-style structure that focused on the operational aspects of ship movements. The quality of customers' experiences received only secondary consideration.

Sealink's managerial weaknesses included a lack of attention to strategic developments in a rapidly evolving industry. There was growing competition from other companies that were purchasing new, high-speed ferries that offered customers a faster and more comfortable ride than traditional ships.

At Sealink, top management exercised tight control, issuing directives to middle managers in each division. The general approach had been to create company-wide standards that could be applied across all divisions, rather than customizing policies to the needs of individual routes. All decisions at the divisional level were subject to head office review. Divisional managers themselves were separated by two levels of management from the functional teams engaged in the actual operation. This organizational structure led to conflicts, slow decision making, and inability to respond quickly to market changes.

Stena's philosophy was very different. The parent company operated a decentralized structure, believing that it was important for each management function to be responsible for its own activities and accountable for the results. Stena wanted management decisions in the new subsidiary to be taken by people who were close to the market and who understood the local variations in competition and demand. Some central functions were moved out to the divisions, including much of the responsibility for marketing activities. New skills and perspectives came from a combination of retraining, transfers, and outside hiring.

Prior to the merger, no priority had been given to punctual or reliable operations. Ferries were often late, but standard excuses were used on the weekly reports, customer complaints were ignored, and there was little pressure from customer service managers to improve the situation. After the takeover, however, the situation started to change. The operational problem of late departures and arrivals was resolved through concentration on individual problem areas.

On one route, for instance, the port manager involved all operational staff and gave each person "ownership" of a specific aspect of the improvement process. They kept detailed records of each sailing, together with reasons for late departures, as well as monitoring competitors to see how their ferries were performing. Apart from helping to solve problems, this participative approach created close liaison between staff members in different job positions; it also helped members of the customer service staff to learn from experience. Within two years, the Stena ferries on this route were operating at close to 100 percent punctuality.

On-board service was another area singled out for improvement. Historically, customer service managers did what was convenient for staff rather than for customers. For instance, staff members would take their meal breaks at times when customer demand for the service was greatest. As one observer noted, "customers were ignored during the first and last half hour on board, when facilities were closed. . . . Customers were left to find their own way around [the ship]. . . . Staff only responded to customers when [they] initiated a direct request and made some effort to attract their attention."

So personnel from each on-board functional area chose a specific area for improvement and worked in small groups to achieve this. In the short run, some teams were more successful than others, resulting in inconsistent levels of service and customer orientation from one ship to another. In time, customer service managers shared ideas and reviewed their experiences, making adaptations where needed for individual ships.

Table 17.3 highlights key changes during the first two years. In combination, these changes contributed to eventual success in achieving consistent service levels on all sailings and all ferries.

TABLE 17.3

Changing Contexts, Competencies, and Performance Following the Takeover

	Inherited Situation	Situation After Two Years
External Context	Inactive competition—"share" market with one competitor	Aggressive competitive activity (two competitors, one operating new, high-speed ferries)
	Static market demand	Growing market
Internal Context	Centralized organization	Decentralized organization
	Centralized decision making	Delegation to specialized decision-making units
	Top management directives	Key manager responsible for each unit team
Managerial Competencies		
Knowledge	General to industry rather than to local market	Understand both industry and local market
Experience	Operational and tactical	Operational and decision making
	General, industry-based	Functional management responsibility
	Noncompetitive environment	Exposed to competitive environment
Expertise	Vague approach to judging situations	Diagnostic judgmental capabilities
	Short-term focus	Longer-term focus
	Generalist competencies	Specific skills for functional tasks
Marketing Decision Making		
Planning	React to internal circumstances, and external threats	Proactive identification of problems
	Minimal information search or evaluation of alternatives	Collect information, consider options
	Focus on tactical issues	Choose between several options
	Inconsistent with other marketing activities	Consistent with other marketing activities
Actions	Follow top management directives	Delegation of responsibility
	Look to next in line for responsibility	Responsibility and ownership for activity
	Minimal or intermittent communication between functions	Liaison between functions
Marketing Efforts		
Pre-purchase	Mostly media advertising	Advertising plus promotions and informational materials
Service delivery	Slow, manual booking system	New computerized reservation system
	Focus on tangible aspects of on-board customer service (e.g., seating, cabins, food, bar)	Better tangibles, sharply improved staff/customer interactions
	Little pressure on operations to improve poor punctuality	Highly reliable, punctual service
	Poor communications at ports and on board ships	Much improved signage, printed guides, electronic message boards, public announcements
	Reactive approach to problem solving	Proactive approach to welcoming customers and solving their problems

Source: Adapted from Audrey Gilmore: "Services Marketing Management Competencies: A Ferry Company Example," *International Journal of Service Industry Management* 9, no. 1 (1998): 74–92.

suggest future trends. Direction setting creates visions and strategies that describe a business, technology, or corporate culture in terms of what it should become over the long term and articulate a feasible way of achieving this goal. Effective leaders have a talent for simplicity in communicating with others who may not share their background or knowledge; they know their audiences and are able to distill their messages, conveying even complicated concepts in just a few phrases.[16]

Many of the best visions and strategies are not brilliantly innovative; rather, they combine some basic insights and translate them into a realistic competitive strategy that serves the interests of customers, employees, and stockholders. Some visions, however, fall into the category that Hamel and Prahalad describe as "stretch"—a challenge to attain new levels of performance and competitive advantage that might, at first sight, seem to be beyond the organization's reach.[17] Stretching to achieve such bold goals requires creative reappraisal of traditional ways of doing business and leverage of existing resources through partnerships. It also requires creating the energy and the will among managers and employees alike to perform at higher levels than they believe themselves able to do.

Planning follows and complements direction setting, serving as a useful reality check and a road map for strategic execution. A good plan provides an action agenda for accomplishing the mission, using existing resources or identifying potential new resources.

Leadership Qualities

What are the characteristics of an effective leader? The qualities that are often ascribed to leaders include vision, charisma, persistence, high expectations, expertise, empathy, persuasiveness, and integrity. Typical prescriptions for leader behavior stress the importance of establishing (or preserving) a culture that is relevant to corporate success, putting in place an effective strategic planning process, instilling a sense of cohesion in the organization, and providing continuing examples of desired behaviors. Leadership has even been described as a service in its own right.[18] For instance, the late Sam Walton, the legendary founder of the Wal-Mart retail chain, highlighted the role of managers as "servant leaders."[19]

Leonard Berry argues that service leadership requires a special perspective. "Regardless of the target markets, the specific services, or the pricing strategy, service leaders visualize quality of service as the foundation for competing."[20] Recognizing the key role of employees in delivering service, he emphasizes that service leaders need to believe in the people who work for them and make communicating with employees a priority. Love of the business is another service leadership characteristic he highlights, to the extent that it combines natural enthusiasm with the right setting in which to express it. Such enthusiasm motivates individuals to teach the business to others and to pass on to them the nuances, secrets, and craft of operating it. Berry also stresses the importance for leaders of being driven by a set of core values that they infuse into the organization, arguing that "A critical role of values-driven leaders is cultivating the leadership qualities of others in the organization." And he notes that "values-driven leaders rely on their values to navigate their companies through difficult periods."[21]

In hierarchical organizations, structured on a military model, it's often assumed that leadership at the top is sufficient. However, as Sandra Vandermerwe points out, forward-looking service businesses need to be more flexible. Today's greater emphasis on using teams within service businesses means that

> [L]eaders are everywhere, disseminated throughout the teams. They are found especially in the customer facing and interfacing jobs in order that decision-making will lead to long-lasting relationships with customers. . .leaders are customer and project champions who energize the group by virtue of their enthusiasm, interest, and know-how.[22]

Many leadership skills can be taught. Educational programs offered by the Center for Creative Leadership help high-potential managers learn how to work more effectively with others.

Leadership in Different Contexts

There are important distinctions between leading a successful organization that is functioning well, redirecting a firm into new areas of activity, and trying to turn around a dysfunctional organization. In the case of Wal-Mart, Sam Walton created both the company and the culture, so his task was to preserve that culture as the company grew and select a successor who would maintain an appropriate culture as the company continued to grow. Herb Kelleher was one of the founders of Southwest Airlines, using his legal skills in his initial role as the company's general counsel; later, he came to deploy his considerable human-relations skills as CEO for two decades, before stepping down in 2001 (he remains chairman). Meg Whitman was recruited as CEO of eBay when it became clear to the founders that the fledgling Internet start-up needed leadership from someone possessing the insights and discipline of an experienced marketer (for her view of leadership, see the box "How eBay's CEO Sees the Role of a Leader").

J.W. (Bill) Marriott, Jr., inherited from his father the position of chief executive of the company that bears the family name. Although it was the son who transformed the company from an emphasis on restaurant and food service into a global hotel corporation, he strove to maintain the corporate culture that flowed from the founder's philosophy and values:

> *"Take care of the employees and customers," my father emphasized . . . My father knew that if he had happy employees, he would have happy customers, and then that would result in a good bottom line.*[23]

Transformation can take place in two different ways. One involves Darwinian-style evolution—constant mutations designed to ensure the survival of the fittest. As described in Chapter 16, Charles Schwab has been very successful in building the innovative brokerage house that bears his name. Over the years, he and his top executives have evolved the focus and strategy of the firm to take advantage of changing conditions and the advent of new technologies. Without a continuing series of mutations, however, it is unlikely that Schwab could have maintained his firm's success in the dynamic marketplace of financial services.

A different type of transformation occurs in turnaround situations. American Express, long an icon in the travel and financial services arena, stumbled in the early 1990s when its attempts to diversify proved unsuccessful. Observers claimed that its elitist culture had insulated it from the changing market environment, where the Amex charge card business faced intense competition from banks that issued Visa and MasterCard credit and debit cards.[24] In 1993, the board forced out Amex's CEO, James Robinson III, the scion of an old Atlanta banking family, and replaced him with the much more down-to-earth Harvey Golub, who immediately insisted that the company start using objective, quantitative measures to gauge performance.

Working closely with Kenneth Chenault, who headed the Amex card business, Golub attacked the company's bloated costs, eliminated lavish perks, and restructured the organization, achieving more than $3 billion in savings. Chenault, who was later named president and chief operating officer, broadened the appeal of Amex cards by offering new features, creating new types of card, and signing up mass-market retailers, including Wal-Mart. When Golub retired in 2001, he handed the baton to Chenault, his chosen successor, who faced the challenge of maintaining the company's global momentum in a continuously evolving marketplace (see the box, "Ken Chenault Takes the Helm at American Express").

A classic example of transformation in the airline industry featured Jan Carlzon, the former chief executive of SAS (Scandinavian Airlines System). Carlzon sought to transform the inappropriate strategy and culture he found at the airline in the 1980s, moving it from an operations focus to a customer focus by highlighting "moments of truth" when customers interacted with the company. He placed particular emphasis on serving the needs of the business traveler.[25] Central to achieving these goals were his efforts to "flatten the pyramid" by delegating authority downwards toward those employees who dealt directly with customers. For some years, his strategy proved highly successful. Unfortunately, he failed to continue adapting the airline as the environment changed to reflect an economic downturn and greater competition within the European airline industry.

Transformational roles have been adopted not only by CEOs of failing companies, but also by many of the chief executives who have worked to wake up sluggish organizations that were previously sheltered and constrained by government ownership, regulation, or protection against foreign competition.

How eBay's CEO Sees the Role of a Leader

"A business leader has to keep her organization focused on the mission. That sounds easy but it can be tremendously challenging in today's competitive and ever-changing business environment. A leader also has to motivate potential partners to join the cause. eBay is successful because we have consistently remained focused on our mission, our customers, and a few key business fundamentals. As a company, we believe that the price of inaction is far greater than the cost of making a mistake."

Meg Whitman, president and CEO, eBay

Source: Deborah Blagg and Susan Young, "What Makes a Good Leader?" *Harvard Business School Bulletin, February 2001*, 32.

One of the traits of successful leaders is their ability to role model the behavior they expect of managers and other employees. Often, this requires the approach known as "management by wandering around," popularized by Peters and Waterman in their book, *In Search of Excellence*.[26] Wandering around involves regular visits, sometimes unannounced, to different areas of the company's operation. It provides insights into both backstage and front stage operations, the ability to observe and meet both employees and customers, and to see how corporate strategy is implemented on the front line. Periodically, it may lead to recognition that changes are needed in that strategy. It can also be motivating for service personnel. No one is surprised to see Herb Kelleher turn up at a Southwest Airlines maintenance hangar at two o'clock in the morning or even to encounter him working an occasional stint as a flight attendant.

In addition to internal leadership, chief executives such as Kelleher, Whitman, Marriott, and Schwab have also assumed external leadership roles, serving as ambassadors for their companies in the public arena and promoting the quality and value of their firms' services. Marriott and Schwab have often appeared in their company's advertising, and Kelleher has done so occasionally.

Ken Chenault Takes the Helm at American Express

The meeting was classic Chenault. Firing off detailed questions about American Express' overseas operations, then quickly moving on to the company's 2001 strategic plan and its newest card offerings, Ken Chenault prodded and probed his top lieutenants for info, occasionally interjecting advice on an upcoming management reshuffle.

But the setting on this June day wasn't Chenault's plush 51st-floor office, with its Master of the Universe views of New York Harbor and the Statue of Liberty. Rather, the 49-year-old executive was presiding from a Midtown hospital bed, his legs encased in ankle-to-hip casts following emergency knee surgery the day before. "Therapists were coming in and out, machines were buzzing, and he was asking me about reorganizing B2B," recalls Ed Gilligan, Amex's president of corporate services. "We were all treading gingerly around the room, but Ken was charging straight ahead." In fact, Chenault, who had ruptured tendons in both knees while playing basketball with his kids, later asked his doctors for the most aggressive rehab schedule possible. By August he was walking again, two months ahead of schedule.

You need that kind of determination and true grit to get to the pinnacle of corporate America. You need them even more if you're black. And Chenault, who earlier this month [January 2001] took over as CEO of the $25-billion-a-year American Express—breaching the concrete ceiling in American business—has no shortage of either. For all the talk about diversity, openness, and inclusion out there, the top ranks of corporate America remain an overwhelmingly white-male preserve. . . .

Unlike some other prominent CEOs, Ken Chenault doesn't have that room-filling, press-the-flesh kind of presence that makes you think of a local Rotary Club president or a candidate for public office. He's much more understated than, say, Howard Schultz of Starbucks or Southwest Airlines' Herb Kelleher. But Chenault has his own brand of charisma, a quiet warmth that puts people at ease and makes them want to be on his team.

Just ask Tom Ryder, who, like Chenault, was an up-and-comer at Amex in the late 1980s and early 1990s and had his eye on the corner office. "He's impossible to dislike, even when you're competing for the top job," says Ryder, who left Amex in 1998 to head Reader's Digest, after it became clear that Chenault had a lock on the No. 1 slot. "If you work around him, you feel like you'd do anything for the guy." Delta CEO Leo Mullin faced off against Chenault in what could have been a tough renegotiation of Delta's partnership with Amex on their co-branded SkyMiles card. There were thorny issues—such as what Amex would pay Delta for frequent-flier miles—but "Ken really kept in mind what would be good for both parties," says Mullin. "He's tough-minded, but there's a great sense of warmth and fairness."

Source: Excerpted from Nelson D. Schwartz, "What's in the Cards for Amex?" *Fortune,* 22 January 2001, 58–70.

There is a risk, of course, that prominent leaders may become too externally focused at the risk of their internal effectiveness. A CEO who enjoys an enormous income (often through exercise of huge stock options), maintains a princely lifestyle, and basks in widespread publicity may even turn off low-paid service workers at the bottom of the organization. Another risk is that a leadership style and focus that has served the company well in the past may become inappropriate for a changing environment. Jan Carlzon—whom management guru Tom Peters once described as a model leader—ignored the need in a changing economic environment to improve productivity and reduce SAS's high costs. Instead, he spent money to expand the company and invest in new acquisitions. As losses mounted during an economic downturn, he was eventually forced out.[27] And family dynasties may come to an end, too, if the successors to the founder prove ineffectual. As noted in the discussion of Club Med in Chapter 4, although Gilbert Trigano and, later, his son Serge were effective leaders for many years, the family was ousted after it proved unable to lead the company in the new directions required by the changing social and economic environment of the 1990s.

Evaluating Leadership Potential

The need for leadership is not confined to chief executives or other top managers. Leadership traits are needed of everyone in a supervisory or managerial position, including those heading teams. Federal Express believes this so strongly that it requires all employees interested in entering the ranks of first-line management to participate in its Leadership Evaluation and Awareness Process (LEAP).[28]

LEAP's first step involves participation in an introductory, one-day class that familiarizes candidates with managerial responsibilities. About one candidate in five con-

The Impact of Leadership Styles on Climate

Daniel Goleman, an applied psychologist at Rutgers University, is known for his work on emotional intelligence—the ability to manage ourselves and our relationships effectively. Having earlier identified six different styles of leadership, he investigated how successful each style has proved to be in affecting climate or working atmosphere, based upon a major study of the behavior and impact on their organizations of thousands of executives.

Coercive leaders demand immediate compliance ("Do what I tell you") and were found to have a negative impact on climate. Goleman comments that this controlling style, often highly confrontational, only has value in a crisis or in dealing with problem employees. *Pacesetting leaders* set high standards for performance and exemplify these through their own energetic behavior; this style can be summarized as "Do as I do, now." Somewhat surprisingly it, too, was found to have a negative impact on climate. In practice, the pacesetting leader may destroy morale by

assuming too much, too soon, of subordinates—expecting them to know already what to do and how to do it. Finding others to be less capable than expected, the leader may lapse into obsessing over details and micromanaging. This style is only likely to work when seeking to get quick results from a highly motivated and competent team.

The research found that the most effective style for achieving a positive change in climate came from *authoritative leaders* who have the skills and personality to mobilize people toward a vision, building confidence and using a "Come with me" approach. The research also found that three other styles had quite positive impacts on climate: *affiliative leaders* who believe that "People come first," seeking to create harmony and build emotional bonds; *democratic leaders* who forge consensus through participation ("What do you think?"); and *coaching leaders* who work to develop people for the future and whose style might be summarized as "Try this."

Source: Daniel Goleman, "Leadership that Gets Results," *Harvard Business Review 78*, March–April 2000, 78–93.

cludes at this point that "management is not for me." The next step is a three-to-six-month period during which the candidate's manager coaches him or her based on a series of leadership attributes identified by the company. A third step involves peer assessment by a number of the candidate's coworkers (selected by the manager). Finally, the candidate must present written and oral arguments regarding specific leadership scenarios to a group of managers trained in LEAP assessment; this panel compares its findings with those from the other sources above.

Federal Express emphasizes leadership at every level through its "Survey Feedback Action" surveys, including the Leadership Index in which subordinates rate their managers along 10 dimensions. Unfortunately, not every company is equally thorough in addressing the role of leadership at all levels in the organization. In many firms, promotional decisions often appear totally haphazard or based on such criteria as duration of tenure in a previous position.

Leadership, Culture, and Climate

To close this chapter, we take a brief look at a theme that runs throughout this chapter and, indeed, the book: the leader's role in nurturing an effective culture within the firm.[29] **Organizational culture** can be defined as including:

> ➤ Shared perceptions or themes regarding what is important in the organization
> ➤ Shared values about what is right and wrong
> ➤ Shared understanding about what works and what doesn't work
> ➤ Shared beliefs, and assumptions about *why* these things are important
> ➤ Shared styles of working and relating to others

organizational culture: shared values, beliefs, and work styles that are based upon an understanding of what is important to the organization and why.

Organizational climate represents the tangible surface layer on top of the organization's underlying culture. Among six key factors that influence an organization's working environment are its *flexibility*—or how free employees feel to innovate; their sense of *responsibility* to the organization; the level of *standards* that people set; the perceived aptness of *rewards*; the *clarity* people have about mission and values; and the level of *commitment* to a common purpose.[30] From an employee perspective, this climate is directly related to managerial policies and procedures, especially those associated with human resource management. In short, climate represents the shared perceptions of employees concerning the practices, procedures, and types of behaviors that get rewarded and supported in a particular setting.

organizational climate: employees' shared perceptions of the practices, procedures, and types of behaviors that get rewarded and supported in a particular setting.

Because multiple climates often exist simultaneously within a single organization, a climate must relate to something specific—for instance, service, support, innovation, or safety. A climate for service refers to employee perceptions of those practices, procedures, and behaviors that are expected with regard to customer service and service quality, and that get rewarded when performed well.

Leaders are responsible for creating cultures and the service climates that go along with them. Transformational leadership may require changing a culture that has become dysfunctional in the context of what it takes to be successful. Why are some leaders more effective than others in bringing about a desired change in climate? As presented in the box, "The Impact of Leadership Styles on Climate," research suggests that it may be a matter of style.

Creating a new climate for service, based upon an understanding of what is needed for market success, may require a radical rethink of human resource management activities, operational procedures, and the firm's reward and recognition policies. Newcomers to an organization must quickly familiarize themselves with the existing culture, otherwise they will find themselves being led by it, rather than leading through it and, if necessary, changing it.

Conclusion

No organization can hope to achieve and maintain market leadership without human leaders who articulate and communicate a vision and are backed by individuals with the management skills to make it happen. Service leadership in an industry requires high performance across a number of dimensions that fall within the scope of the marketing, operations, and HRM functions.

Within any given service organization, marketing has to coexist with operations—traditionally the dominant function—whose concerns are cost and efficiency centered rather than customer centered. Marketing must also coexist with human resource management, which usually recruits and trains service personnel, including those who have direct contact with the customers. An ongoing challenge is to balance the concerns of each function, not only at the head office but also in the field. Ultimately, a company's ability to effectively integrate marketing, operations, and human resource management will determine whether it is classified as a service loser, a service nonentity, a service professional, or a service leader.

Study Questions and Exercises

1. Identify the nature of the tasks that are traditionally assigned to (a) marketing, (b) operations, and (c) human resource management.

2. Describe the causes of tension between the marketing, operations, and human resource functions. Provide specific examples of how these tensions might vary from one service industry to another.

3. Briefly define the four levels of service performance. Based on your own service experiences, provide an example of a company for each category.

4. Which level of service performance do you think best describes Southwest Airlines? Explain your answer using specific examples from the opening story at the beginning of this chapter.

5. What is the difference between leadership and management?

6. Discuss the relationship between leadership, climate, and culture.

7. Profile an individual whose leadership skills have played a significant role in the success of a service organization.

Endnotes

1. From Christopher Lovelock, *Product Plus* (New York: McGraw-Hill, 1994), Chapters 1 and 6; *Southwest Airlines Co. Annual Report* 1999 (Dallas: Southwest Airlines, 2000), Southwest Airlines Web site, www.southwest.com, February 2001; "The Top 25 Managers of the Year," *Business Week*, 8 January 2001, 73; Robert Levering and Milton Moskowitz, "The 100 Best Companies to Work for," *Fortune*, 8 January 2001, 148–168; Ahmad Diba and Lisa Muñoz, "America's Most Admired Companies," *Fortune*, 19 February 2001, 64–66. Note: Herb Kelleher steps down as Southwest's CEO and president in May 2001 on reaching the age of 70, but remains chairman.

2. James L. Heskett, Thomas O. Jones, Gary W. Loveman, W. Earl Sasser, Jr., and Leonard A. Schlesinger, "Putting the Service Profit Chain to Work," *Harvard Business Review*, March-April 1994; and James L. Heskett, W. Earl Sasser, Jr., and Leonard A. Schlesinger, *The Service Profit Chain* (New York: The Free Press, 1997).

3. Note that a relationship between employee satisfaction and customer satisfaction may be more likely in high-contact situations where employee behavior is an important aspect of

the customers' experience. See Rhian Silvestro and Stuart Cross, "Applying the Service Profit Chain in a Retail Environment: Challenging the Satisfaction Mirror," *International Journal of Service Industry Management* 11, no. 3 (2000): 244–68.

4. M. Beer, B. Spector, P. R. Lawrence, D. Q. Mills, and R. E. Walton, *Human Resource Management: A General Manager's Perspective* (New York: The Free Press, 1985).

5. Ibid.

6. David E. Bowen and Edward T. Lawler, III, "The Empowerment of Service Workers: What, Why, How and When," *Sloan Management Review* (Spring 1992): 31–39.

7. See, for example, Jeffrey Pfeffer, *Competitive Advantage through People* (Boston: Harvard Business School Press, 1994).

8. See, for example, Benjamin Schneider and David E. Bowen, *Winning the Service Game* (Boston: Harvard Business School Press, 1995) and Leonard L. Berry, *On Great Service: A Framework for Action.* (New York: The Free Press, 1995), Chapters 8–10.

9. Terri Kabachnick, "The Strategic Role of Human Resources," *Arthur Andersen Retailing Issues Letter* 11, no. 1 (January 1999): 3.

10. Sandra Vandermerwe, *From Tin Soldiers to Russian Dolls*, (Oxford: Butterworth-Heinemann, 1993), 82.

11. Richard B. Chase and Robert H. Hayes, "Beefing Up Operations in Service Firms," *Sloan Management Review* (Fall 1991): 15–26.

12. Claudia H. Deutsch, "Management: Companies Scramble to Fill Shoes at the Top," nytimes.com, 1 November 2000.

13. John P. Kotter, *What Leaders Really Do* (Boston: Harvard Business School Press, 1999), 10–11.

14. Warren Bennis and Burt Nanus, *Leaders: The Strategies for Taking Charge* (New York: Harper and Row, 1985), 92.

15. Kotter, *What Leaders Really Do*, 10–11.

16. Deborah Blagg and Susan Young, "What Makes a Leader?" *Harvard Business School Bulletin*, February 2001, 31–36.

17. Gary Hamel and C. K. Prahalad, *Competing for the Future* (Boston: Harvard Business School Press, 1994).

18. See, for instance, the special issue on "Leadership as a Service" (Celeste Wilderom, guest editor), *International Journal of Service Industry Management*. 3, no. 2 (1992).

19. James L. Heskett, W. Earl Sasser, Jr., and Leonard A. Schlesinger, *The Service Profit Chain*, 236.

20. Leonard L. Berry, *On Great Service*, 9.

21. Leonard L. Berry, *Discovering the Soul of Service* (New York: The Free Press, 1999), 44, 47.

22. Sandra Vandermerwe, *From Tin Soldiers to Russian Dolls*, 129.

23. M. Sheridan, "J. W. Marriot, Jr., Chairman and President, Marriott Corporation," *Sky Magazine*, March 1987, 46–53.

24. Nelson D. Schwartz, "What's in the Cards for Amex?" *Fortune*, 22 January 2001, 58–70.

25. For a discussion of Carlzon's philosophy of leadership, see K. J. Blois, "Carlzon's *Moments of Truth*—A Critical Appraisal," *International Journal of Service Industry Management* 3, no. 3 (1992): 5–17.

26. Thomas J. Peters and Robert H. Waterman, *In Search of Excellence* (New York: Harper & Row, 1982): 122.

27. Michael Maccoby, "Narcissistic Leaders: The Incredible Pros, the Inevitable Cons," *Harvard Business Review*, 78 (January-February 2000): 68–78.

28. Christopher Lovelock, "Federal Express: Quality Improvement Program," IMD case (Cranfield, UK: European Case Clearing House, 1990).

29. This section is based, in part, on Benjamin Schneider and David E. Bowen, *Winning the Service Game* (Boston: Harvard Business School Press, 1995); and David E. Bowen, Benjamin Schneider and Sandra S. Kim, "Shaping Service Cultures through Strategic Human Resource Management," in *Handbook of Services Marketing and Management*, ed. T. Schwartz and D. Iacobucci (Thousand Oaks, CA: Sage Publications, 2000), 439–454.

30. Daniel Goleman, "Leadership that Gets Results," *Harvard Business Review* 78 (March-April, 2000): 78–93.

Arrow Management

"We provide value to our customers in two ways," stated Gary Chamberlain, owner and founder of Arrow Management. "First, we do jobs they could do themselves but don't want to. Second, we help them save money on their equipment and facilities maintenance." After a slow start in Portland, Oregon, in the early 1990s, Chamberlain had found a profitable niche for his company in Menlo Park, California.

Chamberlain's father was a contractor who introduced Gary to the engineering business at an early age. He was a project manager for his father's construction company and then worked in both engineering consulting and mechanical engineering firms. This experience gave him the ability to communicate well with different players in the contracting and maintenance industries. In both appearance and behavior, Chamberlain created an energetic and efficient impression. His athletic activities (he was a national triathlon champion in 1990 and had become an avid mountain biker) kept him physically fit and trim. Chamberlain had no college degree but felt his hands-on training gave him the skills he needed to design and implement his service concept successfully.

Arrow Management did business with 6 to 10 companies a year. Its clients included universities, large biotechnical and pharmaceutical firms, manufacturing plants, and office buildings that had large physical facilities. Chamberlain had two employees (including himself) but had had as many as seven in the past. He preferred to keep his company small because he felt quality was thus easier to control.

ARROW MANAGEMENT'S SERVICES

Chamberlain had developed an effective method for collecting and providing accurate information to businesses about mechanical or electrical equipment at their facilities that requires routine maintenance. He and his employees traveled to clients' sites to locate and inspect their equipment—primarily heating and air-conditioning units or specialized climate control devices—and record data. Arrow Management provided accurate, timely documentation that was presented in a professional, attractive, and user-friendly report. These reports were generated at Arrow's office through computerized mapping techniques and were then delivered to the clients.

Because the task of equipment maintenance was usually outsourced to building contractors at $80 to $90 an hour, clients saved money if they didn't have to pay the contractors to spend time locating the equipment before servicing it. The data could also be used to ensure that contractors who were bidding on maintenance jobs didn't

Prepared by Lauren K. Wright.

overprice their services. Several of Arrow Management's clients would not award maintenance contracts until Chamberlain had analyzed the bids for accuracy.

Prices were calculated and billed on a per-project basis. Chamberlain estimated the costs and labor involved and added a small contingency for unexpected overruns (in case the project took longer to complete or was more expensive than he expected). He had discovered several years earlier that he could make more money by collecting fewer pieces of data and that service quality from the client's perspective actually increased. Based on this information, he streamlined his service delivery processes so he could concentrate on doing a few things well. Reducing the number of services Arrow Management offered had allowed Chamberlain to standardize procedures and improve his profit margins significantly.

WINNING AND KEEPING CUSTOMERS

Much of the company's income was generated from repeat business. For example, Stanford University in Palo Alto, California, used Arrow Management on a regular basis. Chamberlain stated that he had become the "voice of Stanford" for the Athletic Department in quality control for equipment maintenance. Contractors who were hired to maintain the department's equipment did not get paid until he certified that their work had been completed satisfactorily.

Current clients referred many of Arrow Management's new customers. Chamberlain had tried direct mailings to attract additional business but had not been satisfied with the results. He estimated that 800 mailed flyers might generate one or two new clients. Recently he had been experimenting with magnets that displayed the company logo and phone number. These seemed to be more effective because people tended to keep them longer and were more likely to have the information in front of them when a need arose.

Chamberlain encouraged people who were considering his service to check with existing customers and to inspect his work. He sometimes made a preliminary report, using a Polaroid camera to document the location and condition of a company's equipment for potential customers. Chamberlain also attempted to minimize perceived risks by suggesting that potential clients could hire Arrow Management for a small project or the most undesirable jobs so they could judge the quality of its work themselves.

"Anybody can do the technical work," said Chamberlain, "but it's the relationships that make it fun or worthwhile." He believed that relationship management was the key to quality service. It helped him understand what clients needed and expected and also enabled him to complete jobs more efficiently. He used his outgoing manner and aggressive charm to get employees inside his clients' organizations to provide the information he needed in a timely manner so he could complete his own work faster. Chamberlain was aware of small ways in which he could make key employees' lives better so that they would be willing to help him in the future. (An example was the time he fixed a broken heating system in a manager's office for free so that she wouldn't continue to freeze every winter.) Chamberlain was also able to deal very effectively with building contractors who bid on maintenance jobs for his clients. He understood their side of the business and could speak in their terms. Because he was not intimidated by the contractors, he was able to represent his clients' interests well.

WHAT KEEPS THE BOSS UP AT NIGHT?

"Nothing related to work," Chamberlain said with a grin. He believed he had found a niche that was fairly resistant to competition. Chamberlain referred to himself as the "Kelly Boy" of maintenance management (a reference to the international temporary employment agency whose female workers were once popularly referred to as Kelly Girls). Although his clients could do the work themselves, they preferred to hire him because they were typically short-staffed and had difficulty in meeting the necessary maintenance completion dates without additional help. Chamberlain felt that he could outbid larger companies for jobs. He stated that many consulting firms were not interested in doing what Arrow Management does because "it's grunt work and you have to be willing to get dirty."

Chamberlain had no formal business plan and no definite goals for the future. He was satisfied with keeping his company and client base small. "If you're a worrier, being self-employed could eat you alive," he remarked. "You need to have a passion for what you're doing, and customers sense this when selecting a vendor. If I didn't have to work for a living, I'd probably choose my current career as a way to keep occupied anyway."

Questions for Discussion

1. What is the nature of the service that Arrow Management is offering? What processes are involved?

2. How has Arrow Management addressed each of the 8Ps in its overall marketing strategy?

3. What special risks or challenges does Chamberlain face as owner and primary employee of his company? What unique opportunities does he have?

4. Why is relationship management important to the outcome of Chamberlain's work? Is relationship management different for business services than for consumer services?

5. Do you agree with Chamberlain's assessment of his competitive position? Why or why not?

Four Customers in Search of Solutions

Among the many customers of Bell Telephone in Toronto, Ontario, are four individuals living on Willow Street in a middle-class suburb of the city. Each of them has a telephone-related problem and decides to call the company about it.

WINSTON CHEN

Winston Chen grumbles constantly about the amount of his home telephone bill (which is, in fact, in the top 2 percent of all household phone bills in Ontario). There are many calls to countries in Southeast Asia on weekday evenings, almost daily calls to Kingston (a smaller city not far from Toronto) around midday, and calls to Vancouver, BC, most weekends. One day, Chen receives a telephone bill that is even larger than usual. On reviewing the bill, he is convinced that he has been overcharged, so he calls Bell's customer service department to complain and request an adjustment.

MARIE PORTILLO

Marie Portillo has missed several important calls recently because the caller received a busy signal. She phones the telephone company to determine possible solutions to this problem. Portillo's telephone bill is at the median level for a household subscriber. Most

Prepared by Christopher H. Lovelock.

of the calls from her house are local, but there are occasional international calls to Mexico or to countries in South America. She does not subscribe to any value-added services.

ELEANOR VANDERBILT

During the past several weeks, Eleanor Vanderbilt has been distressed to receive a series of obscene telephone calls. It sounds like the same person each time. She calls the telephone company to see if it can stop this harassment. Her phone bill is in the bottom 10 percent of all household subscriber bills and almost all calls are local.

RICHARD ROBBINS

For more than a week, the phone line at Richard Robbins's house has been making strange humming and crackling noises, making it difficult to hear what the other person is saying. After two of his friends comment on these distracting noises, Robbins calls Bell and reports the problem. His guess is that it is being caused by the answering machine, which is getting old and sometimes loses messages. Robbins's phone bill is at the 75th percentile for a household subscriber. Most of the calls are made to locations within Canada, usually during evenings and weekends, although there are a few calls to the United States, too.

Questions for Discussion

1. Based strictly on the information in the case, how many possibilities do you see to segment the telecommunications market?

2. As a customer service representative at the telephone company, how would you address each of the problems and complaints reported?

3. Do you see any marketing opportunities for Bell in any of these complaints?

Dr. Beckett's Dental Office

"I just hope the quality differences are visible to our patients," mused Dr. Barbro Beckett as she surveyed the office that housed her well-established dental practice. She had recently moved to her current location from an office she felt was too cramped to allow her staff to work efficiently—a factor that was becoming increasingly important as the costs of providing dental care continued to rise. Although Beckett realized that productivity gains were necessary, she did not want to compromise the quality of service her patients received.

MANAGEMENT COMES TO DENTISTRY

The classes Beckett took in dental school taught her a lot about the technical side of dentistry but nothing about the business side. She received no formal training in the mechanics of running a business or understanding customers' needs. In fact, professional guidelines discouraged marketing or advertising of any kind. That was not a major problem when Beckett started her practice 22 years ago. In the 1960s and 1970s, profit mar-

Prepared by Lauren K. Wright.

gins were good. But by the 1990s the dental care industry had changed dramatically. Costs rose as a result of labor laws, malpractice insurance, and the constant need to invest in new equipment and staff training as new technologies were introduced. By 1998, Beckett's overhead was between 70 and 80 percent of revenues before accounting for wages or office rental.

As overhead was rising, there was a movement in the United States to reduce health care costs to insurance companies, employers, and patients by offering managed health care through large health maintenance organizations (HMOs). The HMOs set the prices for various services by putting an upper limit on the amount that their doctors and dentists could charge for various procedures. The advantage to patients was that their health insurance covered virtually all costs. But the price limitations meant that HMO doctors and dentists would not be able to offer certain services that might provide better care but were too expensive. Beckett had decided not to become an HMO provider because the reimbursement rate was only 80 to 85 percent of her usual charge. She felt that she could not provide high-quality care to patients at these rates.

These changes presented some significant challenges to Beckett, who wanted to offer the highest level of dental care rather than being a low-cost provider. With the help of a consultant, she decided that her top priority was differentiating the practice on the basis of quality. She and her staff developed an internal mission statement that reflected this goal. The mission statement (which is prominently displayed in the back office) reads, "It is our goal to provide superior dentistry in an efficient, profitable manner within the confines of a caring, quality environment."

Because higher-quality care was more costly, Beckett's patients sometimes had to pay fees for costs that were not covered by their insurance policies. If the quality differences weren't substantial, these patients might decide to switch to an HMO dentist or another lower-cost provider.

REDESIGNING THE SERVICE DELIVERY SYSTEM

The move to a new office gave Beckett a unique opportunity to rethink almost every aspect of her service. She wanted the work environment to reflect her own personality and values, as well as providing a pleasant place for her staff to work.

Facilities and Equipment

Beckett first looked into the office spaces that were available in the Northern California town where she practiced. She didn't find anything she liked, so she hired an architect from San Francisco to design a contemporary office building with lots of light and space. This increased the building costs by $100,000, but Beckett felt that it would be a critical factor in differentiating her service.

Beckett's new office is Scandinavian in design (reflecting her Swedish heritage and attention to detail). The waiting room and reception area are filled with modern furniture in muted shades of brown, grey, green, and purple. Live plants and flowers are abundant, and the walls are covered with art. Classical music plays softly in the background. Patients can enjoy a cup of coffee or tea and browse through the large selection of current magazines while they wait for their appointments.

The treatment areas are both functional and appealing. There is a small conference room with toys for children and a VCR that is used to show patients educational films about different dental procedures. Literature is available to explain what patients need to do to maximize their treatment outcomes.

The chairs in the examining rooms are covered in leather and are very comfortable. Each room has a large window that allows patients to watch birds eating at the feeders that are filled each day. There are also attractive mobiles hanging from the ceiling to distract patients from the unfamiliar sounds and sensations they are experiencing. Headphones are available with a wide selection of music.

The entire back-office staff members (including Beckett) wear matching uniforms in cheerful shades of pink, purple, and blue that match the office décor. All the technical equipment looks very modern and is spotlessly clean. State-of-the-art computerized machinery is used for some procedures. Beckett's dental degrees are prominently displayed in her office, along with certificates from various programs that she and her staff have attended to update their technical skills.

Service Personnel

There are eight employees in the dental practice, including Beckett (who is the only dentist). The seven staff members are separated by job function into front-office and back-office workers. Front-office duties (covered by two employees) include receptionist and secretarial tasks and financial and budgeting work. The back office is divided into hygienists and chair-side assistants.

The three chair-side assistants help the hygienists and Beckett with treatment procedures. They have specialized training for their jobs but do not need a college degree. The two hygienists handle routine exams and teeth cleaning plus some treatment procedures. In many offices, hygienists assume a superior attitude because of their education (a bachelor's degree and specialized training are required) and experience. According to Beckett, this attitude can destroy any possibility of teamwork among the office staff. She feels very fortunate that her hygienists view themselves as part of a larger team whose members are working together to provide quality care to patients.

Beckett values her friendships with the staff members, and she also understands that they are a vital part of the service delivery. "Ninety percent of patients' perceptions of quality comes from their interactions with the front desk and the other employees— not from the staff's technical skills," she states. When the dentist began to redesign her practice, she discussed her goals with the staff and involved them in the decision-making process. The changes meant new expectations and routines for most employees, and some were not willing to adapt. There was some staff turnover (mostly voluntary) as the new office procedures were implemented. The current group works very well as a team.

Beckett and her staff meet briefly each morning to discuss the day's schedule and patients. They also have longer meetings every other week to discuss more strategic issues and resolve any problems that have developed. During these meetings, employees make suggestions about how to improve patient care. Some of the most successful staff suggestions include thank-you cards to patients who refer other patients; follow-up calls to patients after major procedures; a "goodie box" for patients, including toothbrush, toothpaste, mouthwash, and floss; buckwheat pillows and blankets for comfort during long procedures; coffee and tea in the waiting area; and a photo album in the waiting area with pictures of staff members and their families.

The expectations for staff performance (in both technical competence and patient interactions) are very high, but Beckett gives her employees many opportunities to update their skills by attending classes and workshops. She also rewards their hard work by giving monthly bonuses if business is good. Because she shares the financial data with her staff, they can see the difference in revenues if the schedule is slow or patients are dissatisfied. This provides an extra incentive to improve the service delivery. The entire office also goes on trips together once a year (paid for by Beckett), and spouses are welcome (but must cover their own expenses). Past destinations for these excursions have included Hawaii and Washington, D.C.

Procedures and Patients

With the help of a consultant, all the office systems (including billing, ordering, lab work, and patient treatment) have been redesigned. One of the main goals was to standardize some of the routine procedures so that errors were reduced and all patients would receive the same level of care. There are specific times allotted for each procedure, and the staff works very hard to see that these are met. Office policy dictates that patients should be kept waiting no longer than 20 minutes without being given the option to reschedule, and employees often call patients in advance if they know there will be a delay. They also attempt to fill in cancellations to make sure that office capacity is maximized. Staff members will substitute for each other when necessary or help with tasks that are not specifically in their job descriptions to make things run more smoothly.

Beckett's practice includes about 2,000 active patients (and many more who come infrequently). They are mostly white-collar workers with professional jobs (university employees, health care workers, and managers or owners of local establishments). She does no advertising—all of her new business comes from positive word of mouth by current patients.

The dentist believes that the referrals are a real advantage because new patients don't come in cold, they have already been told about her service by friends or family, so she doesn't have to sell herself. All new patients must have an initial exam so that Beckett can perform a needs assessment and educate them about her service. She believes that this is the first indication to patients that her practice is different from others they might have experienced. Patients may then have to wait another three or four months for a routine cleaning and exam because the office is so busy, but they don't seem to mind.

THE BIGGEST CHALLENGE

"Redesigning the business was the easy part," Beckett sighs. "Demonstrating the high level of quality to patients is the hard job." She says it is especially difficult because most people dislike going to the dentist or feel that it's an inconvenience and come in with a negative attitude. Beckett tries to reinforce the idea that high-quality dental care depends on a positive long-term relationship between patients and the dental team. This philosophy is reflected in the patient mission statement hanging in the waiting area: "We are a caring, professional dental team serving motivated, quality-oriented patients interested in keeping healthy smiles for a lifetime. Our goal is to offer a progressive and educational environment. Your concerns are our focus."

Although Beckett enjoys her work, she says it can be difficult to maintain a positive attitude. The job requires precision and attention to detail, and the procedures are often painful to patients. She feels as if she is often "walking on eggshells" because she knows patients are anxious and uncomfortable, which makes them more critical of her service delivery. It is not uncommon for patients to say negative things to Beckett before treatments even begin (as "I really hate going to the dentist—it's not you, but I just don't want to be here."). When this occurs, she reminds herself that she is providing high-quality service whether patients appreciate it or not. "The people will usually have to have the dental work done anyway," Beckett says. "So I just do the best job I can and make them as comfortable as possible." Even though patients seldom express appreciation for her services, she hopes that she has made a positive difference in their health or appearance that will benefit them in the long run.

Questions for Discussion

1. Which of the 8Ps are addressed in this case? Give examples of each.
2. Why do people dislike going to the dentist? Do you feel that Beckett has addressed this problem effectively?
3. How do Beckett and her staff educate patients about the service they are receiving? What else could they do?
4. What supplementary services are offered? How do they enhance service delivery?
5. Contrast your own dental care experiences with those offered by Beckett's practice. What differences do you see? Based on your review of this case, what advice would you give (a) to your current or former dentist and (b) to Beckett?

Mr. Mahaleel Goes to London

It was a Friday in mid-February, and Kadir Mahaleel, a wealthy businessman from the Southeast Asian nation of Tailesia, was visiting London on a trip that combined business and pleasure. Mahaleel was the founder of Eximsa, a major export company in Tailesia. Business brought him to London every two to three months. These trips gave him the opportunity to visit his daughter, Leona, the eldest of his four children, who lived in London. Several of his 10 grandchildren were attending college in Britain, and he was especially proud of his grandson Anson, who was a student at the Royal Academy of Music. In fact, he had scheduled this trip to coincide with a violin recital by Anson at 2 P.M. on this particular Friday.

The primary purpose of Mahaleel's visit was to resolve a delicate matter regarding his company. He had decided that the time had come to retire and wished to make arrangements for the company's future. His son Victor was involved in the business and ran Eximsa's trading office in Europe. However, Victor was in poor health and unable to take over the firm. Mahaleel believed that a group of loyal employees was interested in buying his company if the necessary credit could be arranged.

Before leaving Tailesia, Mahaleel had discussed the possibility of a buyout with Li Sieuw Meng, his trusted financial adviser, who recommended that he talk to several banks in London because of the potential complexity of the business deal: "The London banks are experienced in buyouts. Also, you need a bank that can handle the credit for the interested buyers in New York and London, as well as Asia. Once the buyout takes place, you'll have significant cash to invest. This would be a good time to review your estate plans as well."

Referring Mahaleel to two competing institutions, The Trust Company and Global Private Bank, Li added, "I've met an account officer from Global who called on me several times. Here's his business card; his name is Miguel Kim. I've never done any business with him, but he did seem quite competent. Unfortunately, I don't know anyone at The Trust Company, but here's their address in London."

After checking into his hotel in London the following Wednesday, Mahaleel telephoned Kim's office. Because Kim was out, Mahaleel spoke to the account officer's secretary, described himself briefly, and arranged to stop by Global's Lombard Street office around midmorning on Friday.

On Thursday, Mahaleel visited The Trust Company. The two people he met were extremely pleasant and had spent some time in Tailesia. They seemed very knowledge-

Prepared by Christopher H. Lovelock.

able about managing estates and gave him some good recommendations about handling his complex family affairs. However, they were clearly less experienced in handling business credit, his most urgent need. Without a substantial loan, his employees would not be able to buy the business from him.

The next morning, Mahaleel had breakfast with Leona. As they parted, she said, "I'll meet you at 1:30 P.M. in the lobby of the Savoy Hotel, and we'll go to the recital together. We mustn't be late if we want to get front-row seats."

On his way to Global Private Bank, Mahaleel stopped at Mappin & Webb's jewelry store to buy his wife a present for their anniversary. His shopping was pleasant and leisurely; he purchased a beautiful emerald necklace that he knew his wife would like. When he emerged from the jewelry store, the weather had turned much colder and he was caught in an unexpected snow flurry. He had difficulty finding a taxi and his arthritis started acting up, making walking to the Global office out of the question. At last he caught a taxi and arrived at the Lombard Street location of Global Bancorp about noon. After going into the street-level branch of Global Retail Bank, he was redirected by a security guard to the Private Bank offices on the second floor.

It was 12:15 when he arrived at the nicely appointed reception area of the Private Bank. There he was met by Miguel Kim's secretary, who told him, "Mr. Kim was disappointed that he couldn't be here to greet you, but he had a lunch appointment with one of his clients that was scheduled over a month ago. He expects to return about 1:30. In the meantime, he has asked another senior account officer, Sophia Costa, to assist you."

Sophia Costa, 41, was a vice president of the bank and had worked for Global Bancorp for 14 years (two years longer than Miguel Kim). She had visited Tailesia once but had not met Mahaleel's financial adviser nor any member of the Mahaleel family. An experienced relationship manager, Costa was knowledgeable about offshore investment management and fiduciary services. Kim had looked into her office at 11:45 A.M. and asked her if she would cover for him in case a prospective client, a Mr. Mahaleel, whom he had expected to see earlier, should happen to arrive. He told Costa that Mahaleel was a successful Tailesian businessman planning for his retirement but that he had never met the prospect personally; then he rushed off to lunch.

Questions for Discussion

1. Prepare a flowchart of Mahaleel's service encounters.

2. Putting yourself in Mahaleel's shoes, how do you feel (both physically and mentally) after speaking with the receptionist at Global? What are your priorities right now?

3. As Sophia Costa, what action would you take in your first five minutes with Mahaleel?

4. What would constitute a good outcome of the meeting for both the client and the bank? How should Costa try to bring about such an outcome?

Vick's Pizza Corporation

Victor Firenze, chief executive of Vick's Pizza Corporation, looked somber as he addressed senior executives of the national restaurant chain that bore his nickname. "We're facing yet another lawsuit for injuries because of alleged dangerous driving by

Prepared by Christopher H. Lovelock.

one of our delivery drivers," he announced at the company's head office in Illinois. "It comes on top of some very bad publicity about accidents involving our drivers in recent years."

BACKGROUND

Speed had always been a key strategic thrust for Vick's Pizza, which used the slogan "It's quick at Vick's." Not only was pizza prepared rapidly at the company's restaurants, but home deliveries arrived fast, too. The company's promise to deliver a pizza within 30 minutes of a phone order or to cut $3 off the price had boosted it from a single pizzeria 20 years earlier to the status of a national chain, with thousands of outlets and more than $3 billion in sales. But now a growing number of critics were saying that, in Vick's case at least, speed was a killer.

Vick's executives argued that the system did not promote fast or reckless driving. "The speed takes place in the store—not on the road," declared a spokesperson. "We can custom-make a pizza within 10 to 12 minutes. Our average delivery area is only 1 to 2 miles, so there's enough time to deliver."

THE SAFETY PROBLEM

The company's own records indicated that during the previous year, accidents involving Vick's drivers had cost 20 lives, 18 of them during pizza runs. But it had declined to specify how many of the victims were employees. Randell Meins, Vick's vice president of corporate communications, stated in a TV interview that the company had always encouraged drivers to take care, had never penalized late drivers, was urging franchise owners and store managers to promote safe driving, and would soon implement a new safety course for all Vick's drivers.

Meins cited the owner of several franchises in Ohio, who had declared, "We never ask a driver to break the speed limit. We never want them to do anything unsafe on the road. And we always tell them to fasten their seat belts." While acknowledging that "even one death is too many," Meins noted that with 230 million pizzas delivered last year, this works out to only one death per 11.5 million pies. "We're not minimizing the deaths by any means," Meins said. "But that's what the mathematics show."

Martina Gomes, director of a nonprofit safety research and advocacy group, expressed outrage over Vick's statistic. "Great!" she said. "Now we know the value of the life of a 17-year-old—11.5 million pizzas." Gomes offered her own statistical analysis. Vick's, she said, employed some 75,000 part-time drivers. Assuming that this amounted to the equivalent of 20,000 full-time drivers—four for each of the 5,000 Vick's outlets—she claimed that 20 deaths in one year meant that the company's drivers faced a death rate between three and six times higher than that in the construction industry and twice as high as that of miners. "The point is this," said Gomes. "Would parents let their kids drive for Vick's if they knew they were three times more likely to die doing that job than if they were working in construction?"

Scott and Linda Hurding's 17-year-old son had been the latest Vick's driver to die, the only Vick's employee so far during the current year. Hustling to deliver pizzas in a semirural area near Dallas, Texas, Mike Hurding often covered 100 miles a night. His parents and classmates said he was proud that he almost always made the delivery within the 30-minute limit and was determined never to get the "King of the Lates" badge, allegedly given every week by his franchisor to the driver most often late on deliveries.

Mike died when the company-owned pickup he was driving in a delivery run skidded off a wet road and hit a utility pole in an effort to avoid another car that was braking to make a left-hand turn. A police reconstruction of the accident concluded that Mike had been driving 45 mph on a road with a 30 mph speed limit and was not wearing a seat belt. The other driver was not charged. Vick's subsequently offered the Hurding family about $5,000 in worker's compensation to cover funeral costs. Gomes estimated that the 20 deaths during the previous year had cost Vick's some $90,000 in death benefits. Like many other critics of the company, she argued that Vick's was unconcerned because the cost was so low. Accordingly, she had written to Victor Firenze, asking Vick's to pay $500,000 to each accident victim, abandon the 30-minute rule, and hire only drivers aged 18 or older.

Linda Hurding, Mike's mother, told a TV reporter that Vick's guarantee to deliver each pizza within 30 minutes or knock $3 off the price was just "a license to speed." Blaming this policy for their son's death, the Hurding parents and a group of family friends had started a petition drive, asking for federal restrictions on the policy. Within a month of beginning their drive, the petitioners had delivered the first batch of more than 1,500 signatures to the offices of their U.S. senator. "We're angry and we're fighting," the Hurdings said. Meanwhile, a state agency in Texas was looking into the case to determine whether Vick's policy violated the Occupational Safety and Health Act under its jurisdiction.

Vick's faced criticism and legal action on other fronts as well. In Eugene, Oregon, the widow of a motorcyclist allegedly struck and killed by a Vick's driver nine months earlier had sued the company for damages. In Atlanta, attorney Anders Mundel had just filed suit on behalf of Wilson and Jennifer Groncki, who suffered neck, back, and arm injuries when their car was broadsided by a driver who had run a stop sign as she left a Vick's store with four pizzas for delivery. The Gronckis alleged that the store manager had rushed to the scene of the wreck and yelled, "Let's get this pizza on the road!" In addition to unspecified monetary damages, the suit sought to force Vick's to abandon the 30-minute rule, which the attorney called "a grossly negligent corporate policy."

Mundel was also helping other lawyers around the country to press cases against the company and had organized an information network, including a Web site, to coordinate the filing of cases in different jurisdictions. "Even if Vick's franchisees, managers, and executives do not actively encourage reckless driving," he argued, "the 30-minute rule acts as an inherent encouragement, putting great pressure on the drivers."

As part of her research, safety advocate Gomes had interviewed a number of current and former Vick's employees, several of whom preferred to remain anonymous for fear of reprisals from the managers where they worked. Gomes claimed that her research showed that "the vast majority" of the company's drivers were under 18. Nelson Chen, a 20-year-old college student and former part-time Vick's employee who had worked in several Vick's outlets in southern California over a three-year period, told Gomes that he and other drivers "speeded all the time. I would even run stop signs—anything to make those deliveries." Sue, a 19-year-old driver in Kansas, said managers "get uptight when pizzas are running late and start yelling at everyone to hurry up, hurry up!" A consultant familiar with the industry agreed: "There's a lot of pressure to speed. It's not written in the manuals, but it's there. If a driver goes out with four deliveries and ends up with only a minute to make that last one but figures he's two minutes away, he's going to speed; he's going to cut corners."

RESPONDING TO THE PROBLEM

Two weeks after Mike Hurding's death, Vick's sent a letter to its corporate-owned stores and its franchisees stating that it was company policy to hire drivers 18 or older. This directive, however, was not binding on the franchisees, who operated some 65 percent of all Vick's restaurants.

The newly filed Atlanta lawsuit, together with continuing criticism of the company, had been widely reported in the media. Vick Firenze and his colleagues were worried. Historically, the company had enjoyed a positive public image and a reputation as a generous donor to local community activities. "We definitely have a perception problem," said Randell Meins. "We're taking a lot of heat right now. But the last thing we need to do is to panic," warned the senior vice president of marketing. "The 30-minute guarantee is very, very important to our customers. Sales could be hard hit if we drop it."

Questions for Discussion

1. Make a flowchart of Vick's service delivery system from receipt of the order to delivery of the pizza to the customer. Why are pizzas sometimes delivered late?

2. How important is the 30-minute guarantee?

3. How serious is the present situation for Vick's Pizza Corporation? How well has it handled the situation so far?

4. As a senior manager of Vick's Pizza Corporation, how would you respond to the current situation? Why?

Hampton Inn: The 100% Satisfaction Guarantee

Hampton Inn, a subsidiary of Promus Hotel Corporation (now part of Hilton Hotels), was the first company in the lodging industry to offer its customers an unconditional service guarantee. It read:

HAMPTON INN: 100% SATISFACTION GUARANTEE

We guarantee high quality accommodations, friendly and efficient service, and clean, comfortable surroundings. If you're not completely satisfied, we don't expect you to pay.

Guests were encouraged to act as quality-assurance inspectors by identifying quality deficiencies and reporting them to hotel employees. Reporting systems were set up to track instances where the guarantee was invoked and to monitor the underlying problems.

Following the introduction of the guarantee on a pilot basis at 30 inns, guests who stayed at these hotels were asked whether the guarantee had influenced their decision to stay at that particular Hampton Inn. They were also asked if the 100% Satisfaction Guarantee would influence their decision to return to that same hotel or to another Hampton Inn in the future. Finally, guests were asked what they thought of the guarantee, whether they believed it was truly unconditional, and what changes, if any, they had noticed in the employees' behavior. The most commonly heard comments were:

➢ "It helps ensure I'll get the service I deserve."

➢ "No one else offers this."

➢ "They stand behind what they say."

➢ "I'll get my money's worth."

➢ "It makes their employees try harder."

Later research documented the financial benefits of the guarantee, showing that the revenues from greater patronage greatly exceeded the costs of administering the program. In subsequent years, the guarantee was extended to other hotels operated by Promus, including Hampton Inn & Suites, Embassy Suites, and Homewood Suites. The chairman and other executives emphasized the 100% Satisfaction Guarantee's power to align the organization's processes, systems, and policies to create positive, lasting change.

Soon, a few competing chains started to offer their own guarantees, although Promus executives felt that these competitive programs were often poorly designed and administered.

Among many managers, the 100% Satisfaction Guarantee fostered a proactive attitude toward problem prevention. They saw that it was financially more advantageous for managers and employees to prevent problems from occurring in the first place than to spend money through the reactive response of giving refunds to dissatisfied guests.

In one instance, a manager discovered late one evening that his hotel would lose its water supply overnight. Rather than conjure up a myriad of excuses to offer his guests, he thought hard about how to minimize their dissatisfaction with this potentially disastrous situation. Knowing that his guests would want coffee, he arranged for a caterer to deliver several urns of hot coffee prior to breakfast and guest checkout. He also went to the local Wal-Mart store and purchased over 100 one-gallon jugs, which were filled with water and then placed outside guests' doors so that they could wash and brush their teeth. In the morning, the manager personally called all guests at their appropriate wake-up times, taking responsibility for the problem and apologizing for any inconvenience. His proactive strategy paid off—there were zero guarantee invocations that day.

CONTINUING DOUBTS AMONG HOTEL OWNERS AND MANAGERS

Despite mounting evidence of the guarantee's financial and operational benefits for the chain, many owners and managers of Hampton Inns hotels still had doubts. They overlooked the 100% Satisfaction Guarantee's value as a retention strategy, whose documented return on investment clearly outperformed investment in more traditional marketing and advertising efforts designed to attract new guests. Hotel managers typically had misgivings about "giving the store away" or being taken advantage of by dishonest guests. Further, they viewed guarantee refunds as an expense that should be minimized, rather than seeing them as an investment in building a loyal base of guests who would return in the future.

The general manager of one hotel later recalled his initial reaction to the guarantee:

I didn't agree with it. They were expecting me to give up control of my property and my guests' satisfaction. I didn't want to give my employees full discretion to give away money; I wanted them to check everything through me so that I would have the last say with every guest. Many of us viewed the guarantee solely as an expense item on our profit and loss statements. Given how dedicated I was to managing my bottom line, I viewed the guarantee as an expense line item that I wanted to control and manage. After all, that's the way I had been doing business for years.

At a meeting to promote the benefits of the 100% Service Guarantee, some general managers said they felt more comfortable *negotiating* with customers for what each side felt was a fair remedy to a problem—say, a partial refund, $10 off the guest's bill, or a coupon for the next night, free. Responding to these views, Promus's chairman countered:

But that isn't what guests are paying for! The guests pay for a night's stay. If they aren't satisfied, then they don't pay, pure and simple. Anything further is a compromise of what we stand for—the absolute satisfaction of our customers. This isn't a program to give away money. This is a program to enhance the quality of our hotel system.

Over time, hotel owners and managers came to recognize the value of the 100% Satisfaction Guarantee as a framework for making capital-investment decisions. If they saw a trend of guarantee invocations in a specific area (e.g., numerous complaints about threadbare carpeting), this suggested that priority should be given to making an investment in that area, as opposed to spending money on a more discretionary item, such as the latest telephone technology. The guarantee also freed managers from having to resolve every guest problem themselves. Employees were empowered to resolve customer issues and ensure each guest's total satisfaction, leaving the managers time to dedicate their attention to more strategic issues that might otherwise have been neglected.

THE PROBLEM OF UNCONTROLLABLES

One ongoing barrier to managers' acceptance of the guarantee concept involved "uncontrollables"—problems over which they felt they had no control. During the chain-wide roll-out of the guarantee at Hampton Inn, one general manager expressed concern to a vice president of the company about the numerous guarantee invocations at his property. Many of his guests' visits, he said, were marred by noise from other guests in public areas or other rooms.

"It's just one of those uncontrollables," he ventured. "I've had this problem for years, and I lose a number of people every year to the noise. I consider it a natural part of doing business." He explained that his property was adjacent to a building and sports ground where youth athletic tournaments took place, and said:

> I often have several teams staying here. The kids do get rowdy running upstairs and downstairs, visiting one another, and running down the halls. We try to keep them quiet, but first, they are kids and, second, we need to keep the large volume of business they generate.

Discussing the situation, he and the vice president came up with a solution. The manager would dedicate the bottom floor of one wing to the sports teams, effectively isolating the noise and saving other guests from being disturbed. But, what if the hotel was almost full and a last-minute guest had to be assigned a room in that wing? Their solution was to be proactive: front-desk employees would explain to such guests that it might be noisy and if that was likely to be a problem, they might be more comfortable staying at another hotel. When this procedure was implemented, most guests decided to stay at the Hampton Inn in question, rather than returning to their cars and trying to find other accommodations.

Subsequently, a few people still occasionally invoked the guarantee at that property—even after warnings about noise. However, most guests were satisfied with their stays, and in fact, appreciated the staff's candor. Often, the noise turned out to be less than the receptionist had suggested, resulting in guests who were pleased with their decision to stay.

THE PROBLEM OF FULL-SERVICE FUNCTIONS

One area in which managers and owners still felt overly vulnerable concerned guarantees for functions held at the hotel. They were particularly concerned about the implied obligation to refund the entire cost of a full-service function (e.g., a meeting or wedding banquet) when the guarantee was invoked for any reason. For instance, should customer dissatisfaction with the set-up of a meeting room require a refund of the entire fee? Should the entire wedding banquet fee be refunded because coffee was delivered late? Senior Promus executives debated how best to address these concerns within the spirit of the 100% Satisfaction Guarantee.

Questions for Discussion

1. Evaluate the philosophy behind introduction of the 100% Satisfaction Guarantee. Is this the best way to improve service quality?

2. What are the implications of the 100% Satisfaction Guarantee for (a) guests, (b) managers, (c) owners of hotel buildings, (d) Promus?

3. Since certain events are "uncontrollable," wouldn't it be more realistic to exclude such events from the guarantee?

4. As a member of the Promus senior management team, how would you address hotel managers' concerns about applying guarantees to full-service functions?

Red Lobster

"It felt like a knife going through me!" declared Mary Campbell, 53, after she was fired from her waitressing job at a restaurant in the Red Lobster chain. But instead of suing for what she considered unfair dismissal after 19 years of service, Campbell called for a peer review, seeking to recover her job and three weeks of lost wages.

Three weeks after the firing, a panel of employees from different Red Lobster restaurants was reviewing the evidence and trying to determine whether the server had, in fact, been unjustly fired for allegedly stealing a guest comment card completed by a couple of customers whom she had served.

PEER REVIEW AT DARDEN INDUSTRIES

Red Lobster was owned by Darden Industries, which also owned another large restaurant chain known as the Olive Garden and had a total of 110,000 employees. The company had adopted peer review of disputed employee firings and disciplinary actions in 1994. Key objectives were to limit workers' lawsuits and ease workplace tensions. Advocates of this approach, which had also been adopted at several other companies, believed that it was very effective in channeling in constructive ways the pain and anger that employees felt after being fired or disciplined by their managers. By reducing the incidence of lawsuits, a company could also save on legal expenses.

A Darden spokesperson stated that the peer review program had been "tremendously successful" in keeping valuable employees from unfair dismissal. Each year, about 100 disputes ended up in peer review, with only 10 resulting in lawsuits. Red Lobster managers and many employees also credited peer review with reducing racial tensions. Campbell, who said she had received dozens of calls of support, chose peer review over a lawsuit not only because it was much cheaper but also because "I liked the idea of being judged by people who know how things work in a little restaurant."

THE EVIDENCE

The review panel included a general manager, an assistant manager, a server, a hostess, and a bartender, who had all volunteered to review the circumstances of Campbell's firing. Each panelist had received peer review training and was receiving regular wages plus travel expenses. The instructions to panelists were simply to do what they felt was fair.

This case was prepared by Christopher Lovelock. It is based on a story by Margaret A. Jacobs, "Red Lobster Tale: Peers Decide Fired Waitress's Fate," *The Wall Street Journal*, 20 January 1998. Personal names have been changed.

Mary Campbell had been fired by Jean Larimer, the general manager of the Red Lobster in Marston, where the former worked as a restaurant server. The reason given for the firing was that Campbell had asked the restaurant's hostess, Eve Taunton, for the key to the guest comment box and had stolen a card from it. The card had been completed by a couple of guests whom Campbell had served and who seemed dissatisfied with their experience at the restaurant. Subsequently, the guests learned that their comment card, which complained that their prime rib of beef was too rare and their waitress was "uncooperative," had been removed from the box.

Jean Larimer's Testimony

Larimer, who supervised 100 full- and part-time employees, testified that she had dismissed Campbell after one of the two customers complained angrily to her and her supervisor. "She [the guest] felt violated because her card was taken from the box and her complaint about the food had been ignored." Larimer drew the panel's attention to the company rule book, pointing out that Campbell had violated the policy that forbade removal of company property.

Mary Campbell's Testimony

Campbell testified that the female customer had requested that her prime rib be cooked "well done" and subsequently complained that it was fatty and undercooked. The waitress politely suggested that "prime rib always has fat on it" but arranged to have the meat cooked some more. However, the woman still seemed unhappy with the food. After pouring steak sauce over the meat, she then pushed away her plate without eating it all. When the customer remained displeased, Cambell offered a free dessert. But the guests left after paying the bill, filling out the guest comment card, and dropping it in the box. Admitting that she was consumed by curiosity, Campbell asked Eve Taunton, the restaurant's hostess, for the key to the box. After removing and reading the card, she pocketed it. Her intent, she declared, was to show the card to Larimer, who had been concerned earlier that the prime rib served at the restaurant was overcooked, not undercooked. However, she forgot about the card and later, accidentally, threw it out.

Eve Taunton's Testimony

At the time of the firing, Taunton was a 17-year-old student, working at Red Lobster for the summer. "I didn't think it was a big deal to give her [Campbell] the key," she said. "A lot of people would come up to me to get it."

THE PANEL DELIBERATES

Having heard the testimony, the members of the review panel had to decide whether Ms. Larimer had been justified in firing Ms. Campbell. The panelists' initial reactions were split by rank, with the hourly workers supporting Campbell and the managers supporting Larimer. But then the debate began in earnest in an effort to reach consensus.

Questions for Discussion

1. Evaluate the concept of peer review. What are its strengths and weaknesses? What type of environment is required to make it work well?
2. Review the evidence. Do you believe the testimony presented?
3. What decision would you make and why?

Menton Bank

"I'm concerned about Karen," said Margaret Costanzo to David Reeves. Costanzo was a vice president of Menton Bank and manager of the Victory Square branch, the third largest in Menton's 292-branch network. Reeves, the branch's customer service director, was responsible for coordinating the work of the customer service representatives (CSRs, formerly known as tellers) and the customer assistance representatives (CARs, formerly known as new accounts assistants).

Costanzo and Reeves were discussing Karen Mitchell, a 24-year-old CSR who had applied for the soon-to-be-vacant position of head CSR. Mitchell had been with the bank for three and a half years. She had applied for the position of what had then been called head teller a year earlier, but the job had gone to a candidate with more seniority. Now that individual was leaving—his wife had been transferred to a new job in another city—and the position was once again open. Two other candidates had also applied.

Both Costanzo and Reeves were agreed that according to all the criteria used in the past, Mitchell would have been the obvious choice. She was both fast and accurate in her work, presented a smart and professional appearance, and was well liked by customers and her fellow CSRs. However, the nature of the teller's job had been significantly revised nine months earlier to add a stronger marketing component. They were now required to stimulate customer interest in the broadening array of financial services offered by the bank. "The problem with Karen," as Reeves put it, "is that she simply refuses to sell."

THE NEW FOCUS ON CUSTOMER SERVICE

Facing aggressive competition for retail business from other financial institutions, Menton Bank had taken a number of steps in recent years to strengthen its position. In particular, it had invested heavily in technology, installing the latest generation of automated teller machines (ATMs) and 24-hour automated telephone banking. Customers could also call a central customer service office to speak with a bank representative about service questions or problems with their accounts, as well as to request new account applications or new checkbooks, which would be sent by mail. Recently, Menton had introduced home banking through the Internet. Complementing these new channels was a variety of new retail financial products. Finally, the appearance of the branches was being improved, and a recently implemented pilot program was testing the impact of a radical redesign of the branch interior on the quality of customer service. As more customers switched to electronic banking, the bank planned to close a number of its smaller branches.

In the most recent six months, Menton had seen a significant increase in the number of new accounts opened, as compared to the same period of the previous year. Also, quarterly survey data showed that the bank was steadily increasing its share of new deposits in the region.

CUSTOMER SERVICE ISSUES

Bank officers had found that existing "platform" staff—known as new accounts assistants—were ill equipped to sell many of the new products now offered because they lacked product knowledge and skills in selling. As Costanzo recalled,

> The problem was that they were so used to sitting at their desks waiting for a customer to approach them with a specific request, such as a mortgage or car loan, that it was hard to get them to take a more positive approach that involved actively probing for customer needs. Their whole job seemed to revolve around filling out forms.

Prepared by Christopher H. Lovelock.

Internal research showed that the mix of activities performed by tellers was starting to change. More customers were using the ATMs and automated telephone banking for a broad array of transactions, including cash withdrawals and deposits (from the ATMs), transfers of funds between accounts, and a review of account balances. As home banking caught on, this trend was expected to accelerate. But Costanzo noted that customers who were older or less well educated still seemed to prefer "being served by a real person, rather than a machine."

Three sites were included in the pilot test of "new look" branches, featuring a redesigned interior. One was the Victory Square branch, located in a busy commercial and retail area, about one mile from the central business district and less than 10-minutes' walk from the campus of a major university. The other test branches were in two different metropolitan areas and were located in a shopping mall and next to a big hospital, respectively.

Each of these three branches had previously been remodeled to include at least five ATMs (Victory Square had seven), which could be closed off from the rest of the branch so that they would remain accessible to customers 24 hours a day. Further remodeling was then undertaken to locate a customer service desk near the entrance; close to each desk were two electronic information terminals, featuring color touch screens that customers could activate to obtain information on a variety of banking services. The teller stations were redesigned to provide two levels of service: an express station for simple deposits and cashing of approved checks, and regular stations for the full array of services provided by tellers. The number of stations open at a given time was varied to reflect the volume of anticipated business, and staffing arrangements were changed to ensure that more tellers were on hand to serve customers during the busiest periods.

HUMAN RESOURCES

With the new environment came new staff training programs and new job titles. Frontline staff at all Menton branches received new job descriptions and job titles: customer assistance representatives (for the platform staff), customer service representatives (for the tellers), and customer service director (instead of assistant branch manager). The head teller position was renamed head CSR. The training program for each group began with staff from the three test branches and was being extended to all. It included information about both new and existing retail products (CARs received more extensive training in this area than did CSRs). The CARs also attended a 15-hour course, offered in three separate sessions, on basic selling skills. This program covered key steps in the sales process, including building a relationship, exploring customers' needs, determining a solution, and overcoming objections.

The sales training program for CSRs, in contrast, consisted of just two 2-hour sessions designed to develop skills in recognizing and probing customers' needs, presenting product features and benefits, overcoming objections, and referring customers to CARs. All front-office staff were taught how to improve their communication skills and professional image: Clothing, personal grooming, and interactions with customers were all discussed. Said the trainer, "Remember, people's money is too important to entrust to someone who doesn't look and act the part!"

The CARs were instructed to rise from their seats and shake hands with customers. Both CARs and CSRs were given exercises designed to improve their listening skills and their powers of observation. All employees who were working where they could be seen by customers were ordered to refrain from drinking soda and chewing gum on the job.

Although Menton Bank's management anticipated that most of the increased emphasis on selling would fall to the CSRs, they also foresaw a limited selling role for the CSRs, who would be expected to mention various products and facilities offered by the bank as they served customers at the teller windows. For instance, if a customer happened to say something about an upcoming vacation, the CSR was supposed to mention traveler's checks; if a customer complained about bounced checks, the CSR should recommend speaking to a CAR about opening a personal line of credit that would provide automatic overdraft protection; and if a customer mentioned investments, the CSR was expected to refer him or her to a CAR who could provide information on money market accounts, certificates of deposit, or Menton's discount brokerage service. All CSRs were supplied with their own business cards. When making a referral, they were expected to write the customer's name and the product of interest on the back of a card, give it to the customer, and send that individual to the customer assistance desks.

To motivate CSRs to sell specific financial products, the bank decided to change the process under which employees at the three test branches were evaluated. All CSRs had traditionally been evaluated twice yearly on a variety of criteria, including accuracy, speed, quality of interactions with customers, punctuality, job attitudes, cooperation with other employees, and professional image. The evaluation process assigned a number of points to each criterion, with accuracy and speed being the most heavily weighted. In addition to appraisals by the customer service director and the branch manager, with input from the head CSR, Menton had recently instituted a program of anonymous visits by what was popularly known as the "mystery client." Each CSR was visited at least once a quarter by a professional evaluator, posing as a customer. This individual's appraisal of the CSR's appearance, performance, and attitude was included in the overall evaluation. The number of points scored by each CSR had a direct impact on merit pay raises and on selection for promotion to the head CSR position or to platform jobs.

To encourage improved product knowledge and consultative selling by CSRs, the evaluation process was revised to include points assigned for each individual's success in sales referrals. Under the new evaluation scheme, the maximum number of points assigned for effectiveness in making sales—directly or through referrals to CARs— amounted to 30 percent of the potential total score. Although CSR-initiated sales had risen significantly in the most recent half year, Reeves sensed that morale had dropped among this group, in contrast to the CARs, whose enthusiasm and commitment had risen significantly. He had also noticed an increase in CSR errors. One CSR had quit, complaining about too much pressure.

Karen Mitchell

Under the old scoring system, Karen Mitchell had been the highest scoring teller/CSR for four consecutive half-year periods. But after 12 months under the new system, her ranking had dropped to fourth out of the seven full-time tellers. The top-ranking CSR, Mary Bell, had been with Menton Bank for 16 years but had declined repeated invitations to apply for a head teller position, saying that she was happy where she was, earning at the top of the CSR scale, and did not want "the extra worry and responsibility." Mitchell ranked first on all but one of the operationally related criteria (interactions with customers, where she ranked second) but sixth on selling effectiveness (Exhibit 1).

Costanzo and Reeves had spoken to Mitchell about her performance and expressed disappointment. Mitchell had informed them, respectfully but firmly, that she saw the most important aspect of her job as giving customers fast, accurate, and courteous service:

> *I did try this selling thing but it just seemed to annoy people. Some said they were in a hurry and couldn't talk now; others looked at me as if I were slightly crazy to bring up the subject of a different bank service than the one they were currently transacting. And then, when you got the odd person who seemed interested, you could hear the other customers in the line grumbling about the slow service.*

CSR Name[c]	Length of Full-Time Bank Service	Operational Criteria[a] (max.: 70 points)		Selling Effectiveness[b] (max.: 30 points)		Total Score	
		1st Half	2nd Half	1st Half	2nd Half	1st Half	2nd Half
Mary Bell	16 years, 10 months	65	64	16	20	81	84
Scott Dubois	2 years, 3 months	63	61	15	19	78	80
Bruce Greenfield	12 months	48	42	20	26	68	68
Karen Mitchell	3 years, 7 months	67	67	13	12	80	79
Sharon Rubin	1 year, 4 months	53	55	8	9	61	64
Swee Hoon Chen	7 months	–	50	–	22	–	72
Jean Warshawski	2 years, 1 month	57	55	21	28	79	83

[a]Totals were based on sum of ratings points against various criteria, including accuracy, work production, attendance and punctuality, personal appearance, organization of work, initiative, cooperation with others, problem-solving ability, and quality of interaction with customers.
[b]Points were awarded for both direct sales by CSR (e.g., traveler's checks) and referral selling by CSR to CAR (e.g., debit card, certificates of deposit, and personal line of credit).
[c]These were full-time CSRs only (part-time CSRs were evaluated separately).

EXHIBIT 1

Menton Bank: Summary of Performance Evaluation Scores for Customer Service Representatives at Victory Square Branch for Latest Two Half-Year Periods

Really, the last straw was when I noticed on the computer screen that this woman had several thousand in her savings account so I suggested to her, just as the trainer had told us, that she could earn more interest if she opened a money market account. Well, she told me it was none of my business what she did with her money, and stomped off. Don't get me wrong, I love being able to help customers, and if they ask for my advice, I'll gladly tell them about what the bank has to offer.

Selecting a New Head CSR

Two weeks after this meeting, it was announced that the head CSR was leaving. The job entailed some supervision of the work of the other CSRs (including allocation of work assignments and scheduling part-time CSRs at busy periods or during employees' vacations), consultation on—and, where possible, resolution of—any problems occurring at the teller stations, and handling of large cash deposits and withdrawals by local retailers. When not engaged on such tasks, the head CSR was expected to operate a regular teller window.

The pay scale for a head CSR ranged from $9.00 to $14.50 per hour, depending on qualifications, seniority, and branch size; CSRs earned $6.80 to $11.00 per hour, and CARs earned $7.70 to $12.90. Full-time employees (who were not unionized) worked a 40-hour week, including some evenings until 6 P.M. and certain Saturday mornings. Costanzo indicated that the pay scales were typical for banks in the region, although the average CSR at Menton was better qualified than those at smaller banks and therefore higher on the scale. Mitchell was currently earning $9.90 per hour, reflecting her education, which included a diploma in business administration, three-and-a-half years' experience, and significant past merit increases. If promoted to head CSR, she would qualify for an initial rate of $11.60 an hour. When applications for the positions closed, Mitchell was one of three candidates. The other two candidates were Jean Warshawski, 42, another CSR at the Victory Square branch; and Curtis Richter, 24, the head CSR at one of Menton Bank's small suburban branches, who was seeking more responsibility.

Warshawski was married, with two sons in school. She had started working as a part-time teller at Victory Square some three years previously, switching to full-time work a year later in order, as she said, to put away some money for her boys' college education. Warshawski was a cheerful woman with a jolly laugh. She had a wonderful memory for people's names, and Reeves had often seen her greeting customers on the street or in a restaurant during her lunch hour. Reviewing her evaluations over the previous three years, Reeves noted that she had initially performed poorly on accuracy, and at one point, when she was still a part-timer, had been put on probation because of frequent inaccuracies in the balance in her cash drawer at the end of the day. Although Reeves considered her much improved on this score, he still saw room for improvement. The customer service director had also had occasion to reprimand her for tardiness during the past year. Warshawski attributed this to health problems with her elder son, who, she said, was now responding to treatment.

Both Reeves and Costanzo had observed Warshawski at work and agreed that her interactions with customers were exceptionally good, although she tended to be overly chatty and was not as fast as Mitchell. She seemed to have a natural ability to size up customers and to decide which ones were good prospects for a quick sales pitch on a specific financial product. Although slightly untidy in her personal appearance, she was very well organized in her work and was quick to help her fellow CSRs, especially new ones. She was currently earning $8.80 per hour as a CSR and would qualify for a rate of $11.00 as head CSR. In the most recent six months, Warshawski was ranked ahead of Mitchell as a result of being very successful in consultative selling (Exhibit 1, p. 411).

Richter, the third candidate, was not working in one of the three test branches, so had not been exposed to the consultative selling program and its corresponding evaluation scheme. However, he had received excellent evaluations for his work in Menton's small Longmeadow branch, where he had been employed for three years. A move to Victory Square would increase his earnings from $9.50 to $11.20 per hour. Reeves and Costanzo had interviewed Richter and considered him intelligent and personable. He had joined the bank after dropping out of college midway through his third year but had recently started taking evening courses to complete his degree. The Longmeadow branch was located in an older part of town, where commercial and retail activity was rather stagnant. This branch (which was rumored to be under consideration for closure) had not yet been renovated and had no ATMs, although there was an ATM accessible to Menton customers one block away. Richter supervised three CSRs and reported directly to the branch manager, who spoke very highly of him. Because there were no CARs in this branch, Richter and another experienced CSR took turns in handling new accounts and loan or mortgage applications.

Costanzo and Reeves were troubled by the decision that faced them. Before the bank's shift in focus, Mitchell would have been the natural choice for the head CSR job, which in turn could be a stepping stone to further promotions, including customer assistance representative, customer service director, and eventually manager of a small branch or a management position in the head office. Mitchell had told her superiors that she was interested in making a career in banking and that she was eager to take on further responsibilities.

Compounding the problem was the fact that the three branches that were testing the improved branch design and new customer service program had just completed a full year. Costanzo knew that sales and profits were up significantly at all three branches, relative to the bank's performance as a whole. She anticipated that top management would want to extend the program systemwide after making any modifications that seemed desirable.

Questions for Discussion

1. Identify the steps taken by Menton Bank to develop a stronger customer orientation.

2. Compare and contrast the jobs of CAR and CSR. How important is each to (a) bank operations and (b) customer satisfaction?

3. Evaluate the strengths and weaknesses of Karen Mitchell and other candidates for head CSR.

4. What action do you recommend for filling the position of head CSR?

Museum of Fine Arts, Boston

It was a sunny July day at Boston's Museum of Fine Arts (MFA). Patricia B. Jacoby, deputy director for marketing and development, was lunching with colleagues in the museum's outdoor restaurant and reflecting on the progress made in building up marketing capabilities during the past three years. Sipping her iced tea, she reminded her colleagues of the challenges facing the MFA at the start of a new fiscal year.

> *It's not enough to say that we now have a marketing orientation at the MFA. We must live this orientation through our behavior, as part of our everyday operations. We have to maintain the momentum in our dealings with all the museum's stakeholders—members, current and prospective visitors, the local community, staff, trustees and overseers, volunteers and, of course, the media.*

BACKGROUND

By the late 1990s, Boston's Museum of Fine Arts could boast a permanent collection that ranked it among the best in the United States. *Connoisseur's World* magazine described it as second in quality and scope only to the holdings of New York's Metropolitan Museum of Art. Many art experts saw the MFA as having world-class collections in such fields as French Impressionist paintings; American paintings and decorative arts; Egyptian, classical Greek, and Asian arts; and European silver. However, its modern and contemporary art holdings were generally held to be less significant.

Founded in 1870, the museum was located one mile west of Boston's fashionable Back Bay area and two miles from downtown. There was good access by bus and rapid transit and paid parking was available. Adjacent was the School of the Museum of Fine Arts. The MFA's public facilities included two restaurants, a self-service cafeteria, a large retail store, auditoriums for lectures and other presentations, and two recently renovated outdoor garden courts. Behind the scenes were storage areas, workshops, library facilities, and offices.

Unlike many major American museums, the MFA received no ongoing support from city, state, or federal funds. Government grants were limited to special projects. The basic admissions fee was $10; students and senior citizens paid $8, while accompanied children aged 17 and under entered free. Wednesday evenings were free to all, but donations were welcomed. An admission surcharge was sometimes imposed for major exhibitions. But museum members, who paid an annual fee, could enter without charge at any time.

In mid-1997, the museum employed 700 staff members, divided into three broad areas: curatorial and collections; development and marketing; and operations. The three deputy directors in charge of these areas reported to Malcolm Rogers, the museum's director. In turn, Rogers was responsible to the board of trustees. The MFA also benefited from the services of a large volunteer staff.

The MFA's curators, whom some likened to university faculty (although none had tenure), worked within departments organized around specific art fields and had both programmatic and project responsibilities. Their programmatic tasks involved knowing, managing, and shaping the museum's collections, a role that involved working closely with scholars, collectors, and colleagues and also participating in outside professional activities. Project responsibilities included developing exhibitions, selecting the works of art to display, and deciding how to present them. Curators also presented and interpreted the museum's permanent collection, wrote publications, and conducted lectures and gallery talks.

Prepared by Christopher H. Lovelock. Copyright © 1998 by the J. Paul Getty Trust.

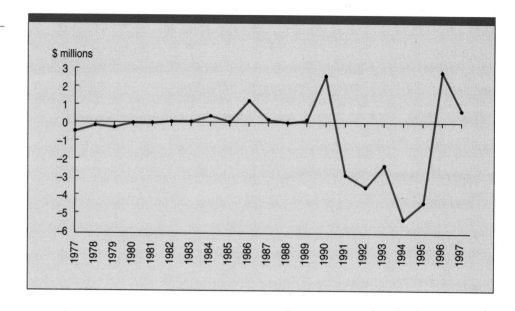

For the fiscal year ending 30 June, 1997, the MFA's operating revenues were $85.2 million (including $12.8 million from the Museum School). After deducting operating expenses, the MFA had ended the year with an estimated surplus of $0.7 million, which would be applied to rebuilding reserves. Exhibit 1 provides a 20-year summary of MFA financial results; Exhibit 2 shows 20-year attendance numbers.

Recent History

During the past quarter-century, the MFA had experienced mixed fortunes. In the late 1960s and early 1970s, it was viewed by some observers as elitist and poorly managed. People accused the MFA of hoarding its remarkable collections, much of them in stor-

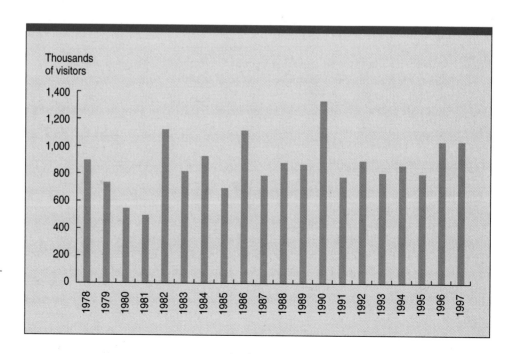

age, rather than inviting visitors to come inside and enjoy them. In 1976, Jan Fontein, curator of the Asiatic Department, was named director of the museum and an experienced manager appointed as deputy director in charge of the institution's business affairs. At its close in 1987, Fontein's 11-year tenure was described as "a huge success" by *The Boston Globe*, which noted:

> The sleepy, dusty mausoleum of the 1960s today is like a thriving city center, bursting with special exhibitions, lectures, and concerts. The shop and restaurants are packed and the line of cars waiting to get in stretches around the block.

The MFA's financial situation improved sharply under Fontein, with the operating results moving into surplus. Reflecting improved marketing and development efforts (aided by a booming economy), donations rose significantly, membership almost tripled over 10 years to 41,049 in 1985–86, and retail and catalog sales leaped from $0.9 million to $11.4 million over the same period. Several "blockbuster" exhibitions fueled the growth in admissions, including *Pompeii: AD 79* (1978), *The Search for Alexander* (1981–82), and *Renoir* (1985–86). Admissions fees rose from $1.75 in 1976 to $4.00 in 1983. The most visible change at the MFA was the new West Wing, which included the Gund Gallery, designed to house large exhibitions.

Reflecting the tighter financial controls and budgetary discipline imposed by the associate director's office, costs were held in check—despite inflation and the greater demands of an enlarged physical plant. The associate director (who left in 1989) also emphasized the need for strategic planning and a stronger marketing orientation.

Fontein was succeeded as director by Alan Shestack, a distinguished art scholar. Shestack served six years as director of the MFA, resigning in September 1993 to become deputy director of the National Gallery of Art in Washington. One highlight of his tenure was the exhibition *Monet in the 90s*, which attracted 537,502 visitors to become the best attended exhibition ever staged at the MFA.

On other fronts, however, these were difficult years. An extended recession hurt fund raising and left the museum with continued heavy indebtedness. Although the Monet show contributed to an operating surplus of $2.4 million in 1989–90, the MFA's financial situation deteriorated sharply thereafter. The previous associate director had left and his successor focused actively on cost cutting, including staff layoffs. An important symbol of the museum's straitened circumstances was the decision in 1991 to close the original grand entrance on Huntington Avenue, thus yielding annual savings of some $100,000. However, critics noted that the MFA was literally closing its face to the local community and leaving only one remaining entrance for visitors on a side street. In a further cost savings, opening hours for visitors were cut back and expenditures on development and public information were sharply curtailed. Yet the annual operating deficit continued to rise, exceeding $5 million in 1993–94 (Exhibit 1, p. 414).

The museum's financial difficulties were compounded by poor budgeting. The MFA had failed to develop a base budget that identified the base number of visitors it could expect, and to prepare incremental budgets for specific projects and exhibitions.

A New Director Arrives

In June 1994, the board appointed Malcolm Rogers, 45, an Oxford educated British art historian who was then deputy director of the National Portrait Gallery in London. Among his many talents was proven skill as a fund raiser. State support for the arts in the United Kingdom had declined sharply, requiring British museums to cut costs but raise funds from corporate and private donors; Rogers had done this with great success. The National Portrait Gallery was also known for its successful merchandising operation, which had brought in substantial revenues and taken the gallery's name around the world.

Arriving in Boston, Rogers found a dispirited institution. Reflecting financial difficulties and recent staff cutbacks, morale was low. Corporate memberships had slumped and attendance had declined since the heady year of the Monet show. The new director lost no time in making his presence felt. One of his first acts was to throw a breakfast for the entire staff. Addressing the crowd, he introduced what would become a central theme:

> We are one museum, not a collection of departments. The museum consists of security guards, curators, technicians, benefactors, volunteers, public relations personnel. We all have our individual professional expertise. And by working cooperatively with colleagues, we all have areas that can be improved.

Rogers's "one museum" theme, repeated at frequent intervals, sent the message that the director's agenda took precedence over that of the traditionally independent curators in terms of setting priorities for acquisitions and exhibitions. The curator of contemporary art subsequently resigned. While recognized for his good humor and friendly, outgoing manner, the new director also showed that he could be blunt and decisive. To address the deficit, he took a tough line with expenditures and began a program to cut staff size by 20 percent.

DEVELOPING A STRONGER MARKETING ORIENTATION

The director's cutbacks did not extend to services for museum visitors. Instead, he set about creating a more welcoming environment. Said Rogers:

> I'm firmly committed to the idea that museums are here to serve the community, and that's going to be one of the keynotes of my work here in Boston—to encourage the MFA to turn out toward its public and to satisfy as broad a constituency as possible.

Early in his tenure, Rogers reopened the Huntington Avenue entrance, making a major publicity event out of the occasion. He reversed the trend of curtailing admission hours. Daily schedules were gradually extended and seven-day operations instituted. On three evenings a week, the museum remained open until almost 10 P.M., with the staff working to make Friday nights at the museum a popular venue for a younger crowd. To mark the 125th anniversary, Rogers initiated a policy of "Community Days," opening the museum free of charge on three Sundays each year. The Education Department offered free programs throughout the day on these occasions.

In each subsequent year, Rogers undertook other, high-profile activities to improve the museum's facilities and image. He raised funds to restore a derelict interior courtyard and installed new exterior lighting for better display of the MFA's imposing facade at night to passersby on busy Huntington Avenue. A second garden courtyard was opened, while the restaurant was extended and a new roof-top terrace added. Making the MFA an evening destination of choice, especially for people living in or close to the city, was another of Rogers's objectives. The broader variety of exhibitions (to encourage multiple visits per year), the upgrading of the restaurants, and the improvement in the museum's overall atmosphere were all designed to help achieve this goal. Rogers enjoyed a much higher public profile than his predecessors. Said Pat Jacoby: "Malcolm personifies marketing: He's accessible, he's an advocate of PR, he cares about the visitors, and he believes that the MFA can set the standard for other museums."

As director, Rogers selected a mix of exhibitions that combined high scholarly content with popular appeal. He believed that museums of the MFA's size and stature needed to mount accessible and popular shows on a regular basis. Rogers's view, shared by the senior staff, was that one show in five should be of a blockbuster nature, which meant hosting such an exhibition at least once every two years. In early 1997, the director personally championed the popular but controversial exhibition, *Herb Ritts: Works*, featuring the black-and-white photographs of the Los Angeles–based artist.

On the other hand, Rogers also recognized the importance of displaying art from the MFA's permanent collection to best advantage, including small revolving shows in a designated gallery. The new curator of European paintings had recently rehung all 15 European galleries in innovative ways designed to stimulate the audience and engage them more actively. The project included new, user-friendly descriptions of the paintings, with captions printed in a larger font and using everyday language rather than heavy academic prose. Commenting on blockbuster shows, the curator noted, "The big shows do bring people to the permanent collection. But the big show is a monster that museums have created. Linking a museum's health to its spectacular exhibitions is a problem."

The Marketing Organization

Overall responsibility for marketing-related activities at the MFA was in the hands of Patricia B. Jacoby, who held the recently created position of deputy director for marketing and development. Jacoby, whose background was in development and external relations, had joined the museum in 1991. She created a team to work on marketing issues throughout the museum: herself, Paul Bessire, associate director of marketing, Dawn Griffin, director of public relations, and Bill Wondriska, senior marketing consultant. Wondriska described the team's work as follows:

Marketing is more than a narrow set of ideas, expressions, and applications. In its broadest sense, it's everything that carries the signature of the institution, how it presents itself both externally, to its guests, and internally, to its staff. We have to ensure that the external strategy is supported by those who work here. We have a multitude of experiences to communicate, but we're trying to speak with a single voice.

Griffin aimed to create the sense that "there's always something going on here. With the variety of programming that we offer, we can appeal to adults and children: 'There's something for *you!*'" Underlying all this was the element of quality, so that people might expect something worth coming to see.

Jacoby and her colleagues were concerned to ensure that the MFA should make itself a welcoming place that visitors found accessible. She had established a department of visitor services, hiring the former chief concierge at the Four Seasons Hotel in Beverly Hills to create a commitment to customer service among the guards, the information booth attendants, the ticket sellers, and everyone who worked with the customers. In another new departure, the MFA commissioned development of a Web site (www.mfa.org), which provided information about the museum and its exhibitions.

In fall 1996, a trustee marketing committee was formed, with membership drawn from all areas of the museum. Objectives included (1) becoming familiar with museum priorities that related to accessibility, new audiences, and the visitor experience; (2) developing a thorough understanding of marketing goals, objectives, strategies, and evaluations; (3) offering advice concerning the marketing program; (4) reviewing the marketing plan and budget and conveying recommendations to the budget and finance committee; and (5) becoming informed advocates for the marketing program and MFA itself. The chair of the committee, Stephen A. Greyser, a marketing professor at the Harvard Business School, believed that museums and other arts organizations should be "mission driven, but market sensitive—blending a strong and clear sense of mission with professional marketing strategy, plans, and programs." He saw effective marketing as a way to help "animate the whole organization" as well as outside target audiences, anticipating that the MFA could reach out to new audiences while also attracting more frequent visits from existing attendees.

At one meeting, a committee member urged the group to focus on making MFA exhibitions "fun and exciting experiences," whereupon a curator expressed discomfort with the word "fun," although she conceded that some exhibitions might be more entertaining than others.

At the MFA, as at other major museums, curators were sometimes uncomfortable with marketing activities. As the deputy director for curatorial affairs explained, promotional activities often overemphasized the most popular and familiar objects at the expense of the most artistically significant, thus giving an unbalanced impression of the collection or exhibition:

> *In a very real sense, the need to stimulate attendance undercuts the educational message (of course, getting people in the door provides the opportunity to deliver that message). Many curators have a hard time understanding why, at some elemental level, the general public don't perceive the magic in the works of art that they do. The reality that the general visitor brings far less to the interaction with a work of art than a highly trained curator often results in the perception that marketing "dumbs down" the object, the project, and the institution. At worst, willfulness on each side undercuts the other, and nasty comments all around are the result. By contrast, in the best possible case, communication and involvement from both sides about goals and means of achieving them, and the explicit acknowledgment of criteria used to come to a solution, ought to create understanding and a positive working relationship.*

The Museum Audience

To understand better the MFA's existing audience, a detailed visitor study was commissioned in 1995. This study involved conducting 100 interviews per month for a total of 12 months. Randomly selected adult visitors were targeted as they exited the museum. Neither school groups nor tour groups (which collectively accounted for one eighth of all museum visitors) were included in these surveys. Goals included obtaining baseline information on demographics, reasons for first and repeat visits, what visitors saw and did at the MFA, and how they experienced the museum. The intention was to use these data to help develop a strategy for increasing attendance. Highlights of the findings, and a comparison with a previous study in 1987, appear in Exhibit 3.

EXHIBIT 3

Museum of Fine Arts:
Highlights of Findings from
1996 and 1987 Visitor
Studies

Demographics
- Visitors to the Museum are still predominantly female, White, affluent and older; Asian visitors are still the single largest group among minority visitors.
- Sixty percent of visitors continue to be drawn from within Massachusetts; New England states, New York, California, and international remain the largest tourist draws.

Members
- Members are more affluent than the average visitor.
- In terms of benefits, members overwhelmingly continue to value unlimited free admission, discount at the Museum Shop, and subscription to *Preview* magazine.

Time & Money Spent
- Although the median number of visits "in the past 12 months" has gone down from 3.8 to 2 visits, visitors today spend the same amount of time (2.5 hours on average) at the Museum as they did in 1987.
- A high percent of visitors still spend money on things other than admission. Spending levels remain highest at the cafe/restaurant and at the Museum Shop.

MFA Collection
- No one part of the Museum dominates as visitors continue to express an interest in a wide range of the Museum's collection. Their reasons for visiting are as varied as the Museum's collection.

Improvements
- Most visitors, then as now, feel positive about the MFA. However, many are still dissatisfied with signage and the difficulties in finding their way around. Visitors continue to want more benches/seating areas in the exhibit halls and around the Museum.
- Unprompted complaints about parking have increased since 1987.

To attract financial support and encourage more frequent visits, the MFA had developed an extensive membership program, with different categories offering an increasing scale of benefits. For instance, a $50 individual membership allowed free admission, whereas a sustaining membership of $900 included invitations to selected opening receptions, reciprocal membership benefits at 21 major art museums around the United States, special programs with curatorial staff, and acknowledgment by name in the annual report. Larger donors received additional privileges. Membership revenues had risen at a much faster rate than the number of members in recent years. In 1996–97, members accounted for 231,000 of the 1.1 million visits recorded at the museum.

Enterprise Activities

In addition to operating revenues from admission fees, memberships, and unrestricted endowment income, the MFA obtained substantial revenues from merchandising and other services collectively known as "Enterprise" activities. In 1996–97, merchandise sales through the museum shop and other channels amounted to $39.5 million. After deducting cost of goods sold and other costs associated with merchandise operations, the MFA realized a net contribution of $1.9 million. Similarly, food service yielded a contribution of $0.8 million on sales of $5.3 million. Parking fees yielded revenues of $1.6 million, but not all related costs, such as security, were broken out separately.

Responsibility for all these activities rested with John Stanley, deputy director of operations. Discussing merchandising, Stanley declared:

We see merchandising as central to the mission of the museum for both philosophical and legal reasons. If we sell items that are unrelated to our collection, we will be liable for unrelated business income tax and will lose our not-for-profit postal rate for mailing items purchased from our catalog.

Merchandise sales included jewelry, children's toys, decorative arts (such as posters, pictures, book ends, and vases), books, and paper products like calendars and note cards. More than half of all sales were catalog orders, handled through the MFA's distribution center outside the city. The main museum store, soon to be expanded, accounted for about 20 percent of sales. A small exhibition shop outside the Gund Gallery catered to visitors attending special exhibitions. There were five satellite stores within the Greater Boston area: Two in central Boston did particularly well because they were located in popular tourist areas. Three other stores (one under construction) were located in sub-urban shopping malls. Planning for merchandise keyed to upcoming exhibitions required a long lead time, because commissioning new items might require as much as two years' advance notification to suppliers.

Development and Sponsorship

A capital campaign had been launched in 1992. The goal of $110 million was designed to boost annual operating support and the museum's endowment, not to finance new construction projects or to fund new acquisitions. Support had been broad, and the campaign was expected to meet or even exceed its target by the closing date of June 1998. Jacoby noted that revenues from the enlarged endowment would eliminate the structural deficit once the campaign was completed.

Rogers was a firm believer in securing corporate sponsorship for exhibitions and other activities. Jacoby observed:

Malcolm is willing to try new things. He's willing to put a corporate logo on the museum banner, if need be, to underwrite an exhibition. Bell Atlantic is underwriting the Picasso show this fall with a million dollars, while Fleet Bank is underwriting the new Monet show the following year with $1.2 million. As hackneyed as the word "partnership" has *become, I think he really understands the concept. He's willing to meet a sponsor half-way, to try to understand their needs as well as the museum's needs and to make things work, rather than saying, "Oh no, we're too pure to display a corporate logo!"*

The MFA had received both funding and marketing assistance for its exhibitions from corporate sponsors. In 1996, a large bank had supported an exhibition of works by Winslow Homer, a popular 19th century American artist. The bank not only donated a large sum to help mount the exhibition, but also offered its customers a credit card featuring a Homer image and promoted Homer within its branches, in mailed statement inserts, and on its ATMs. The exhibition had been very successful, attracting some 270,000 visitors. But critics, including some curators, felt that such actions smacked too much of commercialism. One member of the marketing team commented, "That's always going to happen when you push the envelope."

The Herb Ritts Exhibition

Few major shows at the MFA had generated as much controversy as *Herb Ritts: Works.* It was championed by Malcolm Rogers, who hoped that it would appeal to a wide audience, from newcomers to frequent visitors to the museum. Ritts, 44, had made his name as a photographer of both fashion and celebrities. His images were widely featured in publications such as *Vogue* and *Vanity Fair.* Additionally, he had shaped corporate advertising campaigns for many well-known fashion houses and cosmetics firms. Recently, he had begun directing commercials and music videos.

The exhibition—which would also be shown in Vienna, Ft. Lauderdale, Paris, and Australia—featured some 230 of Ritts's photographs, all in black and white and ranging in size from intimate portraits to ten-foot murals. It was the first time that a show had been sponsored by a major fashion house, Donna Karan of New York. The exhibits included shots of celebrities such as Madonna and other Hollywood stars, images of people, animals, and landscapes from Africa, layouts from the fashion world, and studies of the human form, including some controversial male and female nudes. The MFA budgeted $450,000 to promote the show, advertising it in a wide array of both general and specialist media, ranging from newspapers and magazines to theater programs and public transit vehicles. For the first time, the MFA advertised in national media, encompassing both fashion publications and upscale general audience magazines.

Reviews by the critics were generally unenthusiastic. The *Boston Sunday Herald* review was headlined "Putting on the Glitz." *The Boston Globe* described the show as "fun, all style and little substance, slick and seductive. . . . It's a quick read—art for the attention span of the '90s." Addressing Malcolm Rogers's hope that Ritts would lure new young audiences to the museum, the *Globe's* critic declared, "That might work. . . . But will this show turn young viewers on to *other* art?" One Boston gallery owner remarked: "I don't think that quality should ever be sacrificed in the name of new audiences." Nevertheless, when the show closed on February 9, 1997, it had achieved a total attendance of 253,694, making it the sixth most popular exhibition in MFA history. The press coverage, including national TV, was the broadest ever achieved by the museum.

LOOKING TO THE FUTURE

The next major exhibition scheduled to be held at the MFA was *Picasso: The Early Years, 1892–1906.* Organized by the MFA and the National Gallery of Art in Washington, it was scheduled to run in Boston from early September to the beginning of January, 1998. Surveying the beginnings of the artist's career, the show would include images from Picasso's so-called "Blue" and "Rose" periods. More than 100 paintings, drawings, and sculptures had been selected for display from major collections around the world.

The exhibition was sponsored by a substantial grant from Bell Atlantic, a major regional telecommunications company.

Pat Jacoby recognized that promoting this exhibition was only one of many challenges she faced in seeking to ensure the museum's continued success in serving its many audiences. As she reflected on the future role and responsibilities of marketing at the Museum of Fine Arts, she remembered a recent presentation by Malcolm Rogers, in which he had declared:

> *Marketing is central to the life of a great museum that's trying to get its message out. It's part of our educational outreach, our social outreach. Unfortunately, certain people don't like the word "marketing." What I see out there—and also to a certain extent inside the museum—is a very conservative culture that cannot accept that institutions previously considered "elite" should actually be trying to attract a broader public and also listening to what the public is saying. But it's all to do with fulfilling your mission.*
>
> *Clearly part of a museum's mission is guardianship of precious objects, but unless we're communicating those objects to people effectively and our visitors are enjoying them—and the ambiance of the setting in which they are displayed and interpreted— then we're only operating at 50% effectiveness or less. Having said this, I want to stress that the mission comes first and that marketing is absolutely the servant of our mission. I believe that museums stand for a commitment to certain eternal values that they bring to an ever-broadening public. We're not just in the business of finding out what people want and then giving it to them.*

Questions for Discussion

1. Define the core product and supplementary services of a large museum like the MFA.

2. Prepare a flowchart of a tourist visiting Boston who calls from the hotel to get information about the MFA and then goes to visit it.

3. What differentiates the MFA from a for-profit institution like a department store, a theme park, or a movie theater? How does this distinction affect management priorities and decisions?

4. Evaluate the efforts made by the museum management to make the MFA more marketing oriented. What should be done to get better understanding of marketing and its objectives from curators?

5. Evaluate the role of Malcolm Rogers. Is he a good leader? Has he been an effective service marketer?

Glossary

activity-based costing: an approach to costing based on identifying the activities being performed and then determining the resources that each consumes. (p. 176)

adaptive applications: situations in which the Web supplements a company's existing market arrangements. (p. 359)

adequate service: the minimum level of service that a customer will accept without being dissatisfied. (p. 81)

advertising: any form of nonpersonal communication by a marketer to inform, educate, or persuade members of target audiences. (p. 201)

arm's length transactions: interactions between customers and service suppliers in which mail or telecommunications minimize the need to meet face to face. (p. 247)

auction: a selling procedure managed by a specialist intermediary in which the price is set by allowing prospective purchasers to bid against each other for a product offered by a seller. (p. 180)

augmented product: the core product (a good or a service) plus all supplementary elements that add value for customers. (p. 142)

backstage (or technical core): those aspects of service operations that are hidden from customers. (p. 60)

balking: a decision by a customer not to join a queue because the wait appears too long. (p. 305)

benefit: an advantage or gain that customers obtain from performance of a service or use of a physical good. (p. 6)

benefit-driven pricing: the strategy of relating the price to that aspect of the service that directly creates benefits for customers. (p. 178)

boundary spanning positions: jobs that straddle the boundary between the external environment, where customers are encountered, and the internal operations of the organization. (p. 325)

brand: a name, phrase, design, symbol, or some combination of these elements that identifies a company's services and differentiates it from competitors. (p. 228)

chase demand strategy: adjusting the level of capacity to meet the level of demand at any given time. (p. 291)

clicks and mortar: a strategy of offering service through both physical stores and virtual storefronts via Web sites on the Internet. (p. 350)

competition-based pricing: the practice of setting prices relative to those charged by competitors. (p. 177)

complaint: a formal expression of dissatisfaction with any aspect of a service experience. (p. 120)

complaint log: a detailed record of all customer complaints received by a service provider. (p. 126)

control charts: charts that graph quantitative changes in service performance on a specific variable relative to a predefined standard. (p. 270)

control model of management: an approach based on clearly defined roles, top-down control systems, a hierarchical organizational structure, and the assumption that management knows best. (p. 332)

corporate design: the consistent application of distinctive colors, symbols, and lettering to give a firm an easily recognizable identity. (p. 204)

cost-based pricing: the practice of relating the price to be charged to the costs associated with producing, delivering, and marketing a product. (p. 176)

cost leader: a firm that bases its pricing strategy on achieving the lowest costs in its industry. (p. 179)

credence attributes: product characteristics that customers may not be able to evaluate even after purchase and consumption. (p. 84)

critical incident: a specific encounter between customer and service provider in which the outcome has proved especially satisfying or dissatisfying for one or both parties. (p. 55)

critical incident technique (CIT): a methodology for collecting, categorizing, and analyzing critical incidents that have occurred between customers and service providers. (p. 55)

customer-contact personnel: those service employees who interact directly with individual customers either in person or through mail and telecommunications. (p. 52)

customer satisfaction: a short-term emotional reaction to a specific service performance. (p. 87)

customer service: the provision of supplementary service elements by employees who are not specifically engaged in selling activities. (p. 200)

customer training: formal training courses offered by service firms to teach customers about complex service products. (p. 200)

customization: tailoring service characteristics to meet each customer's specific needs and preferences. (p. 31)

cyberspace: a term used to describe the absence of a definable physical location where electronic transactions or communications occur. (p. 242)

defection: a customer's decision to transfer brand loyalty from a current service provider to a competitor. (p. 105)

delivery channels: the means by which a service firm (sometimes assisted by intermediaries) delivers one or more product elements to its customers. (p. 245)

demand cycle: a period of time during which the level of demand for a service will increase and decrease in a somewhat predictable way before repeating itself. (p. 293)

desired service: the "wished for" level of service quality that a customer believes can and should be delivered. (p. 81)

discounting: a strategy of reducing the price of an item below the normal level. (p. 185)

emotional labor: the act of expressing socially appropriate (but sometimes false) emotions toward customers during service transactions. (p. 326)

empowerment: authorizing employees to find solutions to service problems and make appropriate decisions about responding to customer concerns without having to ask a supervisor's approval. (p. 331)

enablement: providing employees with the skills, tools, and resources they need to use their own discretion confidently and effectively. (p. 331)

enhancing supplementary services: supplementary services that may add extra value for customers. (p. 144)

excess capacity: a firm's capacity to create service output is not fully utilized. (p. 288)

excess demand: demand for a service at a given time exceeds the firm's ability to meet customer needs. (p. 288)

expectations: internal standards that customers use to judge the quality of a service experience. (p. 80)

experience attributes: product performance features that customers can evaluate only during service delivery. (p. 84)

expert systems: interactive computer programs that mimic a human expert's reasoning to draw conclusions from data, solve problems, and give customized advice. (p. 329)

extranets: networks that are reached through a published Web address containing a secured link to a restricted site, whose access is limited by password to authorized users. (p. 357)

facilitating supplementary services: supplementary services that aid in the use of the core product or are required for service delivery. (p. 144)

fail point: a point in a process where there is a significant risk of problems that can damage service quality. (p. 153)

financial outlays: all monetary expenditures incurred by customers in purchasing and consuming a service. (p. 172)

fishbone diagram: a chart-based technique that relates specific service problems to different categories of underlying causes (also known as a cause-and-effect chart). (p. 270)

flat-rate pricing: the strategy of quoting a fixed price for a service in advance of delivery. (p. 178)

flowchart: a visual representation of the steps involved in delivering service to customers. (p. 91)

Flower of Service: a visual framework for understanding the supplementary service elements that surround and add value to the product core. (p. 144)

focus: the provision of a relatively narrow product mix for a particular market segment. (p. 216)

focus groups: groups of customers sharing certain common characteristics who are convened by researchers for in-depth, moderator-led discussions on specific topics. (p. 278)

front stage: those aspects of service operations and delivery that are visible or otherwise apparent to customers. (p. 60)

goods: physical objects or devices that provide benefits for customers through ownership or use. (p. 9)

halo effect: the tendency for consumer ratings of one prominent product characteristic to influence ratings for many other attributes of that same product. (p. 230)

high-contact services: services that involve significant interaction among customers, service personnel, and equipment and facilities. (p. 54)

human resource management (HRM): the coordination of tasks related to job design, employee recruitment, selection, training, and motivation; it also includes planning and administering other employee-related activities. (p. 324)

impersonal communications: one-way communications directed at target audiences who are not in personal contact with the message source (including advertising, promotions, and public relations). (p. 199)

information-based services: all services in which the principal value comes from the transmission of data to customers (includes both mental stimulus processing and information processing). (p. 43)

information processing: intangible actions directed at customers' assets. (p. 35)

in-process wait: a wait that occurs during service delivery. (p. 309)

inputs: all resources (labor, materials, energy, and capital) required to create service offerings. (p. 279)

intangibility: a distinctive characteristic of services that makes it impossible to touch or hold on to them in the same manner as physical goods. (p. 30)

intangible: something that is experienced and cannot be touched or preserved. (p. 10)

integrated service management: the coordinated planning and execution of those marketing, operations, and human resources activities that are essential to a service firm's success. (p. 13)

internal communications: all forms of communication from management to employees in a service organization. (p. 193)

internal customers: employees who receive services from an internal supplier (another employee or department) as a necessary input to performing their own jobs. (p. 324)

internal services: service elements within any type of business that facilitate creation of, or add value to, its final output. (p. 8)

Internet: a public network that includes all e-mail and Web activity that is open and available to any user—around the world. (p. 357)

intranets: e-mail and Web site networks that are internal to specific organizations, available only to authorized employees and other personnel, and protected from outside access. (p. 357)

inventory: for *manufacturing*, physical output stockpiled after production for sale at a later date; for *services*, future output that has not yet been reserved in advance, such as the number of hotel rooms still available for sale on a given day. (p. 288)

involvement model of management: an approach based on the assumption that employees are capable of self-direction and, if properly trained, motivated, and informed—can make good decisions concerning service operations and delivery. (p. 332)

jaycustomer: a customer who acts in a thoughtless or abusive way, causing problems for the firm, its employees, and other customers. (p. 111)

levels of customer contact: the extent to which customers interact directly with elements of the service organization. (p. 53)

low-contact services: services that require minimal or no direct contact between customers and the service organization. (p. 54)

loyalty: a customer's voluntary decision to continue patronizing a specific firm over an extended period of time. (p. 104)

market focus: the extent to which a firm serves few or many markets. (p. 216)

marketing communications mix: the full set of communication tools (both paid and unpaid) available to marketers. (p. 199)

marketplace: a physical location where suppliers and customers meet to do business. (p. 243)

market segmentation: the process of dividing a market into different groups within which all customers share relevant characteristics that distinguish them from customers in other segments. (p. 76)

marketspace: a virtual location in cyberspace, made possible by telephone and Internet linkages, where customers and suppliers conduct business electronically. (p. 243)

mass customization: offering a service with some individualized product elements to a large number of customers at a relatively low price. (p. 77)

maximum capacity: the upper limit to a firm's ability to meet customer demand at a particular time. (p. 288)

medium-contact services: services that involve only a limited amount of contact between customers and elements of the service organization. (p. 54)

membership relationship: a formalized relationship between the firm and a specified customer that may offer special benefits to both parties. (p. 99)

mental stimulus processing: intangible actions directed at people's minds. (p. 35)

Metcalfe's Law: a scientific theory specifying that the utility of a network is the square of its number of users. (p. 354)

molecular model: a framework that uses a chemical analogy to describe the structure of service offerings. (p. 142)

moment of truth: a point in service delivery where customers interact with service employees or self-service equipment and the outcome may affect perceptions of service quality. (p. 55)

Moore's Law: a scientific theory that predicts a doubling of computing power for the same price every 18 months. (p. 354)

mystery shopping: a research technique that employs individuals posing as ordinary customers in order to obtain feedback on the service environment and customer-employee interactions. (p. 278)

needs: subconscious, deeply felt desires that often concern long-term existence and identity issues. (p. 78)

net value: the sum of all perceived benefits (gross value) minus the sum of all perceived outlays. (p. 174)

nonfinancial outlays: the time expenditures, physical and mental effort, and unwanted sensory experiences associated with searching for, buying, and using a service. (p. 173)

opportunity cost: the potential value of the income or other benefits foregone as a result of choosing one course of action instead of other alternatives. (p. 315)

optimum capacity: the point beyond which a firm's efforts to serve additional customers will lead to a perceived decline in service quality. (p. 288)

organizational climate: employees' shared perceptions of the practices, procedures, and types of behaviors that get rewarded and supported in a particular setting. (p. 390)

organizational culture: shared values, beliefs, and work styles that are based upon an understanding of what is important to the organization and why. (p. 390)

outputs: the final outcomes of the service delivery process as perceived and valued by customers. (p. 279)

Pareto analysis: an analytical procedure to identify what proportion of problem events is caused by each of several different factors. (p. 271)

people: customers and employees who are involved in service production. (p. 14)

people processing: services that involve tangible actions to people's bodies. (p. 34)

perceptual map: a visual illustration of how customers perceive competing services. (p. 221)

permission marketing: a marketing communication strategy that encourages customers to voluntarily learn more about a company's products because they anticipate receiving information or something else of value in return. (p. 208)

personal communications: direct communications between marketers and individual customers that involve two-way dialog (including face-to-face conversations, phone calls, and e-mail). (p. 199)

personal selling: two-way communications between service employees and customers designed to directly influence the purchase process. (p. 200)

physical effort: undesired consequences to a customer's body that occur during the service delivery process. (p. 173)

physical evidence: visual or other tangible clues that provide evidence of service quality. (p. 15)

place, cyberspace, and time: management decisions about when, where, and how to deliver services to customers. (p. 14)

positioning: establishing a distinctive place in the minds of customers relative to competing products. (p. 219)

possession processing: tangible actions to goods and other physical possessions belonging to customers. (p. 35)

postprocess wait: a wait that occurs after service delivery has been completed. (p. 309)

postpurchase stage: the final stage in the service purchase process where customers evaluate service quality and their satisfaction/dissatisfaction with the service outcome. (p. 90)

post-transaction surveys: techniques to measure customer satisfaction and perceptions of service quality while a specific service experience is still fresh in the customer's mind. (p. 276)

predicted service: the level of service quality a customer believes a firm will actually deliver. (p. 82)

preprocess wait: a wait before service delivery begins. (p. 309)

prepurchase stage: the first stage in the service purchase process, where customers identify alternatives, weigh benefits and risks, and make a purchase decision. (p. 88)

price and other user outlays: expenditures of money, time, and effort that customers incur in purchasing and consuming services. (p. 15)

price bucket: an allocation of service capacity (for instance, seats) for sale at a particular price. (p. 180)

price bundling: the practice of charging a base price for a core service plus additional fees for optional supplementary elements. (p. 185)

price elasticity: the extent to which a change in price leads to a corresponding change in demand in the opposite direction. (Demand is described as "price inelastic" when changes in price have little or no impact on demand.) (p. 179)

price leader: a firm that takes the initiative on price changes in its market area and is copied by others. (p. 177)

process: a particular method of operations or series of actions, typically involving steps that need to occur in a defined sequence. (p. 14)

product: the core output (either a service or a manufactured good) produced by a firm. (p. 9)

product attributes: all features (both tangible and intangible) of a good or service that can be evaluated by customers. (p. 83)

product elements: all components of the service performance that create value for customers. (p. 14)

productive capacity: the extent of the facilities, equipment, labor, infrastructure, and other assets available to a firm to create output for its customers. (p. 289)

productivity: how efficiently service inputs are transformed into outputs that add value for customers. (p. 14)

promotion and education: all communication activities and incentives designed to build customer preference for a specific service or service provider. (p. 14)

psychological burdens: undesired mental or emotional states experienced by customers as a result of the service delivery process. (p. 173)

public relations: efforts to stimulate positive interest in a company and its products by sending out news releases, holding press conferences, staging special events, and sponsoring newsworthy activities put on by third parties. (p. 203)

purchase process: the stages a customer goes through in choosing, consuming, and evaluating a service. (p. 88)

quality: the degree to which a service satisfies customers by meeting their needs, wants, and expectations. (p. 14)

queue: a line of people, vehicles, other physical objects, or intangible items waiting their turn to be served or processed. (p. 304)

queue configuration: the way in which a waiting line is organized. (p. 305)

rate fences: techniques for separating customers so that segments for whom the service offers high value are unable to take advantage of lower-priced offers. (p. 180)

reciprocal marketing: a marketing communication tactic in which an online retailer allows its paying customers to receive promotions for another online retailer and vice-versa, at no upfront cost to either party. (p. 210)

reengineering: the analysis and redesign of business processes to create dramatic performance improvements in such areas as cost, quality, speed, and customers' service experiences. (p. 162)

relationship marketing: activities aimed at developing long-term, cost-effective links between an organization and its customers for the mutual benefit of both parties. (p. 102)

reneging: a decision by a customer to leave a queue before reaching its end because the wait is longer or more burdensome than originally anticipated. (p. 307)

repositioning: changing the position a firm holds in a consumer's mind relative to competing services. (p. 221)

retail displays: presentations in store windows and other locations of merchandise, service experiences, and benefits. (p. 199)

retail gravity model: a mathematical approach to retail site selection that involves calculating the geographic center of gravity for the target population and then locating a facility to optimize customers' ease of access. (p. 245)

return on quality: the financial return obtained from investing in service quality improvements. (p. 275)

role: a combination of social cues that guides behavior in a specific setting or context. (p. 65)

role congruence: the extent to which both customers and employees act out their prescribed roles during a service encounter. (p. 65)

sales promotion: a short-term incentive offered to customers and intermediaries to stimulate product purchase. (p. 202)

satisfaction-profit chain: a strategic framework that links performance on service attributes to customer satisfaction, then to customer retention, and finally to profits. (p. 266)

scripts: learned sequences of behaviors obtained through personal experience or communications with others. (p. 65)

search attributes: product characteristics that consumers can readily evaluate prior to purchase. (p. 83)

segment: a group of current or prospective customers who share common characteristics, needs, purchasing behavior, or consumption patterns. (p. 76)

sensory burdens: negative sensations experienced through a customer's five senses during the service delivery process. (p. 173)

service: an act or performance that creates benefits for customers by bringing about a desired change in—or on behalf of—the recipient. (p. 6)

service blueprint: a visual map of the sequence of activities required for service delivery that specifies front-stage and backstage elements and the linkages between them. (p. 153)

service delivery system: that part of the total service system where final "assembly" of the elements takes place and the product is delivered to the customer; it includes the visible elements of the service operation. (p. 60)

service encounter: a period of time during which customers interact directly with a service. (p. 53)

service encounter stage: the second stage in the service purchase process where the service delivery takes place through interactions between customers and the service provider. (p. 90)

service factory: the physical site where service operations take place. (p. 35)

service failure: a perception by customers that one or more specific aspects of service delivery have not met their expectations. (p. 120)

service focus: the extent to which a firm offers few or many services. (p. 216)

service guarantee: a promise that if service delivery fails to meet predefined standards, the customer is entitled to one or more forms of compensation. (p. 130)

service marketing system: that part of the total service system where the firm has any form of contact with its customers, from advertising to billing; it includes contacts made at the point of delivery. (p. 60)

service operations system: that part of the total service system where inputs are processed and the elements of the service product are created. (p. 60)

service preview: a demonstration of how a service works to educate customers about the roles they are expected to perform in service delivery. (p. 70)

service-profit chain: a series of hypothesized links between profit; revenue growth; customer loyalty; customer satisfaction; value delivered to customers; and employee capability, satisfaction, loyalty, and productivity. (p. 370)

service quality: customers' long-term, cognitive evaluations of a firm's service delivery. (p. 87)

service quality information system: an ongoing service research process that provides timely, useful data to managers about customer satisfaction, expectations, and perceptions of quality. (p. 275)

service recovery: systematic efforts by a firm after a service failure to correct a problem and retain a customer's goodwill. (p. 127)

servicescape: the design of any physical location where customers come to place orders and obtain service delivery. (p. 206)

service sector: the portion of a nation's economy represented by services of all kinds, including those offered by public and non-profit organizations. (p. 7)

SERVQUAL: a standardized scale that measures expectations and perceptions about critical quality dimensions. (p. 277)

standardization: reducing variation in service operations and delivery. (p. 31)

stickiness: a Web site's ability to encourage repeat visits and purchases by keeping its audience engaged with interactive communication presented in an appealing fashion. (p. 209)

sustainable competitive advantage: a position in the marketplace that can't be taken away or minimized by competitors in the short run. (p. 218)

tangible: capable of being touched, held, or preserved in physical form over time. (p. 30)

target segments: segments selected because their needs and other characteristics fit well with a specific firm's goals and capabilities. (p. 98)

telemarketing: personal selling to prospective customers through the medium of the telephone. (p. 200)

time expenditures: time spent by customers during all aspects of the service delivery process. (p. 173)

total market surveys: periodic measurements of customers' overall evaluations of service quality based on accumulated experience over a period of time. (p. 276)

transaction: an event during which an exchange of value takes place between two parties. (p. 99)

transformative applications: situations in which the Internet becomes the major driver of a firm's strategy. (p. 359)

24/7 service: service that is available 24 hours a day, 7 days a week. (p. 255)

undesirable demand: requests for service that conflict with the organization's mission, priorities, or capabilities. (p. 295)

value-based pricing: the practice of setting prices with reference to what customers are willing to pay for the value they believe they will receive. (p. 177)

variability: a lack of consistency in inputs and outputs during the service production process. (p. 11)

word of mouth: positive or negative comments about a service made by one individual (usually a current or former customer) to another. (p. 200)

yield: the average revenue received per unit of capacity offered for sale. (p. 314)

yield management: a pricing strategy based on charging different prices to different users in order to maximize the revenue yield that can be derived from a firm's available capacity at any specific point in time. (p. 180)

zone of tolerance: the range within which customers are willing to accept variations in service delivery. (p. 82)

Credits

Chapter 1
p. 7: U.S. Department of Commerce. **p. 8:** International Monetary Fund, used with permission. **p. 10:** Churchill & Klehr/Pearson Education/PH College. **p. 20:** Singapore Airlines.

Chapter 2
p. 31: PhotoDisc Inc. **p. 37:** Wolfgang Spunbarg/PhotoEdit. **p. 44:** Used with permission from Flooz.com. **p. 45:** © Lands' End, Inc. Used with permission.

Chapter 3
p. 54: WingspanBank.com. **pp. 56–57:** Copyright © 1990 American Marketing Association. Reprinted by permission. **p. 58:** Copyright © 2000 American Marketing Association. Reprinted by permission. **p. 67:** From *Services Marketing, 4/e,* Christopher Lovelock, p. 65, © 2001. Reprinted by permission of Prentice-Hall, Inc. Upper Saddle River, NJ. **p. 61:** From Services Marketing, 4/e, Christopher Lovelock, p. 67, © 2001. Reprinted by permission of Prentice-Hall, Inc., Upper Saddle River, NJ. **p. 64:** Copyright © 1983 American Marketing Association. Reprinted by permission. **p. 68:** From *Services Marketing, 4/e,* Christopher Lovelock, p. 66, © 2001. Reprinted by permission of Prentice-Hall, Inc., Upper Saddle River, NJ.

Chapter 5
p. 98: Courtesy of Intrawest Corporation, photo by Randy Links. **p. 105:** Reprinted by permission of *Harvard Business Review*. Copyright © 1994 by Harvard Business School Publishing Corporation. **p. 109:** Elena Rooraid/PhotoEdit.

Chapter 6
p. 126: Richard Hutchings/PhotoEdit.

Chapter 7
p. 142: Copyright © 1997 American Marketing Association. Used with permission. **p. 146:** American Express. **pp. 156–159:** From *Services Marketing, 4/e,* Christopher Lovelock, pp. 226–229, © 2001. Reprinted by permission of Prentice-Hall, Inc., Upper Saddle River, NJ.

Chapter 8
p. 170: Reprinted by permission of Travelscape.com, © 2000 O'Gara/Bissell Photography/Las Vegas Stock. **p. 182:** DoveBid and the DoveBid logo are trademarks of DoveBid, Inc. Used with permission. **p. 187:** Reprinted by permission of Clareon. All rights reserved.

Chapter 9
p. 192: Used with permission from Southwest Airlines. **p. 194:** Reprinted by permission from Robins, Kaplan, Miller & Ciresi, L.L.P. **p. 195:** Prudential Insurance Co. of America. **p. 196:** Reprinted by permission of Liberty Mutual. **p. 197:** Radisson Hotels International, Inc. **p. 201:** Williams Communications. **p. 202:** Used with permission of Cleanrite Company. **p. 204:** FedEx service marks used by permission. © 1995–2001 FedEx. All rights reserved. **p. 205:** Merrill Lynch. **p. 209:** PSI Net.

Chapter 10
p. 220: America Online. **p. 228:** AARP. **p. 232:** Starbucks.

Chapter 11
p. 242: Figure from *Services Marketing, 4/e,* by Christopher Lovelock, p. 339, © 2001. Reprinted by permission of Prentice-Hall, Inc., Upper Saddle River, NJ. **p. 249:** New York Convention & Visitors Bureau. **p. 249:** Loews Hotels. **p. 256:** PhotoDisc, Inc.

Chapter 12
p. 272: Reprinted with permission of *Harvard Business Review*. Copyright © 1995 by Harvard Business School Publishing Coporation. **p. 273:** Reprinted with permission of The Free Press, a division of Simon & Schuster, Inc. Copyright © 1997 by James L. Heskett, W. Earl Sasser, Jr., Leonard A. Schlesinger. **p. 280:** United Features. **p. 282:** PhotoDisc, Inc.

Chapter 13
p. 292: Michal Heron/Pearson Education/PH College. **p. 299:** Courtesy of Intrawest Corporation, photo by Randy Links.

Chapter 14
p. 309: Laima E. Druskis Photography/Pearson Education/ PH College. **p. 315:** David Weintraub/Stock Boston.

Chapter 15
p. 326: United Features. **p. 330:** © Fredric Brenner. Reprinted courtesy of United Parcel Service of America, Inc. **p. 332:** Reprinted with

Index